Macmillan Publishing Company
866 Third Avenue, New York, New York 10022

Collier Macmillan Canada, Inc.

LIBRARY OF CONGRESS CATALOGING-IN-PUBLICATION DATA

Johnson, Aaron C.
  Econometrics : basic and applied.
  Bibliography: p.
  Includes index.
  1. Econometrics.   I. Johnson, Marvin B.
II. Buse, Rueben C.   III. Title.
HB139.J63   1987   330'.028   85-29967
ISBN 0-02-360920-6

Printing: 1   2   3   4   5   6   7   8   Year: 7   8   9   0   1   2   3   4   5

ISBN   0-02-360920-6

ECONOMETRICS

BASIC AND APPLIED

Aaron C. Johnson, Jr.
UNIVERSITY OF WISCONSIN, MADISON

Marvin B. Johnson
UNIVERSITY OF WISCONSIN, MADISON

Rueben C. Buse
UNIVERSITY OF WISCONSIN, MADISON

MACMILLAN PUBLISHING COMPANY
NEW YORK
Collier Macmillan Publishers
LONDON

Preface

This book evolved from a set of extended lecture notes distributed each semester to our students under the title "A Tyro's Tryst With Econometrics." The title signaled immediately that what followed was for the newcomer to econometrics, not for the advanced student armed with statistical theory, matrix algebra, and a familiarity with the spirit of applied research. Moreover, the title hinted at pleasure awaiting the tyros. The pleasure was to come, we believed, not from learning abstract regression theory but from seeing regression theory unfold in the broader context of applied research that comprises not only regression, but also social science theory, previous research, common sense, and a lot of hard, often frustrating, work.

Thus our aim has been, and continues to be here, to expose the newcomer to the excitement of applied research. Our objective is not to transform tyros into professional researchers. Instead, our goal is to convey to them as best we can how the applied researcher goes about trying to acquire quantitative knowledge of the world "out there." We recognize that applied research cannot be taught; one can learn only by doing. Nevertheless, we believe that those with experience in doing applied research can impart to beginning students at least some insight into how the applied researcher tries to think through a specific research problem. In teaching, we stress that applied research is more a way of thinking about a problem than it is a mechanical application of techniques learned in a classroom. We hope we have been able to convey by the written word what we convey in the classroom by the spoken word. If we have been even modestly successful in doing so, then this is more than just another regression book. It is an introduction to the exciting, challenging world of applied research.

The book assumes that the student has had a good introductory statistics course and is familiar with the basic concepts of using sample data to estimate population parameters and to test hypotheses. Consequently, this book, unlike many econometrics textbooks, does not cover the fundamentals of statistical theory. A brief, dictionary-like discussion of the basic statistical concepts used in econometrics is included for reference only. A minimum facility with differential calculus is helpful but not essential to understanding the material. Matrix algebra is not required to master this book. However, to make the book potentially useful to a wider audience, the matrix algebra needed for single-equation regression is included in Chapter 20. In addition, the relevant derivations of preceding chapters are reproduced in matrix notation in

Chapter 20. We tried to write the book such that it can be used to teach the material with or without using matrix algebra.

Most important, the book assumes that the student is well grounded in the theory of his or her discipline, be it economics, geography, educational psychology, or business. Throughout the book we stress the singular importance of theory in applied research because we firmly believe the old adage that nothing is as practical as a good theory. The examples used to illustrate various concepts and ways of thinking reflect our formal training and professional responsibilities. However, the technique of regression analysis is not restricted to any particular discipline; it is useful in any applied setting where the researcher wants to make quantitative statements about functional relationships. For example, a political scientist might be interested in testing hypotheses about how certain socioeconomic characteristics affect the way people vote in state elections. Or an educational psychologist might need to examine the effects of certain household characteristics on the performance of schoolchildren. Thus, much of what we say in this book applies full force to many disciplines, the substantive difference being the underlying theory that gives rise to the relationships to be estimated.

We do not cover simultaneous-equation estimation. Although this omission may displease some, it was made based on our teaching experience. As teachers of upper-division undergraduates and beginning graduate students, we concentrate on using regression to actually estimate demand elasticities, income slopes, and the like. Consequently, we had to make a choice: either restrict the subject to single-equation models so that we could develop the theory as a base for applied research, and then spend considerable time on econometric problems, on the procedures of applied research, and on interpreting and evaluating regression results; or else cover the theory of both single-equation and simultaneous-equation models and abandon the applied research emphasis. A one-semester course simply does not provide the time needed to give adequate treatment to both theory and practice.

The book is organized into five parts. Part I, *The Theory,* is made up of seven chapters that form the base of the econometric theory and hypothesis testing used in the book. In Chapter 1 we introduce the principle of least squares. In Chapter 2 we discuss why the study of econometrics is important by going through the steps of applied research and showing how economic theory, mathematics, statistics, and the theory of estimation are combined to permit the applied researcher to make quantitative statements about population parameters. Single-equation regression theory is developed in Chapter 3, using the simple regression model. The results are extended to multiple regression in Chapter 4. In Chapter 5 we deal with correlation as a measure of association and introduce causality via the regression equation to permit interpreting the correlation coefficient as a measure of explained variation. A complete treatment of hypothesis testing is given in Chapter 6. Chapter 7 is a transition chapter that begins by discussing numbers and data sets used in regression and ends by presenting all the least squares computations in matrix notation. The purpose of this chapter is to show the explicit computations embedded in the matrix notation. We believe that this chapter, which can easily and without damage be skipped by anyone so inclined, provides a background sufficient to permit intelligent reading of other books, journals, and the like that use matrix notation.

Part II, *The Practice,* contains four chapters, each developed to address the nitty-gritty of how to think through an applied research problem. Chapter 8, the first of four "how-to-do-it" chapters, shows how to use theory to formulate a problem and identify the type of data needed to get under way. Dummy variables receive extensive treatment in Chapter 9, beginning with how to set up the worksheet and ending with formulating an equation that allows estimating in the presence of structural shifts in the underlying population regression function. In Chapter 10 we address a number of questions that must be answered in applied research. The often neglected subject of functional form is treated in Chapter 11.

Part III, *The Problems,* covers the standard econometric problems. Multicollinearity is discussed in Chapter 12. Omitted relevant variables and included irrelevant variables are covered in Chapter 13. In Chapter 14 we consider heteroscedasticity and autocorrelation. Errors in variables and missing observations are the subject of Chapter 15.

Part IV, *Time,* covers various aspects of using time in applied regression analysis. Chapter 16 covers trend estimation and using time as an independent variable in a regression equation. Chapter 17 shows how to use regression to estimate seasonal indexes. In Chapter 18 we consider forecasting, with primary emphasis on the forecast error.

Part V, *Miscellany,* contains two quite different chapters. The writing of research reports, often a difficult and time-consuming step in applied research, is discussed in Chapter 19. Finally, in Chapter 20 we cover the basic theorems of matrix algebra and present the general treatment of regression theory using matrix notation.

In summary, we have tried to write a book that gives a fair and honest treatment of a subject that contains much that is not intuitive to the beginner. Few start with an innate, intuitive feel for best linear unbiased estimators. Moreover, we are not so old as to have forgotten our first step into the regression jungle, made thick by the underbrush of details, all seemingly unrelated, none making any sense. But slowly things began to take shape for us, to flower into something recognizable, until one day we discovered that the jungle was lush with applications to all sorts of interesting research questions. Suddenly, it made perfect sense to worry about disturbance terms and unbiasedness and minimum variance and omitted variables and heteroscedasticity. At last we could see the practical value of it all. It is to this sudden rush of intuitive grasp, to this excitement of understanding, that we try to lead you in this book. To do this, we have tried to write the book in an informal, low-key way. We take the material seriously, but we do not believe that it has to be presented in a somber, intimidating, impersonal way. We are now ready to lead you through the jungle, flailing away at the underbrush. We know the path, we have traveled it before. If you stick with us to the end, you may agree with us: Regression analysis can be fun.

Many contributed to this book as it evolved from mimeographed class notes, but the greatest contributions came from our former students at the University of Wisconsin and Carleton College. Each class labored, often unwillingly and sometimes angrily, through the current revision of the class notes. We thank these students for the many contributions they unknowingly made, and we apologize for the pain we inflicted on them.

We extend our sincere thanks to Cindy Hoffland, Marcia Verhage, Carmen Ramirez, Karen Denk, Debbie Dutcher, Mary Deitrich, Jack Solock, Madeleine Macho, Jude Grudzina, Linda Chase, Pat Boyd, and Mary Ellen Rodriguez who bore the brunt of manuscript typing and other tasks associated with getting a manuscript in book form. Their patience, diligence, and sense of humor made writing this book much easier.

Dan Bromley, our Department Chairman, supported us in many ways and, more importantly, gave us the encouragement we often needed to keep going. Our colleagues Ron Shaffer and Bill Saupe read various chapters and made many helpful comments.

Two of our former graduate students, Antonio Alvarez and Tera Weitermann, read the entire manuscript. Their suggestions kept us from forgetting our intended audience, namely, newcomers to the study of regression analysis and applied research. Kevin Boyle and Mike Welsh helped us make sure that we were getting the matrix notation and derivations in Chapter 20 correct. Fernando Yepez worked through a number of the exercises.

Paul Koch, David Debertin, Roger Dahlgren, Fred Galloway, Michael Reed, T. A. Hertsgaard, Richard Ashley, Dale Bails, Jeff LaFrance, and Babu Nahata made substantial contributions in their reviews of various versions of the manuscript. We greatly appreciate their criticism and encouragement, which improved the final text.

To all of the above we say thank you, the book is stronger because of your comments, suggestions, and assistance. Errors and weaknesses remaining are attributable only to us.

A. C. J., Jr.

M. B. J.

R. C. B.

Contents

II

The Practice

III

The Problems

V

Miscellany

I

The Theory

To do good applied research, a researcher must have a solid grasp of the theory of estimation. The seven chapters in this part lay out the theory of least squares regression. In Chapter 1 we introduce the notion of measuring economic relationships and the least squares criterion, the underpinning of regression theory, as a mathematical proposition. In Chapter 2 we review the theory of estimation. Single-equation regression theory is developed in Chapter 3, using the simple regression model to illustrate the principles. The results are extended to multiple regression in Chapter 4. Chapter 5 deals with correlation as a measure of explained variation. Hypothesis testing is discussed in Chapter 6. Chapter 7 is a transition chapter that begins with a discussion of numbers and data sets used in regression and ends with a presentation of least squares computations in matrix notation.

1

Introduction to Least Squares

Suppose that a researcher is interested in knowing something about the amount of money that families, or households, spend on food during a typical week. Because no published data on family food expenditures are readily available, the researcher decides to simply ask each of six families how much it spends. Let the data in Table 1.1 represent the responses from the families, where the families are arbitrarily listed by increasing level of food expenditures. These families spend different amounts on food each week. This observation raises the type of interesting question that leads to applied research: Why do different families spend different amounts on food each week? Stated another way: What explains this variation in food expenditures? The key word is "explains": The objective of applied research is often to explain such things as variation in food expenditures among a group of families. Researchers approach this objective by drawing from economic theory, mathematics, and statistics. These three disciplines taken together make up the discipline of *econometrics*, which, as the roots of the words suggest, is concerned with the measurement of economic relationships.

Thus the subject of this book is econometrics, the measurement of economic relationships. The purpose of the book is to develop, from economic theory, statistics, and mathematics, techniques that an applied researcher can use to estimate the economic relationships that are integral to applied economic research. We assume that the reader has had economic theory courses and thus focus primarily on statistics, mathematics, and issues of applied research. However, throughout the book, the dual role of theory in specifying the nature of relationships to be measured ("estimated" is the technically correct term) and in assessing the results obtained by the estimation techniques is emphasized.

In this chapter we introduce the principle of *least squares*. To avoid confusion at the outset, least squares is introduced as a mathematical technique for describing or summarizing the information embedded in a given set of numbers. Once the basic principle of least squares is mastered, the reader is ready for a more rigorous statistical

Table 1.1. Weekly Food Expenditures of Six Families

Family	Weekly Food Expenditure
A	$ 30
B	40
C	40
D	70
E	110
F	130

journey that will lead to estimating population regression parameters and hypothesis testing.

The journey is long, but each step is manageable. Along the way will appear what, at first, seems little more than a maze of nonsensical symbols and manipulations. But understanding will quickly replace bewilderment. Studying econometrics can be fun, and we hope to impart this feeling to you.

Determining a Line of Average Relationship

How do researchers begin to answer such research questions as: What causes different families to spend different amounts on food each week? The first step is to identify factors, called *explanatory variables*, likely to cause (to explain) differences in food expenditures among families. Although it is easy to immediately come up with several candidates for consideration via haphazard guessing, a better, more systematic approach is to turn first to economic theory. Expenditure on food suggests consumption, consumption suggests demand, and demand suggests the theory of consumer choice. Therefore, the theory of consumer choice is a logical place to turn for guidance in selecting variables to explain differences in food expenditures among families.

Of course, many variables are suggested by the theory of consumer choice, but concentration on one variable, consumer income, can keep this presentation as simple as possible. For convenience, assume that when the researcher obtained the food expenditure data from the six families, data on each family's weekly income were also obtained. The complete results of the survey are presented in Table 1.2, where the families again are arrayed by increasing levels of food expenditure.

Now the research question: For these six families, what is the effect of income on food expenditures? Specifically, how much will weekly food expenditure change if income increases by, say, $100 per week? This research question demands a *quantitative* answer, an answer cast in terms of numbers rather than in qualitative terms such as "up" or "down." Providing quantitative answers to research questions is what applied research is all about.

Table 1.2. Weekly Food Expenditures and Weekly Income for Six Families

Family	Food Expenditure	Income
A	$ 30	$100
B	40	200
C	40	300
D	70	200
E	110	400
F	130	600

How to proceed? Simply "eyeballing" the data in Table 1.2 reveals that as income rises, food expenditures tend to rise, a relationship suggested by consumer theory. However, eyeballing is not enough because it does not provide a specific quantitative answer. A more precise method is needed.

The Method of Graphic Analysis

A good beginning is to prepare a graph, commonly referred to as a *scatter diagram*, constructed by plotting paired observations on the *dependent variable* and the *independent variable* for each unit in the data set. This is done in Figure 1.1. It is conventional to place the values of the independent variable (income, in this case)

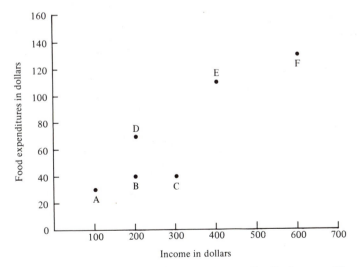

Figure 1.1 Scatter Diagram of Food Expenditures Versus Family Income. (Based on Data from Table 1.2.)

along the horizontal axis and values of the dependent variable (weekly food expenditure) along the vertical axis. For example, the point for family A is plotted at the
intersection of a line drawn vertically from an income of $100 and horizontally from
an expenditure of $30. When the points for each of the remaining families are plotted
in a similar fashion, the result is the scatter diagram in Figure 1.1. This diagram is
nothing more than a way of representing the data in Table 1.2 graphically. Furthermore, as it stands, the graph gets us no closer to the goal of a quantitative answer.
Still missing is some way to summarize the relationship illustrated by the graph.

Figure 1.1 indicates that there is considerable variation in the level of expenditure
among the families. Nevertheless, there seems to be a positive relationship between
expenditure and income: as income rises, expenditures *tend* to rise. The relationship,
however, is not perfect. For example, families B and D have the same income but
different food expenditures, while families B and C have the same level of food
expenditure but different incomes. These differences reflect little more than something
known from economic theory. There are factors other than income (family size, education, and tastes and preferences, to name a few) that affect the amount of money
that a family spends on food. At this point, the problem becomes finding and expressing an average or typical relationship between food expenditures and income.

The ''eyeball'' method was used to draw a line summarizing the average relationship between income and food expenditures in Figure 1.2. ''Eyeball line'' is a shorthand term for a line drawn freehand through the set of data points. Note that the
eyeball line is constructed to represent families with average incomes ($300) as having
average food expenditures ($70); the summary line goes through the midpoint of the
data set, often called the *centroid*. The line of average relationship in Figure 1.2,
located by visual inspection of the scatter of points representing expenditures and
income combinations, provides a quantitative answer to the research question. For

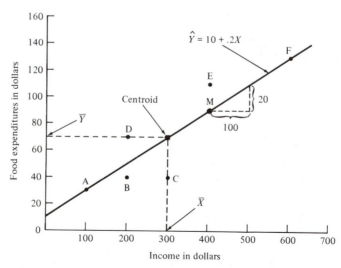

Figure 1.2 ''Eyeball'' Line Representing the Average Relationship Between Weekly Food
Expenditures and Family Income.

example, the summary line says that a family with a weekly income of $400 would, on the average, spend about $90 per week on food (point *M*). In general, Figure 1.2 can be used to determine the average (or expected) level of weekly food consumption for any level of income. Hence lines like that shown in Figure 1.2 can provide a quantitative answer to the research question: How do food expenditures differ with income?

The analysis could stop here. However, a mathematical expression for the line of average relationship is often helpful. The general expression for a straight line is

$$Y = b_0 + b_1X \tag{1.1}$$

where b_0 and b_1 are constants equal to any real number (positive, negative, or zero), Y is the dependent variable, and X is an explanatory or independent variable. The b_0 term is the *intercept*, the value for Y at which the line intersects the vertical axis, or the value for Y where X equals 0. The b_1 term is the *slope* of the line and measures the change in the Y-variable associated with a 1-unit change in the X-variable.

Consider the "eyeball" line in Figure 1.2. First, compute b_1, the slope, by

$$b_1 = \text{slope} = \frac{\text{rise}}{\text{run}} \tag{1.2}$$

This ratio measures the vertical change (change in Y associated with a 1-unit horizontal change (change in X). For Figure 1.2, an income change from $400 to $500 results in a consumption change of $+ \$20$, hence

$$b_1 = \frac{\text{change in expenditure}}{\text{change in income}} = \frac{+20}{+100} = +.2 \tag{1.3}$$

This says that weekly food expenditures increase by .2, or 20 cents, on the average, for every $1.00 increase in income. The intercept, b_0, is the point where the line intersects the Y axis and is calculated by

$$b_0 = \text{intercept} = \overline{Y} - b_1\overline{X} = 10 \tag{1.4}$$

where $\overline{Y} = \$70$ is the average of the dependent variable (average food consumption for the six families) and $\overline{X} = \$300$ is the average of the explanatory variable (average income for the size families), and b_1 is computed by using (1.3). Bringing (1.3) and (1.4) together yields

$$\hat{Y} = 10 + .2X \tag{1.5}$$

as the quantitative expression of the average relationship between food expenditures and income for the six families in Table 1.2. $\hat{Y}$ is the value of consumption on the line of average relationship for a given income level. This $\hat{Y}$-value is usually referred to as the *regression* or the *predicted value* of the dependent variable.

Used by a skillful applied researcher, graphic analysis can be a useful way for obtaining the line of average relationship between Y and X, and in many instances it may be sufficient to meet the research objective. There are, however, several obvious weaknesses of graphic analysis. First, it is a *subjective* method, which means, in simple terms, that two researchers working independently on exactly the same problem and using exactly the same data would undoubtedly get different numerical results.

This is undesirable because of the obvious confusion that would arise regarding what the values of b_0 and b_1 should be. Second, there is a tendency to ignore *outliers*, or extreme values, when eyeballing the line of average relationship. For example, if in the foregoing illustration a seventh observation with expenditures of $160 and income of $200 were plotted on Figure 1.2, it would fall outside the general pattern of the other six observations. There might be a tendency to ignore this outlier when eye-balling the line, hence ignoring some of the information in the data set. Third, and perhaps most important, graphic regression cannot be used to test hypotheses about population parameters because it is done in the absence of any statistical specifications. For these reasons, applied researchers prefer the method of *least squares regression* to determine the line of average relationship. As shown in the following section and in Chapter 3, this method does not possess the weaknesses of graphic regression. Nevertheless, graphic regression has pedagogic value because it gives the newcomer a mental picture of what regression is about and some feeling for what is going on inside the computer as it is computing regression coefficients.

The Method of Least Squares

The method of least squares relies on the objectivity of mathematics to select a line of average relationship, rather than on the subjectivity of a particular researcher's notion of where that line should be located on a scatter diagram. In this section we introduce least squares as a mathematical procedure for fitting a line of average re-lationship between the paired values of Y and X. In Chapter 3 we place least squares in a statistical context and view the method as a procedure for estimating unobservable population parameters.

Figure 1.2 indicates that a straight line typically will not completely describe a relationship between two variables. Some points, such as A and F, may lie directly on the line, but others, such as B and D, may not. Notice also that B and D have the same income ($200) but expenditures of $40 and $70, respectively. The regression value for expenditures on the line $\hat{Y} = 10 + .2X$ for an income of $200 is $10 + (.2)(200) = \$50$. Differences between the actual values of Y and the regression, or predicted, values of Y based on the average relationship, are called *residuals* and denoted by e.

Formally,

$$e_i = Y_i - \hat{Y}_i, \qquad i = 1, \ldots, n \tag{1.6}$$

where Y_i is the value of Y in the data set, $\hat{Y}_i$ is the associated regression or predicted value of Y, and n is the number of observations in the data set. This may be rewritten as

$$Y_i = \hat{Y}_i + e_i \tag{1.7}$$

which expresses the observed value of Y as the sum of the regression value of Y and the residual.

This leads to the *basic regression equation*,

$$Y_i = b_0 + b_1 X_i + e_i \tag{1.8}$$

This basic equation is an identity because, given numerical values of b_0 and b_1, the residual takes on that value which makes the right-hand side of the equation exactly equal to the left-hand side for the ith observation. But a problem arises. For the ith observation, the values of Y_i and X_i are known, but the value of e_i cannot be known until the values for b_0 and b_1 are determined. This raises a fundamental question: Given only the values of Y_i and X_i for each observation, is there any way, other than the eyeball method, to use these observed values to obtain values for b_0 and b_1? The answer is yes, by using the method of least squares.

The basic linear regression can be rewritten as

$$e_i = Y_i - b_0 - b_1 X_i \tag{1.9}$$

For each observation, since the values of Y_i and X_i are known, equation (1.9) expresses the e_i's as a function of b_0 and b_1. To see how residuals depend on the regression coefficients, consider the following illustrative cases:

Obser-vation	Y	X	Value of Residual Case 1: $b_0 = 10$ and $b_1 = .2$		Case 2: $b_0 = 40$ and $b_1 = .1$	
A	30	100	$30 - 10 - .2(100) =$	0	$30 - 40 - .1(100) =$	-20
B	40	200	$40 - 10 - .2(200) =$	-10	$40 - 40 - .1(200) =$	-20

The first set of values for b_0 and b_1 (case 1) yields residual values of 0 and -10 for the A and B observations, respectively. For case 2, the residuals are -20 for each observation. The point is that the numerical values of the residuals depend on the specific values of the regression coefficients b_0 and b_1. It follows that the method used to compute these coefficients is crucial for obtaining the line of average relationship.

The method of *least squares* is used to compute b_0 and b_1. In words, this method first computes the *sum of squared residuals* and then finds values for b_0 and b_1 that minimize this sum, denoted by *ESS*. The ESS is computed by

$$\text{ESS} = \sum_{i=1}^{n} e_i^2 = \sum_{i=1}^{n} (Y_i - b_0 - b_1 X_i)^2 \tag{1.10}$$

The ESS is a number that can be computed from the n paired values of Y and X in the data set *if* the values of b_0 and b_1 are known. But their values are not known at this point and must be computed before the ESS can be computed. There are, in effect, three unknowns in the equation, b_0, b_1, and e, and only two knowns, the paired values of Y and X in the data set. As it stands, not enough information is available to solve the problem. However, a solution is possible if information is added in the form of a restriction on the computation procedure. This is where the principle of least squares enters.

The least squares principle is straightforward: Compute numerical values for the coefficients of the equation using the sample of data at hand such that the resulting sum of squared residuals (ESS) about the regression line $\hat{Y}_i = b_0 + b_1 X_i$ is as small as possible. More succinctly, the principle involves minimizing the sum of the squared residuals.

The necessary conditions for ESS to be a minimum are that the partial derivatives of (1.10) with respect to b_0 and b_1 equal zero. Symbolically,

$$\frac{\partial ESS}{\partial b_0} = 2 \sum_i (Y_i - b_0 - b_1 X_i)(-1) = 0 \tag{1.11}$$

$$\frac{\partial ESS}{\partial b_1} = 2 \sum_i (Y_i - b_0 - b_1 X_i)(-X_i) = 0 \tag{1.12}$$

where "∂" means change. Manipulation of (1.11) and (1.12) yields the *normal equations*,

$$\sum_i Y_i = nb_0 + b_1 \sum_i X_i \tag{1.13}$$

$$\sum_i Y_i X_i = b_0 \sum_i X_i + b_1 \sum_i X_i^2 \tag{1.14}$$

where n is the number of paired values of X and Y. As an exercise, derive (1.13) and (1.14) from (1.11) and (1.12) by removing the parentheses and carrying out the summations.

The normal equations capture the conditions imposed on b_0 and b_1 by the least squares principle. Solving the normal equations for b_0 and b_1 yields formulas for calculating the *regression coefficients*, b_0 and b_1, for any set of observations on Y and X. First, (1.13) is solved for b_0,

$$b_0 = \frac{1}{n} \sum_i Y_i - b_1 \frac{1}{n} \sum_i X_i = \bar{Y} - b_1 \bar{X} \tag{1.15}$$

Note that this is the same formula as that used to calculate the intercept of a line through a scatter of points. Substituting (1.15) for b_0 into (1.14) (and remembering that $n\bar{X} = \sum_i^n X_i$) yields

$$b_1 = \frac{\sum_i Y_i X_i - n\bar{Y}\bar{X}}{\sum_i X_i^2 - n\bar{X}^2} \tag{1.16}$$

An alternative form of (1.16), one often seen in statistics books, is

$$b_1 = \frac{\sum_i (X_i - \bar{X})(Y_i - \bar{Y})}{\sum_i (X_i - \bar{X})^2} \tag{1.17}$$

Equation (1.16) can be obtained from (1.17) by performing the computations indicated. Equation (1.16) is sometimes referred to as the *computational formula*, as it is the one used if b_1 is computed by hand. When discussing regression theory, (1.17) is usually used, as it shows more clearly what b_1 is: If the numerator and denominator of (1.17) are divided by n (an operation that does not change the value of the ratio)

b_1 turns out to be the covariance of Y and X divided by the variance of X, an instructive insight into what a regression coefficient is all about.

An Example of Least Squares Calculations

Consider the data points in Table 1.2. What is the least squares line through these points? While the least squares formulas provide the answers, a table such as Table 1.3 helps keep track of the information. The procedure for developing Table 1.3 follows.

First, the data points are recorded (columns 1 and 2) and the mean values of X and Y are calculated. Next, the differences between the actual and mean values of X and Y are calculated and placed in columns 3 and 5, respectively. The denominator of b_1 is the sum of the squared deviations of X from $\bar{X}$ (column 4) and the numerator is the sum of the *cross products* of the deviations in X and Y from their respective means (column 6). Upon using formula (1.17), the ratio of the two yields the slope of the least squares line, $b_1 = .206$ in this case. Using formula (1.15), we find the inter-

Table 1.3. Information for Least Squares Computations of Data in Table 1.2

(1) Y_i	(2) X_i	(3) $X_i - \bar{X}$	(4) $(X_i - \bar{X})^2$	(5) $Y_i - \bar{Y}$	(6) $(X_i - \bar{X})(Y_i - \bar{Y})$
30	100	-200	40,000	-40	8,000
40	200	-100	10,000	-30	3,000
40	300	0	0	-30	0
70	200	-100	10,000	0	0
110	400	100	10,000	40	4,000
130	600	300	90,000	60	18,000
420	1,800	0	160,000	0	33,000

$$\bar{X} = \frac{1800}{6} = 300$$

$$\bar{Y} = \frac{420}{6} = 70$$

$$b_1 = \frac{\sum (X_i - \bar{X})(Y_i - \bar{Y})}{\sum (X_i - \bar{X})^2} = \frac{33,000}{160,000} = .206$$

$$b_0 = \bar{Y} - b_1\bar{X} = 70 - .206(300) = 8.1$$

The least squares equation is $Y = 8.1 + .21X + e$

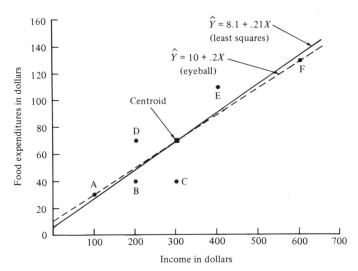

Figure 1.3 Comparison of "Eyeball" and Least Squares Lines of Relationship Between Weekly Food Expenditures and Family Income.

cept term by subtracting b_1 times the mean of X from the mean of Y. In this case, $b_0 = 8.1$. Thus the *least squares regression line* through the points in the example is $\hat{Y} = 8.1 + .206X_i$ and the basic *regression equation* is $Y_i = 8.1 + .206X_i + e_i$. Figure 1.3 shows the least squares line in relation to the eyeball line.

Calculating b_0 and b_1 by hand is a tedious and even difficult exercise, especially with a large number of paired values for X and Y. Fortunately, researchers generally have access to calculators or computers that rapidly perform the least squares calculations for them. When beginning the study of econometrics, however, working through several relatively simple least squares problems is a good idea, for several reasons. First, manually calculating b_0 and b_1 stresses the mechanical nature of the computations and enhances understanding of how the formulas work. Second, after a few simple least squares lines have been calculated manually, the least squares results that appear on computer printouts are less mystical.

Writing Variables in Deviation Form

The normal way to write the regression slope is

$$b_1 = \frac{\sum_i (X_i - \bar{X})(Y_i - \bar{Y})}{\sum_i (X_i - \bar{X})^2} \tag{1.18}$$

because it permits interpreting b_1 as the ratio of a covariance and a variance. However, it takes time and space to write this expression continually, so it is conventional to use a shorthand notation that expresses the variables in the equation as deviations from their respective means.

The *least squares residual* is defined as

$$e_i = Y_i - \hat{Y}_i \tag{1.19}$$

where Y_i is the actual value of Y and $\hat{Y}_i$ is the regression, or predicted, value of Y. Summing both sides yields

$$\Sigma\, e_i = \Sigma\, Y_i - \Sigma\, \hat{Y}_i \tag{1.20}$$

but

$$\begin{aligned}
\Sigma\, \hat{Y}_i &= nb_0 + b_1\, \Sigma\, X_i \\
&= n(\overline{Y} - b_1\overline{X}) + nb_1\overline{X} \\
&= n\overline{Y} \\
&= \Sigma\, Y_i
\end{aligned} \tag{1.21}$$

hence

$$\Sigma\, e_i = \Sigma\, Y_i - \Sigma\, Y_i = 0 \tag{1.22}$$

which says that $(1/n)\, \Sigma\, e_i = 0$. It follows that

$$\overline{Y} = b_0 + b_1\overline{X} \tag{1.23}$$

is the average of

$$Y_i = b_0 + b_1 X_i + e_i \tag{1.24}$$

over the n sample observations. Subtracting the average from each of the individual values yields

$$Y_i - \overline{Y} = (b_0 + b_1 X_i + e_i) - (b_0 + b_1\overline{X}) = b_1(X_i - \overline{X}) + e_i \tag{1.25}$$

The n values on the left-hand side of the equation are computed by subtracting the average of Y from each individual value of Y. The n values on the right-hand side are computed by subtracting the average of X from each individual value of X. In other words, the Y and X values are expressed as deviations from their respective means. Let lowercase letters represent variables expressed in deviation form and write

$$y_i = b_1 x_i + e_i \tag{1.26}$$

as the *regression equation in deviation form*. By manipulations similar to those above, the regression slope can be written as

$$b_1 = \frac{\Sigma\, x_i y_i}{\Sigma\, x_i^2} \tag{1.27}$$

Because (1.27) is quicker and simpler to write, it is used extensively in the remainder of this book. Note, however, that b_0 has not been "lost," as it can always be "recovered" by $(\overline{Y} - b_1\overline{X})$. Lowercase letters are used throughout this book to represent variables measured in deviation form.

Summary

The method of least squares is a mathematical technique for calculating a regression line that summarizes and describes the functional relationship between a set of points. The technique, based on the principle of minimizing the sum of the squared residuals, has the desirable property of mathematical objectivity. But what, if anything, can be said *in general* about family food consumption and disposable income on the basis of a least squares calculation? Answers to such crucial questions require an understanding of the statistical and econometric propositions presented in the remainder of the book.

The purpose of this chapter was to introduce, in an easy and acceptable manner, the principle of least squares. This powerful principle forms the basis of empirical research in many disciplines.

The least squares criterion was invoked in order to get sufficient information to solve the problem of drawing a line of average relationship in a nonsubjective way. But the least squares criterion did not slide down the mountain, etched forever in stone. Least squares is only one of many criteria that could have been chosen. It is possible, for example, to choose b_0 and b_1 to minimize the sum of the absolute value of e_i, or to make all the e_i positive or negative, and so on. It just so happens that the criterion of least squares provides estimates that possess many useful and desirable properties. For this reason, much of the empirical knowledge we have of the world in which we live is based on the least squares principle.

Terms

Centroid	Outlier
Cross product	Regression coefficient
Dependent variable	Regression equation
Deviations	Regression line
Econometrics	Residual
Explanatory variable	Scatter diagram
Intercept	Slope
Least squares	Sum of squared residuals (ESS)
Normal equations	

Exercises

1.1 Use the information in Table 1.2 for parts (a) to (f).
  (a) Plot the six points on a graph where the vertical Y axis represents food consumption and the horizontal X axis represents disposable income.
  (b) Draw the line that appears to "fit" the six points best. (Remember that such lines should go through the centroid.)

(c) What is the equation for the line drawn in part (b)? Specifically, what are the values for the intercept (b_0) and the slope (b_1) of the line?
(d) Use (1.15) and (1.16) to calculate the least squares values for b_0 and b_1. (HINT: See Table 1.3 for one technique.)
(e) Draw the least squares line on the scatter diagram prepared under part (a).
(f) Are the freehand line in parts (b) and (c) and the least squares line in parts (e) and (d) different? Would that always be the case?

1.2 Consider the following five points:

Name	X-Value	Y-Value
H	1	8
J	2	5
K	3	6
L	4	1
M	5	5

(a) Plot the five points and the centroid. Be sure that Y is the vertical axis and X is the horizontal axis.
(b) Draw a line that appears to fit the five points.
(c) Find the b_0 and b_1 for the line you drew in part (b).
(d) Find the residuals. Specifically, calculate $e_i = Y_i - (b_0 + b_1 X_i)$ for $i = H$, J, K, L, and M.
(e) Calculate the sum of the squared residuals ($\Sigma\ e_i^2$) for the line drawn in part (b).
(f) Now calculate the ordinary least squares b_0 and b_1 for the five points. Label them b_0^* and b_1^*.
(g) Find the new residuals. Specifically, find $e_i^* = Y_i - (b_0^* + b_1^* X_i)$ for $i = H$, J, K, L, and M.
(h) Calculate the new sum of squared residuals ($\Sigma\ e_i^{*2}$).
(i) Which line leads to the smaller sum of squared residuals? Does any line exist that leads to a smaller sum of squared residuals?

1.3
(a) In Exercise 1.2, what is the simple sum of all residuals based on the least squares line?
(b) Demonstrate that the sum of residuals is always equal to zero.
(c) Does *any* line through the centroid *always* lead to residuals that sum to zero?

1.4 For four dairy farms, the number of cows and number of acres are known to be as follows:

Name	Cows	Acres
Adams	28	114
Brown	29	122
Cavett	30	116
Davis	37	128

(a) Plot acres (X axis) versus cows (Y axis).

(b) Calculate each of the following numbers: $\Sigma\, X_i Y_i$, n, $\overline{Y}$, $\overline{X}$, and $\Sigma\, X_i^2$.

(c) Find b_1 using (1.16) and b_0 using (1.15).

(d) Plot the least squares line on the scatter plot from part (a).

(e) What is the centroid? Does the line in part (d) pass through the centroid?

(f) Express cows and acres in deviations from their respective means.

(g) Find the least squares b_1 using (1.27).

(h) Are the b_1's in parts (c) and (g) identical?

(i) Plot the deviations (x_i versus y_i) and least squares line on a separate graph. What is the intercept of this line?

(j) How is the graph of part (i) related to the graph of parts (a) and (e)?

1.5 Consider 10 observations on X and Y:

i	X_i	Y_i
1	5	18
2	7	16
3	9	14
4	11	12
5	13	10
6	15	8
7	17	6
8	19	4
9	21	2
10	23	0

What is

(a) $\displaystyle\sum_{i=4}^{7} X_i$?

(b) $\displaystyle\sum_{i} Y_i$?

(c) $\displaystyle\sum_{i=3}^{4} Y_i$?

(d) $\displaystyle\sum_{i=4}^{8} 17Y_i$?

(e) $\displaystyle 12\sum_{i=9}^{10} Y_i$?

(f) $\displaystyle\sum_{i=8}^{10} (X_i + Y_i)$?

(g) $\displaystyle\sum_{i=1}^{3} X_i Y_i$?

1.6 Suppose that a researcher wanted to estimate the parameters in the simple population equation $Y = \beta_0 + \beta_1 X + u$. The actual observations on X and Y are not available, but the following data were calculated from a sample of 10 observations:

$$\begin{array}{llll}
\Sigma\,Y & = & 580 & \Sigma\,y & = & 0 \\
\Sigma\,X & = & 50 & \Sigma\,x & = & 0 \\
\Sigma\,XY & = & 2{,}246 & \Sigma\,xy & = & -654 \\
\Sigma\,Y^2 & = & 41{,}208 & \Sigma\,y^2 & = & 7{,}568 \\
\Sigma\,X^2 & = & 310 & \Sigma\,x^2 & = & 60
\end{array}$$

(a) What is b_1?
(b) What is b_0?

1.7 Four people are allowed to pick pennies from the bottom of a pool. Each finds Y_i dollars worth of pennies during the X_i minutes the four people are allowed in the pool:

Person	Dollars Found, Y_i	Minutes, X_i
A	2.00	1
B	5.00	2
C	6.00	3
D	7.00	6

(a) What is the centroid for this sample?
(b) What is b_1 of the least squares line $Y_i = b_0 + b_1 X_i$?
(c) What is b_0 of the least squares line $Y_i = b_0 + b_1 X_i$?
(d) Interpretation: People tend to find about _____ for each additional minute in the pool.

1.8 A researcher has a set of paired observations on two variables (Y_i, X_i) and is interested in the following sample regression equation:

$$Y_i = b_0 + b_1 X_i + e_i$$

To use the sample of data to compute b_0 and b_1, the researcher proposes to employ the principle of least squares. Using both words and arithmetic expressions, present and discuss the criterion this principle uses to obtain numerical values for b_0 and b_1.

1.9 Let $e_i = Y_i - (b_0 + b_1 X_i)$. If b_0 and b_1 are chosen using the least squares residual principle, we know that for any sample:

(a) $\dfrac{\sum\limits_i y_i x_i}{\sum\limits_i x_i^2} = $ _____

(b) $\bar{Y} - b_1 \bar{X} = $ _____

(c) $\sum\limits_i e_i = $ _____

(d) $e_i = $ _____ if $X_i = \bar{X}$ and $Y_i = \bar{Y} + 8$

1.10 Consider the following data on number of fish caught (Y_i) and hours fished (X_i) by six people:

Person	Fish Caught, Y_i	Hours Fished, X_i
Al	6	4
Betty	12	4
Chuck	8	5
Doris	16	6
Elvis	22	7
Fran	20	10

(a) Plot fish caught $(Y$ axis) versus hours fished $(X$ axis) on a scatter graph and label it "graph 1."

(b) Calculate n, $\sum_i Y_i$, $\sum_i X_i$, $\bar{Y}$, $\bar{X}$, $\sum_i X_i^2$, $\sum_i Y_i X_i$, $n\overline{YX}$, and $n\bar{X}^2$.

(c) Does $\sum_i Y_i X_i = (\sum_i Y_i)(\sum_i X_i)$?

(d) Does $n\bar{X} = \sum_i X_i$? Does $n\bar{Y} = \sum_i Y_i$?

(e) Calculate b_1 using (1.16).

(f) Calculate b_0 using (1.15).

(g) Draw the least squares line on graph 1.

(h) Calculate x_i and y_i for all six people.

(i) Plot y_i versus x_i from part (h) on a new scattergraph and label it "graph 2."

(j) Calculate $\sum_i x_i^2$ and $\sum_i x_i y_i$.

(k) Calculate b_1 from (1.27).

(l) Do the answers in parts (k) and (e) agree?

(m) Would the answer in part (l) be true for all sets of data?

(n) Draw the regression line on graph 2.

(o) What is the intercept and slope of the regression line in graph 2?

(p) What is the intercept and slope of the regression line in graph 1?

(q) Are the slopes in graphs 1 and 2 identical? the intercepts?

(r) What is the centroid in graph 1? in Graph 2?

(s) Does the regression line go through both centroids?

(t) Fill in the blank: Regression analysis reveals that people tend to catch _____ more fish for each additional hour they spend fishing.

2

What Is Econometrics?

Economic theory is a rich source of such statements as the following: "As income increases, the consumption of a normal good increases" and "The competitive firm will reduce its output in response to a fall in market price." These and similar statements derived from theory provide valuable insights into how a market economy attempts to allocate scarce resources among the competing demands for those resources and the products that can be manufactured from them. Theory is the framework that helps us think about and understand how a market economy functions. Moreover, as the two statements above suggest, theory often permits us to make predictions regarding the direction of change in one variable in response to changes in other variables.

For many purposes, the ability to predict the direction of change ("Consumption will increase as income increases") is sufficient. However, it is often necessary to go beyond this to predict how much the change will be (e.g., "Consumption will increase 1 gallon per week as income increases $50 per week"). We must, in other words, measure important economic relationships. Econometrics, as its root words indicate, is the study of methods and procedures that can be used to determine numerical values for these relationships. Econometrics is a subdiscipline of economics, but it draws heavily from mathematics and statistics to achieve its objective of measurement.

Although econometrics is the specific subject of this book, the general subject is applied research, of which econometrics is a part. The basic premise of this book is that theory plays the dominant role in applied research by providing the framework within which the relationships to be measured are identified and the research findings are to be evaluated. Social value attaches to applied research by virtue of its ability to provide quantitative answers to questions posed to policymakers and decision makers.

In Chapter 1 we posed a simple research question by way of motivating interest in the least squares principle. In this chapter we elaborate on the research theme by presenting an overview of how the econometrician blends economic theory, statistics, mathematics, and research philosophy to measure economic relationships. Once the research problem is defined, the researcher proceeds by constructing a logical system of behavior, or model, appropriate to the research objective. Using sample data, the applied researcher tests hypotheses proposed by this economic model. The results of these tests lead to new insights regarding the proper formulation of the model that lead, in turn, to new hypotheses to be tested. This continual back-and-forth between model formulation and hypothesis testing, this act of doing applied research, results in accumulated empirical knowledge of the system being studied. To do this effectively, the researcher must have a solid understanding not only of economics but also of statistical theory, especially the notions of sampling, estimation theory, and hypothesis testing. Data collection and measurement are of little social value unless buttressed by theory and an understanding of accepted research procedures. In the following sections we outline the steps of applied research and review the important statistical concepts and ideas used in subsequent chapters.

Applied Research

The structure of, or sequence of steps in, applied research is discussed in this section. The main objective is to highlight the interrelatedness of theory, mathematics, and statistics in achieving the objective of measurement. The discussion is organized around the flow diagram in Figure 2.1.

Problem Definition

Applied research begins with problem definition. The Secretary of Agriculture needs to know the elasticity of supply response to determine an appropriate price policy. A public official needs to know the income elasticity of food consumption to assess the implications of income changes on the need for food stamps. A community development specialist needs to know the employment multiplier for a proposed investment in a local manufacturing facility. An official of a grain exporting firm needs to know the import demand function for grains in several major countries. As this suggests, much research is initiated in response to the needs of decision makers in both the public and private sectors. But intellectual curiosity is also an important stimulus of research. Investigating new questions and reinvestigating old questions from a new perspective, with different analytical methods or with a new data set, is an integral part of society's research program, even though the results of these endeavors may not have immediate implications for decision makers. Developing new and extending existing theories to gain a deeper understanding of the world in which we live is of great importance. The advent of the computer, with its power of rapid computation, has stimulated research on more effective and efficient estimation procedures for use by the applied researcher who must estimate a supply response elasticity. Thus research begins with problem definition, whether prompted by intellectual curiosity at one end of the spectrum or by the immediate needs of decision makers at the other end of the spectrum. Although clear lines of demarcation cannot be drawn, this spectrum can be said to range from basic research to applied research. This book is directed to the latter.

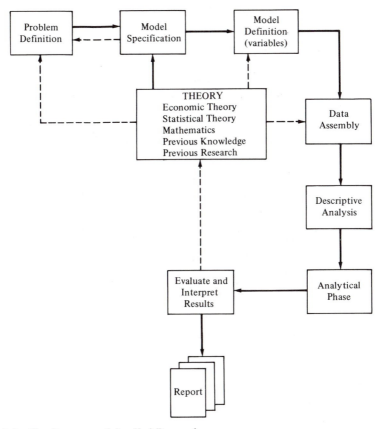

Figure 2.1   The Structure of Applied Research.

Problem definition is, in many ways, the most important and often the most difficult step in applied research. A mixture of skill, extensive reformulation of the problem, and luck is usually required to transform a general question into one that can be meaningfully answered within the constraints of available time and resources. Applied research is more an art than a science because there is no recipe that applies universally. Rather, each research setting casts up its own unique set of problems to be resolved by the applied researcher. In every real sense, "applied research" refers more to a way of thinking about how to answer a question or solve a problem than to a recipe for answering all questions. We try, as best we can, in this book to give you some insights into this way of thinking, but the only way you can really learn how to do applied research is to do applied research.

Model Specification

Given the problem definition, the next step is specifying the economic model appropriate to the research question. This begins with theory, specifically with that aspect of theory pertaining to the problem at hand, such as production theory, demand theory, trade theory, and the like. As suggested by Figure 2.1, theory must be defined broadly to include not only pure theory but also prior, or personal, knowledge and previous research on the problem at hand. Theory is singularly important because it identifies the variables to include in the analysis; it serves as a screening device by sifting out what is not important.

At this point it is helpful to introduce an *implicit* or *generic equation* as a summary device. The result of theorizing about the problem at hand can be summarized by using an implicit equation, written as

$$Y = f(X_1, X_2, \ldots, X_K) \tag{2.1}$$

which says that Y, the variable of interest, depends on or is a function of K independent variables identified by the underlying theory. This equation provides only an abstract view of the relationship being studied, as it says nothing about the explicit functional relationship among the variables. However, the underlying theory often indicates the direction of change in Y resulting from changes in the independent variables. This can be expressed by the partial derivative of (2.1). For example, if Y is the consumption of oranges and X_2 is income, theory predicts that an increase in income will result in an increased consumption of oranges. This can be written mathematically as

$$\frac{\partial Y}{\partial X_2} > 0 \tag{2.2}$$

Similar statements for the other variables in the implicit equation can often be made. Equations such as (2.2) provide one source of hypotheses to be tested by the applied researcher.

In summary, the first step in applied research is to use economic theory, broadly defined, to identify the variables important to the problem at hand. This theorizing is summarized by an implicit function such as (2.1), which expresses the dependent variable as a function of the variables identified by theory as being important in determining how the dependent variable changes. In addition, this stage of the research process typically leads to equations like (2.2) that indicate the direction of change in the dependent variable in response to changes in the independent variables. These *predictions* of theory ultimately become hypotheses to be tested.

Empirical Definition of Model

Although the implicit function is the necessary first step, it must be transformed into an explicit function, or equation, before proceeding to estimation. Two things must be done: Write an explicit mathematical form for the equation and construct empirical measures of the conceptual variables in (2.1). These are discussed briefly in the following two sections.

Role of Mathematics

The important point made here is that an explicit mathematical equation makes a definite economic statement about the system being studied. The applied researcher must be careful regarding the form of the equation to be estimated. Suppose that the *explicit equation* is

$$Y = b_0 + b_1X_1 + b_2X_2 \tag{2.3}$$

where Y = consumption of oranges
     X_1 = price of oranges
     X_2 = consumer income

The change in the consumption of oranges in response to a price change is

$$\frac{\partial Y}{\partial X_1} = b_1 \tag{2.4}$$

and the consumption response to an income change is

$$\frac{\partial Y}{\partial X_2} = b_2 \tag{2.5}$$

Thus the mathematical form of (2.3) makes the following economic statements: The effect of a price change on consumption is the same regardless of the level of income (2.4); the effect of an income change is the same regardless of the price level (2.5). These may be correct statements, but it could be argued that the effect of a given price change on consumption would be different for different levels of income. Similarly,

$$\frac{\partial^2 Y}{\partial X_2^2} = 0 \tag{2.6}$$

This says that a given income change will have the same effect on consumption regardless of the level at which the income change occurs. Yet it is possible that an income change of $1000 at an income level of $8000 will have a different effect on consumption than a $1000 income change at $20,000. If this is the case, (2.6) will not equal zero. Rather, the effect of an income change on consumption will itself be a function of the level of income, as stated by

$$\frac{\partial^2 Y}{\partial X_2^2} = f(X_2) \tag{2.7}$$

The economic statements made by particular mathematical equations are discussed in Chapter 11.

Defining Empirical Variables

Another aspect of defining the empirical model is deciding on empirical measures of the variables identified as important by the underlying theory. The basic idea is that the conceptual variables incorporated in the implicit economic model, (2.1), such as income, production, substitutes, competing crops, tastes and preferences, price, and so on, must be measured in empirical, or observable, terms. For example, the concepts "consumption," "price," and "income" were used above in a meaningful way without giving them any empirical definition. For the theoretical reasoning done prior to estimation, it is sufficient to work with conceptual variables. But if quantitative answers are required, that is, if the research objective is to determine numerical values for b_0, b_1, and b_2 in equation (2.3), it is necessary to define in observable terms precisely what is meant by each of these conceptual variables. In this example, as in most research situations, a number of choices regarding the specific measures to use is available. There is no hard rule for selecting which to use; rather, it depends on the objective of the applied research and on the results of experimenting with alternative measures. For example, the price of oranges can be empirically measured as the season's average price received by all farmers in the United States, as the price for navel oranges received by California farmers, as the price received for processing oranges, or as the price in the export market. The point is that for any conceptual variable defined by theory, there typically exist a number of alternative empirical measures. Choosing which is appropriate to the project at hand is not to be taken lightly. If the empirical measures chosen are not measuring the concepts used in the underlying theory, the quantitative statements subsequently made will be of questionable validity. Certain aspects of this problem, known in regression analysis as measurement error, are discussed in more detail in Chapter 15.

Data Assembly and Worksheets

The values for the empirical variables must be collected and assembled in a systematic way prior to entering them into the computer for analysis. In some cases it may be necessary to conduct a survey to collect the needed data; in other cases, published data may be readily available. The best way to organize and record the values is to use a *worksheet*. The columns of the worksheet identify the variables to be used in the analysis and the rows contain the respective values of the variables for each observation in the data set. Developing a worksheet is discussed in Chapters 7 and 8.

Once the worksheet is completed, the data are ready to enter into the computer. It is good practice, once the data are in the computer, to print out the worksheet immediately and compare it with the original worksheet as a check for errors in data entry. Additional types of data checks should be conducted, such as plotting the variables to detect extreme values. For large data sets, this is useful because it is impossible to rely on a visual check using the two worksheets. The importance of checking the worksheet in the computer cannot be overstressed because seemingly small errors, such as transposition of numbers, can lead to large errors in the resulting estimates.

Descriptive Analysis

Before the formal analysis begins, it is good practice to get a "feel" of the data set you are working with. This requires doing such simple things as computing the averages and standard deviations for the variables to get some idea of the typical values for each variable and of their relative variation. Computing the simple correlations between each pair of variables gives a feel for how much covariation there is between the variables in the data set, an important issue when wrestling with the problem of multicollinearity discussed in Chapter 12. It is also desirable to prepare simple plots of the variables, which not only indicate how the variables change over the observations in the data set, but also help to identify extreme cases that should be checked before proceeding to analysis.

Analytical Phase

Once satisfied that the data have been entered correctly, the researcher is ready to conduct the analysis. Since the remainder of this book is concerned primarily with this phase of research, nothing more will be said about it here.

Evaluation and Interpretation

As evaluation and interpretation also are both primary subjects of this book they need not be discussed in detail here, but two points require emphasis. The primary evaluative criteria are provided by the theory underlying the applied research. Questions such as "Do the signs of the coefficients agree with theoretical expectations?" must be asked and answered to the researcher's satisfaction. Statistical results in the form of hypothesis testing are used to help determine whether the variables in the equation are statistically signficiant.

As suggested by the flow diagram in Figure 2.1, this research phase may or may not lead to preparing the research report. Often it does not. Evaluating the results may reveal problems, such as wrong signs, insignificant variables, or a low proportion of explained variation, that the researcher finds disturbing. As the flow diagram suggests, this means "going back to the drawing board" to think through the problem once again, using the first-round results to ask new questions regarding how the problem might be reformulated, what conceptual variables may have been omitted, whether the mathematical form of the equation is correct, and so on. Once these questions have been resolved to the satisfaction of the researcher, the research report can be prepared.

Theory of Estimation

In the preceding section we discussed the steps followed in doing applied research, emphasizing the respective roles of theory, mathematics, and statistics in formulating the problem, doing the estimation, and evaluating the results. In this section we elaborate on the analytical phase of applied research by reviewing the theory of estimation that provides the framework for estimating the coefficients of an empirical model, such as (2.3). This requires an understanding of statistical theory, which is concerned with methods for using sample data to make quantitative statements about population parameters. Stated alternatively, statistical theory shows how to use sample data to draw inferences about the characteristics of the population from which the sample was drawn. The theory of estimation and the structure of simple hypothesis testing are presented in this and the following section.

Much of the following discussion may appear abstract and quite distant from the nuts and bolts of doing applied research. However, we happen to believe in the old adage that "there is nothing as practical as a good theory": Theory provides the guidelines for empirical work and theory provides the interpretive framework for evaluating the results of empirical work. The theory of estimation is presented in general terms, but each step in the development of the theory is illustrated by using as an example how the sample average of a variable is used to estimate the population average of the variable.

A Population and a Random Variable

A *population* is a collection of elements (people, farms, states, business firms) about which quantitative, or numerical, information is desired. The population of interest is always defined in the context of a specific research question. For example, the population of interest might be all undergraduate students in a university, or all farms in a state, or all consumers of oranges. Typically, the objective of research is making quantitative statements about characteristics of the population: The researcher might want to determine the grade-point average (GPA) of all students, or the average farm size, or the average consumption of oranges. Characteristics of populations, such as GPA, farm size, and consumption of oranges, are called *variables*, signifying that the values of these characteristics are likely to vary across the elements of the population. This leads to a *random variable*, central in estimation theory, defined formally as follows:

> **A random variable is a variable defined on a population that takes on different numerical values in the population with known relative frequencies or probabilities.**

To illustrate, consider the population of farms shown in Table 2.1. In this simple illustration, farm size is the variable defined on the population. It is a "random" variable because it takes on different numerical values over the population elements.

For this population of only 10 elements, a visual examination is sufficient to obtain an idea of farm size and the degree of variation of farm size in the population. However, in most research situations, the population is much larger, and it is not possible to list all the values of the random variable defined on that population. Consequently, a method for describing, or summarizing, the distribution of the values of the variable is needed. Statistical theory offers a number of such summary statistics,

Table 2.1. Population of 10 Farms

Farm Identification	Farm Size (Acres)
1	25
2	338
3	275
4	1450
5	36
6	45
7	21
8	1500
9	350
10	900

or population parameters. You may recall from a statistics course that the mean, variance, standard deviation, median, mode, quartiles, measure of skewness, and so on, were used to describe the distribution of a random variable. In the following, only the mean and variance are used to describe the distribution.

Let X_i represent the value of the random variable for the ith population element. In the population, above, $X_1 = 25$, $X_5 = 36$, and so on, for each of the 10 population elements. By definition

$$\text{mean of } X = \mu = \tfrac{1}{10}(25 + 338 + \cdots + 900) = 494 \tag{2.8}$$

and

$$\text{variance of } X = \sigma^2 = \tfrac{1}{10}[(25 - 494)^2 + \cdots + (900 - 494)^2]$$
$$= 303{,}980 \tag{2.9}$$

where μ is the measure of central tendency of the values and σ^2 is the measure of the dispersion of the individual values of X around μ.

In general, a random variable is defined on a population identified by the research objective. In this and the following chapters, only the mean, μ, and variance, σ^2, of the random variable are used to describe a distribution. Because means and variances of random variables are computed frequently in this book, it is convenient to have a shorthand notation to represent the computations used in (2.8) and (2.9). This notation is developed in the next section, following which we return to estimation theory.

The Expected Value Operator

The formula for computing the mean can be written in a slightly different and instructive way:

$$\mu = (\tfrac{1}{10})25 + (\tfrac{1}{10})338 + \cdots + (\tfrac{1}{10})900 = 494 \tag{2.10}$$

This expresses the mean as the weighted sum of the individual values of the random variable, where the weights are the respective frequencies with which the values occur. Since there are 10 values in the population of Table 2.1, the frequency of each is $\tfrac{1}{10}$. It is also clear that the sum of the weights over the 10 population elements is equal to 1. This leads to the general definition of the *expectation operator*, E. Let Y be a random variable and write

$$E(X) = f_1 X_1 + f_2 X_2 + \cdots + f_N X_N = \sum_i^N f_i X_i \tag{2.11}$$

which says that the *expected value* of the random variable is computed as the *weighted sum* of the individual values of the variable where

1. the weights are the frequencies of occurrence, and
2. the weights sum to 1.0.

In general, the E-operator computes the weighted sum of whatever is included in the term to which it is attached. For example, let the random variable be $[X - E(X)]^2$ and write

$$E[X_i - E(X)]^2 = f_1[X_1 - E(X)]^2 + \cdots + f_N[X_N - E(X)]^2 \tag{2.12}$$

This is the weighted sum, or the average, of the squared deviations of the individual values of X about $E(X)$ and is the variance of X.

If we use standard notation, the population mean is usually denoted as μ and the variance as σ^2. However, there are many instances where it is more convenient to use the expectation operator. From here on, writing the expression $E(X)$ means that the computation shown in (2.11) is to be performed.

If you have two random variables X and Y with expected values μ_x and μ_y and variance σ_x^2 and σ_y^2, the *covariance* of X and Y, σ_{xy}^2, is defined as

$$E[X_i - E(X)][Y_i - E(Y)] = f_1[X_1 - E(X)][Y_1 - E(Y)] + \cdots$$
$$+ f_N[X_N - E(X)][Y_N - E(Y)] \quad (2.13)$$
$$= E(XY) - \mu_x\mu_y$$

A number of theorems regarding the expectation operator are useful. Let X and Y be random variables and a and b be constants.

Theorem 1

$$E(a) = a$$

The expected value of a constant is the constant.

Theorem 2

$$E(aX) = aE(X)$$

The expected value of a constant times a random variable is equal to the constant times the expected value of the random variable.

Theorem 3

$$E(X + Y) = E(X) + E(Y)$$

The expected value of the sum of random variables is equal to the sum of the expected values of the random variables.

Theorem 4

$$E(aX + bY) = aE(X) + bE(Y)$$

Combines Theorems 1 through 3.

Theorem 5

In general, $E(XY)$ is not equal to $E(X)E(Y)$, and $E(X/Y)$ is not equal to $E(X)/E(Y)$.

Population Values and Sample Estimates

Usually, the objective of applied research is to make a quantitative statement about the value of a population parameter, such as the mean, total, proportion, and variance. One method for making such statements is to conduct a *census*. This involves obtaining the value of the random variable from each element in the population and computing the parameter. For example, in the simple population of Table 2.1, acreage would be obtained from each farm, summed over all farms, and divided by the number of farms to obtain the average farm size in the population.

An alternative is to take a *sample*, a subset of the population elements, and use the sample values to compute a number, say the sample mean, to use as an estimate of the population average. Suppose that the research objective is to estimate the average farm size for the population in Table 2.1 using a sample of size 2. The procedure is to select two farms at random and compute that sample mean. Suppose that farms 2 and 7 are selected. The sample mean, and hence the estimate of the population mean, is $(338 + 21)/2 = 179.5$ acres. Two things should be noted. First, this estimate misses the known average of 494 by a wide margin. Second, if farms 4 and 8 had been selected instead of farms 2 and 7, the estimate would have been $(1450 + 1500)/2 = 1475$ acres, which not only is substantially different from the first estimate but is also wide of the mark. This illustrates two important aspects of estimating population parameters: Different samples will yield different estimates of the parameter, and some estimates will be close to the true value whereas others will miss it by a wide margin. This, of course, is no problem in the simple illustration, since the true value of the population mean is known. However, in applied research the true value is not known (if it were, there would be no need to estimate it in the first place). To cope with this problem in applied research, we use the concept of a *sampling distribution* and its parameters.

There are 45 different samples of size 2 that can be drawn from the population of 10 farms in Table 2.2. For each of these samples, a sample mean can be computed and used as an estimate of the population mean. The 45 different samples and sample means are presented in Table 2.2.

Table 2.1 shows the distribution of the random variable "farm size" in the population; Table 2.2 shows the distribution of the random variable "sample mean" for all different samples of size 2 drawn from the population. Like the distribution of farm size in the population, the distribution of sample means has a mean, $E[\overline{X}]$, and a variance, $E[\overline{X}_i - E(\overline{X})]^2$.

This table can be used to elaborate on the definition of a random variable given above. The probability of drawing a particular sample of two farms, and hence obtaining a particular value for the random variable "sample mean," is 1 in 45, as there are 45 different samples of size 2. However, there is no way to know in advance which particular sample will be drawn; each is equally likely to be selected. This aspect of "randomness" has implications for the applied researcher. As Table 2.2 shows, the sample means range widely, from a low of 23.0 (sample 6) to a high of 1475.0 (sample 28). This demonstrates a problem the researcher faces. Typically, only one sample is available for making a statement about the population. Yet the

Table 2.2. Means of All Different Samples of Size $n = 2$ Drawn from the Population in Table 2.1

Sample Number	Sample Elements		Sample Mean
1	25	338	181.5
2	25	275	150.0
3	25	1450	737.5
4	25	36	30.5
5	25	45	35.0
6	25	21	23.0
7	25	1500	762.5
8	25	350	184.5
9	25	900	462.5
10	338	275	306.5
11	338	1450	894.0
12	338	36	187.0
13	338	45	191.5
14	338	21	179.5
15	338	1500	919.0
16	338	350	344.0
17	338	900	619.0
18	275	1450	862.5
19	275	36	155.5
20	275	45	160.0
21	275	21	148.8
22	275	1500	887.5
23	275	350	312.5
24	275	900	587.5
25	1450	36	743.0
26	1450	45	747.5
27	1450	21	735.5
28	1450	1500	1475.0
29	1450	350	900.0
30	1450	900	1174.0
31	36	45	40.5
32	36	21	28.5
33	36	1500	768.0
34	36	350	193.0
35	36	900	468.0
36	45	21	33.0
37	45	1500	772.5
38	45	350	197.5
39	45	900	472.5
40	21	1500	760.5
41	21	350	185.5
42	21	900	460.5
43	1500	350	925.0
44	1500	900	1200.0
45	350	900	625.0

table shows that such statements can be wide of the mark. For this reason, some way is needed to measure how "good" an estimate is. The theory of estimation is very helpful in this regard.

Estimators and Estimates

Using our illustration, we can introduce the general notation of estimation. Let θ be a *population parameter* to be estimated, $\hat{\theta}$ be an *estimator* of θ, and $\hat{\theta}_i$ be an *estimate* of θ based on the *i*th sample. In the context of Table 2.2, θ is μ, the population mean; $\hat{\theta}$ is the formula for computing a sample mean; and $\hat{\theta}_i$ is $\bar{x}_i$, the mean of the *i*th sample. The estimator is defined as

$$\bar{x} = \frac{1}{n} \sum_{i}^{n} x_i = \frac{1}{n} (x_1 + x_2 + \cdots + x_n) \tag{2.14}$$

where the lowercase *x* represents the values in the sample (not deviations from the mean as defined in Chapter 1) and *n* is the sample size. Equation (2.14) illustrates the definition of an estimator:

> **An estimator is a rule, a formula, an algorithm, a recipe that is applied to the data in a specific sample to compute an estimate of the population parameter.**

Sample 2 contains the sample data 25 and 275: Using the rule (the estimator) for computing a sample mean yields an estimate of 150 acres. Similarly, the estimator applied to the data in sample 31 yields an estimate of 40.5 acres. In other words, all the estimates ($\hat{\theta}_i$) in Table 2.2 are generated by the same estimator ($\hat{\theta}$).

An estimate, a number computed by an estimator, is whatever it is (1175 for sample 30), and there is little more that can be said about it. However, something of interest can be said about the estimator that produces the sample estimates. More to the point, we can require the estimator to possess certain desirable properties by specifying the ingredients to be used and how those ingredients are to be combined. The formal properties are stated and then applied to the special case of using the sample mean to estimate the population mean. The properties used in this book follow.

1. The estimator is to be a *linear* function of the sample data:

$$\hat{\theta}_i = w_1 x_{1i} + w_2 x_{2i} + \cdots + w_n x_{ni} = \sum_{j=1}^{n} w_j x_{ji}$$

where the w_j's do not depend on the *x*-values in the sample, *j* goes from 1 to *n* (sample size), and *i* goes from 1 to all different samples of size *n*.

2. The estimator is to be *unbiased*:

$$E(\hat{\theta}_i) = \theta$$

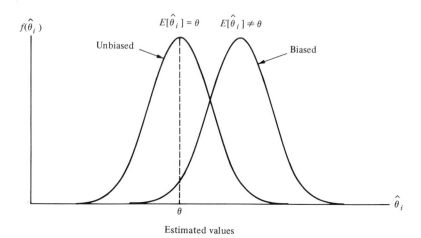

Figure 2.2   Frequency Distribution of Typical "Unbiased" and "Biased" Estimator.

which says that "on average" the estimator is equal to the parameter being estimated. Alternatively, this says that the mean of the sampling distribution is equal to the parameter being estimated. This is illustrated by Figure 2.2.

3. The estimator is a *minimum-variance* estimator. This says that of all possible linear, unbiased estimators of θ, there is no other estimator that has a variance smaller than $E[\hat{\theta}_i - E(\hat{\theta}_i)]^2$, the variance of $\hat{\theta}_i$. The term *efficiency* is often used in reference to the variance of a sampling distribution, the idea being that of two estimators the one with the smaller variance is said to be more efficient. This is illustrated in Figure 2.3. Although the two estimators, $\hat{\theta}_a$ and $\hat{\theta}_b$, are unbiased (their expected values equal the parameter being estimated), $\hat{\theta}_a$ has the smaller variance. The implications of this for the applied researcher are clear: The estimates produced by $\hat{\theta}_a$ tend to cluster much closer around θ, so the researcher is more confident that a particular estimate will be

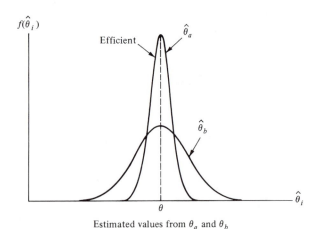

Figure 2.3   Frequency Distribution of Typical "Efficient" and "Inefficient" Estimator.

closer to the "true" value of θ. Hence $\hat{\theta}_a$ is preferred to $\hat{\theta}_b$; $\hat{\theta}_a$ is said to be more efficient.

There are other "nice" properties that can be required of an estimator, but for current purposes these three will suffice. The properties serve as an ideal or standard against which we can evaluate the performance of any estimator and hence determine the degree of confidence we have in the estimates it produces.

Applying these properties to the sample mean yields the following:

$$\bar{x} = \sum_{j=1}^{n} \frac{1}{n} x_j \tag{2.15}$$

where the weights on the sample values, $1/n$, are not dependent on the x-values in the sample. Hence the sample mean is a linear estimator.

For the sample mean to be an unbiased estimator of the population mean, the expected value of the sample mean (the mean of the sampling distribution) must equal the population mean (the parameter being estimated). To see if this is the case, evaluate the following:

$$E(\bar{x}_i) = E\left(\frac{1}{n} \sum_{j}^{n} x_{ji}\right) \tag{2.16}$$

But $E(x_{ji}) = (1/N) \sum_{j}^{N} X_j = \mu$, hence

$$E(\bar{x}_i) = \frac{1}{n} (\mu + \cdots + \mu + \cdots + \mu)$$

$$= \frac{1}{n} (n\mu) \tag{2.17}$$

$$= \mu$$

This general result shows that the sample mean is an unbiased estimator of the population mean. This can be demonstrated in the example above by computing the mean of the 45 sample estimates in Table 2.2:

$$E(\bar{x}_i) = \tfrac{1}{45}(181.5 + 150.0 + \cdots + 625.0) \tag{2.18}$$

$$= 494$$

which is the population mean computed using the population values in Table 2.2.

By definition, the variance of the sampling distribution is

$$\text{Var } (\hat{\theta}) = E[\hat{\theta}_i - E(\hat{\theta})]^2 \tag{2.19}$$

The computation for the sampling distribution in Table 2.2 is

$$\text{Var } (\bar{x}) = \tfrac{1}{45}[(181.5 - 494)^2 + \cdots + (625.0 - 494)^2] \tag{2.20}$$

$$= 135,062$$

The square root of the variance is called the *standard deviation* of the distribution, a statistic used below for constructing confidence intervals and testing hypotheses.

The sample mean is a minimum-variance estimator of the population mean, the proof of which is not offered here. The procedure for proving the minimum variance of an estimator is reserved for Chapter 3, where it is used to demonstrate that a sample regression coefficient is a minimum-variance estimator of a population regression coefficient.

In summary, the applied researcher often uses sample data to make quantitative statements about the values of unobservable population parameters. This is done by using the principles of estimation theory discussed above. Two things were stressed: the general notation of estimation theory and the desired properties of estimators.

Confidence Intervals
and Hypothesis Testing

In practice, the applied researcher computes an estimate, $\hat{\theta}_i$, of θ from the available sample. Although the sample data used to compute this estimate are drawn from the population of interest, the estimate is actually drawn from the sampling distribution of the estimator. In the illustration above, a sample was drawn from the population of farms in Table 2.1 to estimate the average farm size, μ, in the population. Because different samples of size 2 yield different estimates of μ, a particular estimate of μ is drawn from the sampling distribution in Figure 2.3. Consequently, to use $\hat{\theta}_i$ for making a statement about the value of θ requires knowledge of how the sample values of $\hat{\theta}_i$ are distributed.

The *Central Limit Theorem* of statistics tells us that the sampling distribution approaches the *normal distribution* as sample size increases, regardless of the distribution

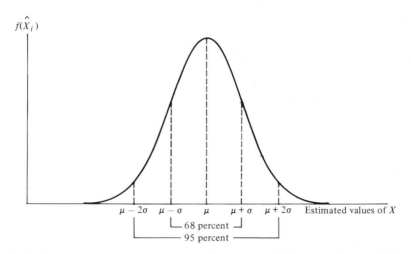

Figure 2.4 The Normal Distribution and Confidence Intervals for a Random Variable X.

of the variable ("farm size") in the population. This theorem is of value to the applied researcher because it allows using the properties of the normal distribution for evaluating an estimator. This is illustrated using the sample mean as an estimator of the population mean.

Figure 2.4 shows the distribution of the sample mean, where $E(\bar{x}) = \mu$ (because the sample mean is an unbiased estimator of the population mean) and s is the standard deviation of the sampling distribution, estimated from the sample.

As shown in Figure 2.4, for the normal distribution, the following statements can be made regarding the relationship between the mean of the sampling distribution and the individual values of the estimates:

68 percent of the estimates lie in the range $\mu \pm 1s$.
95 percent of the estimates lie in the range $\mu \pm 2s$.
99 percent of the estimates lie in the range $\mu \pm 3s$.

In practice, only one sample is available, and these relationships are used in the following way to make probability statements about the value of μ, given a particular estimate $\bar{x}$:

Probability $= .68$ that μ lies in the interval $\bar{x}_i \pm 1s$.
Probability $= .95$ that μ lies in the interval $\bar{x}_i \pm 2s$.
Probability $= .99$ that μ lies in the interval $\bar{x}_i \pm 3s$.

These intervals $\bar{x}_i \pm ks$, where k is the number of standard deviations, are called *confidence intervals* and represent one way that a quantitative statement is made about a population parameter on the basis of sample data. Values of k for different levels of probability are listed in Appendix Table A.1. It is important to note that these are *probability* statements, not *definitive* statements about the value of μ. This "uncertainty" about the true value of μ is the price paid for using a sample rather than a census, a price that normally must be paid in applied research. Confidence intervals are used when the research objective does not predict what the value of μ is or when the researcher is interested only in the range of possible value for the parameter θ.

There are many instances, however, when the researcher is interested in determining the probability that the population parameter θ is equal to a particular value, say θ^*. The source of this particular *hypothesized* value for θ may be the result of previous research, the needs of a policymaker, or the underlying theory guiding the research. This form of the quantitative statement is made in the context of *hypothesis testing*.

The formal structure of an hypothesis test is as follows:

$$H_0: \theta = \theta^* \quad \text{versus} \quad H_a: \theta \neq \theta^*$$

where $H_0 = $ *null hypothesis*
$H_a = $ *alternative hypothesis*
$\theta = $ true but unknown value of the parameter
$\theta^* = $ hypothesized (assumed) numerical value of θ

The decision structure of the test is as follows: Based on a test statistic, the null hypothesis is either *rejected*, in which case the alternative hypothesis is not rejected, or it is *not rejected*, in which case the alternative hypothesis is rejected. The test statistic is computed from the sample as follows:

$$t = \frac{\hat{\theta}_i - \theta^*}{s}$$

where $\hat{\theta}_i$ is the estimate computed from the sample, θ^* is the hypothesized value for θ, and s is the standard deviation computed from the sample. This computed statistic is called the *t-statistic* or the *t-ratio*. It is important to note that the computed *t*-statistic measures the difference between the sample estimate and the hypothesized value for θ in *standard deviation units*, so its structure is similar to that of the confidence interval discussed above. However, as explained in more detail in Chapter 6, the researcher often works with samples that are not "large," which means that the Central Limit Theorem may not apply. In this case, the *t-distribution* is used for hypothesis testing, and the test is conducted by comparing the absolute value of the computed *t*-statistic with the critical *t*-value obtained from a *t-table* showing the critical values of the *t*-distribution for different probability, or confidence, levels. If the computed *t*-statistic is *equal to or less* than the critical *t*-value, the null hypothesis is not rejected; if the computed *t*-statistic is *greater* than the critical *t*-value, the null hypothesis is rejected.

The essence of the test is making a decision on the basis of probabilities. Simply stated, from a given sample an estimate, $\hat{\theta}_i$, is computed, and the question is posed: What is the probability that a sample yielding the number $\hat{\theta}_i$ came from a population where the true value of θ is equal to θ^*? If the probability is "high" that the sample could have been drawn from a population where $\theta = \theta^*$, the null hypothesis is not rejected (and the alternative hypothesis is rejected). If, on the other hand, the probability is "low" that the sample could have been drawn from a population where $\theta = \theta^*$, the null hypothesis is rejected (and the alternative hypothesis is not rejected). In the first case, the applied researcher concludes, on probability grounds, that the sample came from a population where $\theta = \theta^*$; in the second case, the applied researcher concludes, on probability grounds, that the sample came from a population where $\theta \neq \theta^*$. In either case, the number computed from the sample, θ_i, is used as the sample estimate of θ, the unobservable population parameter.

Finally, it is important to understand that one does not prove hypotheses in applied research. This is another way of saying that "fail to reject" is not synonymous with "accept." Observing 10,000 black ravens does not "prove" the hypothesis that "all ravens are black"; the 10,001th raven observed may be white. However, observing 10,000 black ravens makes it difficult to reject the hypothesis that "all ravens are black." In this instance it would be appropriate to accept the hypothesis *conditionally*, the modifier allowing for the possibility of subsequently observing a white raven. Indeed, much of our scientific knowledge of the world we live in comes about not by proving hypotheses but by finding that we cannot reject them. From this perspective, scientific knowledge is conditional—what is scientific truth at any instant of time is a collection of statements that have withstood attempts to reject them.

This discussion of confidence intervals and hypothesis testing is sufficient to make the important point that in applied research we typically make *probability* statements rather than *definitive* statements about the numerical values of unknown population parameters. We return to hypothesis testing in Chapter 6.

Summary

This chapter described the steps in the road from theory to practice that an applied researcher follows in working through a problem using the disciplines of economics, mathematics, and statistics. Particular emphasis was given to the important statistical concepts of random variables, sampling and distribution theory, estimators, estimates, and hypothesis testing. The remainder of the book concentrates on econometric methods falling under the general rubric of "regression analysis."

Terms

Alternative hypothesis	Normal distribution
Best estimator	Null hypothesis
Biased estimators	Parameter
Census	Population
Central Limit Theorem	Random variable
Conceptual variables	Sample
Confidence interval	Sampling distribution
Efficient estimator	Standard deviation
Estimate	Statistic
Estimator	*t*-Statistic
Expectation operator	*t*-Table (*t*-distribution)
Expected value	Unbiased estimator
Implicit equation	Variable
Linear estimator	Variance
Mean	Worksheet
Minimum-variance estimator	

Exercises

2.1 Five families live in Twig. The number of cats each family keeps as pets are indicated in the following table.

Family	Number of Cats
A	0
B	4
C	0
D	0
E	6

(a) What is the parameter "mean number of cats" for the population of Twig families?

(b) Suppose that a researcher took a random sample of two Twig families. What is the sample mean for each of the 10 possible samples of two families?

(c) Calculate the frequency and relative frequency of each possible value of the mean number of cats for all samples of size two in Twig and produce the sampling distribution for $n = 2$.

(d) Suppose that a researcher took a random sample of four Twig families. Calculate the sample mean for each of the five possible samples of four families.

(e) Calculate the frequency and relative frequency of each possible value of the statistic "sample mean for all samples of four Twig families." What is the mean and variance of this sampling distribution?

(f) Will a sample of four families *always* lead to a closer estimate of the population mean than a sample of two families?

(g) Is the mean of the samples an unbiased estimator of the population mean for samples of sizes 2 and 4? Why?

(h) In Twig, what is the variance of "number of cats" about the population mean? (HINT: Use (2.11) and (2.12)—and remember that $E(X) = $ population mean of X).

(i) What is the variance of the sample means in each of the two sampling distributions?

(j) What can you conclude about the variance of the sampling distribution as the sample size increases?

2.2   Some definitions:
(a) $E[X - E(X)]^2 = $ _____ of X.
(b) If the expected value of an estimator is equal to the parameter it is designed to estimate, then the estimator is said to be _____ .
(c) $\sqrt{\text{Variance}} = $ _____ .

2.3   Given the following table of outcomes of an experiment, r, and its corresponding probability of occurrence, what is the expected value of r?

r	P(r)
4	.25
5	.40
8	.25
10	.10

2.4 Consider the following two frequency distributions:

Set 1		Set 2	
X	F(X)	Y	F(Y)
1	.4	1	.1
2	.2	2	.2
3	.3	3	.3
4	.1	4	.4

(a) What is $E(X)$?
(b) What is $E(X^2)$?
(c) What is $E(Y)$?
(d) What is $E(Y^2)$?
(e) What is $E(X)E(Y)$, assuming that X and Y are independent?
(f) What is the variance of X?
(g) What is the standard deviation of X?
(h) What is the variance of Y?
(i) What is the standard deviation of Y?
(j) What is $E(4X)$?
(k) What is $E(X + Y)$?
(l) What is $E(6Y)$?
(m) What is $E(4X + 6Y)$?

2.5 A $1000 investment can result in one of the following possible outcomes. What is the expected *net gain*?

Gross Return	Probability of Obtaining
$10,000	.2
8,000	.4
− 5,000	.4

2.6 Use Theorems 1, 2, and 3 to prove the following (where X is a random variable with $E(X) = \mu$ and $E[X - E(X)]^2 = \sigma^2$):
(a) $E[X - E(X)]^2 = E(X^2) - [E(X)]^2$.
(b) $E(X^2) = \sigma^2 + \mu^2$. (HINT: Expand the expression for σ^2.)

2.7 Use Appendix Table A.1 to calculate the specific confidence interval for the population mean, μ, for samples with the following mean and standard deviation.
(a) $\overline{X} = 50$, $s = 11$ with a 95 percent confidence interval.
(b) $\overline{X} = 50$, $s = 5$ with a 95 percent confidence interval.
(c) $\overline{X} = 50$, $s = 11$ with a 90 percent confidence interval.
(d) $\overline{X} = 50$, $s = 5$ with a 99 percent confidence interval.

2.8 Consider a random variable X that is normally distributed with mean $\mu = 6$ and variance $\sigma^2 = 9$. Answer the following questions with respect to a sample mean $\overline{X}$:

(a) How many standard deviations is $\overline{X} = 4$ from μ?

(b) How many standard deviations is $\overline{X} = 13$ from μ?

(c) What is the probability of getting a sample mean within 1.96 standard deviations of μ?

(d) What is the probability of getting a sample mean more than 2.56 standard deviations above or below μ?

(e) What is the probability of getting a sample mean *larger than* 11.88?

(f) What is the probability of getting a sample mean *less than* zero?

2.9 Suppose that X and Y are both random variables with means μ_x and μ_y; standard deviations of σ_x, σ_y; and covariance of σ_{xy}.

(a) If $S = X + Y$, what is the variance of S?

(b) What is the condition that must hold if

$$\text{var}(S) = \text{var}(X) + \text{var}(Y)?$$

2.10 What is the mean and variance of W in each of the following transformations if $\mu = 6$ and $\sigma^2 = 9$?

(a) $W = 2X + 4$

(b) $W = .2X + 4$

(c) $W = 2X - 4$

2.11 What is the mean and variance of the following transformation of X, where X is a random variable with $E(X) = \mu$, and $\text{var}(X) = \sigma^2$?

(a) $Y = a + bX$

(b) $Z = \dfrac{X - \mu}{\sigma}$

(c) What can you conclude about the mean and variance of a random variable that has been transformed into standard deviation units?

3

Introduction to Least Squares Regression Theory

In Chapter 1 we introduced the method of least squares for computing a "line of average relationship" between two variables. Drawing from the review of estimation theory in Chapter 2, we derive in this chapter the conditions that permit us to interpret the least squares coefficients as estimators of the unobservable population regression coefficients. This combining of estimation theory with a mathematical technique results in the theory of least squares regression. Regression theory is developed and illustrated using the special case of simple regression, a regression equation containing only one independent variable. Simple regression is seldom used in applied research because the workings of most economic systems cannot be adequately represented by such a simple formulation. However, it is an adequate model for expository purposes because the essence of regression theory can be examined with a minimum level of mathematics. A good place to begin is with the important distinction between a *population regression equation* and a *sample regression equation*. Teaching experience indicates that much of the difficulty that beginning students have in understanding and using regression analysis, especially in interpreting empirical results, stems from their failure to recognize and understand the relationship between these two regression equations. In this book we try to make this distinction clear. Using Greek letters for population relations and Arabic letters for sample relations helps to make this distinction.

Population Regression Equation

Consider once again the weekly food expenditure problem of Chapter 1. Economic theory says that food expenditure (Y) depends on weekly household income (X), a

41

Table 3.1. Weekly Food Consumption and Disposable
Income for Six Families

Family	Disposable Income	Food Consumption
A	$100	$ 30
B	200	40
C	200	70
D	300	40
E	400	110
F	600	130

relationship that can be expressed mathematically as

$$Y = \beta_0 + \beta_1 X \qquad (3.1)$$

This is a population equation, indicated by the Greek letters β_0 and β_1. The coefficients β_0 and β_1 are *population parameters*. The objective of applied research is to use sample data to test hypotheses about the values of β_0 and β_1, and it is regression theory that provides the basis for testing these hypotheses.

The observations on food expenditures and income in Chapter 1, repeated here for convenience (Table 3.1), are used here to illustrate a *population* where (3.1) is the expenditure function. It is important to understand that what follows is the *assumed* case in the population. In applied research, populations are never physically "seen"; rather, economic theory provides an abstract view of populations in the form of hypotheses to be tested.

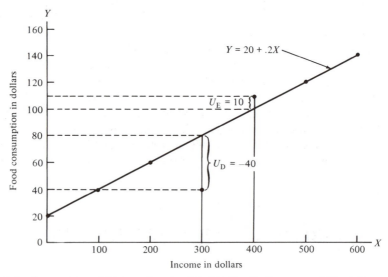

Figure 3.1 Scatter Plot of Observations on Weekly Family Income and Food Consumption.

For this assumed population equation, $\beta_0 = 20$ and $\beta_1 = .2$. The data in Table 3.1 are a sample drawn from this population. How accurately this assumed population equation represents the relationship between Y and X is demonstrated by the scatter diagram in Figure 3.1. Inspection of this diagram shows that β_1 is positive "on average," as expected, but not all of the observations fall on the line $Y = 20 + .2X$. In fact, not a single observation falls on the population line. Mathematically, this means that (3.1) is not an equation, because the left-hand side is not equal to the right-hand side. Consequently, (3.1) must be reformulated to make it an identity. This is done by adding a disturbance term U and defining it in such a way that (3.1) is an exact mathematical expression. The formulated (3.1) is written as

$$Y = \beta_0 + \beta_1 X + U \qquad (3.2)$$

To achieve the identity, the disturbance term is defined as the difference between the observed value and the equation value of Y for a specific value of X. This means that U takes on both positive and negative values. Consider Figure 3.1. For X_D (income equal to \$300), the observed value of Y_D is \$40, the associated *equation value* of Y is \$80, so the disturbance terms for this observation, U_D, is negative ($-\$40$). For X_E (income equal to \$400), the value of U_E is positive (\$10). The population regression equation may be rewritten as

$$Y_i = \beta_0 + \beta_1 X_i + U_i \qquad (3.3)$$

where U_i is the disturbance term added to bring about an equality between the observed value of Y and the equation value of Y on the equation for a given value of X. The subscript i indicates that there is a different value of X, Y, and U for each observation.

Rationale for the Disturbance Term

Adding the disturbance term may seem arbitrary, perhaps even capricious, so a comment on possible reasons for including it might be helpful. Three arguments are typically offered in the econometric literature: omitted variables, the stochastic nature of economic processes, and measurement error in the dependent variable.

One rationale is that variables are *omitted* from the postulated population equation. For example, in the case of family food expenditures, it is reasonable to expect that many variables in addition to household income determine expenditures. Family size, age composition of members, and education are possibilities. In addition, the prices of all nonfood commodities have some impact on food consumption, since food must compete with all other consumption items for the family's dollar. Factors such as changes in packaging and in the tastes and preferences of households also exert an influence on weekly food spending. Other explanatory variables could be suggested. The point is that there are situations where the number of variables that should be included in the equation exceeds the researcher's ability to handle them. It may not be possible to obtain data for all variables, the number of variables could exceed the number of observations available (making estimation impossible), or some of the variables may not be easily quantifiable. Finally, some variables may be left out because the researcher is simply unaware of their importance.

In essence, the omitted variable rationale states that the "true" population equation is

$$Y = f(X_1, X_2, \ldots, X_K) \tag{3.4}$$

with K being a large number, but researchers find it more practical to work with a smaller number of explanatory variables. The population disturbance term, U, is included in the equation to represent the combined effect of all the excluded variables on Y. This carries the assumption that the net effect of all the omitted variables combined is, on average, negligible. (However, see Chapter 13 for the possible consequences of omitting relevant variables when using sample data for estimating a regression equation.)

Another justification for including the disturbance term is based on the reasonable proposition that there is an *inherent randomness* (a "stochastic" element) in the behavior of economic systems. Such randomness is likely because the ultimate units of observation are not planets or machines, but people. Few people, even among econometricians, think the world is completely deterministic. If this assumption of some inherent randomness in the system is true, a random variable must be included in (3.1) if the equation is to describe adequately the behavior of the system.

The third rationale for including U is *measurement error* in the dependent variable, the idea being that the observed Y in (3.1) differs from the "true" value, Y', by an amount equal to U. Measurement error is treated in this book as a problem with the data set used to estimate population regression coefficients and is analyzed in Chapter 15.

In summary, the linear population equation is written as

$$Y_i = \beta_0 + \beta_1 X_i + U_i \quad \text{for } i = 1, \ldots, N \tag{3.5}$$

where Y_i and X_i represent the values of Y and X, the subscript i refers to the ith element in the population, β_0 and β_1 are the unobservable population parameters to be estimated, the U_i's are the unobservable random disturbances, and N is the number of elements in the population.

The Disturbance Term and the Conditional Distribution of Y

Figure 3.1 shows that the value of weekly food expenditures (Y) is not determined exactly by household income (X). Although X and Y are related, the relationship is not perfect. To complete the equation by making the left-hand side of (3.1) equal to the right-hand side, a population disturbance term was added. This leads to the conditional distribution of Y.

Consider the population equation (3.5). There may be many possible values of Y_i for a given value of X, depending on the value of U_i. In other words, for X_i, there exists a distribution for Y_i. Moreover, the distribution of the Y-values can be different for different values of X. Thus it is possible to visualize a conditional distribution of Y for each value of X. For example, Figure 3.2 illustrates the distribution of Y for $X_i = \$200$ and $X_i = \$400$. Note that although the distributions have the same shape, the mean, or expected value, of Y varies with X: $E(Y_i|X_i = \$200) = \$40$ and $E(Y_i|X_i = \$400) = \$60$, where the symbol $(|)$ is read "given that." Note also in

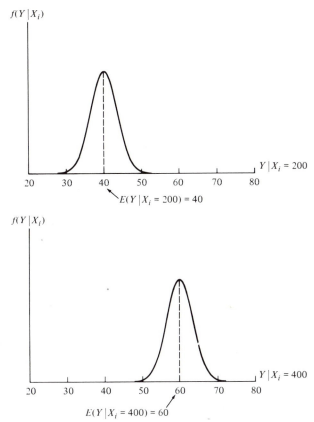

Figure 3.2 Conditional Frequency Distribution of Weekly Food Consumption (Y) for Specific Values of Weekly Family Income (X).

Figure 3.2 that a Y value of 80 is possible for both values of X but is much more likely to occur when X is 400.

There is an alternative way of visualizing the relationship between the conditional distributions and the X-values, as illustrated in Figure 3.2. As samples are drawn from this population with the objective of estimating β_0 and β_1, we can visualize drawing samples from the conditional distributions of Y or the distributions of U associated with the different values of X.

Statistical Assumptions About the Disturbance Term

Regardless of the rationale used to include the U_i's in the population equation, the disturbance term is a random variable because it takes on different values over the elements (households, firms, markets) in the population. This means that the values of U can be described by a distribution with a mean and a variance. Because the U_i are unobservable, the mean and variance of the distribution cannot be computed. Consequently, to provide a basis for estimation, it is necessary to introduce assumptions regarding the statistical properties of the distribution of the population disturbance term.

The following assumptions about the distribution of the disturbance term are necessary to complete the specification of the population regression model. These assumptions, integral to the theory of estimating population parameters, are as follows [where (3.5) is repeated]:

$$Y_i = \beta_0 + \beta_1 X_i + U_i, \qquad i = 1, \ldots, N \tag{3.5}$$

$$E(U_i) = 0 \qquad \text{for all } i \text{ conditional distributions} \tag{3.6}$$

$$E(U_i^2) = \sigma^2 \qquad \begin{array}{l} \text{for all } i \text{ conditional distributions,} \\ \text{where } \sigma^2 \text{ is a constant} \end{array} \tag{3.7}$$

$$E(U_i U_j) = 0 \qquad \text{for all } i \text{ not equal to } j \tag{3.8}$$

$$\text{Values of } X \text{ are fixed in repeated sampling} \tag{3.9}$$

This complete model specifies both the population regression equation and the parameters of the distribution of the population disturbance term. There are two distinct elements in (3.5): an economic statement ($\beta_0 + \beta_1 X_i$) and a statistical statement (U_i and its distribution).

Assumption (3.6) says the expected value, or mean, of each conditional distribution of U is zero. Assumption (3.7) says that the conditional distributions of U associated with different values of X (see Figure 3.2) have the same variance. This is called the *homoscedasticity* specification. Assumption (3.8) states that the disturbance terms are not correlated across the conditional distributions. This means that the value of each U_i is independent of all other values of U. Finally, assumption (3.9) says that the X_i values are not correlated with the U_i values; that is, the X_i are independent of the U_i. Equation (3.5) together with assumptions (3.6) to (3.9) comprise the *linear regression model* considered in this chapter.

Least Squares Estimators of Population Regression Coefficients

In Chapter 2 the distinction was made between an estimator and an estimate. An *estimator* is a formula or computational rule that may be used to compute a number from a given sample of data drawn from the population. The number computed using this formula is an *estimate* of the population parameter based on that sample. In repeated sampling from the population, even though the same estimator is used, the different samples will yield different estimates of the population parameter (recall Table 2.2). It makes no sense to talk about the properties of estimates because each is only a specific number, but it does make sense to consider the properties of the estimator, or the formula, used to generate different estimates. Chapter 2 identified three desirable properties of estimators (linearity, unbiasedness, and minimum variance). These are important in regression, as discussed below.

In this section we have two goals. The first is to derive the least squares coefficients. This is essentially a repeat of what was done in Chapter 1, but here it is done more formally in the context of a fully specified econometric model. The second goal is to prove for the special case of one independent variable that the least squares coefficients can be interpreted as linear, unbiased, minimum-variance estimators of the population regression coefficients.

Deriving the Least Squares Estimators

The population regression equation is

$$Y = \beta_0 + \beta_1 X + U \tag{3.10}$$

In this section we propose using the least squares coefficients derived in Chapter 1 as estimators of the population regression coefficients. The sample regression equation is

$$Y_i = b_0 + b_1 X_i + e_i \tag{3.11}$$

The coefficients, b_0 and b_1, are to be computed from a sample using the least squares criterion. To derive the formulas for computing them, rearrange (3.11), square each value, and sum to obtain the sum of squared residuals:

$$\text{ESS} = \Sigma\, e_i^2 = \Sigma\, (Y_i - b_0 - b_1 X_i)^2 \tag{3.12}$$

The objective is to compute values for b_0 and b_1 from the sample observations on Y_i and X_i such that ESS is a minimum. The solution to this standard minimization problem is obtained by solving the set of equations that result when the partial derivatives of (3.12) with respect to b_0 and b_1 are taken and the resulting two expressions set equal to zero:

$$\frac{\partial \text{ESS}}{\partial b_0} = 2\, \Sigma\, (Y_i - b_0 - b_1 X_i)(-1) = 0 \tag{3.13}$$

$$\frac{\partial \text{ESS}}{\partial b_1} = 2\, \Sigma\, (Y_i - b_0 - b_1 X_i)(-X_i) = 0 \tag{3.14}$$

Divide each of these equations by -2 and rearrange to obtain

$$n b_0 + b_1 \Sigma\, X_i = \Sigma\, Y_i \tag{3.15}$$

$$b_0 \Sigma\, X_i + b_1 \Sigma\, X_i^2 = \Sigma\, X_i Y_i \tag{3.16}$$

Equations (3.15) and (3.16) are two equations with two unknowns that can be solved for the two unknowns b_0 and b_1. These two equations are called the *normal equations*. Dividing (3.15) by n (the sample size) and rearranging terms yields

$$b_0 = \bar{Y} - b_1 \bar{X} \tag{3.17}$$

which, when substituted into (3.16), yields

$$b_1 = \frac{\Sigma\, X_i Y_i - n\bar{X}\bar{Y}}{\Sigma\, X_i^2 - n\bar{X}^2} = \frac{\Sigma\, (X_i - \bar{X})(Y_i - \bar{Y})}{\Sigma\, (X_i - \bar{X})^2} \tag{3.18}$$

In the language of Chapter 2, (3.17) and (3.18) can be viewed as estimators because they are formulas that show how to use sample values of Y and X to compute the intercept (b_0) and the slope (b_1) of a straight line through the Y–X space such that ESS is a minimum.

Before demonstrating that these are linear, unbiased, and minimum-variance estimators, it is useful to introduce some simplifying notation. Equation (3.17) can, given b_1, be used to compute b_0. Either expression on the right-hand side of (3.18) can be used as a computational formula for b_1, but the middle term is easier to use when it is necessary to do the calculation by hand. In any case, b_1 must be computed before b_0 can be computed. But notice that if X and Y are written in terms of deviations from their respective means, $x_i = X_i - \bar{X}$ and $y_i = Y_i - \bar{Y}$, the equation for the slope, (3.18), may be written as (see Chapter 1)

$$b_1 = \frac{\Sigma\, x_i y_i}{\Sigma\, x_i^2} \tag{3.19}$$

The intercept, b_0, can always be recovered by (3.17). Because most of the subsequent material in this book focuses on the slope and not the intercept, extensive use is made of the notational convenience offered by expressing variables as deviations from their respective means.

Properties of the Least Squares Estimators

When both the dependent and independent variables are expressed in deviation form, the population regression equation is written as

$$y_i = \beta_1 x_i + U_i \tag{3.20}$$

to be estimated by the sample regression equation

$$y_i = b_1^* x_i + e_i \tag{3.21}$$

where b_1^* is a general estimator.

First, write the estimator b_1^* as a general *linear* function of Y,

$$b_1^* = w_1 y_1 + \cdots + w_n y_n = \Sigma\, w_i y_i \tag{3.22}$$

where the w_i are arbitrary, fixed weights. As different samples of y of size n are drawn from the population, this estimator will yield different estimates b_1^*. This b_1^* generates a sampling distribution of the estimates of β_1. It is necessary to calculate the mean and variance of this distribution.

The mean of the sampling distribution is $E(b_1^*)$. If this is equal to β_1, then b_1^* is an *unbiased* estimator of β_1. To determine the conditions for b_1^* to be unbiased, write b_1^* as a weighted sum of the unobservable disturbance terms by substituting (3.20) into (3.22). This yields

$$b_1^* = \Sigma\, w_i(\beta_1 x_i + U_i) = \beta_1 \Sigma\, w_i x_i + \Sigma\, w_i U_i \tag{3.23}$$

The expected value of (3.23), the mean of the sampling distribution of b_1^*, is

$$E(b_1^*) = \beta_1 \sum w_i x_i + \sum w_i E(U_i) = \beta_1 \sum w_i x_i \qquad (3.24)$$

Since the w_i are arbitrary constants, the values of X are fixed in repeated sampling by (3.9), and $E(U_i) = 0$ by (3.6). According to (3.24), b_1^* is an unbiased estimator of β_1 if

$$\sum w_i x_i = 1 \qquad (3.25)$$

Once the w_i's are determined, it will be necessary to determine if they satisfy (3.25).

For the moment assume that b_1^* is unbiased (i.e., assume that 3.25 is true) and derive the variance of its sampling distribution. Equation (3.23) may be rewritten as

$$b_1^* = \beta_1 + \sum w_i U_i \qquad (3.26)$$

using (3.23), (3.24), and (3.25). By definition, the variance of the sampling distribution of b_1^* is given by

$$V(b_1^*) = E[b_1^* - E(b_1^*)]^2 = E(\sum w_i U_i)^2 \qquad (3.27)$$

This is evaluated by expanding and taking the expected values as follows:

$$\begin{aligned}
E[(\sum w_i U_i)^2 &= E(w_1^2 U_1^2 + \cdots + w_n^2 U_n^2 + w_1 w_2 U_1 U_2 \\
&\quad + \cdots + w_{n-1} w_n U_{n-1} U_n) \\
&= w_1^2 E(U_1^2) + \cdots + w_n^2 E(U_n^2) + w_1 w_2 E(U_1 U_2) + \cdots \\
&\quad\quad\quad\quad + w_{n-1} w_n E(U_{n-1} U_n) \\
&= w_1^2 \sigma^2 + \cdots + w_n^2 \sigma^2 \quad \text{[using (3.7) and (3.8)]} \\
&= \sigma^2 \sum w_i^2
\end{aligned} \qquad (3.28)$$

Collecting results, we find that the general estimator b_1^* is a linear (3.22), unbiased [(3.24) and (3.25)] estimator of β_1, with variance given by (3.28). Now return to the least squares formula for the regression slope:

$$b_1 = \frac{\sum x_i y_i}{\sum x_i^2} \qquad (3.29)$$

Letting $w_i = x_i / \sum x_i^2$ and substituting into (3.22) yields

$$\begin{aligned}
x b_1^* &= \frac{x_1}{\sum x_i^2} y_1 + \cdots + \frac{x_n}{\sum x_i^2} y_n \\
&= \frac{\sum x_i y_i}{\sum x_i^2} = b_1
\end{aligned} \qquad (3.30)$$

which shows that the weights $x_i / \sum x_i^2$ yield the least squares coefficient, b_1, as a linear estimator. For b_1 to be an unbiased estimator of β_1, condition (3.25) must hold.

Substituting the weights, $x_i/\Sigma x_i^2$, into (3.25) yields

$$\Sigma \frac{x_i}{\Sigma x_i^2} x_i = \frac{\Sigma x_i^2}{\Sigma x_i^2} = 1 \qquad (3.31)$$

Since condition (3.25) holds, b_1 is an unbiased estimator. Alternatively, b_1 can be shown to be unbiased by substituting for w_i in (3.24) to obtain

$$E(b_1) = \beta_1 \Sigma \frac{x_i}{\Sigma x_i^2} x_i = \beta_1 \frac{\Sigma x_i^2}{\Sigma x_i^2} = \beta_1 \qquad (3.32)$$

Finally, substituting the weights, w_i, into (3.28) yields

$$V(b_1) = \sigma^2 \Sigma \left(\frac{x_i}{\Sigma x_i^2} \right)^2 = \sigma^2 \frac{\Sigma x_i^2}{(\Sigma x_i^2)^2} = \sigma^2 \frac{1}{\Sigma x_i^2} \qquad (3.33)$$

as the variance of the least squares estimator.

To see if the least squares estimator is a minimum-variance estimator, define another arbitrary, linear estimator

$$c_1 = w_1^* y_1 + \cdots + w_n^* y_n = \Sigma w_i^* y_i \qquad (3.34)$$

where the weights w_i^* differ from the least squares weights w_i by some amount v_i:

$$w_i^* = w_i + v_i \qquad (3.35)$$

The expected value of the estimator (3.34) is

$$E(c_1) = \beta_1 \Sigma w_i^* x_i = \beta_1 \Sigma (w_i + v_i) x_i = \beta_1 \Sigma w_i x_i + \beta_1 \Sigma v_i x_i \qquad (3.36)$$

Since (3.31) shows that $\Sigma w_i x_i = 1$, the estimator c_1 is unbiased only if

$$\Sigma v_i x_i = 0 \qquad (3.37)$$

Assume that (3.37) holds and consider the variance of c_1 given by

$$V(c_1) = E[c_1 - E(c_1)]^2 = \sigma^2 \Sigma w_i^{*2} = \sigma^2 \Sigma (w_i + v_i)^2 \qquad (3.38)$$

by a derivation similar to (3.28),

$$\Sigma (w_i + v_i)^2 = \Sigma w_i^2 + \Sigma v_i^2 + 2 \Sigma w_i v_i \qquad (3.39)$$

and using the least squares weights yields

$$\Sigma w_i v_i = \Sigma \left(\frac{x_i}{\Sigma x_i^2} \right)^2 v_i = \frac{1}{\Sigma x_i^2} \Sigma x_i v_i = 0 \qquad (3.40)$$

by (3.37). Therefore, the variance of c_1 is

$$V(c_1) = \sigma^2 (\Sigma w_i^2 + \Sigma v_i^2) = V(b_1) + \sigma^2 \Sigma v_i^2 \qquad (3.41)$$

Because Σv_i^2 is zero or positive, the variance of the arbitrary estimator, c_1, is equal to or greater than the variance of the least squares estimator. From this it follows that b_1, the least squares estimator, is a minimum-variance estimator among all linear and unbiased estimators. The word "best" is often used to denote a minimum-variance estimator.

In summary, in this section we have shown that b_1, the least squares coefficient, is, under the assumptions (3.6) to (3.9), a linear, unbiased, minimum-variance estimator of β_1, the population regression slope parameter in (3.5). This confirms, for simple regression, the *Gauss–Markov theorem*, which says that under the assumptions (3.5) to (3.9), the least squares coefficients are *best linear unbiased estimators* (BLUEs) of the population regression coefficients. Although the discussion above has demonstrated the validity of this theorem only for the special case of one independent variable, the Gauss–Markov theorem applies to the case of K independent variables.

Estimating the Variance of a Regression Coefficient

The variance of b_1 is given by (3.33), which is repeated here for convenience:

$$V(b_1) = \sigma^2 \sum \left(\frac{x_i^2}{\sum x_i^2} \right)^2 = \sigma^2 \frac{\sum x_i^2}{(\sum x_i^2)^2} = \sigma^2 \frac{1}{\sum x_i^2} \tag{3.33}$$

Because σ^2, the variance of the population disturbance term, is unobservable, (3.33) cannot be computed from a sample of data. In this section we present a way to estimate the variance of the sampling distribution of b_1.

Estimating σ^2 from Sample Data

The disturbance terms are unobservable and σ^2 cannot be calculated from the sample. However, the least squares residual of the sample regression equation can be calculated by

$$e_i = Y_i - b_0 - b_1 X_i \tag{3.42}$$

The U_i are the unobservable disturbances of the population equation. The e_i are the observable least squares residuals calculated from the sample regression equation. It is reasonable to consider what, if any, relationship exits between the U_i's and the e_i's. In particular, it seems reasonable to explore the possibility of using some function of the e_i as an estimator of the variance of the U_i. The task is made easier by eliminating the constant term from (3.42) by expressing Y and X as deviations from their respective means to obtain

$$e_i = y_i - b_1 x_i \tag{3.43}$$

The idea is to manipulate (3.43) to permit expressing the observable e_i as a function of the unobservable U_i. Sum (3.5) over all sample observations, divide by n (the number of sample observations), and subtract the result from (3.5) to obtain

$$Y_i - \bar{Y} = (\beta_0 - \beta_0) + \beta_1(X_i - \bar{X}) + (U_i - \bar{U}) \tag{3.44}$$

Note that $\overline{U}$ appears in this equation. By assumption the mean of the disturbance term in the population is zero, but here $\overline{U}$ is not necessarily zero because (3.44) includes only the disturbance terms for the population elements selected in a particular sample. Thus it is a particular sample of U_i's that gives rise to the observed e_i's in (3.43).

Equation (3.44), when the variables are written in deviation form,

$$y_i = \beta_1 x_i + (U_i - \overline{U}) \tag{3.45}$$

expresses the dependent variable as a function of the independent variable and the unobservable U_i. Substituting (3.45) into (3.43) yields

$$e_i = (\beta_1 - b_1)x_i + (U_i - \overline{U}) \tag{3.46}$$

which shows that the least squares residuals, e_i, computed from a sample, depend on the values of U_i for the population elements selected into the sample. This important result provides the desired linkage between e and U.

To determine what function of the sample values of e_i can be used to estimate σ^2, sum the squares of (3.46) and expand:

$$\begin{aligned}
\Sigma\, e_i^2 &= \Sigma\, [(\beta_1 - b_1)x_i + (U_i - \overline{U})]^2 \\
&= \Sigma\, [(\beta_1 - b_1)^2 x_i^2 + (U_i - \overline{U})^2 \\
&\qquad + 2(\beta_1 - b_1)x_i(U_i - \overline{U})] \\
&= (\beta_1 - b_1)^2\, \Sigma\, x_i^2 + \Sigma\, (U_i - \overline{U})^2 \\
&\qquad + 2(\beta_1 - b_1)\, \Sigma\, x_i(U_i - \overline{U})
\end{aligned} \tag{3.47}$$

Taking the expected values of each term on the right-hand side of (3.47) yields for the first term

$$\begin{aligned}
E[(\beta_1 - b_1)^2\, \Sigma\, x_i^2] &= \Sigma\, x_i^2 E(\beta_1 - b_1)^2 \\
&= \Sigma\, x_i^2\, \frac{\sigma^2}{\Sigma\, x_i^2} \qquad \text{[by (3.33)]} \\
&= \sigma^2
\end{aligned} \tag{3.48}$$

The expected value of the middle term of (3.47) is

$$E[\Sigma(U_i - \overline{U})^2] = E(\Sigma\, U_i^2 - 2\overline{U}\, \Sigma\, U_i + n\overline{U}^2)$$

Use $\overline{U} = \Sigma\, U_i / n$ to write this as

$$\begin{aligned}
&= E\left[(\Sigma\, U_i^2) - \frac{2(\Sigma\, U_i)^2}{n} + \frac{(\Sigma\, U_i)^2}{n} \right] . \\
&= n\sigma^2 - \sigma^2 \qquad \text{[by (3.7) and (3.8)]} \\
&= (n - 1)\sigma^2
\end{aligned} \tag{3.49}$$

and for the third term is

$$\begin{aligned}
2E[(\beta_1 - b_1)\, \Sigma\, x_i(U_i - \overline{U})] &= 2E[(\beta_1 - b_1)\, \Sigma\, x_i U_i] \\
&\qquad (\text{since } \Sigma\, x_i = 0)
\end{aligned}$$

$$= 2E\left[\frac{-\Sigma\, x_i U_i}{\Sigma\, x_i^2}\, (\Sigma\, x_i U_i)\right]$$

$$= -2E\left[\frac{(\Sigma\, x_i U_i)^2}{\Sigma\, x_i^2}\right] \tag{3.50}$$

$$= -2\sigma^2$$

[by the same argument as (3.28)]

Collecting the results of (3.48), (3.49), and (3.50) and substituting, we obtain the expected value of (3.47):

$$E(\Sigma\, e_i^2) = \sigma^2 + (n - 1)\sigma^2 - 2\sigma^2$$
$$= (n - 2)\sigma^2 \tag{3.51}$$

The manipulations above show that the expected value (over all possible samples of size n) of the sum of the squared residuals, $\Sigma\, e_i^2$, is the variance of the unobserved population disturbance multiplied by $(n - 2)$. Therefore, the following unbiased estimator of σ^2 can be constructed:

$$S^2 = \frac{\Sigma\, e_i^2}{n - 2} \tag{3.52}$$

This is an important result because it shows how to use the least squares residuals to obtain a sample estimate of σ^2, the unobservable variance of the population disturbance term; S^2 is *not* an estimate of the variance of Y. Throughout the book S^2 will be the notation used to indicate the sample estimate of the variance of the population disturbance term.

The positive square root of this estimated variance, denoted by S, is usually referred to as the *standard deviation of the regression* or the *standard error of regression*. The standard deviation of the regression and its relation to the regression line is shown in Figure 3.3. The vertical distance between the regression line and the dashed line represents one standard deviation above and below the regression line. This graph illustrates two important points. First, it shows that S is a measure of the dispersion of the actual Y values about the regression line. The standard error of regression is an indicator of the closeness with which the values of Y may be estimated from the regression line. The closer the dashed lines to the regression line, the better is the equation for predicting Y for given values of X. Conversely, the greater this distance, the less reliable are the predictions. Note, however, that the band representing S relates to the variance of Y about the regression line only when the population parameters β_0 and β_1 are known. When b_0 and b_1 are used as estimates of β_0 and β_1, an additional source of variation must be considered in calculating the variance of Y about the regression line. For practical purposes, S can be visualized as an indication of the deviation in the dependent variable due to changes unrelated to changes in the independent variable X.

The second major point illustrated by Figure 3.3 is that S is measured in the same units as the dependent variable Y. Thus, if Y is measured in dollars of food consumption per week, S is measured in dollars of food consumption per week.

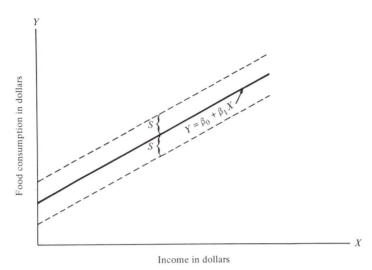

Figure 3.3   Illustration of the Standard Deviation of Regression.

Standard Deviation of the Estimated Coefficient

The variance of b_1 is $\sigma^2/\Sigma\, x_i^2$, a function of the variance of the unobservable population term. However, σ^2 can be estimated from the sample by (3.52) and substituted for σ^2 in the expression of $V(b_1)$, (3.33), to obtain an estimate of the sampling variance of the least squares estimator. The expression for this is

$$S_{b_1}^2 = \frac{S^2}{\Sigma\, x_i^2} = \frac{\Sigma\, e_i^2}{(n-2)(\Sigma\, x_i^2)}$$
(3.53)

The standard error of the estimated regression coefficient, S_{b_1}, is the square root of (3.53) and measures the sampling variability of b_1 about its expected value β_1.

The Intercept Term

Little has been said about the intercept term in the regression equation. It is, of course, important and cannot be ignored. However, because there are relatively few instances in applied research where the intercept has an obvious economic interpretation, major concern is placed, here as elsewhere, on the slope coefficient, which does have an economic interpretation. The intercept term is computed from the sample by

$$b_0 = \bar{Y} - b_1\bar{X}$$
(3.54)

To express b_0 as a function of the sample values of Y, as was done for b_1 [see (3.22)], write

$$\bar{Y} = \frac{1}{n} \Sigma Y \tag{3.55}$$

and

$$b_1 = \frac{\Sigma x_i y_i}{\Sigma x_i^2} = \frac{\Sigma x_i (Y_i - \bar{Y})}{\Sigma x_i^2} = \frac{\Sigma x_i Y_i}{\Sigma x_i^2} - \bar{Y} \frac{\Sigma x_i}{\Sigma x_i^2} \tag{3.56}$$

where the last term is equal is zero (i.e., $\Sigma x_i = 0$). Substitute these two equations into (3.54) to obtain b_0 as a function of the sample values Y_i:

$$b_0 = \frac{1}{n} \Sigma Y_i - \bar{X} \Sigma w_i Y_i = \Sigma \left(\frac{1}{n} - \bar{X} w_i \right) Y_i \tag{3.57}$$

where $w_i = x_i / \Sigma x_i^2$, the least squares weights. Substituting the population regression for Y_i in (3.57) yields

$$b_0 = \Sigma \left(\frac{1}{n} - \bar{X} w_i \right) (\beta_0 + \beta_1 X_i + U_i)$$

$$= \beta_0 \Sigma \left(\frac{1}{n} - \bar{X} w_i \right) + \beta_1 \Sigma \left(\frac{1}{n} - \bar{X} w_i \right) X_i + \Sigma \left(\frac{1}{n} - \bar{X} w_i \right) U_i \tag{3.58}$$

$$= \beta_0 + \Sigma \left(\frac{1}{n} - \bar{X} w_i \right) U_i$$

since $\Sigma w_i = 0$ and $\Sigma w_i X_i = 1$ by manipulating (3.31). Equation (3.58) expresses b_0 as a function of the population disturbance terms U_i. To see that b_0 is an unbiased estimator of β_0, take the expected value of (3.58):

$$E(b_0) = \beta_0 + \Sigma \left(\frac{1}{n} - \bar{X} w_i \right) E(U_i) = \beta_0 \tag{3.59}$$

The variance of b_0 is

$$V(b_0) = E[b_0 - E(b_0)]^2 \tag{3.60}$$

$$= E\left[\Sigma \left(\frac{1}{n} - \bar{X} \right) U_i \right]^2 \qquad \text{[by (3.58) and (3.59)]}$$

Squaring (3.60) and taking the expected value yields

$$V(b_0) = \left(\frac{1}{n} + \frac{\bar{X}^2}{\Sigma x_i^2} \right) \sigma^2 \tag{3.61}$$

as the variance of b_0. This can be written alternatively as

$$V(b_0) = \frac{\sigma^2}{n} + \bar{X}^2 \frac{\sigma^2}{\Sigma x_i^2} = \frac{\sigma^2}{n} + \bar{X}^2 V(b_1) \qquad \text{[by (3.33)]} \tag{3.62}$$

The variance of b_0 is estimated from the sample by substituting S^2 (from 3.52) for σ^2 in (3.62).

Hypothesis Testing

The final item to consider is using the sample values of the least squares coefficients to test hypotheses regarding the values of the population regression coefficients. The general structure of the t-test is discussed in Chapter 2; in this section the t-test is applied to regression coefficients. It is important to recognize that the b_0 and b_1 are numbers computed from a particular sample and hence represent *estimates* of the population parameters. A different sample would, in all likelihood, yield different computed values of b_0 and b_1. However, because an estimate of the variance of the sampling distributions for b_0 and b_1 can be obtained from the sample, it is possible to use the sample data to make probability statements about the values of β_0 and β_1.

At this juncture, the researcher must specify two things: the hypothesis to be tested and the confidence (probability) level at which the test is to be conducted.

Structure of the Hypothesis Test

For convenience, the population regression equation and the sample regression equation are repeated:

$$y_i = \beta_1 x_i + U_i \tag{3.20}$$

$$y_i = b_1 x_i + e_i \tag{3.21}$$

The issue at hand is how to use the value of b_1 in (3.21), computed from the sample, and its standard deviation, computed from the sample by (3.53), to make a quantitative statement about the value of β_1 in (3.20). The desired statement is made in the form of a hypothesis test, where the sample data provide a (probability) basis for rejecting or failing to reject the stated hypothesis. Consequently, structuring the formal statement of the hypothesis is crucial.

There are two elements in the formal statement: the *null hypothesis*, written as H_0, and the *alternative hypothesis*, written as H_a. The null hypothesis states an assumed or hypothesized value for the parameter being estimated, and the alternative hypothesis states the alternative value for that parameter, in the event the null hypothesis is rejected. The idea of the test is to reject H_0 (in which case H_a is not rejected). The actual values used for H_0 and H_a may be drawn from economic theory, broadly defined, or from the specific research objective. Illustrations follow.

A particular variable, say income, is included in a consumption equation because economic theory says that income is an important determinant of consumption behavior. Income is, in other words, an economically significant variable. For regression, this translates into the proposition that the population regression coefficient of income is not equal to zero (if the coefficient were equal to zero, changes in income would not affect consumption behavior, contrary to the prediction of theory). This suggests a test structured as follows:

Example 1

$$H_0: \beta_1 = 0 \quad \text{versus} \quad H_a: \beta_1 \neq 0$$

In words, we hypothesize that $\beta_1 = 0$, and by the test we will either fail to reject H_0 (and hence reject H_a) or reject H_0 (and hence fail to reject H_a). Rejecting H_0 and not rejecting H_a yields a result in accord with economic theory, which says that changes in income will affect consumption expenditures. On the other hand, failing to reject H_0 and rejecting H_a yields a result not in accord with theory. In this case we say that the sample of data used to compute b_1 in (3.21) does not support the prediction of theory that income is an important determinant of expenditures.

This leads to the important distinction between "economic significance" and "statistical significance." The former derives from theory, the latter from a statistical test applied to a specific sample of data. If, in this instance, H_0 is not rejected, a difficult question arises: Is the theory inconsistent with the real world or, conversely, is the real world inconsistent with the theory? To pursue the philosophical implications of this question would take us far beyond the scope of this book. Suffice it to say here that in a given research setting any apparent inconsistency between theory and statistics is resolved in favor of the theory. Moreover, the presence of "wrong" signs can often be attributed to econometric problems, the subject of several subsequent chapters.

In the discussion above, H_a, the alternative hypothesis, specifies only that $\beta_1 \neq 0$; it allows for either a positive or a negative sign on β_1. This is, of course, consistent with demand theory, which does not place a restriction on the sign of the income slope: A positive income slope is associated with a "normal" good, a negative slope is associated with an "inferior" good. This distinction, if H_0 is rejected, is made on the basis of the sign of b_1 in (3.21).

The value used for the null hypothesis need not be zero. Suppose that previous research on essentially the same problem, but for a different geographical region, reported an income slope of 25. The structure of the test to determine whether the income slope in (3.20) is different from the reported value of 25 is

Example 2

$$H_0: \beta_1 = 25 \quad \text{versus} \quad H_a: \beta_1 \neq 25$$

It is more often the case that the researcher has no specific value and uses $H_0: \beta_1 = 0$.

This final illustration draws from the theory of the firm. Under the conventional neoclassical assumptions, the short-run supply curve of the competitive firm is an increasing function of market price. Thus in (3.21), y is the quantity supplied and x is the market price; the underlying theory predicts that β_1 is positive. This leads to the following test.

Example 3

$$H_0: \beta_1 = 0 \quad \text{versus} \quad H_a: \beta_1 > 0$$

Here the test takes advantage of the prediction of theory by specifying the inequality for H_a. In this instance, if H_0 is rejected, the alternative hypothesis of a positive price slope is not rejected. A variation of this particular test might be encountered in doing supply response analysis in developing countries. It is argued (whether correctly or incorrectly is not relevant here) that in subsistence agriculture, farmers will increase production in response to a price decrease in order to maintain their subsistence. This theory leads to the following example.

Example 4

$$H_0: \beta_1 = 0 \quad \text{versus} \quad H_a: \beta_1 < 0$$

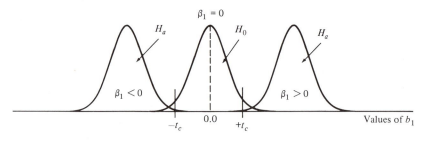

(a) Two-tailed alternative: $\beta_1 = 0$

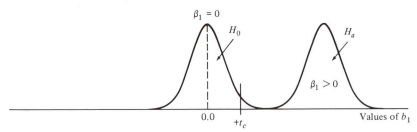

(b) One-tailed alternative: $\beta_1 > 0$

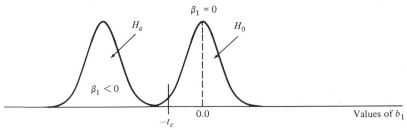

(c) One-tailed alternative: $\beta_1 < 0$

Figure 3.4 Example of the Distribution of b_1, Given a Null Hypothesis that $\beta_1 = 0$ Under One- and Two-Tailed Alternative Hypotheses.

where the rejecting of H_0 results in not rejecting the proposition of a negative supply response.

The simple point of these illustrations is that hypothesis tests are structured on the basis of theory, previous research, or a given research objective. These examples reveal another aspect of hypothesis testing: a *two-tailed test* (examples 1 and 2) and a *one-tailed test* (examples 3 and 4). This distinction is illustrated in Figure 3.4. The basic question is the probability that b_1 in (3.21) came from a sampling distribution where $\beta_1 = 0$. The secondary question is the value or range of values allowed for β_1 in the event that the null hypothesis is rejected. Under the two-tailed test, the researcher is indifferent regarding the sign of β_1 under the alternative hypothesis; under the one-tailed test, a specific sign is imposed by the alternative hypothesis. The practical implication of this distinction rests, as shown in an example below, on the critical t-value that is used to conduct the test. This, however, is of minor consequence. The important point to make here is that the researcher must decide in advance of testing which test to use. If the underlying theory does not predict a sign or if the sign is of no consequence to the research question at hand, the two-tailed test is used. If theory does predict a sign or if the sign is of consequence to the research question at hand, the one-tailed test is used. The choice is governed by the underlying theory and by the research objective.

These ideas can be illustrated with the computations in Table 3.2. From the data in the table, the estimated equation can be written as

$$Y = \underset{(3.26)}{4.223} + \underset{(.047)}{.469X} + e \tag{3.63}$$

Twenty observations were used to estimate the two coefficients, so there are $20 - 2 = 18$ degrees of freedom. The number in parentheses are the standard errors of the coefficients. To illustrate, conduct the test at the .95 level.

Case A

$$H_0: \beta_1 = 0 \quad \text{versus} \quad H_a: \beta_1 \neq 0$$

$$\text{computed } t\text{-statistic} = \frac{.469 - 0}{.047} = \frac{.469}{.047} = 9.98$$

From Appendix Table A.2, the critical t-value for 18 degrees of freedom and a two-tailed test is 2.101. Since the computed value is greater than the critical value, the null hypothesis is rejected and the alternative hypothesis is not rejected.

Case B

$$H_0: \beta_1 = 0 \quad \text{versus} \quad H_a: \beta_1 > 0$$

Note that the computed t-statistic is the same as in case A. The difference is the critical t-value. For the same degrees of freedom and the same level of the test, the t-value for the one-tailed test is 1.734. Again the null hypothesis is rejected and the alternative hypothesis is not rejected.

Table 3.2. Data for Calculating a Simple Regression of Food Expenditures (Y) on Weekly Income (X)

Y	X	X^2	Y^2	XY	e	$\hat{Y}$	e^2
28	54	2,916	784	1,512	− 1.57	29.57	2.47
31	62	3,844	961	1,922	− 2.33	33.33	5.42
36	70	4,900	1,296	2,520	− 1.08	37.08	1.17
37	78	6,084	1,369	2,886	− 3.84	40.84	14.73
41	79	6,241	1,681	3,239	− .31	41.31	.09
40	80	6,400	1,600	3,200	− 1.78	41.78	3.16
44	82	6,724	1,936	3,608	1.28	42.72	1.65
42	85	7,225	1,764	3,570	− 2.12	44.12	4.51
24	45	2,025	576	1,080	− 1.35	25.35	1.81
26	52	2,704	676	1,352	− 2.63	28.63	6.93
24	48	2,304	576	1,152	− 2.76	26.76	7.59
34	56	3,136	1,156	1,904	3.49	30.51	12.17
31	51	2,601	961	1,581	2.84	28.16	8.04
32	64	4,096	1,024	2,048	− 2.27	34.27	5.14
38	66	4,356	1,444	2,508	2.79	35.21	7.81
40	72	5,184	1,600	2,880	1.98	38.02	3.91
46	78	6,084	2,116	3,588	5.16	40.84	26.65
37	60	3,600	1,369	2,220	4.61	32.39	21.27
46	84	7,056	2,116	3,864	2.35	43.65	5.50
44	90	8,100	1,936	3,960	− 2.47	46.47	6.11
721	1,356	95,580	26,941	50,594	0.00	721.00	146.14

Regression slope using (3.18):

$$b_1 = \frac{\Sigma\, XY - n\overline{Y}\overline{X}}{\Sigma\, X - n\overline{X}^2} = \frac{50,594 - (20)(36.05)(67.80)}{95,580 - (20)(67.80)^2}$$

$$= \frac{1710.20}{3643.20} = .469$$

Constant term using (3.17):

$$b_0 = \overline{Y} - b_1\overline{X} = 36.05 - (.469)(67.80)$$

$$= 4.252$$

Standard error of regression using (3.52):

$$S^2 = \frac{\Sigma\, e^2}{n - 2} = \frac{146.14}{20 - 2} = 8.119$$

Standard error of the coefficients (3.53) and (3.57):

$$S_{b_1}^2 = \frac{\Sigma\, e^2}{(n - 2)\,\Sigma\, x^2} = \frac{146.14}{(18)(3643.10)}$$

$$= .00229$$

Table 3.2. *(Continued)*

$$S_{b_1} = .047$$

$$S_{b_0}^2 = \frac{S^2 \; \Sigma \; X^2}{n \; \Sigma \; x^2} = \frac{(8.119)(95,580)}{(20)(3643.20)}$$

$$= 10.650$$

$$S_{b_0} = 3.26$$

It is important to understand that the researcher does not conduct both of these tests and then select the more favorable one. As emphasized above, the structure of the test must evolve from the research at hand. The illustration above simply shows how to construct the test and select the appropriate critical t-value from the t-table. Refer back to Figure 3.4 for a visual representation of the difference between these two tests.

The Confidence Level

To illustrate the structure of the test above, the .95 probability level was arbitrarily used. In applied research, this selection should not be arbitrary. Based on the review of statistical theory in Chapter 2, it is clear that if the null hypothesis, H_0: $\beta_1 = 0$, is true, the sample values of b_1 would lie between minus and plus infinity. Moreover, depending on the degrees of freedom, the probability of the sample value of b_1 being any number of standard deviations above or below $\beta_1 = 0$ can be determined directly from the t-table.

This has the important implication that the null hypothesis can be rejected when it is in fact true. Regardless of the confidence level of the test, which determines the critical value for testing, there exists the chance of getting a computed value larger than the critical value selected and hence rejecting the null hypothesis when it is true. This is called a *type I error:* rejecting the null hypothesis when it is true. Thus when selecting a confidence level for testing, one is really selecting a probability of making a type I error. The conservative way to avoid making this error is to test at a higher confidence level. But this increases the chance of making another error, called a *type II error*: not rejecting the null hypothesis when it is not true. These two types of errors are illustrated in Figure 3.5.

Consider first Figure 3.5(a), which shows the distribution of b_1 when the null hypothesis is true. Let the critical value for the test be $+t_c$. In this case, the probability is .05 of obtaining a sample that yields a b_1 to the right of the critical value. In this case, the null hypothesis would be rejected, yet it is true. The probability of this happening is normally written as α, often referred to as the *level* of the test.

Now consider Figure 3.5(b), which shows the distribution of b_1 when the null hypothesis is not true—$\beta_1 = .75$, for example. In this instance, the null hypothesis should always be rejected, yet for any computed t-statistic up to $+t_c$, it will not be rejected and hence an error is made. Notice in Figure 3.5 that trying to minimize making one error increases the chance of making the other error. Visualize moving

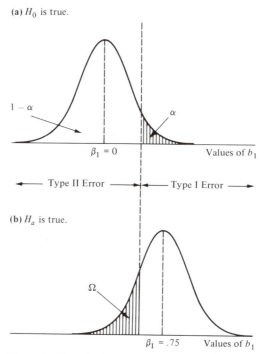

(a) H_0 is true.

$1 - \alpha$

α

$\beta_1 = 0$

Values of b_1

← Type II Error →|← Type I Error →

(b) H_a is true.

Ω

$\beta_1 = .75$ Values of b_1

Figure 3.5 Kinds of Errors in Hypothesis Testing: α = Type I Error; Ω = Type II Error.

the vertical line representing $+t_c$ to the right. This will decrease the probability of rejecting the null hypothesis if it is true, but it increases the probability of not rejecting it if it is not true. These combinations are presented in Table 3.3.

This, in simplified form, is the conundrum facing the applied researcher. Population parameters are seldom known with certainty and must be estimated from sample data. But this permits making only probability statements, in the form of hypothesis tests, about the true values of the parameters. Yet, in testing, the researcher is faced with the probability of rejecting an hypothesis when it should not be rejected. By reducing the chance of making this error, the chances of not rejecting the hypothesis when it should be rejected are increased. We never know whether an error has been committed.

Table 3.3. Results of Hypothesis Tests

True State of Nature	Researcher's Decision	
	Does Not Reject H_0	*Does Reject H_0*
H_0: is true	Correct with probability of $1 - \alpha$ = confidence level	Type I error with probability equal to α
H_0: is false	Type II error with probability equal to Ω	Correct with probability of $1 - \Omega$

An Example

An easy way to see how the least squares regression theory presented in this chapter can be used in practice is to look at a simple example. Suppose that a researcher is interested in the determinants of the stock of money and believes, as a first approximation, that a major determinant is the level of economic activity in the economy. Let M represent the real amount of money per capita in circulation, where money is defined as currency plus balances in checking and saving deposits. Let E represent the real gross national product per capita. (How and why some variables should be expressed in real and per capita terms is discussed, together with other basic techniques in applied regression, in Chapter 10.) Quarterly data on these variables for 1973 to 1984 are presented in Table 3.4.

Table 3.4. Macroeconomic Data on Money and GNP in the United States, Quarterly, 1973 to 1984.

Year	Quarter	Money in Circulation[a]	Gross National Product[b]	Year	Quarter	Money in Circulation	Gross National Product
1973	1	$3757.46	$5906.00	1979	1	$3948.54	$6572.00
	2	3745.98	5900.00		2	3950.87	6540.00
	3	3731.80	5921.00		3	3951.72	6598.00
	4	3697.10	5954.00		4	3927.40	6590.00
1974	1	3691.12	5882.00	1980	1	3898.45	6603.00
	2	3639.59	5876.00		2	3828.78	6430.00
	3	3578.33	5825.00		3	3864.24	6423.00
	4	3519.28	5732.00		4	3841.62	6464.00
1975	1	3485.62	5600.00	1981	1	3800.71	6606.00
	2	3561.57	5655.00		2	3830.58	6583.00
	3	3613.96	5764.00		3	3805.05	6611.00
	4	3627.03	5800.00		4	3814.52	6502.00
1976	1	3702.14	5915.00	1982	1	3855.81	6410.00
	2	3774.49	5943.00		2	3863.20	6383.00
	3	3821.48	5962.00		3	3911.66	6352.00
	4	3890.87	6001.00		4	3971.52	6343.00
1977	1	3960.97	6115.00	1983	1	4113.35	6381.00
	2	3994.99	6201.00		2	4187.54	6512.00
	3	4019.67	6286.00		3	4216.75	6605.00
	4	4035.00	6279.00		4	4249.31	6684.00
1978	1	4049.00	6317.00	1984	1	4267.61	6832.00
	2	4007.15	6468.00		2	4301.03	6949.00
	3	3988.18	6502.00				
	4	3973.23	6570.00				

Source: Business Statistics, various editions.

[a] Real per capita M2.
[b] Real GNP per capita.

The starting point is a simple linear equation of the form

$$M = \beta_0 + \beta_1 E + U \tag{3.64}$$

The ordinary least squares (OLS) estimates of the β-parameters in (3.64), using the data in Table 3.4 and equations (3.17), (3.18), (3.52), (3.53), and (3.62), are

$$\begin{array}{cc} M = 991.3 + .460E + e & S = 118.4 \\ (321.9) \quad (.051) \end{array} \tag{3.65}$$

where the numbers in parentheses are the standard errors of the regression coefficients. An interpretation of the β_1 (.460) term is straightforward: Between 1973 and 1984, each additional dollar of real per capita GNP tended to be associated with a 46 cent increase in the real per capita stock of money. As stated above, the intercept term is included to force the regression line through the midpoint of the data set used to estimate (3.64). It has no economic interpretation in this illustration. The value for S, the estimated standard error of regression says that about 68 percent of the values of M will fall within plus or minus \$118.40 around the population regression equation.

The value for b_1 (.460) in (3.65) is the OLS estimate of the β_1 parameter in (3.64) obtained from the 1973–1984 data set. One possible research question is whether the level of economic activity affects the money stock; that is, does M change as E changes? If the answer is no, then β_1 would be zero and b_1 "close to" zero. But is .460 "close enough" to zero in this case to conclude that E does not affect M? Hypothesis testing is used to provide probabalistic answers to such questions. The null hypothesis in this case is that "E does not affect M," stated formally as

$$H_0: \beta_1 = 0 \tag{3.66}$$

and the alternative hypothesis is that "E does affect M," stated formally as

$$H_0: \beta_1 \neq 0 \tag{3.67}$$

The next step is to construct a confidence interval around the slope estimate of .460. Using a two-tailed 95 percent confidence interval involves finding the critical t-value for 44 degrees of freedom (46-2) shown in Appendix Table A.2. This table shows that the critical t-value is 2.021 for 40 degrees of freedom and 2.000 for 60 degrees of freedom. Using the more conservative value (2.021) to construct a confidence interval yields

$$.460 \pm (2.021)(.051) \tag{3.68}$$

or

$$P[.357 \leq \beta_1 \leq .563] = .95 \tag{3.69}$$

Since zero does not fall within this confidence interval, the null hypothesis is rejected and the alternative hypothesis is not rejected. The level of statistical significance is found by subtracting the confidence level from 1: $1 - .95 = .05$. The conclusion is that β_1, the marginal effect of E on M, is significantly different from zero at the .05 (or 5 percent) level.

What we have just described is a two-tailed confidence interval. If the researcher had good reason to believe that β_1 should be positive, this extra information could be used to develop the one-tailed confidence interval. Here the formal statement is

$$H_0: \beta_1 = 0 \quad \text{versus} \quad H_a: \beta_1 > 0 \tag{3.70}$$

The appropriate one-tailed confidence interval would be

$$\beta_1 > [.460 - (1.684)(.051)] \quad \text{or} \quad \beta_1 > .374 \tag{3.71}$$

Since the lower boundary of this interval is above zero, the null hypothesis would again be rejected and the alternative hypothesis would not be rejected.

The easiest and most common way to conduct hypothesis tests is to construct a t-ratio using the value of b_1 and its standard error:

$$t = \frac{b_1 - \beta_1}{S_{b_1}} = \frac{.460 - 0}{.051} = 9.02 \tag{3.72}$$

Since the (absolute) value of this t-ratio is greater than either the one- or two-tailed critical t-values, the null hypothesis would be rejected. This t-ratio is frequently printed out by computer programs and used by researchers to check for coefficients that are significantly different from zero or, in common researcher parlance, "significant."

Summary

In this chapter we have presented the basic theory of least squares regression. Although everything was presented in terms of a simple regression equation (an equation with only one independent variable), the content of this chapter can be generalized to multiple regression.

Whatever regression model is being used, it is important for the applied researcher to understand the distinction between a population regression equation and the sample regression equation that is used to estimate it. Population regression functions include disturbance terms because some relevant independent variables may be omitted from the regression equation, because there is an inherently stochastic element to social behavior, or because the dependent variable might be measured incorrectly. Because of the disturbance term, the dependent variable can never be known with certainty. Instead, the applied researcher must accept that the observed values for the dependent variable are themselves random variables that depend both on the level of the independent variable(s) and the values of the disturbance term. The regression model assumes that the disturbance terms are "well behaved" in that their expected value is zero, their variance is constant, and they are not correlated with each other. The problems that arise when disturbance terms are not well behaved are discussed in later chapters.

The least squares formulas for computing the slope and intercept of a straight line developed in Chapter 1 turn out to have desirable properties: Using the statistical assumptions specified by (3.6) to (3.9), the least squares coefficients computed from a sample are minimum-variance, linear, unbiased estimators of the population regression coefficients. The Gauss–Markov theorem (which is proven above for the special case of simple regression) says that the least squares coefficients are best linear un-biased estimators (BLUEs) of the parameters in the regression model. The ultimate goal of applied research is to learn something about the values of population param-eters. Least squares regression, when combined with statistical theory, is the basis for much applied work.

In this chapter we have examined least squares regression. In advanced economet-rics literature, one encounters *generalized least squares* (often denoted GLS) and *two-stage least squares* (often denoted 2SLS or TSLS). To avoid confusion, the least squares regression model of this chapter is usually referred to as *ordinary least squares* (denoted OLS). This term is used in the remainder of the book.

Terms

BLUE (best linear unbiased
   estimator)
Conditional distribution
Disturbance term (U)
Error sum of squares
Estimated error variance
Gauss–Markov theorem
Homoscedasticity
Linear regression model
Measurement error
OLS (ordinary least squares)
Omitted variables
One-tailed test

Population parameter
Population regression equation
   (PRE)
Sample regression equation
Standard deviation of
   regression
Standard error of regression
Stochastic disturbance
Two-tailed test
Type I error
Type II error
Variance of the regression
   coefficients

Exercises

3.1 What is the equation and four assumptions that comprise the simple classical linear regression model?

3.2 Show that if $y_i = b_1 x_1 + e_i$, then $\Sigma\, x_i e_i = 0$. (HINT: Substitute for e_i and b_1.)

3.3 Find the critical t-values in the following cases:
  (a) $n = 34$ $K = 3$ $\alpha = .05$ two-tailed test
  (b) $n = 24$ $K = 1$ $\alpha = .05$ one-tailed test
  (c) $n = 180$ $K = 6$ $\alpha = .05$ one-tailed test

(d) $n = 67$	$K = 6$	$\alpha = .05$	two-tailed test
(e) $n = 24$	$K = 2$	$\alpha = .01$	one-tailed test
(f) $n = 24$	$K = 3$	$\alpha = .01$	two-tailed test
(g) $n = 246$	$K = 6$	$\alpha = .01$	two-tailed test
(h) $n = 582$	$K = 18$	$\alpha = .01$	one-tailed test
(i) $n = 582$	$K = 18$	$\alpha = .05$	one-tailed test

3.4 Consider the model $Y = f(X)$, where

$$Y = \text{consumption of purple oongs, pounds per person}$$

$$X = \text{consumer income, hundreds of dollars per person}$$

$$n = 20 \qquad \Sigma (Y - \bar{Y})(X - \bar{X}) = -66.5$$

$$\Sigma X = 300 \qquad \Sigma x^2 = 500$$

$$\Sigma Y = 120 \qquad \Sigma e^2 = 3.6$$

(a) Write the general linear form of the population regression function.
(b) Write the general linear form of the sample regression function.
(c) Compute the sample regression coefficients b_0 and b_1.
(d) Compute the estimated variance of the regression.
(e) Compute the standard error of the regression.
(f) Compute the estimated variance of b_1.
(g) Compute the standard error of b_1.

3.5 Suppose that a researcher is studying the relationship between gallons of milk consumed by the Jones family per month (Y) and the price of milk each month (X in dollars per gallon). The sample consists of observations in 12 consecutive months. Analysis of the data reveals the following:

$$\Sigma Y = 480 \qquad \Sigma X = 36$$

$$\Sigma xy = -440 \qquad \Sigma x^2 = 20$$

$$\Sigma e_i^2 = 528, \text{ given } \hat{b}_0 \text{ and } \hat{b}_1$$

For this sample, find the following values. (HINT: Show formulas and units in your answers.)

(a) $\bar{X} = $ _____
(b) $\bar{Y} = $ _____
(c) Least squares slope = _____
(d) Least squares intercept = _____
(e) Estimated error variance (S^2) = _____
(f) Standard error of regression (S) = _____
(g) Estimated variance of b_1 ($S_{b_1}^2$) = _____
(h) Standard error of b_1 (S_{b_1}) = _____
(i) Test the hypothesis that $b_1 = 0$ at the 5 percent confidence level.

3.6 Suppose that a researcher is studying the relationship between grade points on an exam (Y_i) and hours studied for the exam (X_i) for a group of 20 students. Analysis of the data reveals the following:

$$\Sigma\, Y = 1600 \qquad \Sigma\, X = 400$$

$$\Sigma\, xy = 1800 \qquad \Sigma\, x^2 = 600$$

$$\Sigma\, e_i^2 = 43{,}200, \text{ given } \hat{b}_0 \text{ and } \hat{b}_1$$

Find the following values. (HINT: Show formulas and units in your answers.)

(a) $\overline{X}$ = _____

(b) $\overline{Y}$ = _____

(c) Least squares slope = _____

(d) Least squares intercept = _____

(e) Standard error of regression (S) = _____

(f) Standard error of b_1 (S_{b_1}) = _____

(g) What is the meaning of b_1?

(h) Interpret S, the standard deviation of regression.

(i) Test the hypothesis that hours studied has no impact on exam points against the alternative hypothesis that b_1 is positive at the 5 percent level of significance.

3.7 The following four observations yield, via OLS, the sample regression function $Y_i = .5 + .8X_i + e_i$.

i	Y	X	$\hat{Y}$	e	e^2
1	1	1			
2	3	2			
3	2	3			
4	4	4			
	10	10			

(a) Complete the table by calculating $\hat{Y} = .5 + .8X$, e_i, and e_i^2.

(b) Calculate S^2, the BLUE of the variance of the population disturbance term, σ^2.

(c) What is S, the square root of S^2, called? What is its value in this case?

(d) Use another possible line, $\hat{Y} = 1 + .6X$, and recalculate the table.

(e) Compare the sums of the Y, e, and e^2 columns in the answers to parts (a) and (d).

(f) Can we draw any line through these four observations that yields a similar sum of e_i^2 as the line used in part (a)? How or why not?

3.8

(a) What is known about $\hat{Y}$ if $S^2 = 0$?

(b) What is known about $\hat{Y}$ if S^2 = estimated variance of Y?

(c) What would be the values for b_0 and b_1 in part (b)?

3.9 Use the data in the following table to calculate the regression coefficients for
$Y = b_0 + b_1 X + e$.
  (a) Complete the table.

Y	X	x_i	y_i	$x_i y_i$	x_i^2	y_i^2
0	0					
2	1					
1	2					
3	1					
1	0					
3	3					
4	4					
2	2					
1	2					
2	1					
19	16					

  (b) b_1 = _____
  (c) b_0 = _____
  (d) Calculate the sum of squared errors without calculating each e_i. [HINT: From
      (3.43) note that $\Sigma\, e_i^2 = \Sigma\, y^2 - b_1\, \Sigma\, yx_1.$]
  (e) What is the standard error of regression?

3.10 Using (3.52), show that $E(S^2) = \sigma^2$.

3.11 Show that

$$\frac{\Sigma\, x_i y_i}{\Sigma\, x_i^2} = \frac{\Sigma\, XY - \Sigma\, X\, \Sigma\, Y/n}{\Sigma\, X^2 - \Sigma\, (X)^2/n}$$

4

Multiple Least Squares Regression

The theory of least squares regression was developed in Chapter 3 using simple regression to illustrate the derivation of the least squares estimators and their properties. In this chapter we turn to *multiple regression* and consider an equation containing several independent variables. Explicit formulas for computing the least squares coefficients are not derived here as they were in Chapter 3, because matrix algebra is required and we have chosen not to introduce matrix algebra at this point. The advanced reader is encouraged to turn to Chapter 20 for the general treatment of multiple regression.

Multiple regression, especially interpreting the least squares coefficients, is not always easy to comprehend on first reading. To provide some interpretative insight, in the next section we return to the research theme of previous chapters to make the important distinction between *experimental* and *nonexperimental research*. The former refers to research settings in which the applied researcher generates under controlled, or experimental, conditions the data needed for hypothesis testing. The latter refers to research settings in which the researcher cannot generate the needed data but, rather, must use data already generated by the system under study.

With this as background, the general regression model is presented and the normal equations are derived. At this juncture, the Gauss–Markov theorem is invoked to claim the best linear unbiased properties for the least squares estimators. To give some insight into the computational procedures, the estimators are derived for the two-independent-variable case. This model, like the one-independent-variable model, is not particularly useful to the applied researcher. However, working through the derivations gives some intuitive insight into the general case. In addition, the two-independent-variable model is used for expository purposes in later chapters to illustrate several econometric problems encountered by the applied researcher.

Experimental Versus Nonexperimental Research

Interpreting a simple regression equation is straightforward. In the simple regresssion equation

$$Y = b_0 + b_1 X + e \qquad (4.1)$$

b_0 is the intercept, the point where the linear equation intersects the Y axis, and b_1 is the slope coefficient, which says that a 1-unit change in the value of X results in a b_1-unit change in Y. The interpretation of the coefficients in a multiple regression is not necessarily as obvious. Consider the multiple regression equation

$$Y = b_0 + b_1 X_1 + b_2 X_2 + \cdots + b_K X_K + e \qquad (4.2)$$

where X_1 is the same variable as in (4.1). Again, the coefficient of X_1, b_1, is the change in Y for a 1-unit change in X_1; but is this all it says, or is there something more to be said, given that there are a number of other independent variables in the equation? To develop an understanding of how the applied researcher interprets the coefficients in (4.2), it is helpful to return to the research theme to consider ways by which the researcher attempts to measure the effect of a change in one or another variable.

To experiment is to use data to test the validity of an hypothesis derived from some underlying theory. So, in this sense, all applied research is experimental. However, an important distinction can be made regarding how the sample data used for hypothesis testing are obtained. This distinction and its implications for interpreting the coefficients of a multiple regression equation are discussed here.

Suppose that a plant scientist is interested in measuring the effect of a herbicide on corn yield; that is, the research objective is to determine whether increased application rates of the herbicide will result in increased yields. This can be expressed as

$$Y = f(H) \qquad (4.3)$$

where Y is corn yield and H is herbicide application. To keep the illustration simple, assume that the underlying theory identifies the following relationship regarding the factors that affect corn yield:

$$Y = f(H, F, W, C) \qquad (4.4)$$

where Y = corn yield
  H = rate of herbicide application
  F = level and composition of fertilizer
  W = water availability during growing season
  C = cultural practices during planting, growing, and harvesting

This theory makes clear that the researcher must somehow account for, or control for, the effect of all four independent variables on corn yield, even though the research objective is to measure only the yield–herbicide relationship.

Thus the equation

$$Y = f(H|F, W, C) \tag{4.5}$$

represents the immediate research objective of measuring the effect of herbicide on yield, "given" (or controlling for) the effect of F, W, and C on corn yield.

To proceed, the researcher prepares a small experimental plot, perhaps as small as a few square yards. The plot is divided into subplots, each of the same size, as shown in Figure 4.1. Three levels of herbicide application are selected for the experiment, $H = 5$, 10, and 15. The plots to receive these different treatment levels are selected at random. Each subplot receives the same amount of fertilizer of the same composition, the same amount of water during the growing season, and each is planted and harvested at the same time. In other words, and this is the important point, each subplot is treated the same regarding the variables identified by the underlying theory, except for the level of herbicide application. Consequently, any difference in corn yield among the plots will be due to the difference in the level of herbicide application, H, plus any random variation that nature may introduce.

At the end of the growing season, the researcher harvests the crop, being careful to record the yields for each of the nine subplots. The worksheet to summarize the results is shown in Table 4.1. In this simple illustration, there are three observations

No. 1	No. 2	No. 3
$H = 5$	$H = 15$	$H = 5$
No. 4	No. 5	No. 6
$H = 10$	$H = 15$	$H = 10$
No. 7	No. 8	No. 9
$H = 15$	$H = 5$	$H = 10$

Underlying theory: $Y = f(H, F, W, C)$
Research equation: $Y = f(H|F, W, C)$
where
  Y = corn yield
  H = herbicide application
  F = fertilizer level
  W = water availability
  C = cultural practices on the plots
Research objective: Measure the yield–herbicide relationship.

Figure 4.1 Illustration of an Experimental Design to Measure the Effect of Herbicide on Corn Yield.

Table 4.1. Worksheet Used to Record Yield Data

Level of Herbicide, H	Yield of Subplots	Average Yield by Herbicide Level
5	Y_1, Y_3, Y_8	$\bar{Y}_5$
10	Y_4, Y_6, Y_9	$\bar{Y}_{10}$
15	Y_2, Y_5, Y_7	$\bar{Y}_{15}$

on yield for reach of the three levels of herbicide application. Because of the likelihood of some random variation in the system, the corn yields for a given value of H will not be the same, but will vary around the true yield for that value of H. Consequently, the *conditional mean* for corn yield for each H is computed, as shown in the last column of Table 4.1. The differences in the conditional means measure the effect of herbicide on corn yield. Finally, using the appropriate statistical procedures, the researcher tests the *null hypothesis* that H has no effect on corn yield, holding constant the effect of F, W, and C on corn yield.

This example illustrates the concept of experimental research mentioned above: The researcher *generates* the data under experimental conditions that control for (or hold constant) the effect of all variables on corn yields except for H, the variable of interest.

The social sciences cannot be viewed as experimental sciences in this sense because applied researchers can seldom, if ever, generate under controlled conditions the data needed to test hypotheses. Rather, like astronomy, the social sciences must use for hypothesis testing the data generated by the underlying system being studied, data over which the applied researcher has no control.

Suppose that an agricultural economist is interested in measuring the effect of income change on food expenditures, written as

$$Y = f(I) \tag{4.6}$$

Drawing from the theory of consumer choice, we formulate the following implicit function:

$$Y = f(I, P_0, P_i, T) \tag{4.7}$$

where Y = food expenditures
  I = consumer income
  P_0 = price of food
  P_i = price of commodities competing for food dollar
  T = consumer tastes and preferences

Given this theory, the equation representing the specific research question is

$$Y = f(I|P_0, P_i, T) \tag{4.8}$$

where the objective is to measure the effect of income on food expenditures, holding constant the effect of P_0, P_i, and T.

The agricultural economist begins, as does any scientist, by drawing on theory to develop the empirical model appropriate to the research objective. However, at this point, a substantive difference is encountered. It is not possible to assign consumers to a number of subgroups, each with the same tastes and preferences, each confronted by the same set of prices, each with a different income, and then compute the conditional means of food expenditures for each income level. In other words, the researcher cannot experimentally control for the effect of P_0, P_i, and T on food expenditures. Rather, the effect of these variables on expenditures must be estimated, and thereby "controlled for" within the experiment, together with the variable of interest. This is accomplished by using sample data to estimate the following equation:

$$Y = b_0 + b_1 I + b_2 P_0 + b_3 P_i + b_4 T + e \tag{4.9}$$

where the variables are defined above and e is added to allow for random variation in food expenditures.

To determine how the conditional mean for food expenditures changes as income changes, obtain the mean expenditure by

$$E(Y) = b_0 + b_1 E(I) + b_2 E(P_0) + b_3 E(P_i) + b_4 E(T) \tag{4.10}$$

since $E(e) = 0$. Next, assign a specific value of P_0, P_i, and T and rewrite (4.10) as

$$E(Y) = b_0 + b_2 P_0^* + b_3 P_i^* + b_4 T^* + b_1 I$$
$$= b_0^* + b_1 I \tag{4.11}$$

where $b_0^* = b_2 P_0^* + b_3 P_i^* + b_4 T^*$ is the intercept, or constant term, because P_0^*, P_i^*, and T^* are assigned specific numerical values. Thus (4.11) measures the change in the conditional mean of food expenditures as a function of income, holding constant the effect of P_0, P_i, and T. This can be expressed mathematically as

$$\frac{\partial E(Y)}{\partial I} = b_1 \tag{4.12}$$

a relationship that holds for any preassigned values for P_0, P_i, and T.

This illustration provides the basis for the general interpretation of the coefficients of the X-variables in (4.2). The coefficient, b_i, of the ith independent variable measures the change in Y for a 1-unit change in X_i, holding constant the effect on Y of the other variables in the equation. For this reason, the coefficients are often called *partial* or *net regression coefficients*. In some cases, the notation b_1 is sufficient to denote a partial or net regression coefficient. In other cases, to avoid any confusion it is necessary to make clear that the coefficient is a partial coefficient. The conventional notation for this is $b_{y1.234}$, which in (4.11) is read as "the effect of income on food expenditures, holding constant the effect of food price, other prices, and consumer tastes and preferences on food expenditures."

In summary, the applied researcher in agricultural economics and economics cannot, in general, generate under controlled or experimental conditions the data needed to test hypotheses. Rather, the researcher must use the data generated by the system being studied, and the effects of *all* the variables identified by the underlying theory must be included in (4.2). This is so even though only one variable is of interest to the research objective. The least squares coefficient of a particular independent variable measures the effect of that variable on the dependent variable, holding constant the effects of the other independent variables in the equation. In most research settings the researcher is, of course, interested in the effect of all the variables in the equation, not just one as in the illustration above. This does not alter the interpretation of the individual coefficients, they remain partial or net coefficients.

Multiple Regression

The general multiple regression equation is written as

$$Y = \beta_0 + \beta_1 X_1 + \cdots + \beta_K X_K + U \qquad (4.13)$$

which differs from (3.5) in that it allows for K independent variables. This general equation cannot be shown graphically as easily as was the simple regression equation in Chapter 3. In technical language, simple regression, with its one independent variable, can be represented by a line in "2-space," while the general equation must be represented by planes in "$K + 1$-space." The special case of two independent variables is illustrated in Figure 4.2. This shows the *plane* (rather than the line) of average relationship between Y and the two independent variables X_1 and X_2. The mathematical expression for this plane is

$$\hat{Y} = \beta_0 + \beta_1 X_1 + \beta_2 X_2$$

Given the population regression coefficients, specific values for X_1 and X_2 yield unique values for Y, namely $\hat{Y}$. These values for the range of combinations of X_1 and X_2 trace out the plane of average relationship shown in Figure 4.2. The actual, or observed,

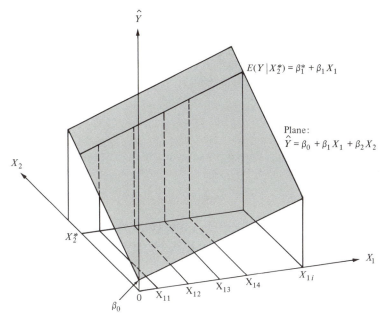

Figure 4.2 Typical Regression Plane for $K = 2$.

values of Y will fall above and below this plane, depending on the values of U. The sample counterpart of U, the OLS residual e, is what is minimized in developing the estimators of the coefficients in (4.13). Finally, the conditional mean of Y, holding constant X_2, traces on a path on the plane that shows how Y changes with X_1. This conditional mean can be written as

$$E(Y|X_2) = \beta_0^* + \beta_1 X_1$$

Adding another independent variable to (4.13) requires an added spatial dimension, making graphic representation difficult. About all one can do is imagine that somewhere in K-space there exists a plane (actually a hyperplane) that summarizes the average relationship between Y and K-independent variables. Fortunately, as described in the preceding section, (4.13) is easily interpreted without resort to this multidimensional visualization.

The disturbance term is included in (4.13) for the same reasons given for including it in (3.5). To complete the regression model, the following statistical assumptions are made:

$$E(U) = 0 \tag{4.14}$$

$$E(U) = \sigma^2 \tag{4.15}$$

$$E(U_i U_j) = 0, \qquad \text{all } i \text{ not equal to } j \tag{4.16}$$

X-values fixed in repeated sampling $\tag{4.17}$

No exact linear relationship exists among the independent variables $\tag{4.18}$

Assumptions (4.14) to (4.17) are identical to the assumptions (3.6) to (3.9) and carry the same interpretation. Assumption (4.18), the new assumption, says that there is no linear dependence among the independent variables. The implications of this assumption for estimation, on both theoretical and practical grounds, are not explored here but are treated in Chapters 12 and 13.

The population regression equation, (4.13), is estimated by the sample regression equation:

$$Y = b_0 + b_1 X_1 + \cdots + b_K X_K + e \tag{4.19}$$

The first step toward finding the OLS estimator of the β-coefficients is writing the sum of squared residuals:

$$\text{ESS} = \Sigma\, e_i^2 = \Sigma\, (Y_i - b_0 - b_1 X_{1i} - \cdots - b_K X_{Ki})^2 \tag{4.20}$$

The second step is to take the derivatives of (4.20) with respect to each of the b-coefficients and then equate each derivative to zero. This step yields the set of $K + 1$ *normal equations*:

$$\frac{\partial \text{ESS}}{\partial b_0} = 2\, \Sigma\, (Y_i - b_0 - b_1 X_{1i} - \cdots - b_K X_{Ki})(-1) = 0$$

$$\frac{\partial ESS}{\partial b_1} = 2 \Sigma (Y_i - b_0 - b_1 X_{1i} - \cdots - b_K X_{Ki})(-X_{1i}) = 0 \qquad (4.21)$$

$$\frac{\partial ESS}{\partial b_K} = 2 \Sigma (Y_i - b_0 - b_1 X_{1i} - \cdots - b_K X_{Ki})(-X_{Ki}) = 0$$

There are $K + 1$ equations and $K + 1$ unknowns (the least squares coefficients), so a solution to the normal equations exists. Because of the number of equations in the system, however, the computational formulas for the b's cannot be written as easily as they were in Chapter 3. The one exception to this is the formula for b_0, the intercept. Slight manipulation of the first normal equation yields

$$b_0 = \overline{Y} - b_1 \overline{X}_1 - \cdots - b_K \overline{X}_K \qquad (4.22)$$

Given that b_0 can always be obtained from (4.22), the variables in (4.21) can be written in deviation form. Using deviation notation, multiplying out (4.21), and rearranging terms yields

$$\Sigma y_i x_{1i} = b_1 \Sigma x_{1i}^2 + b_2 \Sigma x_{1i} x_{2i} + \cdots + b_K \Sigma x_{1i} x_{Ki}$$

$$\Sigma y_i x_{2i} = b_1 \Sigma x_{1i} x_{2i} + b_2 \Sigma x_{2i}^2 + \cdots + b_K \Sigma x_{2i} x_{Ki}$$

$$\qquad (4.23)$$

$$\Sigma y_i x_{Ki} = b_1 \Sigma x_{1i} x_{Ki} + b_2 \Sigma x_{2i} x_{Ki} + \cdots + b_K \Sigma x_{Ki}^2$$

There are K equations to be solved for the K regression slopes. Matrix algebra is requried to write out the full set of computational formulas; the derivation is illustrated here for the special case of two independent variables.

Computations for $K = 2$

The ESS in deviation form for the $K = 2$ is

$$ESS = \Sigma e_i^2 = \Sigma (y_i - b_1 x_{1i} - b_2 x_{2i})^2 \qquad (4.24)$$

The necessary conditions for ESS to have a minimum value, found by taking the first derivative of (4.24) with respect to b_1 and b_2 and equating to zero, are

$$\frac{\partial ESS}{\partial b_1} = 2 \Sigma (y_i - b_1 x_{1i} - b_2 x_{2i})(-x_{1i}) = 0 \qquad (4.25)$$

$$\frac{\partial ESS}{\partial b_2} = 2 \Sigma (y_i - b_1 x_{1i} - b_2 x_{2i})(-x_{2i}) = 0 \qquad (4.26)$$

Dividing by 2, expanding, removing the parentheses, and rearranging terms in both (4.25) and (4.26) yields the two *normal equations* to be solved for b_1 and b_2:

$$\Sigma\ yx_1 = b_1\ \Sigma\ x_1^2 + b_2\ \Sigma\ x_1x_2 \tag{4.27}$$

$$\Sigma\ yx_2 = b_1\ \Sigma\ x_1x_2 + b_2\ \Sigma\ x_2^2 \tag{4.28}$$

where the i subscripts are suppressed and the summations are over the sample of n observations.

Multiplying (4.27) by $(\Sigma\ x_2^2)$ and (4.28) by $(\Sigma\ x_1x_2)$ yields

$$(\Sigma\ x_2^2)(\Sigma\ yx_1) = b_1(\Sigma\ x_1^2)(\Sigma\ x_2^2) + b_2(\Sigma\ x_1x_2)(\Sigma\ x_2^2) \tag{4.29}$$

$$(\Sigma\ x_1x_2)(\Sigma\ yx_2) = b_1(\Sigma x_1x_2)^2 + b_2(\Sigma\ x_1x_2)(\Sigma\ x_2^2) \tag{4.30}$$

Subtracting (4.30) from (4.29) to eliminate b_2 yields

$$(\Sigma\ x_2^2)(\Sigma\ yx_1) - (\Sigma\ x_1x_2)(\Sigma\ yx_2)^2 = b_1[(\Sigma\ x_1^2)(\Sigma\ x_2^2) - (\Sigma\ x_1x_2)^2]$$

which can be written as

$$b_1 = \frac{(\Sigma\ x_2^2)(\Sigma\ yx_1) - (\Sigma\ x_1x_2)(\Sigma\ yx_2)}{(\Sigma\ x_1^2)(\Sigma\ x_2^2) - (\Sigma\ x_1x_2)^2} \tag{4.31}$$

Equation (4.31) is the estimator of β_1. By a similar technique, the normal equations can be solved for b_2, the estimator of β_2, as

$$b_2 = \frac{(\Sigma\ x_1^2)(\Sigma\ yx_2) - (\Sigma\ x_1x_2)(\Sigma\ yx_1)}{(\Sigma\ x_1^2)(\Sigma\ x_2^2) - (\Sigma\ x_1x_2)^2} \tag{4.32}$$

These *slope estimators* can be used to obtain the estimator of β_0 as

$$b_0 = \overline{Y} - b_1\overline{X}_1 - b_2\overline{X}_2 \tag{4.33}$$

The variances of these estimators are derived as follows. By definition, the variance of b_1 is given by

$$\text{Var } b_1 = E[b_1 - E(b_1)]^2 \tag{4.34}$$

Because b_1 is an unbiased estimator of β_1, (4.34) may be written as

$$\text{Var } b_1 = E(b_1 - \beta_1)^2 \tag{4.35}$$

Substituting the population regression equation where $K = 2$ for y in (4.31) and rearranging terms yields

$$b_1 - \beta_1 = \frac{(\Sigma\ x_2^2)(\Sigma\ x_1U) - (\Sigma\ x_1x_2)(\Sigma\ x_2U)}{(\Sigma\ x_1^2)(\Sigma\ x_2^2) - (\Sigma\ x_1x_2)^2} \tag{4.36}$$

Substituting (4.36) into (4.35) and performing the required manipulations yields

$$\text{Var } b_1 = \frac{\Sigma\ x_2^2}{(\Sigma\ x_1^2)(\Sigma\ x_2^2) - (\Sigma\ x_1x_2)^2}\ \sigma^2 \tag{4.37}$$

By a similar manipulation,

$$\text{Var } b_2 = \frac{\Sigma x_1^2}{(\Sigma x_1^2)(\Sigma x_2^2) - (\Sigma x_1 x_2)^2} \sigma^2 \tag{4.38}$$

The important thing to note about (4.37) and (4.38) is that the variances of b_1 and b_2 depend on the variance of the disturbance term, σ^2, which is unknown and must be estimated from the sample.

In Chapter 3 we derived an unbiased estimator of the variance of the population disturbance for $K = 1$:

$$\text{estimator of } \sigma^2 = S^2 = \frac{\Sigma e^2}{N - 2} \tag{4.39}$$

The generalized version of this unbiased estimator for $K > 1$ is given by

$$\text{estimator of } \sigma^2 = S^2 = \frac{\Sigma e^2}{n - (K + 1)} \tag{4.40}$$

where n is the number of observations in the sample, K is the number of independent variables in the equation, the $+1$ picks up the constant term in the equation, and $K + 1$ is the total number of parameters estimated in the regression of Y on $X_1, \ldots, X_K$. S^2 is the sample estimate of the variance of the population disturbance term. The square root, S, is called the *standard deviation of the regression equation*, the *standard deviation of the estimate*, or most commonly the *standard error of regression*.

Substituting this result in equations (4.37) and (4.38) yields

$$S_{b_1}^2 = \frac{\Sigma e^2}{n - 3} \frac{\Sigma x_2^2}{(\Sigma x_1^2)(\Sigma x_2^2) - (\Sigma x_1 x_2)^2} \tag{4.41}$$

$$S_{b_2}^2 = \frac{\Sigma e^2}{n - 3} \frac{\Sigma x_1^2}{(\Sigma x_1^2)(\Sigma x_2^2) - (\Sigma x_1 x_2)^2} \tag{4.42}$$

as the estimated variances of the OLS coefficients in the two-independent-variable case. The square roots of these estimated variances are referred to as *standard deviations of the coefficients*.

Multiple Regression Computations: An Example

Suppose that a researcher is trying to evaluate the potential benefits of a proposed irrigation project on corn yields in a developing country. From the previous discussion it is clear that in investigating the effect of water on yield, the effect of all other variables must be held constant. Since the local farmers use little fertilizer, the only other factor considered important in the research is temperature during the growing season. Consequently, data on yields, rainfall, and average temperature are collected. The data are shown in Table 4.2.

Table 4.2. Observed Yield, Rainfall, and Temperature for Eight Years

Year	Yield, Y (Bushels/acre)	Total Rainfall, R (Inches)	Average Temperature, T (Degrees)
1972	55	19	49
1973	65	17	58
1974	80	21	55
1975	75	17	58
1976	70	19	55
1977	50	18	49
1978	60	20	46
1979	65	21	46

The equation to be estimated by multiple linear regression is

$$Y = b_0 + b_1R + b_2T + e \tag{4.43}$$

where R is rainfall measured in inches and T is average temperature measured in degrees. In this equation, T is not of immediate interest but must be included to control for the effect of temperature on yield.

The computations needed to calculate the OLS coefficients in (4.43) are tabulated in Table 4.3. The results required by the OLS estimators are

$$\bar{Y} = 65 \quad \Sigma y^2 = 700 \quad \Sigma yx_1 = 20$$

$$\bar{X}_1 = 19 \quad \Sigma x_1^2 = 18 \quad \Sigma yx_2 = 225$$

$$\bar{X}_2 = 52 \quad \Sigma x_2^2 = 180 \quad \Sigma x_1x_2 = -33$$

The estimates of the regression coefficients are

$$b_1 = \frac{(180)(20) - (-33)(225)}{(18)(180) - (-33)^2} = \frac{11{,}026}{2151} = 5.13$$

$$b_2 = \frac{(18)(225) - (-33)(20)}{(18)(180) - (-33)^2} = \frac{4710}{2151} = 2.19$$

$$b_0 = 65 - (5.13)(19) - (2.19)(52) = -146.35$$

The variances of the estimators are

$$S^2 = \frac{104.48}{8 - 3} = 20.9$$

$$S_{b_1}^2 = \frac{180}{(18)(180) - (-33)^2}(20.9) = 1.749$$

$$S_{b_2}^2 = \frac{18}{(18)(180) - (-33)^2}(20.9) = .175$$

Table 4.3. Information for Least Squares Computation of Data in Table 4.2

Year	(1) Yield, Y	(2) Rain, X_1	(3) Temp., X_2	(4) Y	(5) x_1	(6) x_2	(7) y^2	(8) x_1^2	(9) x_2^2	(10) yx_1	(11) yx_2	(12) x_1x_2	(13) $\hat{Y}$	(14) e	(15) e^2
1972	55	19	49	−10	0	−3	100	0	9	0	30	0	58.4	−3.4	11.56
1973	65	17	58	0	−2	6	0	4	36	0	0	−12	67.9	−2.9	8.41
1974	80	21	55	15	2	3	225	4	9	30	45	6	81.8	−1.8	3.24
1975	75	17	58	10	−2	6	100	4	36	−20	60	−12	67.9	7.1	50.41
1976	70	19	55	5	0	3	25	0	9	0	15	0	71.6	−1.6	2.56
1977	50	18	49	−15	−1	−3	225	1	9	15	45	3	53.3	−3.3	10.89
1978	60	20	46	−5	1	−6	25	1	36	−5	30	−6	57.0	3.0	9.00
1979	65	21	46	0	2	−6	0	4	36	0	0	−12	62.1	2.9	8.41
	520	152	416	0	0	0	700	18	180	20	225	−33	520.0	0.0	104.48

The estimated regression equation, with standard deviations of the coefficients in parentheses, is

$$Y = -146.35 + 5.13R + 2.19T + e \qquad S = 4.6 \qquad (4.44)$$
$$(1.32) \quad (.42)$$

The estimated equation says that a 1-inch increase in rainfall increases yield by 5.14 bushels per acre, holding temperature constant. A 1-degree increase in average temperature increases yields by 2.2 bushels per acre with no change in rainfall. The researcher can use these results to project the economic benefits of an irrigation project that delivers additional water to the corn-growing region.

To determine if R, the variable of interest in this particular research, is a significant variable, the critical t-value is compared to the computed t-statistic. From Appendix Table A.2, the critical t-value for $8 - 3 = 5$ degrees of freedom and a .025 two-tailed test is 2.571. The calculated t-value is

$$t = \frac{5.13}{1.32} = 3.9$$

Because the computed t-statistic is larger than the critical t-value, the null hypothesis, $\beta_1 = 0$, is rejected and the alternative hypothesis that β_1 is not zero is not rejected.

The confidence interval can be used to develop a lower and an upper bound on the estimated benefit of additional water provided by the proposed irrigation project. Using the estimated coefficient of water application, 5.13, and the critical t-value for 5 degrees of freedom at the .95 level, 2.571, the confidence interval around the true value of β_1 is

$$5.13 - (2.571)(1.32) \leq \beta_1 \leq 5.13 + (2.571)(1.32)$$

$$1.75 \leq \beta_1 \leq 8.52$$

Consequently, the researcher can say that the probability is .95 that each additional inch of water will increase corn yield between 1.74 and 8.52 bushels per acre.

Summary

This completes the discussion of the multiple regression model. Because this chapter illustrated the computations only for the special case of two independent variables, the validity of the contents of Chapters 3 and 4 for the general K-variable case must be taken on faith for the time being, or by resort to the Gauss–Markov theorem. It is easy to see from the two-independent-variable model that adding independent variables to the regression equation just makes the computational formulas more complicated. For skeptics, an intuitive treatment of the general K-variable model is given in Chapter 7 and a mathematical proof of the Gauss–Markov theorem is presented in Chapter 20.

Terms

Conditional mean	Slope coefficients
Estimated variance of	Standard error of b_i
regression	Standard error of estimate
Multiple regression	Variance of OLS estimators
Partial regression coefficient, b_i	

Exercises

4.1 For the two-independent-variable case:
  (a) What are the equation and assumptions comprising the classical regression model?
  (b) What are the OLS formulas for b_0 and b_1, and b_2?
  (c) What does the Gauss–Markov theorem say about the properties of the OLS estimators of β_0, β_1, and β_2?

4.2 Use the data in the following table to answer parts (a) to (e).

i	Y	X_1	X_2
1	10	2	1
2	20	5	0
3	40	3	1
4	30	8	2
5	50	7	1

  (a) Create a table with six rows (one for each observation plus one for the total) and the following columns: y, x_1, x_2, yx_1, yx_2, x_1x_2, x_1^2, and x_2^2. Use the data in this table to answer parts (b) to (d).
  (b) What are the OLS estimates of b_0 and b_1 in $Y = b_0 + b_1x_1 + e$?
  (c) What are the OLS estimates of b_0 and b_2 in $Y = b_0 + b_2x_2 + e$?
  (d) What are the OLS estimates of b_0, $b_{y1.2}$, and $b_{y2.1}$ in

$$Y = b_0 + b_{y1.2}x_1 + b_{y2.1}x_2 + e?$$

  (e) Interpret $b_{y1.2}$ and $b_{y2.1}$ in part (d).
  (f) Why is $b_{y2.1}$ not equal to b_2?

4.3 Use the following data to answer parts (a) to (e) in Exercise 4.2.

Parcel of Land	Value (Thousands)	Size (Acres)	Distance from Nearest City (Miles)
1	$ 40	40	30
2	60	40	30
3	100	10	20
4	150	50	20
5	150	60	0

4.4 Consider the following data:

Parcel of Land	Y Value (Thousands)	X_1 Size (Acres)	X_2 Distance from Nearest City (Miles)
1	$ 52	26	22
2	60	12	22
3	122	5	11
4	126	19	5
5	140	18	0

(a) Calculate the OLS equation for the relationship of value to size of parcel and distance from city.
(b) What are the values for $\hat{Y}_i$ and e_i for each observation?
(c) Calculate the ESS by using equation (4.20).
(d) Calculate the variance of the regression (S^2) and interpret its meaning.
(e) Calculate the variances of $b_{1.2}$ and $b_{2.1}$.
(f) Interpret the partial regression parameters of part (a).

4.5 Consider the following computer printout.

```
THE REGRESSION EQUATION IS
Y = 21.3 + 0.109X₁ - 0.388X₂
```

VARIABLE	COEFFICIENT	ST. DEV. OF COEFF.	T-RATIO = COEFF./S.D.
CONST	21.316	8.626	2.47
X1	.10905	.0105	10.35
X2	-.3878	.1076	-3.60

```
THE ST. DEV. OF Y ABOUT THE REGRESSION LINE IS
S = 1.418 WITH (14 - 3) = 11 DEGREES OF FREEDOM
```

(a) What is the estimated error variance of the regression?
(b) What are the standard deviations of the partial regression coefficients?
(c) How many observations were included in the analysis?
(d) What is the regression value for Y when $X_1 = 430.8$ and $X_2 = 99.0$?
(e) What is the mean value of Y in the data set if $\bar{X}_1 = 333.39$ and $\bar{X}_2 = 97.829$?

4.6 What is the estimate of the standard deviation of regression under the following circumstances?

(a) $\Sigma\, e^2 =$ 1,440 $n =$ 24 $K = $ 2
(b) $\Sigma\, e_i^2 =$ 0 $n =$ 12 $K = $ 12
(c) $\Sigma\, e_i^2 =$ 51,150 $n = $ 3,546 $K = $ 4
(d) $\Sigma\, e_i^2 =$ 51,150 $n =$ 24 $K = $ 3
(e) $\Sigma\, e_i^2 =$ 19,761,984 $n =$ 48 $K = $ 7

4.7 A researcher incorrectly reports that $S_{b_1} = 4$ and $S_{b_2} = 12$ based on an incorrect calculation that the standard error of regression was 10. What are the correct S_{b_1} and S_{b_2} if the correct value for S is

(a) $S = 20$?
(b) $S = 5$?
(c) $S = 100$?
(d) $S = 25$?
(e) $S = K$?

4.8 Suppose that the following model is estimated for school districts in Wisconsin during 1976–1977:

$$C = b_0 + b_1 W + b_2 N + b_3 X + U$$

where C = average annual teacher compensation
("teacher salaries")
W = average monthly compensation of workers in the private sector of the local labor market ("opportunity wage")
N = number of teachers per 1000 students ("class size")
X = average years of experience of teachers ("experience")

The OLS regression results are

$$C = 9734.26 + 4.80W - 14.37N + 235.77X + e$$
$$\qquad\qquad\;\; (1.23) \qquad (6.47) \qquad (101.01)$$

with the standard errors in parentheses.
(a) Carefully interpret b_0, b_1, b_2 and b_3 in terms of teacher salaries, opportunity wage, class size, and experience.
(b) What do the results indicate about a $1000 increase in the annual compensation of private-sector workers in the local labor market?
(c) Are the b's above, below, or equal to their respective β's?

5

Correlation: A Measure of Association in Regression Analysis

In Chapters 3 and 4 we concentrated on the *nature* of the relationship between a dependent variable and a set of independent variables in the context of a regression equation. In this chapter we focus on the *degree* of relationship between variables, customarily measured by the correlation coefficient. The major purpose of this chapter is to show the conditions under which the correlation coefficient can be interpreted as a measure of the variation in the dependent variable associated with, or explained by, variation in the independent variables.

Correlation Coefficient

The Rationale

Consider any two variables X_1 and X_2 that may or may not be associated in any causal way. For example, let X_1 be runs scored by the Milwaukee Brewers baseball team and X_2 be the high temperature during the day in Nome, Alaska. The *correlation model* answers a simple question: Are these two variables linearly related? It is important to understand that the correlation model measures only the degree of covariation between the corresponding values of any two variables. No functional relationship between X_1 and X_2 is assumed or required for the use of the correlation model, and the existence of mutual variation between two variables in no way implies that the variation in one variable, say X_1, is "caused by" variation in X_2.

Table 5.1. Sample Observations on Runs Scored by the Milwaukee Brewers Team and the High Temperature Recorded in Nome, Alaska, for 10 Days in July

Date	Runs (X_1)	Temperature (X_2)
1	4	76
2	5	72
3	1	66
4	7	70
5	12	82
6	11	84
7	7	74
8	2	62
9	3	70
10	8	84

Suppose that a researcher wishes to examine the degree of covariation between the variables X_1 and X_2 in Table 5.1. A possible approach is to look for covariation by plotting the values of X_1 and X_2 on a scatter diagram like Figure 5.1. The nature of the scatter of points suggests that the two variables do vary together. The task here is to develop a quantitative measure of this covariation.

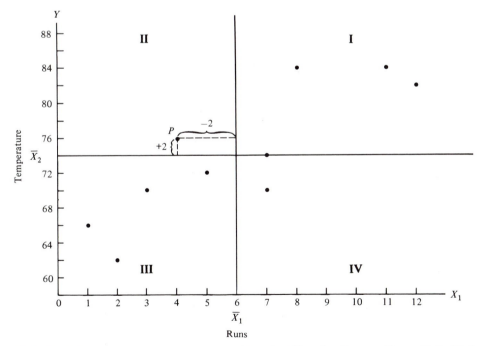

FIGURE 5.1 Scatter Diagram of Runs Scored by the Milwaukee Brewers Versus Daily High Temperatures in Nome, Alaska.

At the outset it is important to recognize that the relationship between two variables can vary considerably from one set of data to the next or from one pair of variables to another. Figure 5.2 illustrates four of many possible degrees of relationship among variables. Case A shows perfect (positive) correlation where all observations lie exactly on a straight line. Case B shows an imperfect, but relatively strong (negative) correlation where the points are tightly bunched about, but do not lie exactly on, a line. In case C, some rather weak (negative) correlation appears to exist. Finally, the points in case D seem randomly scattered and no covariation is apparent.

One Measure of Covariation

To begin developing a quantitative measure of association, return to Figure 5.1 and divide it into four quadrants by erecting perpendiculars to the X_1 and X_2 axes at their respective means $(\bar{X}_1, \bar{X}_2)$. The effect is to move the origin to the centroid. Any point on the scatter diagram can then be expressed as a deviation from the centroid. For example, point P (the observations on X_1 and X_2 for July 1) can be expressed in deviation form as $(-2, 2)$. These paired values of x_{1i} and x_{2i} (where $x_{1i} = X_{1i} - \bar{X}_1$

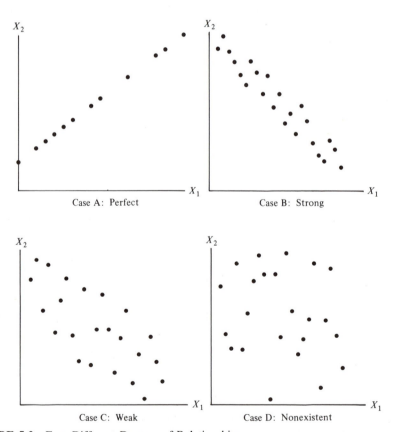

FIGURE 5.2   Four Different Degrees of Relationship.

and $x_{2i} = X_{2i} - \overline{X}_2$) can be multiplied together and this product may be summed over all observations in that quadrant. The resulting sum of cross products will be positive in quadrants I and III and negative in quadrants II and IV.

Most of the observations in Figure 5.1 fall in quadrants I and III, so the *total sum* of cross products over all four quadrants is likely to be positive. If, on the other hand, most of the observations had fallen in quadrants II and IV, the total sum of cross products would probably be negative. Finally, if the points had been evenly distributed among the four quadrants, the positive quantities would tend to be offset by the negative quantities and the total sum would be near zero.

The above suggests that the sum of cross products of the deviations over all sample observations $(\Sigma\, x_{1i}x_{2i})$ could serve as a measure of the degree of association between X_1 and X_2. As suggested by Figure 5.2, if the variables are related in a positive way, this sum will be large and positive. If the variables are inversely related, the sum of the cross products will be large and negative. If, on the other hand, the points are scattered somewhat randomly throughout all four quadrants, the sum of the cross products would be close to zero.

Often, researchers wish to make a quantitative comparison of the degree of association between two different samples or between two different sets of variables. For example, is the association between food consumption and family income stronger or weaker than the association between Brewer scores and Nome temperatures? Using the sum of cross products would have two weaknesses as a method for answering this and similar questions. First, the sum of cross products as a measure of association is affected by the *scale of measurement*. In the example above, the sum of cross products would be one number if temperature were measured in degrees Celsius and another if it were measured in degrees Fahrenheit. Moreover, the units of measurement can vary from problem to problem and from variable to variable. Feet, pounds, dollars, grade points, miles per hour, acres, bushels, degrees, and runs scored are just a few of the large number of measurement units encountered in quantitative economic research. Meaningful comparisons of sums of cross products across such units are difficult. An ideal measure of association would put all observations on a standard scale to aid comparability.

Second, the numerical value of the sum of cross products can be affected by the *number of observations*. For example, if the sample of observations of X_1 and X_2 in Table 5.1 were enlarged, most of the new observations probably would fall in quadrants I or III and only a few would fall in quadrants II and IV. In this case it therefore seems reasonable to expect that for a given level of association the sum of the cross products will increase with the size of the sample (n). Alternatively, many of the new observations might fall in quadrants II and IV, in which case the sum of cross products would decrease. The point simply is that adding new observations to the data set can greatly affect the numerical values of the sum being used as a measure of covariation. Since researchers often wish to compare levels of association across samples of different sizes, the sum of cross products again falls short of being an acceptable measure. An ideal measure of association between two variables would avoid the problems of differences in measurement scale and differences in the number of observations. The most commonly used statistical measure of association in applied research, the Pearson correlation coefficient, successfully avoids both pitfalls.

The Pearson Correlation Coefficient

The *Pearson correlation coefficient*, (*r*), sometimes called the *product moment correlation coefficient* or simply the *correlation coefficient*, is the standard measure of the degree of association between two variables. This statistic, based on *standardized variables*, eliminates the unit-of-measurement problem and mitigates sensitivity to extreme values. Variation is standardized by expressing each value of the variable as a deviation from its mean divided by its standard error. The relevant standardized variable is based on the following computation:

$$\text{standardized values of } X = \frac{X_i - \overline{X}}{S_x} = \frac{x_i}{S_x}$$

for $i = 1, \ldots, n$ observations on X, where S_x is the standard deviation of X. The standard deviation of X can be calculated by taking the square root of any one of the following three equivalent formulas:

$$S_x^2 = \frac{1}{n} \Sigma (X_i - \overline{X})^2 = \frac{\Sigma X_i^2}{n} - \overline{X}^2 = \frac{\Sigma x_i^2}{n}$$

The correlation coefficient is calculated by summing the cross products of the standardized variables and dividing by the sample size:

$$r = \frac{\dfrac{x_{11}}{S_1} \dfrac{x_{21}}{S_2} + \dfrac{x_{12}}{S_1} \dfrac{x_{22}}{S_2} + \cdots + \dfrac{x_{1n}}{S_1} \dfrac{x_{2n}}{S_2}}{n} \tag{5.1}$$

where x_{1i}/S_1 is the *i*th standardized value of X_1, x_{2i}/S_2 is the *i*th standardized value of X_2, S_1 is the standard deviation of X_1, and S_2 is the standard deviation of X_2. A more compact formula is

$$r = \frac{\Sigma x_{1i} x_{2i}}{n S_1 S_2} \tag{5.2}$$

Dividing by n to generate the *average* cross product of standardized variables frees the correlation coefficient from the unit-of-measurement problem and mitigates, if not eliminates, the effect of the number of observations on the computed value. Alternative computational formulas for calculating the correlation coefficient are

$$r = \frac{\Sigma x_{1i} x_{2i}}{\sqrt{(\Sigma x_{1i}^2)(\Sigma x_{2i}^2)}} \tag{5.3}$$

and

$$r = \frac{n \Sigma X_{1i} X_{2i} - (\Sigma X_{1i})(\Sigma X_{2i})}{\sqrt{[n \Sigma X_{1i}^2 - (\Sigma X_{1i})^2][n \Sigma X_{2i}^2 - (\Sigma X_{2i})^2]}} \tag{5.4}$$

However calculated, the Pearson correlation coefficient is a pure number in that the original measurement units of X_1 and X_2 do not affect its value. No matter what the units of measurement may be, or how many observations may be included, the r statistic ranges between -1 and 1. When small values of X_1 are associated with small values of X_2 and large values of X_1 with large values of X_2, the value of r should be positive. The correlation coefficient would be $+1$ for the case of perfect positive correlation (case A of Figure 5.2), an imperfect negative correlation would lead to an r between 0 and -1 (case B of Figure 5.2), and an r near zero would indicate little or no correlation (case D of Figure 5.2).

It is important to remember that the correlation coefficient implies nothing about *causal* relationships. The correlation model thus requires fewer assumptions than does the regression model derived from economic theory, which requires the naming of a dependent and independent variables and, by implication, makes an assumption about causality. The absence of implied causality in the correlation model is reinforced by observing that X_1 and X_2 enter the formulas for calculating r in a symmetric fashion. For example, calling Nome temperatures X_1 and baseball runs X_2 (rather than the other way, as was done in the beginning) would have absolutely no effect on the value of the correlation coefficient.

In summary, the correlation coefficient, r, is a measure of association, or covariation, between any two variables. The variables are treated in a symmetric fashion, implying no causality and permitting none to be deduced from the empirical results. To use the correlation coefficient in the context of causality requires the introduction of the regression model.

Correlation and Regression

Although the correlation coefficient is only a descriptive statistic measuring the degree of covariation between any two variables, it plays an important role in regression models. In this section we place the correlation coefficient in the context of the regression model and show the conditions under which it is appropriate to interpret the correlation coefficient as a measure of the strength of a causal relationship. The best place to begin is with a derivation of a fundamental identity frequently used in statistics.

Decomposition of Sum of Squares

Figure 5.3 illustrates for a simple regression equation how any particular value of the dependent variable, Y_i, can be decomposed into three components:

1. The sample mean of the dependent variable, $\overline{Y}$.
2. The difference between the regression value $\hat{Y}_i$ and $\overline{Y}$.
3. The difference between the actual value of Y_i and its regression value, $\hat{Y}_i$.

Formally, we find that

$$Y_i = \overline{Y} + (\hat{Y}_i - \overline{Y}) + (Y_i - \hat{Y}_i) \tag{5.5}$$

or, rearranging terms,

$$(Y_i - \overline{Y}) = (\hat{Y}_i - \overline{Y}) + (Y_i - \hat{Y}_i) \tag{5.6}$$

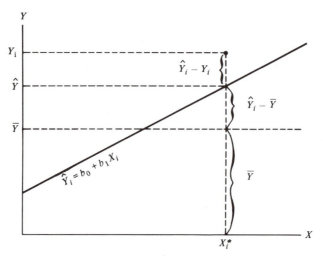

FIGURE 5.3   Decomposition of Sample Variation in the Dependent Variable.

Squaring (5.6) and summing over the n sample points yields

$$\Sigma \, (Y_i - \overline{Y})^2 = \Sigma \, (\hat{Y}_i - \overline{Y})^2 + \Sigma \, (Y_i - \hat{Y}_i)^2 + 2 \, \Sigma \, (\hat{Y}_i - \overline{Y})(Y_i - \hat{Y}_i) \quad (5.7)$$

Since $(\hat{Y}_i - \overline{Y}) = (b_0 + b_1 X_i) - (b_0 + b_1 \overline{X}) = b_1 (X_i - \overline{X})$ and $(Y_i - \hat{Y}_i) = e_i$,

$$\Sigma \, (\hat{Y}_i - \overline{Y})(Y_i - \hat{Y}_i) = b_1 \, \Sigma \, (X_i - \overline{X}) e_i = 0 \quad (5.8)$$

since X and e are independent by assumption. Thus the fundamental identity is

$$\Sigma \, (Y_i - \overline{Y})^2 = \Sigma \, (\hat{Y}_i - \overline{Y})^2 + \Sigma \, (Y_i - \hat{Y}_i)^2 \quad (5.9)$$

This result may be expressed using the following notation:

$$\Sigma \, (Y_i - \overline{Y})^2 = \text{TSS} = \textit{total sum of squared deviations}$$
$$\text{of the sample values of } Y \text{ about the} \quad (5.10)$$
$$\text{mean of } Y.$$

(Note that dividing TSS by n, the sample size, yields the variance of Y in the sample.)

$$\Sigma (\hat{Y}_i - \overline{Y})^2 = \text{RSS} = \textit{sum of squared deviations} \text{ of}$$
$$\text{the regression values of } Y, \quad (5.11)$$
$$\text{the } \hat{Y}_i, \text{ about the mean of } Y.$$

(Note that the mean of $\hat{Y}$ equals the mean of Y.)

$$\Sigma \, (Y_i - \hat{Y}_i)^2 = \text{ESS} = \textit{sum of squared residuals} \quad (5.12)$$

(Note that the mean of the residuals is zero.) Since identity (5.9) may be written as

$$\text{TSS} = \text{RSS} + \text{ESS} \quad (5.13)$$

equation (5.13) is the fundamental decomposition of variance for the regression model. The values for TSS, RSS, and ESS can be computed from the sample regression results *if* the constant term, b_0, is included in the equation; if it is not, (5.13) does not hold.

An alternative interpretation is that the variance of Y in the sample [the terms in (5.13) are variances if each is divided by n] is equal to the sum of the variance due to regression plus the variance due to random variation. In easy-to-remember terms, total variation equals explained variation plus unexplained variation. This could have been demonstrated more quickly if the decomposition started with the basic regression equation

$$Y_i = b_0 + b_1X_i + e_i = \hat{Y}_i + e_i \qquad (5.14)$$

which, via appropriate theorems plus the assumption that X and e are independent, would have led to

$$V(Y_i) = V(\hat{Y}_i) + V(e_i) \qquad (5.15)$$

The more lengthy derivation is necessary because it makes clearer what is going on and because the TSS, RSS, and ESS notation appears below and in the following chapters.

R^2 *as a Measure of Explained Variance*

Suppose that two estimated versions of the population regression equation are available. All else constant, a researcher probably would prefer the equation that "explains" more. The most common measure of how much is "explained" is the *coefficient of multiple determination*, or as it is more commonly known, the R^2. Lest this seem arcane, note that in the case of simple regression, the R^2 is nothing more than the square of the Pearson correlation coefficient between the independent and dependent variables. In fact, in the case of both simple and multiple regression, the R^2 is nothing more than the square of the Pearson correlation coefficient between the observed and expected values for the dependent variable. The R^2 can be viewed as a measure of the explanatory power of a regression equation based on the fundamental decomposition developed above.

Return to (5.9) and divide through by the sample size to get

$$\frac{\Sigma (Y_i - \overline{Y})^2}{n} = \frac{\Sigma (\hat{Y}_i - \overline{Y})^2}{n} + \frac{\Sigma (Y_i - \hat{Y}_i)^2}{n} \qquad (5.16)$$

This says that the variance of Y in the sample is equal to the variance of regression values of Y plus the variance of the error term. Dividing through by the variance of Y yields

$$1 = \frac{\Sigma (\hat{Y}_i - \overline{Y})^2}{\Sigma (Y_i - \overline{Y})^2} + \frac{\Sigma (Y_i - \hat{Y}_i)^2}{\Sigma (Y_i - \overline{Y})^2} \qquad (5.17)$$

If we use the notation of (5.10) to (5.12), this may be rewritten

$$1 = \frac{\text{RSS}}{\text{TSS}} + \frac{\text{ESS}}{\text{TSS}} \qquad (5.18)$$

where RSS/TSS is the percent of the variance of Y in the sample associated with the regression equation and ESS/TSS is the percent associated with random variation.

Let R^2 stand for RSS/TSS, substitute into (5.18), and rearrange terms to obtain

$$R^2 = 1 - \frac{ESS}{TSS} \qquad (5.19)$$

Thus R^2, the coefficient of multiple determination, is the percent of variation in the dependent variable associated with variation in the independent variables in the equation. Alternatively, the R^2 is the percent of the variation in the dependent variables "explained" by the regression portion of the equation. In terms of (5.19), R^2 is 1 minus the percent of variation in the dependent variable due to random variation. If the equation explains none of the variation in Y, then $R^2 = 0$. If the equation explains all the variation, then $R^2 = 1$. In most research situations, the R^2 will fall somewhere between these two extremes.

Now return to the problem of choosing between two estimated versions of the same population regression equation. A possible criterion is to select the version that explains the larger percent of the observed variation in the dependent variable. In other words, choose the version that has higher R^2. However, this is only one of several criteria used in evaluating estimated regression equations and not a particularly good one at that.

Adjusted Coefficient of Determination

One purpose of the R^2 is to compare the explanatory power of different regressions, but different regressions may involve different numbers of observations and different combinations of independent variables. As discussed below, comparing R^2's is treacherous in the best of circumstances without some correction for differences in observations and number of included independent variables and is foolhardy. To facilitate meaningful comparisons across equations using different explanatory variables and different sample sizes, applied researchers therefore often use a corrected or adjusted R^2, computed as

$$\bar{R}^2 = R^2 - \frac{K}{n - (K + 1)} (1 - R^2) \qquad (5.20)$$

where K is the number of independent variables in the equation, $K + 1$ is the number of estimated coefficients, and n is the number of observations. Note that the adjusted R^2 is equal to or less than the unadjusted R^2,

$$\bar{R}^2 \leq R^2 \qquad (5.21)$$

Unless all the sample variance in Y is explained by the independent variables in the equation, the adjusted R^2 is always lower than the unadjusted R^2. Many computer programs print out both the unadjusted and the adjusted R^2. It is possible to get a negative value for $\bar{R}^2$ if the the value of R^2 is low and degrees of freedom are few.

Are Low R^2's a Problem?

Although R^2 is one statistic used for evaluating the "goodness" of an estimated regression equation, it is best used with caution. Experienced researchers are not alarmed if their R^2's are not as high as those of fellow researchers who are working on a different research issue and using different data. For example, time-series data generally lead to much higher R^2's than do cross-sectional data. In the former case, the units of observation are essentially aggregates, such as season's average price or annual average consumer disposable income. A lot of variation is "averaged out" by the process of aggregation. Cross-sectional data are typically based on micro units where such variation has not been "averaged out." Furthermore, and more important, there is no such thing as a good, best, optimal, or acceptable R^2. In applied research settings, the R^2 is a summary statistic, not a scoreboard.

Two Examples

In the first example, the data on yields, rainfall, and temperature in Table 4.2 are used to illustrate the calculation and interpretation of the correlation coefficient and the coefficient of multiple determination. Table 5.2 on page 96 contains the necessary information from Table 4.2 to calculate the simple correlation coefficients. Most computer programs display the simple correlation coefficients as a matrix that looks like the following:

	Y	X_i	X_2
Y	1.00	.18	.63
X_1		1.00	-.58
X_2			1.00

The correlation between Y and X_1 indicates that there is not much covariation between them. In contrast, the association between Y and X_2 is much stronger. The $r_{y1} = .18$ and the $r_{y2} = .63$ means that variation in yields is much more closely associated with temperature. The r_{12} of $-.58$ means that X_1 and X_2 are negatively associated (i.e., as rainfall increases average daily temperatures decrease). The result is reasonable in that when it rains the sun does not shine.

The simple correlation coefficient is measure of *gross* association between any two variables. It carries no implication of causality. Based on a theory, the OLS model permits inferences with respect to the direction and strength of causality between a dependent and a set of independent variables. The R^2 is a measure of the strength of that relationship. It describes the percent of variation in the dependent variable explained by the independent variables.

Based on the correlation matrix, the beginning researcher might assume that X_1 does not affect yield. In actuality, our model works quite well. The coefficient of multiple determination shows that both variables jointly explain 85 percent of the variation in yields.

The calculations for R^2 are shown in Table 5.3. The calculated values of Y, called *Y-hat* (column 4), are obtained by inserting the values of X_1 and X_2 into the calculated

Table 5.2. Worksheet to Calculate Pearson Correlation Coefficients (From Data in Table 4.2)

Year	(1) Yield, Y	(2) Rain, X_1	(3) Temp., X_2	(4) y^2	(5) x_1^2	(6) x_2^2	(7) yx_1	(8) yx_2	(9) x_1x_2
1972	55	19	49	100	0	9	0	30	0
1973	65	17	58	0	4	36	0	0	-12
1974	80	21	55	225	4	9	30	45	6
1975	75	17	58	100	4	36	-20	60	-12
1976	70	19	55	25	0	9	0	15	0
1977	50	18	49	225	1	9	15	45	3
1978	60	20	46	25	1	36	-5	30	-6
1979	65	21	46	0	4	36	0	0	-12
	520	152	416	700	18	180	20	225	-33

Correlation coefficients [from (5.3)]:
Between Y and X_1:

$$r_{Y1} = \frac{\Sigma\ yx_1}{\sqrt{(\Sigma\ y^2)(\Sigma\ x_1^2)}} = \frac{20}{\sqrt{(700)(18)}} = .18$$

Between Y and X_2:

$$r_{Y2} = \frac{\Sigma\ yx_2}{\sqrt{(\Sigma\ y^2)(\Sigma\ x_2^2)}} = \frac{225}{\sqrt{(700)(180)}} = .63$$

Between X_1 and X_2:

$$r_{12} = \frac{\Sigma\ x_1x_2}{\sqrt{(\Sigma\ x_1^2)(\Sigma\ x_2^2)}} = \frac{-33}{\sqrt{(18)(180)}} = -.58$$

regression equation:

$$\hat{Y} = -146.75 + 5.13X_1 + 2.19X_2$$

and the residuals (column 5) by

$$e = Y - \hat{Y}$$

As a second example, the correlation coefficient is illustrated using an expanded version of equations (3.64). In that equation, M, the stock of money (cash plus balances in checking and savings accounts), was expressed as a function of E, the level of economic activity in the economy as measured by per capita real GNP. This example expands on the original model by adding two new independent variables to the equation, the interest rate (R) and the unemployment rate (J):

$$M = \beta_0 + \beta_1E + \beta_2R + \beta_3J + U \tag{5.22}$$

The independent variable R, measured by the real (nominal rate less inflation rate) interest rate of Treasury bills, is included to control for the opportunity cost of holding

Table 5.3. Worksheet to Calculate the Coefficient of Multiple Determination (from Yield Data in Table 4.2)

Year	(1) Yield, Y	(2) Rain, X_1	(3) Temp., X_2	(4) $\hat{Y}$	(5) e	(6) e^2
	(1)	(2)	(3)	(4)	(5)	(6)
1972	55	19	49	58.4	− 3.4	11.56
1973	65	17	58	67.9	− 2.9	8.41
1974	80	21	55	81.8	− 1.8	3.24
1975	75	17	58	67.9	7.1	50.41
1976	70	19	55	71.6	− 1.6	2.56
1977	50	18	49	53.3	− 3.3	10.89
1978	60	20	46	57.0	3.0	9.00
1979	65	21	46	62.1	2.9	8.41
	520	152	416	520.0		104.48

TSS $= \Sigma y^2 = 700$ (from Table 5.2)
ESS $= \Sigma e^2 = 104.48$

From (5.19):
$$R^2 = 1 - \frac{\text{ESS}}{\text{TSS}} = 1 - \frac{104.48}{700.00} = .85$$

From (5.20):
$$\bar{R}^2 = R^2 - \frac{K}{n - (K + 1)} (1 - R^2)$$

$$= .85 - \frac{2}{8 - 3} (.15)$$

$$= .79$$

cash balances. The independent variable J, the percent of people in the labor force without jobs, is included as a leading indicator of the direction of the economy in the near term.

Using quarterly data from 1973 through the second quarter of 1984 yields the following equation:

$$M = -286.1 + .679E - 41.973R + 26.159J + e$$
$$\quad (262.1) \quad (.045) \quad (5.463) \quad (7.457)$$

$$n = 46 \quad S = 76.0 \quad \begin{aligned} R^2 &= .861 \\ \bar{R}^2 &= .851 \end{aligned}$$

$$\text{TSS} = \Sigma y^2 = 1,745,000 \hspace{2cm} (5.23)$$

$$\text{RSS} = \Sigma \hat{y}^2 = 1,502,900$$

$$\text{ESS} = \Sigma e^2 = 242,544$$

The numbers in parentheses are the standard errors of the regression coefficients.

TSS is the total sample variation in the dependent variable. As shown above, this coefficient of multiple correlation can be calculated as the ratio of the variance in M explained by (5.23) to the total variation:

$$R^2 = \frac{RSS}{TSS} = \frac{1,502,900}{1,745,000} = .861 \tag{5.24}$$

Based on the framework developed above for interpreting the correlation coefficient, (5.24) says that 86.1 percent of the variation in M during the 1973 to 1984 period is explained by variation in E, R, and J.

Summary

The correlation coefficient is a computed measure of the degree of covariation between any two variables. It is only a measure of covariation. In particular, there is absolutely no way that the concept of causality can be used in connection with a correlation coefficient. However, in the context of regression analysis, where a researcher bestows a regression equation with causality derived from some guiding theory, the variance of the dependent variable can be decomposed into explained and unexplained elements. The percent of the variance associated with or "explained by" the regression equation is called the coefficient of determination and identified symbolically as R^2. Causability enters at this juncture. Some researchers, recognizing that philosophers of science still argue over the meaning of "causality," prefer to interpret R^2 as the percent of observed variation in Y associated with (not necessarily caused by) variation in the X-variables.

Terms

Adjusted coefficient of multiple
  determination ($\bar{R}^2$)
Coefficient of multiple
  determination (R^2)
Correlation coefficient (r)
Error sum of squares (ESS)

Pearson correlation coefficient
  (r)
Regression sum of squares
  (RSS)
Standardized variable
Total sum of squares (TSS)

Exercises

5.1 Using the data presented in Table 5.1, calculate the simple correlation coefficient between
(a) Date and runs.

(b) Date and temperature.
(c) Temperature and runs.

5.2 The following data were plotted as cases B, C, and D in Figure 5.2.

X	Y_1	Y_2	Y_3
1	12	11	12
2	9	3	11
3	7	5	9
4	12	14	11
5	4	9	8
6	3	12	6
7	10	15	5
8	2	4	4
9	9	8	5
10	4	1	2
11	6	13	3
12	1	6	1

(a) "Eyeball" the data and guess whether the correlation is strong or weak for each pair of X and Y_i and then relate to cases B, C, and D in Figure 5.2.
(b) Calculate the simple correlation coefficient between each pair of variables and present your results in a correlation matrix like the following:

	X	Y_1	Y_2	Y_3
X	——	——	——	——
Y_1		——	——	——
Y_2			——	——
Y_3				——

5.3 OLS yields $\hat{Y} = 10 + 2X$, where $\overline{X} = 4$. Decompose the observed values of Y_i into three components according to equation (5.5).

$$Y_i = \overline{Y} + (\hat{Y}_i - \overline{Y}) + (Y_i - \hat{Y}_i) \tag{5.5}$$

(a) $X = 4$ $Y = 22$
(b) $X = 6$ $Y = 30$
(c) $X = 8$ $Y = 26$
(d) $X = 10$ $Y = 24$
(e) $X = 1$ $Y = 8$
(f) $X = 2$ $Y = 14$
(g) $X = 3$ $Y = 18$
(h) $X = 0$ $Y = 16$

100 THE THEORY

5.4 Consider the following data set:

i	Y	X
1	15	1
2	10	2
3	14	3
4	8	4
5	3	5

(a) Calculate the OLS for b_0 and b_1 for $Y = b_0 + b_1X + e$.
(b) Calculate $\hat{Y}$ for each i.
(c) Calculate TSS, ESS, and RSS.
(d) Calculate R^2.
(e) Calculate the correlation coefficient between $\hat{Y}$ and Y_i.
(f) Calculate r_{YX}.
(g) How does R^2 relate to $r_{\hat{Y}Y}$?
(h) How does R^2 relate to r_{YX} in *simple* regression?
(i) Does $r_{YX} = r_{\hat{Y}Y}$ in simple regression?

5.5 Consider the following information from a multiple regression equation:

$$\Sigma e_i^2 = 94$$

$$Y = 10, 12, 14, 9, 7, 8, 2, 22, 4, 12$$

(a) What is the R^2?
(b) What is TSS, ESS, and RSS?
(c) What is the variance of Y, (S_y^2)? The *sample* variance of the error term (S_e^2)? Note that $S_e^2 \neq S^2$.
(d) Show the relationship between S_y^2, S_e^2, and R^2? Verify your relationship by calculating R^2.
(e) What is the relationship between S_e^2 and S^2?

5.6 Calculate $\bar{R}^2$ under the following conditions:
(a) $R^2 = .60$, $N = 25$, $K = 2$
(b) $R^2 = .60$, $N = 125$, $K = 2$
(c) $R^2 = .60$, $N = 25$, $K = 12$
(d) $R^2 = .60$, $N = 20$, $K = 12$
(e) $R^2 = .90$, $N = 200$, $K = 6$

6

Distribution Theory and Hypothesis Testing

Suppose that the government establishes a new food-stamp plan to provide assistance to families whose food consumption is below the average consumption level in the community where they live. The total amount of money available for the plan is to be allocated among a number of communities on the basis of the average food expenditure level in each community. The law stipulates that a particular community cannot apply for assistance funds until that community has determined its average level of food expenditure. Although the law does not stipulate specifically how the average is to be determined, it does stipulate that the method used must conform to accepted statistical procedures. What would constitute an acceptable statistical procedure for determining the average family food expenditure in, say, the tiny town of Twig?

The problem of determining the value of population parameters is the essence of applied research, as discussed in previous chapters. In Chapter 1 we presented the least squares method for mathematically fitting a straight line through a set of data points. In Chapter 2 we introduced the concept of a random variable, discussed the distribution of sample estimates, reviewed estimation theory, and developed the fundamentals of hypothesis testing. This introductory material provided sufficient background for introducing regression theory, deriving the OLS estimators, examining their properties, and conducting simple hypothesis tests. In the first part of this chapter we amplify the basic concepts in Chapter 2. This is followed by a discussion of the basic statistical distributions essential for hypothesis testing. In the final section we develop the framework for hypothesis testing in regression analysis.

Populations and Population Parameters

A population is a collection of elements (e.g., people, farms, states, business firms) about which quantitative, or numerical, information is desired. The population of interest is always defined in the context of a specific research question. For the hypothetical situation presented at the beginning of this chapter, the population of interest is the collection of all families residing in the town of Twig. Other research situations might refer to the population of all farms in Dane County or all school districts in California. Populations are often difficult to define unambiguously. It could happen, for example, that a family's house straddles the town line between Twig and Trunk, raising the issue of residency. Furthermore, and more important, many concepts are difficult to define empirically. What is a family? Does it include single-person units? If a married son and his wife live with his parents, are they one family or two families? Despite such definitional problems, as well as some conceptual problems described later, in this chapter we assume that the population has been accurately identified and all concepts appropriately defined.

Applied research involves studying characteristics of a population that can be quantified, or expressed in numerical terms. These quantified characteristics are called *variables*, signifying that the values of these characteristics typically vary across the elements of the population. For example, the variable "food expenditure" could take on a large value (say, $100 per week) for a family with a high income level and a small value (say, $30 per week) for a family with a low income level. There are, of course, other variables that could be defined for the Twig household population, such as number of dependent children, size of dwelling, and length of trip to work.

Some characteristics of a population are not so easily quantified, such as the sex of the head of household, whether the family has a pet, or the political party of the household members. Fortunately for applied researchers, such qualitative characteristics can be quantified and used in regression analysis (see Chapter 9).

A population parameter refers to some aspect of a particular variable. As pointed out in Chapter 2, there are a number of parameters of interest, such as the mean, the mode, the median, the variance, and so on. Statistical theory is concerned with using sample data to test hypotheses regarding the population value of such parameters. These procedures are developed in the following sections.

Determining the Value of a Population Parameter

There are two approaches for determining the value of a population parameter, the *census* approach and the *sampling* approach. Although the focus of this book is on using sample data, the census approach is worth discussing both to make the presentation complete and to reveal the nature of the "cost" the applied researcher must pay for working with sample data.

Using a Census

A census involves obtaining the desired information from each element in the population. For the example above, a census would involve obtaining food expenditure data from each family in Twig. These data would be used to compute the mean, or average, expenditure (a population parameter). Suppose that the population of Twig consists of five families, with expenditures shown in Table 6.1. To determine average weekly food expenditure, a researcher needs only to add the responses over all families and divide by the number of families in the population. For Twig, this leads to a value of $58 for the average family food expenditure.

Thus the census method involves obtaining the needed data for each element in the population and then *computing* the value of the population parameter of interest. Although straightforward, the census method is not often used in practice. Conducting a census is expensive and time consuming; the results often are not available in time to aid decision makers; and experience has shown that it is difficult to control the errors, often referred to as *nonsampling* or *survey errors*, that creep into census work. Let the "true" expenditures, the values a researcher desires, for the five households in Twig be represented by $v_1, v_2, \ldots, v_5$. Let $z_1, z_2, \ldots, z_5$ represent the actual values ("survey values") obtained by the survey. There is nothing to guarantee that the true values and the survey values will be equal. Indeed, there is good reason to suspect that they may differ substantially. The survey values could differ from the true values because different households compute expenditures differently. Some families may misstate expenditures for personal reasons. Other families may not have a clear understanding of what is meant by "expenditures," and so on. The point is simply that what respondents tell survey takers may differ, for whatever reason, from the value researchers are seeking. In addition to these response errors, data handling can give rise to substantial errors if responses are incorrectly recorded, coded, or entered into the computer. Regardless of the source of nonsampling errors, however, any difference between the survey value and the true value constitutes a bias, which

Table 6.1. Weekly Food Expenditures for the Five Families in the Town of Twig

Family	True Value of Food Expenditures
A	$ 30
B	40
C	70
D	40
E	110
Population mean =	$58

can be expressed as

$$d_i = z_i - v_i \tag{6.1}$$

Of course, the survey value can equal the true value, in which case the bias (d_i) would be zero.

This result is a source for concern because any biases that occur in the observations are likely to be reflected in the computed value of the population parameter. To see this, sum (6.1) over all households in the population, divide by N (the number of elements in the population), and rearrange slightly to get

$$\frac{\Sigma z_i}{N} = \frac{\Sigma v_i}{N} + \frac{\Sigma d_i}{N} \tag{6.2}$$

In words, the computed mean, based on the survey data, equals the true mean plus the average bias. Only if Σd_i is zero, which would happen if all the d_i's were exactly zero or if individual biases happen to cancel each other out, would the census (computed) mean be identical to the true (desired) mean.

Such survey errors are likely to be present in both census and sample data. Because a sample is smaller (often much smaller) than a population, surveyors can take more precautions to assure that nonsampling errors are kept to a minimum.

Using a Sample

In most practical situations a researcher uses survey data collected not by a census but by a sample. For the moment simply view a sample as consisting of a subset of observations drawn from the population of interest. The method by which these observations are drawn from the population is extremely important, and there are a number of sophisticated selection procedures that can be used. However, it is sufficient here to assume that each element in the population has a known chance of being included in the sample and that the population elements are selected at random. Finally, it is necessary to assume that nonsampling errors, as discussed above, are absent. These assumptions make it possible to focus on *sampling error*, or *sampling variability*, a form of variation that underlies all subsequent work.

Return to the problem of determining the average food expenditure in Twig. In such a small town, it would be possible to rely on either a census or a sample. If a census were taken, and nonsampling errors were avoided, the census would reveal the true average expenditure in Twig to be $58, as shown in Table 6.1.

Alternatively, an estimate of the population average could be developed from a sample of, say, two Twig households. Suppose that two families were drawn at random. If families A and C (refer to Table 6.1) were chosen, the two sample values would be 30 and 70. The average of these sample values (or sample average) is $50. This number, sometimes referred to as a *sample statistic*, can be used to estimate the population mean. However, two points need to be stressed. First, the sample statistic would, in some sense, be a "wrong" number. The sample statistic is $50, but in this simple case the true average is $58. Second, a different pair of families would produce a different sample mean and hence a different estimate of the population mean.

To see the latter and very important point more clearly, refer to Table 6.2, where the sample means are calculated for each of the 10 possible samples of size 2 that

Table 6.2. Sampling Errors for All Possible Samples of Two Families in Twig Where the Population Mean Is 58

Sample	Sample Statistic (Mean)	Sampling Error (Actual − Estimate)
AB	35	23
AC	50	8
AD	35	23
AE	70	− 12
BC	55	3
BD	40	18
BE	75	− 17
CD	55	3
CE	90	− 32
DE	75	− 17

can be drawn from the population of Twig. Observe that the difference between the sample statistic and the population parameter being estimated can vary considerably from one sample to another, yielding in some cases substantial differences. Compare, for example, the estimates based on samples AB and AD with the estimate based on sample CE.

Table 6.2 reveals the nature of sampling variability, or sampling error. Different samples from the same population yield different numerical estimates of the population parameter. Because the applied researcher really wants to make a statement about the population, sampling variability raises the central question of *statistical inference*: What can be said about a population parameter on the basis of a sample statistic computed from one sample drawn from the population? The answer is based on an understanding of random variables.

On Random Variables
and Experiments

Central to statistical inference is the concept of a *random variable*, defined as a variable that takes on different values over a number of experiments. In probability theory, a random variable arises from an experiment in the following way. Suppose that 10 cards were drawn at random from a standard deck of playing cards. This could be viewed as an experiment for which such random variables as "number of spades obtained" or "number of face cards obtained" could be defined. The experiment could be repeated and the value of the random variable "number of spades obtained" would probably differ from the value obtained from the first experiment. The random variable "number of face cards obtained" would also be likely to take on a different value. Now consider repeating the experiment many times, each time recording the value of the random variable. It is clear that the random variable takes on different numerical values over the set of experiments.

Table 6.3. Possible Outcomes for Random Variable =
Number of Heads Obtained from an Experiment of Flipping
Two Fair Coins

Coin 1	Coin 2	Number of Heads	Probability of Occurring
T	T	0	1/4
T	H	1	1/4
H	T	1	1/4
H	H	2	1/4

This gives rise to the *distribution* of a random variable. The distribution combines the set of values the random variable can take on and the probability of each of these values occurring. For example, suppose that two fair coins are tossed and define "number of heads obtained" as the random variable. For this experiment, the random variable can take on the value of 0, 1, or 2. This is shown in Table 6.3. Since the coins are assumed to be fair, each of the four possible outcomes of the experiment has an equal probability of occurring. The distribution of the random variable "number of heads obtained" is summarized in Table 6.4.

A random variable is a variable defined on an experiment that takes on different values over the set of experiments and the distribution of the random variable states the probability of occurrence for each value the random variable can take on. Two important points in connection with random variables must be addressed.

In the examples used here, it is easy to define in advance the possible values the random variable can take on over a set of experiments. These values, often referred to as the *population* of sample points, or experimental outcomes, are important in the theory of estimation. However, in many applied research settings there is no a priori basis for identifying the values that a random variable can take on. Rather, a researcher must conduct a number of experiments, observe the values obtained for the random variable and their frequency of occurrence, and then make a (statistical) statement about the probable set of sample points. This, as observed above, is what statistical inference is all about. But there is an important distinction that needs to be made regarding the distribution of a random variable.

In the preceding discussion, the term "probability" was introduced but not defined. Although a thorough discussion of this concept, which stirred to life in the seventeenth

Table 6.4. Probability or Relative Frequency Distribution of Number of Heads Obtained from Flipping Two Fair Coins

Value of the Random Variable	Probability
0	1/4
1	2/4
2	1/4

century in connection with games of chance, is beyond the scope of this book, a couple of observations are in order. In mathematics, *probability* is a mathematical model constructed on a set of axioms that provides a theory of processes that have uncertain outcomes. Much of the purely theoretical work focuses on processes where the population of sample points (or experimental outcomes, as discussed above) can be determined a priori. This theory provides the foundation of statistics. However, as statisticians have become increasingly active in studying real-world processes (e.g., the spread of epidemics or the incidence of poverty) where there is seldom an a priori basis for determining the population of sample points for random variables, they have been forced to distinguish between a theoretical model, with *probability* of occurrence, and an empirical model, with (observed) *relative frequency* of occurrence. These two concepts are linked by theorems known as *laws of large numbers* that define probability as the limit outcome of relative frequencies observed over a large number of experiments. That is, if the "experiment" of drawing 10 cards at random and recording for each experiment the number of face cards obtained were repeated many times, the observed frequencies would approach in numerical terms the probability of obtaining a particular number of face cards in a random sample of 10 cards. In all that follows, "probability" and "relative frequency" are freely interchanged. However, it is important to understand the distinction sketched briefly here.

Random Variables Illustrated

In this section we apply the ideas of the preceding section to the Twig data by distinguishing between the distribution of a variable in the population and the distribution of a sample statistic used to estimate a population parameter.

Distribution of a Random Variable Defined on a Population

The random variable "weekly food expenditures" has been defined on the population of Twig families. The distribution for this random variable, based on Table 6.1, is presented in Table 6.5. For the moment, the important point is that the relative frequencies (probabilities) of the values of the random variable necessarily sum to 1, although the frequencies need not be the same for each value of the random variable.

Table 6.5. Distribution of the Random Variable "Expenditures" for the Population of Twig

Possible Values of the Random Variable	Relative Frequency of Occurrence (Probability)
30	1/5
40	2/5
70	1/5
110	1/5
	1

Distribution of a Sample Statistic

Table 6.2 illustrates how different samples of size 2 yield different estimates of the population average. This means that the sample average is a random variable. Different values for the variable "sample average" are obtained over a set of experiments involving the drawing of samples of size 2 and computing the sample average. The distribution of this random variable can be constructed from the data in Table in 6.2 and is summarized in Table 6.6. Again note that the relative frequencies sum to 1, but different values for the variable have different frequencies of occurrence.

The distribution in Table 6.6 can be used in a way that anticipates some things that are important later and uses the knowledge of the population presented in Tables 6.1, 6.2, 6.5, and 6.6. (Unfortunately, in applied research such knowledge is never available.) If a sample of size 2 were drawn from the population of Twig, the probability is 2/10 (or .20) that the estimate of the population mean would be $35. Similarly, the probability of getting an estimate of $70 is 1/10 (or .10). Notice that the probability of getting an estimate of $58 (the actual population average) is zero. Although this situation (the sample statistic is never right!) can understandably be disturbing to a newcomer to applied research, it is really only a reminder that a sample does not contain as much information about a population as a census does. This, in turn, means that a sample does not permit researchers to make statements about a population parameter that are as precise as statements based on a census, a situation that should not be too surprising. Moreover, it is shown below how researchers using sample data can make only probability, not definitive, statements about the values of population parameters. This is what statistical inference is all about.

Describing a Distribution

As defined in the preceding section and illustrated in this section, the distribution of a random variable involves both the values of random variable can take on and the frequency of occurrence of each value. The distribution of a random variable may be presented in tabular form, as in Table 6.6, or it may be presented graphically by plotting the values of the random variable on the horizontal axis and the frequency of

Table 6.6. Relative Frequency of Sample Means for Samples of Size 2 Drawn from the Population of Twig

Values of Random Variables (Sample Mean)	Relative Frequency of Occurrence (Probability)
35	2/10
40	1/10
50	1/10
55	2/10
70	1/10
75	2/10
90	1/10
	10/10 = 1

occurrence on the vertical axis. In either case, it is rather difficult to talk about a distribution. Because of this, it is conventional to use descriptive, or summary, measures to characterize a distribution. There are a number of such terms in statistical theory such as mean, mode, median, variance, skewness, and so on.

As discussed in Chapter 2, only two of these measures, the mean (or average) and the variance, are used here. The mean of a distribution is a measure of its *central tendency*, a numerically defined point about which the individual values of the random variable tend to cluster. The variance of a distribution is a measure of its *dispersion*. It is a quantitative measure of the degree to which the individual values of the random variable tend to cluster around the mean. These two descriptive measures of a distribution will be considered more thoroughly after some new concepts have been developed.

Some Statistical Distributions

Now that the notion of a random variable and its distribution has been developed, it is time to discuss some important statistical distributions needed for hypothesis testing. Here these distributions are developed only to the extent necessary to provide a basis for hypothesis testing. A more complete treatment is available in any good basic statistics book.

Normal Distribution

Consider first a random variable that is normally distributed with a mean of μ and a variance of σ^2. This distribution is shown in Figure 6.1, where the values the variable

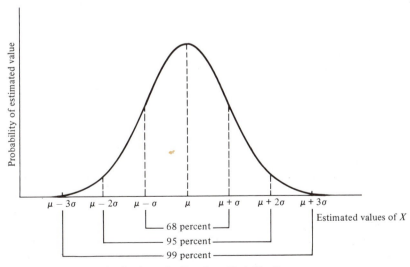

FIGURE 6.1 Normal Distribution of a Random Variable X.

takes on are plotted on the horizontal axis and the frequency of occurrence for each value is plotted on the vertical axis. Notice that this distribution is symmetrical about its mean μ, the maximum point of the distribution. Because of the symmetry of the normal distribution, statistical theory can be used to show that

About 68 percent of the values of X fall in the interval $(\mu - \sigma)$ to $(\mu + \sigma)$.
About 95 percent of the values of X fall in the interval $(\mu - 2\sigma)$ to $(\mu - 2\sigma)$.
About 99 percent of the values of X fall in the interval $(\mu - 3\sigma)$ to $(\mu + 3\sigma)$.

This symmetry therefore has the important implications for experiments as defined above. If one number were to be drawn repeatedly at random from this distribution, about 68 percent of the time the number obtained would have a value in the range $(\mu - \sigma)$ to $(\mu + \sigma)$. Similarly, probability statements can be made for the 2- and 3-standard-deviation ranges.

The probability of getting a value larger than or smaller than some prestated value can also be determined. For example, the probability of getting a value that is more than 2 standard deviations from the mean of the distribution is about $1 - .95 = .05$. The probability of getting a value greater than $(\mu + 2\sigma)$ is about .025 and the probability of getting a value less than $(\mu - 2\sigma)$ is also about .025.

Standardized Normal Distribution

The *standardized normal variable*, also used for hypothesis testing, is defined as

$$Z_i = \frac{X_i - \mu}{\sigma} \tag{6.3}$$

where X is the random variable with a mean of μ and a variance σ^2. Note that all (6.3) does is express in standard deviation units the distance between each value of the random variable X and the mean of the distribution. The distribution of Z has a mean of 0 and a variance of 1. To see this, consider

$$E(Z) = E\left(\frac{X - \mu}{\sigma}\right) = \frac{E(X - \mu)}{\sigma} = \frac{E(X) - \mu}{\sigma} = \frac{\mu - \mu}{\sigma} = 0 \tag{6.4}$$

since μ and σ are constants. The variance of the standard normal variable is

$$E[Z - E(Z)]^2 = E(Z^2) = \frac{E(X - \mu)^2}{\sigma^2} = \frac{\sigma^2}{\sigma^2} = 1 \tag{6.5}$$

since, by definition, $E(X - \mu)^2 = E[X - E(X)]^2 = \sigma^2$.

The standard normal distribution, shown in Figure 6.2, is directly comparable to the normal distribution in Figure 6.1, except that the unit of measurement has been changed to the standardized values of X. Its interpretation is also similar. For example, the probability of getting a value for Z larger than $+2$ is about .025, the same as getting a value of X larger than $(\mu + 2\sigma)$ in Figure 6.1. Often it is more convenient to think in terms of the standardized normal distribution because specific values, such as 2, rather than general values, such as $\mu + 2\sigma$, can be used.

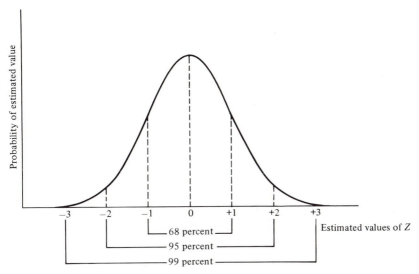

FIGURE 6.2　Normal Distribution of a Standardized Random Variable Z.

Distributions of Sample Statistics

The following three distributions, the chi-square distribution, the t-distribution, and the F-distribution, are used for hypothesis testing. They pertain not to the distribution of a random variable defined on a population, as do the normal and standard normal distributions, but to the distribution of sample statistics, the values of which vary across a set of samples drawn from a normal population. All three require a new concept called *degrees of freedom*. Formally, degrees of freedom is defined as the size of the sample minus the number of parameters estimated from the sample. For example, if a sample of size n is used to estimate the population mean μ, there are $n - 1$ degrees of freedom.

The Chi-Square Distribution

Let $Z_1, \ldots, Z_n$ be independent standardized normal variables and write

$$SS = Z_1^2 + Z_2^2 + \cdots + Z_n^2 \tag{6.6}$$

as the sum of squares. Since SS is computed from sample values, it follows that it is a random variable and it will take on different values in repeated sampling. This sum-of-squares random variable follows a *chi-square distribution*, the exact shape of which depends on degrees of freedom. The standard notation for this distribution is $\chi^2(n)$, where n is the degrees of freedom. The range of values for this distribution is 0 to ∞. Although the chi-square distribution is highly skewed to the right when n is

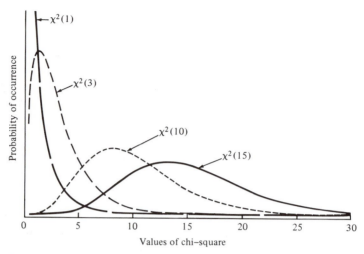

FIGURE 6.3   Chi-Square Distribution for Selected Degrees of Freedom.

small, the distribution becomes increasingly symmetric as the degrees of freedom increase. This is illustrated in Figure 6.3.

The t-Distribution

Suppose that a random sample of size n is drawn from a normal distribution and the sample mean $(\overline{X})$ is computed. The standardized value of this sample mean may be written as

$$Z = \frac{\overline{X} - E(\overline{X})}{\sigma_{\overline{X}}} \tag{6.7}$$

where $\sigma_{\overline{X}}$ is the standard deviation of the sampling distribution. Assuming that $\overline{X}$ is an unbiased estimator of μ, this can be written as

$$Z = \frac{\overline{X} - \mu}{\sigma_{\overline{X}}} \tag{6.8}$$

The sample mean, $\overline{X}$, is a random variable, so Z is a random variable and will take on different values in repeated sampling. Usually, the researcher does not know the standard deviation of the sampling distribution and must estimate it from the sample. Let S be the estimated value, substitute into (6.8), and write

$$t = \frac{\overline{X} - \mu}{S_{\overline{X}}} \tag{6.9}$$

Because the standard deviation has to be estimated, this variable does not have a normal distribution. Rather, it has a *t-distribution* and the computed value is called a *t-statistic*. It does look like a standardized normal variable, and it does have a mean of 0. However, unlike a standardized normal variable, a *t*-statistic does not have variance of 1. Instead, the variance of a *t*-statistic is a function of the degrees of freedom.

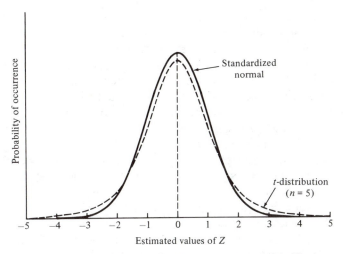

FIGURE 6.4 Comparison of the Standardized Normal and the *t*-Distribution.

The relationship between the distribution of a standardized normal variable and the distribution of the *t*-statistic is shown in Figure 6.4. Both distributions have mean of zero, but the *t*-distribution is "wider in the tails," the price paid for having to use an estimate of the standard deviation of the sampling distribution. Statistical theory indicates that the *t*-distribution approaches the standardized normal distribution as the degrees of freedom increase.

The F-Distribution

The *F*-statistic is the ratio of two chi-square variables, each divided by its respective degrees of freedom, and follows the *F*-distribution. The *F*-distribution is more complex than the previous distributions and there is no simple illustration of what it looks like. The distribution is complex because the probability of getting a particular *F*-value from a sample depends on *two* sets of degrees of freedom, one for the numerator and one for the denominator.

Decomposition of the Variance of Y: the Analysis-of-Variance Table

The fundamental decomposition of the variance of the dependent variable in regression was shown in Chapter 5 to be

$$\Sigma \, (Y_i - \overline{Y})^2 = \Sigma \, (\hat{Y} - \overline{Y})^2 + \Sigma \, (Y_i - \hat{Y})^2 \tag{6.10}$$

or

$$\text{TSS} = \text{RSS} + \text{ESS} \tag{6.11}$$

Testing hypotheses involves understanding the relationship between total variance, explained variance, and unexplained variance, so the sum-of-squares terms in (6.10) and (6.11) are useful. Because in applied work these sum-of-squares terms are estimated from sample data, they are random variables. Thus different samples from the same population would be expected to yield different numerical values for these terms. Consequently, in order to make probability statements about the results of applied research, it is necessary to know how the sample values of these sum-of-squares terms are distributed and what the probabilities are of getting different values for these terms. These sum-of-squares variables have the *chi-square distribution*.

One question the researcher usually asks is whether RSS, the variance associated with the regression equation, is "larger" than ESS, the variance associated with random disturbances. If it is not, the variables in the model do not really explain anything. The answer to this question involves computing an F-ratio using the formula $F = \text{RSS}/\text{ESS}$, with RSS and ESS divided by their respective degrees of freedom. Because RSS and ESS are random variables with a chi-square distribution, F is also a random variable. It follows that different samples from the same population would be expected to yield different numerical values for the computed F-statistic. However, for a sum-of-squares variable to follow a chi-square distribution the underlying variable (the one forming the sum of squares) must be normally distributed. In Chapter 3 we showed that the random variable $(Y_i - \bar{Y})$ can be written as a function of the population disturbance term. Because $(Y_i - \bar{Y})$ will take on different values across the samples as U takes on different samples, the sum of squares of $(Y_i - \bar{Y})$ will depend on the sum of squares of U. It is therefore necessary to make the important assumption that the population disturbance term is a normally distributed random variable. With this assumption, it is appropriate to use the chi-square and F-distributions for testing hypotheses about regression coefficients.

In Chapter 5 we showed how the variance of the dependent variable can be decomposed into the sum of two components, the variance due to regression and the variance due to random variation. This decomposition is integral to hypothesis testing. An *analysis-of-variance table* offers an instructive view of the decomposition of variance because it shows the basic structure of the test statistics used in applied research. Most computer programs produce this table, either as a part of the standard regression output or as an option available to the researcher. It is an important table, one all applied researchers must be able to read with ease. The general format for an analysis-of-variance table is shown in Table 6.7.

As discussed in the preceding section, the TSS, RSS, and ESS terms are estimated from a sample and are therefore random variables. Because of this, it is important when using these sample statistics for hypothesis testing first to adjust them for degrees of freedom, or for the amount of information available in the sample for estimating statistics. This is why the columns headed "degrees of freedom" and "mean square" appear in Table 6.7. The first column, "source of variation," lists the components of variation and the total variation. Remember that RSS (regression sum of squares) is the variation of the dependent variable associated with sample variation in X_1, X_2, . . ., X_K, the independent variables in the regression equation. Similarly, ESS is the variation associated with e_i, the random (unexplained) variation in the dependent variable.

Table 6.7. Basic Analysis-of-Variance Table

Source of Variation	Degrees of Freedom	Sum of Squares[a]	Mean Square	Computed F-Ratio or F-Statistic
Regression equation, $X_1, X_2, \ldots, X_k$	K	RSS	RSS/K	Ratio of mean squares appropriate to the specific test
Random variation, e_i	$n - (K + 1)$	ESS	ESS/$n - k - 1$	
Total, Y_i	$n - 1$	TSS	TSS/$n - 1$	

[a] $\text{RSS} = \Sigma (\hat{Y}_i - \bar{Y})^2 = \Sigma (b_j \Sigma x_{ij} Y_i)^2$; $\text{ESS} = \Sigma (\hat{Y}_i - Y_i)^2 = \Sigma e_i^2$; $\text{TSS} = \Sigma (Y_i - \hat{Y})^2$.

The second column lists the degrees of freedom appropriate to each element in the variance equation. Because the regression coefficients, b_k, $k = 1, 2, \ldots, K$, are estimated directly from the sample observations, each coefficient estimate uses up 1 degree of freedom, for a total of K degrees of freedom in the general case. The last row of this column shows $n - 1$ degrees of freedom for computing the total sum of squares, TSS. Remember that all the observations are used to calculate TSS, but one degree of freedom is lost in computing the $\overline{Y}$ term used in the TSS formula. Finally, the degrees of freedom for ESS is determined by subtracting $n - 1$, the regression degrees of freedom, K, from the total degrees of freedom. This yields $n - 1 - K$ or $n - (K + 1)$ degrees of freedom for ESS, where $K + 1$ is the number of parameters estimated (β_0, β_1, \ldots, β_K).

The third column presents the sum of squares used in the calculations, and below the table there is a reminder of how the actual computations are made.

The fourth column, "mean square," shows the sum of squares divided by its degrees of freedom. Note two important points: (1) The mean square $TSS/(n - 1)$ is an unbiased estimator of the variance of the *dependent variable* in the *population* from which the sample is drawn, and (2) the mean square $ESS/[n - (K + 1)]$ is an unbiased estimator of σ^2, the variance of the *population disturbance term*.

The final column of the table contains the computed F-ratio, or F-statistic, used for hypothesis testing. In this case it is computed as the ratio of the appropriate sum of squares, each adjusted for degrees of freedom or, more simply, the ratio of the appropriate mean squares. Which sum of squares is appropriate depends on the specific hypothesis to be tested.

The analysis-of-variance table in Table 6.7 provides the basis for hypothesis testing. The following discussion is organized around three basic classes of tests: (1) tests on a regression equation and on individual coefficients within a given equation, (2) tests on restrictions imposed on coefficients, and (3) tests across two or more equations.

Hypothesis Testing
in Regression Analysis

To set the stage for hypothesis testing, which can be rather intimidating on first contact, suppose that a sample of data is used to estimate the following regression equation:

$$Y = 7559.0 - 2.086X_1 + .603X_2 + e \qquad (6.12)$$

These results say that a 1-unit increase in X_1 will cause Y to decrease by 2.086 units, while a 1-unit increase in X_2 will cause Y to increase by .603 unit. These estimates of the slope coefficients computed from the sample are random variables and it is not at all clear what can be said about their "correctness." This is where hypothesis testing enters. Hypothesis testing permits researchers to use one sample as a basis for making probability statements about the "true" values of population regression coefficients.

Before going on, it is important to remember from Chapters 3 and 4 that the OLS estimators are unbiased, a property associated with computing estimates from each of all possible samples of size n from the population. So biasedness is not the issue here. Rather, the problem is that applied researchers typically have estimates from only one sample drawn from the population under study.

In Chapter 4 the variance of the distribution of b_1 was shown to be

$$\text{Var } b_1 = \frac{\Sigma x_2^2}{(\Sigma x_1^2)(\Sigma x_2^2) - (\Sigma x_1 x_2)^2} \sigma^2 \qquad (6.13)$$

and the variance of b_2 is

$$\text{Var } b_2 = \frac{\Sigma x_1^2}{(\Sigma x_1^2)(\Sigma x_2^2) - (\Sigma x_1 x_2)^2} \sigma^2 \qquad (6.14)$$

where σ^2 is the variance of the population disturbance term. Equations (6.13) and (6.14) are estimated from sample data by

$$S_{b_1}^2 = \frac{\Sigma e^2}{n-3} \frac{\Sigma x_2^2}{(\Sigma x_1^2)(\Sigma x_2^2) - (\Sigma x_1 x_2)^2} \qquad (6.15)$$

and

$$S_{b_2}^2 = \frac{\Sigma e^2}{n-3} = \frac{\Sigma x_1^2}{(\Sigma x_1^2)(\Sigma x_2^2) - (\Sigma x_1 x_2)^2} \qquad (6.16)$$

where $\Sigma e^2/(n-3)$ is the sample estimate of σ^2, the population variance. These estimates permits rewriting (6.12) as

$$\begin{array}{cccc} Y = 7559 & - 2.086 X_1 & + .603 X_2 + e \\ (519) & (.168) & (.036) \end{array} \qquad (6.17)$$

where the numbers in parentheses are the estimated standard deviations of the least squares coefficients computed from the sample. Equation (6.17) contains the necessary ingredients for constructing an hypothesis test about the value of a population regression coefficient, an estimate of the coefficient and its standard deviation.

The formal structure of hypothesis testing can be illustrated using β_1:

$$H_0: \beta_1 = \beta_1^* \quad \text{versus} \quad H_a: \beta_1 \neq \beta_1^*$$

where H_0 is the *null hypothesis*, H_a is the *alternative hypothesis*, and β_1^* is what the researcher thinks is the likely value of β_1 in the population. The purpose of the test is to use the evidence available from the sample to draw some conclusions about the value of β_1. If the null hypothesis is rejected, the alternative hypothesis is not rejected; if the null is not rejected, the alternative hypothesis is rejected.

Because the variance of b_1 is estimated, the normal distribution is not appropriate for hypothesis testing. Instead, the t-statistic and the t-distribution must be used. The t-statistic is computed from the sample by

$$t = \frac{b_1 - \beta_1^*}{S_{b_1}} \qquad (6.18)$$

where b_1 is the estimated (sample) value of β_1, β_1^* is the hypothesized value of β_1, and S_{b_1} is the estimated standard error of the regression coefficient. Suppose that the proposition to be tested is that X_1 is not a "relevant" variable in the sense that changes in X_1 do not result in changes in Y. Formally, the null hypothesis would be

$$H_0: \beta_1 = 0 \quad \text{versus} \quad H_a: \beta_1 \neq 0 \qquad (6.19)$$

and the computed t-statistic would be

$$t = \frac{-2.086}{.168} = -12.38 \qquad (6.20)$$

A t-statistic of -12.38 says that the value for the sample estimate, -2.086, is 12.38 standard deviations below the hypothesized value of 0 for β_1.

Now for the fundamental question: What are the chances of getting an estimate that yields a computed t-statistic of -12.38 from a distribution where the "true" value of β_1 is zero? The first step toward answering this question is to turn to a t-table and obtain the appropriate critical t-value. If the computed t-statistic is less than the critical t-value, the b_1 value is acceptably close to the hypothesized value and the null hypothesis is not rejected. In contrast, if the computed t-statistic is greater in absolute value than the critical t-value, then b_1 is "too far" from β_1^* and the null hypothesis is rejected and the alternative hypothesis is not rejected.

Suppose, for example, that the results shown in (6.20) were based on 52 observations. The degrees of freedom would be $52 - 3 = 49$, since three parameters are estimated in (6.17). The t-table, using 40 degrees of freedom, shows a critical t-value $= 2.021$ for the .05 (.95 probability) level with a two-tailed test. The critical t-value, or tabled t-value, of 2.021 may be interpreted in different ways. Under the null hypothesis that $\beta_1 = 0$, the probability of getting a computed t-value of less than 2.021 is .95. Alternatively, the probability of getting a computed t-value that is larger than 2.021 is .05. Because the probability of getting a computed t-statistic greater than 2.021 from a population where the true value of β_1 is zero is equal to or less than .05, the probability is equal to or greater than .95 that the sample came from a population where β_1 is *not* equal to zero. Consequently, a t-statistic of -12.38 would lead a researcher to reject the null hypothesis and not reject the alternative hypothesis.

Now consider X_2 in (6.17). Suppose that one objective of the research is to determine whether the slope of X_2 is equal to .65, where perhaps this particular value was found in previous research or is important in the context of some policy debate. The formal structure of the appropriate hypothesis test is

$$H_0: \beta_2 = .65 \quad \text{versus} \quad H_a: \beta_2 \neq .65$$

and the computed t-statistic is

$$t = \frac{.603 - .65}{.036} = -.47 \qquad (6.21)$$

In this case, the computed t-statistic is less than the critical t-value for a two-tailed test at the .05 level, which says that the observed value is acceptably close to the hypothesized value. Consequently, the null hypothesis would not be rejected and the alternative hypothesis would be rejected.

In summary, the applied researcher typically has only one sample available for making estimates of the unobservable population regression coefficients. Because these estimates are random variables (different samples for the same population are expected to yield different numerical estimates), the researcher must resort to hypothesis testing, which involves comparing computed t-statistics with critical t-values to determine whether to not reject or to reject the null hypothesis being tested. The upshot is that applied researchers end up making probability, not deterministic, statements about the value of unobservable population parameters. The remainder of the chapter presents the formal treatment of hypothesis testing.

Tests on a Regression Equation and on Individual Coefficients

The following regression equation was estimated using n sample observations.

$$Y = b_0 + b_1X_1 + b_2X_2 + b_3X_3 + b_4X_4 + e \qquad (6.22)$$

A researcher might be interested in whether (1) all the population coefficients taken together are significantly different from zero (this is a significance test on the equation itself); (2) a subset of coefficients, say for X_3 and X_4, are simultaneously ("taken together") significantly different from zero; or (3) one particular population regression coefficient is significantly different from zero.

Although these three hypotheses ask different economic questions, the formal structure is the same for each test. All three hypothesis tests follow from the analysis-of-variance table in Table 6.8. This table differs slightly from Table 6.7. First, it allows for a breakdown of the sum of squares due to regression according to the number of independent variables in the equation. This involves two terms, RSS_2 and RSS_1. RSS_2 refers to the equation with the full set of K independent variables, while RSS_1 refers to a second equation based on a subset of L independent variables. For equation (6.22), K is 4, but L could be 1, 2, 3, or 4, depending on the particular hypothesis being tested. The various hypotheses were explained in detail below.

Table 6.8 also introduces a new term called *difference*. This allows for testing, as columns 3 and 4 suggest, whether the regression sum of squares, RSS, is different depending on whether all K independent variables are included in the equation. The principle is to test whether the regression sum of squares increases significantly (or the error sum of squares decreases significantly) when $K - L$ variables are added to the equation.

Testing the Regression Equation

Using the equation above, we obtain the formal statement of the hypothesis test:

$$H_0: \beta_1 = \beta_2 = \beta_3 = \beta_4 = 0 \quad \text{versus} \quad H_a: \text{at least one } \beta_k \neq 0. \quad (6.23)$$

Table 6.8. General Analysis-of-Variance Table for Regression

(1) Source of Variation	(2) Degrees of Freedom	(3) Sum of Squares	(4) Mean Square	(5) Computed F-Statistic
All K variables, $X_1, \ldots, X_L, X_{L+1}, \ldots, X_K$	K	RSS_2	RSS_2/K	$F = \dfrac{RSS_2/K}{Q_2}$
First L variables, $X_1, \ldots, X_L$	L	RSS_1	RSS_1/L	$F = \dfrac{RSS_1/L}{Q_2}$
Difference	$K - L$	$RSS_2 - RSS_1$	$\dfrac{RSS_2 - RSS_1}{K - L} = Q_1$	$F = \dfrac{Q_1}{Q_2}$
Residual	$n - (K + 1)$	ESS	$\dfrac{ESS}{n - (K + 1)} = Q_2$	
Total	$n - 1$	TSS		

In words, H_0 says that all the population coefficients are simultaneously equal to zero. In more familiar terms, it says that the four variables taken together do not explain any of the observed variation in the dependent variable. In this instance, $L = 0$ in Table 6.8 because the full set of independent variables is being used. Consequently, the appropriate sum of squares for the numerator of the ratio, Q_1, is RSS_2. The appropriate statistic for this test is

$$\text{computed } F = \frac{RSS_2/K}{ESS/[n - (K + 1)]} \tag{6.24}$$

with K degrees of freedom in the numerator [4 for (6.23)] and $n - (K + 1)$ degrees of freedom in the denominator [$n - 5$ for (6.23)], written as $F_{K, n-(K+1)}$. A word of caution: The F-statistic is sometimes shown as

$$\text{computed } F = \frac{RSS_2[n - (K + 1)]}{ESS[K]}$$

which can be confusing, especially with regard to the degrees of freedom for numerator and denominator. The form shown in (6.24) makes it easier to keep degrees of freedom straight.

What is this test doing? The null hypothesis is that the coefficients of all the independent variables taken jointly are not different from zero. Another way of stating the null hypothesis is that TSS, the variation of Y in the sample, is due only to random variation (i.e., that TSS = ESS). Now notice that the numerator of (6.24) is RSS_2 (sum of squares due to the regression) and the denominator is ESS (sum-of-squared residuals). Hence, if H_0 is true, then, in the extreme, RSS_2 will be zero and the computed F-statistic will be zero. In practice, if H_0 is true, the F-statistic will be "small"; if H_0 is not true, the F-statistic will be "large." Testing this hypothesis formally involves comparing the "computed" F [equation (6.24)] with a "critical" or "tabled" F value, which is found using the F-distribution.

This is easily demonstrated using a numerical example. For (6.24), 4 degrees of freedom are needed for the numerator. If the sample size equals 25, there are [25 − (4 + 1)] or 20 degrees of freedom in the denominator. Consider Appendix Table A.3, which identifies F for the "upper 5 percent points." At the intersection of column 5 and row 20 is the number 2.87. This says that under the hypothesis being tested, the probability of getting a computed F-statistic larger than 2.87 is .05. Conversely, if the null hypothesis is true, the probability of getting a computed F-statistic less than 2.87 is .95.

Suppose that the computed F-statistic were 1.2. H_0 would not be rejected at this probability level since 1.2 is less than 2.87. Remember that not rejecting the null hypothesis means only that the null hypothesis is reasonably consistent with the data, not that the data have proved the null hypothesis to be true. On the other hand, if the computed F-statistic were 5.14, the probability is less than .05 that the sample came from a population characterized by all the β's being simultaneously equal to zero. This implies that the probability is at least .95 that the sample came from a population where at least one of the β's is different from zero. Consequently, H_0 would be rejected and H_a would not be rejected. Thus the essence of hypothesis testing is to compare the "computed" statistic with the "critical" (or "tabled") statistic, and then, depending on the probabilities, either to reject or not to reject H_0.

Most computer regression programs print out either the computed F-statistic or the value of RSS and ESS from which the F-statistic can be computed. Many, however, print out both pieces of information because, as is shown below, RSS and ESS are needed for other tests. The F-statistic can also be computed using the R^2. Chapter 5 showed that the relationship between TSS, RSS, and ESS, and R^2 can be written as follows:

$$R^2 = 1 - \frac{ESS}{TSS} = \frac{RSS}{TSS}$$

Dividing both numerator and denominator of F as defined by (6.24) by TSS and rearranging terms yields

$$\text{computed } F = \frac{RSS/K}{ESS/[n - (K + 1)]} = \frac{RSS/TSS}{ESS/TSS} \frac{n - (K + 1)}{K}$$

$$= \frac{R^2}{1 - R^2} \frac{n - (K + 1)}{K}$$

(6.25)

with K degrees of freedom in the numerator and $n = (K + 1)$ in the denominator.

The joint test of all coefficients is used infrequently in applied research. To understand why, consider H_a: at least one $\beta_k \neq 0$. It says that the decision will be to reject H_0 if *any one* of the four coefficients in (6.22) is significantly different from zero. There is a method, developed below, for testing whether any single coefficient is significantly different from zero. If at least one of these tests shows a $\beta_k \neq 0$ in (6.22), H_0 would, in principle at least, be rejected, in which case there is little need for testing (6.23) in the first place.

There is, however, one situation where the joint test can be helpful. It is possible that no one of the individual coefficients is significantly different from zero according to the simple tests, yet the joint test could show a statistically significant regression equation. This can occur when there is severe multicollinearity in the data set (see Chapter 12).

Testing a Subset of Coefficients

Return to (6.22), and assume that the formal statement is

$$H_0: \beta_2 = \beta_4 = 0 \quad \text{versus} \quad H_a: \text{either } \beta_2 \neq 0 \text{ or } \beta_4 \neq 0 \quad (6.26)$$

To test this hypothesis, first estimate the two-variable equations

$$Y = b_0 + b_1 X_1 + b_3 X_3 + e \quad (6.27)$$

and then consider what happens, statistically speaking, if the variables X_2 and X_4 are added to this equation. In effect, the joint test proposed in (6.26) is commonly viewed as testing the effect of adding two or more variables to an equation already estimated. The alternative would be first to estimate the equation with all four independent variables, and then ask what would happen, statistically speaking, if X_2 and X_4 were deleted from the equation. The formal structure of this joint test is the same under either approach.

In the analysis-of-variance table, Table 6.8, the difference from adding $K - L$ variables to the first L variables is the key to testing (6.26). First estimate the equation with L variables and compute RSS_1, then add the $K - L$ variables, reestimate the equation, and compute RSS_2. This yields an F-statistic

$$\text{computed } F = \frac{(RSS_2 - RSS_1)/K - L}{ESS/[n - (K + 1)]} = \frac{Q_1}{Q_2} \qquad (6.28)$$

to compare to the tabled F-statistic with $K - L$ degrees of freedom in the numerator and $n - (K + 1)$ degrees of freedom in the denominator. If the computed F is less than the critical F, do not reject H_0. If the computed F is larger than the critical F, reject H_0. Notice that the test is whether the RSS_2, with all variables in the equation, is significantly larger than the RSS_1, with a subset of the variables. This test is sometimes written with $(ESS_1 - ESS_2)$ in the numerator, in which case the test is whether the *error sum of squares* significantly decreases when variables are added to the equation. The test is equivalent to that of (6.28).

Testing an Individual Coefficient

A test of an individual coefficient is a special case of the previous test where $L = 1$ and only one variable, rather than two or more, is added to the equation. So, in the context of the general equation

$$Y = b_0 + b_1 X_1 + \cdots + b_K X_K + e \qquad (6.29)$$

the test on any one coefficient, b_k, is simply testing whether adding the kth variable to an equation containing the other $K - 1$ variables results in a significant increase in RSS. The structure of the computed F would be identical to (6.28) used in the preceding section, but there is an important practical difference. The degrees of freedom in the numerator, $K - L$, is $K - (K - L) = 1$, since in this case only one variable is added to the equation. Consequently, the F-statistic when testing on a subset of only one coefficient has 1 degree of freedom in the numerator and $n - (K + 1)$ degrees of freedom in the denominator. The square root of this F-statistic (1 degree of freedom in the numerator) is the t-statistic, which follows the t-distribution. The formal test here is

$$H_0: \beta_k = 0 \quad \text{versus} \quad H_a: \beta_k \neq 0 \qquad \text{for any } k \qquad (6.30)$$

The null hypothesis is that X_k is not a (statistically) significant variable. In other words, a 1-unit change in X_k does not result in a change in the dependent variable.

In this special case of testing one coefficient, the appropriate test statistics are

$$\text{computed } F = \frac{(RSS_2 - RSS_1)/1}{ESS/[n - (K + 1)]} \qquad (6.31)$$

$$\text{computed } t = \frac{b_k - \beta_k}{S_{b_k}} = \frac{b_k}{S_{b_k}} \qquad \text{since } \beta_k = 0 \text{ by (6.30)}$$

$$(6.32)$$

To illustrate, assume that there are 20 degrees of freedom for the denominator. Appendix Table A.3 reveals that, for the .05 level,

$$\text{critical } F = 4.35 \tag{6.33}$$

From Appendix Table A.2, for the two-tailed test at the .05 level,

$$\text{critical } t = 2.086 \tag{6.34}$$

The square root of 4.35 is 2.086. Thus either the critical F or the critical t can be used to test H_0 in (6.30).

In summary, it is possible to test whether all population coefficients are simultaneously equal to zero, a subset is equal to zero, or any one coefficient is equal to zero. These tests and their associated test statistics are summarized in Table 6.9.

Table 6.9. Summary Table: Hypothesis Testing of Regression Parameters (Unconstrained Estimation)

Substance of Test	*Test Statistic*[a]
H_0: $\beta_1 = \beta_2 = \cdots = \beta_k = 0$	Computed $F = \dfrac{\text{RSS}_2/K}{\text{ESS}/n - (K + 1)}$
H_0: $\beta_l = \beta_j = 0$	Computed $F = \dfrac{(\text{RSS}_2 - \text{RSS}_1)/K - 1}{\text{ESS}/n - (K + 1)}$
H_0: $\beta_k = 0$	Computed $F = \dfrac{(\text{RSS}_2 - \text{RSS}_1)/1}{\text{ESS}/n - (K + 1)}$
	or
	Computed $t = \dfrac{b_k - 0}{S_{b_k}}$

[a] The critical value for the F-test is obtained from an F-table and the critical value for the t-test is obtained from a *t-table*.

Testing Restrictions on Coefficients

In multiple regression, either linear or nonlinear restrictions (constraints) can be imposed on coefficients. This technique leads to *constrained estimation*. Examples of linear restrictions are $\beta_k = 5$, or $\beta_k = \beta_j$, or $\beta_h + \beta_j = c$. Examples of nonlinear constraints are $\beta_k > 5$, or $\beta_k + \beta_j < c$, and so on. Estimation procedures for nonlinear constraints are beyond the scope of this book, so the case of nonlinear restrictions will be left for more advanced textbooks. Tests on linear restrictions, described below, are straightforward.

The formal structure for testing linear restrictions on coefficients is similar to the structure used in the previous sections, but the procedure for computing the required sum-of-squares terms is slightly different. The procedure is illustrated with two examples.

$\beta_k = c$, *a Constant*

Estimation using a particular data set, say, a food consumption survey conducted in a particular town, Twig, yields

$$Y = b_0 + b_1X_1 + b_2X_2 + e$$

where Y is weekly food expenditure, X_1 is age of head of household, and X_2 is income.

Suppose that the estimated value of b_2 turns out to be .31, indicating that a \$10.00 increase in income results in a \$3.10 increase in weekly food expenditure. Suppose that later a survey conducted in another town, say Trunk, yields a different data set where the variables are defined in the same manner and are reported using the same measurement scale. One possible research question is whether the income slope in Trunk equals .31. Formally, the hypothesis to be tested can be expressed

$$H_0\colon \beta_2 = .31 \quad \text{versus} \quad H_a\colon \beta_2 \neq .31$$

To test the null hypothesis, use the RSS_2 and RSS_1 terms in Table 6.8, but interpret them in a slightly different way. In this case, RSS_2, which involves all the variables, is called the *unrestricted sum of squares* because there are no restrictions placed on the coefficients of any of the K variables. The RSS_1 term is called the *restricted sum of squares* because of the restrictions on some coefficients. Actually, in the preceding section, RSS_1 involved the restriction of zero on one or more coefficients simultaneously, depending on the particular test. In that case it was easy to impose such restrictions simply by not including the variable(s) in the equation. Imposing restrictions here involves more manipulations.

To test $H_0\colon \beta_2 = .31 \quad \text{versus} \quad H_a\colon \beta_2 \neq .31$, estimate

$$Y = b_0 + b_1X_1 + b_2X_2 + e \tag{6.35}$$

to obtain RSS_2. Then impose the condition $\beta_2 = .31$ by

$$Y = b_0 + b_1X_1 + .31X_2 + U \tag{6.36}$$

where the restricting value, .31, replaces β_2 in the population regression equation. Estimate the restricted equation

$$(Y - .31X_2) = b_0 + b_1X_1 + e \tag{6.37}$$

to obtain RSS_1. Note that the "assumed" value of β_2 is used to create a transformed dependent variable to use in (6.37). The computed F is given by Table 6.8 as

$$\text{computed } F = \frac{(RSS_2 - RSS_1)/P}{ESS/[n - (K + 1)]}$$

where P is the number of restrictions imposed on the coefficients, one in this case. This is the formal test. But, as we noted in the preceding section, an F-statistic with 1 degree of freedom in the numerator follows the t-distribution. Therefore, H_0 can also be tested using the simple t-test. The null hypothesis in this case would be that β_2 was some nonzero constant: H_0: $\beta_2 = \beta_2^* = .31$. The test statistic would be

$$\text{computed } t = \frac{b_2 - .31}{S_{b_2}}$$

where b_2 and S_{b_2} are obtained directly from estimating (6.35).

Equality of Coefficients

Consider a marketing year, price-dependent equation for a feed grain, say corn. For a given year, total available supply comes from two different sources, quantity produced in the current year and stocks carried over from the previous year. These quantities are measured in the same units, usually million bushels, and for all practical purposes corn from one source is a perfect substitute for corn from an other.

These particular market characteristics suggest the hypothesis that the slopes of the two variables are the same. The population regression function is

$$Y = \beta_0 + \beta_1 X_1 + \beta_2 X_2 + U$$

where Y is corn price, X_1 is corn production, and X_2 is carry-in stocks, and the formal test is H_0: $\beta_1 = \beta_2$ versus H_a: $\beta_1 \neq \beta_2$. As before, RSS$_2$ is obtained by estimating the unrestricted equation

$$Y = b_0 + b_1 X_1 + b_2 X_2 + e \tag{6.38}$$

To obtain RSS$_1$, the restricted sum of squares, the restriction $\beta_1 = \beta_2$ is used to rewrite the population regression equation as

$$Y = \beta_0 + \beta_1 X_1 + \beta_1 X_2 + U \tag{6.39}$$

or

$$Y = \beta_0 + \beta_1 (X_1 + X_2) + U \tag{6.40}$$

which may be estimated using the transformed variable $X^* = (X_1 + X_2)$ to obtain

$$Y = b_0 + b_1 X^* + e \tag{6.41}$$

which yields the RSS$_1$ to compute the required F-statistic. Again there is only one restriction on the coefficients, so again there is an F-statistic with 1 degree of freedom in the numerator.

In the special case of only one restriction, the null hypothesis $\beta_1 = \beta_2$, which can be written as $(\beta_1 - \beta_2) = 0$, can be tested using the t-test. To test H_0 with the t-statistic requires a specification of the distribution of the difference between two OLS coefficients, that is, the mean and variance of the variable $(b_1 - b_2)$. The mean is given by

$$E(b_1 - b_2) = E(b_1) - E(b_2) = \beta_1 - \beta_2 \tag{6.42}$$

and the variance by

$$E(b_1 - b_2)^2 = V(b_1) + V(b_2) - 2 \text{ Cov } (b_1, b_2) \tag{6.43}$$

The relevant test statistic is

$$\text{computed } t = \frac{(b_1 - b_2) - 0}{S_{(b_1 + b_2)}} = \frac{b_1 - b_2}{S_{(b_1 + b_2)}} \tag{6.44}$$

where the denominator is computed from the sample by taking the square root of

$$S_{b_1}^2 + S_{b_2}^2 - 2 \operatorname{Cov}(b_1, b_2) \tag{6.45}$$

Not all computer regression programs produce the covariance terms of the OLS estimates, needed for this test. In such cases the F-test described above is useful. In any event, (6.44) is simply the t-test to be compared to the appropriate tabled t with $n - (K + 1)$ degrees of freedom. In the case of more than one set of equalities, the F-test is the appropriate test with 1 degree of freedom for each set of constraints.

Sum of Coefficients

A related test is on the sum of two or more coefficients. The simplest example is the Cobb–Douglas production function, which can be written as

$$Y = b_0 + b_1 X_1 + b_2 X_2 + e \tag{6.46}$$

where the output, Y, and the inputs, X_1 and X_2, are written in logarithmic form. (See Chapter 11 for a discussion of log forms for variables.) Suppose that a researcher wants to test the proposition that the function exhibits constant returns to scale. This suggests

$$H_0: \beta_1 + \beta_2 = 1 \quad \text{versus} \quad H_a: \beta_1 + \beta_2 \neq 1$$

In this case H_0 can be tested with either the F-test or the t-test, because there is only one restriction. For the t-test, the researcher would first calculate

$$S_{b_1}^2 + S_{b_2}^2 + 2 \operatorname{Cov}(b_1, b_2) \tag{6.47}$$

and then use it to form the appropriate test statistic,

$$\text{computed } t = \frac{(b_1 + b_2) - 1}{S_{(b_1 + b_2)}} \tag{6.48}$$

The example is based on a specific case, but the structure of the test is general, so the procedure can be used to test any set of coefficients against any assumed value for the sum of the coefficients. Remember that if the computer output does not yield $\operatorname{Cov}(b_1, b_2)$, it is necessary to use the F-test.

Testing the Equality of Two Regression Equations

The final test considered involves the equality of two regression equations, an interesting situation that often occurs in applied work. Suppose, for example, that a researcher is using time-series data to estimate a regression equation. Suppose further that at about the midpoint of the time period, something occurred that might have caused a change in the structure (a change in the population regression coefficients) of the system being studied. For instance, the government institutes a new policy, a trade embargo is imposed, or a high-yielding variety is introduced. Often there is reason to question whether the underlying structure of the equation is different between the two time periods.

The possibility of different structures is not restricted to time series. A researcher may be estimating a production function where the data come from two quite different geographic regions, in which case a relevant question is whether the input elasticities are different between the two regions. In estimating consumption functions, a researcher might use a data set that includes families living in urban areas and families living in rural areas and ask the question of whether the structure of consumption differs between urban and rural residents.

In many research settings there is a "natural" grouping within the sample data that raises the question of different structural relationships between the groups. When considering this question, exactly the same structure (variables included, units of measurement on the variables, and functional form, and so on) must be used. Comparing a consumption function with a production function, or comparing two consumption functions with different combinations of variables or with different functional forms, is not valid.

Suppose that the equation to be estimated is

$$Y = \beta_0 + \beta_1 X_1 + \beta_2 X_2 + U \tag{6.49}$$

but there is a "natural" grouping within the data set that gives rise to

$$\hat{Y} = \beta_0^a + \beta_1^a X_1 + \beta_2^a X_2 \qquad \text{for one subgroup} \tag{6.50}$$

$$\hat{Y} = \beta_0^b + \beta_1^b S_1 + \beta_2^b X_2 \qquad \text{for the other} \tag{6.51}$$

To test the equality of these two equations (i.e., to test whether the structure of the two equations is the same) the hypothesis to be tested is

$$H_0: \beta_0^a = \beta_0^b \text{ and } \beta_1^a = \beta_1^b \text{ and } \beta_2^a = \beta_2^b \tag{6.52}$$

There are four basic steps to conducting the test.

1. Estimate the equation using only the observations (assume that there are n of them) in group a to obtain ESS_a.
2. Estimate the equation using only the observations (assume that there are m of them) in group b to obtain ESS_b.
3. Estimate the equation using all observations to obtain ESS_c, the combined ESS.
4. Computed $F = \dfrac{[\text{ESS}_c - (\text{ESS}_a + \text{ESS}_b)]/(K + 1)}{(\text{ESS}_a + \text{ESS}_b/[n + m - 2(K + 1)]}$

as the F-statistic with $(K + 1)$ degrees of freedom in the numerator and $[n + m - 2(K + 1)]$ degrees of freedom in the denominator.

This test, although appealing, may have a limitation. Notice in (6.52) that the test requires each pair of coefficients to be equal. Consequently, if this does not hold for any one pair, the conclusion must be that the structure is different between the two groups. For example, an equation with five independent variables, for a total of six coefficients, would require only $\beta_k^a \neq \beta_k^b$ to reject H_0, even if the coefficients between the two groups would be the same in five of the six cases.

In applied work, this might be considered too restrictive in the sense that it can suppress important information, such as a number of the coefficients not being significantly different. Because of this, applied researchers often prefer an alternative procedure for testing the equality of regression equations, namely, analysis of covariance. This is discussed in Chapter 9.

Some Examples

The tests of hypotheses described in this chapter can be illustrated using the demand for money example presented in Chapter 5. To review, that equation took the form

$$M = \beta_0 + \beta_1 E + \beta_2 R + \beta_3 J + U$$

where M = real per capita money
E = real per capita gross national product ($1000)
R = real interest rate
J = unemployment rate

The regression output for this equation applied to quarterly U.S. data for 1973 to 1984 is presented in Table 6.10.

Table 6.10. Results of Equation (5.23) on the U.S. Demand for Money, Quarterly, 1972 to 1984

a. Regression Equation

Variable	Coefficient	St. Dev. of Coeff.	t-Ratio = Coeff./S.D.
	−286.1	262.1	−1.09
E	678.89	44.95	15.10
R	−41.973	5.463	−7.68
J	26.159	7.457	3.51

$S = 75.99$
$R^2 = 86.1\%$
$\bar{R}^2 = 85.1\%$, adjusted for d.f.

b. Analysis of Variance

Due to	d.f.	SS	MS = SS/d.f.
Regression	3	1,502,900	500,967
Residual	42	242,544	5,775
	45	1,745,444	

The first hypothesis a researcher might test is that the population coefficients are jointly equal to zero. The alternative hypothesis is that at least one of the parameters is different from zero. Formally,

$$H_0: \beta_1 = \beta_2 = \beta_3 = 0$$

$$H_a: \text{at least one } \beta_k \neq 0$$

The critical F-value, at the 1 percent level of significance and with 3 and 42 degrees of freedom, is approximately 4.32. The calculated F-statistic is

$$F = \frac{\text{RSS}_2/k}{\text{ESS}/(N - k - 1)} = \frac{1,502,900/3}{242,544/42} = 86.7 \tag{6.53}$$

Since the computed F is larger than 4.32, the null hypothesis would be rejected and the alternative hypothesis not rejected.

A second test might be whether the basic components of GNP (consumption, investment, and government spending) all had the same marginal effect on the stock of money. Such a test would involve using the identity $C + I + G$ to form three new independent variables. For this test, the first step would be to estimate the equation

$$M = \beta_0 + \beta_1 C + \beta_2 I + \beta_3 G + \beta_4 R + \beta_5 J + U \tag{6.54}$$

where C = real per capita personal consumption expenditures
I = real per capita domestic investment
G = real per capita government spending

and M, R, and J are as before. A formal statement of the null hypothesis and its alternative would be

$$H_0: \beta_1 = \beta_2 = \beta_3 = \beta*$$

$$H_a: \beta_1 \neq \beta_2 \neq \beta_3$$

There are three steps to testing the hypothesis above. First, equation (6.54) must be estimated to obtain RSS_1, the unconstrained sum of squares. These results are shown in Table 6.11. Second, the constrained equation

$$M = b_0 + b_1^* E + b_2 R + b_3 J + e \tag{6.55}$$

which incorporates the null hypothesis by making use of the identity $E = C + I = G$, must be estimated to obtain RSS_2. Note that $E = \text{GNP} = C + I + G$ and that b_1^* is the estimated value for the constrained parameter. These results are shown in Table 6.10. The third step is to use these results to calculate the F-statistic:

$$F = \frac{(\text{RSS}_1 - \text{RSS}_2)/P}{\text{ESS}_1/(N - k - 1)} = \frac{142,773/3}{99,771/40} = 19.08 \tag{6.56}$$

where P is the number of restrictions on the coefficients. Since this calculated F-value is greater than the critical F-value with 3 and 40 degrees of freedom (4.31 at the 1 percent significance level), the null hypothesis would be rejected and the alternative hypothesis would not be rejected.

These two examples are suggestive of other hypotheses that may be tested. For

Table 6.11. Results of Equation (6.54), the Demand for Money

a. Regression Equation

Variable	Coefficient	St. Dev. of Coeff.	t-Ratio = Coeff./S.D.
	2577.1	662.7	3.89
C	.77515	.09525	8.14
I	.4891	.1850	2.64
G	− 1.7929	.6252	− 2.87
R	− 30.585	3.541	− 8.64
J	24.70	12.92	1.91

$$S = 49.94$$
$$R^2 = 94.3\%$$
$$\overline{R}_2 = 93.6\%, \text{ adjusted for d.f.}$$

b. Analysis of Variance

Due to	d.f.	SS	MS = SS/d.f.
Regression	5	1,645,673	329,135
Residual	40	99,771	2,494
	45	1,745,444	

example, one might wonder whether the coefficients in the basic demand for money equation (6.54) changed after President Reagan took office. This hypothesis, as well as many other hypotheses that a researcher might dream up, are testable using the techniques presented in this chapter.

Summary

Often researchers are interested in testing hypotheses about regression parameters. Traditionally, applied researchers test a null hypothesis about the value of a parameter. The most common null hypothesis probably is that an individual coefficient is equal to zero. To test this (and other hypotheses), applied researchers first use regression to obtain an estimage of the parameter and then ask whether this estimate is "close enough" to the value specified in the null hypothesis. If the estimate is close enough to the hypothesized value, the researcher does not reject the null hypothesis. If, however, the estimate is "too far" from the hypothesized value for the regression parameter, the null hypothesis is rejected as being unreasonable. For the most common case, the hypothesis test is stated formally as H_0: $\beta_k = 0$ versus H_a: $\beta_k \neq 0$ and the conclusion is either to not reject H_0 and reject H_a or reject H_0 and not reject H_a.

The essence of testing hypothesis is determining whether an estimate is close enough to the value of the parameter specified in the null hypothesis for it to be reasonable to conclude that the sample was drawn from a population where the null hypothesis is true. Statistical theory is used to conduct such tests. First, the variance of the statistic being considered is estimated. Then a test statistic is calculated, a t-statistic in the specific case when only one regression coefficient is being tested and an *F*-statistic in all other cases. Statistical tables, such as those printed in the Appendix, inform researchers how large *F*- and *t*-statistics can get and still permit one to reasonably assume that the null hypothesis is true. If the *F*- or *t*-statistic calculated from the sample is larger than the critical *F*- or *t*-value, the null hypothesis is rejected. Usually, applied researchers want to be 95 percent confident in any decision to reject a null hypothesis, so they choose critical values such that there is only a 5 percent chance of incorrectly rejecting a null hypothesis.

Terms

Analysis-of-variance table	Nonsampling error
Chi-square distribution	Probability
Constrained estimation	Random variable
Critical value	Sampling error
Degrees of freedom	Sources of variation
F-distribution	Standardized normal variable
Law of Large Numbers	Statistical inference
Mean square	*t*-distribution

Exercises

6.1 Are the following statements true or false? If false, why?
   (a) Statistics, properly used, provides definitive answers to a wide variety of questions about parameters.
   (b) OLS estimators cannot be BLUE unless the disturbance term is normally distributed about zero.
   (c) Conventional hypothesis testing in regression analysis is based on an assumption that the disturbance term is normally distributed.
   (d) The Central Limit Theorem tells us that as sample size increases, the distribution of the sample statistics generated in regression analysis will approach the normal distribution regardless of the distribution of the variable of interest in the population.
   (e) Hypothesis testing in applied work involves the normal, the *t*, the chi-squared, and the *F*-distributions.
   (f) As degrees of freedom increase, the *t*-distribution approaches the chi-squared distribution.
   (g) The ratio of two variables that are distributed according to a chi-squared distribution is distributed according to an *F*-distribution.
   (h) The normal distribution, the *t*-distribution and the *F*-distribution are based on one measure of degrees of freedom, whereas two measures of degrees of freedom are required for the chi-squared distribution.

(i) Sum-of-squares terms, such as TSS, RSS, or ESS, follow an F-distribution.

(j) The ratio of two sum-of-squares terms, each an estimate of a variable with a chi-squared distribution, follows an F-distribution.

(k) All the conventional hypothesis tests presented in this chapter are based on the assumption of unbiased estimators.

6.2 Consider the following basic analysis-of-variance table based on an OLS regression.

Source of Variation	Degrees of Freedom	Sum of Squares
Regression equation	—	800
Error	45	—
Total	49	1200

(a) How many observations are in the sample?

(b) How many independent variables are used in the regression equation?

(c) What is $\Sigma\ e^2$?

(d) What is the variance explained by the regression equation?

(e) What is an unbiased *estimator* of the variance of the disturbance term?

(f) What is the estimate of σ^2?

(g) What is the standard error of regression?

(h) What is the unbiased *estimator* of the variance of the dependent variable in the population?

(i) What is the estimate of Var (Y)?

(j) What is the R^2?

(k) Calculate the F-statistic to test the null hypothesis that all four β_i's are equal to zero at the 5 percent level.

6.3 Find the critical t-value in the following cases.

(a) $n = 34 \quad K = 3 \quad \alpha = .05 \quad$ two-tailed test
(b) $n = 24 \quad K = 1 \quad \alpha = .05 \quad$ one-tailed test
(c) $n = 180 \quad K = 6 \quad \alpha = .05 \quad$ two-tailed test
(d) $n = 67 \quad K = 6 \quad \alpha = .05 \quad$ two-tailed test
(e) $n = 24 \quad K = 2 \quad \alpha = .01 \quad$ one-tailed test
(f) $n = 24 \quad K = 3 \quad \alpha = .01 \quad$ two-tailed test
(g) $n = 246 \quad K = 6 \quad \alpha = .01 \quad$ two-tailed test
(h) $n = 582 \quad K = 18 \quad \alpha = .01 \quad$ one-tailed test
(i) $n = 582 \quad K = 18 \quad \alpha = .05 \quad$ one-tailed test

6.4 Find the critical F-value in each of the cases in Exercise 6.3. (Ignore the information on number of tails in test.)

6.5 Consider the following OLS regression results:

$$\hat{Y} = 16.5 + 2.1X_1 + 50.0X_2 \qquad R^2 = .333$$
$$\quad\quad (10.0) \quad (.5) \quad\; (20.0) \qquad n = 28$$
$$F = 18.75$$

The numbers in parentheses are the standard errors of the regression coefficients. In each of the following, specify both the test statistics as well as the appropriate critical value.

(a) Construct a 95 percent two-sided confidence interval for β_1.
(b) Would you reject H_0: $\beta_1 = 0$ and not reject H_a: $\beta_1 \neq 0$ at the 5 percent level of significance?
(c) Would you reject H_0: $\beta_1 = 1$ and not reject H_a: $\beta_1 > 1$ at the 5 percent level of significance?
(d) Would you reject H_0: $\beta_2 = 0$ and not reject H_a: $\beta_2 \neq 0$ at the 1 percent level of significance?

6.6 Consider the following computer printout, where a faulty printer failed to print some of the regression information.

```
THE REGRESSION EQUATION IS
Y = ?? + ??X₁ + ??X₂
```

	COEFFICIENT	ST. DEV. OF COEFF.	T-RATIO= COEFF./S.S.
constant	-7.6682	–	-.584
X₁	51.0918	–	6.80
X₂	41.4607	–	1.12

```
THE ST. DEV. OF Y ABOUT THE REGRESSION LINE IS
S = ??
R-SQUARED =$#&&&& PERCENT
R-SQUARED =*¢¢%$# PERCENT, ADJUSTED FOR D.F.
```

ANALYSIS OF VARIANCE

DUE TO	DF	SS.	MS=SS/DF
REGRESSION	2	17023.	8511.
RESIDUAL	17	6262.	368.
TOTAL	19	23285.	

(a) What are b_0, b_1, and b_2 in the regression equation?
(b) How many observations are there in the sample?
(c) What is the standard deviation of regression?
(d) What are the standard errors for each of the regression coefficients?
(e) One can be 95 percent confident that β_1 is between _____ and _____ .

(f) What is the 95 percent confidence interval for β_2?
(g) Test H_0: $\beta_1 = 25$ versus H_a: $\beta_1 \neq 25$ at $\alpha = .01$.
(h) Test H_0: $\beta_2 = 0$ versus H_a: $\beta_2 \neq 0$ at $\alpha = .05$.
(i) Test H_0: $\beta_2 = 100$ versus H_a: $\beta_2 \neq 100$ at $\alpha = .05$.
(j) What is the coefficient of multiple determination?
(k) What is the adjusted coefficient of multiple determination?
(l) Test H_0: $\beta_1 = \beta_2 = 0$ versus H_a: $\beta_1 \neq 0$, or $\beta_2 \neq 0$, or both using the F-statistic at $\alpha = .05$.

6.7 Consider the following general analysis-of-variance table:

Source of Variation	Degrees of Freedom	Sum of Squares	Mean Squares
All variables (X_1, X_2, X_3, X_4)		800	
First variables (X_1, X_2)		300	
Difference			
Residual			
Total	25	1500	

(a) Complete the table by filling in the missing information.
(b) Test H_0: $\beta_1 = \beta_2 = \beta_3 = \beta_4 = 0$
   H_a: at least one $\beta_k \neq 0$ at the 5 percent significance level.
(c) Test H_0: $\beta_1 = \beta_2 = 0$
   H_a: $\beta_1 \neq 0$ or $\beta_2 \neq 0$ at 5 percent significance level.
(d) Test H_0: $\beta_3 = \beta_4 = 0$
   H_a: $\beta_3 \neq 0$ or $\beta_4 \neq 0$ at the 1 percent significance level.

6.8 Let Y = family food spending
   X_1 = income
   X_2 = family size

Data:

Family	Y	X_1	X_2
1	40	100	1
2	50	150	1
3	50	100	2
4	70	300	1
5	80	200	4
6	100	400	2
7	110	300	4
8	140	300	6
9	160	850	1
10	200	300	8

Calculate the following.
(a) Find r_{y1}, r_{y2}, and r_{12}.
(b) Find b_{01} and b_{y1} in $Y = b_{01} + b_{y1}X_1 + e_1$.
(c) Find b_{02} and b_{y2} in $Y = b_{02} + b_{y2}X_2 + e_2$.
(d) Find b_0, $b_{y1.2}$ and $b_{y2.1}$ in $Y = b_0 + b_{y1.2}X_1 + b_{y2.1}X_2 + e_{y.12}$.

For the equation in part (d),
(e) Find S^2.

(f) Find the standard deviation of $b_{y1.2}$ and $b_{y2.1}$.

(g) Find R^2 and $\overline{R}^2$.

(h) Test H_0: $\beta_1 = 0$ versus H_a: $\beta_1 \neq 0$ at $\alpha = .05$.

(i) Test H_0: $\beta_2 = 0$ versus H_a: $\beta_2 \neq 0$ at $\alpha = .05$.

(j) Test the following null hypothesis:

$$H_0: \beta_1 = \beta_2 = 0$$

$$H_a: \beta_1 \neq 0 \text{ or } \beta_2 \neq 0 \text{ or both}$$

6.9 The following model of household housing expenditures was estimated for a sample of two-earner households living in the northeastern and the western United States. Test the hypothesis that the structure is the same in the two regions.

$$Y = \text{total annual housing expenditures}$$

$$X_1 = \text{total annual income of the primary earner}$$

$$X_2 = \text{total annual income of the secondary earner}$$

Northeastern sample:

$$\hat{Y} = -183.80 + .326X_1 + .163X_2 \qquad R^2 = .823$$
$$\phantom{\hat{Y} = -183.80 + } (1.04) \qquad (.065)$$

Western sample:

$$\hat{Y} = -129.930 + .636X_1 + .105X_2 \qquad R^2 = .681$$
$$\phantom{\hat{Y} = -129.930 + } (.452) \qquad (.021)$$

Analysis-of-Variance Tables

Source of Variation	Degrees of Freedom	Sum of Squares	Mean Square	F
Northeastern sample				
Regression	2	31.8072	15.904	11.6
Residual	111	152.1810	1.371	
Total	113	183.9882		
Western sample				
Regression	2	337.0302	168.515	3.9
Residual	111	4,796.1990	43.209	
Total	113	5,133.2292		
Pooled set				
Regression	2	2,525.0544	1,262.527	26.4
Residual	225	10,760.1750	47.823	
Total	227	13,285,2294		

CHAPTER
7

Data Sets, Worksheets, and a Tyro's Treatment of Matrix Algebra

Since first probing into the eating habits of families in the tiny town of Twig in the beginning of Chapter 1, this book has covered a lot of material. Among the topics considered have been scatter diagrams and least squares lines, populations and samples, parameters and estimators, linearity and unbiasedness and minimum variance, disturbances and residuals, homoscedasticity and statistical independence, simple and multiple regression, variance decomposition and correlation, covariation and causation, definitive statements and probability statements, null hypotheses and alternative hypotheses, the normal, chi-square, and F-distributions, t-tests and F-tests, confidence intervals and probability levels, not rejecting and rejecting, and critical values and computed values. All of which can seem abstract and intimidating.

In this chapter we begin by talking about numbers, or, more technically, "data sets," a seemingly trivial subject, but one that is important to the applied researcher. For the beginning researcher, the gap between theory and working with numbers in an applied research setting can be difficult to bridge. However, once it has been bridged, the student's ability to do applied research improves quickly and dramatically. Suddenly, this whole business seems to make sense.

Consequently, it is worthwhile at this juncture to spend some time on data sets and worksheets. As a fringe benefit, a comfortable familiarity with data sets and worksheets provides an easy transition into the arcane world of matrix algebra. That transition is made in this chapter, taking a low-key, casual approach. Of course, matrix algebra is not essential to understanding this book or to conducting good applied research. Yet some idea of what matrix algebra is all about, particularly how its notation relates to the computations of previous and subsequent chapters, is helpful background information. In this chapter we offer enough understanding of matrix

137

algebra to enable an interested researcher to make sense of other books, journal articles, or research reports that use the matrix notation.

We begin by presenting and discussing, in the language of previous chapters, the output of an actual computer run. The format of the output is that of a computer program called MINITAB. Other regression programs use different formats, yet the substance of the output is the same.

The regression output discussed here, using a real-world data set described completely in Chapter 8, has hog price as the dependent variable and pork production (a "supply shifter") and consumer income (a "demand shifter") as the two independent variables. Formally, the equation to be estimated is

$$Y = \beta_0 + \beta_1 X_1 + \beta_2 X_2 + U$$

where Y = hog price
X_1 = pork production
X_2 = consumer income
U = population disturbance term

The goal is OLS estimates, b_0, b_1, and b_2, of the population parameters β_0, β_1, and β_2. The regression output is presented in Table 7.1.

Table 7.1. Computer Output of the Regression of Pork Price on Production and Income

THE REGRESSION EQUATION IS
    PIGPRICE = 75.6 − 20.9 PIGPRO + 6.03PCPI   (A)

COLUMN	COEFFICIENT	ST. DEV. OF COEFF.	T-RATIO = COEFF./S.D.	
	75.587	5.190	14.57	
PIGPRO	− 20.858	1.684	− 12.39	(B)
PCPI	6.0328	.3563	16.93	

THE STANDARD DEVIATION OF Y ABOUT THE   (C)
REGRESSION LINE IS
    S = 4.425

WITH (52 − 3) = 49 DEGREES OF FREEDOM   (D)

R-SQUARED = 86.4 PERCENT   (E)
R-SQUARED = 85.6 PERCENT, ADJUSTED FOR D.F.   (F)

ANALYSIS OF VARIANCE

DUE TO:	DF	SS	MS = SS/DF	
REGRESSION	2	6113.0	3056.5	
RESIDUAL	49	959.5	19.6	(G)
TOTAL	51	7072.5		

Item (A) presents the equation in the familiar form, with $b_0 = 75.6$, $b_1 = -20.9$, and $b_2 = 6.03$ being the OLS estimates of the respective population regression coefficients. More informative is the table (B). The first column, COLUMN, is simply a listing of the independent variables presented in the order in which they were fed into the machine. The first row contains information on the constant, b_0 (MINITAB leaves this cell blank). The second row pertains to the first independent variable (pork production, or PIGPRO), and the third row, the second independent variable (consumer income, or PCPI). The next column, COEFFICIENT, gives the estimated coefficients of the variables. Because this is a two-independent-variable equation, b_0, b_1, and b_2 were respectively computed according to equations (4.33), (4.31), and (4.32). Next, ST. DEV. OF COEFF. contains the standard deviations of the respective coefficients computed by formulas (4.41) and (4.42). Finally, T-RATIO = COEFF./S.D. is the computed t-ratio on the assumption that $\beta_k = 0$ (i.e., H_0: $\beta_k = 0$ versus H_a: $\beta_k \neq 0$), as discussed in Chapter 6.

Item (C) is the standard deviation of the dependent variable about the regression line. The square of this standard deviation, identified by S^2 in previous chapters, is the estimate of σ^2, the variance of the population disturbance term. This number is computed by equation (4.39).

There are 52 observations in the data set used to estimate β_0, β_1, and β_2. Consequently, there are $52 - 3 = 49$ degrees of freedom, as shown by (D). Items (E) and (F) are, respectively, the R^2 and $\bar{R}^2$ terms computed by equations (5.19) and (5.20).

The table (G) is a slightly modified version of the analysis-of-variance table discussed in Chapter 6. The first column identifies the components of variance, the second column shows the degrees of freedom associated with each, and the third column presents the computed sum of squares for each item. Upon using the notation of previous chapters, the first number in this column is RSS, the second is ESS, and the third is TSS. Note that TSS = RSS + ESS, in accord with equation (5.13). The final column shows the MEAN SQUARE, the sum of squares divided by the degrees of freedom. The square root of the mean square of RESIDUAL is 4.425, the number shown above as S. This table does not include the F-statistic for the test of the significance of the regression equation (H_0: $\beta_1 = \beta_2 = 0$) developed in Chapter 6. However, it can be easily computed as (mean square for regression)/(mean square for residual) = 155.94. In Chapter 5 [equation (5.19)] it was shown that $R^2 = 1 - $ ESS/TSS, which can be computed from this table as $1 - (6113.0)/(7072.5) = $ RSS/TSS = .8643, the number shown above by (E). Finally, the last column, T-RATIO, gives the computed t-statistics for testing the significance of the respective coefficients. It is important to note that these t-ratios are constructed on the null hypothesis that the population regression coefficients are zero. This interpretation of a computer printout was designed to make the derivations of the previous chapters less abstract and to introduce the subject of this chapter.

Both ends of a spectrum, the theory of least squares and a computer printout of computations made on the basis of that theory, have been presented. It is time to fill in the gap between these two extremes by looking at how applied researchers select the variables to be used in the analysis and how they get the numbers into the computer to do the computations. The various aspects of selecting variables are woven into the fabric of the rest of this book, especially Chapter 8. Preparing data for computers is discussed in this chapter.

On Data Sets

In applied research, there are time-series data sets and cross-sectional data sets. This distinction, far from being sophisticated, simply refers to the unit of observation on which the data are measured. Consider, as an example, the research problem of how to estimate the effect of corn production and corn exports on the season's average price of corn received by farmers. A relevant data set might consist of annual values for the three variables, where price (P) would be the average price for a particular year, quantity (Q) would be corn production for that year, and exports (E) would be corn exports for the year. The researcher might accumulate the data for, say, 20 years, covering the period from 1961 to 1980. A data set structured in this fashion, where the data are identified by time units ("years" in this example), is called a *time-series data set*.

Consider another example. As part of a research project a researcher wants to estimate the effect of property valuations and school enrollments on educational expenditures by local school districts in a particular state. In this case, the researcher collects the required data from each local school district in the state for a particular year, say 1984. In this case, the data would be identified by cross-sectional units ("school districts" in this example) for a specific time period and would be called a *cross-sectional data set*.

Worksheets are the means by which researchers structure their data sets so that the data sets make sense and can be entered into the computer. Constructing a worksheet is the topic of this section.

Before a worksheet can be prepared it is, of course, necessary to know what data are needed. The relevant data are determined by the specific research question being examined. Developing a regression equation to be estimated as a prelude to data collection is discussed in detail in the following chapter. For now assume that the research question focuses on the population equation

$$C = f(I, S) \tag{7.1}$$

where C is weekly food expenditures, I is family income, and S is family size. The sample regression equation to be estimated by OLS procedures is

$$C_i = b_0 + b_1 I_i + b_2 S_i + e_i, \qquad i = 1, \ldots, n \tag{7.2}$$

Estimating (7.2) requires a worksheet consisting of information on expenditures, income, and family size for each of the n families in the sample. The data in Table 3.1, which are reproduced as a worksheet in Table 7.2, can be used as an illustration.

The first column identifies the observations, families in this case. Note that this is a cross-sectional data set. If a time-series data set were being used, the appropriate time identification would be in the first column. It is important to identify each observation in the data set, as will become clear in later chapters. Most researchers put the identification in the first column, but this is strictly a matter of personal preference. The content of the remaining three columns is clear from the column headings. The columns of the worksheet refer to the variables in the equation being estimated and the rows contain the values of these variables for each observation in the sample.

Table 7.2. Worksheet: Cross-Sectional Data Set on Weekly Food Expenditures, Family Income, and Family Size

Family Identification	Weekly Food Expenditures	Family Income	Family Size (Number)
01	$130	$600	2
02	40	200	2
03	70	200	1
04	40	300	6
05	110	400	4
06	30	100	3

This worksheet and equation (7.2) are related in the following way. There are six families ($n = 6$), so (7.2) comprises six equations, one for each family. This can be expressed as follows:

Family	Equation	
01	$130 = b_0 + b_1(600) + b_2(2) + e_1$	
02	$40 = b_0 + b_1(200) + b_2(2) + e_2$	
03	$70 = b_0 + b_1(200) + b_2(1) + e_3$	(7.3)
04	$40 = b_0 + b_1(300) + b_2(6) + e_4$	
05	$110 = b_0 + b_1(400) + b_2(4) + e_5$	
06	$30 = b_0 + b_1(100) + b_2(3) + e_6$	

where the OLS residuals, e_i, take on values such that (7.2) is an exact equation (an identity) for each of the six families. Notice that the values of the variables C, I, and S and the value of the OLS residuals vary across the six families in the sample, but the values of the OLS coefficients b_0, b_1, and b_2 do not. The latter point says in formal terms that the structure of the equation (the underlying population regression coefficients) is constant over the sample observations, a point used in subsequent chapters that need not deter us here.

The material above illustrates the structure of a worksheet and the relationship between the worksheet and the regression equation being estimated for a simple example. Consider now the more general case,

$$Y_i = b_0 + b_1 X_{1i} + b_2 X_{2i} + \cdots + b_K X_{Ki} + e_i, \qquad i = 1, \ldots, n \quad (7.4)$$

where the columns of the worksheet would refer to Y, the dependent variable, and the K independent variables, and the rows would contain the values of these variables for each of the n observations in the sample. To show the connection between the worksheet and (7.4), all of these n equations in (7.4) could be written out in the manner of (7.3) for the example of six families. That task, however would be tedious and not very enlightening. It is at this juncture that matrix algebra enters as an extremely powerful *notational* device for expressing succinctly the general regression equation and for carrying out the kinds of manipulations done in Chapters 3 to 6.

The remainder of this chapter attempts to provide some appreciation for the use of matrix algebra in regression analysis. What follows does not provide a basis for using matrix algebra in an analytical way (this is done in Chapter 20), but it is designed to make matrix algebra less intimidating to the newcomer.

To move to the general case, it is convenient to adopt the conventional notation of Y for the dependent variable and X_k for the kth independent variable in the regression equation. The manipulations will be illustrated with the data in the worksheet (Table 7.2), so Y represents food expenditures, X_1 family income, and X_2 family size.

Sliding into a Matrix

Now that a worksheet has been introduced, return to (7.3) and start again, this time with the goal of writing (7.3) in a different, more succinct way. Begin by writing

$$Y \text{ for } \begin{bmatrix} Y_1 \\ Y_2 \\ Y_3 \\ Y_4 \\ Y_5 \\ Y_6 \end{bmatrix}, \quad X_1 \text{ for } \begin{bmatrix} X_{11} \\ X_{21} \\ X_{31} \\ X_{41} \\ X_{51} \\ X_{61} \end{bmatrix}, \quad X_2 \text{ for } \begin{bmatrix} X_{12} \\ X_{22} \\ X_{32} \\ X_{42} \\ X_{52} \\ X_{62} \end{bmatrix}, \quad e \text{ for } \begin{bmatrix} e_1 \\ e_2 \\ e_3 \\ e_4 \\ e_5 \\ e_6 \end{bmatrix} \quad (7.5)$$

where a letter (Y, X_K, or e) represents a column in the worksheet. The double subscript ik refers the ith observation on the kth independent variable. By using this shorthand, (7.2) may be written

$$Y = b_0 + b_1 X_1 + b_2 X_2 + e \quad (7.6)$$

where Y is the column of expenditures over the sample of observations, X_1 is the associated column of income, X_2 is the column of family size, and e is the column of OLS residuals. Note that the e's are only implicitly on the worksheet. In the language of matrix algebra, the worksheet columns are referred to as *column vectors*. Researchers often say such things as "Let Y be the vector of weekly food expenditures, X_1 be the vector of family income," and so on. This notation saves some time in writing because now the single letter Y represents a column of numbers on the worksheet headed "Weekly Food Expenditures." Similarly, the terms X_1, X_2, and e should immediately evoke images of columns of data.

To see the full extent of the gains in notation, work back from (7.6) through (7.5) to (7.3). Consider first a term in (7.6), say $b_1 X_1$, where X_1 is the vector of the values for family income over the six families and b_1, as shown in (7.3), is a constant. Thus the term $b_1 X_1$ represents the *multiplication* of a *column vector* by a *constant*. This is accomplished by multiplying *each element* of the vector by the constant, which yields another column vector:

$$b_1 X_1 = b_1 * \begin{bmatrix} X_{11} \\ X_{21} \\ X_{31} \\ X_{41} \\ X_{51} \\ X_{61} \end{bmatrix} = \begin{bmatrix} b_1 X_{11} \\ b_1 X_{21} \\ b_1 X_{31} \\ b_1 X_{41} \\ b_1 X_{51} \\ b_1 X_{61} \end{bmatrix} \tag{7.7}$$

where "*" is used to denote multiplication. The right-hand side of (7.7) looks exactly like the appropriate part of (7.3). Similar computations can be made for $b_2 X_2$ in (7.5). Remaining is b_0 without a vector, but (7.3) indicates that b_0 is a constant over the sample observations. Multiplying b_0 by 1 does not change its value. Hence define a vector where each element is a 1 and write

$$\begin{aligned} Y_1 &= b_0(1) + b_1 X_{11} + b_2 X_{12} + e_1 \\ Y_2 &= b_0(1) + b_1 X_{21} + b_2 X_{22} + e_2 \end{aligned} \tag{7.8}$$

$$Y_6 = b_0(1) + b_1 X_{61} + b_2 X_{62} + e_6$$

which is (7.3) in general notation.

To summarize quickly, the relationship between the worksheet and the regression equation can be expressed in one of three ways. The first way is (7.2), which uses the subbscript i to denote changing values of the variables over the sample observations. The second way is shown in (7.3), which "writes out" the n equations for the sample. The third way is (7.6), which uses column vectors to represent the columns of the worksheet and involves the multiplication of a vector by a constant. Notationally, (7.6) is the simplest. In fact, the subscript i can be suppressed without any loss in content. Most important, (7.6) connects regression to matrix algebra with its powerful arithmetic operations. This link can be made after a new concept is introduced.

The worksheet in Table 7.2 now can be viewed as a series of column vectors presented side by side. If a new vector is added, where each element in the new vector is a 1 associated with b_0, it is possible to write the X-variables in the worksheet as

$$X\text{-matrix} = \begin{array}{c} \begin{array}{ccc} X_0 & X_1 & X_2 \end{array} \\ \begin{bmatrix} 1 & 600 & 2 \\ 1 & 200 & 2 \\ 1 & 200 & 1 \\ 1 & 300 & 6 \\ 1 & 400 & 4 \\ 1 & 100 & 3 \end{bmatrix} \end{array} \tag{7.9}$$

Enclosing a series of column vectors within a set of brackets in this fashion creates a *matrix*. Conversely, a matrix can be viewed as a set of column vectors treated as an entity. The right-hand side of (7.9) contains all the values of the independent variables for (7.2), so it is natural to call it the X-matrix. Generally, "X-matrix" refers to the matrix of the values of the independent variables, regardless of the number of variables in the equation or the number of observations in the sample. Finally, note that (7.9) includes the independent variable X_0 associated with the b_0 in the regression equation. Because only 1's are involved in X_0, it is superfluous to include X_0 when writing an equation such as (7.6), and it is not necessary to include this column on the worksheet. Nearly all computer programs automatically include this intercept column for purposes of computing the OLS coefficients. Thus X_0 is always there, just as b_0 is always there when variables are expressed as deviations from their respective means in the previous chapters.

The dependent variable is expressed in (7.6) as the weighted sum of column vectors, where b_0 is the weight for X_0, b_1 is the weight for X_1, and b_2 is the weight for X_2. The first three terms on the right-hand side of (7.6) involve the same elements as (7.9). The question to address now is how to use (7.9) in (7.6). More specifically, the problem is how to get the weights matched up with the proper columns in the X-matrix. This requires matrix multiplication, which is best shown via an example.

A special case of matrix multiplication is multiplying a column vector by a constant, shown in (7.7). In principle, the general version of matrix multiplication is identical to the special case. In practice, however, the general case is a little trickier. Suppose that there are two columns of data on a worksheet, say

Column 1	Column 2
1	6
2	7
3	8
4	9
5	10

and the problem is to find the sum of the cross-products, that is, the value of the term $[(1 \times 6) + (2 \times 7) + (3 \times 8) + (4 \times 9) + (5 \times 10)]$. In this simple case it would be easy to write $6 + 14 + 24 + 36 + 50 = 130 = \Sigma X_1 X_2$.

Write the two columns as

$$[1 \quad 2 \quad 3 \quad 4 \quad 5] \begin{bmatrix} 6 \\ 7 \\ 8 \\ 9 \\ 10 \end{bmatrix} = 130 \qquad (7.10)$$

The second term on the left-hand side of this expression is the now familiar column vector (the second column above). The new expression in brackets, which contains the numbers in the first column above, strings the numbers out in a row rather than stacking them. The configuration $[1 \quad 2 \quad 3 \quad 4 \quad 5]$ is called a *row vector*. So (7.10) is a row vector times a column vector. Let X_1 stand for the first column above and let X_2 stand for the second column. In (7.10), X_1 is presented as a row vector with the elements strung out rather than stacked up. The technical name for writing a column vector as a row vector is *transposing* a column vector. The resulting row vector is called the *transpose* of the column vector. Notationally, if X_1 is a column vector, X_1' (read "X_1-prime") is its transpose. So for (7.10), the general expression may be written in matrix notation as

$$X_1'X_2 = \text{sum of cross products of elements in the vectors } X_1 \text{ and } X_2 \quad (7.11)$$

This is nothing more than a shorthand expression for performing the operation above: $(1 \times 6) + (2 \times 7) + (3 \times 8) + (4 \times 9) + (5 \times 10)$, an expression much more time consuming to write than $X_1'X_2$. The expression (7.11) is simply a shorthand way of expressing the arithmetic operations to be performed on the numbers at hand.

The basic data (the worksheet) are already written as the X-matrix (7.9). Now the problem is to find a way to multiply each column of the X-matrix by its appropriate coefficient shown in (7.3). Specifically, the problem is to develop a notation that indicates the multiplication of the column of 1's in the X-matrix by b_0, the elements in the X_1 column by b_1, and the elements in the X_2 column by b_2. The conventional solution is

$$\begin{bmatrix} 1 & 600 & 2 \\ 1 & 200 & 2 \\ 1 & 200 & 1 \\ 1 & 300 & 6 \\ 1 & 400 & 4 \\ 1 & 100 & 3 \end{bmatrix} * \begin{bmatrix} b_0 \\ b_1 \\ b_2 \end{bmatrix} \quad (7.12)$$

where the first term is the X-matrix, the second term contains the OLS coefficients as a column vector, and $*$ denotes multiplication. The $*$ is usually suppressed in matrix notation. Expression (7.12) calls for multiplying a column vector by a matrix. If the first row of the X-matrix is treated as a row vector and (7.11) applied, the result would be

$$b_0(1) + b_1(600) + b_2(2) \quad \text{or} \quad b_0 + b_1(600) + b_2(2) \quad (7.13)$$

Similarly, treating the second row of the X-matrix as a row vector and applying (7.11) yields

$$b_0 + b_1(200) + b_2(2) \quad (7.14)$$

Repeating the treatment for each row of the X-matrix yields

$$\begin{aligned} &b_0 + b_1(600) + b_2(2) \\ &b_0 + b_1(200) + b_2(2) \\ &b_0 + b_1(200) + b_2(1) \\ &b_0 + b_1(300) + b_2(6) \\ &b_0 + b_1(400) + b_2(4) \\ &b_0 + b_1(100) + b_2(3) \end{aligned} \quad (7.15)$$

which is the right-hand side of (7.3), except for the residuals. But (7.15) is tiresome to write, and it would be next to impossible if there were, say, eight independent variables in the equation and 50 observations in the sample. However, a shorthand notation is now accessible. The term X has already been used to represent the matrix of independent variables. If b represents the column vector of OLS coefficients, the general case for (7.15) can be written compactly as Xb. Combining the general shorthand version of (7.15) with (7.5) yields

$$Y = Xb + e \qquad\qquad (7.16)$$

where Y = column vector of n observations on the dependent variable
$\quad\;\; X$ = matrix of n observations on K independent variables that
$\qquad\quad$ includes a column of 1's for b_0
$\quad\;\; e$ = column vector of the n OLS residuals

Comparing (7.16) with (7.4), the general regression equation, reveals the notational power of (7.16). With this background, the remainder of this chapter applies matrix algebra to the manipulations in Chapter 4 to illustrate further its notational power.

Matrix Algebra and Regression Theory

Begin with equations (4.31) and (4.32), reproduced here for convenience:

$$b_1 = \frac{(\Sigma \, x_2^2)(\Sigma \, x_1 y) - (\Sigma \, x_1 x_2)(\Sigma \, x_2 y)}{(\Sigma \, x_1^2)(\Sigma \, x_2^2) - (\Sigma \, x_1 x_2)^2} \qquad\qquad (4.31)$$

$$b_2 = \frac{(\Sigma \, x_1^2)(\Sigma \, x_2 y) - (\Sigma \, x_1 x_2)(\Sigma \, x_1 y)}{(\Sigma \, x_1^2)(\Sigma \, x_2^2) - (\Sigma \, x_1 x_2)^2} \qquad\qquad (4.32)$$

where the variables are measured as deviations from means and b_1 and b_2 are the OLS coefficients. A close inspection of these equations reveals that the various components are nothing more than sums of cross products, such as x_1 with y, x_1 with x_2, and x_1 with x_1. (The cross product of x_1 with itself is called the *sum of squares.*) Such expressions can easily be written in matrix shorthand. For example, $\Sigma \, x_1 y$ can be written as $x_1' y$, where x_1' is the transpose (row vector) of the numbers under the column headed "X_1," *after these numbers are expressed as deviations from their mean.* A first goal is to write (4.23) and (4.24) using matrix notation.

The terms in (4.31) and (4.32) involve two sets of cross products, one set involving the x-variables and y, the other set involving only the x-variables. Furthermore, the denominator is the same in both equations and involves only the x-variables. Now recall a notational convenience from arithmetic. The expression $8/2 = 4$ says "eight *divided* by two equals four." The same relationship can be expressed $8 \times \frac{1}{2} = 4$, which says "eight *multiplied* by one-half equals four." In other words, division may be viewed as multiplication, where the divisor is written as the inverse of the denominator. Another point to recall is that a number such as $\frac{1}{2}$ can be written as 2^{-1}. Thus the above could have been written as $8 \times 2^{-1} = 4$. Writing a number with the superscript -1 indicates that the number must be inverted before it is used in an arithmetic operation. That is, the number must be flipped over so that $2/1$ becomes $1/2 = 2^{-1}$. Technically, 2^{-1} is the *inverse* of 2.

Now back to the problem of expressing (4.31) and (4.32) in matrix notation. Note that the denominator in these equations has terms only in the x-variables. Using the above equations, we can either leave the denominator as it is or write it in the inverse form, as was done with "2" above. This is the form needed here, but the first task is to see how to write the number itself in the new shorthand.

The x-variables can be written in matrix form as above, except to keep things simple the values of X are written as deviations from their respective means:

$$
\begin{array}{cc}
\underline{X_1} & \underline{X_2} \\
x_{11} & x_{12} \\
x_{21} & x_{22} \\
\cdot & \cdot \\
\cdot & \cdot \\
\cdot & \cdot \\
x_{n1} & x_{n2}
\end{array}
$$

What is needed are the sums of cross products of x_1 with x_2, x_1 with x_1, and x_2 and x_2. Notationally, this is the X-matrix, as before. From (7.11) the cross products are formed by multiplying a row vector into a column vector, so the x-matrix needs to be *transposed* and written

$$
\begin{bmatrix} x_{11} & x_{21} & \cdots & x_{n1} \\ x_{12} & x_{22} & \cdots & x_{n2} \end{bmatrix}
\begin{bmatrix} x_{11} & x_{12} \\ x_{21} & x_{22} \\ x_{n1} & x_{n2} \end{bmatrix} = X'X \text{ in matrix notation}
$$

or more succinctly as $X'X$, read "the X-prime X matrix." This is an important matrix in regression theory.

A new wrinkle appears above, one that needs to be ironed out. To compute the product $X'X$, the first row of X' is viewed as a row vector and the first column of X as a column vector. Then (7.11) is applied to get

$$
(x_{11}x_{11} + x_{21}x_{21} + \cdots + x_{n1}x_{n1}) \quad \text{or} \quad \Sigma\, x_{i1}^2
$$

The wrinkle is that there is a second column in the X-matrix. This must be treated as a column vector and multiplied with the first row of X'. Applying (7.11) as above yields the number $\Sigma\, x_{i1}x_{i2}$, which are terms in (4.31) and (4.32). The process can be repeated by using the second row of X' as a row vector and applying (7.11). The results may be summarized by

$$
\begin{bmatrix} x_{11} & x_{21} & \cdots & x_{n1} \\ x_{12} & x_{22} & \cdots & x_{n2} \end{bmatrix}
\begin{bmatrix} x_{11} & x_{12} \\ x_{21} & x_{22} \\ \cdot & \cdot \\ \cdot & \cdot \\ \cdot & \cdot \\ x_{n1} & x_{n2} \end{bmatrix} =
\begin{bmatrix} \Sigma\, x_{i1}^2 & \Sigma\, x_{i1}x_{i2} \\ \Sigma\, x_{i1}x_{i2} & \Sigma\, x_{i2}^2 \end{bmatrix} = X'X
$$

The $X'X$ matrix contains the sums of squares and cross products of independent variables on the worksheet. It is these sums of squares and cross products that appear in the denominator of the formulas used to compute the OLS coefficients from sample data. To signify this division, use the "inverse" notation discussed above and write $(X'X)^{-1}$. At this point, readers without training in matrix algebra must accept on faith that this can be written

$$(X'X)^{-1} = \begin{bmatrix} \dfrac{\Sigma\, x_2^2}{(\Sigma\, x_1^2)(\Sigma\, x_2^2) - (\Sigma\, x_1 x_2)^2} & \dfrac{-\Sigma\, x_1 x_2}{(\Sigma\, x_1^2)(\Sigma\, x_2^2) - (\Sigma\, x_1 x_2)^2} \\[3mm] \dfrac{-\Sigma\, x_1 x_2}{(\Sigma\, x_1^2)(\Sigma\, x_2^2) - (\Sigma\, x_1 x_2)^2} & \dfrac{\Sigma\, x_1^2}{(\Sigma\, x_1^2)(\Sigma\, x_2^2) - (\Sigma\, x_1 x_2)^2} \end{bmatrix} \qquad (7.17)$$

Remaining are the cross-product terms of the X and Y variables that appear in the numerator of the OLS computations. Using the procedure above gives us

$$\begin{bmatrix} x_{11} & x_{21} & \cdots & x_{n1} \\ x_{12} & x_{22} & \cdots & x_{n2} \end{bmatrix} \begin{bmatrix} y_1 \\ y_2 \\ \cdot \\ \cdot \\ \cdot \\ y_n \end{bmatrix} = \begin{bmatrix} \Sigma\, x_{i1} y_i \\ \Sigma\, x_{i2} y_i \end{bmatrix} = X'Y \text{ in matrix notation} \qquad (7.18)$$

Putting (7.17) and (7.18) together yields

$$\begin{bmatrix} b_1 \\ b_2 \end{bmatrix} = \begin{bmatrix} \dfrac{\Sigma\, x_2^2}{(\Sigma\, x_1^2)(\Sigma\, x_2^2) - (\Sigma\, x_1 x_2)^2} & \dfrac{-\Sigma\, x_1 x_2}{(\Sigma\, x_1^2)(\Sigma\, x_2^2) - (\Sigma\, x_1 x_2)^2} \\[3mm] \dfrac{-\Sigma\, x_1 x_2}{(\Sigma\, x_1^2)(\Sigma\, x_1^2) - (\Sigma\, x_1 x_2)^2} & \dfrac{\Sigma\, x_1^2}{(\Sigma\, x_1^2)(\Sigma\, x_2^2) - (\Sigma\, x_1 x_2)^2} \end{bmatrix}^{-1} \begin{bmatrix} \Sigma\, x_1 y \\ \Sigma\, x_2 y \end{bmatrix}$$

$$(7.19)$$

which, using the familiar procedure for matrix multiplication, yields

$$b_1 = \frac{(\Sigma\, x_1 y)(\Sigma\, x_2^2) - (\Sigma\, x_2 y)(\Sigma\, x_1 x_2)}{(\Sigma\, x_1^2)(\Sigma\, x_2^2) - (\Sigma\, x_1 x_2)^2} = \text{equation (4.31)} \qquad (7.20)$$

$$b_2 = \frac{(\Sigma\, x_2 y)(\Sigma\, x_1^2) - (\Sigma\, x_1 y)(\Sigma\, x_1 x_2)}{(\Sigma\, x_1^2)(\Sigma\, x_1^2) - (\Sigma\, x_1 x_2)^2} = \text{equation (4.32)} \qquad (7.21)$$

All this can be written compactly using the multiplication rules developed above as

$$b = (X'X)^{-1} X'Y \qquad (7.22)$$

where b = column vector of OLS coefficient
$\quad\;\; Y$ = column vector of observations on the dependent variable
$\quad\;\; X$ = matrix of observations on the independent variables

Equation (7.22) is obviously much more compact than (7.20) and (7.21) taken together.

The variances for b_1 and b_2 in the two-independent variable equation were derived from equations illustrated by equation (4.41).

$$b_1 - \beta_1 = \frac{(\Sigma\, x_2^2)(\Sigma\, x_1 U) - (\Sigma\, x_1 x_2)(\Sigma\, x_2 U)}{(\Sigma\, x_1^2)(\Sigma\, x_2^2) - (\Sigma\, x_1 x_2)^2} \qquad (7.23)$$

and by analogy

$$b_2 - \beta_2 = \frac{(\Sigma\, x_1^2)(\Sigma\, x_2 U) - (\Sigma\, x_1 X_2)(\Sigma\, x_1 U)}{(\Sigma\, x_1^2)(\Sigma\, x_2^2) - (\Sigma\, x_1 x_2)^2} \qquad (7.24)$$

with the variances being obtained by squaring both sides of these equations and then taking expected values. Notice two things. First, these equations are of the same structure as (7.20) and (7.21), except that the cross-product terms in x and y are replaced by cross-product terms in x and U, the population disturbance term. Second, when these equations are squared and the expected values are taken, the E-operator will apply only to terms containing U, since the X-values are, by the classical assumptions, fixed in repeated sampling.

By virtue of the comparability of (7.23) and (7.24) with (7.20) and (7.21), the derivation above, especially (7.22) and (7.19), can be the basis for writing

$$b - \beta = (X'X)^{-1}X'U \tag{7.25}$$

where

$$b - \beta = \begin{bmatrix} b_1 - \beta_1 \\ b_2 - \beta_2 \end{bmatrix}$$

terms in X are defined above, and U is the column vector of population disturbance terms.

The variances of the OLS coefficients are obtained by evaluating $E(b - \beta)^2$. After considerable manipulation, this can be written as

$$V(b) = (X'X)^{-1}\sigma^2 \tag{7.26}$$

For the two-independent-variable case, with variables expressed as deviations from means, $V(b)$ can be written out as

$$V(b) = \begin{bmatrix} V(b_1) & \text{Cov } (b_1, b_2) \\ \text{Cov } (b_1, b_2) & V(b_2) \end{bmatrix}$$

where the diagonal elements are the variances of the coefficients and the off-diagonal elements are the covariances of the coefficients. Because of this structure, (7.15) is called the *variance-covariance matrix*. In applied research, the diagonal elements (the variances) are of prime importance. However, the covariance terms are used in certain types of hypothesis tests (see Chapter 6).

Recall that (7.26) cannot be used as is because it requires knowledge of the unobservable σ^2. However, (4.40) showed that an unbiased estimate of σ^2 can be obtained from

$$S^2 = \frac{\Sigma e^2}{n - (K + 1)} \tag{7.27}$$

where Σe^2 is the sum of squares of the OLS residual, which can be written as $e'e$ in matrix notation. Hence

$$S^2 = \frac{e'e}{n - (K + 1)} \tag{7.28}$$

which, when substituted into (7.26), yields

$$S^2(b) = (X'X)^{-1} \frac{e'e}{n - (K + 1)} \tag{7.29}$$

Table 7.3. Summary of Results from Chapter 7

	Longhand	Shorthand
Population regression:	$Y_i = \beta_0 + \beta_1 X_{1i} + \cdots + \beta_K K_{Ki} + U_i,$ $i = 1, \ldots, n$	$Y = X\beta + U$
Classical assumptions:	$E(U_i) = 0,\ i = 1, \ldots, n$ $E(U_i^2) = \sigma^2,$ all i $E(U_i U_j) = 0,$ all $i \neq j$ X-values fixed in repeated sampling or $E(X_k U) = 0,$ all k	$E(U) = 0$ $E(UU') = \sigma^2 I = \sigma^2$ $E(X'U) = 0$
Sample regression:	$Y_i = b_0 + b_1 X_{1i} + \cdots + b_K X_{Ki} + e_i$	$Y = Xb + e$
OLS estimates:	*Two-independent-variable case* $b_1 = \dfrac{(\sum x_1 y)(\sum x_2^2) - (\sum x_1 x_2)(\sum x_1^2)}{(\sum x_1^2)(\sum x_2^2) - (\sum x_1 x_2)^2}$ $b_2 = \dfrac{(\sum x_2 y)(\sum x_1^2) - (\sum x_1 x_2)(\sum x_2^2)}{(\sum x_1^2)(\sum x_2^2) - (\sum x_1 x_2)^2}$	*General case* $b = (X'X)^{-1} X'Y$
Variance-covariance of OLS estimates:	*Two-independent-variable case* $V(b_1) = \dfrac{\sum x_2^2}{(\sum x_1^2)(\sum x_2^2) - (\sum x_1 x_2)^2}\, \sigma^2$ $V(b_2) = \dfrac{\sum x_1^2}{(\sum x_1^2)(\sum x_2^2) - (\sum x_1 x_2)^2}\, \sigma^2$	*General case* $V(b) = (X'X)^{-1} \sigma^2$
Estimates of variance-covariance:	*Two-independent-variable case* $S_{b_1}^2 = \dfrac{\sum x_2^2}{(\sum x_1^2)(\sum x_2^2) - (\sum x_1 x_2)^2}\; \dfrac{\sum e^2}{n-3}$ $S_{b_2}^2 = \dfrac{\sum x_1^2}{(\sum x_1^2)(\sum x_2^2) - (\sum x_1 x_2)^2}\; \dfrac{\sum e^2}{n-3}$	*General case* $S^2(b) = (X'X)^{-1} e'e / [n - (K+1)]$

where $S^2(b)$ is the vector of estimated variance-covariance matrix of the OLS coefficients.

All that has been done here is summarized in Table 7.3, where a distinction is maintained between the population and sample equation.

Matrix Manipulations for the Regression Equation

In this section we give empirical substance to the matrix expressions in Table 7.3 based on the 52 observations used to estimate the regression equation in Table 7.1. From the basic worksheet (Table 8.1) we have

Y = matrix (column vector)
  of dependent variables X = matrix of independent variables

		(Pork	(Consumer
(Price)	(Constant)	Production)	Income)

$$Y = \begin{bmatrix} 28.23 \\ 23.53 \\ \cdot \\ \cdot \\ \cdot \\ 63.13 \\ 53.59 \end{bmatrix} \qquad X = \begin{bmatrix} 1 & 3.056 & 3.272 \\ 1 & 3.133 & 3.353 \\ \cdot & \cdot & \cdot \\ \cdot & \cdot & \cdot \\ \cdot & \cdot & \cdot \\ 1 & 3.240 & 9.461 \\ 1 & 3.638 & 9.549 \end{bmatrix}$$

where a column of 1's is included in the X-matrix to allow for the intercept term. The X'-matrix is written as

$$X' = \begin{bmatrix} 1 & 1 & \cdots & 1 & 1 \\ 3.056 & 3.133 & \cdots & 3.240 & 3.638 \\ 3.272 & 3.353 & \cdots & 9.461 & 9.549 \end{bmatrix}$$

Note that the X-matrix has 52 rows (number of observations on the worksheet) and three columns (the number of parameters to estimate, allowing for the intercept term). The X'-matrix, the transpose of the X-matrix, has three rows and 52 columns. The 3×3 $X'X$-matrix is computed as

$$X'X = \begin{bmatrix} 1 & 1 & \cdots & 1 & 1 \\ 3.056 & 3.133 & & 3.240 & 3.638 \\ 3.272 & 3.352 & & 9.461 & 9.049 \end{bmatrix} \begin{bmatrix} 1 & 3.056 & 3.272 \\ 1 & 3.133 & 3.353 \\ \cdot & & \\ \cdot & & \\ \cdot & & \\ 1 & 3.240 & 9.461 \\ 1 & 3.638 & 9.549 \end{bmatrix}$$

$$= \begin{bmatrix} 52.00 & 178.81 & 306.34 \\ 178.81 & 623.72 & 1072.99 \\ 306.34 & 1072.99 & 2002.29 \end{bmatrix}$$

using the matrix multiplication rules discussed above.

The inverse of this matrix is

$$(X'X) = \begin{bmatrix} 1.37528 & -.41343 & .01114 \\ -.41343 & .14481 & -.01435 \\ .01114 & -.01435 & -.00648 \end{bmatrix}$$

The method for computing this inverse matrix was not laid out above. However, the inverse matrix was defined such that the product of the inverse matrix times the original matrix yields the *identity*, or *unit matrix*. This is a matrix with 1's on the northwest-southwest diagonal and 0's elsewhere. In the example at hand, we have

$$(X'X)^{-1}(X'X) = \begin{bmatrix} 1.37528 & -.41343 & .01114 \\ -.41343 & .14481 & -.01435 \\ .01114 & -.01435 & .00648 \end{bmatrix} \begin{bmatrix} 52.00 & 178.81 & 306.34 \\ 178.81 & 623.72 & 1072.99 \\ 306.34 & 1072.99 & 2002.29 \end{bmatrix}$$

$$= \begin{bmatrix} 1.0000061 & -.0000005 & .0000001 \\ .0000078 & 1.0000030 & -.0000003 \\ .0000358 & -.00000024 & 1.0000002 \end{bmatrix}$$

which, except for rounding error, satisfies the stated condition.

The final product needed for computing the least squares coefficients is

$$X'Y = \begin{bmatrix} 1 & 1 & \cdots & 1 & 1 \\ 3.056 & 3.133 & \cdots & 3.240 & 3.638 \\ 3.272 & 3.352 & \cdots & 9.461 & 9.549 \end{bmatrix} \begin{bmatrix} 28.23 \\ 23.53 \\ \cdot \\ \cdot \\ \cdot \\ 63.13 \\ 53.49 \end{bmatrix} = \begin{bmatrix} 2{,}049.0 \\ 6{,}979.4 \\ 12{,}854.6 \end{bmatrix}$$

The least squares coefficients are provided by

$$b = (X'X)^{-1}X'Y = \begin{bmatrix} 1.37528 & -.41343 & .01114 \\ -.41343 & .14481 & -.01435 \\ .01114 & -.01435 & .00648 \end{bmatrix} \begin{bmatrix} 2{,}049.0 \\ 6{,}979.4 \\ 12{,}854.6 \end{bmatrix}$$

$$= \begin{bmatrix} 75.5873 \\ -20.8581 \\ 6.0328 \end{bmatrix}$$

where $b_0 = 75.587$
$\quad\;\; b_1 = -20.858$
$\quad\;\; b_2 = 6.0328$

as shown in Table 7.1.

The variance-covariance matrix of the least squares coefficients is given by

$$S^2(b) = (X'X)^{-1} \frac{e'e}{n - (K + 1)}$$

$$= \begin{bmatrix} 1.37528 & -.41343 & .01114 \\ -.41343 & .14481 & -.01435 \\ .01114 & -.01435 & .00648 \end{bmatrix} \begin{bmatrix} \dfrac{959.545}{52 - (2 + 1)} \end{bmatrix}$$

$$= \begin{bmatrix} 26.9316 & -8.0961 & .2181 \\ -8.0961 & 2.8357 & -.2809 \\ .2181 & .2809 & .1269 \end{bmatrix}$$

and

$$S_{b_0}^2 = 26.9316 \quad \text{and} \quad S_{b_0} = 5.190$$

$$S_{b_1}^2 = 2.8357 \quad \text{and} \quad S_{b_1} = 1.684$$

$$S_{b_2}^2 = 0.1269 \quad \text{and} \quad S_{b_2} = 0.3563$$

where the standard deviations of the coefficients are as presented in Table 7.1.

Summary

This chapter introduced matrix notation by beginning with the basic data in the worksheet and moving on to the OLS equation and formulas, illustrating at each step a shorthand method for writing the cumbersome equations developed in the previous six chapters. Viewing matrix notation as only a shorthand device is valid, but it turns out that there also are tremendous gains in computational power because matrices and vectors have a mathematics all their own. This mathematics is presented in Chapter 20 for those who are interested in such things. For those not so inclined, this chapter provides sufficient understanding to read books, journal articles, and research reports that use matrix notation. All applied researchers should, at a minimum, have an intuitive feeling for the implied manipulations presented here.

Terms

Column vector

Cross-sectional data

Matrix

Row vector

Time-series data

Transpose (vector or matrix)

Exercises

7.1 Consider the following MINITAB printout:

```
THE REGRESSION EQUATION IS
Y = -7.67 + 51.1X₁ + 41.5X₂
                                    ST. DEV.        T-RATIO=
           COLUMN    COEFFICIENT    OF COEFF.       COEFF./S.D.
X₀          --        -7.6682        13.1408         -.584
X₁          C2        51.0918         7.5179          6.80
X₂          C3        41.4607        36.9885          1.12
THE ST. DEV. OF Y ABOUT REGRESSION
LINE IS
S = 19.2
WITH (20-3) = 17 DEGREES OF FREEDOM
R-SQUARED = 73.1 PERCENT
R-SQUARED = 69.9 PERCENT, ADJUSTED
FOR D.F.
ANALYSIS OF VARIANCE
DUE TO                  DF              DD              MS=SS/DF
REGRESSION               2           17023.             8511.
RESIDUAL                17            6262.              368.
TOTAL                   19           23285.
```

(a) What are b_0, b_1, and b_2?
(b) What is the standard error of estimate?
(c) What are the standard errors for each of the regression coefficients?
(d) How many observations are in the data set?
(e) A researcher is 95 percent confident that β_1 is between _____ and

_____ .

(f) Test H_0: $\beta_1 = 25$ versus H_a: $\beta_1 \neq 25$ at $\alpha = .01$.
(g) Test H_0: $\beta_2 = 0$ versus H_a: $\beta_2 \neq 0$ at $\alpha = .05$.
(h) Test H_0: $\beta_2 = 100$ versus H_a: $\beta_2 \neq 100$ at $\alpha = .05$.
(i) The 99% confidence interval for β_2 is _____ $\leq \beta_2 \leq$ _____ .
(j) What is the coefficient of multiple determination?
(k) What is the adjusted coefficient of multiple determination?
(l) Test H_0: $\beta_1 = \beta_2 = 0$ versus H_a: $\beta_1 \neq 0$, $\beta_2 \neq 0$, or both, using an F-statistic
at $\alpha = .05$.

7.2 Explain the difference between cross-sectional and time-series data sets.

7.3 Classify each of the following data sets as time-series or cross-sectional.
  (a) U.S. cotton exports, 1971 to 1984.
  (b) 1982 profit-and-loss statements of a sample of 75 U.S. businesses.
  (c) Monthly U.S. imports of raw natural rubber, 1980 to 1984.

(d) Power generated during the first quarter in each of the 48 states in millions of kilowatts.

(e) July 1982 recreational expenditures of a sample of 2020 U.S. households.

(f) 1982 transportation expenditures for a sample of 75 Chicago households.

7.4

(a) Construct a hypothetical worksheet containing the information on the name, height, weight, age, sex, and amount spent for lunch during the previous five days by yourself and five friends. Pay particular attention to how you will record the information.

(b) Construct another hypothetical worksheet that contains information on the amount you spent for lunch each of the past five days.

(c) Which of the data sets above is time-series and which is cross-sectional?

7.5 Given

$$V_1 = \begin{bmatrix} 3 \\ 5 \\ 8 \end{bmatrix} \quad \text{and} \quad V_2 = \begin{bmatrix} 2 \\ 4 \\ 6 \end{bmatrix}$$

calculate the following.

(a) $V_1 + V_2$
(b) $V_1 - V_2$
(c) $2V_2$
(d) $2V_1 + V_2$
(e) V_1'
(f) $V_1'V_2$

7.6 Given $V_1 = [2 \quad 3]$ and $V_2 = [4 \quad 5]$, calculate the following.

(a) $V_1 + V_2$
(b) $V_1 - V_2$
(c) $V_2 - V_1$
(d) $2V_2 - 3V_1$
(e) $V_1 + 12$
(f) $V_1 + V_2'$
(g) V_2V_1'
(h) V_1V_2'

7.7 Given $X_1 = [1 \quad 3 \quad 2]$, $X_2 = [a_1 \quad a_2 \quad a_3]$, and $X_3 = [3 \quad 6 \quad 7]$, what are the values for X_2 if the following vector equation is true?

$$X_1' + X_2' = X_3'$$

7.8 Suppose that a lunch group buys 6 colas at 30 cents each, 10 root beers at 25 cents each, and 5 yogurts at 50 cents each.

(a) Write the row vector Q for the quantities and the row vector P for the prices.

(b) Calculate $PQ' = $ total cost of group's lunch.

7.9 Given

$$X_1 = \begin{bmatrix} 3 \\ 5 \\ 10 \end{bmatrix} \quad \text{and} \quad X_2 = \begin{bmatrix} 5 \\ 1 \\ 2 \end{bmatrix}$$

calculate the following.
(a) $(X_1 + X_2)'$
(b) $X_1' + X_2'$
(c) $(X_1 + X_2)'X_1$
(d) $X_1'X_1 + X_2'X_1$
(e) $(X_1 + X_2)'(X_1 + X_2)$
(f) $X_1'X_1 + X_2'X_1 + X_1'X_2 + X_2'X_2$
(g) Compare your answers to parts (a) and (b); (c) and (d); and (e) and (f). What do you conclude?

7.10 Use the following matrices to calculate parts (a) to (i).

$$A_1 = \begin{bmatrix} 2 & 3 \\ 4 & 5 \end{bmatrix} \quad X_1 = \begin{bmatrix} 6 & 4 \\ 2 & -3 \end{bmatrix}$$

$$A_2 = \begin{bmatrix} 3 & 4 & 2 \\ 6 & 5 & 7 \end{bmatrix} \quad X_2 = \begin{bmatrix} 6 & 4 & 1 \\ 2 & -3 & 3 \\ 1 & 2 & 3 \end{bmatrix}$$

(a) $A_1 + X_1$
(b) $A_1 - X_1$
(c) $X_1 - A_1$
(d) $A_1 + A_2$
(e) A_1X_1
(f) X_1A_1
(g) A_2X_2
(h) X_2A_2
(i) X_2A_2'

7.11

$$A = \begin{bmatrix} 2 & 3 \\ 4 & 5 \end{bmatrix} \quad \text{and} \quad B = \begin{bmatrix} 3 & 1 \\ 2 & 5 \end{bmatrix}$$

Write the following.
(a) A'
(b) B'
(c) $(A + B)'$
(d) $A' + B'$
(e) $(AB)'$
(f) $B'A'$
(g) What rule is suggested by a comparison of parts (c) and (d)? Parts (e) and (f)?

7.12 Use the following data to answer parts (a) to (h). Let Y, X_1, and X_2 be column vectors. Let $b_1 = 5.5$ and $b_2 = -9.4$.

Observation	Y	X_1	X_2
1	420	40	1
2	360	20	6
3	180	10	2
4	120	0	3
5	100	30	5

(a) What is $b_1 X_1$?
(b) What is $b_2 X_2$?
(c) What is $b_1 X_1 + b_2 X_2$?
(d) What is $\hat{Y}_1$ if $b_0 = 165.7$?
(e) What is e_1?
(f) What is the X-matrix?
(g) Express $Y = Xb + e$ using matrices.
(h) Express $Y = Xb + e$ as an equation in three column vectors.

II

The Practice

In this section we discuss many often-overlooked aspects of applied research. In Chapter 8 we show how to use theory to identify the type of data needed to get underway. Using dummy variables for incorporating qualitative variables in a regression equation receives extensive treatment in Chapter 9. In Chapter 10 we address a number of questions encountered in applied research. Finally, in Chapter 11 we treat the important issue of functional form.

8

Getting Started
in Applied Research

Suppose that it is the first day at work for an assistant economist in the Department of Agriculture, and the new applied researcher is meeting with the senior economist. After the usual informalities, discussion turns to the beginner's first assignment as a professional. The state's Pork Producers Cooperative is interested in developing a marketing strategy for enhancing the quarterly prices received by their producer members, and the cooperative has asked the department to help. The senior economist has already designed the overall research project, one component of which is an analysis of factors that affect market price. The beginning researcher is assigned responsibility for conducting this aspect of the project, with specific instructions to use regression analysis to analyze how various market forces affect hog price. The project must be completed in a month.

Panic sets in. Despite having taken courses in economic theory, agricultural marketing, and price analysis, having been exposed to regression, and having done a couple of homework problems using the computer to estimate regression coefficients, the beginning applied researcher has no experience working on a problem like this, not a real problem. How to proceed? How to use that formal training to come up with a quantitative answer to this research question in only one month?

In this chapter we attempt the transition from the abstract regression theory of the first seven chapters to the practical regression techniques needed to obtain quantitative answers to research questions such as the one posed above. This and the following three chapters provide a flavor of the ins and outs, the ups and down, the starts and stops of applied research. More concretely, these four chapters are designed to show how regression theory can be used in practice and to give some insights into the thought processes that guide applied research.

In this chapter we discuss typical questions encountered when starting a research project. In Chapter 9 we introduce "dummy" variables, which allow researchers to use qualitative as well as quantitative variables in a regression equation. In Chapter 10 we address a range of questions relating to the specific form of the variables to use in a regression equation. Suggestive of the questions addressed there are: What units of measurement should be used? Should quantity and income variables be measured in per capita terms? Should variables be lagged? In Chapter 11 we consider an important but often overlooked aspect of applied research, the proper functional (mathematical) form for the regression equation.

The subject of these "how-to-do-it" chapters is difficult to grasp because these chapters introduce a special way of thinking about applied research. Thinking through a research project for the first (or fourteenth) time is difficult. Anyone with minimal training can estimate regression equations and mechanically interpret the statistical results. Yet how to really do applied research can be learned only by doing it. However, many of the problems the applied researcher must resolve are illustrated in these four chapters.

The Model

Theory as the Starting Point

Still somewhat shaky, the new applied researcher returns to an empty office and agonizes over the question faced by all applied researchers: How do I get started? Surprising as it may seem, when faced with a practical problem, the researcher's only real beginning point is a good theory, the same classroom theory that so many students feel, at least on first encounter, is unrelated to the real world. "Theory" in applied research means more than classroom theory, however. It includes the previous research done on the project at hand, personal knowledge, and introspection. (Beginning researchers are often surprised by how much they know about a lot of topics once they sit down and think about them.) In all that follows, "theory" is used in this broader sense.

Theory is the place to begin because its purpose is to help sift out the unimportant and retain that which is important. For example, researchers need some "numbers" to complete the task of estimating the effect of various market forces on hog prices. But what numbers? Prices of ball-point pens? Imports of automobiles? Consumption of orange juice? Production of beef? At this point, students of general equilibrium theory recall that in a market economy, all prices and quantities are interrelated and, consequently, may be tempted to answer yes to these questions. But as a practical matter, not everything can be included in the analysis. Moreover, everyday shopping experience shows that whereas changes in the price of ball-point pens do not have much effect on how much bacon consumers buy, changes in the price of beef often do. Thus a researcher begins to blend classroom theory, practical considerations, and experience to help screen out things that are unlikely to be particularly relevant to the research project. In other words, a theory is forming to help the researcher select from all possible variables that subset most likely to be important for answering the specific research question. In other words, theory enables researchers to abstract from the complexity of the real world. It may, of course, turn out that the theory developed to guide the research is terrible, but some theory, good or bad, is necessary to beginning research. Whether a theory is good or bad is partly an empirical question, one that can be investigated later with the help of regression analysis. Theories evolve, sometimes substantially, as empirical work proceeds.

Single-Equation and Simultaneous-Equation Systems

We return to the issue of collecting the necessary numbers. Based on formal training and personal knowledge, an applied researcher might begin with the very general proposition that the quarterly price of hogs depends on the quantity of pork produced, consumer income, and the quantity of substitute and complementary products available. Thus the first equation may be written

$$P = f(Q, I, Q_j) \tag{8.1}$$

where P = price of good X
Q = quantity of good X
I = income
Q_j = quantity of substitute or complementary good, j

When assessing this equation, the applied researcher suddenly recalls that market theory involves supply and demand curves, and that it is through the interaction of supply and demand that market price is determined. Because this theory says that the equilibrium price and quantity traded are jointly determined, (8.1) does not appear to be a fruitful beginning point. However, this theory is based on the assumption that the current quantity of the commodity can instantaneously change in response to a current change in market price. (Theory texts often mention something about a widget factory being constantly switched from fast to slow to fast production as market price changes.) Knowing little about the technical aspects of the hog production, the applied researcher calls a professor of animal science who says that because of the underlying biological production function, *current* hog supply can respond little, if any, to *current* market price. Rather, once the hog production process is started, the supply must move to market regardless of the market price at the time of marketing.

This argument justifying the use of (8.1) deserves some elaboration. The theory of market pricing expresses the equilibrium price as the intersection of the market demand and supply curves. Consequently, when studying factors affecting the price of some commodity, it is necessary to specify both a demand curve (function) and a supply curve (function). In the theory of the firm, from which the market supply curve is derived, a distinction is made between the "long run," the "short run," and the "very short run." The *long run* is defined as a period of time sufficient to permit all factors of production, both fixed and variable, to respond to changes in market price. The *short run* is a period of time during which the fixed factors of production do not change but the variable factors of production do change in response to market price. The key in each of these definitions is the notion that *current* output, or supply, responds to *current* market price. Finally, the *very short run* is defined as a period of time during which current output, or supply, cannot be varied in response to changes in current market prices. This means that supply is *predetermined*; it cannot be changed during the pricing period. By the equilibrium condition that the quantity demanded is equal to the quantity supplied, it follows that quantity demanded is also *predetermined*. This is usually shown graphically as the intersection of the downward-sloping demand curve and the vertical supply curve. In this setting, the only thing the market must "solve" for is the equilibrium, or market-clearing, price. Consequently, the research focuses on factors affecting price during the very short run.

Because agriculture is based on a biological production function, the very short run model is a workably accurate characterization of the pricing mechanism for many farm commodities. This is especially the case for crop agriculture, where crops are generally harvested annually yielding a predetermined supply (and hence quantity to be consumed) that moves to the market, which determines the equilibrium price. Thus in many research settings a *single-equation model* is a workably acceptable statement regarding price determination. Things do, of course, get complicated if storage is possible, but the fundamental point remains.

The situation in animal agriculture is not as clear. In the illustration above, where quarterly prices are specified by the research objective, the very short run is probably appropriate, since supply coming to the market in any given quarter cannot respond much to price during that quarter. However, if the research objective had called for annual average prices, it would not be appropriate to use the very short run specification because the quantity coming to market over a year's time can respond to price changes during the year. In this case the researcher would need to worry about both a supply and a demand curve. This leads to what is called a *simultaneous-equation system*, where both price and quantity are determined by market forces. Methods for estimating this type of system are left for more advanced texts. The important point of this digression is simply that doing good applied research requires an understanding of the production-marketing characteristics of the commodity being studied, and these characteristics must be incorporated in the analysis.

Thus the theory suggests that (8.1), a single-equation characterization of the hog market, may be an acceptable beginning point, but how short is "very short"?

Implementing the Model

Now something is on paper, but there is still much work to do before it is time to collect data. Specifically, the *conceptual variables*, descriptive of a general class of variables, must be empirically defined. Applied researchers need to define variables precisely in the everyday terminology of markets. For example, pork researchers will not find numbers reported for a variable called "substitutes." Developing *empirical measures* of conceptual variables is largely an interactive procedure. The first step is a general definition, say "hog price." The next step might be to go to the library stacks and browse through statistical (data) publications to see what data can be found that resemble "hog price." In this particular case, there are all kinds of prices, defined on several dimensions of the market: prices for heavy hogs, prices for light hogs; prices for individual states, for regions, for the country; prices for boars, prices for sows, prices for barrows and gilts; prices for live hogs, prices for carcass hogs; prices at the farm, prices at the slaughter plant; monthly prices, quarterly prices, annual prices; and more. The list of possible hog prices seems endless. Similar lists would be encountered for each of the conceptual variables in the initial formulation of the research question shown in (8.1).

The point of the discussion above, and it is an important point in applied research, is that identifying empirical measures of conceptual variables is not a trivial exercise. Instead, it involves a lot of hard work and often many frustrations. There can be no precise rule to follow in defining variables. All an applied researcher can do is work in the context of the guiding theory, the specific objective of the project, and the constraints imposed by the data that are available. This aspect of applied research cannot be overemphasized.

Chapter 7 made the distinction between time-series and cross-sectional data sets. So, while staring at the equation and the list of variables, the applied research must decide which type of data set to use. This may be one of the easier decisions, because very often in applied work there is only one type of data set available. In this example the applied researcher decides to work with a time-series data set.

The next decision is the level of aggregation for the data. The researcher could focus on a single state, on a larger region (such as the Corn Belt states), or on the national level by aggregating over all states. Given a level of geographical aggregation, the researcher has to decide whether to study price at the retail, wholesale, or farm level. Again, these decisions rest heavily on the specific research question, conditioned by the type of data available. The example in the following sections uses national data at the farm level.

More decisions before moving on. A time unit of observation, such as a week, a month, a quarter, or a year, is required, as well as the time period for the analysis. In light of the very short run model being used to guide this research, the researcher decides to use quarterly data to ensure that (8.1) is an acceptable characterization of the market. A time-series data set consisting of the 52 quarters from January 1970 to December 1982 will therefore be used to estimate the equation. Finally, the researcher decides to use beef and chicken as substitutes for pork.

Collecting the Data

At last the researcher is ready to collect data. But first a quick look back. The researcher was given a specific project by the senior economist: Use regression analysis to estimate the effect of various market factors on the quarterly price of hogs. Back in an empty office, the new researcher began to develop a theory to help decide which of the large number of possible price determinants should be considered. Based on market theory and the technical aspects of hog production, the researcher chose a single-equation characterization of the market. An equation using conceptual variables to help identify the specific variables for which data were needed helped formalize the model. A trip to the library stacks sent the researcher back to the office to wrestle further with the problems of developing empirical measures of the conceptual variables appropriate to the problem. This led to a series of decisions regarding specific prices, level of geographical aggregation, stage of the marketing system, and so on. Out of this emerged a list of precisely defined variables that measure, as well as possible under the circumstances, the conceptual variables of the guiding theory.

Earlier, we introduced the *worksheet* as a useful way for recording the data needed for regression. The completed worksheet for the hog-price project, based on the decisions made above, is presented in Table 8.1. This, of course, is an initial worksheet. As the analysis unfolds, better empirical measures of conceptual variables may arise, and the appropriate changes will have to be made. It is also possible that additional variables will have to be added. But it is time for the data collection to begin; adjustments can be made for new problems as they are encountered. It is impossible to foresee all possible contingencies in applied research. Experienced researchers accept this as a way of life.

Notice that the worksheet shown in Table 8.1 contains three kinds of important information. First is the list of *variable symbols and names and meanings*. It is important to keep careful track of exactly what the specific variables measure and the units (e.g., cents per pound or dollars per pound) used for counting. Second are the actual *numbers*. Third is a summary of the *sources* of the data. The complete citations need not be on the actual worksheet (a separate page will do nicely), but a researcher must be able to find and check all data sources. Equally important, other researchers should be able to find the sources and verify the numbers. With all three parts of the worksheet in good order, the researcher is ready to enter the numbers into the computer.

Before entering the data into the computer, consider a few hints on using worksheets, based on the authors' many mistakes over the years. One suggestion is to save room on the worksheet for additional variables. Often in the course of research (or even data collection) new variables appear that should be included. In the next three chapters, for example, there appear good reasons for adding three new variables to the data set: population, the Consumer Price Index, and "time." Finally, never do any manipulation on the basic data set. The computer can change units, compute ratios, or do any other arithmetic operation far more quickly and accurately that people can. Moreover, entering basic data directly into the computer makes it much easier to verify the numbers in the computer against the original sources, something that needs to be done.

All researchers need to record the exact sources of their data clearly so that other researchers can find the numbers used in the regressions. Reproducibility requires, among other things, careful documentation of data sources. Many researchers are in such a hurry to get on with the "real work" on the computer that they are tempted to make skimpy notes and assume that the sources of the data are easy to remember. Researchers who do this, unless blessed with terrific memories, are prone to becoming utterly exasperated at their inability to document their own data set. Do as other researchers say, not as they all too often do: Record your sources carefully as you go along.

Table 8.1. Worksheet Containing Data for Pork Price Analysis, United States, Quarterly, 1970 to 1982

Year	Quarter	$P_P{}^a$	$Q_P{}^b$	$Q_B{}^c$	$Q_C{}^d$	I^e
1970	1	28.23	3.056	5.276	2.130	3.272
	2	23.53	3.133	5.326	2.413	3.353
	3	22.12	3.154	5.410	2.915	3.395
	4	15.69	3.905	5.460	2.784	3.410
1971	1	19.43	3.671	5.300	2.229	3.517
	2	17.43	3.678	5.446	2.400	3.592
	3	19.05	3.441	5.575	2.932	3.620
	4	19.39	3.816	5.378	2.814	3.649
1972	1	25.61	3.503	5.370	2.374	3.711
	2	25.32	3.386	5.566	2.596	3.765
	3	28.86	3.064	5.559	3.012	3.831
	4	27.79	3.507	5.723	2.901	3.955
1973	1	36.23	3.262	5.394	2.327	4.143
	2	36.35	3.178	5.049	2.504	4.244
	3	56.68	2.791	4.998	2.876	4.339
	4	40.97	3.347	5.648	2.942	4.452
1974	1	39.73	3.378	5.434	2.505	4.513
	2	26.09	3.531	5.637	2.696	4.574
	3	37.67	3.242	5.751	2.923	4.697
	4	38.34	3.431	6.021	2.583	4.779
1975	1	39.61	3.044	5.842	2.193	4.809
	2	46.44	2.923	5.593	2.540	5.102
	3	58.10	2.512	5.942	2.887	5.105
	4	49.74	2.836	6.295	2.815	5.227
1976	1	48.85	2.896	6.492	2.527	5.374
	2	48.89	2.782	6.145	2.884	5.462
	3	44.00	2.951	6.618	3.285	5.540
	4	32.05	3.589	6.412	3.043	5.665
1977	1	40.18	3.294	6.287	2.567	5.772
	2	41.79	3.185	6.158	2.978	5.934
	3	44.38	3.073	6.321	3.282	6.077
	4	39.33	3.500	6.220	3.089	6.250

[a] P_P = seven-market price for barrows and gilts (dollars per hundred weight), middle month of each quarter (*Source: Livestock and Meat Statistics*).
[b] Q_P = quarterly production of pork (billions of pounds): Total for 1970–1972 (48 states), Excluding farm slaughter and lard and rendered pork fat, packer style as of January 1981 (*Source: Livestock and Poultry Outlook and Situation*).
[c] Q_B = quarterly production of beef (billions of pounds) (*Source: Livestock and Meat Statistics*).
[d] Q_C = quarterly production of poultry (billions of pounds) (*Source: Poultry and Egg Situation*).
[e] I = quarterly per capita disposable person income (thousands of current dollars) (*Source: Economic Indicators and Agricultural Outlook*).

Table 8.1.   *(Continued)*

Year	Quarter	$P_P{}^a$	$Q_P{}^b$	$Q_B{}^c$	$Q_C{}^d$	I^e
1978	1	48.83	3.243	6.106	2.744	6.402
	2	49.17	3.265	5.938	3.116	6.584
	3	48.77	3.160	5.923	3.405	6.749
	4	48.36	3.541	6.042	3.289	6.955
1979	1	54.42	3.395	5.547	2.998	7.186
	2	43.79	3.754	5.076	3.493	7.320
	3	38.21	3.775	5.222	3.760	7.533
	4	36.01	4.347	5.417	3.569	7.722
1980	1	37.51	4.126	5.249	3.298	7.785
	2	29.50	4.299	5.251	3.615	7.848
	3	48.30	3.756	5.384	3.596	8.074
	4	46.38	4.252	5.585	3.539	8.299
1981	1	42.43	4.076	5.559	3.401	8.551
	2	42.05	3.880	5.438	3.814	8.698
	3	50.92	3.606	5.541	3.998	8.951
	4	42.40	4.155	5.676	3.795	9.107
1982	1	49.49	3.695	5.449	3.439	9.155
	2	58.14	3.550	5.363	3.786	9.285
	3	63.13	3.240	5.730	4.023	9.461
	4	53.49	3.638	5.818	3.797	9.549

Entering the Data

One more step is required before the researcher is ready to do some empirical economic analysis. The data set must be entered into the computer and verified. There are few surer ways of getting seemingly perverse results than making an error while entering data and then not catching and correcting it. The computer does only what it is told. Saying "you know what I mean!" may cover errors made while speaking with friends, but the phrase will not help in dealing with a computer. If, for example, a researcher tells a computer that the price of pork in the first three quarters of 1971 was 28.23, 2352 (no decimal), and 22.12, the computer takes the information literally and uses the bad information to do the calculations, and reports goofy results without apology. Data sets can be checked manually or with some computerized verification program, but they must be checked. One good check, especially with a large data set, is to record column totals and row totals on the worksheet, enter the data, and use the computer to compute column totals and row totals as a check on errors of entering the data. If possible, have someone else do the checking, as others are not predisposed to making the same mistakes as the one who originally entered the data. In any event, checking is an ounce of prevention always worth applying.

Getting a "Feel" for the Data

When starting a new project or when working with a new data set, applied researchers often like to get a feel for the data before running regressions. There are any number of things an experienced researcher might do at this point, and it is impossible to cover all of them here. Instead, this section offers a couple of illustrations of how a researcher might try to acquire this subjective feel for the data.

Descriptive Statistics

One thing to look at is the descriptive statistics of the variables on the worksheet. The means, standard deviations, minima, and maxima for the variables in the worksheet above are presented in Table 8.2. It is possible to check for recording errors or special cases by looking at the minimum and maximum values. For example, if the maximum value for pork price happened to be $163.13 instead of $63.13, a recording error of some sort is highly probable. Comparisons of means, where appropriate, can also provide useful background information. Notice, for example, that pork production over the time period averaged slightly more than chicken production but only half of beef production. The standard deviation of a variable offers some idea of how much it varied during the period of study. Because the standard deviation is measured in the same units as the variable, it is difficult to compare the degree of variation across variables. However, such a comparison can be made by using the *coefficient of variation* (computed by dividing the standard deviation by the mean), a measure of relative variation. These figures are given in the last column of Table 8.2. Notice, for example, that over the 52 quarters, the relative variation of pork production was twice that of the relative variation of beef production.

Time-Series Plots

It is also a good idea to prepare a time-series plot for each of the variables on the worksheet. Before tackling a complicated question such as why pork price goes up and down, it makes sense first to get some feel for how much pork prices actually went up and down during the period of analysis. A visual inspection of Figure 8.1, the time-series plot for quarterly hog prices from 1970 to 1983, reveals several useful points. There is clear evidence of an upward trend in price over time, with considerable price deviation around this general upward trend. The sharp rise from mid-1970 to late 1973 was, as many old hands know, due to a host of things that hit the markets in the early 1970s, the oil embargo and the devaluation of the dollar being particularly important. Finally, the plot shows that pork price can change rather dramatically over a very short period of time. A beginning researcher should take the time and effort to prepare these time-series plots to check for trends, reversals, extreme values, and the like. Although this can be done quickly with the computer, beginning researchers should pay their dues by preparing a number of time-series plots by hand. The physical act of plotting data tends to reveal things the unexperienced eye does not pick up when scanning computer output.

Scatter Plots

Finally, it is a good idea to prepare a series of scatter plots with the dependent variable plotted on the vertical axis and the independent variables plotted on the horizontal

Table 8.2. Basic Summary Statistics for Pork Price Data Set

	Minimum	Mean	Maximum	Standard Deviation	Coefficient of Variation
P_P = pork prices (dollars per hundredweight)	15.69	39.40	6.13 nt11.78	.75	
Q_P = pork production (billions of pounds)	2.512	3.439	4.347	.416	.17
Q_B = beef production (billions of pounds)	4.998	5.672	6.618	.393	.08
Q_C = chicken production (billions of pounds)	2.130	3.027	4.023	.504	.24
I = income (dollars per capita)	3.272	5.891	9.549	1.968	.60

170

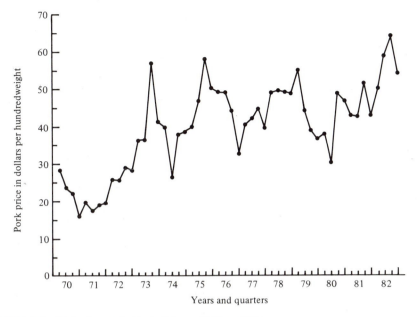

FIGURE 8.1 U.S. Quarterly Pork Prices, 1970 to 1982.

axis. With experience, this can be done easily with the computer, but again it is wise that you do it laboriously by hand for a few times because manual plotting gives a better feel for what is going on. An example is given in Figure 8.2, which shows a plot of pork price against pork production using the data in the worksheet. Note that for reasons that will be clear in a moment, the year appears next to each point. At first glance, Figure 8.2 gives the impression of an inverse relation between pork prices and quantity. After awhile, however, this inverse relationship seems to be a mirage, disappearing before an anxious observer's eye. Even closer inspection reveals that the relationship seems to be "drifting" over time. Note how all the plots to the left are for the early part of the period and the plots to the right are for the later part of the period. Indeed, except for three quarters in 1978 and one quarter in 1979, there appear to be two separate relationships separated by time, with an outward movement over time. Figure 8.2 will never indicate *why* this drift occurred, but it does suggest to the researcher that a simple linear functional form for Figure 8.1 is not appropriate.

By now, even a novice researcher would have some feel for the data. Specifically, these simple steps enable a researcher to have some idea of the average levels of the variables, as well as their ranges and variation. Moreover, a researcher will have seen the time pattern of the price variable and know something about how the relation between pork price and pork production has shifted over time. These are only illustrations of the kinds of things that might be done before starting formal analysis. With experience from doing their own research and from studying what other researchers have done, individual researchers acquire their own personal gimmicks to help them get a feel for the data.

172

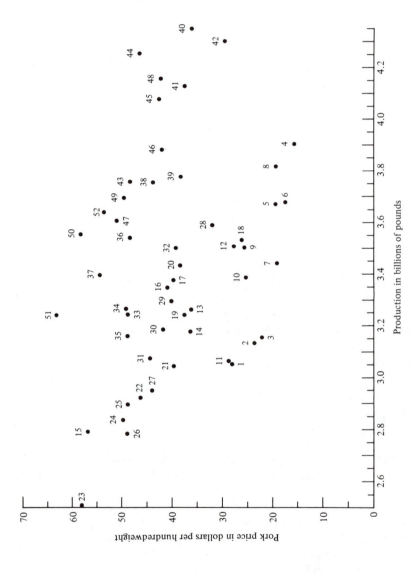

FIGURE 8.2 Scatter Diagram of U.S. Pork Price Versus Pork Production, Quarterly, 1970 to 1982.

Estimating the Model

Prompted by the need for data, a beginning researcher began theorizing about the hog market in order to identify and define specifically the variables needed to do empirical analysis. Theory was the guide to data collection. Now it is time to start the analysis, and again theory is the place to turn. In particular, it suggests what regression results should look like. Although theory, as defined earlier, is quite rich in identifying important relationships, it says little about the numerical values of regression coefficients. Theory often does, however, have something to say about the direction of the relationship between the dependent variable and the independent variables. For example, more pork available (higher Q_p) means lower pork prices, other things equal. After all, the law of demand says that demand curves shall slope downward. Increases in consumer income (higher I) shift the demand curve outward, causing price to increase. Since income increased over time, this might explain the drift observed in Figure 8.2. Finally, increased quantities of substitutes, meats like beef and chicken, means lower demand for pork and consequently, lower pork prices.

Thus conventional microeconomic theory suggests that holding other things constant, pork price (P_p) should be expected to be negatively associated with the available quantity of pork (Q_p), positively associated with consumer income (I), and negatively associated with the available quantity of substitutes such as beef (Q_b) and chicken (Q_c). A review of previous applied research would probably confirm these expectations.

The First Regression Equation

With still slightly over two weeks before the deadline, the researcher is ready to estimate a regression equation. Formally, the first step is to specify the population regression function

$$P = \beta_0 + \beta_1 Q_p + \beta_2 Q_b + \beta_3 Q_c + \beta_4 I + U \qquad (8.2)$$

as was done in previous chapters. If the disturbance term is assumed to satisfy the classical assumptions, the sample regression function may be written

$$P = b_0 + b_1 Q_p + b_2 Q_b + b_3 Q_c + b_4 I + e \qquad (8.3)$$

Then, with some trepidation, the researcher sits down at the computer, runs the regression program, and obtains the following results:

$$P = 92.60 - 21.27 Q_p - 1.62 Q_b - 3.92 Q_c + 6.96 I + e \qquad S = \$4.37$$
$$ (1.89) \qquad (1.77) \qquad (1.57) \qquad (0.65) \qquad R^2 = .873$$
$$(8.4)$$

where the numbers in parentheses are the standard deviations of the coefficients.

The R^2 of .87 indicates that 87% of the quarterly variation in pork price over the 13 years is associated with the variation in four independent variables in the equation. The standard error of the regression, $S = \$4.37$ per hundredweight, says that any point on the population regression line plus or minus 2 standard errors (about $8.74) includes 95 percent of the values of pork price. The square of this term is an estimate of the variance of the population disturbance term. One way to put some perspective on S is to express the standard error as a percent of the mean of the dependent variable, $4.37/39.40 = .111$, a measure of relative variation.

From an economic standpoint, the results are pleasing, because the sign of each independent variable is as predicted by theory. An increase in the quantity of pork or in one of the substitutes, all else constant, results in a decrease in pork price; an increase in consumer income, all else constant, causes the demand function to shift outward, resulting in a price increase. This income effect is a likely explanation for the drift observed in Figure 8.2.

Hypothesis Tests

The next step is to use these sample results to test hypotheses about the values of the population regression coefficients. Remember that the numbers in (8.4) are only estimates of the population regression coefficients. Moreover, the regression coefficients obtained depend on the specific sample used. A different sample would, in all likelihood, have generated different values. Fortunately, an estimate of the sampling variation for each of coefficients is available via their standard deviations (shown in parentheses). Consequently, the results in (8.4) plus the material in Chapter 6 can be combined into probability statements about the values of the population regression coefficients. These are computed as follows:

Variable	Coefficient	Standard Deviation	t-ratio
Q_p	-21.27	1.89	-11.25
Q_b	-1.62	1.77	$-.92$
Q_c	-3.92	1.57	-2.50
I	6.96	.65	10.71

At this juncture the researcher needs to make two basic decisions: exactly what hypotheses is to be tested and at what confidence level to test. The income variable can be used to illustrate the issues involved.

The strand of economic theory that has guided the research says that income is an important determinant of consumer purchases in the marketplace. But it says more. The purchases of some goods increase as income increases; these are called *normal goods*. In a regression equation, the income coefficient is expected to be positive for a normal good. On the other hand, the purchases of some goods decrease as income decreases; these are called *inferior goods*. In a regression equation, the income coefficient would be expected to be negative for an inferior good.

Thus a researcher faces a choice. One possible approach is to test whether income is an "important" variable in the following way. If the coefficient is zero (statistically speaking), a researcher might conclude that income is not an important variable in the analysis. If the income coefficient is significantly different from zero, a researcher would conclude that income is an important variable. Moreover, if the coefficient is positive, pork is a normal good; if the coefficient is negative, pork is an inferior good.

A researcher is, in a sense, asking two questions: Is income important in the analysis? If it is, is the sign of the coefficient positive or negative? The structure of the formal test is

$$H_0: \beta = 0 \quad \text{versus} \quad H_a: \beta \neq 0$$

This requires a two-tailed test because the researcher is interested in knowing whether the coefficient, if it is significantly different from zero, is positive or negative.

On the other hand, a researcher might want to test whether the income slope is positive. The specific objective of the research can require this test. For example, the Pork Producers Cooperative might have said that if income has a positive effect on price, the cooperative will adopt a particular marketing strategy and it will do something different if the income slope is not positive. In this case, the research objective' would be to determine one thing only, namely, whether the slope is positive. If it is not, then whether it is significant and negative is irrelevant to the objective. The formal test is

$$H_0: \beta = 0 \quad \text{versus} \quad H_a: \beta > 0$$

This requires a one-tailed test because the researcher is interested in knowing only if the slope is positive.

Consult the t-table for the critical t to reject the null hypothesis. Note that a lower value is required for the one-tailed test at the same confidence level. It is tempting to conclude that it is "easier to get significance" with a one-tailed test and decide to always use a one-tailed test. Resist this temptation. The one-tailed test requires less "information" from a sample—for example, only whether the coefficient is significantly positive, not whether it is significantly positive or significantly negative. As a result, researchers must "pay" less in the form of a lower critical t-value. It follows that less information is available from the sample. Specifically, a researcher can make a (probability) statement about whether the coefficient is positive, but not about whether it is positive *or* negative. This decision must be made prior to hypothesis testing and in the context of the specific research objective.

A second decision involves the probability, or confidence, level at which to conduct the test. There are no hard and fast rules for deciding what level is appropriate. Many applied researchers test at the .95 confidence (or .05 significance) level, but this is by no means followed by all researchers. Some use a higher level, some use a lower level. Often the context of the research (as well as the uses to be made of the results) will make clear how much confidence needs to be placed on the estimates. The implications of using different levels, by testing at the .95 level and at the .90 level, are illustrated below. This is *not* a legitimate procedure in applied research. In practice, a researcher must choose a confidence level before looking at the results and must live with the outcome of the test.

Although theory can help identify some of the "important" variables to use in research, as it has in this chapter, it seldom, if ever, has anything to say about the quantitative effect (think "regression coefficient") of the variables. Moreover, as the foregoing discussion of the income variable suggests, theory can be ambiguous about the direction (think "sign" of regression coefficient) of the effect, as theoretical analysis often shows that the effect will be positive under one set of conditions and negative under another set of conditions. For this reason, it is conventional, but only conventional, to use two-tailed tests to get as much information as possible from the sample. Finally, because testing at the .95 level is common, and because the critical *t*-value at this level is close to 2 for the two-tailed test, researchers often use the value 2 as a rule of thumb in examining regression results. This is at best a rough approximation, one that should be used only after considerable experience with *t*-tables.

The researcher has used 52 observations to estimate five parameters, which yields $52 - 5 = 47$ degrees of freedom for testing. The *t*-table does not list critical *t*-values for 47, but it does list them for 40 and 60. Rather than attempt an interpolation, we will use 40 degrees of freedom, a slightly conservative test, since the critical value for 47 degrees of freedom would be slightly smaller. From Appendix Table A.2, for a one-tailed test at the .95 level, the absolute value of the critical *t* is 1.684. Upon comparing this to the computed *t* above, the appropriate conclusion is that there is a high probability that the population regression coefficient on pork production is negative and the coefficient on consumer income is positive. Researchers would say that these coefficients are *statistically significant*; they are on statistical grounds different from zero. Because the computed *t*-values for beef and chicken are below the critical *t*-values, researchers would say that these coefficients are *not statistically significant*. If originally the decision had been to test at the .90 level, the critical value of *t* would be 1.303. In this case, the appropriate conclusion would be that the coefficients of pork production, chicken production, and consumer income were statistically significant, but the coefficient of beef is not statistically significant. The structure of the two-tailed test is identical, but there are larger critical *t*-values for rejecting the null hypothesis.

Researchers must select the probability level before looking at the results and researchers cannot use the same data set to test at several different confidence levels. As the discussion above clearly suggests, by continually testing at successively lower levels one can ultimately end up with all statistically significant results!

A Final Look

Now the beginning researcher has an equation, has evaluated the various summary statistics, such as the correlation coefficient and the standard deviation of the equation, and has tested some hypotheses. Time for a sigh of relief. With about two weeks to deadline, results are in hand. But the researcher does not dare spend too much time sighing because there is still lots of work to do. Are the variables measured properly? Is there a seasonal pattern that needs to be recognized? Has the proper functional form been used? These questions and many others like them are addressed in the following three chapters. But first consider another diagnostic applied researchers quickly get in the habit of using in regression analysis.

In Chapter 3 we introduced the population disturbance term, a random variable with mean of zero and variance of σ^2. Chapter 3 also showed how to use the OLS residuals to estimate σ^2. The square root of σ^2, σ, is the standard deviation of Y about

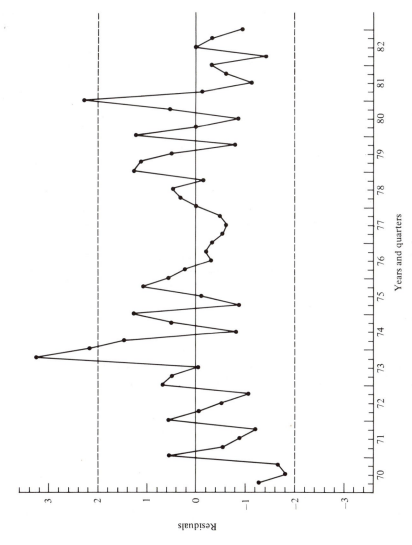

FIGURE 8.3   Times-Series Plot of Residuals from Equation (8.4).

177

the regression line. This is estimated by the "$S = 4.37$" of equation (8.4). Based on the normal distribution, it is reasonable to expect that about 95 percent of the residuals of (8.4), when divided by S, will fall with plus or minus two standard deviations from the regression line. Moreover, the residuals are expected to be randomly distributed around the regression equation. Thus one additional check on the appropriateness of (8.4) is to look at the residuals to see if there are any extreme values, called outliers, and if there appears to be a systematic pattern in the residuals.

Because time-series data are being used here, it is convenient to plot the residuals against time, as shown in Figure 8.3. The value of the residual is plotted on the vertical axis, where both positive and negative values are possible, and time is plotted on the horizontal axis. Figure 8.3 shows the plus and minus 2-standard-deviation lines.

There are three outliers (values that are two or more standard deviations from the regression line), two in late 1973 and one in the fourth quarter of 1980. Since three observations make up about 5 percent of the total number of observations, the sample seems to fit on the "statistical borderline" mentioned above. That is, this many outliers are expected on probability grounds alone. Nevertheless, it is always good practice to examine outliers to see whether there may be something that explains them. For example, the quantity of pork production in the third quarter of 1973 was the second lowest for the 52 quarters of the data set. This may, in part, explain the extreme, positive value of the residual. In addition, 1973 was the year when so many shocks hit the markets, such as the oil embargo and the devaluation of the dollar, and prices skyrocketed. Markets soon stabilized, however, as the initial shock wore off. These two phenomena, low pork production and rapidly rising prices, may explain the large, positive residuals during late 1973 and early 1974. No rationale for the positive outlier in 1980 comes to mind.

Visual examination cannot determine whether the residuals in Figure 8.3 are randomly distributed around zero. However, there is a suggestion of a positive trend in the early period, followed by an overall decline, except for the one-quarter extreme in 1980. Moreover, there may be a seasonal pattern in these quarterly prices.

This brief illustration suggests the value of looking at residual plots as an additional evaluation of an estimated equation. However, looking at these plots is much like reading tea leaves. By staring long enough, one can always discover interesting configurations, but the meaning of these configurations is not always clear. There is not much more to be said here about looking at residuals because there are no rules to follow. It is simply something that applied researchers do and, by doing it, gain understanding. With experience, a researcher's proficiency at reading residuals improves.

Summary

In this chapter we followed a beginning researcher the first few steps down the road from regression theory to regression in practice. We also offered a glimpse of how an applied researcher tries to work through a problem. Although both the research question and the data set in this chapter were relatively simple, both were real. When faced with an empirical question, a beginning or experienced researcher takes the steps discussed in this chapter to get off to a practical start.

In summary, the basic steps are:

1. Ask a question.
2. Develop a theory.
3. Make a worksheet.
4. Collect a data set.
5. Get a feel for the data using summary statistics, time-series plots, scatter diagrams, and other tricks.
6. Run some regressions.
7. Record the results on a summary sheet.
8. Think about what is being done. (Do your results make sense? Why? Why not?)

In the following three chapters we introduce some new techniques and raise some new questions that will flesh out the outline developed here.

Terms

Coefficient of variation   Specific variable
Generic variable

Exercises

8.1   Consider one or more of the following possible dependent variables.
    I. Grades on exams in this course.
    II. Household income.
    III. Price of corn.
    IV. Value of houses.
    V. Quantity of steel produced.
    VI. Gross national product.
    VII. Baseball players' salaries.
    VIII. Annual mobile home sales.
    IX. Annual city spending per capita.
    X. State sales tax collections.
For each dependent variable, think about how you would begin doing empirical research on each of these topics by answering the following questions.
(a) What would be your research question?
(b) What independent variables would you use?
(c) Would you need time-series or cross-sectional data?
(d) What time period would you consider?

(e) From what group would you take your sample?

(f) What signs would you expect on each independent variable, and why?

8.2 Jesse Johnson has been wondering if his gasoline consumption and efforts to drive more conservatively as prices per gallon increased have been successful. He has collected data from his personal records for the past eight years.

Year	Consumption, Y (Gallons)	Price per Gallon, X_1	Miles Traveled, X_2
1977	164.50	$ .48	2222.2
1978	156.00	.57	2261.9
1979	180.25	.58	2428.1
1980	156.17	.69	2404.8
1981	135.58	.88	2264.2
1982	120.25	1.04	2063.3
1983	136.42	1.22	2376.5
1984	125.67	1.38	2611.0

(a) Plot all three variables against time. Are there trends?

(b) Plot Y against both of the independent variables. Which independent variable seems to be most closely related to Jesse's gasoline consumption?

(c) Calculate the regression of Y on X_1 and X_2 and test the hypothesis that gasoline price has influenced his consumption.

8.3. The following data set hypothesizes that the monthly natural gas consumption of a Minnesota family is a function of the price of gas, and the number of degree days in the month.

Year	Month	Time Period	Monthly Gas Usage, Y	Average Gas Price, X_1	Total Degree Days, X_2
1976	1	1	215	$ .20	1391
	2	2	188	.21	1415
	3	3	92	.22	1001
	4	4	56	.25	816
	5	5	52	.26	470
	6	6	48	.26	239
	7	7	49	.26	18
	8	8	40	.26	9
	9	9	141	.22	52
	10	10	269	.23	272
	11	11	390	.24	710
	12	12	434	.24	1226
1977	1	13	291	.24	1790
	2	14	160	.25	1674
	3	15	107	.28	1166

Year	Month	Time Period	Monthly Gas Usage, Y	Average Gas Price, X_1	Total Degree Days, X_2
	4	16	34	.32	771
	5	17	36	.32	272
	6	18	33	.32	108
	7	19	41	.31	61
	8	20	46	.30	6
	9	21	95	.27	101
	10	22	273	.26	250
	11	23	335	.26	492
	12	24	421	.26	1064
1978	1	25	340	.26	1543
	2	26	212	.26	1650
	3	27	124	.28	1488
	4	28	64	.31	915
	5	29	45	.32	593
	6	30	47	.32	170
	7	31	48	.32	38
	8	32	52	.32	34
	9	33	106	.29	7
	10	34	276	.26	208
	11	35	387	.28	539
	12	36	462	.28	1140

(a) Plot Y against time.
(b) Plot X_1 against time.
(c) Plot X_2 against time.
(d) Find maximum, mean, and minimum for Y, X_1, and X_2.
(e) Find standard deviations for Y, X_1, and X_2.
(f) Find coefficient of variation for Y, X_1, and X_2.
(g) Find correlations among Y, X_1, and X_2.

8.4 Run the following regression on the data in Exercise 8.3:

$$Y = b_0 + b_1 X_1 + b_2 X_2 + e$$

(a) Test $\beta_1 = 0$ versus $\beta_1 \neq 0$ at the 5 percent significance level.
(b) Test $\beta_2 = 0$ versus $\beta_2 \neq 0$ at the 5 percent significance level.
(c) Redo parts (a) and (b) at the 80 percent confidence level.

9

Dummy Variables, Covariance Analysis, and Pooling Data

In deriving the least squares estimators in Chapters 3 and 4, and in discussing econometric problems in subsequent chapters, we made no explicit reference to the measurement scale of the variables appearing in the regression equation. In this chapter we make the important distinction between quantitative variables and qualitative (sometimes called categorical or classificatory) variables. Quantitative variables, such as pork prices, traffic accidents, or GNP, are measured on a numerical scale that implies a definite positional ordering among the values of the variable. A budget deficit of $200 billion is twice as large as a deficit of $100 billion. Qualitative variables, such as sex of head of household or political preference, involve grouping elements into mutually exclusive and exhaustive categories, such as "female" and "male" or "Republican," "Democrat," and "Other." These variables are measured on an ordinal scale, which means that the differences between the categories of the variable possess no useful numerical information. For example, "Republican" is not twice as large as "Democrat."

In Chapter 8 we showed that working with quantitative variables creates no problem in regression estimation because the recorded values of the variables are simply used in the appropriate formulas to compute the OLS estimates. However, researchers often encounter classificatory variables in applied work and want to measure their effect on the dependent variable, just as they want to measure the effect of continuous variables on the dependent variable. In this chapter we present the conventional method used by applied researchers to "quantify" and use in regression analysis qualitative variables such as "political preference" and "sex of head of household." This method is referred to by a number of terms, such as zero-one variables, binary variables, and most commonly, dummy variables.

A Classificatory Variable

After reviewing the regression equation developed in Chapter 8, the researcher's supervisor points out that the system being studied is based on a biological production function. This suggests the possibility of a seasonal pattern in price because of a likely seasonal pattern in breeding practices, the biologically determined length of the gestation period, and the nonstorability of the finished product that prohibits adding to or drawing from stocks to smooth out the flow of product to market. In other words, perhaps an important variable, "seasonality," has been omitted from the analysis. The researcher receives directions to use regression analysis to determine if there is a seasonal pattern in hog prices.

Seasonal price analysis provides a useful example for showing how dummy variables are incorporated in a regression equation and how the coefficients are interpreted. This section is concerned strictly with technique. The substance of the equations presented below will be considered in subsequent sections of this chapter.

The implicit function to make explicit an estimate by OLS procedures is

$$\text{price} = f(\text{season}) \tag{9.1}$$

which says that price will change as the season changes. Two questions need to be addressed: What general characteristics should the estimating equation possess? How can be the variable called "season" be quantified (expressed in numerical terms)?

Estimating seasonals using regression analysis is developed in detail in Chapter 17. It is adequate here to note that a *seasonal pattern* is defined as a regularly recurring pattern in a variable, such as housing starts or the unemployment rate, that works itself out over a 12-month period. A seasonal is computed to measure how much the value of the variable, say housing starts, in a particular period (a week, a month, a quarter) deviates from the average of the variable over the 12-month period. If, for example, the July seasonal for housing starts is 110.5, housing starts in July are 10.5 percent higher than annual average housing starts. Thus what is needed is an estimated equation that reproduces the actual seasonal price pattern and in doing this yields regression coefficients that are easily interpreted.

The second question concerns how to measure the variable "season" in a way that permits using the OLS formulas for computing the regression coefficients. "Season" is a classificatory variable because the values of the variable "price" in (9.1) can be assigned to a set of mutually exclusive and exhaustive categories—52 weeks, 12 months, or four quarters, depending on the research objective and the data available. The conventional procedure in applied regression is first to assign a unique, numerical value to each category of the classificatory variable and then code each observation in the sample according to its category of the variable. For example, if "season" were defined on monthly data, a researcher might code all January observations in the sample with a 1, February observations with a 2, and end with a 12 for December. These code values are then used as the independent variable in the regression equation.

Thus the fundamental problem is finding a coding scheme for the categories that yields an estimated equation that satisfies the criterion stated above.

At this juncture it is possible to go directly to dummy variables. However, in teaching beginning students, the authors have found that a leisurely approach to dummy variables tends to be more efficient in the long run because it answers the obvious first question: Why dummy variables rather than some other coding scheme? By first seeing that an intuitively appealing coding scheme yields regression results that are difficult to interpret and that do not satisfy the criterion above, students can readily accept dummy variables and, more important, they have less trouble interpreting them. This section works with the basic equation

$$\text{price} = b_0 + b_1(\text{season}) + e \tag{9.2}$$

using the quarterly data in the worksheet in Figure 8.1.

An Intuitively Appealing Coding Scheme

Perhaps the most obvious coding scheme is to assign a value of 1 to all first-quarter observations, a value of 2 to second-quarter observations, a value of 3 to third-quarter observations, and a value of 4 to fourth-quarter observations. This would result in the worksheet shown in Table 9.1.

Table 9.1. Worksheet for Q1 = 1, Q2 = 2, Q3 = 3, Q4 = 4

Year	Quarterly Average Price	Season
1970	28.23	1
	23.53	2
	22.12	3
	15.69	4
1971	19.43	1
	17.43	2
	19.05	3
	19.39	4
.	.	.
.	.	.
.	.	.
1982	49.49	1
	58.14	2
	63.13	3
	53.49	4

The data in Table 9.1 permit the estimation of equation (9.2) by regressing "quarterly average price" on the variable "season." In anticipation of checking the estimated equation against the criterion above (average of seasonal prices equal overall average price), the quarterly average prices and the overall average price for the 52 observations in the sample are presented in Table 9.2.

Table 9.2. Quarterly Average Prices and Overall Average Price

Quarter	Average Price
1	$39.273
2	37.576
3	43.092
4	37.672
Overall	$39.403

The estimated regression equation and the implied seasonal prices are presented in Table 9.3. The estimated equation has an intercept of 39.224 and a slope of .071, which says that price tends to increase by $.071 per hundredweight from quarter to quarter during the calendar year.

Table 9.3. Estimated Seasonal Regression Equation Where Q1 = 1, Q2 = 2, Q3 = 3, Q4 = 4[a]

Quarter	Implied Quarterly Average Price	Actual
1	$39.224 + .071(1) = $39.295	$39.273
2	39.224 + .071(2) = 39.366	37.576
3	39.224 + .071(3) = 39.437	43.092
4	39.224 + .071(4) = 39.508	39.508
	Average = $39.402	$39.403

[a] Estimated equation: price = 39.224 + .71(season).

The average of the regression values of the seasonal prices, $39.402, is equal to the actual average price, except for rounding error. Of paramount concern is the failure of the estimated seasonal prices to trace out the actual seasonal price pattern. The estimated equation shown shows prices rising seasonally throughout the year, while the actual pattern shows a seasonal high in the third quarter and a seasonal low in the second quarter. For this reason, the coding scheme is unacceptable and it is necessary to search for something better.

Dummy Variables and the Dummy Variable Trap

The general rule for a qualitative variable is to create a *dummy variable* for each category of the variable. This variable takes on a value of either one or zero, as illustrated below. For example, the classificatory variable "season" has four categories, so four dummy variables are needed, one for each of the four quarters. The dummy variables for season may be defined as follows:

$$D_1 = 1 \text{ for all first-quarter prices}$$

$$= 0 \text{ for all other-quarter prices}$$

$$D_2 = 1 \text{ for all second-quarter prices}$$

$$= 0 \text{ for all other-quarter prices}$$

$$D_3 = 1 \text{ for all third-quarter prices}$$

$$= 0 \text{ for all other-quarter prices}$$

$$D_4 = 1 \text{ for all fourth-quarter prices}$$

$$= 0 \text{ for all other-quarter prices}$$

Note that although only *one variable*, "season," has been defined, there are *four categories* for this variable. Thus in general, several *empirical variables* ("dummies")

Table 9.4. Example of Worksheet for Incorporating Four Seasonal Dummy Variables

Year	Quarter	Pork Price	D_1	D_2	D_3	D_4
1970	1	$28.23	1	0	0	0
	2	23.53	0	1	0	0
	3	22.12	0	0	1	0
	4	15.69	0	0	0	1
1971	1	19.43	1	0	0	0
	2	17.43	0	1	0	0
	3	19.05	0	0	1	0
	4	19.39	0	0	0	1
.	.	.	.	.	.	.
.	.	.	.	.	.	.
.	.	.	.	.	.	.
1982	1	49.49	1	0	0	0
	2	58.14	0	1	0	0
	3	63.13	0	0	1	0
	4	53.49	0	0	0	1

are required to incorporate one *conceptual variable* into the regression equation; one empirical variable for *each* class of the conceptual variable.

The worksheet for this coding scheme is structured as in Table 9.4, where the data are from Table 8.1. The equation to be estimated with the data in this worksheet is

$$P = b_0 + b_1 D_1 + b_2 D_2 + b_3 D_3 + b_4 D_4 + e \qquad (9.3)$$

Before interpreting this equation, consider the so-called *dummy variable trap*. Remember that the computer uses a slightly different worksheet than the one used for assembling the data. Usually, the computer automatically inserts a column of 1's to account for the intercept term. By compressing the worksheet above and omitting the price column, the worksheet used by the computer has the following general structure:

Category	Intercept Term	D_1	D_2	D_3	D_4
Q1	1	1	0	0	0
Q2	1	0	1	0	0
Q3	1	0	0	1	0
Q4	1	0	0	0	1

This worksheet calls for estimating five coefficients, one for the intercept term and one for each of the four dummy variables.

The dummy variable trap is sprung. Summing over the values in columns D_1 to D_4 yields a column of 1's, which is equal to the column of 1's for the intercept. Recall from Chapter 4 that the OLS procedure is based on the assumption that there is no exact linear relation among the independent variables. In the case at hand, one of the variables (the implicit X_0 for the intercept) is the sum of the other independent variables. In technical language, this is a case of perfect linear dependence among the independent variables. Since this linear dependence violates one of the assumptions underlying OLS estimation, the regression coefficients cannot be obtained. Researchers who include all dummy variables fall into this dummy variable trap. Consequently, a condition (restriction) needs to be imposed on the coefficients of (9.3) in order to permit estimation and avoid the dummy variable trap.

Restrictions on Dummy Variable Coefficients

In this section we consider two types of restrictions that are imposed on the coefficients of dummy variables to avoid the dummy variable trap, show the structure of the associated worksheet, and interpret the coefficients. Remember for now that the focus is strictly on the technique of dummy variables, not on substantive interpretation of the regression results.

Coefficients Sum to Zero

The basic equation, repeated here for convenience, is

$$P = b_0 + b_1 D_1 + b_2 D_2 + b_3 D_3 + b_4 D_4 + e \qquad (9.3)$$

As defined above, a seasonal is computed as the amount by which the value of a variable, price in this case, deviates in a particular "season" from the 12-month average of the variable. In the context of (9.2), this suggests that b_k should measure how much the price in the kth quarter deviates from the overall average price. Moreover, if each coefficient measures the deviation from the overall average, the sum of the seasonal coefficients should be zero because, on average over the 12-month period, there is no seasonality. From this it follows that the intercept, b_0, would equal the overall average.

To get this result, impose the following restriction:

$$b_1 + b_2 + b_3 + b_4 = 0 \quad \text{or} \quad b_1 = (-b_2 - b_3 - b_4) \qquad (9.4)$$

which, when substituted into (9.3), yields

$$P = b_0 + (-b_2 - b_3 - b_4)D_1 + b_2 D_2 + b_3 D_3 + b_4 D_4 \qquad (9.5)$$

Collecting terms gives us

$$P = b_0 + b_2(D_2 - D_1) + b_3(D_3 - D_1) + b_4(D_4 - D_1) \qquad (9.6)$$

as the form of the equation to estimate. It is important to distinguish between (9.3) and (9.6). Equation (9.3) is interpreted under the restriction as follows: b_0 is the overall average price, b_1 is the amount that the first-quarter price deviates from the average price, b_2 is the deviation of the second-quarter price, b_3 is the deviation of the third-quarter price, and b_4 is the deviation of the fourth-quarter price. Equation (9.6), on the other hand, shows how to estimate the coefficients of (9.3) such that the restriction given by (9.4) holds. Two steps are involved: First estimate (9.6) to get b_0, b_2, b_3, and b_4; then "recover" b_1 by (9.4). The restriction in effect dictates estimating (9.3) using "transformed" variables. In other words, instead of regressing price on D_1, D_2, D_3, and D_4, regress price on the variables $D_2^* = (D_2 - D_1)$, $D_3^* = (D_3 - D_1)$, and $D_4^* = (D_4 - D_1)$.

These transformations are easy to compute. Suppose that the computer contains the worksheet shown in Table 9.4, complete with four seasonal dummies. All a researcher needs to do is tell the computer to subtract column D_1 from each of the following three columns and put the results in three separate columns. The resulting worksheet will look as shown in Table 9.5. The first-quarter observations are coded -1 for each of the transformed variables, the second-quarter variables are coded 1 for $D_2 - D_1$ and 0 for the other transformed variables, and the third- and fourth-quarter observations are coded in a similar fashion.

Two comments on this worksheet are in order. First, the sum over the values for the three independent variables is not equal to the suppressed column of 1's for the intercept term, the case in Table 9.4, so the dummy variable trap is avoided. Second, this coding scheme may seem bizarre, but it simply "falls out" of the restriction imposed on the coefficients of (9.3) by (9.4). It is nothing more than a means to the end of estimating (9.3).

Table 9.5. Worksheet when Sum of Coefficients Is Constrained to Zero

Year	Quarter	Price	$D_2 - D_1$	$D_3 - D_1$	$D_4 - D_1$
1970	1	$28.23	−1	−1	−1
	2	23.53	1	0	0
	3	22.12	0	1	0
	4	15.69	0	0	1
1971	1	19.43	−1	−1	−1
	2	17.43	1	0	0
	3	19.05	0	1	0
	4	19.39	0	0	1
.		.	.	.	.
.		.	.	.	.
.		.	.	.	.
1982	1	49.49	−1	−1	−1
	2	58.14	1	0	0
	3	63.13	0	1	0
	4	53.49	0	0	1

The results of the estimation are presented in Table 9.6. These results seem quite acceptable. The intercept term is equal to the overall average price, each coefficient shows how much price in a particular quarter deviates from the overall average, and the estimated equation reproduces the observed seasonal pattern.

In general, using this coding scheme when estimating an equation of the form (9.3) yields an intercept term equal to the overall average of the dependent variable and slope coefficients that measure the amount by which their respective categories deviate from the average over all categories. Note, however, that this result on the intercept term holds only for equations where there are no continuous variables in the equation.

Table 9.6. Regression Results when Coefficients Constrained to Sum to Zero

	Implied Seasonal Price[a]	Actual
Q1	$39.403 - .131(1) - 1.827(0) + 3.688(0) - 1.730(0) = 39.272$	$39.273
Q2	$39.403 - .131(0) - 1.827(1) + 3.688(0) - 1.730(0) = 37.576$	37.576
Q3	$39.403 - .131(0) - 1.827(0) + 3.688(1) - 1.730(0) = 43.091$	43.092
Q4	$39.403 - .131(0) - 1.827(0) + 3.688(0) - 1.730(1) = 37.673$	37.672
	Average $= \$39.403$	$39.403

[a] Estimated equation:

$$\text{price} = 39.403 - 1.827(D_2 - D_1) + 3.688(D_3 - D_1) - 1.730(D_4 - D_1)$$

By the restriction (9.4) imposed we have

$$-(-1.827 + 3.688 - 1.730) = -0.131 = b_1$$

which permits us to write

$$\text{price} = 39.403 - .131(D_1) - 1.827(D_2) + 3.688(D_3) - 1.730(D_4)$$

as the estimate of (9.3).

The case of continuous and dummy variables in the same equation is considered in a later section.

Delete One Category

The second, and perhaps more commonly used, method for avoiding the dummy variable trap is "deleting" one category of the variable. The effect on the worksheet in Table 9.4 is to exclude one of the dummy variables from the regression equation, as shown below. This is done by defining the dummy variable for "season" as follows, where the first quarter is omitted:

$$D_2 = 1 \text{ for all second-quarter prices; } 0 \text{ otherwise}$$

$$D_3 = 1 \text{ for all third-quarter prices; } 0 \text{ otherwise}$$

$$D_4 = 1 \text{ for all fourth-quarter prices; } 0 \text{ otherwise}$$

This results in a worksheet structured as follows:

Category	Intercept	D_2	D_3	D_4
Q1	1	0	0	0
Q2	1	1	0	0
Q3	1	0	1	0
Q4	1	0	0	1

In this case the three dummy variables are coded 0 for all first quarter (the omitted category) observations. This is the substantive difference from the previous worksheet since the remaining categories are coded in the same manner. The equation to estimate from this worksheet is

$$\text{price} = b_0 + b_2 D_2 + b_3 D_3 + b_4 D_4 + e \quad (9.7)$$

The implied seasonal prices for this equation are

Category	Implied Seasonal Price
Q1	$P = b_0 + b_2(0) + b_3(0) + b_4(0) = b_0$
Q2	$P = b_0 + b_2(1) + b_3(0) + b_4(0) = b_0 + b_2$
Q3	$P = b_0 + b_2(0) + b_3(1) + b_4(0) = b_0 + b_3$
Q4	$P = b_0 + b_2(0) + b_3(0) + b_4(1) = b_0 + b_4$

In this particular formulation, the estimated intercept term is interpreted as the price of the omitted category and the coefficient for a particular category shows how much the price for that category differs from that of the omitted category. For example, price in the second quarter minus the price in the first quarter is $(b_0 + b_2) - b_0 = b_2$, the coefficient of D_2. This interpretation of the coefficients differs from that of the previous case where the intercept was equal to the overall average price and the coefficients measured deviations from average.

Table 9.7. Estimating Dummy Variable Coefficients for Pork Price by Omitting One Category

Equation	Intercept	D_1	D_2	D_3	D_4
1	39.273	(omitted)	−1.696	3.818	−1.600
2	37.576	1.696	(omitted)	5.515	.096
3	43.091	−3.818	−5.515	(omitted)	−5.419
4	37.672	1.600	−.096	5.419	(omitted)

	Calculated Average Prices			
Equation	Quarter 1	Quarter 2	Quarter 3	Quarter 4
1	39.273	37.577	43.091	37.673
2	39.272	37.576	43.091	37.672
3	39.273	37.576	43.091	37.672
4	39.272	37.576	43.091	37.672
Actual	39.273	37.576	43.092	37.672

Does it make any difference which category is omitted? Not really, as shown by Table 9.7, which presents four equations, one for each category omitted. The bottom part of Table 9.7 shows that the implied quarterly prices are the same regardless of which seasonal category is omitted for purpose of estimating the equation.

There is also no real difference with regard to the coefficients. Consider equation 1, where D_1 is omitted. The coefficient of D_2 says that price in the second quarter is −$1.696 less than price in the first quarter. It follows that price in the first quarter (the omitted category) is $1.696 higher than price in the second quarter. Now look at the coefficient of D_1 in equation 2, where the second quarter is the omitted category: It says that price in the first quarter is $1.696 higher than price in the second quarter (the omitted quarter). Similar results obtain for any set of coefficients. Consequently, *it makes no difference which category is omitted; different numbers are obtained but the relationships among the coefficients are the same.*

Summary

Researchers can use either of two restrictions on the coefficients of the dummy variables to avoid the dummy variable trap. It really does not make any difference which restriction is used. As the example above shows, the same results are obtained from both methods with regard to the implied seasonal price pattern. The methods do differ, of course, in terms of interpreting the estimated coefficients. In one case the coefficients measure the deviation from the overall average; in the other case the coefficients measure the deviation from the omitted category. So the choice of which to use is largely a matter of personal choice, conditioned perhaps by the specific research problem and how the results are to be presented. In practice, however, the second method is used more frequently. This is due in large part to the easier interpretation of the coefficients in more complex equations that contain two or more classificatory variables plus continuous variables. In this case, the nice interpretation on the intercept term for the first method tends to get lost and it becomes easier to interpret the dummy variable coefficient in terms of difference from the omitted category for a particular classificatory variable.

Covariance Analysis

In the previous sections we showed how to code dummy variables and to interpret their coefficients. In this section we show how to use dummy variables where the equation contains both classificatory and numerical variables. The terms *analysis of covariance* or *covariance analysis* are sometimes used to characterize this type of regression equation.

Suppose that a researcher wants to estimate

$$Y = b_0 + b_1 X_1 + d_1 D_1 + d_2 D_2 + e \qquad (9.8)$$

where X_1 is a quantitative variable and D_1 and D_2 are the two dummy variables for a classificatory variable with three categories. D_3 in (9.8) is set to zero, or the third category of the variable (D_3) has been omitted. The coefficient b_1 is interpreted in the usual fashion: a 1-unit increase in X_1 causes Y to change b_1 units. Because of the restriction that $D_3 = 0$, it is also possible to interpret d_1 and d_2. However, the interpretations of the coefficients on the dummy variables are not quite as straightforward as they were in the preceding section because of the presence of the numerical variable X_1. However, the rationale in the previous section can still be followed.

In the preceding section, where "season" was the only variable in the equation, it was possible to interpret the coefficients of the dummy variables in terms of a seasonal pattern. How should the dummy variable coefficients in (9.8) be interpreted? Consider first what (9.8) looks like over the three categories of the classificatory variable:

Category	Specific Form of (9.8)
1. D_1	$Y = b_0 + b_1 X_1 + d_1(1) + d_2(0)$ or $Y = (b_0 + d_1) + b_1 X_1$
2. D_2	$Y = b_0 + b_1 X_1 + d_1(0) + d_2(1)$ or $Y = (b_0 + d_2) + b_1 X_1$
3. (omit)	$Y = b_0 + b_1 X_1 + d_1(0) + d_2(0)$ or $Y = b_0 \qquad\quad + b_1 X_1$

These results, obtained from the coding scheme used for the classificatory variable, show that (9.8) effectively represents three equations, one for each of the three categories of the variable. Although these equations have the same slope coefficient for the quantitative variable, they have different intercepts: $(b_0 + d_1)$ for the first category, $(b_0 + d_2)$ for the second category, and b_0 for the third, or omitted, category. Consequently, the coefficients of the two dummy variables in (9.8) can be interpreted as follows. The d_1 coefficient measures the difference in the intercept between the first category and the third (omitted) category. The d_2 coefficient measures the difference in the intercept between the second category and the third (omitted) category.

This partly answers the question of how to interpret dummy variable coefficients when there is a quantitative variable in the equation. The coefficients on the dummy variables can be interpreted as *intercept shifters*. Dummy variables also can be used as *slope shifters*, where a single estimated equation represents two equations with the same intercept but different slopes for each of the categories. Rather than elaborate on these in the abstract, consider a concrete example based on an actual data set of observations on 50 school districts in Wisconsin.

Intercept Shifters

Suppose that the research problem is estimating the effect of certain variables on per pupil school expenditures. Based on theory and previous research, the analysis begins with

$$Y = b_0 + b_1X_1 + b_2X_2 + dD + e \qquad (9.9)$$

where Y = annual per pupil expenditures in a school district

X_1 = number of pupils in the school district

X_2 = tax valuation per pupil in the school district

D = type of school district

The sample contains data from 50 school districts in Wisconsin. This equation has two numerical variables, X_1 and X_2, and one classificatory variable, D.

There are three types of school districts in the sample: K-12 districts, the modern, consolidated school districts that provide education through high school graduation; K-8 districts, usually located in rural areas, that provide education through eighth grade; UHS, unified high school districts that offer high school education to K-8 graduates. Since there are three categories of the variable "type of school district," the coding scheme is

$$D_1 = 1 \text{ if a K-12 district; } 0 \text{ otherwise}$$

$$D_2 = 1 \text{ if a K-8 district; } 0 \text{ otherwise}$$

$$D_3 = 1 \text{ if a UHS district; } 0 \text{ otherwise}$$

To avoid the dummy trap, one of these categories must be omitted from the estimating equation. In the preceding section we showed that it makes no difference which category is omitted, since the relationships among the dummy variable coefficients are unaffected and the only difference is the category of the variable used to interpret the estimated coefficients. However, many times there is a category that seems a "natural" for omission in the sense of interpreting the estimated equation. Here that category is the K-12 school district. Because K-12 is the predominant type of district in Wisconsin, it seems natural to test whether the intercepts of the equations for the other types of districts differ significantly from the intercept of the predominant district. We must reemphasize that it is a matter of personal choice which is left out.

The results of estimating an equation that allows the intercept to shift across the three categories of the variable "type of school" are presented in Table 9.8. The first equation assumes that the intercept is the same for each category, whereas equation 2 allows for intercept shifts, with K-12 schools as the omitted category. The three

Table 9.8. Regression Equations Explaining Expenditure per Pupil in 50 Wisconsin School Districts, 1977 to 1978, with Intercept Shifts[a]

Equation	$\bar{R}^2$	Intercept	Number of Pupils, X_1	Valuation per Pupil, X_2	Intercept Shifter X_3	X_4	X_5
1	.162	1699*	.01246	.00131*	—	—	—
		(55)	(.00717)	(.00045)			
2	.332	1686*	.00883	.00185*	−290*	−27	—
		(61)	(.00650)	(.00065)	(84)	(153)	
3	.362	1666*	.00578	.00186*	−318*	−67	92
		(61)	(.00658)	(.00063)	(84)	(151)	(52)

[a] Numbers in parentheses are standard deviations of coefficients; an asterisk denotes a computed t-statistic greater than the 5% critical t-statistic of $t_{40} = 2.021$.

equations implied by equation 2 are

$$\text{K-12 schools: } Y = (1686 + 0) + .00883X_1 + .00185X_2 + e$$
$$(55) \quad\quad (.0065) \quad\quad (.00065)$$

$$\text{K-8 schools: } Y = (1686 - 290) + .00883X_1 + .00185X_2 + e$$
$$(61)\ (84) \quad\quad (.0065) \quad\quad (.00065)$$

$$\text{UHS schools: } Y = (1686 - 27) + .00883X_1 + .00185X_2 + e$$
$$(61)\ (153) \quad\quad (.0065) \quad\quad + (.00065)$$

The t-tests on the individual intercept shifters indicate that the intercept for K-8 schools is significantly less than the intercept for K-12 schools, whereas the intercept for UHS schools is not significantly different from the intercept for K-12 schools. These statistical results say that the intercept term for UHS schools is not significantly different from the intercept term for K-12 schools and the intercept term for K-8 schools. Thus there are really only two equations with different intercepts but the same slopes on X_1 and X_2:

K-12 and UHS schools:

$$Y = 1686 + .00883X_1 + .00185X_2 + e$$

K-8 schools:

$$Y = 1396 + .00883X_1 + .00185X_2 + e$$

To illustrate an equation with two dummy variables for intercept shifters, consider the research problem of determining whether a school district located in a Standard Metropolitan Statistical Area (SMSA) has an intercept different from a school district not located in an SMSA. Since a school district either is or is not in an SMSA, "SMSA" is a classificatory variable. In this case, if the category "is not in an SMSA" is omitted, the dummy variable would be coded 1 for SMSA districts and 0 otherwise. Now there are two classificatory variables in the equation, one for type of school district and one for location of school district. The first variable has three categories, so one category is omitted and the coefficients of the two included categories are interpreted relative to the coefficient for the omitted category. The second variable has two categories, so one category is omitted and the coefficient of the included category is interpreted relative to the coefficient for the omitted category.

The results from estimating this equation are shown as equation 3 in Table 9.8. There are six equations here, as many as there are different combinations of "type of school" and "SMSA." For example, the equation for a K-8 school located in an SMSA is

$$Y = (1666 - 318 + 92) + .00578X_1 + .00186X_2 + e$$

Note, however, that the intercept for a school located in an SMSA is not significantly different from the intercept for an SMSA school.

Slope Shifters

In the preceding section we used a formulation that *assumed* the slopes on the numerical variables were the same for each category and *tested the hypothesis* that the intercepts were the same for each category. This section develops a formulation that *assumes* that the intercepts are the same and uses dummy variables to *test the hypothesis* that the slope of "tax valuation per pupil" (X_2) is the same for each category of "type of school district." In other words, this new formulation allows for the possibility that the slopes are different across the categories.

Before conducting this test on the school district data set, consider a simple example of how dummy variables can be used to structure such a test. Start with the simple equation

$$Y = b_0 + b_1X_1 + d_1D_1 + e \tag{9.10}$$

where X_1 is a numerical variable and D_1 is the included category of a classificatory variable with two categories.

The test to be made on the slope coefficients implies two equations:

$$\text{Category 1: } \hat{Y} = b_0 + b_1^*X_1$$
$$\text{Category 2: } \hat{Y} = b_0 + b_1X_1 \tag{9.11}$$

where the intercept, b_0, is the same, but it is possible that the slope for X_1 is different, b_1^* versus b_1. To incorporate (9.10) into (9.9) requires a new variable, Z, defined by

$$Z = X_1D_1 \tag{9.12}$$

This is called an *interaction variable* because it is the product of two variables. To construct Z, the values of X_1 are multiplied by the respective (i.e., same observation) values of D_1. The resulting worksheet, in compressed form, has the following structure:

Category	Y	Constant	X_1	D_1	$Z = X_1D_1$
1	Y	1	X_1	1	X_1
2	Y	1	X_1	0	0

To see the result, write the equation to estimate as

$$\hat{Y} = b_0 + b_1X_1 + d_1Z \qquad \text{where } Z = X_1D_1 \tag{9.13}$$

For sample observations in category 1, $Z = X_1D_1 = X_1$, since $D_1 = 1$, and (9.13) is written as

$$\text{Category 1: } \hat{Y} = b_0 + b_1X_1 + d_1X_1 = b_0 + (b_1 + d_1)X_1 \tag{9.14}$$

Similarly, for sample observations in category 2, the omitted category, $Z = X_1D_1 = 0$, since $D_1 = 0$, and (9.14) is written as

$$\text{Category 2: } \hat{Y} = b_0 + b_1X_1 + d_1(0) = b_0 + b_1X_1 \tag{9.15}$$

Thus the slope associated with the numerical variable differs by the amount d_1 between the two categories. Applying this formulation to the school district data set, we obtain the equation to estimate:

$$\hat{Y} = b_0 + b_1X_1 + b_2X_2 + z_2Z_2 + z_3Z_3 \tag{9.16}$$

where Y = per pupil school expenditure
X_1 = number of pupils in district
X_2 = tax valuation per pupil
$Z_2 = X_2D_2$, where D_2 is the dummy for K-8 districts
$Z_3 = X_2D_3$, where D_3 is the dummy for UHS districts

The results of estimating (9.16) are given in Table 9.9.

Table 9.9. Regression Equation Explaining Expenditures per Pupil in 50 Wisconsin School Districts, 1977 to 1978, with Slope Shifts in X_2[a]

Equation	$\bar{R}^2$	Intercept	Number of Pupils, X_1	Valuation per Pupil, X_2	Slope Shifter for X_2 K-8, X_2	Slope Shifter for X_2 UHS; X_4
1	.162	1699*	.01246	.00131*	—	—
		(55)	(.00717)	(.00045)		
2	.303	1630*	.00876	.00246*	−.00200*	−.00054
		(92)	(.00668)	(.00107)	(.00071)	(.00085)

[a] Numbers in parentheses are standard deviations of coefficients; an asterisk denotes a computed t-statistic greater than the 5% critical t-statistic of $t_{40} = 2.021$.

The implied equations are:

$$\text{K-12: } \hat{Y} = 1630 + .00876X_1 + .00246X_2$$

$$\text{K-8: } \hat{Y} = 1630 + .00876X_1 + (.00246 - .00200)X_2$$

$$\text{UHS: } \hat{Y} = 1630 + .00876X_1 + (.00246 - .00054)X_2$$

On statistical grounds, the X_2-slope for K-8 schools is significantly different from the X_2-slope for K-12 schools, the omitted categories, whereas the slope for UHS schools is not. This means that increases in property values per pupil have the same impact

Table 9.10. Regression Equation Explaining Expenditures per Pupil in 50 Wisconsin School Districts, 1977 to 1978 Fiscal Year, with Both Intercept Shifts and Slope Changes on X_2

$\bar{R}^2$	Intercept	Number of Pupils, X_1	Valuation per Pupil, X_2	Intercept Shifter		Slope Shift on X_2	
				K-8, X_3	UHS, X_4	K-8, X_5	UHS, X_6
.303	1685	.00883	.00186	−346	16	.00037	−.00016
	(109)	(.0012)	(.00125)	(252)	(285)	(.00191)	(.00155)

197

on per pupil expenditures in K-8 and UHS districts, but the effect is less on K-8 school districts.

Table 9.10 illustrates how both intercept shifters and slope shifters can be used in the same equation, where again K-12 is the omitted category. Although this is equivalent to estimating a separate equation for each category (except for rounding error, the separate estimates would give the same coefficients as implied by the equation in Table 9.10), it has the advantage of providing a test (t-test on the shifters) on whether the intercepts and slopes are significantly different among the categories. This is a version of "pooling data," the subject of the next section.

Pooling Data:
Testing for Structural Differences

Another use of dummy variables is similar in structure to what has already been done, but it differs by the types of hypotheses to be tested. The full worksheet for the school district data comprises a cross-section-over-time data set because it contains data on all the variables for 50 school districts for each of the fiscal years from 1977–1978 to 1981–1982. Several questions arise when using such a data set: Should an equation for each year be estimated separately? If so, do researchers in any sense fail to use all the information contained in the full data set? Does it make sense simply to assume that there are 250 observations and estimate the equation? Should the cross-sectional averages for each year be computed and the resulting five observations (one for each year in the sample) be used to estimate the equation? The point here is that it is not immediately obvious what to do with such a data set.

It is possible, of course, to wade through all the possibilities suggested above, hoping that the estimated results will give some clue as to the appropriate procedure. As usual, however, it is more efficient to think through the problem before rushing to estimation. Because what is done below is so similar to what was done above, it is not necessary to spend much time on the technique of pooling data. A better approach is simply to discuss the issues involved and illustrate with the data set used throughout in this section.

Begin by looking at two extremes: (1) Estimate five separate cross-section equations, and (2) *pool the data* by concatenating the five years of 50 cross-sectional observations into a single data set with 250 observations and then estimate a single equation. The results for both approaches are presented in Table 9.11. Note that the fit as measured by the R^2 is not particularly good, either for the individual equations or the pooled-1 equation at the 5 percent level. The intercept terms and the slopes on "valuation per pupil" are significantly different from zero in all cases.

The pooled equation assumes that the coefficients (the structure of the underlying equation) did not change over the five years of the analysis. It is certainly possible that this is the case. However, in applied research, one should make only those assumptions needed to get the job done. When the data permit testing what would

Table 9.11. Summary of Regression with Separate and Pooled Data for Five Fiscal Years, 50 Wisconsin School Districts[a]
Dependent Variable: Expenditure per Pupil (Dollars)

Equation	Sample Size	$\bar{R}^2$	Intercept	Number of Pupils, X_1	Valuation per Pupil, X_2	Dummy Variable Shifter			
						1978–1979 (X_3)	1979–1980 (X_4)	1980–1981 (X_5)	1981–1982 (X_6)
1977–1978	50	.162	1699* (55)	.01246 (.00717)	.00131* (.00045)	—	—	—	—
1978–1979	50	.191	1905* (55)	.01031 (.00717)	.00126* (.00036)	—	—	—	—
1979–1980	50	.104	2211* (70)	.00690 (.01049)	.00101* (.00037)	—	—	—	—
1980–1981	50	.183	2156* (62)	.01031 (.00925)	.00101* (.00029)	—	—	—	—
1981–1982	50	.231	2360* (77)	.00945 (.01199)	.00135 (.00033)	—	—	—	—
Pooled-1[b]	250	.260	1957* (38)	.00925 (.00580)	.00191* (.00020)	—	—	—	—
Pooled-2[c]	250	.628	1718* (36)	.01002* (.00412)	.0117* (.00015)	199* (44)	463* (45)	411* (45)	674* (15)
Pooled-3[d]	250	.523	2074* (32)	.00989* (.00412)	−.00141* (.00037)	.00168* (.00038)	.00303* (.00036)	.00276* (.00036)	.00385* (.00035)

[a] Numbers in parentheses are standard deviations of coefficients; an asterisk denotes a computed t-statistic greater than the critical t-statistic.
[b] No structural shift over time.
[c] Intercept shift over time.
[d] Slope shift on X_2 over time.

otherwise be an assumption, the test should be made. In this way, as much information as possible is extracted from the data set.

For illustrative purposes, consider an approach that is not appropriate in an actual research setting (where hypotheses should be stated before looking at the data). A close examination of the coefficients of the five annual equations suggests an upward trend in the intercept term, a fluctuating value for the coefficient of "number of pupils" and a relatively constant value for the coefficient of "valuation per pupil." With the benefit of this hindsight, and to illustrate a slightly different use of dummy variables, it is possible to test the hypothesis that the intercept term did not change over the five-year period. This is done by introducing a dummy variable for time, coded with 1977–1978 as the omitted category. The results of estimating this equation are presented as "pooled-2" in Table 9.11.

By allowing the intercepts to shift over time, the R^2 of the equation increases substantially, suggesting a better fit of the data. Moreover, not only are the coefficients of the intercept dummies significantly different from the intercept for 1977–1978 (the omitted category), but their magnitude increases over time. This, of course, confirms what is evidenced by the individual-year equations. (Remember that in practice it is not appropriate to "peek" at the data and then suggest hypotheses to test.) Thus it seems that a structural shift of the underlying equation occurred with regard to the intercept over the five years of the analysis.

A similar test for a structural shift with regard to the slopes of the numerical variables can be constructed. Consider the slope of X_2 and the results shown in the last equation in Table 9.11. Again a structural shift, this time in the slope coefficient, seems to have occurred. In both cases, it seems that 1979–1980 and 1980–1981 are not much different and could be combined.

Given the similarity between this section and the previous sections, this should clearly demonstrate the method of pooling data in a covariance framework. It really involves testing for structural differences in the coefficients of the underlying equation. The illustrations have all involved time, but the procedure would be the same for any natural grouping within the data where structural differences might occur. Indeed, as suggested above, the equation in Table 9.11 provides a framework for testing for structural differences across type of school district.

The importance of testing for structural differences derives from the implications of how to treat a sample where natural groupings are present, as in the sample used here. If there are no structural differences, all the observations in the sample can be pooled and one equation be estimated. However, if structural differences are present, this should not be done because incorrect inferences may be drawn from the analysis. This is easily seen by comparing the pooled-1 with the pooled-2 or pooled-3 equations in Table 9.11. Failure to allow for the possibility of structural shifts (pooled-1) results in accepting the null hypothesis the "number of pupils" is not a statistically significant variable. However, as the other two equations show, it is a significant variable when the possibility of shifts is allowed for.

Finally, note that all of the foregoing manipulations and tests implicitly assume that the variance of the disturbance term is constant across all formulations. In applied work, this assumption should be tested before constructing the types of hypothesis test discussed above. If the variances are not constant, adjustments must be made, as discussed in Chapter 14 under heteroscedasticity.

Summary

In this chapter we considered a powerful tool, dummy variables. The large amount of space dedicated to dummy variables reflects their importance in applied research. A thorough understanding of and the ability to use dummy variables wisely give the applied researcher an enormous amount of flexibility to incorporate a wide range of classificatory variables in the regression equation and, consequently, the ability to test a wide range of hypotheses. Remember, however, that dummy variables, like all powerful tools, can easily be used indiscriminately and lead to nonsensical results. As is the case in all aspects of applied research, the applied researcher must first think through a problem, trying to recognize all possible theoretical ramifications, and only then turn to estimation. Before using dummy variables, a researcher must know exactly why dummy variables are being used and what they are expected to reveal.

Terms

Covariance analysis

Dummy variable

Dummy variable trap

Intercept dummy

Pooled data

Qualitative (classificatory) variable

Quantitative variable

Slope dummy

Structural shift

Exercises

9.1 Are the following variables continuous or classificatory in nature?
  (a) Age of consumer.
  (b) Income of household.
  (c) Sex of head of household.
  (d) Price of corn.
  (e) Gross national product.
  (f) Political party affiliation.
  (g) Season of year.
  (h) Country of birth.
  (i) Wheat production per acre.
  (j) Profits.

9.2 Explain the dummy variable trap.

9.3 Consider the following OLS regression results:

$$S = 12{,}000 - 3000X_1 + 8000X_2 + e \qquad R^2 = .75$$
$$\phantom{S = 12{,}000 -} (4{,}000) \quad (1000) \qquad (2000) \qquad\qquad n = 25$$

where S = annual salary for economists with B.A. or higher degree
$X_1 = 1$ if M.S. is highest degree; 0 otherwise
$X_2 = 1$ if Ph.D. is highest degree; 0 otherwise
$X_3 = 1$ if B.A. is highest degree; 0 otherwise

and the standard errors are in parentheses.
(a) Why is X_3 not included in the equation?
(b) What is the estimated annual salary ($\hat{S}$) for economists whose highest degree is a B.A.?
(c) What is the estimated annual salary ($\hat{S}$) for economists whose highest degree is an M.S.?
(d) What is the estimated annual salary ($\hat{S}$) for economists whose highest degree is a Ph.D.?
(e) At the 5 percent level of significance, would you conclude that economists with M.S.'s have different earnings from those with a B.A.?
(f) At the 5 percent level of significance, would you conclude that economists with Ph.D.'s have different earnings from those with B.A.'s?
(g) Suppose that the same model were used to estimate $S = \beta_0 + \beta_1 X_3 + \beta_2 X_1 + U$. What would b_0, b_1, and b_2 be?
(h) Suppose that you used the same model to estimate $S = \beta_0 + \beta_1 X_2 + \beta_2 X_3 + U$. How would b_1 and b_2 be interpreted?

9.4 Consider the following regression results:

$$S = \$18{,}000 - \$2500(W) + \$1000(D) + \$500(DW) + e$$

where S = starting salary for economists
$W = 1$ if person is woman; 0 otherwise
$D = 1$ if person had Ph.D.; 0 otherwise

$$R^2 = .48$$
$$n = 52$$

(a) What is $\hat{S}$ for a man with a Ph.D.?
(b) What is $\hat{S}$ for a woman with a Ph.D.?
(c) What is $\hat{S}$ for a man without a Ph.D.?
(d) What is $\hat{S}$ for a woman without a Ph.D.?
(e) According to these results, is a Ph.D. worth more or less to a woman than to a man? How much?

9.5 Consider following OLS regression results with standard errors in parentheses:

$$S = 12{,}000 - 3000X_1 + 8000(X_1 + X_2) + e \qquad R^2 = .74$$
$$\phantom{S = 12{,}000 -} (1000) \qquad (3000) \qquad\qquad\qquad n = 25$$

where S = annual salary of economists with B.A. or higher degree
X_1 = 1 if M.A. is highest degree; 0 otherwise
X_2 = 1 if Ph.D. is highest degree; 0 otherwise

(a) What is $\hat{S}$ for economists with an M.A.?
(b) What is $\hat{S}$ for economists with a Ph.D.?
(c) What is the difference in $\hat{S}$ between M.A.'s and Ph.D.'s?
(d) At the 5 percent level of significance, would you conclude that Ph.D.'s earn more per year than M.A.'s?
(e) At the 1 percent level of significance, would you conclude that economists with graduate degrees earn more than $3000 per year more than B.A.'s?

9.6 Suppose theory suggested that annual income (Y) depended on sex (S), highest degree received (D), and years of experience (E): $Y = f(S, D, E)$. We define five variables:

$$D_1 = 1 \text{ if highest degree is high school or less; } 0 \text{ otherwise}$$

$$D_2 = 1 \text{ if highest degree is B.A. or higher degree; } 0 \text{ otherwise}$$

$$S_1 = 1 \text{ if person is a man; } 0 \text{ otherwise}$$

$$S_2 = 1 \text{ if person is a woman; } 0 \text{ otherwise}$$

$$E = \text{years of experience}$$

The following results were obtained:

$$\hat{Y} = \$8000 - 1500S_2 \qquad R^2 = .16$$
$$\phantom{\hat{Y} = \$} (2000) \quad (600) \qquad n = 25$$

(a) What is the mean income for men in the sample? for women?
(b) Do women earn significantly less than men? $(\alpha = .05.)$
(c) What is the Pearson correlation coefficient between S_2 and Y?
(d) What would b_0 and b_1 be if the same sample was used to estimate

$$Y = b_0 + b_1 S_1 + e$$

9.7 To control for educational attainment and years of experience as well as sex, the following estimates were obtained from the same sample used in Exercise 9.6:

$$Y = \$7000 - 2000S_2 + 6000D_2 + 500E + 1600S_2D_2 - 200S_2E + e$$
$$ (1200) \quad (2000) \quad (150) \quad (500) \quad (150)$$

$$R^2 = .78$$

$$n = 25$$

(a) What is $\hat{S}$ for a man with no college degree and no experience?
(b) What is $\hat{S}$ for a woman with a college degree and 10 years of experience?
(c) Does getting a college degree significantly $(\alpha = .05)$ increase the expected income for men?

(d) How much does a woman gain in expected salary from earning an advanced degree?
(e) Do women get a significantly different (α = .05) salary increase from earning an advanced degree than men?
(f) Do women get significantly (α = .05) different income raises for years of experience than men?

9.8 An economist is interested in the relationship between household expenditures on food in restaurants (Y) and household disposable income (X). Data are collected from a sample of two person families and plotted on a scatter diagram. The scatter diagram reveals that the data fall into two clearly *distinct* clusters, one corresponding to households where both members work outside the home and another to households where the one member does not work outside the home.

(a) Draw a picture illustrating what the scatter plot might look like. (HINT: Draw a graph with Y on the vertical axis and X on the horizontal axis and use ovals to indicate the areas in which the two clusters of points might be found.)
(b) Based on the answer to part (a), specify a model that incorporates the difference between households with and without both members working outside the house.
(c) What is the result likely to be if Y is regressed on X with no allowance for the effect of different work circumstances?

9.9 The following equation was estimated for quarterly sales of automobiles for the past 10 years.

$$\hat{S} = 592 - .47P + 96(Q_2 - Q_1) + 74(Q_3 - Q_1) - 25(Q_4 - Q_1)$$
$$\phantom{\hat{S} = 592 -} (.13) \quad (21) \qquad\qquad (16) \qquad\qquad (12)$$

$N = 40$
$R^2 = .62$

where S = sales, thousands of units
P = price, thousands of dollars
Q_i = i for quarter i; 0 otherwise

(a) What is the average sales in each quarter if P = \$8000?
(b) How much below the average are sales in the first quarter of the year?

10

Some Basic Techniques in Regression Analysis

In Chapter 8 we introduced applied research, and stressed the importance of turning to theory, broadly defined, for guidance in thinking through a research problem. It was also argued that applied research is not a mechanical exercise but an art requiring a lot of abstract theorizing, a lot of practical theorizing, and a lot of hard work. In Chapter 9 we introduced classificatory variables and their use in regression analysis, both separately and in conjunction with numerical variables. Using dummy variables provides considerable flexibility for testing hypotheses. In this chapter we discuss still more problems encountered in applied research and offer various methods to resolve them.

Changing Measurement Units: Scaling Variables

The first regression equations run for Chapter 8 involved using the data in Table 8.1 to estimate the following equation:

$$P = 65.22 - .007508Q_p + e \qquad (10.1)$$

where P (price) is measured in dollars per hundredweight and Q (pork quantity) is measured in million-pound units. The estimated slope quantity (b_1) says: "A 1-million-pound (1-unit) increase in quantity will tend to cause price to decrease \$.007508 per hundredweight." Some might find an expression like "\$.007508" or "75/10,000 of a dollar" awkward, as it is not commonly used in everyday conversation. Depending on the regression software used, one can easily get estimated coefficients written with a number of leading zeros (.000001234) or in scientific notation (1.234×10^{-6}). In either event, the researcher often finds such numbers clumsy to work with and tries to avoid them by *scaling the variables*. For example, in equation (10.1) the quantity measurement scale was changed from million-pound units to billion-pound units by dividing the original values of quantity by 1000. The equation was reestimated to obtain

$$P = 65.22 - 7.508Q_p + e \qquad (10.2)$$

which says that a 1-unit (billion-pound) increase in quantity decreases price by about $7.51 per hundredweight, an expression that is easier to comprehend.

In this section we show that changing measurement units, or scaling variables, affects the numerical values of the coefficients but does not alter the "economic statement" of the estimated equation. The objective is simply to show how an applied researcher can control the numerical values of coefficients. Although a simple regression equation is used to estimate the technique, the results apply directly to multiple regression equations.

Scaling an Independent Variable

Consider

$$Y = b_0 + b_1X + e \qquad (10.3)$$

where Y and X are measured in original units, whatever they may be. Scale the values of X by a factor a, where a can take on any value (excluding 0, for which the result is obvious), and regress Y on (aX):

$$Y = b_0^* + b_1^*(aX) + e \qquad (10.4)$$

The OLS coefficients are obtained by regressing Y on the "new" independent variable (aX). Substituting into the OLS formulas in Chapter 3 yields

$$b_1^* = \frac{\Sigma (ax)y}{\Sigma (ax)^2} = \frac{a \Sigma xy}{a^2 \Sigma x^2} = \frac{1}{a} b_1 = \frac{b_1}{a} \qquad (10.5)$$

This says that if X in (10.3) is scaled by a factor a, b_1 in (10.3) is changed by the factor $1/a$, the inverse of the factor used to scale the independent variable. The intercept term is given by

$$b_0^* = \overline{Y} - b_1^*(a\overline{X}) = \overline{Y} - \frac{b_1}{a} a\overline{X} = \overline{Y} - b_1\overline{X} = b_0 \qquad (10.6)$$

which shows that the intercept is unaffected by scaling the independent variable.

As an example, compare (10.1) and (10.2). In going from the first to the second equation, the original values of Q_p were scaled by the factor $1/1000$. That is, quantity was converted to billion-pound units by dividing the million-pound units by 1000. The effect of this was to change the slope by the inverse of the scaling factor:

$$(1000)(.007508) = 7.508$$

The intercept remained unchanged at 65.22. However, the "economic statement" of the equations is the same: for (10.1), where quantity is measured in million-pound units, a change of 1 billion pounds (or 1000 units) yields

$$\hat{P} = 65.22 - (.007508)(1000) = 57.712$$

while for (10.2) a change of 1 billion pounds (1 unit) yields

$$\hat{P} = 65.22 - (7.508)(1) = 57.712$$

Scaling the Dependent Variable

Now change the original unit of Y by a factor a and leave the scale of X unchanged. The equation to estimate is

$$Y^* = (aY) = b_0^* + b_1^* X + e \tag{10.7}$$

The slope coefficient is

$$b_1^* = \frac{\Sigma\, x(ay)}{\Sigma\, x^2} = a\,\frac{\Sigma\, xy}{\Sigma\, x^2} = a\,\frac{\Sigma\, xy}{\Sigma\, x^2} = ab_1 \tag{10.8}$$

and the intercept is

$$b_0^* = a\bar{Y} - b_1^*\bar{X} = a\bar{Y} - ab_1\bar{X} = a(\bar{Y} - b_1\bar{X}) = ab_0 \tag{10.9}$$

Substituting into (10.7) yields

$$aY = ab_0 + (ab_1)X + e \tag{10.10}$$

Comparing (10.10) and (10.3) shows that scaling the dependent variable, with the scale of the independent variable unchanged, also changes the original intercept and slope coefficient by the scaling factor a.

Scaling Both the Independent and Dependent Variables

Finally, consider scaling Y in (10.3) by a_1 and X by a_2. The equation to be estimated is written in terms of the original units as

$$a_1 Y = b_0^* + b_1^*(a_2 X) + e \tag{10.11}$$

The OLS estimator of the slope in this equation is

$$b_1^* = \frac{\Sigma\, (a_2 x)(a_1 y)}{\Sigma\, (a_2 x^2)} = \frac{a_1 a_2}{a_2^2}\,\frac{\Sigma\, xy}{\Sigma\, x^2} = \frac{a_1}{a_2}\, b_1 \tag{10.12}$$

and the OLS estimator of the intercept is

$$b_0^* = a_1\bar{Y} - b_1^*(a_2\bar{X}) = a_1\bar{Y} - \frac{a_1}{a_2}\, b_1(a_2\bar{X}) = a_1(\bar{Y} - b_1\bar{X}) = a_1 b_0 \tag{10.13}$$

When both variables are scaled, the original intercept is changed directly by the scaling factor for the dependent variable [see (10.9)] and the slope is changed by the ratio of the scaling factors.

Finally, scaling the variables does not affect any of the test statistics. For example, if S_{b_1} is the estimated standard deviation with the independent in the original measurements, then S_{b_1}/a is the standard devision of the coefficient in (10.5), with $t = [b_1/a]/[S_{b_1}/a] = b_1/S_{b_1}$, the same as the t-ratio for the original units. Similarly, if the dependent variable is scaled, the standard deviation for the coefficient of X in (10.7) is aS_{b_1}, with $t = ab_1/aS_{b_1} = b_1/S_{b_1}$ as for the original case. In other words, scaling variables does not suddenly yield "significance" where none existed before. A similar relation holds for R^2 and $\bar{R}^2$.

Since scaling variables is a matter of convenience, there is no rule for selecting an "optimum" scaling factor. In practice, it is probably easiest first to estimate the equation using the data as measured in the source from which they were obtained, and then if any coefficients seem awkward scale the variables accordingly.

Relative Importance of Independent Variables

It may be tempting to rank the independent variables in an estimated equation in order of their importance in explaining observed changes in the dependent variable. In this section we consider some alternative criteria for making such rankings and conclude that no one of them is particularly attractive.

Comparing Coefficients

An appealing basis for identifying the "most important" variable in the equation is comparing the magnitude of the regression coefficients. There is little to be said for this ranking method. As demonstrated in the preceding section, the absolute value of a coefficient is easily controlled by simply scaling the variable. Consider the following regression results:

$$Y = 6.3 + 63.05X_1 + 20.2X_2 + e \qquad (10.14)$$

Using the "size" criterion, X_1 is "more important" than X_2. Change the measurement scale of X_1 and reestimate the equation:

$$Y = 6.3 + .6305X_1 + 20.2X_2 + e \qquad (10.15)$$

Now X_2 is the "more important" variable.

As a matter of practice, the absolute values of coefficients should not be used to make statements about the relative importance of the variables in the equation. A possible exception is when all variables are measured in percentage terms. Another possible case is when all the independent variables are measured in exactly the same numerical units, but even here it is treacherous to make direct comparisons.

Simple Correlation Coefficients

Another possible basis for ranking variables is the simple correlation between each of the independent variables and the dependent variable. This follows because correlation coefficients are based on standardized values; thus apparently solving the measurement unit problem. However, to see the serious problems with this use of simple correlation coefficients, consider the simple correlations of pork price with the independent variables in Table 8.1 printed in Table 10.1.

Using those correlation coefficients to rank variables would rank income the most important, chicken second, beef third, and pork last. Remember, however, that in testing hypotheses in Chapter 8, the coefficient of beef was not statistically significant and the coefficient of chicken was statistically significant at a low probability level. Notice also that the simple price correlations with beef and chicken are positive, yet in the equation in Chapter 8, the signs of these coefficients were negative, as expected on theoretical grounds. These inconsistencies reflect the important point that simple correlation coefficients are computed without controlling for the effect on the dependent variable of the other relevant variables in the equation.

t-Ratios

A third basis for assigning relative importance is comparing t-ratios. The presumption in this case might be that a coefficient with a higher t-ratio is in some sense more significant and therefore the variable is more important in explaining variation in the dependent variable. This is an improper interpretation of the t-ratio. All the t-ratio does is test the probability that the estimated coefficient came from a population where the population regression coefficient has the value assumed by the null hypothesis. If, on statistical grounds, the coefficient of one variable is not significantly different from zero and the coefficient of another variable is significantly different from zero, a researcher may conclude that one is not important and the other is important. However, if one coefficient has a t-ratio of 12.8 and another a t-ratio of 6.4, it does not follow that the former is twice as "important" as the latter in explaining variation. All the two t-ratios say is that the relative variance of one estimated coefficient is smaller than the relative variance of the other estimated coefficient. As long as the computed t-ratio exceeds the critical t-ratio for the confidence level of the test, one can reject the null hypothesis, *but that is all*.

Table 10.1. Simple Personian Correlation Coefficients for Pork Price Data in Table 8.1

	Price	Pork	Beef	Chicken	Income
Price	1.00				
Pork	− .26	1.00			
Beef	.29	− .40	1.00		
Chicken	.49	.47	− .03	1.00	
Income	.66	.47	.03	.87	1.00

Standardized Regression

The method of *beta coefficients* (not to be confused with the β_k's used for population parameters), or standardized regression, offers the possibility for making direct comparisons of the relative importance of the independent variables. This method involves first standardizing each variable by converting it to a variable with mean of zero and variance of 1 and then estimating the equation using these standardized values. A comparison, using the data in Table 8.1, between regression with natural values and with standardized values is given in Table 10.2.

The R^2's are the same, as they should be since all standardization does is shift the origin of measurement. The standard deviation of the regression, S, and the coefficients are different because the measurement unit is different. Finally, the intercept in the standardized equation is zero because all the variables in the equation have zero mean.

Because all the variables are measured on the same (standardized) scale, direct comparisons are possible. For example, income is more important that pork quantity in explaining price variation. But be careful because beta coefficients have a unique interpretation. A regression coefficient must be interpreted in terms of the measurement units of the variables. For the first equation, "a change of 1 billion pounds (1 unit) in quantity will result in a price change of $21.27 per hundredweight." For the second equation, "a change of *1 standard deviation* (1 unit) in quantity will result in a *.75 standard deviation change* in price." To the extent that one does not think in terms of standard deviation changes, beta coefficients can be awkward to interpret.

Beta coefficients are directly related to OLS coefficients in the following way. Let S_y and S_x be the standard deviation of Y and X respectively; then the standardized coefficient is

$$\text{beta coefficient} = \frac{S_x}{S_y} b_{yx}$$

Consequently, a researcher can always use the sample data to convert OLS coefficients to standardized coefficients. Beta coefficients are part of the standard output of many computer software packages because standardized variables are widely used in applied research where the basic variables do not have a "natural" unit of measurement, as is often the case when studying psychological and sociological relationships.

Elasticities

The final ranking method discussed here is using percentage changes, or *elasticities*. As a general proposition, if

$$Y = f(X) \tag{10.16}$$

then the elasticity of Y with respect to X is defined as

$$E_{Y/X} = \frac{\% \text{ change in } Y}{\% \text{ change in } X} \tag{10.17}$$

Table 10.2. Beta Coefficients, or Standardized Regression, Compared to Normal Regression[a]

	S	R^2	Constant	Pork	Beef	Chicken	Income
Normal[b]	4.37	.87	92.60	−21.27*	−1.62	−3.92	6.96 *
			(14.2)	(1.9)	(1.8)	(2.5)	(.65)
Standardized	.37	.87	0	−.752*	−.054	−.168	1.163*
				(.07)	(.06)	(.11)	(.11)

[a] An asterisk denotes a computed t-ratio greater than the critical t-ratio at the .05 level; standard errors are in parentheses.
[b] Pork price in dollars per hundredweight; pork, beef, chicken in billions of pounds; and income in thousands of dollars per capita.

or

$$E_{Y/X} = \frac{\partial Y/Y}{\partial X/X} = \frac{\partial Y}{\partial X} \frac{X}{Y} \qquad (10.18)$$

where "∂" means "small change." In the general linear regression equation,

$$\frac{\partial Y}{\partial X_k} = b_k \qquad (10.19)$$

where b_k is the regression slope of X_k. Substituting into (10.18) yields

$$E_{Y/X_k} = b_k \frac{X_k}{Y} \qquad (10.20)$$

An elasticity is "dimensionless" because it is a ratio of two percentages, so (10.20) may be interpreted as the percent change in Y for a 1 percent increase in X_k.

To compute the elasticity, a point on the linear regression line must be specified in order to get the numerical values for Y and X_k needed to compute (10.20). Any point can be selected, but in applied work it is conventional to compute the elasticity at the means of the variables. This choice is, of course, arbitrary. Consequently, using elasticities does not provide an unequivocal answer to the question: What is the most important variable in the regression equation?

Table 10.3 shows the regression equation estimated in Table 10.2 and the elasticities for each independent variable computed at the means. These are percentages and can be interpreted as such. For example, a 1 percent increase in pork quantity is associated with a 1.86 percent decrease in price. Because elasticities are easy to compute and to interpret, they are often used in applied research to make relative comparisons among variables.

Table 10.3. Elasticities Measured at Means of Variables for Pork Price Equation

	S	R^2	Constant	Pork	Beef	Chicken	Income
Coefficients	4.37	.86	92.60	−21.27*	−1.62	−3.92	6.96*
				(1.89)	(1.77)	(2.49)	(.65)

Variable	Sample Mean	Elasticity
Price	39.40	—
Pork	3.44	$-21.27 \dfrac{3.44}{39.40} = -1.86$
Beef	5.67	$-1.62 \dfrac{5.67}{39.40} = -.23$
Chicken	3.03	$-3.92 \dfrac{3.03}{39.40} = -.30$
Income	5.89	$6.96 \dfrac{5.89}{39.40} = 1.04$

Empirical Specification
of a Conceptual Equation

In Chapter 8 we made a distinction between a conceptual variable and an empirical measure of the variable. Recall, for example, that the conceptual variable "price" appeared in the theory used to guide the research. Yet the library contains several empirical measures of price, each defined on different aspects of the market. The conceptual-empirical distinction reappears, applied here to equations rather than variables. In this section we start with the conceptual equation specified by theory and then focus on the proper empirical specification of the equation. There are two aspects of empirically specifying equations. The first is how to incorporate the variables in the equation. The second, and the subject of the remainder of this chapter, is empirically specifying equations. Choosing the proper mathematical form for the equation is the subject of Chapter 11.

Absolute and Per Capita Quantities

The objective in Chapter 8 was to illustrate how an applied researcher approaches a research question by using theory to help identify the data needed to get the job done. In Chapter 8 we ignored a number of important questions. For example, total quantities and per capita income were used without any fanfare even though important "population adjustment" issues are involved in the choice of each variable.

Since consumer demand theory underlies the research in Chapter 8, a quick review of that theory for clues regarding the proper way to measure quantity variables in a regression equation is in order here. Remember that the theory of consumer choice is cast in terms of the individual consumer. The objective of the theory is to explain how the consumer's budget is allocated among commodities. From the theoretical analysis is derived the consumer's demand curve, a behavioral relationship showing the quantity of a particular commodity that the consumer will purchase as the price of that commodity changes, all else constant. To get from the individual consumer to the market demand for the commodity requires that the demand curve for each of the n consumers be derived and that these demand curves be added over the population of n consumers to get the market demand curve.

Although the above says nothing explicit about measuring quantity variables for regression analysis, it does suggest the following line of reasoning linking the theoretical demand curve to the demand curve of real-world markets. Visualize a market initially in equilibrium, where the population of n consumers is buying pork, beef, and chicken. Let population increase to $n + m$. If we assume that these additional m consumers will also buy pork, beef, and chicken, and assume for the moment that all else in the system remains unchanged, it follows that the market demand curve, now added over $n + m$ consumers, will move to the right. More of the commodity will be purchased at the same price as the number of consumers increase. Of course, the real world never stands still long enough to permit exact observation of the phenomena described above. Nevertheless, these population pressures are at work in the market-place.

It follows from the above that the conceptual equation used to study factors causing price to change must include population. Thus the conceptual equation may be re-written

$$P_p = f(Q_p, Q_b, Q_c, I, \text{POP}) \qquad (10.21)$$

where the Q variables are the quantities of pork, beef, and chicken, I is per capita income, and POP is population. The question now is how to incorporate POP in the empirical equation to be estimated. This can be done in one of two ways: (1) by including POP as an additional independent variable in the equation, or (2) by dividing each quantity variable in the equation by population and regress price on the per capita quantities. To do this, the variable "POP" must be added to the worksheet, a portion of which would look as follows:

Year-Quarter	Q_p (Millions of Pounds)	POP (Millions of People)	Q_p/POP (Pounds of Pork per Person)
1970-1	3056	200.662	15.23
1970-2	3133	201.294	15.56
1970-3	3154	202.158	15.60
1970-4	3905	202.980	19.24

This worksheet permits the two different approaches to handling population change in a time-series data set. The structure of the worksheet and regression equations would be the same if a cross-sectional data set were being studied.

The results of estimating the two equations are presented in Table 10.4. The im-portant point to be made is that these results represent two empirical formulations of the same conceptual equation (10.21). Both estimating equations contain the variables specified by this conceptual equation, but the empirical specifications differ. The choice between the two empirical specifications depends on the research question at hand. In some situations, equation 1 would be better; in other situations, equation 2 would be better. However, it is important to explicitly recognize that the equations do make a different empirical statement about how the effect of population change on price works itself out.

Consider the coefficients of pork quantity and population in the two equations. In equation 1, the change in price associated with a 1-billion-pound increase in quantity is given by

$$\frac{\partial P}{\partial Q_p} = -20.80 \qquad (10.22)$$

Notice that since population does not appear in (10.22), price decreases by \$20.81 per hundredweight regardless of the level of population at which the quantity change occurs. Similarly, in equation 1 the marginal effect on price of a 1-unit (1000 persons) increase in population is given by

$$\frac{\partial P}{\partial \text{POP}} = .0018 \qquad (10.23)$$

Table 10.4. Two Alternatives for Adjusting Quantity Variables for Population Differences in the Pork Price Model[a]

Equation[b]	S	$\bar{R}^2$	Constant	Pork	Beef	Chicken	Income	Population
1	$3.86	.89	-237.50*	-20.80*	-5.08*	-3.17	-4.78	.0018*
			(83.00)	(1.67)	(1.81)	(2.21)	(8.50)	(.0004)
2	$4.13	.89	113.01*	-4.67*	-.63	-.80	4.84*	—
			(15.56)	(.38)	(.38)	(.50)	(.49)	

[a] An asterisk denotes a computed t-ratio larger than the critical t-value for $\alpha = .05$.
[b] In equation 1, pork, beef, and chicken are measured in billion-pound units; income in trillion-dollar units; and population in thousand-person units. In equation 2, pork, beef, and chicken are measured in pounds per person and income in dollars per person.

This says that all else constant, an increase in population causes price to increase, a result consistent with the theory sketched above. The magnitude of the price change is, in this case, independent of the level of pork quantity at which the change in population occurs because pork quantity does not appear in (10.23).

Now consider equation 2, where pork production is measured as pounds per capita. In this case

$$\frac{\partial P}{\partial (Q_p/\text{capita})} = -4.67 \tag{10.24}$$

which represents the change in price associated with a 1-unit change in per capita quantity. This result differs from (10.22) because population is present in (10.24). To see this, write out just the pork quantity portion of equation 2:

$$P = 113.01 - 4.67 \frac{Q_p}{\text{POP}} \tag{10.25}$$

In this case, the marginal effect of pork prices of an increase in the level of *total* pork quantity is

$$\frac{\partial P}{\partial Q_p} = -\frac{4.67}{\text{POP}} \tag{10.26}$$

which says that the effect of a given change in total quantity depends on the level of population at which the quantity change occurs. In particular, (10.26) says that a given change in quantity will have a smaller negative effect on price the higher the level of population at which the quantity change occurs. This result is in accord with the proposition that population increases are likely to cause a price increase, all else constant.

In parallel fashion, the marginal effect of a population increase on price for a given total quantity is given by

$$\frac{\partial P}{\partial \text{POP}} = 4.67 \frac{Q_P}{(\text{POP})^2} \tag{10.27}$$

which again shows the positive effect on price of a population increase. Equation (10.27) also says that while a population increase results in a price increase, the magnitude of the price increase grows smaller as population increases.

In summary, equations 1 and 2 are alternative empirical specifications of the same conceptual equation, and in this sense they are the same. However, as shown by (10.22) to (10.27), they make different empirical statements about how the price effects get worked out. In other words, the two equations make different statements about how markets work. The choice between the two has to be made in the context of the specific research question under study.

Deflating Prices and Income

In this section we address the question of adjusting for differences in the general price level across the sample observations. This is typically of concern when using time-series data sets since the general price level can change substantially over time, but it also can arise with cross-sectional data sets because prices can differ across geographical regions due to such things as regional differences in economic conditions and transportation costs. However, it is often the case that regional prices are not available, so what follows is keyed to time-series data sets. Nevertheless, the nature of the issue and its resolution are the same for cross-sectional data.

The general level of all prices tends to change over time due to forces operating in the economy, such as government policies, management of the money supply, and international conditions. This suggests that when studying the price for a particular commodity, researchers need to recognize two sets of market forces, those operating in the economy at large and those specific to the market for the commodity. Let Z refer collectively to general market forces and X refer collectively to the specific market forces and write

$$P = f(X, Z) \qquad (10.28)$$

as the properly specified, implicit form of the equation to estimate. As discussed in detail in Chapter 13, if the Z-variables are omitted, a misspecified equation will result, one likely consequence of which would be biased estimators of the coefficients. Consequently, the Z-variables should be included in the equation.

In principle, the Z-variables can be included directly in the equation. However, this raises a number of difficult questions: What specific variables should be included? Do they lend themselves easily to estimation? Are data available for them? Would you end up with too many variables to handle in the regression equation? Because of questions such as these, a practical expedient often followed in applied research is to use an appropriate *price index* based on the argument that this is an acceptable summary measure of the working out of general economic forces.

There is no "optimum" price index and the one chosen from the many price indexes available depends heavily on the research objective. To "remove" the effect of general economic conditions, researchers often use the Consumer Price Index or the gross national product implicit price deflator. If, on the other hand, the objective is to look at pork price in the context of all agricultural prices, an index of prices received by farmers for all commodities might be more appropriate. In other instances, an index of wholesale prices might be best.

Adjusting for the general price level can be illustrated using the Consumer Price Index (CPI), an index widely used to adjust variables expressed in dollars for changes in the general price level. As in the preceding section, there are two ways to proceed. A researcher can (1) introduce the CPI as a separate independent variable, or (2) divide all nominal variables (prices, income, taxes, interest rates, and the like) by the CPI and run the equation using these "deflated" values. To get some feel for what deflation can do to the values of price and income, see Figures 10.1 and 10.2.

The results of using the two procedures are presented in Table 10.5, where the quantity variables are in per capita terms. The situation here is identical to that of the preceding section, where alternative empirical formulations of the same conceptual equation were presented. Again, these equations make different empirical statements about how market forces work. (Interpreting these different empirical statements is left as an exercise.) The choice between the two equations must be made in the context

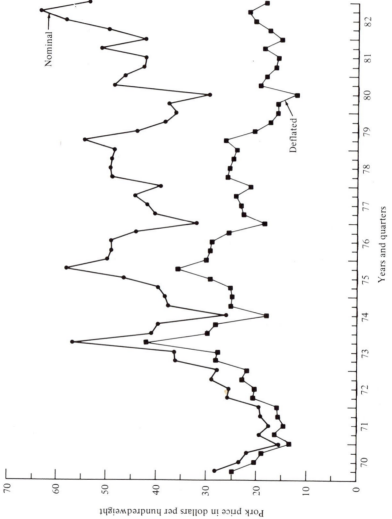

FIGURE 10.1 U.S. Pork Price, Nominal and Deflated by the Consumer Price Index, Quarterly 1970 to 1982.

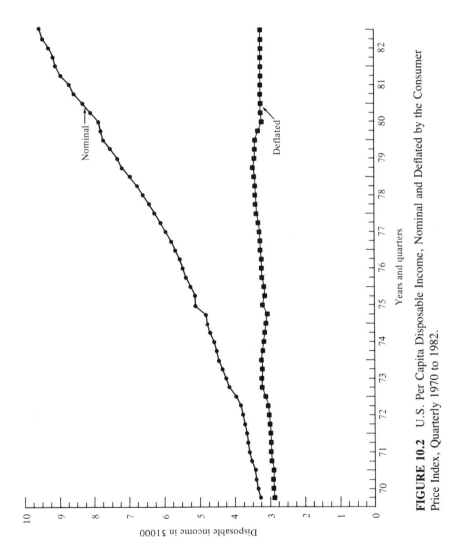

FIGURE 10.2 U.S. Per Capita Disposable Income, Nominal and Deflated by the Consumer Price Index, Quarterly 1970 to 1982.

of the specific research question. However, it is important to recall that the equilibrium solutions in neoclassical theory are stated in terms of real prices and income.

Lagged Variables

The final topic of this chapter is lagged variables. The worksheet in Chapter 8 contains time-series data with each variable measured at time t, where t stands for a particular quarter in a particular year. Consequently, all the equations estimated so far use variables measured at t. When all the variables in the equation are measured at t, the implied economic statement is that the effects of the independent variables on the dependent variable completely work themselves out during the period t. Whether this is a correct statement depends, of course, on the particular system being studied. It is true in many markets that time is required before the market responds fully to changes in market forces. Equations containing lagged variables are sometimes called *dynamic equations* to denote the presence of this time lag in market response.

The treatment of how to use lagged variables will not be complete in this section because lagging variables, especially if the lagged dependent variable appears as an "independent" variable, as it does in many lagged models, calls for more advanced estimation procedures than those covered in this book. The problem derives from the relationship between the lagged variables and the disturbance term in the equation. If a lagged dependent variable is used as an independent variable, the classical assumptions (see Chapters 3 and 4) may not be satisfied, and more sophisticated assumptions are required. For this reason the disturbance term is ignored in the following discussion and emphasis is placed on the economics issues. Readers interested in proofs of the validity of some of the results shown below are referred to more advanced textbooks.

Simple Lags

One of the earliest uses of lagged variables in applied research was in agricultural supply analysis. Because of the biologically determined time period between planting and harvesting field crops, the price for a particular marketing year cannot be known at the time the planting decision is made. In other words, production in t is not affected by price in t because price in t cannot be determined until production in t is harvested and moved to market. To do supply analysis in the context of production theory, which says that output is a function of market price, applied researchers used the assumption that output in t (this year) depends on price received by producers in $t - 1$ (last year), which suggests the following equation:

$$Q_t = b_0 + b_1 P_{t-1} + e_t \tag{10.29}$$

P_{t-1} is a lagged variable.

This type of formulation, which is more widely applicable than suggested by the example, is referred to in present-day terminology as an *expectations model*. When a decision maker must make a decision at t, the outcome of which will not be realized

Table 10.5. Comparison of Methods for Adjusting of Price Level in Pork Price Equations[a]

| | S | $\bar{R}^2$ | Constant | Per Capita Consumption | | | Per Capita | |
				Pork	Beef	Chicken	Income	CPI
1. Price index included	$3.90	.89	116.65* (14.75)	−4.54* (.36)	−.71 (.36)	−.76 (.47)	12.12* (2.83)	−.26* (.10)
2. Deflated by CPI	$2.90	.78	70.49* (14.58)	−2.68* (.27)	−.54* (.26)	−1.19* (.27)	7.87* (3.07)	

[a] An asterisk denotes a computed *t*-ratio greater than the critical *t*-ratio at $\alpha = .05$.

221

until $t + 1$, or some other future period, the decision at t is based on the "expected" value of the decision variable. Thus in (10.29) the expected price used for decision making is quantified as the price received in the preceding production period. This simple formulation is the *cobweb model*, often used in economic textbooks as an illustration of a dynamic model. The expectation argument embedded in (10.29) is still widely used in applied research, but more sophisticated methods are used in an attempt to get a better quantitative measure of expected price. One example in supply analysis is the use of the planting-time price of a futures market contract that matures at harvest time. This can be used only where a futures market exists for the commodity. Perhaps the most important point to be made about this formulation is that it is rooted in production theory and therefore has an interpretive framework.

Another simple lag formulation arises in the context of habit or persistence in behavior. For example, the amount of a commodity consumers buy in t may in part be influenced by the amount they purchased in $t - 1$. This suggests the following simple formulation:

$$Y_t = b_0 + b_1 Y_{t-1} + e_t \qquad (10.30)$$

where Y_{t-1} is a lagged dependent variable used as an independent variable. There are at least two problems with this simple formulation. First, the interpretive framework, or theory, is not particularly rigorous. Second, it may pose a problem for estimation by OLS procedures. A key assumption used in Chapters 3 and 4 was that of independence between the independent variables and the disturbance term. This assumption is not applicable here, since the independent variable is the dependent variable, albeit lagged one period. An evaluation of this case shows that the OLS coefficients of (10.30) may be biased in small samples, which suggests that some other estimating procedure must be used if BLUE estimates are desired. However, if the research objective is forecasting, where the predictive power of the equation is often viewed as more important than the properties of the coefficient estimates, an equation like (10.30) is rewarding in the sense that it usually has a high multiple correlation coefficient and a low standard error of regression. There is a bit of the history-repeating-itself argument here, which although not helpful in explaining change, can be helpful in forecasting the degree of change. Forecasting is considered more fully in Chapter 18.

The final method to consider is

$$Y_t = b_0 + b_1 X_{t-1} + b_2 X_{t-2} + b_3 X_{t-3} + \cdots + e_t \qquad (10.31)$$

which posits an infinite lag. Because it is not possible to estimate an infinite lag, the practical suggestion would be to estimate a series of equations, the first with X_{t-1}, the second with X_{t-2}, and so on. The first problem with this is that it has no theoretical framework, hence there is no way of really knowing when to stop lagging the variable. In addition, because of the likelihood of multicollinearity (see Chapter 12), the values of the coefficients and their respective standard deviations are likely to change as additional lags are added, compounding the problem of selecting the best lag formulation.

However, part of the problem above can be solved by introducing the following assumptions. Assume that the population regression coefficients, β_k, are all positive and have a finite sum. Assume further that the values of the β_k decline over time in a geometric pattern. Applying these assumptions to (10.31) and grinding through their implications yields the following equation to estimate:

$$Y_t = \beta(1 - \lambda)X_t + \lambda Y_{t-1} + e_t \qquad (10.32)$$

This is called the *Koyck distributed lag formulation*, where λ, which is assumed to fall in the interval from zero to 1, is the weight for the geometric decline, and β and λ are parameters to estimate from the sample. The model says that the effect of a change in X is distributed over a number of periods, depending on the size of λ. If λ equals zero, there is no lag, and a change in X_t is fully reflected in Y_t. On the other hand, if λ is small, a change in X in period t takes a long time to be fully reflected as a change in Y. A potential problem with the underlying assumptions is the appearance of the lagged dependent variable as an independent variable, posing possible estimation problems, as mentioned above.

Partial Adjustment and Expectation Models

The search for an interpretive framework for lagged specifications led to what are called *partial adjustment and expectation models*, sometimes referred to as *Nerlove models* in recognition of the researcher who first used them extensively in applied research. These models, or variations of them, are often used in applied research. In this section we present the underlying theory, show what the estimating equations look like, and interpret the coefficients. Proper estimating procedures are left for more advanced texts.

The partial adjustment model is illustrated by the following equation:

$$Y_t^* = b_0 + b_1 X_t + e_t \qquad (10.33)$$

where X_t might be a predetermined price, say, by government policy or a contract signed at decision-making time t. The dependent variable, Y_t^*, is viewed as the desired or optimum output for the price X_t. Because of technological or institutional rigidities, say, lack of adequate financing, the decision maker is unable to move immediately to Y_t^*. Only a partial move, or a partial adjustment, is possible. Let Y_t be the observed output. The problem in estimating (10.33) is that Y_t^* is not observable. However, Y_t is observable, so the task is to introduce a second equation that links the observable Y_t to the unobservable Y_t^*. One way of doing this is specifying

$$Y_t - Y_{t-1} = \delta(Y_t^* - Y_{t-1}), \qquad 0 < \delta \leq 1 \qquad (10.34)$$

which says that the observed adjustment from Y_{t-1} to Y_t is proportional, by the factor δ, to the desired move from Y_{t-1} to Y_t^*. Thus the observed change $(Y_t - Y_{t-1})$ is the partial adjustment caused by technological or institutional rigidities. Manipulating (10.34) yields

$$Y_t^* = \frac{1}{\delta} Y_t + \frac{\delta - 1}{\delta} Y_{t-1} \qquad (10.35)$$

which expresses the unobservable Y^* in terms of the observable Y. Substituting this into (10.33) yields

$$Y_t = \delta b_0 + \delta b_1 X_t + (1 - \delta)Y_{t-1} + e_t \qquad (10.36)$$

where all variables are observable. Notice that the lagged dependent variable appears on the right-hand side of the equation and that the coefficients in (10.36) are multiplicative expressions of the coefficients in (10.32) and (10.33). Rewrite the equation as

$$Y_t = d_0 + d_1 X_t + d_2 Y_{t-1} + e_t \qquad (10.37)$$

Treating these as OLS coefficients, we can write

$$\hat{\delta} = 1 - d_2 \qquad (10.38)$$

$$b_0 = \frac{d_0}{\hat{\delta}} \qquad (10.39)$$

$$b_1 = \frac{d_1}{\hat{\delta}} \qquad (10.40)$$

As we stated above, this model is used in those cases where technological and institutional rigidities result in only a partial adjustment. Equation (10.37) provides estimates of both the economic equation, (10.33) and the partial adjustment equation (10.34). If Y is consumption of a commodity and X is its price, then b_1 is the long-run demand response to a change in price, and d_1 in (10.37) is an estimate of the short-run demand response. The ability of this model to yield estimates of both short-run and long-run coefficients is one reason why it is of considerable interest to the applied researcher.

The adaptive expectations model can be illustrated by

$$Y_t = b_0 + b_1 X_t^* + e_t \qquad (10.41)$$

which differs from the partial adjustment model in that the observed outcome, Y_t, depends on expectations concerning the decision variable, X_t. The estimation problem is present because the independent variable is unobservable. If X_t^* were an expected price, it could be quantified (as above) by using price received in the previous period or an appropriate futures market price. The adaptive expectations model makes the following assumption:

$$X_t^* - X_{t-1}^* = \delta(X_t - X_{t-1}^*), \qquad 0 < \delta < = 1 \qquad (10.42)$$

which says that expectations are adjusted from $t - 1$ to t proportional, by the factor δ, to the difference between expectations held in $(t - 1)$ and the actual value of X in t. Other specifications could be made, but this form will be used to illustrate the model. Using (10.42) to express X^* in terms of X and substituting into (10.41) yields

$$Y_t = (1 - \delta)b_0 + (1 - \delta)b_1 X_t + \delta Y_{t-1} + (e_t - \delta e_{t-1}) \qquad (10.43)$$

which is formally equivalent to (10.36), differing only by the structure of the coefficients and error term in the equation. The OLS version of (10.43) is

$$Y_t = d_0 + d_1 X_t + d_2 Y_{t-1} + e_t^* \tag{10.44}$$

where d_2 is the estimate of δ. Appropriate substitution of d_2 in d_0 and d_1 yields b_0 and b_1.

The attractive feature of these models is their explicit recognition of rigidities and expectations. As a consequence, they yield both short-run and long-run coefficients. The models have been illustrated using the simplest formulation, but more complicated versions, some incorporating rigidities and expectations in the same equation, are found in the literature. However, the newcomer should be judicious in using these models because of the estimation problems mentioned before and discussed in more advanced textbooks.

To illustrate some of the formulations above, suppose that a researcher were interested in developing and estimating a simple model of monthly gas consumption for home heating. An ad hoc approach would be to specify

$$Q_t = b_0 + b_1 P_t + b_2 Q_{t-1} + e_t \tag{10.45}$$

where Q_t is gas use in the current period, P_t is gas price in the current period, and Q_{t-1} is gas use in the preceding period. This lag specification might be justified on the "habit" argument discussed in connection with (10.30).

Another approach would be to argue that there exists an optimum quantity of gas use for a given price. This can be written as

$$Q_t^* = c_0 + c_1 P_t + e_t \tag{10.46}$$

where the dependent variable is not actual gas use in t but the optimum gas use given P_t. Because this variable is not observable, (10.46) cannot be estimated. However, by adding to this model a statement of changes in the optimum use according to (10.34), the following estimating equation for the coefficients of (10.46) can be obtained:

$$Q_t = d_0 + d_1 P_t + d_2 Q_{t-1} + e_t \tag{10.47}$$

Equation (10.45) is an ad hoc model and equation (10.46) is a stock adjustment model. It is clear that each makes a different economic statement about how the underlying system (gas use for home heating) works itself out; thus the coefficients in each have different interpretations.

As an aside, note that the estimating equations (10.45) and (10.47) involve the same operation: regress current gas use on current price and gas use in the previous period. Thus, regardless of the economic model used, the coefficients of the estimating equation will be identical. But the estimating equations are not identical on statistical grounds. In the derivations above we ignored the all-important error term. It turns out that applying the transformations to the error term, as was done to the variables, yields substantially different specifications on the error terms. The implications of these specifications is beyond the level of this book. Be sure to refer to more advanced sources before using partial adjustment or adaptive expectations in applied work.

The data set used to obtain the coefficients of the estimating equation consisted of monthly observations on gas use, measured in 100 cubic feet, and monthly gas price from January 1976 to December 1983. The data were from the personal files of one of the authors. The estimated equation is

$$\hat{Q}_t = \begin{matrix} 41.88 \\ (26.8) \end{matrix} - \begin{matrix} 30.15 P_t \\ (49.7) \end{matrix} + \begin{matrix} .8092 Q_{t-1} \\ (.064) \end{matrix} \qquad \begin{matrix} R^2 = .66 \\ S = 73.9 \end{matrix} \qquad (10.48)$$

where standard errors are in parentheses.

Under the ad hoc model, this equation says that a 1-unit change in gas price will result in a 30.15-unit decrease in gas use and a 1-unit change in gas use in $t - 1$ is associated with a .8092-unit change in gas use in t. To interpret (10.48) in the context of a partial adjustment model, the transformations given by equations (10.38) to (10.40) are:

$$\text{estimate of adjustment coefficient} = 1 - .8092 = .1908$$

$$\text{estimate of } b_0 \text{ in (10.45)} = \frac{41.88}{.1908} = 219.50$$

$$\text{estimate of } b_1 \text{ in (10.45)} = \frac{-30.15}{.1908} = -158.02$$

Consequently, the estimated version of (10.46) is

$$\hat{Q}_t^* = 219.50 - 158.02 P_t, \qquad \text{partial adjustment} = .1908 \qquad (10.49)$$

As pointed out above, the short-run price response is obtained from (10.48) as -30.15, and the long-run price response is obtained from (10.49) as -158.02.

Probably the most important message of this simple illustration is the role of theory prior to estimation. As shown, two different theoretical arguments (ad hoc versus partial adjustment) yielded exactly the same "set of numbers." Yet these numbers produce a different economic statement because they had to be interpreted in different contexts.

Summary

A theory is the starting point for empirical work. Theory, not data, not techniques, not high R^2, is the guiding light for applied research. The questions addressed in this chapter are only suggestive of the many faced by applied researchers whenever they do the hard work necessary to go from abstract theory to a precise, practical estimating equation. Although we have shown how these techniques can be used, we have offered little in the way of guidance with respect to when they should be used. A platitude has to suffice: Do whatever best fits your theory and your research objective. Reading and understanding what others have done before you when faced with similar problems is a good beginning point, so always review the literature on your research topic. But real learning comes only with practice and experience.

Terms

Adaptive expectations model	Partial adjustment model
Beta coefficient	Per capita
Cobweb model	Real
Deflation	Scaling
Elasticity	Standardized coefficient
Lagged variable	Standardized regression
Nominal	

Exercises

10.1 Consider the following OLS regression results:

$$Y^* = 3 + 2X^* + e^*$$

where X and Y were transformed to X^* and Y^* before estimating the regression. The results in terms of the original units would be

$$Y = b_0 + b_1X + e$$

What would b_0 and b_1 be in each of the following cases?

(a) $Y^* = Y$ $X^* = .10X$
(b) $Y^* = 100Y$ $X^* = X$
(c) $Y^* = Y$ $X^* = X + 5$
(d) $Y^* = Y + 2$ $X^* = X$
(e) $Y^* = Y + 2$ $X^* = X + 5$
(f) $Y^* = 100Y$ $X^* = 10X$
(g) $Y^* = 100Y + 2$ $X^* = X$
(h) $Y^* = Y$ $X^* = 10X + 5$
(i) $Y^* = 100Y + 2$ $X^* = 10X + 5$

10.2 Consider the general OLS regression equation

$$Y = b_0 + b_1X + e$$

After linear transformation on Y and X, you could obtain the estimated equation

$$Y^* = b_0^* + b_1^*X^* + e^*$$

Express b_1^* and b_0^* in terms of b_0 and b_1 in each of the following cases. (Note: f, g, h, and k are constants.)

(a) $Y^* = Y$ $X^* = fX$
(b) $Y^* = gY$ $X^* = X$
(c) $Y^* = Y$ $X^* = X + h$
(d) $Y^* = y + k$ $X^* = X$

(e) $Y^* = Y + k$ $X^* = X + h$
(f) $Y^* = gY$ $X^* = fX$
(g) $Y^* = gY + k$ $X^* = fX$
(h) $Y^* = Y$ $X^* = fX + h$
(i) $Y^* = gY + k$ $X^* = fX + h$

10.3 Consider the following regression results:

$$S = 2 + 1.20I + .15T + 1.50K + e$$

where S = amount family spends on refreshments during a
            day on the beach, dollars
       I = annual family income, thousands of dollars
       T = temperature, degrees Fahrenheit
       K = number of kids along

Using the same sample data.
(a) What would b_I be if "income" were measured in dollars?
(b) What would b_t be if "temperature" were measured in degrees Celsius? (HINT: $C° = -17.78 + .5556 F°$.)
(c) What would b_K be if S were measured in pennies?
(d) What would b_0 be if S were measured in pennies?

10.4 Are each of the following methods for determining which variable is "most important" in the regression equation valid? Why?
(a) The variable with the largest regression coefficient is the most important.
(b) The variable with the highest correlation coefficient with the dependent variable is the most important.
(c) The variable with the highest t-ratio is the most important.
(d) The variable with the highest standardized regression coefficient is the most important.
(e) The variable with the largest response elasticity with respect to the dependent variable is the most important.

10.5 Consider the following cross-sectional data set for a sample of cities.

City	Government Spending for Safety, G (Thousands)	Population, P (Hundreds)	Property Value, V (Millions)
Appleton	$10	10	$200
Bentpine	14	15	220
Culver	20	18	240
Duluth	28	30	260
Edgerton	40	45	280
Franklin	60	70	300

Suppose that you were interested in determining how "property valuation" affected spending for public safety. (NOTE: A computer may help in doing the necessary calculations.)

(a) What are the simple correlation coefficients among G, P, and V?
(b) What are the simple correlation coefficients among per capita G, per capita V, and P?
(c) Estimate $G = b_0 + b_1 V + e$. What effect do property values have on government spending for public safety? Is it statistically significant?
(d) Estimate $G = b_0 + b_1 V + b_2 P + e$. What effect do property values have on city spending for public safety if population is held constant? Is it statistically significant?
(e) Estimate $G/P = b_0 + b_1 V/P + e$. What effect does per capita property valuation have on per capita public safety spending? Is it statistically significant?
(f) Which model [from part (c), (d), or (e)] is most useful for addressing the basic question?

10.6 Consider the following time-series data set for a small county:

Year	Rice Consumption, R (Pounds)	Income, I (Thousands)	Population, P
1900	1000	$200	10
1910	1100	205	9
1920	900	210	8
1930	800	215	9
1940	900	220	6
1950	600	225	4
1960	700	230	5

(a) Compare the correlation coefficients among R, I, P, and the corresponding per capita variables.
(b) Calculate $R = b_0 + b_1 I + e$. What effect does I have on R if population is not held constant?
(c) Calculate $R = b_0 + b_1 I + b_2 P + e$. What effect does I have on R if population is held constant?
(d) Calculate $R/P = b_0 + b_1(I/P) + e$. What effect does per capita income have on per capita rice consumption?
(e) How do you explain the difference between your conclusions in parts (d) and (c)? Are the two results consistent?

10.7 Consider the following time-series data on quantities (Q), price (P), and a general price index (G).

Year, Y	Q	P	G
1972	10	21	1.0
1973	11	22	1.0
1974	12	25	1.2
1975	14	23	1.4
1976	16	28	1.9
1977	13	24	2.3

Year, Y	Q	P	G
1978	15	26	2.6
1979	19	30	2.7
1980	16	27	2.9
1981	20	29	3.0
1982	17	32	3.2

(a) Plot P versus Y, Q versus Y, and P versus Q. What do you think is the likely form of the relationship between Q and P?

(b) Calculate $Q = b_0 + b_1 P + e$ and interpret your result.

(c) Plot P/G versus Y and Q versus P/G. What do you conclude about the relationship of Q and P/G?

(d) Calculate $Q = b_0 + b_1(P/G) + e$.

(e) What conclusions can you draw from looking at the plots and the OLS equations?

(f) Calculate $Q = b_0 + b_1 P + b_2 Q + e$ and compare the results to part (d).

10.8 Consider the following time-series data set.

Year, Y	Output, Q	Price, P
1976	100	2
1977	50	10
1978	120	3
1979	60	9
1980	90	4
1981	60	8
1982	80	5
1983	70	6

(a) Plot Q_t versus P_t and label each observation. Connect the observations. What do you conclude?

(b) What is the correlation between Q_t and P_t?

(c) Calculate $Q_t = b_0 + b_1 P_t + e$.

(d) What is the correlation between Q_t and P_{t-1}?

(e) Estimate the coefficients of a simple cobweb model:

$$Q_t = b_0 + b_t P_{t-1} + e$$

(f) Compare the models and decide which seems most appropriate.

11

Functional Form

In Chapter 8 we began with the basic regression equation (8.1) and quickly went on to consider the specific variables to include in the equation, how to collect the data, and so on. In this chapter we consider the mathematical form of various equations from the standpoint of the economic statement they make about the system being studied by the applied researcher. The basic message of this chapter is that when the applied researcher writes an explicit form for the population regression equation to be estimated, a specific statement is made about the economics of the system, be it the consumption of peanuts or the multiplier effect of retail sales on regional employment levels. The population regression equation makes two statements: an *economic statement* about how the variables in the equation are related and a *statistical statement* about the distribution of the population disturbance term. The economic statement is discussed in this chapter.

After making the distinction between a mathematical and an econometric equation, this chapter uses a simple example to illustrate how theory and functional form are interrelated. The illustration stresses that by first thinking through the economics of the research problem, the applied researcher is, in most cases, able to write an explicit mathematical equation that possesses the desired economic properties. This example is followed by a brief discussion of the basic mathematical properties of linearity and additivity of an equation that have economic implications. With the stage thus set, various functional forms enjoy their moment on center stage, one by one. Those in the audience with little or no facility in differential calculus may find the script difficult to follow, but with a little work and a lot of patience the lines will make enough sense that the message can be transferred to applied research.

An Important Distinction

Consider first the important but often underemphasized distinction between a *mathematical equation* and an *econometric equation*. Failure to recognize this distinction in applied research can lead to serious consequences, notably the inability to claim the BLUE properties of the OLS estimators. This distinction arises in the following way. Consider the mathematical equation

$$Y = \beta_0 + \beta_1 X \tag{11.1}$$

The property of this equation germane to the present discussion is *reversibility*. By simple algebraic manipulation, this equation can be rewritten as

$$X = \frac{Y - \beta_0}{\beta_1} \tag{11.2}$$

without changing anything of substance. Only the presentation of the relationship between Y and X is changed. As a general proposition, if $Y = f(X)$, it is possible to write $X = f^{-1}(Y)$, where $f^{-1}(\ )$ is the inverse function notation.

Now consider an econometric equation,

$$Y = f(X, U) \tag{11.3}$$

where U is the population disturbance term. In regression theory, U is included as the measure of the combined effect of all the independent variables that are not, for whatever reason, included in (11.3). Moreover, (11.3) is specified and interpreted in the context of economic theory. In particular, on the basis of theory, defined broadly as in Chapter 8, (11.3) is a *causal* relationship, with the direction of causality running from X to Y, not Y to X. Moreover, estimating the parameters of (11.3) is based on the crucial assumption of no correlation between X, the independent variable, and U in (11.3). Indeed, this lack of correlation between X and U, this independence of X from the random variation in the system as measured by U, is one of the things that makes X the independent variable.

The upshot is that if (11.3) is the properly specified population regression equation, as it is assumed to be here, it would be improper to estimate

$$X = f^{-1}(Y, U) \tag{11.4}$$

by OLS procedures because, by (11.3), Y and U are not independent. That the relationship between causality derived from the underlying theory and the stochastic component of the equation is crucial for estimation is something that often receives little attention in applied research. Typically, applied researchers experiment with various explicit equations without paying much, if any, attention to the disturbance term. Then, willy-nilly, they tack a disturbance term on to the end of the equation and estimate the regression equation. Although there may be nothing wrong with doing this, the distinction here suggests that some thought should be given to where in the manipulations U should be introduced. When and where the disturbance term is added matters because it also says something about which variables in the equation are dependent and which are independent, and it says something about the distribution of the disturbance term. How the disturbance term is handled affects the properties of the resulting estimates.

Having said all this, the disturbance term is ignored in the remainder of this chapter. Although the importance of the disturbance term and related statistical properties and problems must be recognized, the intent in this chapter is to concentrate on the economics of various functional forms without getting mired in metaphysical propositions about unobservable disturbance terms.

Theory and Functional Form: An Illustration

Suppose that a researcher wanted to estimate the production function for corn. Microeconomic theory says that output is a function of the amounts of inputs used in production. Let land, labor, and capital be the major inputs and write the production function as

$$Q = f(L, H, K) \qquad (11.5)$$

where Q is corn output, L is the amount of land, H is the amount of human input (labor), and K is the amount of capital (machinery) used in production. This general statement of the underlying relationship among the variables is the beginning of quantitative work. Estimation of this production function, however, requires researchers to go from the general equation (11.5) to a specific mathematical function.

After laboring through the first 10 chapters of this book, one might write the following equation:

$$Y = \beta_0 + \beta_1 X_1 + \beta_2 X_2 + \beta_3 X_3 \qquad (11.6)$$

where X_1 is land, X_2 is labor, and X_3 is capital. There is nothing wrong with this function mathematically, but the specific statements (11.6) makes about the production function are another matter.

Taking the partial derivatives of (11.6) with respect to each input yields

β_1 = marginal physical product of land in corn production

β_2 = marginal physical product of labor in corn production

β_3 = marginal physical product of capital in corn production

These results make two important, explicit statements. First, the marginal physical product of each input is constant with respect to its level of application. Equation (11.6) states that output increases by the same amount (β_i) in response to a 1-unit change in X_i, no matter how large or small the application of X_i to which the marginal application is made. This is bothersome because production theory says that inputs (at least over the economically viable stage 2 of the production function) have positive but *declining* marginal physical products. Neoclassical production theory assumes that the eighty-first hired hand is not likely to add as much to output as the second hired hand. Equation (11.6) disagrees.

Second, (11.6) says that the marginal physical product of each input is independent of the application level of the other inputs. It is, of course, possible that an added laborer can contribute as much to corn production with a shovel as with a tractor, but it is not very likely. Similarly, the contribution a large piece of capital, such as a tractor, can make to production is likely to vary with the amount of land available to till. Equation (11.6) says "not so."

These results are a consequence of writing (11.6) to represent (11.5) without thinking through what production theory has to say about the nature of marginal physical products. As mentioned previously, theory suggests that as the use of an input increases there comes a point where marginal physical product begins to decline, where an added unit of input will contribute *less* to total output than the previous unit of input. Moreover, it seems reasonable to expect the productivity (marginal physical product) of an input to differ depending on the application level of all other inputs.

The point is that not spending enough time theorizing before writing the equation to estimate can get applied researchers in a bit of trouble. An important implication for applied researchers is to think through the research problem to determine exactly what kind of statement is desired *before* writing the equation.

What is needed is a mathematical form that exhibits two properties: (1) a positive but declining marginal physical product, and (2) a marginal physical product that depends on the application level of all inputs. Although many equations will yield these results, the following equation is a good form for illustrating the desired properties:

$$Y = \beta_0 X_1^{\beta_1} X_2^{\beta_2} X_3^{\beta_3} \tag{11.7}$$

This is the *Cobb–Douglass function*, frequently seen in economics textbooks. To demonstrate that this equation has the properties stated above, examine the case for X_1 and claim similar results for X_2 and X_3. [How to estimate the parameters of (11.7) is discussed later in the chapter.] The marginal physical product of X_1 is

$$\frac{\partial Y}{\partial X_1} = \beta_0 \beta_1 X_1^{\beta_1 - 1} X_2^{\beta_2} X_3^{\beta_3} = \frac{\beta_0 \beta_1 X_2^{\beta_2} X_3^{\beta_3}}{X_1^{1 - \beta_1}} \tag{11.8}$$

Assuming that the β_i's are all positive and less than 1, (11.8) shows two things. First, as X_1 increases with, X_2 and X_3 held constant, the rate of increase in Y decreases because X_1 appears in the denominator of the equation. Second, the marginal physical product of X_1 depends on the application level of X_2 and X_3 since both appear in the equation. These are the desired results, but it is important to recognize that they are based on the restrictions that $0 < \beta_1 < 1$, $0 < \beta_2 < 1$, and $0 < \beta_3 < 1$.

The point of this simple example is that it is necessary to think through a theory carefully and completely before writing the mathematical form of the equation to be estimated. An estimating equation must be consistent with the underlying theory in order to get the desired estimates.

Two Mathematical Concepts

Before examining the economic properties of various mathematical forms commonly used in applied research, two concepts essential to understanding the mathematical characteristics of an equation must be defined. These concepts, used frequently hereafter, are "linear in the variables" and "additive in the variables." Each is discussed separately below.

Linear in the Variables

To say that an equation is *linear in an independent variable* is to say that the marginal effect of that variable on the dependent variable does not depend on the level of the independent variable at which the marginal change occurs. An equation consisting of two independent variables provides an adequate example for demonstrating three propositions: (1) An equation may be linear in all variables, (2) an equation may be linear in some variables but not in others, and (3) an equation may be nonlinear in all variables.

Linear in All Variables

Consider the equation used throughout most of this book:

$$Y = \beta_0 + \beta_1 X_1 + \beta_2 X_2 \qquad (11.9)$$

This basic equation is linear in X_1 and in X_2 because the marginal effect of each does not depend on the level at which the marginal effect is calculated. To see this mathematically, write the partial derivatives

$$\frac{\partial Y}{\partial X_1} = \beta_1 \qquad (11.10)$$

and

$$\frac{\partial Y}{\partial X_2} = \beta_2 \qquad (11.11)$$

The two important characteristics to note are that X_1 does not appear on the right-hand side of (11.10), the equation that expresses the marginal effect of X_1 on Y; and X_2 does not appear on the right-hand side of (11.11), the equation that expresses the marginal effect of X_2 on Y. Mathematically, this indicates that the marginal effect of each independent variable is not a function of the variable itself.

Nonlinear in One Variable, Linear in the Other

An equation can be linear in one variable and nonlinear in another. An economic example might be a study of income determinants. Suppose there is reason to believe that income increases with age up to some age level and then decreases at higher age levels, and that income increases linearly with education. This could be expressed by

$$I = \beta_0 + \beta_1 A + \beta_2 A^2 + \beta_3 E \qquad (11.12)$$

The marginal effect of age (A) on income (I) is given by

$$\frac{\partial I}{\partial A} = \beta_1 + 2\beta_2 A \tag{11.13}$$

and the marginal effect of education (E) is given by

$$\frac{\partial I}{\partial E} = \beta_3 \tag{11.14}$$

The age variable (A) appears on the right-hand side of (11.13), which says that the marginal effect of age on income depends on the age level at which the marginal effect is measured. In other words, the marginal effect of age is itself a function of age. Hence income is *nonlinear* in age. According to the definition above, equation (11.14) shows income to be *linear* in education. Thus (11.12) is nonlinear in age and linear in education.

Nonlinear in All Variables

Finally, consider

$$Y = \beta_0 + \beta_1 X_1 + \beta_2 X_1^2 + \beta_3 \frac{1}{X_2} \tag{11.15}$$

Spinning a plausible theory to rationalize this equation is admittedly difficult, but it does have the property being illustrated.

From the discussion above, it is easy to see that (11.15) is nonlinear in X_1. The marginal effect of X_2 is

$$\frac{\partial Y}{\partial X_2} = -\beta_3 \frac{1}{X_2^2} \tag{11.16}$$

which, since X_2 appears on the right-hand side, shows the marginal effect of X_2 on Y to depend on the level of X_2 at which the marginal effect is measured. Thus (11.15) is nonlinear in both X_1 and X_2.

The General Case

Consider a general case. Let

$$Y = f(X_k), \qquad k = 1, \ldots, K \tag{11.17}$$

be the general form of the regression equation. If

$$\frac{\partial Y}{\partial X_k} \neq g(X_k) \tag{11.18}$$

that is, if X_k does not appear on the right-hand side of (11.18), then (11.17) is *linear* in X_k. If, on the other hand,

$$\frac{\partial Y}{\partial X_k} = g(X_k) \tag{11.19}$$

that is, if X_k does appear on the right-hand side of (11.19), then (11.17) is *nonlinear* in X_k.

Additive in the Variables

Additivity is similar to linearity in that it pertains to the marginal effect of a particular independent variable on the dependent variable. Additivity differs from linearity in that additivity is present if the marginal effect of a variable is not a function of any other variable in the equation. Because the treatment of additivity parallels that of linearity, examples are not necessary. Instead, the general results, using (11.17) as the base equation, may be stated directly. If

$$\frac{\partial Y}{\partial X_k} \neq g(X_i), \qquad i \neq k \qquad (11.20)$$

that is, if no X_i appears on the right-hand side of (11.20), then the marginal effect of X_k on Y does not depend on the level of X_i. Therefore, (11.20) is not a function of X_i. In this case, (11.17) is *additive* in X_k. If, on the other hand,

$$\frac{\partial Y}{\partial X_k} = g(X_i), \qquad i \neq k \qquad (11.21)$$

that is, if an X_i does appear in the right-hand side of (11.21), then the marginal effect of X_k on Y depends on the level of X_i [i.e., (11.21) is a function of X_i]. In this case (11.17) is *nonadditive* in X_k. Thus, as with linearity, an equation can be additive in all variables, additive in some variables and nonadditive in others, or nonadditive in all variables.

Equations (11.18) and (11.19) with (11.20) and (11.21) show both the similarity and difference between linearity and additivity. Loosely speaking, linearity is concerned with "own," or "direct," effects, while additivity is concerned with "cross effects."

Intrinsically Linear and Additive Equations

One final matter needs to be addressed before considering specific functional forms. As demonstrated in the previous sections, an equation may be linear or nonlinear and additive or nonadditive in one or more independent variables. A review of Chapters 3 to 6 reveals that the estimation theory developed there was applied to equations that are linear and additive in all variables. Yet the example used at the beginning of this chapter to illustrate the role of theory in specifying an equation to estimate led to equation (11.7), one that is not linear and additive in the three independent variables. In this section we discuss the conditions where OLS procedures can be used to estimate equations that are neither linear nor additive, such as (11.7).

A nonlinear, nonadditive equation can be estimated by OLS procedures if *two* conditions are satisfied. First, there must exist a transformation of the variables such that when the equation is rewritten using the transformed variables, the equation is linear and additive in the *transformed* variables. Second, the sample must provide sufficient information to permit computing the transformed variables. Two examples illustrate these two conditions.

Suppose that a researcher wants to estimate

$$Y = \beta_0 + \beta_1 X_1 + \beta_2 X_1^2 + \beta_3 X_1 X_2 \qquad (11.22)$$

which is nonlinear and nonadditive. Transforming the original variables as

$$X_2^* = X_1^2 \qquad (11.23)$$

and

$$X_3^* = X_1 X_2 \qquad (11.24)$$

the equation may be rewritten in terms of these transformed variables as

$$Y = \beta_0 + \beta_1 X_1 + \beta_2 X_2^* + \beta_3 X_3^* \qquad (11.25)$$

This equation is linear and additive in the transformed variables. The first condition for OLS estimation is satisfied. Moreover, the second condition is satisfied because X_2^* and X_3^* can easily be computed from the sample by (11.23) and (11.24), respectively.

By contrast, suppose that a researcher wanted to estimate

$$Y = \beta_0 + \frac{\beta_1}{X + \beta_2} \qquad (11.26)$$

Transform according to

$$X^* = \frac{1}{X + \beta_2} \qquad (11.27)$$

and rewrite the equation as

$$Y = \beta_0 + \beta_1 X^* \qquad (11.28)$$

which is linear and additive in the independent variable. However, the observations on Y and X in the data set provide no information about the value of β_2. Hence the transformed variable X^* cannot be computed from the sample, and therefore equation (11.26) cannot be estimated by OLS procedures.

In summary, an equation that is not linear and additive in all variables can still be estimated by OLS procedures if there exists a transformation on the variables that leads to a linear and additive equation and if the sample data permit the computation of the transformed variables. An equation is *intrinsically linear and additive* if both conditions hold. An equation that is not intrinsically linear and additive cannot be estimated by OLS. Such equations usually can be estimated by nonlinear estimation procedures, advanced techniques beyond the scope of this book.

Simple Functional Forms

In this section we use a one-independent variable equation to illustrate six specifications frequently encountered in applied research. Simple regression equations are used to analyze the economics of each specification. In the next section we demonstrate the flexibility of functional form with examples that combine two or more of the simple specifications considered here. More sophisticated functional forms, such as the trans-log function, are considered in more advanced texts.

In this section we consider three cases where the variables are measured in their natural units and three cases where the variables are measured in logarithms. Each functional form is first discussed in general terms and then estimated with the same data set in order to illustrate the difference in the underlying economic statements made by each specification.

Variables Measured in Natural Units

Linear

Begin with the linear equation, the easiest and most commonly used specification, written as

$$Y = \beta_0 + \beta_1 X \qquad (11.29)$$

This relationship between Y and X is demonstrated in Figure 11.1. The derivative, or slope, of the equation, β_1, is a constant, which means that Y changes β_1 units in response to a 1-unit change in X. If β_1 is positive, Y changes in the same direction that X changes. If β_1 is negative, Y changes in the opposite direction. If β_1 is zero, Y does not change as X changes and thus Y is a constant. In sum, this specification is linear in X because the marginal effect of X on Y is constant and does not depend on the value of X at which the marginal effect is evaluated.

In Chapter 10 we introduced the elasticity measure as one way to make comparisons regarding the relative effect of the independent variables on the dependent variable. The elasticity of Y with respect to X is defined as

$$E_{YX} = \frac{\% \text{ change in } Y}{\% \text{ change in } X} = \frac{\partial Y/Y}{\partial X/X} = \frac{\partial Y}{\partial X} \frac{X}{Y} \qquad (11.30)$$

which shows it to be a ratio of two percentages. An elasticity is computed by multiplying the slope of the line, $\partial Y/\partial X$, by the ratio X/Y, where the paired values for Y and X may be chosen from any point on the linear relationship. In Chapter 10 the elasticity was computed at the means of Y and X. However, the elasticity may be evaluated at other X/Y points on the line.

A fundamental characteristic of a linear function is a changing elasticity in X. To see this, consider case 1 in Figure 11.1, which specifies $Y = 20 + 10X$. The marginal effect of X is always 10, which means that a 1-unit change in X will result in a 10-unit change in Y, regardless of the level of X at which the change occurs. For example, if X increases from 2 to 3, then Y increases from 40 to 50, and if X increases from

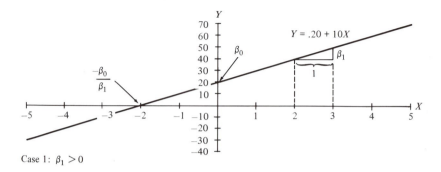

Case 1: $\beta_1 > 0$

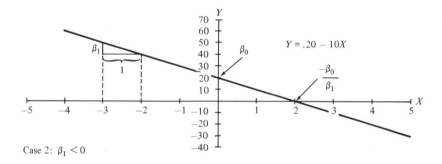

Case 2: $\beta_1 < 0$

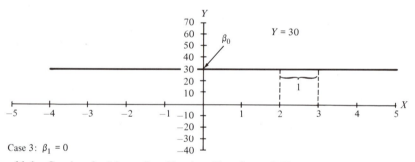

Case 3: $\beta_1 = 0$

Figure 11.1 Graphs of a Linear Specification: $Y = \beta_0 + \beta_1 X_1$.

30 to 31, then Y increases from 320 to 330. Now consider the elasticities at these points. When $X = 2$, Y must equal 40, and the elasticity of Y with respect to X at this point on the line is computed as $(10)(2/40) = .50$. On the other hand, at the point $X = 30$ and $Y = 320$ the elasticity is $(10)(30/320) = .94$. This demonstrates two important points: (1) the elasticity of Y with respect to X changes on a linear relationship, and (2) the sign of the elasticity is the same as the sign of the slope of the relationship. If the slope is positive, the elasticity is positive, and if the slope is negative, the elasticity is negative.

Now consider the *price elasticity* of a linear demand function. Let Y be the quantity demanded, Q, and X be the price, P. The elasticity of Q with respect to P, the price elasticity of demand, is the percent change in Q for a 1-percent increase in P. There will be points on the demand function where the absolute value of the elasticity will be greater than 1. At these points, a 1 percent change in P will result in an opposite (since the slope of the demand function is negative) change of more than 1 percent in the quantity demanded. Economists say that "demand is price elastic" in this portion of the demand function because the percentage change in Q is greater than the percentage change in P. Similarly, there are points on the demand function where the absolute value of the elasticity will be less than one. At these points, a 1 percent change in P will result in an opposite change of less than 1 percent in the quantity demanded. Economists say that "demand is price inelastic" in this portion of the demand function because the percentage change in Q is less than the percentage change in P. Finally, there will be one point where the absolute value of the elasticity is 1 because the percentage change in Q is equal to the percentage change in P. This is the point of *unitary price elasticity*.

In sum, a linear specification carries with it two statements of economic importance: (1) The marginal effect of X on Y is constant, and (2) the elasticity of Y with respect to X changes along the function. These statements may or may not be appropriate to a researcher's particular research objective.

Reciprocal

The reciprocal function is

$$Y = \beta_0 + \beta_1 \frac{1}{X} \qquad (11.31)$$

An examination of the examples in Figure 11.2 suggests why the reciprocal function might be of interest. If β_1 is positive (case 1), the function decreases at a decreasing rate as X increases. Technically, this function is a hyperbola. Notice that as X increases, $1/X$ decreases toward zero. Thus this function has a lower limit, called an *asymptote*, of β_0. Similarly, if β_1 is negative, the function has an upper asymptote of β_0.

The marginal effect of X on Y is given by

$$\frac{\partial Y}{\partial X} = -\beta_1 \frac{1}{X^2} \qquad (11.32)$$

and the elasticity is

$$E_{Y/X} = \frac{\partial Y}{\partial X} \frac{X}{Y} = -\beta_1 \frac{1}{X^2} \frac{X}{Y} = -\beta_1 \frac{1}{XY} \qquad (11.33)$$

A common use of reciprocal transformations is modeling systems with *satiation* or "minimum acceptable" levels for the dependent variable. Consider a satiation example from consumer theory. Let Y be the pounds of meat consumed per family member per week and let X be income. Other things constant, it is possible that as family income increases, meat consumption increases, but a smaller proportion of each increment in income would be spent on meat. In other words, meat consumption would increase at a decreasing rate. Moreover, it is possible that as income continues

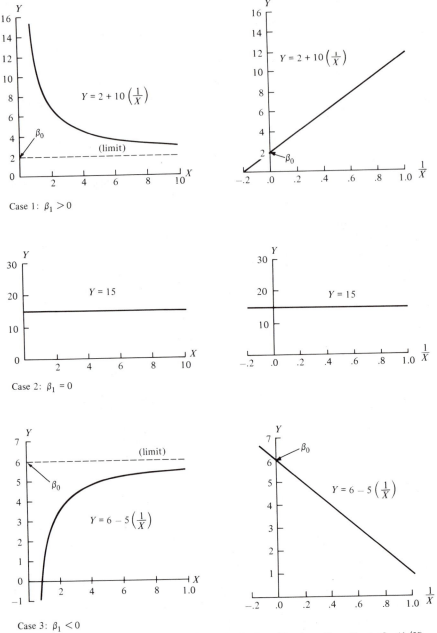

Figure 11.2 Graphs of a Reciprocal or Hyperbolic Specification: $Y = \beta_0 + \beta_1 (1/X)$.

to increase a point of satiation would be reached where additional income would not result in increased purchases of meat. A reciprocal specification would capture this relationship nicely.

Quadratic

The quadratic differs from the specifications above in that two empirical variables are required to measure the one generic variable X. The form is

$$Y = \beta_0 + \beta_1 X + \beta_2 X^2 \tag{11.34}$$

with examples given in Figure 11.3. The marginal effect of X is

$$\frac{\partial Y}{\partial X} = \beta_1 + 2\beta_2 X \tag{11.35}$$

and the elasticity is

$$E_{Y/X} = (\beta_1 + 2\beta_2 X)\frac{X}{Y} \tag{11.36}$$

There are three major reasons for using the quadratic. The first, and perhaps most prominent, reason is to capture *turning points*. Turning points occur when the effect of an additional unit of X causes a change in the direction of the effect of X on Y. Consider the familiar U-shaped marginal cost curve illustrated in case 2 of Figure 11.3. The marginal cost decreases first as additional units are produced. As output increases, the marginal cost of producing additional units begins to increase, and the slope of the marginal cost curve eventually goes from negative to zero to positive as output increases. In the marginal cost case, the quadratic parameters would take values such that $\beta_0 > 0$, $\beta_1 < 0$, and $\beta_2 > 0$. As X increases, X^2 will increase faster than X and eventually the positive value of $\beta_2 X^2$ will outweigh the negative influence of $\beta_1 X$, causing the function to turn up.

Finding the exact level of X at which the turning point occurs is simple. A turning point is the point at which the curve is flat or, more technically, where the first derivative of the dependent variable with respect to the single generic independent variable (X) is zero. For a simple quadratic, one without any other independent variables except X and X^2, the turning point occurs at the value for X such that $b_1 + 2b_2 X = 0$. More directly, the turning point occurs where $X = -b_1/2b_2$. If b_1 and b_2 have the same sign, there is no turning point at positive values for X (see cases 3 and 4 of Figure 11.3).

The second major reason for using a quadratic is to allow for a nonlinear relation between the independent and dependent variables. Often researchers are unwilling to accept the stronger assumptions required to use other nonlinear specifications, either on economic grounds or because of reduced flexibility. Moreover, over the range of observed values in the sample, the quadratic is often a good approximation of more complicated nonlinear functions.

A third reason for using a quadratic is related to the second. A quadratic also aproximates a linear relationship quite well. In fact, when β_2 is close to zero, the more general quadratic specification reduces to a linear specification (case 3). The null hypothesis that the relationship between X and Y is linear may be tested by regressing Y against X_1 and X_1^2 and then testing H_0: $\beta_2 = 0$. If the null hypothesis is rejected, a researcher may conclude that a relationship is nonlinear and give further thought to the appropriate nonlinear specification.

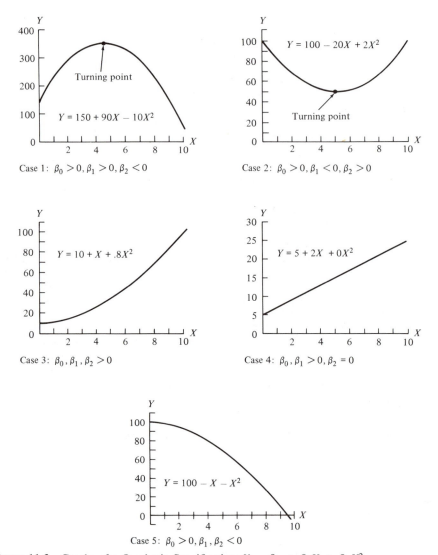

Figure 11.3 Graphs of a Quadratic Specification: $Y = \beta_0 + \beta_1 X + \beta_2 X^2$.

There are, however, costs as well as benefits associated with using a quadratic specification. First is the danger of introducing multicollinearity and its concomitant problems (see Chapter 12). Second is the loss of a degree of freedom for an "extra" independent variable. Although this might be a problem for small data sets, most economic data sets are large enough to handle the quadratic specification.

Variables Measured in Logarithms to the Base e

Log-Log
The example at the beginning of this chapter led to an equation of the form

$$Y = \beta_0 X^{\beta_1} \tag{11.37}$$

Consider whether (11.37) is linear in X by determining if the effect of X on Y depends on the level of X. Taking the first derivative of (11.37) yields

$$\frac{\partial Y}{\partial X} = \beta_1\beta_0 X^{\beta_1 - 1} = \beta_1\beta_0 X^{\beta_1 - 1}\frac{X}{X} = \frac{\beta_1\beta_0 X^{\beta_1}}{X}$$

$$= \beta_1\frac{Y}{X} \tag{11.38}$$

which shows that the effect of a 1-unit change in X on Y does depend on where the change in X occurs. In other words, the marginal effect of X changes as the level of X changes. Consequently, (11.37) is not linear in X.

Next consider the elasticity of (11.37), written as

$$E_{YX} = \frac{\partial Y}{\partial X}\frac{X}{Y} = \left(\beta_1\frac{Y}{X}\right)\frac{X}{Y} = \beta_1 \tag{11.39}$$

This shows that (11.37) is a constant elasticity function.

For the *linear* specification, the marginal effect of the X-variable is constant, but the elasticity changes as the X-variable changes. For the *multiplicative* specification, the marginal effect of the X-variable changes as the X-variable changes, but the elasticity is constant.

The multiplicative function is nonlinear and nonadditive in the variables and cannot, as it stands, be estimated by OLS procedures. However, the function is intrinsically linear because there exists a transformation that yields a linear and additive specification. The secret is to take the natural logarithm (denoted by ''ln'') of both sides of (11.37) to obtain

$$\ln Y = \ln \beta_0 + \beta_1 \ln X \tag{11.40}$$

After two transformations, $Y^* = \ln Y$ and $X^* = \ln X$, (11.40) may be rewritten

$$Y^* = \ln \beta_0 + \beta_1 X^* \tag{11.41}$$

which is linear and additive in the transformed variables.

It remains to consider whether the sample provides enough information to transform the variables according to the scheme above. In this case it does: define $Y^* = \ln Y$ and $X^* = \ln X$. Regressing Y^* on X^* will yield BLUE estimates of the coefficients of (11.37). Graphs of the original and transformed equation are shown in Figure 11.4.

In summary, the log-log specification has a number of appealing features. It allows for nonlinearity and nonadditivity in the variables, an economic property important in many instances. It is easy to understand, to estimate, and to interpret. Often the constant elasticity property is useful. Finally, a reminder: Logs of zero and of negative numbers are not defined.

Linear-Log

The linear-log function differs from the log-log function in that Y, the dependent variable, is measured in natural units, whereas X is measured in logarithms. Unlike the log-log function, the base of the logarithm for X does matter in the linear-log specification. Convention dictates using base e, the natural log, rather than logarithms

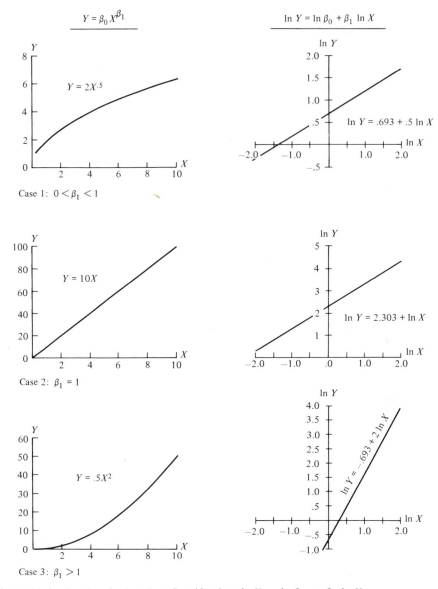

Figure 11.4 Graphs of a Log-Log Specification: $\ln Y = \ln \beta_0 + \beta_1 \ln X$.

to the base 10. An example of a linear-log function is given by

$$Y = \beta_0 + \beta_1 \ln X \qquad (11.42)$$

The marginal effect of X on Y is

$$\frac{\partial Y}{\partial X} = \beta_1 \frac{1}{X} \qquad (11.43)$$

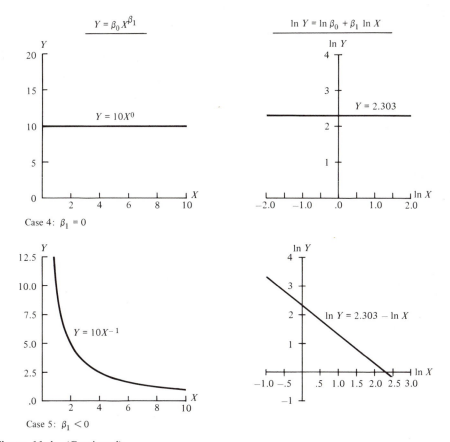

Figure 11.4 (Continued)

which shows (11.42) to be nonlinear in X. If β_1 is positive (case 1, Figure 11.5), as X increases Y continues to increase but at a decreasing rate. The opposite is the case if β_1 is negative (case 3). Note that (11.42) can be estimated by OLS using the transformation $X^* = \ln X$.

This functional form is a little tricky to interpret. It says that a given "percentage" change in X results in the same "absolute" change in Y. Let X in (11.42) change by some percent, say λ (for a 23 percent change, λ would be written .23), to give

$$Y' = \beta_0 + \beta_1 \ln (X + \lambda X) \tag{11.44}$$

Subtracting (11.42) from (11.44) yields

$$Y' - Y = \beta_1\{\ln [X(1 + \lambda)] - \ln X\} = \beta_1 \ln \frac{X(1 + \lambda)}{X} \tag{11.45}$$

$$= \beta_1 \ln (1 + \lambda)$$

which shows the change in Y for a given percentage change in X is constant, regardless of the actual level of X. Suppose that the regression equation is

$$Y = 16 + 29(\ln X) \tag{11.46}$$

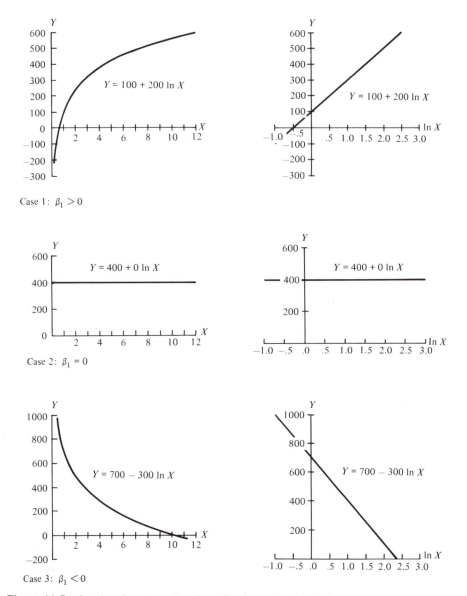

Figure 11.5 Graphs of a Linear-Log Specification: $Y = \beta_0 + \beta_1 \ln X$.

where X is in natural logs. According to (11.45), a 20 percent increase in X will cause a change in Y of

$$29 \ln (1 + .20) = 5.28732 \qquad (11.47)$$

This can be checked. If $X = 15$, $Y = 94.53346$; if X increases by 20 percent to 18, $Y = 99.82078$, for an increase of 5.28732. Now start with $X = 25$, with $Y =$

109.3474. Let X increase by 20 percent to 30, which means that $Y = 114.63472$, for an increase of 5.28732. Thus a 1 percent change in X will result in the same "absolute" change in Y regardless of the value of X at which the change in X occurs.

Finally, the elasticity of the linear-log function is

$$E_{Y/X} = \frac{\beta_1}{X} \frac{X}{Y} = \frac{\beta_1}{Y} \tag{11.48}$$

which shows that the elasticity is not constant, but instead changes inversely with Y. A given percent increase in X will result in the same *absolute* change in Y, regardless of where on the function the increase in X occurs, but the *percent* increase in Y will decrease as X increases. Other examples of the linear-log function are given in Figure 11.5. Notice that this function gives results similar to the reciprocal function, except that it does not have an aysmptote. Thus researchers who want a function in X that increases at a decreasing rate can choose between one that approaches a limit and one that does not.

Log-Linear

The log-linear function is written as

$$\ln Y = \beta_0 + \beta_1 X \tag{11.49}$$

and is illustrated in Figure 11.6. The log-linear specification is similar to the linear-log function, except that the dependent variable is measured in natural logs. This can also be written as

$$Y = e^{\beta_0 + B_1 X} \tag{11.50}$$

the familiar exponential function. The parameters of this equation are estimated by regressing $Y^* = \ln Y$ on X as shown in (11.49). The marginal change is given by

$$\frac{\partial Y}{\partial X} = \beta_1 e^{\beta_0 + \beta_1 X} \tag{11.51}$$

The elasticity of (11.50) is

$$\frac{\partial Y}{\partial X} \frac{X}{Y} = \beta_1 e^{\beta_0 + \beta_1 X} \frac{X}{e^{\beta_0 + \beta_1 X}} = \beta_1 X \tag{11.52}$$

An Example and a Comparison

The results of the previous sections are summarized in Table 11.1, which shows the nonlinear form of the equation, the linear form to estimate, the marginal effect on Y of a 1-unit change in X, and the elasticity, which expresses the percent change in Y for a 1 percent change in X. It is important to understand that the same general function, namely $Y = f(X)$, applies to each of the six functional forms shown in the Table 11.1. What differs is, of course, the specific mathematical formulation of this equation. As the text above pointed out and as this table reinforces, each functional form makes a different economic statement about the relationship between Y and X. This can be seen by observing the marginal effect of X for each equation. Some of

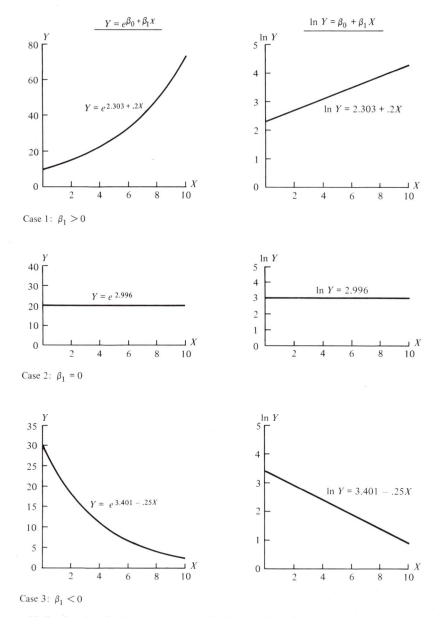

Figure 11.6 Graphs of a Log-Linear Specification: $\ln Y = \beta_0 + \beta_1 \ln X$.

these marginal effects are quite easy to interpret, the linear case being the easiest, whereas others are quite difficult to interpret, the log-linear being the most difficult.

The table also points out a problem for the applied researcher. The values for all the elasticities, except for the log-log specifications, depend on where the elasticity is evaluated. Alternatively, only the log-log is a constant-elasticity specification. This raises the question of where the elasticity should be measured. It is possible that the

Table 11.1. Comparison of Common Function Forms

Name	Nonlinear Form	Linear and Additive Form	Marginal Effect $\partial Y/\partial X$	Elasticity, $(\partial Y/\partial X)/(Y/X)$
Linear	—	$Y = \beta_0 + \beta_1 X$	β_1	$\beta_1 \dfrac{X}{Y}$
Reciprocal (hyperbola)	—	$Y = \beta_0 + \beta_1 \dfrac{1}{X}$	$-\beta_1 \dfrac{1}{X^2}$	$-\beta \dfrac{1}{XY}$
Quadratic (polynomial degree 2)	—	$Y = \beta_0 + \beta_1 X + \beta_2 X^2$	$\beta_1 + 2\beta_2 X$	$(\beta_1 + 2\beta_2 X)\dfrac{X}{Y}$
Log-log	$Y = \beta_0 X^{\beta_1}$	$\ln Y = \ln \beta_0 + \beta_1 \ln X$	$\beta_1 \dfrac{Y}{X}$	β_1
Linear-log (semilog)	$e^Y = e^{\beta_0} X_1^{\beta_1}$	$Y = \beta_0 + \beta_1 \ln X_1$	$\beta_1 \dfrac{1}{X}$	$\beta_1 \dfrac{1}{Y}$
Log-linear (exponential)	$Y = e^{\beta_0 + \beta_1 X_1}$	$\ln Y = \beta_0 + \beta_1 X_1$	$\beta_1 e^{\beta_0 + \beta_1 X}$	$\beta_1 X$

research objective may specify a measurement point, but more likely it will not. For this reason, in applied research elasticities are usually measured at the sample means of the variables.

To give some empirical substance to these general relationships, consider estimates for the simple regression equation

$$Y = f(X) \tag{11.53}$$

where Y = weekly food expenditures on food at home, $1 units
$\quad\quad X$ = average weekly income, $100 units

using each of the six functional forms. The estimated equations are presented in Table 11.2, which shows the linear and additive form of each and the nonlinear form where appropriate. All estimated coefficients are statistically significant at the .95 level.

The marginal effects and the elasticities for the equation in Table 11.2, computed according to the equations in Table 11.1, are presented in Table 11.3.

The important message in this table is that different formulations make different economic statements about the effect of a change in weekly income on weekly food expenditures. If, for example, a researcher believes that the linear specification is appropriate, a change of $100 in income will cause an increase of $2.30 per week in food expenditures. On the other hand, if the reciprocal function, with its asymptote, is deemed appropriate, a change of $100 in income will result in an increase of $.85 in weekly food expenditures. Similar statements can be made for the other functional forms.

Remember, however, that making comparisons such as these is of questionable validity because, in general, the marginal effect is determined by the specific point on the function where it is measured. For example, if the marginal effect of income

Table 11.2. Alternative Specifications of Same Simple Regression: $Y = f(X)$

Functional Form	Estimated Equation[a]
Linear	$Y = 40.81 + 2.2968X$ (2.69) (.5466)
Reciprocal	$Y = 55.34 - 13.4040X$ (2.28) (4.037)
Quadratic	$Y = 35.22 + 4.4720X - .1262X^2$ (3.91) (1.235) (.0644)
Log-log	$\ln Y = 3.54 + .2069 \ln X$ or $Y = 3.54X^{.2069}$ (.21) (.0484)
Linear-log	$Y = 37.50 + 10.6190X$ or $e^Y = e^{37.50}X^{10.6190}$ (3.17) (2.347)
Log-linear	$\ln Y = 3.61 + .0442X$ or $Y = e^{3.61 + .0442X}$ (.06) (.0113)

[a] Numbers in parentheses are standard deviations of estimates. Y = Weekly expenditures on food at home = \$1 units (sample mean = \$49.93); X = average weekly income = \$100 units (sample mean = 3.9718).

is measured at an income level of \$225 per week rather than at the sample mean (\$397 per week), the marginal effect of an income change on food expenditure for the *linear* specification would still be +\$2.30, but it would be +\$2.62 for the *reciprocal* specification. In one case, the marginal effect of an income change for the linear specification is greater than for the reciprocal specification. In the other case, the marginal effect is smaller for the linear specification. A relationship such as this can be quite troublesome if the research results are to be used in policy analysis, say in analyzing how income changes will affect food expenditures. For this reason, theory and the specific research objective must play the paramount role in specifying the functional form to estimate, while standard statistics, such as correlation coefficients and *t*-ratios, are of secondary importance.

Table 11.3. Marginal Effect of X on Y and Elasticities for Equations in Table 11.2[a]

Functional Form	Marginal Effect	Elasticity
Linear	2.30	.183
Reciprocal	.85	.068
Quadratic	3.47	.276
Log-log	2.60	.207
Linear-log	2.67	.213
Log-linear	.58	.175

[a] All computations at sample means.

Alternative Functional Forms

In the preceding section we considered only simple regression, to stress the economic aspect of the functional form. However, applied researchers typically work with more than one independent variable and may want to estimate an equation that is linear in one variable and nonlinear in another. Presented below are three examples with different specifications on the independent variables. Remember, however, that such specifications should be undertaken with extreme care and only after considerable thought with regard to justifying what is done, the form of error term, and how the results are to be interpreted and used.

The following illustrations are presented in the context of the general equation:

$$Y = f(\text{INC, HHS}) \tag{11.54}$$

where Y = weekly family expenditures on food consumed at home
INC = weekly average family income
HHS = number of family members eating at home

The linear and additive version of (11.54) is

$$Y = b_0 + b_1\text{INC} + b_2\text{HHS} + e \tag{11.55}$$

The estimated coefficients of this are given as equation 1 in Table 11.4. An increase of \$100 in income results in an increase of \$1.65 in weekly food expenditures, all else constant. An increase of one family member results in an increase of \$11.23 in weekly food expenditure, all else constant. Using the definitions of linearity and additivity, we find that this equation says that (1) a change of \$100 in income has the same effect on expenditure regardless of the level of income at which the \$100 change occurs (linearity), and (2) a change of \$100 in income has the same effect on expenditure regardless of family size (additivity). A similar interpretation obtains for the coefficients of HHS. This, as pointed out above, is the standard economic interpretation of a linear and additive specification.

Table 11.4. Regression Results Using Alternative Functional Forms for $Y = F(\text{INC, HHS})$[a]

Equation	Intercept	INC	ln (INC)	HHS	INC*HHS	HHS²	$\overline{R}^2$
1. Linear	2.35	1.65	—	11.23	—	—	.46
		(3.91)		(12.91)			
2. Interaction	42.32	−6.17	—	—	2.14	—	.38
		(−6.95)			(11.03)		
3. Linear-log	1.15	—	6.97	11.11	—	—	.45
			(3.80)	(12.69)			
4. Quadratic	10.54	1.68	—	6.78	—	.52	.46
		(3.99)		(1.92)		(1.30)	

[a] Standard errors in parentheses. Y = Weekly family expenditures of food eaten at home; INC = weekly average family income; HHS = number of family members eating at home.

There can be many instances where this may not be an appropriate economic interpretation. For example, it is possible to argue that the effect of a given income change on food expenditure varies by family size. In mathematical terms, this calls for an equation in which the derivative of food expenditures with respect to income is a function of family size. Although a number of equations can be written to satisfy this condition, consider a formulation that is often used in applied research. Write

$$Y = b_0 + b_1 INC + b_2 INC*HHS + e \qquad (11.56)$$

where INC*HHS is called an interaction variable. It is computed by multiplying the paired values of income and household size for each family in the data set. The marginal effect of income on food expenditure is then given by

$$\frac{\partial Y}{\partial INC} = b_1 + b_2 HHS \qquad (11.57)$$

which shows it to be a function of family size. The estimated equation, presented as equation 2 in Table 11.4, shows the marginal effect of income increasing as family size increases. However, the results have an implication that may be disturbing: The marginal income effect is negative for one-member and two-member households. Whether this is acceptable depends, of course, on the specific research question. The goal here is simply to demonstrate the use of an interaction variable.

The linearity property of income in the linear and additive formulation may not be acceptable. Instead, it might be argued that the amount of each additional dollar of income spent on food at home decreases as income increases. In this case, the expenditure function should be nonlinear in income. This suggests the following equation:

$$Y = b_0 + b_1 \ln (INC) + b_2 HHS + e \qquad (11.58)$$

where ln (INC) is the natural log of income and HHS is defined in natural units. In this case, the equation is linear-log in income and linear in family size. The estimate is shown as equation 3 in Table 11.4. The marginal effect of income on expenditure for this estimated equation is

$$\frac{\partial Y}{\partial INC} = 6.97 \left(\frac{1}{INC} \right) \qquad [\text{by } (11.43)] \qquad (11.59)$$

which shows the marginal income effect to decrease as income increases.

The final example is similar in that it specifies nonlinearity in the family size variable but differs by using a quadratic specification to capture the nonlinearity. The estimate of this form is given as equation 4 in Table 11.4. Since the coefficients of HHS and HHS-squared are both positive, the equation says that the marginal effect of an increase in family size on food expenditure increases at an increasing rate as family size increases (see Figure 11.3). This result may be acceptable, but it is certainly contrary to the experience of the authors of this book. That the t-ratio on the squared terms shows that it is not statistically significant suggests that either food expenditure is linear in family size or that the quadratic is not the proper specification to capture the nonlinearity.

Many combinations other than those illustrated above can be used in applied research. However, in all cases, a researcher should think through very carefully the justification for using combinations of functional forms. As the examples above suggest, even very simple formulations may yield results with unacceptable implications.

Summary

In this chapter we considered functional forms, an important but sometimes neglected issue in applied research. Only simple cases have been considered here, leaving the more complicated form for advanced texts. Nevertheless, there is enough material in this chapter to enable a researcher to evaluate any functional form that might seem important. The important thing is first to think through, in the context of the specific research question, the type of economic statement required of the functional form. Often this is most easily done by evaluating the expressions for the marginal effects of the variables and their elasticities. In this regard, it often helps to sketch out the function to see what it looks like.

This completes the four how-to-do-it chapters, which have tried to provide some ideas and hints on how to go about this creative activity known as applied research. The best way to learn the material in these chapters is to do some applied research.

Terms

Additive in X	Linear in X
Causal relationship	Linear-log
Cobb–Douglas function	Log-linear
Econometric equation	Log-log
Functional form	Mathematical form
General form	Nonlinear in X
Interaction variable	Quadratic in X
Intrinsically linear and additive	Reciprocal in X
Linear form	Reversibility

Exercises

11.1 Are the following functions implicit or specific?
(a) $Y = f(X_1 X_2)$
(b) $Y = \beta_0 + \beta_1 X_1 + \beta_2 X_2$
(c) $Y = \beta_0 + \beta_1 X_1 X_2$

(d) $Y = f(X_1, X_2/X_1)$
(e) $Y = \beta_0 + \beta_2(1/X_1) + \beta_3X_2^2$

11.2 Are the following equations mathematical or econometric?
(a) $Y = \beta_0 + \beta_1X + U$
(b) $Y = \beta_0 + \beta_1X$
(c) $y = \beta_1x$
(d) $x = \beta_1y + u$

11.3 Which of the following equations are linear in X_1?
(a) $Y = \beta_0 + \beta_1X_1 + \beta_2X_2$
(b) $Y = \beta_0 + \beta_1X_1 + \beta_2X_2 + \beta_3X_2^2$
(c) $y = \beta_1x_1 + \beta_2x_2 + \beta_3x_2^2$
(d) $y = \beta_1x_1 + \beta_2x_2x_1$
(e) $y = \beta_1(1/x_1) + \beta_2x_2$
(f) $\ln Y = \beta_0 + \beta_1 \ln X_1 + \beta_2 \ln X_2$
(g) $Y = \beta_0 + \beta_1 \ln X_1 + \beta_2X_2$

11.4 Which of the equations listed in Exercise 11.3 are linear in X_2?

11.5 Which of the equations listed in Exercise 11.3 are additive in X_1 *and* X_2?

11.6 Consider the following regression results:

$$Q = 10 + .88P + e$$

where Q = quantity demanded
P = price

(a) What do these estimates suggest about the elasticity of Q with respect to P, (E_{QP}), at the centroid ($\overline{Q} = 32$, $\overline{P} = 16$)?
(b) Would your estimate of E_{QP} be different if you used the same sample of observations on Q and P but the log-log functional form: $\ln Q = b_0 + b_1(\ln P) + U$? Why?

11.7 Three runners agree that best times in a mile run (T) decrease with each mile of training (M), $T = f(M)$, but they have different ideas about how miles trained influence times. Plodder says that each mile trained reduces T by a fraction of a second. Skeptic thinks that each mile lowers T, but not as much as the previous mile, and argues that no human runner can ever run a mile under 3:45. Champ argues that each 1 percent increase in miles trained causes T to drop by .2 percent. Specify a functional form, the expected signs, and null hypothesis for
(a) Plodder.
(b) Skeptic.
(c) Champ.

11.8 You have a theory that the number of season tickets for the local college basketball games (A) depends on the dollar price for individual games (P) and the number of games won the previous year (W): $A = f(P, W)$. You have data for the past 20 years and use OLS to estimate the two functional forms listed below:

    I. $A = 11,400 + 1200(W) - 1000(P) + e$

    II. $(A^*) = 8.6 + .9(W^*) - .6(P^*)$

where

$$\overline{A} = 8000 \qquad A^* = \ln A$$
$$\overline{W} = 8 \qquad W^* = \ln W$$
$$\overline{P} = 12 \qquad P^* = \ln P$$

(a) What is the estimated *marginal impact* on A of a $1 increase in P in model I? in model II?

(b) What is the estimated elasticity of A with respect to P in model I? in model II?

(c) What is the marginal impact of an additional win in the preceding year in each model?

(d) Which is the "correct" elasticity? Which is the "correct" marginal impact of price increase? Which is the "correct" marginal impact of an additional win?

11.9 Moe, Larry, Curly, and colleagues are arguing about what determines final exam grades (G). They agree that hours (H) studied somehow is important, but some think that weight (W) of students might matter too.

Moe says that W doesn't matter, but that G goes up 10 points every time H is doubled.

Larry says that W doesn't matter and that G goes up 10 percent for every 20 percent increase in H.

Curly thinks that W doesn't matter and that studying helps G, but diminishing returns are expected.

Shemp thinks that the first few hours of studying improves grades, but that additional hours just confuse and tire students and lower grades. Weight doesn't matter.

Laurel joins the argument because he thinks that weight matters. Every pound and every hour both help increase grades at a constant rate, but the heavier you are, the more effectively you study, because you move around less.

Hardy claims that all the hypotheses above are nonsense: neither weight nor hours studied influence grades because grades are random events.

(a) For each of the six scholars listed above, specify the functional form as well as the null and alternative hypotheses on H and W.

(b) Use the following data to test each of the null hypotheses indentified in part (a) at the 5 percent level of significance.

G	H	W
100	20	140
95	11	180
94	12	200
90	9	120
88	6	170
85	4	150
80	5	190
80	2	160
70	3	130
60	1	110

[NOTE: You may wish to use a computer for part (b) to avoid tedious calculations.]

11.10 After the hypotheses test in Exercise 11.9 our students are still arguing. All now agree that only hours studied (H) affects grades (G), but now the point of controversy is the appropriate functional form of that relationship. The estimated statistical models of Moe, Larry, Curly, and Shemp are presented below with their standard errors in parentheses:

Moe's model:

$$G = 63.278 + 12.567 \ln H + e \qquad \bar{R}^2 = .861$$
$$\quad (3.13) \qquad (1.67) \qquad\qquad S = 4.54$$

Larry's model:

$$\ln G = 4.1601 + .1578 \ln H + e \qquad \bar{R}^2 = .835$$
$$\qquad (.043) \qquad (.023) \qquad\qquad S = .063$$

Curly's model:

$$G = 94.587 - 37.293\left(\frac{1}{H}\right) + e \qquad \bar{R}^2 = .061$$
$$\quad (2.75) \qquad (7.05) \qquad\qquad S = 6.09$$

Shemp's model:

$$G = 63.531 + 4.253H - .1241H^2 + e \qquad \bar{R}^2 = .783$$
$$\quad (4.52) \quad (1.13) \qquad (.054) \qquad\qquad S = 5.66$$

(a) What is the marginal affect of an additional hour of study in each model? (Evaluate at six hours of study.)
(b) Shemp argues that Moe's and Larry's models are suspect because they imply that the longer your study, the higher the grade (i.e., there is no function

maximum), and that Curly's model is suspect because it does not permit a perfect exam score of 100. Check if Shemp's points are true by finding the maximum grade in each model.

(c) Larry argues that his model is better than Curly's and Shemp's because he has a higher adjusted coefficient of multiple determination. Is his model better?

(d) In Shemp's model, what number of hours will produce the highest grade?

(e) Which model do you think is the most reasonable representation of the population function generating exam grades? Why?

III

The Problems

The chapters in this section cover the standard econometric problems. Multicollinearity is discussed in Chapter 12. Omitted relevant variables and included irrelevant variables are covered in Chapter 13. Heteroscedasticity and autocorrelation are considered in Chapter 14. Errors in variables and missing observations are the subjects of Chapter 15. In each case, the nature of the problem is spelled out, its implications for the properties of the OLS estimators are assessed, and possible solutions to the problem are offered.

12

Multicollinearity

Applied researchers usually want to estimate the separate influence(s) of one or more variables on the dependent variable. For example, a researcher might be interested in the influence of income and education on consumption patterns, where the specific objective is estimating the effect of income on consumption, holding the effect of education constant, and the effect of education on consumption, holding the effect of income constant. This is expressed formally by the population regression function

$$Y = \beta_0 + \beta_1 X_1 + \beta_2 X_2 + U \tag{12.1}$$

where Y is consumption, X_1 is income, and X_2 is education. In this equation, β_1 is the change in consumption resulting from a unit change in income, and β_2 is the change in consumption resulting from a unit change in education. In the language of calculus, β_1 is the partial derivative of Y with respect to X_1, and β_2 is the partial derivative of Y with respect to X_2. A partial derivative measures the change in the value of Y with respect to a change in one independent variable, holding constant the effect of all other variables in the equation. It is these partial, or net, effects that need to be estimated.

At this juncture it is instructive to recall the discussion in Chapter 4 regarding the distinction between experimental and nonexperimental research. The experimental researcher is able to measure, or estimate, the net effect by analyzing the effect of one variable, say X_1, on Y, holding constant the effect on Y of all other variables by assigning them fixed values over all experiments involving the response of Y to changes in X_1. The important characteristic of experimental research is the researcher's ability to generate under controlled conditions the data needed for hypothesis testing. For (12.1), the ideal experimental design would permit the study of the consumption-income relation holding education constant, and the consumption–education relation holding income constant. In this way, the net effects of these two variables on consumption would be estimated. This ideal experimental design can seldom be used in the social sciences. Rather, the researcher must work with a sample of data generated by the economic system being studied, and this can pose a practical problem. Since the variables are generated by the same basic system, their values are likely to vary together in the sample.

In cross-sectional data, for example, people with high incomes will tend to be well educated. With time-series data, the situation is likely to be even worse because most economic variables move together, albeit imperfectly, as a result of underlying trends, business cycles, and the like. The practical implication of this is that the explanatory variables in a *particular* sample may exhibit some degree of incidental covariation. This is another way of saying that there may not be a substantial degree of independent movement of the explanatory variables in the sample the researcher is using to estimate regression coefficients. This lack of independent movement in the sample is called *multicollinearity*.

The implication of multicollinearity is easy to perceive intuitively. Suppose that Y is assumed to be a function of two variables, X_1 and X_2. If the values of the variables tend to move together in the sample at hand, the researcher may not be able to obtain a very precise estimate of the effect of a change in X_1 on Y, holding X_2 constant, since X_2 changes concomitantly with X_1. In the extreme, if perfect correlation exists between the two variables, either could be used to predict Y and the other would be superfluous. Usually, perfect correlation in the sample is not encountered, but sufficiently high correlations are frequently present to make it difficult to obtain precise estimates of the individual regression coefficients.

Multicollinearity is a *sample* problem, not a *population* problem. Multicollinearity does not arise if X_1 and X_2 are functionally related in the *population*, say by $X_1 = f(X_2)$. If that were the case, the functional relationship should be incorporated directly in (12.1) via a simultaneous-equation model. Multicollinearity arises because of nature's experimental design. Researchers in the social sciences must take the data as they are; they typically cannot conduct controlled experiments. As a result of nature's uncontrolled experiment, X_1 and X_2 *may* be correlated in a particular sample used to estimate population regression coefficients.

A major practical problem that multicollinearity poses is large standard errors of the estimated regression coefficients. This leads to what is often referred to as instability of the regression estimates. Although economic theory is helpful in identifying the variables to include in a particular analysis, these guidelines are usually quite general, particularly with regard to the specific empirical variables to include. Demand theory says that *substitutes* are important determinants of the demand for a particular commodity, but it does not indicate what the substitutes might be for a specific commodity such as apples, for example. Consequently, when working with a particular sample, it is customary to experiment with alternative specifications of the same basic equation. For example, in studying the demand for apples, the researcher might estimate a number of formulations of the demand function that differ by the specific substitutes used, such as pears, peaches, bananas, and the like, together with other variables specified by theory. If there is correlation among the variables in the sample, it can happen that the coefficients of some variables will be significant in some formulations and not significant in others. It is in this setting that the estimates are said to be *unstable*. This means that it may be difficult to reject a wide array of hypotheses concerning the values of the population coefficients. In this chapter we explore the problem of multicollinearity in applied regression analysis.

Effect on Regression Coefficients

The easiest way to see the effect of multicollinearity is to compare a simple regression and a multiple regression. The two basic equations may be written succinctly by expressing the variables in deviation form,

$$y = b_{y1}x_1 + e_1 \tag{12.2}$$

$$y = b_{y1.2}x_1 + b_{y2.1}x_2 + e_{12} \tag{12.3}$$

where b_{y1} and e_1 denote the simple regression with only X_1, and the "12" subscripts in (12.3) denote the multiple regression that includes the X_1 of (12.2) plus X_2. The separating period in "1.2" denotes the effect of X_1, holding constant the effect of X_2. The coefficient on X_2 is interpreted in a parallel fashion. In a pristine world, where the experiment is constructed, it seems reasonable to expect b_{y1} to equal $b_{y1.2}$. That is, the effect of X_1 on Y would be the same with or without X_2 in the equation since X_1 and X_2 are not, by assumption, functionally related in the population. To see the exact relation between these two OLS coefficients, start with basic OLS formulas from Chapters 3 and 4,

$$b_{y1} = \frac{\Sigma\, x_1 y}{\Sigma\, x_1^2} \tag{12.4}$$

$$b_{y1.2} = \frac{(\Sigma\, x_1 y)(\Sigma\, x_2^2) - (\Sigma\, x_1 x_2)(\Sigma\, x_2 y)}{(\Sigma\, x_1^2)(\Sigma\, x_2^2) - (\Sigma\, x_1 x_2)^2} \tag{12.5}$$

Then consider the relationship between b_{y1} and $b_{y1.2}$ in two slightly different but equally informative ways, first in terms of simple correlation coefficients and then in terms of regression coefficients.

Using the formula in Chapter 5 for a simple correlation coefficient between two variables, we can write terms such as $\Sigma\, x_1 y$ in (12.5) as $r_{y1}S_y S_1$, where r_{y1} is the sample correlation between Y and X_1, S_y is the sample standard deviation of Y, and S_1 is the sample standard deviation of X_1. Applying this formula to each of the cross-product terms in (12.4) and (12.5), respectively, yields

$$b_{y1} = r_{y1} \frac{S_y}{S_1} \tag{12.6}$$

$$b_{y1.2} = \frac{r_{y1} - r_{12}r_{y2}}{1 - r_{12}^2} \frac{S_y}{S_1} \tag{12.7}$$

Careful examination of (12.7) shows that the relationship between the coefficients of X_1 in (12.6) and (12.7) depends on r_{12}, the correlation between X_1 and X_2 in the sample. In other words, the relationship between b_{y1} and $b_{y1.2}$ depends on the degree of correlation between X_1 and X_2 (multicollinearity) in the sample. At one extreme, where r_{12} is zero, (12.7) collapses to (12.6). At the other extreme, where r_{12} is 1, (12.7) cannot be computed, since division by zero is undefined. In practice, r_{12} will be somewhere between these extremes, in which case (12.6) will not equal (12.7), depending on the specific values of the correlation coefficients.

Alternatively, by manipulations and substitutions similar to those above, (12.5) may be rewritten as

$$b_{y1.2} = b_{y1} - b_{21}b_{y2.1} \qquad (12.8)$$

or

$$b_{y1} = b_{y1.2} + b_{21}b_{y2.1} \qquad (12.9)$$

which provides a link between b_{y1} and $b_{y1.2}$

The simple and multiple regression coefficients for X_1 differ by the term $b_{21}b_{y2.1}$. Consider first $b_{y2.1}$, the effect of X_2 on Y with X_1 in the equation. Remember from Chapter 4 that $E(b_{y2.1}) = \beta_2$. If X_2 is a significant variable, as it is assumed to be by (12.1), then $\beta_2 \neq 0$, and $b_{y2.1}$ would not be expected to be zero. Consequently, the relation of interest hinges on b_{21}. But this coefficient is nothing more than the OLS regression of X_2 on X_1 using the sample data. Figure 12.1 illustrates this relationship. If X_1 is the only variable in the equation, b_{y1} is the direct effect on X_1 on Y, as shown by the horizontal arrow at the top. If X_2 is added to the equation and if X_1 and X_2 are correlated in the sample, the relationship is captured by b_{21} or through the sample regression of X_2 and X_1. This is shown by the vertical arrow. This effect is in turn transmitted to Y by $b_{y2.1}$. So the key to the relationship between b_{y1} and $b_{y1.2}$ is b_{21}, the sample regression coefficient with X_2 as a dependent variable and X_1 as an independent variable. If X_1 and X_2 are not related in this sample, b_{21} is zero and $b_{y1} = b_{y1.2}$. In other words, if multicollinearity exists in the sample because $b_{21} \neq 0$, it is difficult to measure the separate (net) effect of one explanatory variable because the OLS estimate of that effect will reflect that variable's relationship with the other explanatory variables in the sample.

Equation (12.9), sometimes called an *auxiliary regression*, is *descriptive*, since under the classical regression assumptions the X-values are fixed in repeated sampling and thus are nonstochastic. However, in a particular sample, X_1 and X_2 can exhibit covariation. So b_{21} is a sample phenomenon. Such auxiliary regressions are encountered in later chapters.

In the population, represented by (12.1), X_1 and X_2 are not assumed to be func-

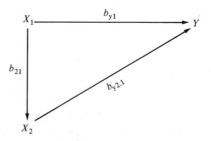

Figure 12.1 Simple, Partial, and Auxiliary Regression Coefficients.

tionally related. If there are a priori grounds for arguing that X_1 and X_2 are functionally related, then (12.1), written as a single-equation model, would not be properly specified because the functional relationship between X_1 and X_2 in the population is not explicitly recognized. However, many of the variables used in applied regression analysis are generated by the same underlying system ("nature's" experimental design), and researchers are likely to find in the sample linear relationships among the independent variables as manifested by $b_{21} \neq 0$ in the auxiliary regression (12.8). When this occurs, multicollinearity exists in the sample. One consequence of this is that the estimate $b_{y1.2}$ will not in general equal the estimate, b_{y1}, as shown by (12.7) or (12.9). This is one reason why in applied work coefficients may change as alternative formulations of the basic equation are estimated from the same sample of data.

Multicollinearity is really a matter of degree. In the extreme case where the linear relation between X_1 and X_2 in the sample is exact, the estimating procedure breaks down [see equation (12.7)]. This is why it is necessary that there be no exact linear relationship between X_1 and X_2. At the other extreme, if $b_{21} = 0$, then $b_{y1} = b_{y1.2}$. Typically, researchers encounter something in between the two cases. Multicollinearity is almost always a fact of life in applied research, but it varies in degree, depending on the sample at hand.

Effect on Coefficient Variances

The estimators of the variances of $b_{y1.2}$ and $b_{y2.1}$ [(4.41) and (4.42)] can be rewritten in terms of the simple correlation between the two independent variables:

$$S^2_{b_{y1.2}} = \frac{\Sigma\, e^2}{n - 3} \frac{1}{\Sigma\, x_1^2\, (1 - r_{12}^2)} \tag{12.10}$$

and

$$S^2_{b_{y2.1}} = \frac{\Sigma\, e^2}{n - 3} \frac{1}{\Sigma\, x_2^2(1 - r_{12}^2)} \tag{12.11}$$

where r_{12}^2 is the square of the correlation between X_1 and X_2 in this particular sample. For the extreme case where $r_{12}^2 = 0$, there is no linear relation between X_1 and X_2, and these equations reduce to

$$S^2_{b_{y1.2}} = \frac{\Sigma\, e^2}{n - 3} \frac{1}{\Sigma\, x_1^2} \tag{12.12}$$

and

$$S^2_{b_{y2.1}} = \frac{\Sigma\, e^2}{n - 3} \frac{1}{\Sigma\, x_2^2} \tag{12.13}$$

as the estimated variances. For the other extreme case, where $r_{12}^2 = 1$, the denominator in (12.10) and in (12.11) is zero, resulting in an undefined computation. Thus, as was observed in the preceding section, the entire estimating procedure breaks down in the case of perfect multicollinearity.

For the case typically encountered in research, $0 < r_{12}^2 < 1$, equations (12.10) and (12.11) provide the variances of the regression coefficients. A comparison of these equations with (12.12) and (12.13) reveals that multicollinearity in the sample increases the variances of the coefficients. Moreover, the greater the degree of multicollinearity (the greater the value of r_{12}^2), the larger the variances. As r_{12}^2 approaches 1, the denominator in (12.10) and (12.11) decreases and, consequently, the estimate of the variance increases. In sum, the greater the degree of multicollinearity the less precise will be the estimates of the parameters.

This matter of the precision of the estimates is crucial in hypothesis testing. The t-test for $b_{y1.2}$ is

$$\text{computed } t = \frac{b_{y1.2} - \beta_1^*}{S_{b_{y1.2}}} \tag{12.14}$$

where β_1^* is the hypothesized value for β_1. If, due to a high degree of multicollinearity in the sample, the denominator of this ratio is very large relative to the numerator, the t-ratio will tend to be small. Consequently, it will be necessary to not reject a wide range of hypotheses concerning the value of β_1. To state the converse, it will be difficult to reject rather diverse hypotheses concerning the value of β_1.

An alternative way to visualize this problem is to construct a confidence interval around $b_{y1.2}$ for a significance level α, as

$$\text{confidence interval} = b_{y1.2} \pm t_\alpha S_{b_{y1.2}} \tag{12.15}$$

which will include β_1 with a probability $(1 - \alpha)$. Since the upper and lower limits of this interval are a function of $S_{b_{y1.2}}$, it is clear that the larger the estimated variance, the greater the range of possible values for β_1. Thus the effect of multicollinearity is to widen the confidence interval and thereby reduce the precision of the OLS estimates.

An important point must be made before moving on. The analysis shows that multicollinearity causes the standard error to be larger than it would be otherwise and, thereby, the t-ratio to be smaller than it would be otherwise. Although this makes it more difficult to discriminate among alternative hypotheses concerning the value of β_1, it does not imply that the computed t-ratio *must necessarily* be less than the critical t-ratio. The null hypothesis is not perforce not rejected whenever multicollinearity appears in a sample. All it says is that the t-ratio will be lower in the presence of multicollinearity. For example, the t-ratio might be, say, 6.92 rather than 8.40, in which case the null hypothesis is still rejected. Multicollinearity is a fact of life for applied researchers, one that researchers do not worry much about unless it causes a serious problem, such as a t-ratio below the critical value. Then researchers worry about it, but not too much. There is really nothing that can be done about multicollinearity, other than make compromises. But even these compromises, some of which are mentioned below, do not make the problem go away.

Detecting Multicollinearity

The major signal of the multicollinearity problem is the presence of high values for the variance of the estimated coefficients since, as shown in the preceding section, the effect of multicollinearity is to increase the variance estimates. Again, it must be emphasized that this is only a warning because it may well be that the variables in the equation are not appropriate to the system being studied. With this caveat, a large value for the variance is in practice often used as an indicator of the presence of the problem. In fact, it can happen that none of the coefficients are significantly different from zero because of multicollinearity, yet the R^2 for the equation may be quite large (or the F-test rejects H_0 that the variables taken together equal zero), indicating that a substantial portion of the variance in the dependent variable has been "explained" by the independent variables. In such a case, severe multicollinearity exists and poses an obvious problem when interpreting the coefficients.

For the *two*-explanatory-variable case, the r_{12}^2 is a measure of multicollinearity. However, even in such a simple case there is no benchmark for what level of r_{12} is "too high." There is no magic level signifying the presence of "severe" multicollinearity and hence a problem. Further, when more than two explanatory variables are involved, detecting multicollinearity is complex. It is quite possible that although none of the simple correlation coefficients (these can be printed out as a correlation matrix by most computer programs) are large, substantial multicollinearity may exist because one of the variables is highly correlated with some *subset* of the other variables. That is, a multiple correlation coefficient, say $R_{2.46}^2$ from the sample regression of X_2 on X_4 and X_6, may be quite large. Thus one should derive little comfort from observing no large values in the matrix of simple correlations. Another possibility is to regress *each* independent variable against *all* other independent variables and use the resulting R^2's as measures of multicollinearity. If one or more of these R^2's is "large," there is evidence of multicollinearity in the sample. In this case, the dependent variable of this artificial sample regression does not add any new information and can, on *statistical* grounds, be removed from the basic equation.

A variation of this multiple R^2 method for detecting a potential problem of multicollinearity, called the *variance inflation factor* (VIF), is computed as part of the standard output by some regression software packages. The VIF is developed as follows. Rewrite (12.10) slightly to obtain

$$S_{b_{y1.2}}^2 = \frac{\Sigma\, e^2}{\Sigma x_1^2\,(n\,-\,3)} \frac{1}{1\,-\,r_{12}^2} \tag{12.16}$$

It was shown above that as r_{12}^2 increases, the ratio $1/(1\,-\,r_{12}^2)$ increases and consequently $S_{b_{y1.2}}^2$ increases. Hence $1/(1\,-\,r_{12}^2)$ is a *variance inflation*. This, of course, is not very interesting in this two-variable case because it is possible to "see" immediately what is going on simply by looking at r_{12} in the correlation matrix. However, this VIF is much more difficult to see in the case of a larger number of independent variables. In this case, the VIF, computed as $1/(1\,-\,R_{i.1,\ldots,j}^2)$ where

$R^2_{i,1,...,j}$ is the multiple correlation of X_i with all other independent variables in the regression, can be helpful. There is no firm guideline for how large the VIF should be; it is left to the researcher to consult the literature or more experienced econometricians for help in making a decision.

Remedies

Because the presence of multicollinearity results in a loss of precision in the estimates, it is natural to search for a means of addressing the problem. Unfortunately, there are not many solutions. A few that may be helpful in *some* situations are mentioned below.

In this chapter we have emphasized that multicollinearity is a problem with the sample being used. Therefore, one possible way to resolve the problem is to *obtain a new sample*. This is easier said than done. In cross-sectional studies it may be possible to take a new sample from the population being studied, but it is seldom practical to do so. Data collection by the interview method is an expensive undertaking and the cost of resampling is usually prohibitive. In time-series studies, where the number of years of observations is limited at the outset, there is little one can do in terms of obtaining a new sample. In either event, there is no guarantee that the new sample will be free of multicollinearity.

A second possible means of coping with the problem of multicollinearity is to *eliminate one or more of the variables*. Such action might reduce multicollinearity, but it might also introduce other problems. When only two explanatory variables are used in the equation, one can simply delete one or the other. Of course, there is the question of which to delete. When there are several explanatory variables in the equation, the problem is more difficult. It may not be easy to determine which of the variables are correlated with which other variables. Also, it may be that more than one variable is highly correlated with the same or a different subset of the remaining variables, raising the question of which two or more variables to delete. An even more serious potential problem is that deleting relevant variables can result in the introduction of bias into the estimates of the coefficients of the variables retained in the equation. This omitted relevant variable problem is developed in Chapter 13.

To illustrate what can happen in applied research, suppose that the research objective requires estimating the equation

$$Y = f(I, I2, A, \text{ALT19}, \text{HHS}) \tag{12.17}$$

where Y = weekly household expenditures for food consumed at home
I = weekly houshold income
$I2$ = income squared
A = age of head of household
HHS = household size
ALT19 = number of children under age 19 living at home

The quadratic specification on income assumes that food expenditures increase at a decreasing rate as income increases, a relationship supported by theory and by many empirical studies. Age of head of the houshold is an empirical measure of the conceptual variable "stage in family life cycle." The number of children under age 19 living at home is included as a distributional variable on household size, the idea being that, all else constant, the greater the number of children in the household, the larger the expenditures on food consumed at home.

This equation was estimated using a randomly selected subset of 235 households from a nationwide survey of U.S. households conducted in 1977 and 1978 by the U.S. Department of Agriculture. The estimated equation is

$$\hat{Y} = -10.45 + 2.16I^* - .04I2 + .19A + 13.03HHS^* - 2.03ALT19 \qquad R^2 = .463$$
$$\phantom{\hat{Y} = -}(6.45)\quad (.98)\quad\ (.05)\quad (.12)\quad (1.75)\qquad (1.98)$$

$$(12.18)$$

where the numbers below the coefficients are standard deviations of the estimates and an asterisk denotes a computed t-ratio larger than the critical t-ratio.

The coefficient on income has the expected positive sign and is statistically significant, and the coefficient on income squared has the expected negative sign but is not statistically significant, suggesting that the quadratic specification may not be appropriate for this data set. On the other hand, income and income squared may be highly correlated in the sample, causing high standard deviations of the coefficients. The household size variable has the expected sign and is statistically significant. Of economic concern, at least for those who have had the pleasure of raising a family, is the negative coefficient of ALT19. However, with the benefit of hindsight, it seems clear that there could be considerable sample correlation among the age, household size, and number of children under 19 variables. This, as the previous sections show, could explain the reverse sign on ALT19.

The correlation matrix for these independent variables is presented in Table 12.1. The obvious is documented. The sample correlation between income and income squared is very high. There is also substantial sample correlation between household size and the number of children in the household. Moreover, there is some correlation between the age of the head of the household and household size, not a particularly surprising result. However, as argued above, the presence of simple correlation in the sample does not necessarily mean that the "multicorrelation problem" exists. To

Table 12.1. Correlation Matrix of Independent Variables in Equation (12.18)

	I	I2	A	ALT19
I2	.898			
A	.165	.146		
ALT19	0	− .010	− .328	
HHS	.120	.057	− .167	.853

determine whether multicollinearity exists in the present case, a little experimentation is warranted.

Table 12.2 contains the base equation, (12.18), for reference, and two additional equations, one with ALT19 but not HHS (equation 1) and one with HHS but not ALT19 (equation 2). When ALT19 is used alone, it has the expected positive sign and is statistically significant. A similar result obtains when HHS is used alone. Note also that the age coefficient is of the right sign and statistically significant in both equations 1 and 2.

The base equation (12.18) contains both variables. A comparison of this with equations 1 and 2 reveals the effect of the sample correlation. In equation 1, the coefficient of ALT19 is positive and statistically significant, with a standard deviation of 1.11. In the base equation, this coefficient becomes negative with a standard deviation of 1.98, a 75 percent increase. In equation 2, the standard deviation of HHS is .88, and it doubles to 1.75 in the base equation. Changes of this magnitude when variables are added to or deleted from an equation are clear signals of the multicollinearity problem. In the present case, it is quite clear that HHS and ALT19 should not be in the same equation. In this particular sample, HHS increases primarily because there are more children in the household. Hence the sample does not permit testing hypothesis on *both* variables.

There is little more to be said regarding this type of experimenting for detecting and coping with multicollinearity. Ultimately, if a problem exists in a particular data set, there is nothing the applied researcher can do to make the problem go away. As in this example, the researcher may be forced to accept a final equation different from the one called for by the research objective. That is, it may not always be possible to test the hypotheses specified by the objective of the study. In other cases, two of which are demonstrated below, the researcher may be able to mitigate the problem by using information from outside the given sample, but this can result is a substantive recasting of the original objective of the study.

Another method for mitigating the effect of multicollinearity is to introduce *extraneous information*, information obtained from a source other than the sample being used. One possibility would be to estimate a parameter from one sample and then use it in such a way that only one parameter need to be estimated with another sample.

Table 12.2. Alternative Regression Equations Explaining Weekly Household Food Expenditure on 235 Households in 1977 and 1978[a]

Equation	Intercept	I	I^2	A	ALT19	HHS	$\bar{R}^2$
Base	− 10.45	2.16*	− .04	.19	− 2.03	13.03*	.463
	(6.45)	(.98)	(.05)	(.12)	(1.98)	(1.75)	
1	6.18	3.98*	− .11	.36*	10.66*	—	.336
	(6.72)	(1.05)	(.05)	(.13)	(1.11)		
2	− 9.97	2.35*	− .05	.23*	—	11.47*	.463
	(6.43)	(.96)	(.05)	(.11)		(.88)	

[a] An asterisk denotes a computed *t*-ratio greater than the critical *t*-ratio at $\alpha = .05$.

Suppose that a researcher wanted to estimate the effect of price and income on the purchases of a particular commodity. Price and income would probably be correlated in a time-series data set, raising the problem of multicollinearity. Let

$$C = b_0 + b_1 P + b_2 I + e \qquad (12.19)$$

where C is the purchases of a commodity, P is the price of the commodity, and I is income, be the equation to estimate. Assume that there is a cross-sectional data set, which is "outside" or "extraneous to" a time-series data set, that permits the estimation of the income effect by

$$C = d_0 + d_1 I + e \qquad (12.20)$$

For each year in the data set, use the I-values in the time-series data set to compute the consumption due to income by

$$\hat{C} = d_0 + d_1 I \qquad (12.21)$$

then estimate with the time-series data set

$$(C - \hat{C}) = c_0 + c_1 P \qquad (12.22)$$

where C is the time-series value of purchases and $(C - \hat{C})$ is the "income-adjusted" purchases.

This yields d_1 in (12.20) as the estimate of b_2 in (12.19) and c_1 in (12.22) as the estimate of b_1 in (12.18). To ensure that (12.18) goes through the midpoint of the time-series data set, compute b_0 in (12.18) by

$$b_0 = \overline{C} - c_1 \overline{P} - d_1 \overline{I} \qquad (12.23)$$

where $\overline{C}$, $\overline{P}$, and $\overline{I}$ are the sample means. This, however, assumes that d_1 is *known*. More likely, it will be an estimate of the income slope from some other research.

Another form of extraneous information that can be used is a constraint, or restriction, on the parameters being estimated. For example, in the estimation of a Cobb–Douglas production function it is possible to restrict it to be homogeneous of degree 1. Suppose that a researcher estimated

$$Y = b_0 X_1^{b_1} X_2^{b_2} \qquad (12.24)$$

where Y is the output, X_1 is input 1, and X_2 is input 2, with a sample where X_1 and X_2 are "highly" correlated. Introduce the constraint

$$b_1 + b_2 = 1 \qquad (12.25)$$

which states that (12.24) is homogeneous of degree one. This permits the equation to be rewritten

$$Y = b_0 X_1^{(1 - b_2)} X_2^{b_2} \qquad (12.26)$$

or

$$Y^* = C_0 + (1 - b_2) X_1^* + b_2 X_2^* \qquad (12.27)$$

where the asterisks denote the natural logs of the variables and $C_0 = \ln b_0$. This yields

$$Y^* = C_0 + X_1^* + b_2(X_2^* - X_1^*) \qquad (12.28)$$

or

$$(Y^* - X_1^*) = C_0 + b_2(X_2^* - X_1^*) \qquad (12.29)$$

Let $Q = (Y^* - X_1^*)$ and $I = (X_2^* - X_1^*)$ and obtain an estimate of b_2 from

$$Q = C_0 + b_2 I \qquad (12.30)$$

and obtain the estimate of b_1 from (12.25).

Other types of extraneous information and restrictions on the parameters might be introduced to permit estimation. Doing this does not purge the sample of multicollinearity. Although multicollinearity still exists, such manipulation may mitigate its effect. One example of this is expressing quantity data on a per capita basis and deflating prices and income by a price index as discussed in Chapter 10. However, such manipulations also may alter the research statement. There should always be an economic justification for imposing constraints. Constraints should not be imposed willy-nilly in an attempt to solve the multicollinearity problem. These constraints can be tested with the t-tests of F-tests discussed earlier.

Finally, more-advanced literature describes several techniques, such as ridge regression and principal components analysis, designed to mitigate the impact of multicollinearity. An applied researcher may or may not care to make the compromises necessary to use these techniques. They do not make multicollinearity go away.

A Concluding Observation

It is extremely unlikely that any applied researcher will ever enjoy the luxury of working with a data set free of any degree of multicollinearity. One way to avoid the attendant problems thereto is to avoid doing applied research involving regression analysis, but this is obviously not a real solution. If one chooses to engage in (or even read about) applied research, there is one important point concerning multicollinearity that must be understood; To use multicollinearity as an excuse for insignificant results is not valid. The confidence intervals, because of relatively large standard errors of the coefficients, are so wide as to preclude, or at least make difficult, discriminating among competing hypotheses. This could occur precisely because the variables in the equation are not the "right" variables. Moreover, to attribute the large standard errors to multicollinearity is to imply that in the absence of multicollinearity, significant results would be forthcoming. This is pure conjecture, unsupportable by the sample at hand. If the sample produces large variances, then there are large variances. If the sample does not permit discrimination among competing hypotheses, one cannot discriminate among competing hypotheses. That is all that can be said.

Summary

All data sets used in applied regression analysis are afflicted with multicollinearity. The problem is a matter of degree: Sometimes it is high, sometimes it is low, but multicollinearity is always there. The consequences of its presence in the sample are differences in the computed coefficient of a particular independent variable, depending on what other variables happen to be present in a particular equation, and standard errors larger than they would be in the absence of multicollinearity. The implications of the latter for hypothesis testing are obvious, but it is important to remember that although researchers obtain t-ratios lower than they would be otherwise, it does not necessarily follow that the computed t-ratios will be lower than the critical t-ratios. Detection of multicollinearity is difficult. Simple correlations among pairs of independent variables are suggestive but not conclusive. Large standard errors are probably the best indicator of the problem, especially if the magnitude of the standard error on a particular coefficient changes dramatically as other variables are added to or deleted from the equation. There is no solution to the problem, short of never doing applied regression. In the end, the nature of the problem and its resolution depend on the particular research at hand and the proclivity of the researcher.

Terms

Multicollinearity
Auxiliary regression

Exercises

12.1 True or false? If false, why?
  (a) Multicollinearity between independent variables means that the OLS estimators of regression coefficients are biased.
  (b) Multicollinearity makes it easier to get estimates of coefficients that are statistically significant.
  (c) Researchers should try to purge their regression models and data of all traces of multicollinearity before reporting their results.
  (d) If all simple correlations between included relevant variables are less than .5, multicollinearity definitely is not a problem.

12.2 Make up a set of five observations on X_1 and X_2 such that $r_{12} = 0$. Are such "independent" ($r = 0$) variables likely to occur naturally? Explain.

12.3 Consider the following regression results, where standard deviations are in parentheses.

$$Y = 16 + 8X_1 + 12X_2 + e \qquad R^2 = .64$$
$$\quad\;\; (6) \quad\;\; (8)$$

$$F = 6.98$$

$$n = 20$$

The researcher is disappointed because the theory suggested that both b_1 and b_2 should be positive and significantly different from zero and wonders if the sample suffers from severe multicollinearity. What evidence of severe multicollinearity is there in these results?

12.4 Assume that a researcher wants to estimate the following model:

$$Y = \beta_0 + \beta_1 X_1 + \beta_2 X_2 + U$$

Unfortunately, the correlation between X_1 and X_2 in the sample is very high and the b coefficients are very unsatisfactory. The multicollinearity problem could be resolved in one of two ways: Case I: Use extraneous information from other data, such as

$$Y = 14 + 4X_2$$

Case II: Introduce a restriction, such as

$$\beta_1 = 3 + 4\beta_2$$

yielding the following OLS equation:

$$Y^* = \beta_0^* + \beta_1^* X^*$$

(a) What is the definition of Y^* and X^* in each case?
(b) What are the implicit values for b_0, b_1, and b_2 of the model in each case?

12.5 Consider the following results:

$$\hat{Y} = 182 - 16X_1 + 2X_2 \qquad R^2 = .47$$
$$\qquad\quad (2) \qquad (1) \qquad n = 57$$

and $r_{12} = .75$. Theory suggested the signs on both coefficients should be negative. Are the following approaches reasonable? Why or why not?
(a) Collect new data on X_1, X_2, and Y_2.
(b) Reject H_0: $\beta_1 = 0$ and do not reject H_0: $\beta_2 = 0$ and go on with work.
(c) Do not reject H_0: $\beta_1 = 0$ because multicollinearity makes a t-test unreliable.
(d) Reject H_0: $\beta_2 = 0$ because multicollinearity made the confidence intervals too wide.
(e) Add some X_3 that will clear up the collinearity that exists between X_1 and X_2.
(f) Find a different specific variable to represent the generic variable behind X_1 and X_2.

12.6 Suppose that a researcher is trying to estimate the following consumption function, where consumption is hypothesized to depend on current income (Y_t), habit or past income (Y_{t-1}), and expectations or change in income ΔY_t:

$$E_t = b_0 + b_1 Y_t + b_2 Y_{t-1} + b_3(\Delta Y_t) + e_t$$

where E_t = current expenditure

   Y_t = current income

   Y_{t-1} = past income

   $\Delta Y_t = Y_t - Y_{t-1}$

(a) Show that without further information it is impossible to estimate b_1, b_2, and b_3.

(b) Put the equation in a form that could be estimated.

(c) Can all the parameters in the original equation be determined? Why or why not?

12.7 Assume that the following production function is to be estimated from annual data on a firm:

$$Q = \beta_0 + \beta_1 L_1 + \beta_2 L_2 + \beta_3 K$$

where L_1 = acres of land

   L_2 = dollars of labor

   K = dollars of capital equipment

Suppose that the firm always budgets $30,000 a year for labor and capital (i.e. $L_2 + K = 30,000$).

(a) Is there a multicolinearity problem?

(b) Can β_1, β_2, and β_3 be estimated? Explain.

CHAPTER 13

Omitted Relevant Variables and Included Irrelevant Variables

One justification for including a disturbance term in the regression equation is to incorporate the combined effect of all the variables not explicitly included (see Chapter 3). This, of course, assumes that the effect of any one of these variables by itself is negligible. This assumption is another way of saying that any particular omitted variable is not relevant in the equation being estimated. In this chapter we investigate the effect of omitting a variable that may, in fact, be relevant, and this raises the obvious question of what is meant by "relevant." Unfortunately for the confusion it causes, there are two distinct meanings of "relevant" in regression analysis: economic relevance and statistical relevance. *Economic relevance* derives from the underlying theory guiding the research. Variables are included in the analysis because economic theory says that they should be there—they are "relevant." *Statistical relevance* derives from the hypothesis test in the sense that if the null hypothesis is not rejected, we say that the coefficient is not on statistical grounds different from zero.

In this chapter we present the standard treatment of the implications for estimating equations that are misspecified on the basis of economic theory. The issue is investigated by positing a theoretically correct specification and then determining the conseuences of estimating an equation that does not include one or more of the variables specified by theory, or of estimating an equation that includes a variable that is not specified by the underlying theory. This immediately raises the obvious question of why the theoretically correct equation is not estimated in the first place. In principle, the correct equation would always be estimated, but there is often considerable slippage between principle and practice. It is possible, for example, that a researcher, being human, does not spend sufficient time carefully working through the underlying theory and fails to identify a variable. More likely, theoretically relevant variables may be identified but not included in the empirical analysis for lack of data. But even if we assume the best of all possible worlds, we must candidly admit that it is intellectually satisfying to know what would have happened if the job had not been well done.

Omitting Relevant Variables

To investigate the issue at hand requires distinguishing between a *correctly specified equation* and an *incorrectly specified equation*. This can be demonstrated by the following two specifications:

$$\text{Correct specification: } y = \beta_1 x_1 + \beta_2 x_2 + \beta_3 x_3 + U \qquad (13.1)$$

$$\text{Estimated equation: } \quad y = b_1 x_1 + e \qquad (13.2)$$

The least squares estimate for b_1 in (13.2) is given by

$$b_1 = \frac{\Sigma\, x_1 y}{\Sigma\, x_1^2} \qquad (13.3)$$

Substituting (13.1) for y yields

$$b_1 = \frac{\Sigma\, x_1(\beta_1 x_1 + \beta_2 x_2 + \beta_3 x_3 + U)}{\Sigma\, x_1^2} \qquad (13.4)$$

or

$$b_1 = \beta_1 \frac{\Sigma\, x_1^2}{\Sigma\, x_1^2} + \beta_2 \frac{\Sigma\, x_1 x_2}{\Sigma\, x_1^2} + \beta_3 \frac{\Sigma\, x_1 x_3}{\Sigma\, x_1^2} + \frac{\Sigma\, x_1 U}{\Sigma\, x_1^2} \qquad (13.5)$$

Take the expected value of (13.5) and use the assumption that $E(U) = 0$ to obtain

$$E(b_1) = \beta_1 + \left(\beta_2 \frac{\Sigma\, x_1 x_2}{\Sigma\, x_1^2} + \beta_3 \frac{\Sigma x_1 x_3}{\Sigma\, x_1^2}\right) \qquad (13.6)$$

Equation (13.6) shows that if relevant variables are omitted from the analysis, the expected value of the coefficient of the included variable may not equal the population parameter that it is estimating. Specifically, (13.6) shows the expected value of b_1 to be equal to the population parameter β_1 plus a *bias factor* composed of a linear combination of the population parameters of the omitted variables. In other words, if the expression in brackets is not equal to zero, b_1 will be a biased estimator of β_1.

To evaluate the bias, consider the *weights* attached to β_2 and β_3 in (13.6). Note that $\Sigma\, x_1 x_2 / \Sigma\, x_1^2$, the weight attached to β_2, is the sample OLS regression coefficient obtained by regressing X_2 on X_1. Similarly, the weight associated with β_3 is the OLS coefficient obtained from the regression of X_3 on X_1. These are the auxiliary regressions encountered in Chapter 12, which permit (13.6) to be rewritten as

$$E(b_1) = \beta_1 + (\beta_2 b_{21} + \beta_3 b_{31}) \qquad (13.7)$$

where b_{21} and b_{31} are the respective slopes. Thus the bias in b_1 as an estimator of β_1 is a linear combination (weighted sum) of the "population" coefficients of the omitted relevant variables, where the weights are the slopes from the auxiliary regression of each of the omitted relevant variables on the included variable. Figure 13.1 illustrates this relationship. The dashed lines represent the population regression coefficients that measure the net effect of each of the independent variables on Y. When X_2 and X_3

$$E(b_1) = \beta_1 + [\beta_2 b_{21} + \beta_3 b_{31}]$$

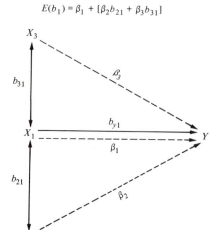

Figure 13.1   Effect of Omitted Variables on the Included Regression Coefficients.

are omitted, b_{y1} is the OLS estimate of β_1. However, X_2 and X_3 are related to X_1 via the auxiliary regression coefficients b_{21} and b_{31}. This means that when X_1 changes, there are concomitant changes in X_2 and X_3. The magnitude of the change depends on the respective values of b_{21} and b_{31}. Consequently, the OLS coefficient b_{y1} is picking up not only the effect of X_1, but also the effect of the concomitant changes in X_2 and X_3, where the respective population effects, β_2 and β_3, are weighted by the auxiliary coefficients. It is in this sense that b_{y1} is said to "pick up" the effect of the omitted variables.

Under certain conditions the bias term in (13.7) could be equal to zero. Observe that since X_2 and X_3 were assumed to be relevant variables in (13.1), β_2 and β_3 are not equal to zero. If β_2 and β_3 did equal zero, then by definition, X_2 and X_3 would not be relevant variables. Since the degree of the bias depends on the auxiliary regression coefficients, one set of conditions for no bias would be $b_{21} = b_{31} = 0$. In other words, if there is no linear relationship between X_2 and X_3 (the omitted variables) and the included variable X_1, the bias term in (13.7) would be zero. In this special case the omission of relevant variables does not result in a biased estimate of β_1.

Now look at (13.7) in a slightly different way. As was shown in Chapter 12, the simple regression coefficients may be written

$$b_{21} = \frac{\sum x_2 x_1}{\sum x_1^2} = \frac{S_2}{S_1} r_{12} \tag{13.8}$$

and

$$b_{31} = \frac{\sum x_3 x_1}{\sum x_1^2} = \frac{S_3}{S_1} r_{13} \tag{13.9}$$

If (13.8) and (13.9) are substituted into (13.7), the condition for unbiasedness can be restated: The bias will be zero if the correlations between the included variable and *all* of the omitted variables are equal to zero.

There is one other very special condition which, if satisfied, would result in a zero bias term. If in (13.7) the terms $\beta_2 b_{21}$ and $\beta_3 b_{31}$ happen to be exactly equal in magnitude but of opposite sign, then their sum, and hence the bias term, would be zero. Obviously, this is a rather extreme situation, one rarely encountered in practice.

At this point it is instructive to introduce the intercept term:

$$\text{Correct specification: } Y = \beta_0 + \beta_1 X_1 + \beta_2 X_2 + \beta_3 X_3 + U \qquad (13.10)$$

$$\text{Incorrect: } \qquad Y = b_0 + b_1 X_1 + e \qquad (13.11)$$

The OLS estimate of β_0 in (13.11) is

$$b_0 = \overline{Y} - b_1 \overline{X}_1 \qquad (13.12)$$

with

$$E(b_0) = E(\overline{Y}) - E(b_1)\overline{X}_1 \qquad (13.13)$$
$$= \beta_0 + \beta_1 \overline{X}_1 + \beta_2 \overline{X}_2 + \beta_3 \overline{X}_3 - (\beta_1 + \beta_2 b_{21} + \beta_3 b_{31})\overline{X}_1$$

Multiplying out and rearranging terms yields

$$E(b_0) = \beta_0 + (\overline{X}_2 - b_{21}\overline{X}_1)\beta_2 + (\overline{X}_3 - b_{31}\overline{X}_1)\beta_3 \qquad (13.14)$$

which shows that b_0, as well as b_1, is biased. But more than that, if relevant variables (X_2 and X_3) are omitted, b_0 is biased even if b_{21} and b_{31} in the sample are zero.

Consequences of Bias

The presence of bias in the estimates has several consequences relevant to empirical research. First, the standard tests of significance are not appropriate since these tests require that estimates of the parameters be unbiased. In terms of an earlier example above, this means that it is not appropriate to use the standard t-test to test hypotheses concerning the value of β_1 in the population.

Second, the presence of bias may result in estimated coefficients that are substantially different from what was expected in terms of sign or magnitude. For example, in an analysis of the factors affecting the price of an agricultural commodity, say potatoes, it might be hypothesized that the slope of the income variable would be positive, on the argument that income is a demand shifter that shifts the demand for potatoes to the right. However, in an empirical analysis one might obtain a negative sign for the income coefficient. One interpretation would be that potatoes are an inferior good in that as income increases, the demand curve for potatoes shifts to the left. On the other hand, the negative income coefficient could reflect a bias due to correlation of income with omitted relevant variables.

Note that the foregoing argument works both ways. Specifically, the estimated coefficient could have the expected sign, but because a bias term masks the true (and unexpected) value of the coefficient, it would be quite wrong.

Solution: The Multicollinearity Problem

The solution to the problem of omitted relevant variables seems to be straightforward: Simply include the relevant variables. Such a solution is seldom available, however. First, the investigator may be doubtful as to the specific variables to include in a particular equation. Although the theories used to guide empirical research are rather powerful in identifying the variable to use, the problem in applied research is that the proper measures of these are open to question.

Second, the conceptual form of the variable as used in the theory must be linked to the available data before estimation is possible. Yet real-world measurements and theoretical constructs seldom coincide (see Chapter 15). This fact, combined with the practical considerations in a specific research situation, frequently forces the researcher to work with incorrectly specified equations. The theory of consumer choice provides one illustration of the practical considerations that can affect the list of variables included in empirical analyses. Consumer demand theory suggests that a consumer's demand function for a commodity is a function of all commodity prices and the consumer's income. Yet in a particular research situation, say a study of the factors affecting the demand for felt-tip pens, it is impossible to include the prices of all other commodities in the analysis. Thus the researcher is forced to select a subset of prices. Unfortunately, the appropriate subset is not always obvious and relevant variables may be omitted.

Finally, variables may be omitted because of lack of available data. For example, in an analysis of family budgets, theory may indicate that family size and the education of the housewife are relevant variables in explaining observed consumption expenditure patterns, yet there may be no information available on these two variables. Consequently, the investigator is forced to work with an incorrectly specified equation.

On the basis of these arguments, the typical research situation is likely to involve equations that omit relevant variables and are thus misspecified. To the extent that these omitted relevant variables are correlated with the included variables, biased estimates of the coefficients will be obtained. It is quite possible that the omitted relevant variables will be correlated with the included variables since all the economic variables with which researchers generally work are generated by the same economic system.

Suppose, however, that one could include the omitted relevant variable involved in the bias term. According to the analysis above, this should eliminate the bias in the estimate of the coefficient of the included variable. But the elimination of one problem has created a new one: multicollinearity is likely present because the new explanatory variable is probably correlated with the initial explanatory variable in the sample. Consequently, the problems of multicollinearity (discussed in Chapter 12) must be dealt with. This interrelation between omitted relevant variables and multicollinearity creates a dilemma. One can mitigate the impact of multicollinearity by eliminating one of the variables, but in doing so obtain biased estimates. Alternatively, one may eliminate the bias by introducing the relevant variable, but then face the problems associated with multicollinearity.

Including Irrelevant Variables

Another possible danger associated with adding variables to the equation is that the added variables might be irrelevant. Faced with the problem of bias if relevant variables are omitted from the estimating equation, a researcher may be tempted to try the "kitchen sink" approach by including any variables that just might be relevant. However, some such included variables may, in fact, be irrelevant.

The consequences of including irrelevant variables can be explored using a relatively simple case. Suppose that the correct economic specification is

$$y = \beta_1 x_1 + U \tag{13.15}$$

but a researcher estimates the following misspecified equation by OLS:

$$y = b_1 x_1 + b_2 x_2 + e \tag{13.16}$$

where y = dependent variable
x_1 = relevant independent variable
x_2 = irrelevant independent variable

all variables being measured in deviations from their means. By including X_2 as an independent variable, the researcher inadvertently ignores the true parameter restriction implicit in (13.15), that $\beta_2 = 0$, and instead generates an estimate (b_2) from available data.

The OLS estimator b_1, the coefficient of the relevant variable, is

$$b_1 = \frac{(\Sigma\, x_1 y)(\Sigma\, x_2^2) - (\Sigma\, x_2 y)(\Sigma\, x_1 x_2)}{(\Sigma\, x_1^2)(\Sigma\, x_2^2) - (\Sigma\, x_1 x_2)^2} \tag{13.17}$$

Substitute (13.15) for y and take the expected value to obtain

$$E(b_1) = \frac{\beta_1(\Sigma\, x_1^2)(\Sigma\, x_2^2) - \beta_1(\Sigma\, x_1 x_2)^2}{(\Sigma\, x_1^2)(\Sigma\, x_2^2) - (\Sigma\, x_1 x_2)^2} = \beta_1 \tag{13.18}$$

which shows the estimator of the coefficient of the relevant variable to be unbiased. Similarly, b_2, the estimator of the coefficient of the irrelevant variable is given by

$$b_2 = \frac{(\Sigma\, x_2 y)(\Sigma\, x_1^2) - (\Sigma\, x_1 y)(\Sigma\, x_1 x_2)}{(\Sigma\, x_1^2)(\Sigma\, x_2^2) - (\Sigma\, x_1 x_2)^2} \tag{13.19}$$

with an expected value of

$$E(b_2) = \frac{\beta_1\,(\Sigma\, x_1 x_2)(\Sigma\, x_1^2) - \beta_1\,(\Sigma\, x_1 x_2)(\Sigma\, x_1^2)}{(\Sigma\, x_1^2)(\Sigma\, x_2^2) - (\Sigma\, x_1 x_2)^2} = 0 \tag{13.20}$$

as it should be, since $\beta_2 = 0$ by specification.

In general, then, including irrelevant variables in the equation does not affect the unbiasedness property of the coefficient estimators of either the relevant or irrelevant variables. However, the price to be paid for using the kitchen sink regression equations is inefficient estimators; that is, the OLS estimators are not minimum-variance. The variance of b_1 when the irrelevant variable, X_2, is not in equation (13.16) is given by

$$\mathrm{Var}\,(b_1^*) = \frac{1}{\Sigma\, x_1^2}\,\sigma^2 \tag{13.21}$$

and when X_2 is included in the equation,

$$\mathrm{Var}\,(b_1) = \frac{\Sigma\, x_2^2}{(\Sigma\, x_1^2)(\Sigma\, x_2^2) - (\Sigma\, x_1 x_2)^2}\,\sigma^2 \tag{13.22}$$

Since (13.22) is larger than (13.21), the variance of b_1 is larger when the irrelevant variable X_2 is added to the equation.

In summary, the consequence of including irrelevant variables is *inefficient* OLS coefficient estimators for included relevant variables. In this case, the standard statistical tests remain valid, but their computed values are smaller than they should be, decreasing the chances of rejecting the null hypothesis. Because the variance is increased by the inclusion of irrelevant variables, it becomes unnecessarily difficult to reject the null hypothesis that β_1 equals zero. Since including irrelevant variables can lead to not rejecting the null hypothesis when it should be rejected, researchers should beware of the kitchen sink approach.

What Are "Relevant" and "Irrelevant" Variables?

The previous sections showed what happens to the properties of OLS estimators in the presence of a misspecified equation, whether the misspecification is omitting a relevant variable or including an irrelevant variable. But there remains the question of what is an economically relevant (or irrelevant) variable. The answer must be found in the theory underlying the specific research question. For example, a particular variable, say population, may be economically "relevant" in one research setting (estimating demand functions) and economically "irrelevant" in another research setting (estimating production functions). Hence the determination must always be made in the context of a given research question, using general guidelines provided by the underlying theory. Moreover, there can be a conflict between economic relevance and statistical significance. For example, income is an economically relevant variable in a demand equation based on theory, yet the statistical results obtained from a given sample might call for not rejecting the null hypothesis that income is a statistically insignificant variable.

An Illustration

In the following discussion, we illustrate how an applied researcher might try to arrive at such a judgment. The data used to estimate the equations are from the worksheet in Table 8.1.

The illustration involves estimating an equation that explains changes in the level of pork prices, using pork production, beef production, and chicken production, where the latter two are assumed to be substitutes in consumption. The correlation matrix for the variables is presented in Table 13.1 and the equations of interest are given in Table 13.2.

Suppose that equation 1, using only pork production, is estimated first. Two things are to be noted. First, the sign of the independent variable is negative, as expected from the underlying theory, lending support to the proposition that quantity is a

Table 13.1. Correlation Matrix: Pork Price Data from Chapter 8[a]

	P	Q_p	Q_b
Q_p	−.266		
Q_b	.288	−.399	
Q_c	.484	.472	−.033

[a] P = pork price; Q_p = pork quantity; Q_b = beef quantity; Q_c = chicken quantity.

relevant variable. Second, the relatively high standard deviation of this estimate yields a computed t-ratio of −1.94, which is less than the critical t-ratio for rejecting the null hypothesis at the .95 level, lending support to the proposition that quantity is an irrelevant variable.

Although these results send mixed signals concerning the *statistical* "relevance" of pork quantity, the equation is not very interesting because an economically relevant variable, substitutes, is omitted from the equation. There is no way of knowing precisely what the substitutes might be, but beef and chicken are certanly possibilities worthy of consideration. The question of whether to include them in separate equations or together in the same equation is examined in equations 2 to 4.

Adding the beef variable does little for the equation. Although pork quantity remains *economically* significant (the coefficient has the expected sign), it is still *statistically* nonsignificant. The beef coefficient fails on two counts: It has the "wrong" sign and it is not statistically significant. Consequently, it is a candidate for the discard basket. The slight increase in the standard deviation of the pork coefficient when the beef variable is added to the equation (a result expected when an irrelevant variable is added to an equation) supports this candidacy.

When chicken quantity is used as the empirical measure of substitutes in equation 3, some interesting things happen. The coefficient of pork quantity is now statistically significant, with a smaller standard deviation than in the preceding two equations,

Table 13.2. Preliminary Pork Price Regression Results Showing the Effect of Omitting Variables[a]

Equation	Intercept	Q_p	Q_b	Q_c	$\bar{R}^2$
1	65.22*	−7.508	—	—	.052
	(13.35)	(3.855)			
2	20.03	−5.066	6.485	—	.074
	(33.41)	(4.156)	(4.406)		
3	45.56*	−18.074*	—	18.497*	.539
	(9.69)	(3.05)		(2.520)	
4	30.69	−17.057*	2.185	18.157*	.534
	(23.75)	(3.406)	(3.184)	(2.583)	

[a] Numbers below coefficients are respective standard errors of coefficients; an asterisk indicates a computed t-ratio greater than the critical t-ratio at α = .05.

lending even further support to the proposition that the beef variable may not be an appropriate variable. Now for the enigma shrouding the coefficient of chicken quantity. The coefficient is statistically significant, but more important, it has the "wrong" sign. All else constant, if chicken is a substitute for pork, then as chicken production increases chicken price will decrease, including a shift in demand away from pork and to chicken, in which case pork price should decrease.

Finally, equation 4 contains both empirical measures of substitutes. For practical purposes, equations 3 and 4 are identical with regard to the pork and chicken coefficients. The only difference of interest between the two is the increase in the standard deviation of the pork coefficient when beef quantity is added to the equation.

In summary, at this point there is a temptation to conclude that pork quantity is a relevant variable, as it has the correct sign and is statistically significant. The beef coefficient is troublesome on two grounds: It has the wrong sign and is also statistically nonsignificant. Moreover, its effect on the standard deviation of the pork coefficient supports the proposition that beef quantity adds no information to the equation. The chicken coefficient remains a mystery, as it has the wrong sign yet is statistically significant. If, for whatever reason, the analysis had to stop at this point and an equation be selected from Table 13.2 for use in, say policy analysis, a researcher would be hard put to choose one. Fortunately, the analysis does not have to cease.

Turning to demand theory, which implicitly underlies the equations in Table 13.2, it is obvious that a variable of theoretical importance is omitted, namely, consumer income. If this is a relevant variable, its omission may at least partially explain the results above.

The correlation matrix extended to include income is presented in Table 13.3 and the regression equations of Table 13.2 with the income variable added are shown in Table 13.4. A quick examination of Table 13.3 shows that chicken quantity and income are, for whatever reason, highly correlated in the sample. From the analysis of the omitted relevant variable case outlined above, experienced researchers know that if a relevant variable is omitted from the equation and if the omitted variable is correlated with one or more of the included variables, the coefficients of the included variables may be biased by picking up the effect of the omitted variable [equation (13.7)].

To see if this is the case, compare equation 4 of Table 13.4 with equation 4 of Table 13.2. The income coefficient in Table 13.4 is positive, as would be expected on theoretical grounds, and it is also statistically significant, suggesting that it is a relevant variable. Moreover, adding income to the equation causes the beef and chicken coefficients to have the correct signs, suggesting the presence of bias in the coefficients

Table 13.3. Augmented Correlation Matrix: Pork Price Data[a]

	P	Q_p	Q_b	Q_c
Q_p	$-.266$			
Q_b	.288	$-.399$		
Q_c	.489	.472	$-.033$	
I	.663	.468	.031	.869

[a] P, Q_p, Q_b, and Q_c are defined in Table 13.1; $I =$ per capita disposable income.

Table 13.4. Pork Price Regression Results[a]

Equation	Intercept	Q_p	Q_b	Q_c	I	$\bar{R}^2$
1	75.59*	− 20.858*	—	—	6.033*	.859
	(5.19)	(1.683)			(3.56)	
2	95.84*	− 21.583*	− 1.452	—	6.113*	.856
	(13.68)	(1.912)	(1.792)		(.371)	
3	80.99*	− 20.475*	—	− 3.782	6.836*	.862
	(6.22)	(1.680)		(2.482)	(.634)	
4	92.60*	− 21.270*	− 1.617	− 3.917	6.955*	.862
	(14.15)	(1.89)	(1.768)	(2.490)	(.648)	

[a] Standard errors are in parentheses; an asterisk indicates a computed t-ratio greater than the critical t-ratio at $\alpha = .05$.

shown in Table 13.2. However, neither of the coefficients is statistically significant. But are they economically relevant? This question can only be answered by the researcher in the context of the specific research question. In some cases, this might lead the researcher to include an economically relevant variable even though it is statistically irrelevant.

Summary and Implications

This chapter has shown how omitting relevant economic variables leads to biased estimators of the regression slopes of the included relevant variables if the omitted relevant variables are correlated with the included variables. This bias invalidates the standard methods of hypothesis testing and can even lead to estimates with the wrong sign. The solution to the problems associated with omitting economic relevant variables appears simple: Include all possible relevant variables. However, this solution is difficult to achieve in practice because many relevant variables are imprecisely defined, difficult to measure, or characterized by a lack of appropriate data. If data are available, including relevant variables can cure the bias illness. However, the cure can cause a new illness—multicollinearity—if the new variables are highly correlated with the old in the sample. Including irrelevant variables in the empirical analysis occasionally causes researchers to conclude (wrongly) that (1) an irrelevant variable is statistically significant, and (2) a relevant economic variable is statistically insignificant.

The researcher faced with the problem of whether to include a variable is left with an unpleasant dilemma. To leave the perhaps relevant variable out is to risk biasing the empirical results and thus ruining the validity of the standard statistical tests. Including the questionable variable may introduce multicollinearity problems if the variable is relevant, making statistical tests more conservative. If the questionable variable is indeed irrelevant, its inclusion opens the door to two types of wrong conclusions: The irrelevant variable is significant and a relevant variable is not significant. This dilemma defies a general solution beyond the basic platitude "make good theories." In practice, decisions on whether to include a specific variable must be made on the basis of theory, insight, experience, and intuition.

Terms

Irrelevant variables   Relevant variables

Exercises

13.1 Suppose that the correct model is

$$Y = \beta_0 + \beta_1 X_1 + \beta_2 X_2 + U, \qquad \beta_1 \neq 0, \quad \beta_2 \neq 0$$

but a researcher estimates

$$Y = b_0 + b_1 X_1 + e$$

(a) Is $E(b_1) = \beta_1$?
(b) If you are using the same sample to estimate

$$Y = b_0^* + b_1^* X_1 + b_2^* X_2 + e^*$$

under what condition would $b_1 = b_1^*$?

13.2 Suppose that the correct model is

$$Y = \beta_0 + \beta_1 X_1 + U$$

but a researcher estimates

$$Y = b_0 + b_1 X_1 + b_2 X_2 + e$$

(a) Is $E(b_1) = \beta_1$?
(b) What is β_2?
(c) What is $E(b_2)$?
(d) What possible harm is there in including X_2?

13.3
(a) How does a researcher know if a variable is relevant?
(b) Does rejecting the null hypothesis $B_i = 0$ mean that a variable is theoretically relevant?

13.4 Suppose that the population regression function is

$$Y = \beta_0 + \beta_1 X_1 + \beta_2 X_2 + U, \qquad \beta_1 = 5, \quad \beta_2 \neq 0$$

but a researcher thinks the appropriate model is

$$Y = b_0 + b_1 X_1 + e$$

What would be the $E(b_1)$ under the following circumstances?
(a) $\beta_2 = 2$ and $b_{21} = 3$
(b) $\beta_2 = 2$ and $b_{21} = -3$
(c) $\beta_2 = 2$ and $b_{21} = 0$
(d) $\beta_2 = -35$ and $b_{21} = 0$

13.5 As part of a study of food consumption patterns in Stetson a researcher obtains the following regression results:

$$C = 200 - \underset{(.35)}{.025Y} + e \qquad \begin{array}{l} R^2 = .69 \\ n = 350 \end{array}$$

where C = weekly spending on food
$\qquad$ Y = average weekly income

and the standard deviation of the regression coefficient is in parentheses. The researcher could not obtain data on family size (F), which the researcher believes to be negatively correlated with Y and, holding Y constant, positively related to C. Explain why you would agree or disagree with the following observations.
(a) The unexpected sign for b_y is due to the omitted relevant variable.
(b) b_y is based on an estimator that has a negative bias.
(c) Including F in the equation would make b_y positive and statistically significant.
(d) Every effort should be made to include data on F in the equation.

13.6 Suppose that you estimate, based on a survey of your classmates, the following:

$$S = 70 + \underset{(.8)}{1.2H} + \underset{(1)}{4P} + e$$

where S = score on midterm exam
$\qquad$ H = hours studies
$\qquad$ P = number of pennies on person when taking the exam

and the standard deviations are in parentheses. The correlation coefficient, r_{hp}, is .80. Explain why each of the following statements is true or false.
(a) Pennies are a significant determinant of grades.
(b) b_H is biased downward.
(c) P should be omitted from the equation.

13.7 Suppose that a researcher is studying the productivity of electronics firms in Silicon Valley and obtains the following estimate of the output function of 291 firms:

$$P_i = 5.0 + .53W_i + .50K_i + e_i$$

where P_i = value of output

W_i = wage and salaries of the firm

K_i = value of plant and equipment

The researcher knows that the level of management is an important variable, but knows of no way to measure management, and yet would like to allow for the effect of management (M_i) in evaluating the estimated equation and making recommendations. Other studies in the literature indicate that management is related to wages and plant size by the following equation:

$$M = a_0 + b_{mw}W + b_{mk}K + v$$

Assuming that capital-intensive firms have a more highly skilled management staff than those with labor-intensive operations, the sign of b_{mw} would be negative and b_{mk} positive.

(a) Write the equations for the expected values of b_{pw} and b_{pk}.
(b) What can be said about the bias of the estimator for the coefficient of W_i ($b_1 = .53$) in the equation? Why?
(c) What can you say about the bias of the estimator for the coefficient of K_i ($b_2 = .50$)? Why?

13.8 The population regression function is

$$Y = \beta_1 x_1 + \beta_2 x_2 + \beta_3 x_3 + U$$

but a researcher runs the regression

$$y = b_1 x_1 + b_3 x_3 + e$$

(a) Given that $r_{13} = 0$ and r_{12} is positive, what is the bias inherent in the estimator of the slope of b_1?
(b) Assume that $X_2 = -22 + 11X_1$.
  (i) Show that $E(b_1) < \beta_1$, given $\beta_2 = -.5$, $\beta_1 = 8.0$, and $r_{13} = 0$.
  (ii) Show that $E(b_1) > \beta_1$, given $\beta_2 = -.5$, $\beta_1 = 8.0$, $B_3 = 2.4$, $r_{13} = .5$, and $S_3^2 = 2500$ and $S_1^2 = 25$.

13.9 As part of a study of residential property values in Hermantown, a researcher obtains the following regression results:

$$V = 20,000 + 220\,S + e \qquad R^2 = .48$$
$$ (250) \qquad\qquad m = 400$$

where V = value of parcel of property

S = size of house (square feet)

and the standard deviation of the regression coefficient is in parentheses. The researcher could not include information for two relevant variables, distance for the local school (D) and parcel size (A). Both D and A are positively correlated with S and, other things equal, D is negatively related to V and A is positively related to V. Explain why you agree or disagree with each of the following observations.

(a) b_{vs} is not significantly different from zero.
(b) b_{vs} is an unbiased estimate of β_s.
(c) b_{vs} is an underestimate of β_s.
(d) Including D would cause b_{vs} to decrease.
(e) Including A would cause b_{vs} to increase.
(f) D and A should be included in equation.

14

Misspecified Disturbance Terms: Heteroscedasticity and Autocorrelation

The subject of this chapter is *generalized least squares*, the estimation procedure often used in applied research when the assumptions $E(U_i^2) = \sigma^2$ for all i or $E(U_iU_j) = 0$ for all $i \neq j$ are violated. Following the scheme of previous chapters, this chapter examines the subject using special cases. A general treatment, using matrix algebra, is given in Chapter 20.

When deriving the OLS estimators, Chapters 3 and 4 used the following assumptions on the population disturbance term:

$$E(U) = 0 \tag{14.1}$$

$$E(U^2) = \sigma^2 \tag{14.2}$$

$$E(U_iU_j) = 0, \qquad i \neq j \tag{14.3}$$

where (14.2) is the homoscedasticity assumption that the variances of the conditional distributions associated with the fixed values of X are the same and equal to σ^2. Assumption (14.3) says that in repeated sampling from the population, the correlation between any pair of disturbance terms across the conditional distributions is zero. This assumption is referred to as *lack of serial correlation* or *absence of autoregressiveness* in the disturbance term. On the basis of these assumptions, the minimum-variance, linear, unbiased properties may be claimed of the least squares estimators.

In this chapter we do two things: (1) show the importance of these assumptions, and (2) consider what happens to the properties of the OLS estimators if (14.2) and (14.3) are violated. We begin by examining the properties of the OLS estimator without using assumptions (14.2) and (14.3). This derivation will reveal the importance of these assumptions to the properties of the OLS estimators and, at the same time, identify the implications of using OLS estimators when the assumptions are violated. Having done this, the discussion turns to some alternative estimation procedures often used in applied research.

A General Treatment

The population regression function in deviation form is

$$y = \beta_1 x + U \qquad (14.4)$$

First, evaluate the properties of the OLS estimator of β_1 using only the following assumptions:

$$E(U) = 0 \qquad (14.5)$$

$$X\text{-values fixed in repeated sampling} \qquad (14.6)$$

Given this specification, it is possible to examine the OLS estimator for β_1 in (14.4).

Expected Value of b_1

$$b_1 = \frac{\Sigma\, xy}{\Sigma\, x^2} = \frac{\Sigma\, x(\beta_1 x + U)}{\Sigma\, x^2} = \beta_1 + \frac{\Sigma\, xU}{\Sigma\, x^2} \qquad (14.7)$$

with expected value

$$E(b_1) = \beta_1 + \frac{\Sigma\, xE(U)}{\Sigma\, x^2} = \beta_1 \qquad [\text{by } (14.5)] \qquad (14.8)$$

This gives the first important result: The unbiasedness property of the OLS estimator depends only on assumptions (14.5) and (14.6); it does not depend on the distributional properties (variance, or serial correlation) of the population disturbance term. Alternatively, whatever assumptions are made about the variance and covariance of the disturbance term, it is still possible to use the OLS estimator to obtain an unbiased estimate of β_1. Note, however, that this result does require the $E(U) = 0$ assumption. If this assumption does not hold, the OLS estimator yields biased estimates of the population regression coefficients.

Variance of b_1

By definition, the variance of b_1 is

$$\text{Var}(b_1) = E(b_1 - \beta_1)^2$$

$$= E\left(\frac{\Sigma\, xU}{\Sigma\, x^2}\right)^2 \qquad [\text{by } (14.8)]$$

$$= \frac{1}{(\Sigma\, x^2)^2}\, [x_1^2 E(U_1^2) + \cdots + x_n^2 E(U_n^2) \qquad (14.9)$$

$$+ \Sigma\, x_1 x_2 E(U_1 U_2) + \Sigma\, x_2 x_1 E(U_2 U_1) \cdots]$$

$$= \frac{1}{(\Sigma \, x^2)^2} \, [\Sigma \, x_i^2 E(U_i^2) + \sum_{i \neq j} x_i x_j E(U_i U_j)]$$

Chapter 3 showed the U_i's to be the values of U from repeated sampling from the ith conditional distribution. By assumption, the mean of this distribution is $E(U_i) = 0$, so it is possible to write

$$E(U_i^2) = E(U_i - 0)^2 = E[U_i - E(U_i)]^2 = \sigma_i^2 \qquad (14.10)$$

But (14.10) is the variance of U for the ith conditional distribution. Consequently, (14.9) may be rewritten

$$V(b_1) = \frac{1}{(\Sigma \, x^2)^2} \, [\Sigma \, x_i^2 \sigma_i^2 + \sum_{i \neq j} x_i x_j E(U_i U_j)] \qquad (14.11)$$

By definition, (14.11) is the variance of b_1, where it is assumed that $E(U) = 0$ and the X-values are fixed in repeated sampling. The variance of b_1 is seen to depend on two things: (1) the variance of the conditional distributions of the population disturbance term, and (2) the covariance of disturbance terms across these distributions. This equation is the *generalized variance* of the OLS estimator, b_1.

Now substitute the assumptions $E(U_i^2) = \sigma^2$, for all i, and $E(U_i U_j) = 0$, all $i \neq j$, into (14.11) to obtain

$$V(b_1) = \frac{1}{(\Sigma \, x^2)^2} \, (\Sigma \, x^2 \sigma^2) = \frac{\Sigma \, x^2}{(\Sigma \, x^2)^2} \, \sigma^2 = \frac{1}{\Sigma \, x^2} \, \sigma^2 \qquad (14.12)$$

which is exactly the result obtained in Chapter 3 under the classical assumptions. Chapter 3 showed that (14.7) is a minimum-variance estimator, with variance given by (14.12). The analysis here, using only assumptions (14.5) and (14.6), shows the minimum variance to be (14.11). Since (14.12) is not the same as (14.11), we get the second important result: If the classical distributional properties of the disturbance term do not hold, the OLS estimator is not a minimum-variance estimator.

Estimating σ^2

In Chapter 3 it was shown that under the classical assumptions an unbiased estimator of the population variance, needed to estimate the variance of b_1, is

$$\text{estimate of } \sigma^2 = S^2 = \frac{\Sigma \, e^2}{n - 2} \qquad (14.13)$$

which permits the estimation of Var (b_1) by

$$S_{b_1}^2 = \frac{\Sigma \, e^2}{\Sigma \, x^2(n - 2)} \qquad (14.14)$$

In the present case, using only the assumptions (14.5) and (14.6), it can be shown that (14.13), the OLS estimator of the variance, is a biased estimator of σ^2. It follows that the OLS estimator of $V(b_1)$, which depends on the estimate of σ^2, is a biased estimator. This third important result is of concern on both theoretical and practical grounds.

Theoretically, hypotheses cannot be tested using OLS procedures when the classical distributional assumptions do not hold. This follows because the conventional test statistics are derived on the assumption of, and therefore have validity only for, unbiased estimators. Since OLS procedures produce a biased estimator of the population variance, a key assumption underlying the conventional test is violated.

Even if the foregoing theoretical niceties are ignored, practical problems await the applied researcher. There is no theoretical basis for determining whether the bias in the estimate of the population variance is positive or negative. If it is negative, the computed confidence intervals will be narrower than they should be, in which case the applied researcher will be predisposed to reject the null hypothesis when it should not be rejected. This, in turn, can lead to an ill-founded belief in the precision of the OLS estimates. If the bias is positive, the opposite obtains.

Summary

If OLS procedures are used when the classical assumptions on the population disturbance term do not hold, several problems arise. The OLS estimators provide unbiased estimates of the population regression parameters, but they are not minimum-variance estimates. Moreover, the estimated variance of the OLS coefficient estimates will be biased, quite likely negatively biased, in which case the regression results will appear more precise than they actually are.

For these reasons, the applied researcher should guard against the unquestioned use of OLS estimators. In the following sections we suggest that OLS equations estimated from cross-sectional data sets often yield residuals that exhibit heteroscedastic (non-constant variance) patterns. Similarly, OLS residuals estimated from time-series data sets often exhibit autoregressiveness. In the following two sections we discuss heteroscedasticity and autocorrelation, suggest tests for detecting their presence in the data, and outline estimation procedures used in applied research. An exhaustive theoretical and practical treatment of these two problems is beyond the scope of this chapter, but a complete theoretical treatment of generalized least squares is given in Chapter 20.

Heteroscedasticity

In this section we focus on (14.2), the assumption of a homoscedastic disturbance term, which assumes that the variance of the disturbance terms is the same for all values of X (see Figure 3.3). Figure 14.1(a) is a scatter diagram that illustrates the relationship that would be expected between Y and X in a simple regression with homoscedastic disturbances. Note that the observed Y's have a constant variance around the expected Y's, represented by the simple regression line.

The assumption of a homoscedastic disturbance term is not always valid. For example, the variance of food expenditures among families may increase as family

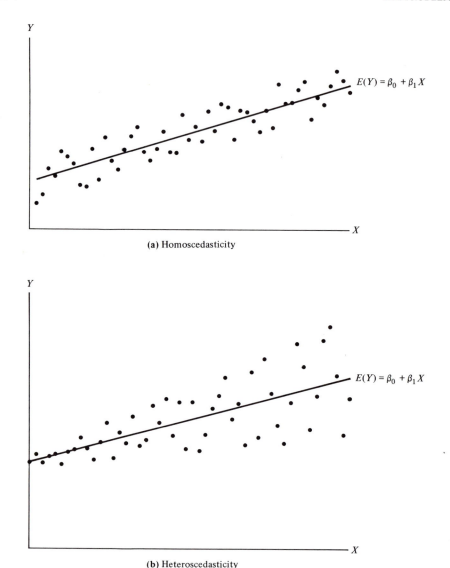

Figure 14.1 Homoscedasticity and Heteroscedasticity in a Simple Regression Model.

income increases. Similarly, the variance of profits may increase with firm size, and the variance of public spending may increase with city size. *Heteroscedasticity* is the formal name for the case of nonconstant variance in the disturbance term. Figure 14.1(b) suggests what heteroscedasticity might look like. This illustration shows the variance increasing as X increases, the most common case, but there is no necessary reason why the variance could not decrease as X increases.

In applied research, heteroscedasticity is usually associated with cross-sectional data. In cross-sectional data on such units as families, firms, or cities, the range in the values of the variables is often very large. Consider, for example, the range in family income between the poorest and richest family in town, the range in annual sales between a corner drugstore and General Motors, or the range in city spending between Peoria and New York City. Even when using units of analysis with less dramatic ranges in the relevant variables, cross-sectional data generally involve many different-sized units, and the heteroscedastic problem is likely present. Heteroscedastic disturbances are possible, of course, in time-series data sets, but experience suggests that it is of minor consequence, especially relative to autoregressiveness, the subject of the next section. As a practical matter, heteroscedasticity is treated here as a problem faced by researchers using cross-sectional data sets.

The Theory

Formally, heteroscedasticity may be denoted by rewriting (14.2) as

$$E(U_i^2) = \sigma_i^2, \qquad i = 1, \ldots, n \tag{14.15}$$

to say that the variance of the conditional distributions is different across the values of the independent variable. In the previous section we saw that using OLS procedures when (14.15) holds results in unbiased estimates of regression coefficients, but that these estimates are not minimum-variance estimates, and the estimates of their variances are biased. In this section we consider the possibility of correcting for heteroscedasticity in a way that will permit the use of OLS procedures for estimating the population regression function. Specifically, what is needed is a transformation of the original values of the variables such that OLS procedures applied to the transformed values of the variables yield best, linear, unbiased estimates of the population parameters.

Consider the following specification with two independent variables:

$$Y = \beta_0 + \beta_1 X_1 + \beta_2 X_2 + U \tag{14.16}$$

$$E(U_i) = 0, \qquad \text{all } i \tag{14.17}$$

$$E(U_i^2) = k_i^2 \sigma^2, \qquad \text{all } i \tag{14.18}$$

$$E(U_i U_j) = 0, \qquad \text{all } i \neq j \tag{14.19}$$

$$X_i\text{-values fixed in repeated sampling} \tag{14.20}$$

This differs from the classical specification by (14.18), the heteroscedastic assumption, where the subscript i on k_i^2 signifies that the $E(U_i^2)$ varies across the sample observations. There are no restrictions on the value of k. If k is zero, the population disturbance term is zero, an unlikely case. If all k_i are 1 (or any constant, for that matter), homoscedasticity returns. The practical procedure to remove the heteroscedasticity is to transform (14.16) in such a way that the transformed equation has a disturbance term that satisfies the classical assumptions, the idea being that OLS procedures can be applied to the transformed equation.

The first step toward correction for heteroscedasticity is to divide (14.16) by k_i to obtain

$$\frac{Y_i}{k_i} = \beta_0 \frac{1}{k_i} + \beta_1 \frac{X_{1i}}{k_i} + \beta_2 \frac{X_{2i}}{k_i} + \frac{U_i}{k_i} \tag{14.21}$$

and evaluate the properties of the disturbance term, U_i/k_i, in the transformed equation (14.21):

$$E\left(\frac{U_i}{k_i}\right) = \frac{1}{k_i} E(U_i) = 0 \qquad \text{[by (14.17)]} \tag{14.22}$$

$$E\left(\frac{U_i}{k_i}\right)^2 = \frac{1}{k_i^2} E(U_i^2) = \frac{1}{k_i^2} k_i^2 \sigma^2 = \sigma^2 \qquad \text{[by (14.18)]} \tag{14.23}$$

$$E\left(\frac{U_i}{k_i}\frac{U_j}{k_j}\right) = \frac{1}{k_i k_j} E(U_i U_j) = 0 \qquad \text{[by (14.19)]} \tag{14.24}$$

These results show that the disturbance term in the transformed equation satisfies the classical assumptions. Consequently, OLS procedures are appropriate for estimating (14.21).

In sum, we began by specifying a heteroscedastic disturbance term, (14.18), that allows the variance of U to vary across the conditional distributions according to the square of some number k_i. Next, the population regression equation (14.16) was divided by the number k_i. Finally, equations (14.22) to (14.24) showed that the resulting disturbance term in the transformed equation, U_i/k_i, satisfies the classical assumptions. This means that (14.21), expressed in terms of transformed variables, can be estimated by OLS procedures. It is important to note that the parameters to be estimated, β_0, β_1, and β_2, are the same in (14.16) and (14.21).

In essence, OLS estimation under (14.16) to (14.20) is a two-step process. The first step is to "weight" each of the n observations by $1/k_i$ (where k_i comes from is discussed below). The second step is to apply OLS to the weighted observations. This method has the effect of creating the three new variables, Y^*, X_1^*, and X_2^*, in the worksheet used to estimate the coefficients. A worksheet of this type might look like Table 14.1, where Y, X_1, and X_2 are the observed values in the sample, $1/k_i$ are values assumed for illustration, and Y^*, X_1^*, and X_2^* are the original values transformed

Table 14.1. Example of a Transformation to Correct for Heteroscedasticity

	Original Values				Transformed Values		
Observation	Y	X_1	X_2	k_i	$Y^* = \dfrac{Y}{k_i}$	$X_1^* = \dfrac{X_1}{k_i}$	$X_2^* = \dfrac{X_2}{k_i}$
A	30	10	50	1.9	15.79	5.26	26.32
B	80	20	40	3.2	25.00	6.25	12.50
C	50	30	70	3.9	12.82	7.69	17.95
D	140	40	60	5.5	25.45	7.27	10.91
E	70	50	30	4.1	17.07	12.20	7.32
F	200	60	50	4.7	42.55	12.77	10.64
G	90	70	50	2.8	32.14	25.00	17.86

according to the heteroscedastic transformation (14.21). To get the desired estimates in this illustration, a researcher would instruct the computer to regress Y^* on X_1^* and X_2^*. Because the effect of the transformation is to weight the original observations, this is sometimes referred to as *weighted regression*. Note in passing that all the regressions done thus far in the book have been weighted regressions for the special case where all the weights have the value of one.

To get an intuitive feel for what is going on, notice that the weights depend on the variance of the disturbance term of the ith observation. Observations with large variances, large k_i^2 in (14.18), are weighted lightly, whereas those with small variances are weighted heavily. This transformation has the effect in regression computations of decreasing the relative size of observations with larger variances and increasing the relative size of observations with smaller variances, the net effect being to make the transformed variances more equal in size. Loosely speaking, it makes the scatter plot in Figure 14.1(b) look more like the scatter plot in Figure 14.1(a).

The difficulty in applied research is finding the k_i for performing the transformation required to remove the heteroscedasticity problem. Practical approaches to fixing heteroscedasticity follow the discussion of testing for heteroscedasticity in the next section.

Tests For Heteroscedasticity

Two tests for heteroscedasticity are presented in this section, the Goldfeld–Quandt test and the Breusch–Pagan test. Note from the outset, however, that an applied researcher should not feel overly secure in using these tests. As demonstrated in the following section, these tests involve considerable judgment in determining which of the independent variables is at the root of the problem. Moreover, there is no guarantee that only one independent variable is involved. These issues are explored with an example in the next section, following the formal statement of the tests in this section.

Consider the structure of the *Goldfeld–Quandt test*. First select a suspect independent variable, where the selection procedure is necessarily ad hoc. One way to detect a possible problem is to plot the computed OLS residuals against each of the independent variables in the equation to obtain diagrams similar to those in Figure 14.1, where the OLS residuals, rather than Y, are plotted on the vertical axis. Plots similar to those in Figure 14.1(b) would suggest heteroscedasticity. On the other hand, there may be a priori grounds for suspecting an independent variable for being guilty of heteroscedasticity. For example, the variance of certain types of consumer expenditures is likely to increase as consumer income increases. But whatever method may be used, a suspect X_k must be identified.

Given X_k, restructure the worksheet so that the sample observations are sequenced according to increasing values of X_k. Then delete the middle portion of the observations. The "middle portion" should consist of somewhere between, say, 20 and 30 percent of the sample. The precise number is arbitrary. Estimate two separate OLS regressions, one using the observations associated with the small values of X_k and one using the observations associated with the large values of X_k. From each, obtain the respective residual sum of squares, ESS_1 and ESS_h. Divide each by its appropriate degrees of freedom to obtain MSE_1 and MSE_h. Under the normality assumption, the ratio MSE_h/MSE_1 follows the F-distribution with $[n - d - 2(K + 1)]/2$ degrees of freedom in both numerator and denominator, where n is the sample size, d is the number of deleted sample observations, and $(K + 1)$ is the number of parameters estimated. If the computed F-statistic is greater than the critical F-statistic at the chosen probability level, the null hypothesis of no heteroscedasticity is rejected and a heteroscedastic transformation is required. The test above assumes an equal number of observations in each of the two subgroups. If for some reason there are unequal numbers in the two groups, the degrees of freedom must be adjusted accordingly.

The *Breusch–Pagan test* may be viewed as more general than the Goldfeld–Quandt test since it allows the researcher to test for more than one independent variable simultaneously. However, it remains as subjective as the Goldfeld–Quandt test in selecting the suspect independent variables. Let the basic equation be

$$Y = b_0 + b_1X_1 + b_2X_2 + b_3X_3 + b_4X_4 + e \qquad (14.25)$$

where X_1 and X_4 are suspect variables. The test procedure is as follows.

1. Obtain the OLS estimates of (14.25).
2. Calculate the OLS residuals for the sample observations, $e_i = Y_i - \hat{Y}_i$, where $\hat{Y}_i$ is the regression value of Y in (14.25).
3. Compute the variance of these residuals as $S_e^2 = \Sigma\, e_i^2/n$, where n is the sample size.
4. Standardize the residuals by e_i/S_e^2.
5. Estimate the equation $e_i/S_e^2 = a_0 + a_1X_{1i} + a_2X_{4i}$, where X_1 and X_4 are the suspect variables.
6. The statistic $(TSS - ESS)/2$ is distributed as chi-squared with K degrees of freedom, where K is the number of independent variables, TSS is the total sum of squares, and ESS is the error sum of squares from the equation in step 5.

If the computed statistic in step 6 is less than the critical chi-square value, do not reject the null hypothesis of no heteroscedasticity on X_1 and X_4 taken together. If the computed statistic is greater than the critical value, reject the null hypothesis.

These tests, together with alternative heteroscedastic transformations on the variables, are illustrated in the next section.

Remedies

A physicist, a chemist, and an economist are stranded and hungry on a barren island. A can of beans washes ashore and discussion immediately turns to opening it. "Smash it with a stick," cries the physicist. "Heat it over a fire," exclaims the chemist. "Wait!" commands the economist sagely. "Let's assume that we have a can opener. . . ." This anecdote captures the essence of the quandary of the applied researcher faced with heteroscedasticity. Assumptions about the specific nature of heteroscedasticity must be made if the problem is to be mitigated.

This section offers two general examples to illustrate how the applied researcher might specify the k_i appropriate to the data set at hand. These are illustrated below with a specific equation.

Suppose that the population regression function is

$$Y = \beta_0 + \beta_1 X_1 + \beta_2 X_2 + U \tag{14.26}$$

where we might suspect that U is heteroscedastic on X_2. First, estimate (14.26) by OLS and then plot the residual against X_2. This might yield something like Figure 14.2, which suggests that the variance is increasing with X_2. Moreover, the plot suggests that the variance of U_i increases linearly with X_2. It seems plausible therefore, to write (14.18) as

$$E(U_i^2) = X_{2i}\sigma^2 \tag{14.27}$$

where $k_i = \sqrt{X_{2i}}$. Dividing (14.26) by $\sqrt{X_{2i}}$ yields

$$\frac{Y_i}{\sqrt{X_{2i}}} = \beta_0 \frac{1}{\sqrt{X_{2i}}} + \beta_1 \frac{X_{1i}}{\sqrt{X_{2i}}} + \beta_2 \frac{X_{2i}}{\sqrt{X_{2i}}} + \frac{U_i}{\sqrt{X_{2i}}} \tag{14.28}$$

where demonstrating that the disturbance term in (14.28) satisfies the classical assumptions is left as an exercise. Applying OLS to (14.28) yields the desired estimates of (14.26). It is important to note that because of the assumption and transformation on (14.26), (14.28) has no constant term, so the regression must be estimated without one. However, it is best to return to (14.26) for interpreting the results. The estimate of β_0 is recovered as the estimated coefficient of the variable $1/\sqrt{X_{2i}}$ in (14.28).

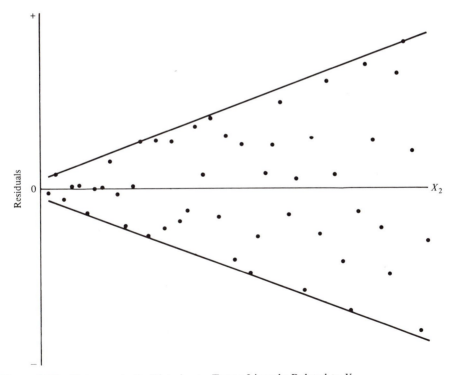

Figure 14.2   Heteroscedastic Disturbance Terms Linearly Related to X_2.

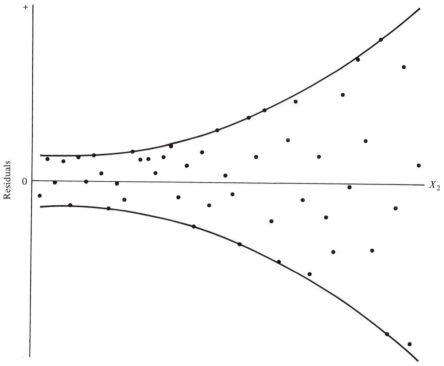

Figure 14.3 Heteroscedastic Disturbance Terms Proportional to X_2.

An alternative specification often used in applied research is a variance that increases proportional to X_{2i}^2. This implies a scatter plot of OLS residuals similar to that shown in Figure 14.3. The procedure in this case is exactly as above, except that $k_i^2 = X_{2i}^2$, and the transformed equation becomes

$$\frac{Y_i}{X_{2i}} = \beta_0 \frac{1}{X_{2i}} + \beta_1 \frac{X_{1i}}{X_{2i}} + \beta_2 \frac{X_{2i}}{X_{2i}} + \frac{U_i}{X_{2i}} \tag{14.29}$$

where the error term satisfies the classical assumptions.

To see more clearly how to interpret the OLS estimates of (14.29), it is instructive to examine the worksheet for (14.29), shown in Table 14.2. The important point is the treatment of the column of 1's.

Table 14.2. Example Worksheet Illustrating an Adjustment for Heteroscedasticity Using X_{2i}

Original Values				Transformed Values				
Y	C	X_1	X_2	Y^*	C	C^*	X_1^*	X_2^*
Y_1	1	X_{11}	X_{21}	Y_1/X_{21}	1	$1/X_{21}$	X_{11}/X_{22}	$X_{21}/X_{21} = 1$
Y_2	1	X_{12}	X_{22}	Y_2/X_{22}	1	$1/X_{22}$	X_{12}/X_{22}	$X_{22}/X_{22} = 1$
.	.	.	.	.	.	.	.	.
.	.	.	.	.	.	.	.	.
.	.	.	.	.	.	.	.	.

If the original values of the variables were used, the instructions to the computer would be to regress Y on X_1 and X_2. The computer automatically includes the constant C as a variable (at least most regression software packages do), the OLS coefficient of which is the estimate of the population intercept. After transforming the original values according to (14.29), we have on the worksheet Y^*, C^*, X_1^*, and X_2^*. But under this specific transformation, X_2^* is a column of 1's, so the computer "sees" two such columns, C and X_2^*. So care must be shown in instructing the computer to perform the analysis. Specifically, tell it to regress Y^* on C^* and X_1^*, and the computer uses C, C^*, and X_1^*. (This assumes regression software that does not have a "generalized least squares" routine; if it does have such a routine, be sure to read the manual to see how to set up the regression run.)

The OLS coefficients from this estimation must be interpreted carefully. The "constant" term in (14.29) is actually the slope of X_2 in (14.26), the values of X_2 in (14.29) being a column of 1's. The coefficient of C^*, the values of which are $1/X_{2i}$, is by (14.26) the estimate of the intercept. The coefficient of X_1^* is the estimate of the slope of X_1 in (14.26). These "re-transformations" must be made before making statements about the coefficients.

Although these examples illustrate the nature of the heteroscedastic transformation, they are based on the simple expedient of subjectively examining the pattern of OLS residuals against one of the independent variables. When working with a large number of independent variables, this procedure may not be very practical. For this reason, applied researchers sometimes use slightly more complicated, but not necessarily less arbitrary, procedures. One procedure uses $k_i = \hat{Y}_i$, where the $\hat{Y}_i$ are the OLS regression values of Y_i obtained from first regressing Y on X_1 and X_2. This particular transformation assumes that $k_i = b_0 + b_1X_1 + b_2X_2$, which in turn assumes that the adjustment factors k_i and Y are the same function (the b_i's are the same) of X_1 and X_2. A variation of this transformation is to first regress Y on X_1 and X_2, and then use the OLS residuals to estimate $e_i = c_0 + c_1X_1 + c_2X_2$, where $c_i \neq b_i$, and use $k_i = \hat{e}_i$ for the transformation. The t-tests on the c_i give a check on the presence of heteroscedasticity. These are illustrated below.

The following example is used to illustrate the two test procedures discussed in the preceding section and to illustrate what happens when various heteroscedastic transformations are used. The data used are those discussed in Chapter 12.

The equation of interest is

$$Y = \beta_0 + \beta_1 I + \beta_2 N + \beta_3 A + U \tag{14.30}$$

where Y = weekly food expenditures
I = weekly household income
N = household size
A = age of head of household.

The estimated equation is

$$Y = -8.25 + 1.48I^* + 11.58N^* + .24A^* + e \tag{14.31}$$
$$(6.35) \quad (.423) \quad\quad (.877) \quad\quad (.114)$$

where numbers in parentheses are standard deviations and an asterisk denotes a t-ratio greater than 2. Since each of the slope coefficients is statistically significant, complacency would let it go at that. However, a cross-sectional data set was used to estimate the equation and a test for heteroscedasticity should be conducted. If heteroscedasticity is present, the estimates of the standard deviations of the coefficients in (14.31) may be biased, in which case the t-ratios are invalid.

To illustrate the Goldfeld–Quandt test, income was taken as the suspect variable, and the test was conducted as follows:

1. The 235 observations were ordered by increasing income.
2. The middle 55 observations were deleted, leaving 90 observations for the "low"-income households and 90 observations for the "high"-income households.
3. An OLS equation using all independent variables was estimated for each of the two subgroups.
4. The ESS for the low-income group was 22,604, and ESS for the high-income group was 40,479.
5. Computed F-statistic $= (40,479/22,604) \times (86/86) = 1.79$.
6. The critical F-statistic for 86 degrees of freedom in the numerator and 86 degrees of freedom in the denominator is approximately 1.4.

Because the computed F-statistic is greater than the critical F-statistic at the .05 level, the null hypothesis of no heteroscedasticity is rejected. (It is important to keep in mind that this result assumes that income is the "problem" variable.) A similar test was conducted using age of household head as the suspect variable, and the null hypothesis was not rejected. This illustrates two facts regarding the Goldfeld–Quandt test. First, the test is conducted on only one independent variable and if by chance the wrong variable is selected for the test, the null hypothesis may not be rejected, yet heteroscedasticity remains.

Second, there may be compelling reasons for believing that two or more independent variables are jointly suspect, in which case the Goldfeld–Quandt test is not applicable. In this case the Breusch–Pagan test can be used. However, it does require prior identification of the suspect variables. To illustrate the Breusch–Pagan test, use income and family size as suspect variables and conduct the following:

1. Compute the OLS residuals from (14.27) according to $(Y_i - \hat{Y}_i)$, where $\hat{Y}$ are the regression values of (14.27).
2. Calculate e_i^2/S_e^2, where $S_e^2 = \Sigma\, e_i^2/n$.
3. Regress these standardized OLS residuals, e_i^2/S_e^2, on I_i and N_i.
4. The estimated equation is $e_i^2/S_e^2 = .079 + .050I_i + .197N_i$, where TSS $= 539.916$ and ESS $= 514.708$.
5. The test statistic $= (539.916 - 514.708)/2 = 12.6$.
6. The critical value of the chi-square distribution at the .05 level with 2 degrees of freedom is 5.99.

The computed test statistic is larger than the critical value of the statistic and the null hypothesis of homoscedasticity is rejected.

To reaffirm the sensitivity of these tests to the suspect variables identified, the Breusch–Pagan test was conducted using I and A, rather than I and N, as the suspect variables. The computed test statistic was 4.2. In this case the null hypothesis of homoscedasticity was not rejected. This reenforces the comment above that considerable subjectivity is involved in testing for heteroscedasticity.

Given the presence of heteroscedasticity, the researcher must search for a transformation of the equation such that the disturbance term of the transformed equation is homoscedastic. The search is illustrated here with four different specifications on the variance of the disturbance term. In each case, the transformation implied by the specification is shown, the equation is reestimated using the transformed variables, and the Breusch–Pagan test is used to determine if the disturbance term of the resulting equation is homoscedastic. The important lesson to be learned is that the nature of the search process is ad hoc and that the empirical results can be quite sensitive to the assumptions made on the disturbance term. The equations and the transformations are presented, followed by a summary table with the estimates of the equations.

Basic Model Assumes That $E(U_i^2) = \sigma^2$

$$Y_i = \beta_0 + \beta_1 I_i + \beta_2 N_i + \beta_3 A_i + U_i$$

to be estimated directly by OLS.

Model I Assumes That $E(U_i^2) = I_i \sigma^2$

This assumes that the variance is a linear function of income. The transformed equation to be estimated by OLS is

$$\frac{Y_i}{\sqrt{I_i}} = \beta_0 \frac{1}{\sqrt{I_i}} + \beta_1 \frac{I_i}{\sqrt{I_i}} + \beta_2 \frac{N_i}{\sqrt{I_i}} + \beta_3 \frac{A_i}{\sqrt{I_i}} + \frac{U_i}{\sqrt{I_i}}$$

Model II Assumes That $E(U_i^2) = I_i^2 \sigma^2$

This assumes that the variance changes at an increasing rate as income changes. The transformed equation to be estimated by OLS is

$$\frac{Y_i}{I_i} = \beta_0 \frac{1}{I_i} + \beta_1 + \beta_2 \frac{N_i}{I_i} + \beta_3 \frac{A_i}{I_i} + \frac{U_i}{I_i}$$

These two models are those discussed above under the theoretical treatment of heteroscedasticity.

Model III Assumes That $E(U_i^2) = \hat{Y}_i^2 \sigma^2$

This assumes that the variance is proportional to the regression, or estimated, values of Y obtained from the OLS estimation of the basic model. The transformed equation is

$$\frac{Y_i}{\hat{Y}_i} = \beta_0 \frac{1}{\hat{Y}_i} + \beta_1 \frac{I_i}{\hat{Y}_i} + \beta_2 \frac{N_i}{\hat{Y}_i} + \beta_3 \frac{A_i}{\hat{Y}_i} + \frac{U_i}{\hat{Y}_i}$$

Model IV Assumes That $E(U_i^2) = |e_i| \sigma^2$

This assumes that the variance is a linear function of the OLS residuals. Two versions of this are considered: Type IV-a uses the residuals from regressing Y on I and N;

type IV-b uses the residuals from regressing Y on I, N, and A. In either case the structure of the transformed equation is

$$\frac{Y_i}{\sqrt{|e_i|}} = \beta_0 \frac{1}{\sqrt{|e_i|}} + \beta_1 \frac{I_i}{\sqrt{|e_i|}} + \beta_2 \frac{N_i}{\sqrt{|e_i|}} + \beta_3 \frac{A_i}{\sqrt{|e_i|}} + \frac{U_i}{|e_i|}$$

The results of estimating these six equations are presented in Table 14.3. The final column of the table shows the computed value of the Breusch–Pagan statistic for the estimated equation constructed using I, N, and A. Consequently, there are three degrees of freedom for testing, and the critical chi-square value at the .05 level is 7.81.

The value of the computed statistic for each equation exceeds the critical value, which means that the null hypothesis of no heteroscedasticity must be rejected. In other words, none of the five transformations has completely removed the heteroscedastic problem. However, the Breusch–Pagan test is conservative in that it rejects the null hypothesis in instances where the hypothesis should be accepted. Consequently, as a practical matter, the two versions of Model IV are acceptable for applied work.

In summary, testing for heteroscedasticity is important, especially when working with cross-sectional data sets; otherwise, the estimated variances of the coefficients may be biased and the t-ratios invalid. As the illustration shows, testing is somewhat arbitrary with regard to the suspect variables, and finding an appropriate transformation is equally arbitrary. As Table 14.3 shows, the results can be quite sensitive to the heteroscedastic assumption used. Moreover, there is no guarantee that a transformation will correct for the problem.

A final warning is in order. The illustrations above, plus many other transformations, are essentially based on an examination of the OLS residuals. This examination can be dangerous to the health of an otherwise robust equation. Chapter 3 showed the relation in the sample between the observable e_i, the unobservable U_i, and the X-values to be

$$\Sigma \, e_i^2 = \Sigma \, (\beta_1 - b_1)^2 x_i^2 + \Sigma \, (U_i - \overline{U})^2 \tag{14.32}$$

which on dividing by $n - 1$ yields

$$\text{Var} \, (e_i) = (\beta_1 - b_1)^2 \, \text{Var} \, (X_i) + \text{Var} \, (U_i) \tag{14.33}$$

as the sample relationship. This shows that the scatter plot of e_i is affected not only by the variance of U but also by the variance of X in the sample. Thus what might appear to be heteroscedasticity in the OLS residuals may be due not to a heteroscedastic disturbance term, but to the sample variance in X, in which case no transformation is called for.

Suppose that a heteroscedastic transformation is applied to healthy (homoscedastic) relationship. Specify a simple heteroscedastic relationship

$$E(U_i^2) = X_i^2 \sigma^2 \tag{14.34}$$

when in fact $E(U_i^2)$ is the constant σ^2. According to the illustrations above, the appropriate weight is $1/X_i$, which yields

$$U_i^* = \frac{U_i}{X_i} \tag{14.35}$$

Table 14.3. Parameter Estimates Under Different Assumed Models of Heteroscedasticity

Model	Assumed Hetero-scedasticity	Constant	Income	Size	Age	S	Breusch–Pagan Value
		OLS Parameter Estimates[a]					
Base	$E(U^2) = \sigma^2$	−8.25	1.48	11.58	.24	18.4	27.1
		(1.3)	(3.5)	(13.2)	(2.1)		
I	$E(U^2) = I\sigma^2$	−1.43	2.28	10.50	.09	10.5	25.6
		(.2)	(4.0)	(12.2)	(1.0)		
II	$E(U^2) = I^2\sigma^2$	8.95	3.20	9.34	−.11	7.8	118.0
		(1.7)	(4.4)	(10.5)	(1.5)		
III	$E(U^2) = \hat{Y}^2\sigma^2$	−5.28	1.42	10.91	.23	.38	16.8
		(1.0)	(2.9)	(10.9)	(2.6)		
IV-a	$E(U^2) = |e|\sigma^2$	−7.31	1.50	11.35	.23	4.8	8.9
		(1.2)	(3.2)	(12.4)	(2.2)		
IV-b	$E(U^2) = |e|\sigma^2$	−7.81	1.48	11.36	.24	4.8	7.1
		(1.3)	(3.2)	(12.4)	(2.3)		

[a] The t-values are in parentheses. IV-a, $|e| = F(I, N)$; IV-b, $|e| = F(I, N, A)$. The critical value of chi-square for 3 degrees of freedom is 7.81.

This disturbance term has an expected value of zero,

$$E(U_i^*) = E\left(\frac{U_i}{X_i}\right) = \frac{1}{X_i} E(U_i) = 0 \qquad (14.36)$$

and a variance of

$$E\left(\frac{U_i}{X_i}\right)^2 = \frac{1}{X_i^2} E(U_i^2) = \frac{1}{X_i^2} \sigma^2 \qquad (14.37)$$

This shows that by attempting to correct a homoscedast model for heteroscedasticity, a researcher can introduce heteroscedasticity where it did not exist before. All of which is simply to say that heteroscedastistic transformations should not be applied willy-nilly.

As the discussion and examples above illustrate, in applied research, there is no foolproof way to detect the heteroscedasticity problem. Moreover, even if its presence is suspected, it is not clear how to correct for it. The best the researcher can do is to prepare and examine plots like those suggested above to determine if heteroscedasticity may be present. If it may be, then various transformations should be examined, using plots and statistical tests to assess the results.

Autocorrelation

Suppose that a researcher is using time-series data to estimate the quarterly supply function for hog slaughter. One of the winter quarters during the period of analysis was extremely cold. As a consequence, the number of pigs saved per litter was less than the number saved during any other quarter in the data set. Several quarters would be required for the effect of this single-period shock to work itself out. The reduction of the number of pigs saved in one quarter means that the breeeding stock would be below "normal" in the immediately following quarters and that the inventory of slaughter hogs would be below normal in subsequent quarters. The effect of a "random shock" in one time period is carried forward into subsequent time periods, causing a ripple effect to occur much like the waves that radiate outward when a rock is dropped into calm waters. In cases such as this, the successive disturbance terms in the equation being estimated are likely to be correlated. If this is the case, then ordinary least squares procedures will not yield best, linear, unbiased estimates because the $E(U_iU_j) = 0$ assumption is violated.

In the absence of autocorrelation, which in applied work we associate with time-series data set, the plot of the OLS residuals against time should exhibit no obvious pattern. This is illustrated in Figure 14.4(a). On the other hand, autocorrelation should result in a pronounced pattern in the OLS residuals over time since, by specification, the population disturbance terms are not statistically independent. What the pattern may be is, of course, an empirical proposition; it depends on the specific data set. Parts (b) and (c) of Figure 14.4 are only suggestive of the types of time patterns in residuals when autocorrelation is a problem.

Before considering how to handle autocorrelation in applied research, an alternative argument for the presence of autocorrelation in the disturbance term when using time-series data for estimating regression coefficients should be mentioned. Recall that a major rationale for including the disturbance term is to measure the combined effect of all the variables not included in the equation being estimated. Many socioeconomic variables are autocorrelated, which is to say that contemporaneous values of the variables are correlated with their respective past values. Since the disturbance term is included to measure the combined effect of these omitted variables, it follows that if they are autocorrelated, the disturbance term will be autocorrelated.

The Theory

The solution to the autoregressive problem is analogous to that of heteroscedasticity: Transform the equation with the autoregressive disturbance term into an equation with a nonautoregressive disturbance term so as to permit the use of OLS procedures. In this section we first illustrate a general transformation and then consider two specific approaches that can be used in applied research. A general theoretical treatment is given in Chapter 20.

Consider the population regression function, where the t subscript denotes time, since autoregression is usually associated with time-series data sets:

$$Y_t = \beta_0 + \beta_1 X_t + U_t, \qquad t = 1, \ldots, T \qquad (14.38)$$

with a *first-order* autoregressive specification on U:

$$U_t = \rho U_{t-1} + V_t, \qquad -1 \le \rho \le 1 \qquad (14.39)$$

$$E(U_t) = 0 \qquad (14.40)$$

$$E(U_t^2) = \sigma^2 \qquad (14.41)$$

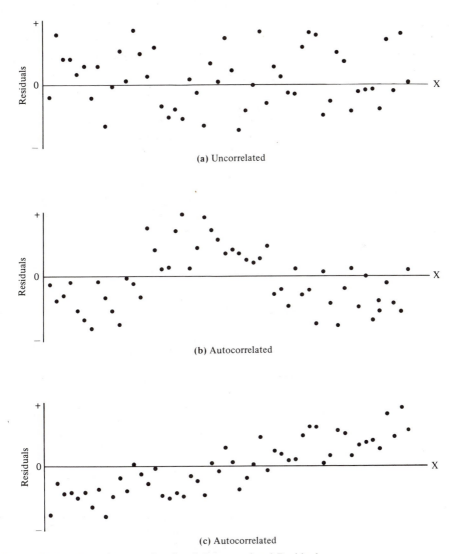

Figure 14.4 Plots of Uncorrelated and Autocorrelated Residuals.

$$E(V_t V_{t-s}) = 0, \quad \text{all } t \neq s \tag{14.42}$$

$$E(V_t U_{t-s}) = 0, \quad \text{all } s \neq 0 \tag{14.43}$$

Equations (14.39) to (14.43) taken together define a first-order autoregressive model, with equation (14.39) as the autoregressive specification, which relates the contemporaneous U to the preceding U. Note carefully that this is a first-order specification and all that follows is based on this specification. There is nothing sacred about this specification (perhaps simplicity of exposition is its main virtue). Any order of specification is possible, and the lag structure need not be continuous over time. For example, when working with quarterly data, a researcher might specify $U_t = \rho U_{t-4} + V_t$, or with monthly data, $U_t = \rho U_{t-12} + V_t$. The *form* of the analysis based on (14.39) that follows can be applied to any autoregressive specification, but the *specifics* are different. If in applied research there arises a need to work with some other specification, the researcher must derive the implications of that specification before estimating the equation.

The objective is to find a transformation of (14.38) that yields an equation with a disturbance term that is not autocorrelated. Before proceeding, consider carefully what this specification is saying. Equation (14.39) states that the contemporaneous disturbance term, U_t, is a simple linear function of its immediately preceding value, U_{t-1}, plus a random variable, V_t. Two things are to be noted. First, the coefficient of U_{t-1}, ρ (rho), called the *autoregression coefficient*, is interpreted as the change in U_t for a 1-unit change in U_{t-1}, and it can range between -1 and $+1$. Second, the disturbance term, V_t, has the classical statistical specifications and it is uncorrelated with U_t.

Since (14.38) holds for all t, it holds for $t - 1$, and it is possible to lag (14.38) one period to obtain

$$Y_{t-1} = \beta_0 + \beta_1 X_{t-1} + U_{t-1} \tag{14.44}$$

On the assumption that the autoregressive coefficient is not equal to zero, the next step is to multiply (14.44) by ρ to obtain

$$\rho Y_{t-1} = \rho \beta_0 + \rho \beta_1 X_{t-1} + \rho U_{t-1} \tag{14.45}$$

Observe that (14.38) and (14.45) involve U_t, U_{t-1}, and ρ, the same terms that appear in (14.39). Subtract (14.45) from (14.38) to obtain

$$Y_t - \rho Y_{t-1} = (1 - \rho)\beta_0 + \beta_1(X_t - \rho X_{t-1}) + U_t - \rho U_{t-1} \tag{14.46}$$

By (14.39),

$$U_t - \rho U_{t-1} = V_t \tag{14.47}$$

which on substitution into (14.46) yields

$$Y_t - \rho Y_{t-1} = (1 - \rho)\beta_0 + \beta_1(X_t - \rho X_{t-1}) + V_t \tag{14.48}$$

For the moment, let $Y_t^* = Y_t - \rho Y_{t-1}$ and $X_t^* = X_t - \rho X_{t-1}$ and write

$$Y_t^* = (1 - \rho)\beta_0 + \beta_1 X_t^* + V_t \tag{14.49}$$

This is a linear expression of Y_t^* as a function of X_t^*. More important, the disturbance term in (14.49), V_t, has the classical OLS assumptions, and the OLS estimator of β_1 in (14.49) will have the desired properties.

This suggests the following procedure. If the "true" specification is (14.38) to (14.43) and BLUE estimators are desired, researchers should use a two-step procedure. First, create the variables Y_t^* and X_t^* on the worksheet according to the following:

Transforming Y and X to Y^* and X^*

$$Y_2^* = Y_2 - \rho Y_1 \qquad X_2^* = X_2 - \rho X_1$$

$$Y_3^* = Y_3 - \rho Y_2 \qquad X_3^* = X_3 - \rho X_2$$

$$\vdots \qquad\qquad \vdots$$

Second, apply OLS procedures to these transformed variables [estimate (14.49)] to obtain the desired results. In concept, the solution to the autocorrelation problem involves the simple, straightforward two-step procedure.

A Test for Autocorrelation

The Durbin–Watson test is commonly used in applied research to test for the presence of autoregressiveness. It is important to understand that this test is appropriate *only* for the first-order specification and where the lagged dependent variable does not appear in the equations.

To use this test, a *d*-statistic is computed from the sample according to

$$d = \frac{\sum\limits_{t=2}^{T} (e_t - e_{t-1})^2}{\sum\limits_{t=1}^{T} e_t^2} \tag{14.50}$$

where the *e*'s are the OLS residuals computed from the sample. To get an intuitive feel for this test, recall that the *e*'s take on both positive and negative values, with an average of zero over the sample observations. If the series has a positive autocorrelation, the typical case with time-series data sets, the value of e_t will be close to the value of e_{t-1}, and the value of the first differences, $(e_t - e_{t-1})$, in the numerator of (14.49) will tend to be quite small relative to the values of e_t in the denominator of (14.50). Consequently, the *d*-statistic will tend to be small. The opposite argument holds for the case of negative, first-order autocorrelation. Thus *d* will tend to be small for positive autocorrelation, *d* will tend to be large for negative autocorrelation, and *d* will fall somewhere between these two limits for a random series (i.e., one with no autocorrelation).

To get some idea of these relationships, we expand (14.50) to obtain

$$d = \frac{\sum\limits_{t=2}^{T} e_t^2 - 2 \sum\limits_{t=2}^{T} e_t e_{t-1} + \sum\limits_{t=2}^{T} e_{t-1}^2}{\sum\limits_{t=1}^{T} e_t^2} \tag{14.51}$$

As a practical matter, the squared terms summed over $t = 1$ and $t = 2$ will be nearly equal, so we rewrite this as

$$d \approx \frac{\sum e_t^2 - 2 \sum e_t e_{t-1} + \sum e_t^2}{\sum e_t^2}$$

$$\approx \frac{2 \sum e_t^2 - 2 \sum e_t e_{t-1}}{\sum e_t^2} \tag{14.52}$$

$$\approx 2\left(1 - \frac{\Sigma\, e_t e_{t-1}}{\Sigma\, e_t^2}\right)$$

but $\Sigma\, e_t e_{t-1}/\Sigma\, e_t^2 = \hat{\rho}$, so

$$d \approx 2(1 - \hat{\rho}) \qquad (14.53)$$

If there is no first-order autocorrelation $\rho = 0$, in which case

$$d \approx 2 \qquad (14.54)$$

The distribution of the Durbin–Watson d-statistic is based on this approximation, so the d-distribution does not provide a unique critical value for testing as does the t-distribution, for example. Rather, there is an "inconclusive" range, which means that if the computed d-statistic falls in this range a researcher can neither reject or not reject the null hypothesis of no positive autocorrelation. Consequently, a Durbin–Watson table shows two critical values, d_L and d_U, for different sample sizes, where d_L is the "lower" value and d_U is the "upper" value. The formal test for positive autocorrelation is

H_0: no positive autocorrelation   versus H_a: positive autocorrelation

The decision rules are

1. If $d < d_L$, reject H_0, do not reject H_a.
2. If $d > d_U$, do not reject H_0.
3. If $d_L < d < d_U$, inconclusive.

Here d is computed from the sample and d_L and d_U are critical values from the table. Because this test is only approximate and because of the consequences of using OLS estimators in the presence of autocorrelation, applied researchers may test on the basis of $d < d_U$, a more conservative test than the one above.

In summary, the critical d-values are a function of the number of sample observations used to estimate the equation, the number of parameters estimated by the equation, and the confidence level for the test.

The formal test above is for positive autocorrelation, the typical case. However, if a researcher has no a priori basis for this test, it is possible to to test the more general hypothesis of no autocorrelation, positive or negative. The decision rules for $H_0 =$ no autocorrelation are

1. Reject H_0 if $d < d_L$ (positive) or if $d > 4 - d_L$ (negative).
2. Do not reject H_0 if $d_U < d < 4 - d_U$.
3. Test inconclusive if $d_L < d < d_U$ or $4 - d_U < d < 4 - d_L$.

This can be depicted schematically as in Figure 14.5.

Many computer programs provide the d-statistic as part of the standard regression output. Other programs do not offer the d-statistic as part of the standard output, but do have it as an option. When using time-series data sets it is a good idea to obtain the statistic and conduct the test in order to get some information about a possible autocorrelation problem.

Although the Durbin–Watson statistic is widely used in applied research, it has

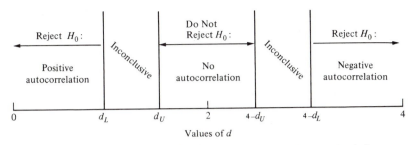

Figure 14.5   Acceptance and Rejection Regions for the Durbin-Watson Statistic.

several shortcomings. It is appropriate to testing *only* for first-order autocorrelation. Technically, it is valid only if the population disturbance terms V_i are observable, which they are not. Moreover, as (14.33) shows, the e_i computed from the sample are a function not only of V_i but also of the regressors in the equation. As a practical matter, a time-series plot of the OLS residuals may be as good a method for detecting the possibility of the autocorrelation problem.

Finally, the Durbin–Watson test is not applicable to regression equations where one of the explanatory variables is the lagged value of the dependent variable, such as Y_{t-1} or Y_{t-2}. For this case Durbin has developed the *h*-statistic to test for serial correlation in the residuals:

$$h = \hat{\rho} \sqrt{\frac{n}{1 - nS_{b_1}}} \qquad (14.55)$$

where $\hat{\rho}$ is given in equation (14.52) or could be calculated as $1 - \frac{1}{2} d$ [equation (14.53)]. S_{b_1} is the least squares estimate of the coefficient of Y_{t-1}. The value h is normally distributed with a mean of zero and a variance of 1 and n is the sample size. Thus the critical values for the null hypothesis are in Appendix Table A.1.

In the case where $nS_{b_1} > 1.0$, the *h*-statistic cannot be calculated using (14.55). Durbin has developed another version of the foregoing test to handle this situation. A researcher first regresses the least squares residual e_t on e_{t-1} plus all the independent variables, including the lagged dependent variable. The null hypothesis of no serial correlation is tested by the significance of the coefficient of e_{t-1} using the *t*-test applicable to ordinary least squares regression coefficients.

Remedies

While the theoretical solution is straightforward, the practical solution is not because of the need to know ρ in order to create the transformed variables. More advanced texts examine a number of proposals for determining ρ from the sample, particularly with regard to their statistical properties. Two practical procedures are demonstrated here. One offers computational ease; the other, more commonly used, procedure has more desirable statistical properties. The latter is highly recommended if a computer program is available to do the calculations.

The simple procedure uses the Durbin–Watson statistic (d-statistic) to compute ρ, the autoregressive coefficient. Because d is standard output of most least squares programs, it is a simple matter to calculate $\hat{\rho}$ by (14.53).

$$\rho \approx 1 - \tfrac{1}{2}(d) \tag{14.56}$$

The money demand equation (6.54) can illustrate. The equation is reproduced below for convience.

$$\hat{Y} = 2577.1 + .755C + .489I - 1.793G - 30.585INT + 24.70UNEMP$$
$$\quad\;\; (662.7) \quad (.095) \quad (.185) \quad (.625) \quad\;\; (3.541) \quad\quad (12.92)$$

$$S = 42.6$$

$$R^2 = .936$$

$$d = 1.10$$

$$\tag{14.57}$$

The Durbin–Watson statistic for this equation is 1.10. From Appendix Table A.4, with $k = 1$ and $n = 46$, $d_L = 1.48$, $d_U = 1.57$, $4 - d_L = 2.52$, and $4 - d_U = 2.43$. (Using $n = 45$ produces a slightly conservative test.) The decision intervals are:

1. $d < 1.48$; reject H_0: positive autocorrelation.
2. $1.48 < d < 1.57$; inconclusive.
3. $1.57 < d < 2.43$; do not reject H_0: no autocorrelation.
4. $2.43 < d < 2.52$; inconclusive.
5. $2.52 < d$; reject H_0: negative autocorrelation.

According to the criterion above, reject H_0: and do not reject the alternative hypotheses of positive autocorrelation. The parameter estimates in (14.57) are unbiased, but their variances are underestimated. This means that the parameters appear to be significant when, in fact, they may not be. To obtain the correct variances, the error term must be adjusted in the spirit of (14.47) to (14.48). This requires three steps:

1. Calculate $\hat{\rho}$.
2. Transform the data via equation (14.48) to obtain Y^* and X^*.
3. Regress Y^* on X^* to obtain BLU estimates of α and β_i.

In the first step, $\hat{\rho}$ is calculated from d:

$$\hat{\rho} = 1 - \tfrac{1}{2}(d) = 1 - \tfrac{1}{2}(1.10) = .45 \tag{14.58}$$

The second step uses $\hat{\rho}$ to transform the data, that is,

$$Y^*_t = Y_t - .45Y_{t-1}$$
$$X^*_t = X_t - .45X_{t-1} \tag{14.59}$$

Note that since the first available observation for the transformed variables is Y^*_2 and X^*_2, one observation is lost in the transformation. To preserve the first observation, the following transformations are used:

Table 14.4. Illustration of Transformation for First-Order Autocorrelation of Data for the Demand for Money, Equation (14.57)

Year	Quarter	M	C	I	G	INT	UNEMP
1973	1	3757.46	3641.88	1021.79	1206.06	2.69	4.9
	2	3745.98	3621.46	1026.46	1186.67	4.86	4.9
	3	3731.80	3628.95	1015.56	1184.82	6.69	4.8
	4	3697.10	3606.30	1043.27	1206.02	5.39	4.8
1974	1	3691.13	3572.03	968.09	1208.35	5.78	5.1
	2	3639.59	3578.92	940.98	1221.55	5.78	5.2
	3	.	.	.	.	.	.
		.	.	.	.	.	.
		.	.	.	.	.	.
		.	.	.	.	.	.

Transformed data ($\hat{\rho} = .45$)

Year	Quarter	M	C	I	G	INT	UNEMP
1973	1	3355.52	3252.30	912.49	1077.05	2.40	4.38
	2	2055.12	1982.61	566.66	643.94	3.65	2.70
	3	2046.11	1999.29	553.65	650.82	4.50	2.60
	4	2017.79	1973.28	586.27	672.85	2.37	2.64
1974	1	2027.43	1949.20	498.62	665.64	3.56	2.94
	2	1978.59	1971.51	505.34	667.79	3.18	2.90
	3	.	.	.	.	.	.
		.	.	.	.	.	.
		.	.	.	.	.	.
		.	.	.	.	.	.

$$Y_1^* = Y_1 \sqrt{1 - \hat{\rho}^2} \tag{14.60}$$

$$X_1^* = X_1 \sqrt{1 - \hat{\rho}^2}$$

Table 14.4 shows the original and transformed data for the first few observations. The estimated equation using the transformed variables is

$$\hat{Y}^* = 62.00 + .685C^* + .503I^* - .541G^* - 27.721INT^* + 12.510\ UNEMP^*$$
$$\phantom{\hat{Y}^* =} (90.74)\quad (.124)\quad\ \ (.227)\quad\ \ (.237)\quad\ \ (5.162)\quad\quad\ (18.47) \tag{14.61}$$

$$S = 50.4$$

$$R^2 = .950$$

$$d = 1.55$$

The *new* d-value for the transformed equation is 1.55, which is inconclusive. This is at least an improvement over this original equation. If the researcher is not satisfied with the Durbin–Watson value, a new autocorrelation coefficient can be estimated based on the transformed equation as $\hat{\rho} = 1 - (\frac{1}{2})1.55 = .225$. This is much smaller than the original estimate (.45). Using the original values of Y_t, X_t^*, and the new ρ, we can calculate a new set of transformed values and use them to reestimate (14.61) and, if necessary, proceed to a third and a fourth interation. In fact, the process can be continued, one step at a time, until the value of ρ does not change.

Changes in (14.57) when compared to (14,61) are instructive. The estimate of S was biased downward in the original data (42.6 versus 50.4). The result is overstated values of the coefficient of multiple determination and understated values of the variance estimates. They have all increased. Thus, in the original equation, the t-values for testing significance are too low.

In transforming the variables, equation (14.49) shows that the estimated intercept is $(1 - \rho)\beta_0$. Therefore, if the correct intercept is to be used, the estimate of β_0 and Var (β_0) must be multiplied by $1/(1 - \rho)$. The other parameters and their respective variances are not affected by the transformation procedure.

Finally, the procedure above can easily be extended to higher-order autoregressive schemes by calculating $\hat{\rho}_1$, $\hat{\rho}_2$, $\hat{\rho}_3$, and so on, using the following adjustment to (14.39):

$$U_t = \rho_1 U_{t-1} + \rho_2 U_{t-2} + \rho_3 U_{t-3} + \cdots + V_t$$

Then

$$Y_t^* = Y_t - \hat{\rho}_1 Y_{t-1} - \hat{\rho}_2 Y_{t-2} - \hat{\rho}_3 Y_{t-3} - \cdots$$

and

$$X_t^* = X_t - \hat{\rho}_1 X_{i,t-1} - \hat{\rho}_2 X_{i,t-2} - \hat{\rho}_3 X_{i,t-3} - \cdots$$

where

$$\hat{\rho}_1 = r_{e,e_{t-1}}; \quad \hat{\rho}_2 = r_{e,e_{t-2}}; \quad \hat{\rho}_3 = r_{e,e_{t-3}}; \quad \cdots$$

The second practical solution is the Hildreth–Lu, or grid procedure. The Hildreth–Lu procedure is chosen here not because it is necessarily the best in any sense, but because it is intuitively appealing, fairly easy to use, and does possess desirable statistical properties. In addition, some software packages use a grid procedure for estimating ρ from the sample.

The grid method works as follows. Set $\rho = +1.0$ in (14.48), create the transformed variables, estimate the OLS regression using the transformed variables, and compute the sum of squared residuals, SSE. Repeat the process with $\rho = +.9$, then with $\rho = +.8$, and so on, through $\rho = -1.0$. Then select as the "best" value of ρ that value which yields the estimated equation with the smallest SSE. As a practical matter, the classical properties can be claimed for the resulting estimate.

Following is an example of this procedure for the autoregressive transformation. The following equation was estimated by OLS using the 52 quarterly observations in the worksheet in Chapter 8:

$$Y = 92.60 - 21.27X_1 - 1.62X_2 - 3.92X_3 + 6.96X_4 + e$$
$$\quad\quad\quad\quad (1.89) \quad\quad (1.77) \quad\quad (2.49) \quad\quad (.65)$$
$$d = 1.28 \quad\quad\quad\quad\quad\quad\quad\quad\quad\quad\quad\quad\quad\quad (14.62)$$

where Y = quarterly average pork price
$\quad\quad X_1$ = quarterly pork production

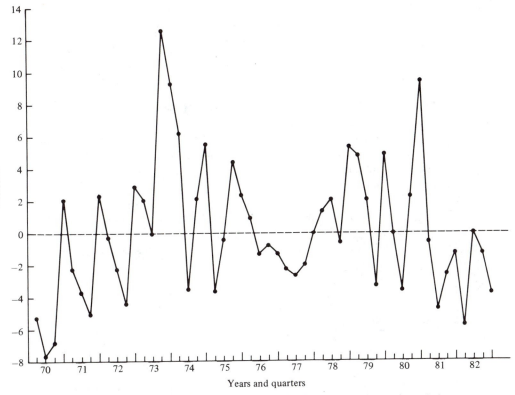

Figure 14.6   Residuals of Pork Price Equation (14.62), Demonstrating Autocorrelation.

X_2 = quarterly beef production
X_3 = quarterly broiler production
X_4 = quarterly per capita disposable income

The numbers in parentheses are the standard deviations of the estimated regression coefficients. The Durbin–Watson statistic, d, is 1.28. From Appendix Table A.4, for 55 observations and four independent variables, $d_L = 1.41$ and $d_U = 1.72$. Since the computed d of 1.28 is less than d_L for the null hypothesis of no positive autocorrelation, the null hypothesis is rejected and the alternative hypothesis of positive autocorrelation is not rejected.

The time-series plot of the OLS residuals is shown in Figure 14.6. There is a suggestion of positive autocorrelation in the residual as evidenced by the tendency of positive residuals to be followed by positive residuals and negative residuals to be followed by negative residuals.

In the first stage of the grid search, rho was set to $+1.0$ and incremented to 0 by increments of $-.1$. For each value of rho, the equation was estimated by OLS on the transformed values of the variable, and the ESS was recorded. The results of this search are presented on the left-hand side of Table 14.5. As rho decreased, ESS decreased until rho reached .4, at which point it began to increase. This suggests that the "best" value of rho lies between .5 and .3. The second search incremented rho from .5 to .3 by increments of $-.01$. The results are shown on the right-hand side of Table 14.5. Using a rho of .39, the estimated equation is

$$Y = 50.88 - 19.65X_1 - .77X_2 - 3.50X_3 + 6.56X_4 + e \qquad (14.63)$$
$$(1.93) \quad (2.10) \quad (2.28) \quad (.71)$$

where the numbers in parentheses are the standard deviations. The d-statistic for this equation is 1.93.

The theoretical analysis above showed that in the presence of autoregression, the OLS estimators are not minimum-variance estimators. Moreover, the OLS estimate of the population variance, needed to compute the standard deviations of the OLS coefficients, is a biased estimate. Consequently, the standard tests are invalid. If the validity of the procedure illustrated above is accepted, then (14.63) is preferred to (14.66) because the desired properties can be claimed for the estimators in the former.

The constant term for (14.63) is not correct. However, as (14.49) shows, the estimate of β_0 can be obtained by $b_0/(1 - \rho)$, where b_0 is the computer output for the "constant" term.

Table 14.5. Grid Search for the Optimum Rho in a Data Set with Autocorrelation

Incrementing Rho from +1.0 to 0 by −.1		Incrementing Rho from +.50 to +.30 by −.01	
Rho	ESS	Rho	ESS
1.0	1052	.50	765.38
.9	975	.49	763.72
.8	895	.48	762.21
.7	834	.47	760.87
.6	791	.46	759.68
.5	765	.45	758.66
.4	756—minimum	.44	757.68
.3	762	.43	757.08
.2	782	.42	756.52
.1	818	.41	756.12
.0	868	.40	755.87
		.39	755.78—minimum
		.38	755.84
		.37	756.06
		.36	756.42
		.35	756.94
		.34	757.60
		.33	758.42
		.32	759.38
		.31	760.50
		.30	761.76

Summary

In this chapter we have investigated the implications of specification errors on the population disturbance terms, heteroscedasticity and autocorrelation. The formal analysis of the problem revealed that in the presence of either misspecification, the use of OLS procedures will yield unbiased estimates of the population regression coefficients but that these estimates will not be minimum-variance estimates. Moreover, and of greater consequence, the OLS estimate of the variance of the population disturbance term is a biased estimator. Formally, this means that a researcher cannot conduct tests, since the tests are valid only when using unbiased estimators. Furthermore, there is no a priori basis for determining the direction of the bias, so there is no way of knowing whether the variances of the coefficients are overestimated or underestimated. However, experience in working with data sets strongly suggests that the bias will be negative, in which case researchers will underestimate the variance of the coefficients when improperly using OLS procedures. This means that the confidence intervals will be narrower than they should be and, consequently, researchers will overstate the precision of their parameter estimates. The result will be the rejection of the null hypothesis when it should not be rejected.

In principle, the solution to the specification error is straightforward: Transform the primary equation into one that has a disturbance term satisfying the classical assumptions and use OLS procedures on the resulting transformed variables to obtain estimates with the desired properties. In practice, the solution is difficult because researchers simply do not know, and have no unequivocal way of knowing, what the optimum transformation is. Consequently, applied researchers must resort to rather ad hoc procedures, do whatever seems best, and then discuss clearly in the resulting research report the procedures followed to mitigate the specification error.

Finally, we have treated the two problems separately by investigating the heteroscedastic problem assuming no autocorrelation, and vice versa. These two problems can occur simultaneously, in which case both transformations are called for. In principle this is straightforward; in practice it is messy and great care must be exercised in interpreting the coefficients.

Terms

Autocorrelation

Autoregression coefficient

Breusch–Pagan test

Durbin–Watson statistic

First-order autoregression

Goldfeld–Quandt test

Heteroscedasticity

Hildreth–Lu procedure

Homoscedasticity

Serial correlation

Weighted regression

Exercises

14.1

(a) What is the name for the problem associated with the assumption that $E(U^2) = \sigma^2$ is not true?

(b) What is the name for the problem associated with the assumption that $E(U_iU_j) = 0$ for all $i \neq j$ is not true?

(c) Do the problems named in parts (a) and (b) invalidate the best, the linear, or the unbiased part of the OLS estimators?

(d) For which of the problems described in parts (a) and (b) are the OLS estimators of S_{b_i} unbiased?

(e) Which type of misspecified disturbance term is more likely to occur in time-series data? in cross-sectional data?

(f) Is the variance of the disturbance term more likely to be positively or negatively correlated with the independent variables?

(g) Is autocorrelation more likely to be positive or negative?

14.2 The following regression model is heteroscedastic:

$$Y = \beta_0 + \beta_1 X_1 + \beta_2 X_2 + U \tag{1}$$

where Y = dollars spent by consumers on food in a city in a week
X_1 = dollars of income earned by consumers in a city during a week
X_2 = population of a city

A researcher uses OLS to estimate (1) by the following equation, assuming that $E(U^2) = \sigma^2$:

$$Y = b_0 + b_1 X_1 + b_2 X_2 + e \tag{2}$$

(a) Is $E(b_0) = \beta_0$? $E(b_1) = \beta_1$? $E(b_2) = \beta_2$? $E(S^2) = \sigma^2$?

(b) Are the estimators of b_0, b_1, b_2, and S^2 best estimators?

(c) Assuming that b_0, b_1, and b_2 are unbiased estimators of the parameters in (1), can S_{b_i} be used to test hypothesis?

14.3 Assume that the variance of the disturbance term increases linearly with population (X_2) in Exercise 14.2.

(a) What is $E(e^2)$ in (2)?

(b) What is the appropriate transformation of (2) so that it can be estimated by OLS?

(c) If a researcher estimated the equation

$$Y^* = b_0^* X_0^* + b_1^* X_1^* + b_2^* X_2^* + e \tag{3}$$

where X_i^* and Y^* are the appropriate transformations specified in part (b), what are the statistical properties of b_0^*, b_i^*, and $(S^*)^2$?

(d) Is $E(S_{b_i}^{*2}) = E(b_i^* - \beta_i)^2$?

(e) Set up the worksheet and show the transformation for (3).

Following are the first three observations in the data set:

Y	X_1	X_2
100,000	484,000	1,225
36,000	192,000	529
10,418,000	49,612,000	99,225

14.4 Assume that the model is the same as (1) except the variance of the disturbance term increases proportionally with the square of population.

(a) What is $E(e^2)$?

(b) In order to estimate b_0, b_1, and b_2 by using OLS on $Y^* = b_0X_0^* + b_1X^* + b_2X_2^*$, how would you define Y^*, X_0^*, X_1^*, and X_2^* in terms of X_1, X_2, and Y?

(c) Create the worksheet necessary to do part (b) for the three observations.

14.5 Suppose that you want to estimate the following consumption function:

$$C_t = b_0 + b_1I_t + b_2W_t + e_t \qquad (4)$$

where C_t = consumption in year t

I_t = income in year t

W_t = wealth in year t

Assume that $E(e_t) = 0$ and $E(e_t^2) = (C_t^2)\sigma^2$. Transform equation (4) into one in which the disturbance term is homoscedastic and describe the steps required to estimate it.

14.6 Apply the Goldfeld–Quandt test to the following data and comment on the results. (HINT: Drop the middle six observations.)

Obs.	Y	X
1	30.5	49.6
2	32.8	55.7
3	39.4	63.3
4	50.8	75.4
5	55.7	78.3
6	74.2	96.7
7	81.4	109.3
8	88.2	115.8
9	90.1	118.8
10	107.3	133.0
11	116.1	140.2
12	122.5	150.7
13	138.4	167.3

14	155.3	181.3
15	173.0	207.9
16	197.5	235.0
17	217.6	258.9
18	225.7	227.7
19	253.0	297.6
20	269.6	309.4

14.7 Consider the following regression equation:

$$A_t = 44 + 18N_t \qquad R^2 = .78$$
$$\quad\ (3)\quad (6) \qquad\quad n = 40$$
$$\qquad\qquad\qquad\qquad\quad d = 1.40$$

where A_t = number of accidents on a highway during day t

N_t = number of cars traveling the highway on day t

and the number in parentheses is the standard error.

(a) Does autocorrelation exist at 5 percent level of significance?
(b) Is the autocorrelation positive or negative?
(c) Is X a significant determinant of Y at the 10 percent level of significance?

14.8 Suppose that the following regression model has a serially correlated disturbance term:

$$Y_t = \beta_0 + \beta_1 X_{1t} + U_t \qquad (5)$$

where $U_t = \rho U_{t-1} + V_t$. The first three observations in the data set are as follows:

Y_t	X_t
100	14
210	17
362	22

(a) If you estimate (5) by OLS, would $E(b_1) = \beta_1$?
(b) Using OLS to estimate, would Var (b_1) be the minimum for linear and unbiased estimators of β_1?
(c) Would $E(S_{b_1}^2) = E(b_1 - \beta_1)^2$?
(d) Write the appropriate OLS model for estimating (5).
(e) If $\rho = .5$, write the general transformation for Y^* and X^* and then calculate the values for three observations above.
(f) If $\rho = .2$, what are Y^* and X^* for the observations above?
(g) If ρ is correct, would $E(b_1^*) = \beta_1$?
(h) If ρ is correct, is $E(b_1^* - \beta_1)^2 = $ minimum?
(i) If ρ was correct, would $E(S_{b_1}^2) = E(b_1^* - \beta_1)^2$?
(j) If ρ is correctly estimated, is $E(b_0^*) = \beta_0$?

14.9   The population regression equation is

$$Y_t = \beta_0 + \beta_1 X_t + U_t \tag{6}$$

(a) The researcher assumes that U_t is autoregressive with $\rho = 1$. Write the appropriate autoregressive transformation to estimate (6) by OLS.

(b) What is different about the transformed equation?

(c) Suppose that the researcher had estimated the equation

$$Y_t^* = b_0^* + b_1 X_t^* + e_t^*$$

which included a constant term? How might b_0^* be correctly included in the equation?

14.10

(a) Can $|\rho| > 1$ in a first-order serial correlation model?

(b) What would $|\rho| > 1$ imply about the stability of the structure being studied?

14.11 Given the model

$$Y_t = a + bX_t + e_t$$

with the following data:

Obs.	Y	X
1	2.4	1
2	2.5	2
3	2.5	3
4	1.6	4
5	3.7	5
6	5.8	6
7	6.9	7
8	7.0	8
9	11.1	9
10	11.2	10
11	11.3	11
12	13.4	12
13	16.5	13
14	11.5	14
15	12.6	15

The OLS estimate of the equation above is

$$Y_t = 0 + 1.0X_t + e_t$$

Calculate the Durbin–Watson statistic to test for first-order autocorrelation at the .05 significance level.

15

Sample Deficiencies: Measurement Error and Missing Data

In Chapter 12 we discussed multicollinearity, a sample problem frequently encountered in the data sets used in applied research. In Chapters 13 and 14 we discussed omitting relevant and including irrelevant variables, the issue of specifying the correct variables to include in the equation to be estimated, and heteroscedasticity and autocorrelation, misspecifications of the statistical properties of the disturbance term. In this chapter we return to sample problems, this time to measurement errors and missing data. Each of these has implications for the properties of the OLS coefficients used to estimate population regression coefficients. As in previous chapters, the plan here is first to determine the specific implications of the problem and then to consider what, if anything, can be done to alleviate them. As might be expected from studying Chapter 12, there is little the applied researcher can do about these sample problems. Nevertheless, it is important to understand them, as such understanding can often assist in assessing regression results.

Measurement Error

Everything done to this point has been based on the important, implicit assumption that the variables Y_i and X_i are measured without error across the sample observations. In Chapter 3 we noted that one of the reasons often given in econometrics books for including the population disturbance term is measurement error in the dependent variable. The approach taken in this book is to treat measurement error as a separate topic in this chapter. Although little, if anything, can be done to correct for measurement error in a given sample, it is a problem worthy of some discussion if for no other reason than to generate some skepticism about sample data. Such skepticism is important because it keeps applied researchers humble when making claims for their results.

The numbers used in applied research must come from somewhere. Data must be collected by some method and as stressed in previous chapters, especially Chapter 8, they should be collected in the context of an underlying theory. The term *data system* is used to refer collectively to the institutions, methods, and procedures involved in producing much of the data available to applied researchers. For the current discussion, it is reasonable to assume that the function of the data system is to provide a statistical picture, a symbolic representation, of a population of interest, such as the inventory of market hogs on December 1, the number of people unemployed in a particular month, the number of acres under irrigation in a country, the number of families living in poverty, and so on. Two questions should be raised in this context: Do the available data measure the exact concept ("market hogs," "families in poverty," "irrigated acres") needed to answer the research question at hand? How accurately is the concept measured? Underlying these questions are some fundamental philosophical issues that should be considered.

Types of Errors

Three types of errors may be present in data: conceptual, operational, and measurement. Although measurement error is the main subject of this chapter, it is important to discuss briefly the other two potential sources of error, if only to put measurement error in proper perspective.

Conceptualization

Conceptual error is difficult to define in a precise way. In Chapters 2 and 8 we stressed that theory is the beginning point, where theory is defined broadly to include not only theory as such but also existing knowledge, common sense, and the like. Theory provides a world view that helps sort out the complexities of everyday life. It helps to identify what is and what is not important to a particular question. Theory identifies, in other words, the concepts relevant to our research. Applied researchers build empirical knowledge of the world on the basis of these concepts. Against this background, conceptual errors occur if the data used do not measure the relevant conceptual variables identified by the theory used to guide the applied research.

To determine the variables needed to estimate the first regression equation in Chapter 8, the beginning researcher drew on, among other things, the theory of the competitive market. There the researcher encountered the concept of "price," which has a well-defined meaning in the theory. Price is the *equilibrium price*, the price at which the quantity demanded by buyers is equal to the quantity supplied by sellers. It is a price that arises as a consequence of the competitive conditions assumed to exist in the market. Thus, answering the research question required finding a price that occurred as a consequence of competitive market-clearing activities. But suppose that the price actually used in the analysis was a price that occurred as a consequence of market power exercised by the buyers or the sellers in the marketplace? In price theory, this is often referred to as a *monopoly price*, a concept quite different from a "competitive equilibrium price." If, knowingly or unknowingly, a researcher uses a price based on the concept of a monopoly price, then according to the definition above, a conceptual error occurs because the researcher is using a variable based on a concept different from the concept called for by the guiding theory. It is an error because the variable is not measuring the "correct" concept and the resulting interpretation of the regression results would be incorrect.

Before moving on, it is important to stress that conceptual error arises in the context of a specific research question, as illustrated above. It is conceivable that in another research project, the guiding theory could call for the concept of a monopoly price, in which case a researcher would not want to use a price based on the concept of a competitive equilibrium price. In summary, applied researchers, in any particular research setting, determine first the concepts called for by the theory and then make sure to the extent possible that the variables used are based on these concepts.

Operationalization

Given the proper conceptual (or theoretical) variable to be measured, the next potential source of error lies in the *rules of correspondence*, or guidelines, used to link the theoretical variable to an empirical variable. This is easiest seen with an example. In the theory of consumer choice, "income" is an important determinant of individual consumer behavior. In this theory, *income* is defined precisely as the consumer's command over goods and services in the marketplace. To "operationalize" this variable means to develop a linkage between the concept of "income" and possible real-world measures of income. The basic question is: What specific rules, or definitions, are used to obtain an empirical measure of the concept of "income" in theory? Is total family income used? Is the income of children, such as money received from baby-sitting and lawn mowing, and Social Security payments and other forms of transfer income included? Is gross income or income after taxes used? What taxes? How about income from assets owned? Are adjustments made for expenses incurred in earning income? Are adjustments made for the dollar value for goods produced and consumed at home? Is imputed rental income for a homeowner included? How about the value of the house work and farm work of the wife? Does it make sense even to use money income? Perhaps real income should be used (whatever that is), or perhaps some ratio of money income to the income needs (how defined?) of the family would be a better measure of purchasing power.

The answers certainly are not obvious. What is obvious is the importance of the answer. Applied researchers are likely to get quite different results depending on which empirical measure of income is used. The problem is that if the rules do not lead to an income variable that measures the "consumer's command over goods and services," the correct concept of income is not being measured and an operational error has occurred. Consequently, researchers must be concerned not only about the underlying concepts but also about the rules used to link these concepts to the empirical variables used in applied research.

Measurement

Given the appropriate conceptual variables and their appropriate empirical measures, errors can creep into data sets by the very act of collecting the data. Measurement errors may be classified into nonsampling errors and sampling errors. *Nonsampling errors* arise from a number of sources: improperly structured questionnaires; improperly trained interviewers; scales, thermometers, and other such measuring devices improperly calibrated; reporting and recording errors; and so on. Common sense suggests and experiments confirm that errors of this type are unavoidable when large quantities of data are collected and processed prior to publication, whether census data or sample data. *Sampling errors* are present as a consequence of using a sample statistic to estimate a population parameter. Chapter 2 treats this type of error.

In summary, a researcher must ascertain to the extent possible how the data to be used in the research were produced. A good researcher is concerned with the conceptual base of the data, the rules of correspondence used to link the concepts with the data, and the accuracy of the data. Unfortunately, there is little of a practical nature one can do when confronted with a data set that must be used to conduct the research. Not all statistical agencies and research organizations publish information pertaining to the issues discussed here, and when they do the information may be difficult to find and it is often highly technical in nature. About the best an applied researcher can do is recognize that the data being used are likely to be afflicted with errors, examine to the extent possible the implications of these errors for the analysis, and assume an attitude of humility when drawing conclusions based on the sample.

Econometric Effects of Measurement Error

In this section we consider measurement error, the third type of error discussed in the preceding section. Begin again with the population regression function, expressed in deviation form,

$$y_i^t = \beta_1 x_i^t + U_i \tag{15.1}$$

to illustrate the implications of measurement error, where the superscript t denotes the "true" values of the variables. This makes explicit the implicit assumption used to this point.

Before moving on, notice that there is an "error" in (15.1), the U_i that has always been part of the regression model. This is referred to as *error in equation*. Traditionally, the econometrics literature has focused on the error in equations and paid much less attention to *error in variables*. This reflects in part that little can be done about the latter. The various types of measurement errors are discussed in the following sections.

Error in Y

Begin with the simple assumption that only Y, expressed in deviation form, is measured with error according to

$$y_i^0 = y_i^t + v_i \tag{15.2}$$

where y_i^t is the true value of Y in (15.1), y_i^0 is the observed value of y in the sample, and v_i is the measurement error in y_i^0. Assume that

$$E(v_i) = 0 \tag{15.3}$$

$$E(v_i^2) = \sigma_v^2 \tag{15.4}$$

$$E(v_i, U_i) = 0 \tag{15.5}$$

$$E(v_i, x_i) = 0 \tag{15.6}$$

Assumptions (15.3) and (15.4) state that the measurement error has mean zero and a positive variance. Equations (15.5) and (15.6) state that the measurement error is uncorrelated with the population disturbance term and with the independent variable. Substituting (15.2) into (15.1) yields

$$y_i^0 - v_i = \beta_1 x_i' + U_i \quad \text{or} \quad y_i^0 = \beta_1 x_i' + (U_i + v_i) \tag{15.7}$$

In this case, the OLS estimator, b_1, is given by

$$b_1 = \frac{\Sigma x_i' y_i^0}{\Sigma x_i'^2} = \frac{\Sigma x_i'[\beta_1 x_i' + (U_i + v_i)]}{\Sigma x_i'^2} = \beta_1 + \frac{\Sigma x_i'(U_i + v_i)}{\Sigma x_i'^2} \tag{15.8}$$

with expected value of

$$E(b_1) = \beta_1 + \frac{\Sigma x_i'[E(U_i) + E(v_i)]}{\Sigma x_i'^2} = \beta_1 \tag{15.9}$$

by the classical assumptions on U_i and (15.3). This demonstrates that measurement error in the dependent variable does not bias the estimate of the slope coefficient. It is important to note that this result is based on the strong assumption that $E(v_i) = 0$. Moreover, it does not bias the estimate of the intercept term. Write

$$Y' = \beta_0 + \beta_1 X + U \tag{15.10}$$

The OLS estimator of β_0 in (15.10) is

$$b_0 = \bar{Y}^0 - b_1 \bar{X} \tag{15.11}$$

From (15.2) write

$$\bar{Y}^0 = \bar{Y}' + \bar{v} \tag{15.12}$$

and

$$b_0 = (\bar{Y}' + \bar{v}) - b_1 \bar{X} = (\beta_0 + \beta_1 \bar{X} + \bar{U} + \bar{v}) - b_1 \bar{X} \tag{15.13}$$

$$= \beta_0 + (\beta_1 - b_1)\bar{X}$$

and $\tag{15.14}$

$$E(b_0) = \beta_0 + \bar{X}E(\beta_1 - b_1) = \beta_0.$$

Again, it is important to note the role of $E(v) = 0$.

Based on the assumptions (15.3) to (15.6), we find that the measurement error in the dependent variable has no implications for the unbiasedness property of the OLS estimates. It does, however, have implications for the estimated variances of these coefficients and for the multiple correlation coefficient of the estimated equation. While deriving the OLS estimator for the population variance in Chapter 3, we showed the relationship between the observable OLS residuals and the unobservable population disturbance terms to be

$$\Sigma e^2 = \Sigma [(\beta_1 - b_1)X + (U - \bar{U})]^2 \tag{15.15}$$

If the analysis were repeated under the assumption of measurement error in the dependent variable, the following expression for the OLS residuals would be generated:

$$\Sigma\ e^2 = \Sigma\ [(\beta_1 - b_1)X + (U - \bar{U}) + (v - \bar{v})]^2 \tag{15.16}$$

Since the variance of v is positive by assumption, the computed OLS residual is larger in the presence of measurement error in the dependent variable. This means that the OLS estimate of the variance of the disturbance term, given by

$$S^2 = \frac{\Sigma\ e^2}{n - 2} \tag{15.17}$$

is larger by the variance of the measurement error. This, in turn, means that the OLS of the variance of the slope coefficient, given by

$$S_{b_1}^2 = \frac{1}{\Sigma\ x^2} \frac{\Sigma\ e^2}{n - 2} \tag{15.18}$$

will be larger. A similar result can be obtained for the variance of the intercept estimator. The implication of this for hypothesis testing is a decreased chance of rejecting the null hypothesis.

A second practical consequence is a lower multiple correlation coefficient for the estimated equation. In Chapter 5 we showed that $R^2 = 1 - \text{ESS/TSS}$. Because the measurement error increases the value of ESS, the R^2-value will be lower.

In summary, the effect of measurement error in the dependent variable is to increase the error term by the amount of the variance in the measurement error. The estimates of the population regression coefficients remain unbiased, but their estimated variances are larger than in the absence of measurement error, and the multiple correlation coefficient is lower.

Error in X

Life is less pleasant when the independent variable is measured with error. Again, assume that the "true" equation is (15.1) with

$$x_i^0 = x_i^t + w_i \tag{15.19}$$

where x_i^0 is the observed value of X, x_i^t is the true value, and w_i is the measurement error in the independent variable. Assume the following specifications:

$$E(w_i) = 0 \tag{15.20}$$

$$E(w_i^2) = \sigma_w^2 \tag{15.21}$$

$$E(w_i U_i) = 0 \tag{15.22}$$

$$E(x_i^t U_i) = 0 \tag{15.23}$$

$$E(x_i^t w_i) = 0 \tag{15.24}$$

Substituting (15.19) into (15.1) yields

$$y_i^t = \beta_1(x_i^0 - w_i) + U_i = \beta_1 x_i^0 + (U_i - \beta_1 w_i) \tag{15.25}$$

Here the OLS procedure breaks down because the regressor in (15.25), x^0, is not independent of the disturbance term of (15.25). To see this, evaluate

$$E[(U_i - \beta_1 w_i)x_i^0] = E[(U_i - \beta_1 w_i)(x_i^t + w_i)]$$

$$= E[U_i x_i^t + U_i w_i - \beta_1 w_i x_i^t - \beta_1 w_i^2] \qquad (15.26)$$

$$= -\beta_1 \sigma_w^2$$

which shows that the regressor and the disturbance term in (15.25) are not statistically independent.

Since this violates the OLS assumption of independence between the independent variable and the disturbance term, the OLS estimator of β_1 in (15.25) will be biased. This is a consequence of (15.19), which says that the observed X-values, the values in the data set, are not fixed in repeated sampling. Instead, the values are generated by a random process as reflected by w_i in (15.19). In other words, the "observed" independent variable is a random variable, called a *stochastic regressor*, that is not independent of the disturbance term.

In this case, the expected value of the OLS estimator is

$$E(b_1) = \frac{\beta_1}{1 + \sigma_w^2/\sigma_x^2} \qquad (15.27)$$

where σ_w^2 is the variance of the measurement error in X and σ_x^2 is the variance of X. This says that measurement error in the independent variable yields an OLS estimator that is biased downward. On average the OLS estimator will understate the true value of β_1. If the variance of the measurement error is "small" relative to the variance of X, the bias in b_1 will be small. Thus, if some information on the measurement error, such as a confidence interval for the published values of X, is available, a researcher could at least approximate the degree of bias in the estimate. However, such an aproximation would be tenuous.

If there are two or more independent variables in the equation, the precise nature of the bias is difficult to assess. If only one variable is measured with error, its coefficient will be biased downward, but the bias in the coefficients of the other variables can be in either direction. There are, however, methods available in more advanced texts for calculating and correcting for the bias. If, on the other hand, two or more independent variables are measured with error, the situation is extremely complex, as there is a really no way to determine even the direction of the bias, much less its magnitude.

A second problem with measurement error in the independent variable is that the OLS estimator of the variance of the disturbance term, needed for computing test statistics, is biased and overstates the true value of the variance. This follows from the presence of the measurement error in the disturbance term. Consequently, the calculated t and F-statistics used for hypothesis testing are not correct and the tests are not valid. However, if the multiple correlation for the estimated equation is "high," the bias in the estimated variance is "small" and perhaps not worth worrying about.

Advanced econometric literature does consider one procedure for estimating in the presence of measurement error. This is known as *instrumental variable estimation*.

The interested reader may refer to more advanced textbooks for a treatment of this technique.

Before moving on, consider one other issue in connection with measurement error. Many published variables are revised as independent means of checking the data become available. This is particularly true with agricultural data. For example, original crop production and livestock inventory estimates are usually revised, sometimes a year or two later, as marketing data become available. As another example, many time-series variables across all sectors of the economy are revised as census data become available. Which are the "true" values of the variables, the original or the revised values? Presumably, the revised are "more true," in which case the revised values should be used to minimize the measurement-error bias in the OLS estimators. However, decisions in the real world are made on the basis of the original, reported values of the variable because decision makers cannot wait two years for revised data. Hence it is not obvious which value of the variable to use in regression analysis, the original value or the revised value.

Stated alternatively, do agricultural markets, labor markets, financial markets, households, and the like respond to current values of variables, or do they respond to revised values? Because time is irreversible, it seems unlikely that markets ignore the current values and respond to the currently unknown revised values. On the other hand, individuals in the markets may know something the producers of statistical data do not know and automatically adjust the original values.

In summary, applied researchers use data that may be afflicted with measurement error (as well as conceptual and operational errors). This chapter's treatment of the problem suggests that there may be many biased estimates floating in the sea of applied research. It is unfortunate that there is little the applied researcher can do to correct for the problem. The situation is not, however, as bleak as these comments might suggest. Most, if not all, professional data-producing agencies are working hard, within the confines of limited budgets, to improve the quality of their output. Because of these endeavors, the quality of the data used by applied researchers has been improving and will continue to improve. Moreover, some agencies, such as the Statistical Reporting Service of the U.S. Department of Agriculture, are beginning to publish confidence intervals for their estimates that give users a measure of the sampling error in the data. This trend will continue, and as it does applied researchers will be able to improve the quality of applied regression work. The most important thing to take away from this discussion of measurement error is a healthy suspicion of numbers, and a commitment to be critical, in a positive way, of the data used in applied research.

Finally, more advanced texts contain suggestions for dealing with measurement error in the independent variables. These suggestions assume, of course, that the measurement error actually exists, and in many applied research situations there is no way of independently assessing the validity of this assumption. Given this, the suggested treatments focus on the correlation between the regressor and the disturbance term [see equation (15.26)]. The idea here, as in Chapter 14, is to reformulate the basic equation in such a way that the classical OLS assumptions are satisfied and then estimate the transformed equation. One widely used procedure is the use of instrumental variables. To treat this approach adequately here would introduce such new concepts as consistent estimators and two-stage least squares, concepts best left for more advanced texts.

Missing Data

The second sample deficiency discussed here is missing data, a problem often encountered in applied research involving either time-series or cross-sectional data sets. Missing data simply means that values of one or more variables (including the dependent variable) are missing from the data set. Alternatively, there are gaps or holes in the worksheet. Such gaps may occur for any number of reasons. With time-series data sets it is not uncommon to find more current values for some variables than for others. For example, a researcher may have values for one variable through 1983 and values for another only through 1981. It is possible that data on a particular variable may not have been published prior to a particular year. For example, the time period of analysis might be 1960 to 1982, but one variable is available only from 1965 to 1982. Gaps often occur with cross-sectional data sets as well, such as the failure of a household to record its income or its food expenditures. Often there is an added problem in cross-sectional data with regard to missing values of the dependent variable. Suppose that the dependent variable is recreational expenditures and the data set contains one or more instances of missing responses. They might be missing simply because of a reporting or recording error, but they might be missing because the families simply did not spend any money on recreation.

The point is that gaps in the worksheet are often encountered in applied work, raising the question of how to proceed with regression analysis. Naturally enough, missing data raise serious problems, and what to do about these problems is not obvious. Much depends on such fundamental questions as why the data are missing, whether they are missing as a result of random forces or as a result of systematic forces, and whether it is reasonable to treat the independent variables as nonstochastic (fixed in repeated sampling) or as stochastic (random variables). For these reasons, a complete treatment of the missing data problem is beyond the scope of this book. Here it is possible to sketch the nature of the problem, its implications, and suggest some possible methods that can be used in applied research. No detailed statistical treatment of these methods is offered because many of them get quite complicated. In order to use one of the particular methods to handle the missing data problem in an actual research setting, it would be wise to refer to a more advanced book for a complete treatment of the problem.

The method for coping with missing data in applied research depends on two things: the reason for the missing values and the type of data set, cross-sectional or time-series. A distinction can be made between data missing at random and data missing due to systematic forces. Suppose, for example, that a researcher was putting together a worksheet and the library did not have two publications, say for the years 1971 and 1982, in the series being used to find the values for one of the variables. In this case, a researcher could say that the values were missing at random in the sense that somebody just happened not to return the publications to their proper place in the library. In other words, there would be nothing systematic in the relation between the fact that the values were missing and the values themselves. Suppose, on the other hand, that the researcher was getting data from a published survey and knew that the interviewers had systematically neglected to collect income data from, say, low-income families. In this case, there would be a relation between the fact that the values were missing and the values themselves. The problem of missing data in this case is very difficult to handle in applied research and will not be considered here. The methods discussed below are applicable only to the case where the data are missing at random.

An illustration of the methods used to handle missing data starts with the following worksheet:

Number of Observations	Y	X	Z
n_1	Y_1	X_1	Z_1
n_2	Y_2	X_2	
n_3	Y_3		Z_3
n_4		X_4	Z_4
n_5		X_5	
n_6			Z_6
n_7	Y_7		

This worksheet contains n_1 complete observations, n_2 observations on Y and X only, n_3 observations on Y and Z only, n_4 observations on X and Z only, and so on. This is indeed a serious case of missing data, one unlikely to be encountered in practice. However, it will illustrate the problem nicely. There are three ways used in practice to proceed with estimation:

1. Classical least squares.
2. Regression estimates using variables in the base equation.
3. Regression estimates using variables not in the base equation.

The classical least squares approach involves using only the subset of complete observations, n_1 in this sample, to estimate the regression equation. Because the values are assumed to be missing at random (there is no relation between the fact that the values are missing and the values themselves), the OLS estimator will be unbiased. This property is not lost by using only the complete observations. However, the variance of the estimator, in terms of expected values, is larger than it would be if there were no missing observations simply because there is not as much information on which to base the estimate. From a practical standpoint, the fruitfulness of using this method depends, in part, on the number of missing observations relative to the total number of observations. For example, if a cross-sectional data set of 500 observations had only 10 observations missing at random, very little would be lost by just using the 490 complete observations. On the other hand, if a time-series data set of 22 observations were missing 5 observations, a researcher might want to devote some time to determining if there is some way to find these missing values.

The second method uses regression estimates to replace the missing values. To illustrate, suppose that the worksheet was made up of just the n_1 and n_2 observations in the illustration above. In this case, a researcher could first use the n_1 observations to regress Z on X_1 and then use the n_2 observations on X_2 in this regression to calculate the regression values of Z for each value of X_1 and use the estimated Z-values this to replace the missing Z_2-values. The regression equation is then estimated using the $n_1 + n_2$ observations. Whether this yields results that are more efficient (smaller-variance) estimators depends on specific assumptions regarding the reasons for missing data. However, this method is often an acceptable practical expedient for minimizing the effect of missing observations.

The third method also uses regression estimates to replace the missing values, but it differs in that the regression is based on a variable not included in the equation to be estimated. In this case, the researcher tries to find a variable W that is highly correlated with Z (using the $n_1 + n_2$ data set), regresses the sample values of Z in the n_1 portion of the data set on W, then uses this regression to compute the missing values of Z for the n_2 portion of the data set. In general, this method yields more efficient estimators than simply using the complete observations to estimate the regression equation.

A final method used only with time-series data sets is interpolation. If you have 40 quarterly observations and the value in one quarter for one variable is missing, replace it with the simple average of the preceding and following quarters. Although this is a useful expedient, it is not a cure-all. If there are missing observations for two or more quarters in a row, it is not a good idea to interpolate. Moreover, even if there are only one-quarter gaps in the worksheet, there is a limit to the number of quarters that should be filled in with interpolations.

A slightly more sophisticated way to fill in the gaps of a time-series data set is to regress the available observations on time (see Chapter 17), use the estimated trend equation to interpolate or extrapolate the missing values, and then run the equation on the full set of observations in the worksheet. This method recognizes that many variables show a trend over time, and for that reason it is appealing. However, because this method does require the assumption of no correlation between the trend variable and the disturbance term, it should be used with some caution.

Finally, with all these methods for filling in missing values, the degrees of freedom for hypothesis testing must be reduced by one for each missing value that is replaced. Researchers must adjust the regression output before constructing the test statistics.

Notice that all of the suggestions above consider missing observations on the independent variables. Using the methods described in this section to replace missing values of the dependent variable is *not* appropriate. Consequently, the researcher usually discards all observations with missing Y-values.

One final issue needs to be discussed, but not resolved. Suppose that a researcher is using a cross-sectional data set on households to estimate the effect on recreational expenditures of certain socioeconomic variables. It turns out that many families, perhaps low-income families, do not spend money on recreation. In essence, this means a number of 0's in the data set that have economic meaning, namely, zero expenditures. This raises the important question of whether these observations with a zero value for the dependent variable should be included or whether they should be deleted from the sample prior to estimation. Situations of this type give rise to estimation procedures known as logit, probit, tobit, and similar procedures designed to permit estimation using the full data set. See a more advanced text for a derivation and discussion of these estimation methods.

Summary

The missing data problem, just like every problem discussed in this book, is a serious problem in that it affects the properties of the OLS estimators, yet there is precious little that applied researchers can do about it. There are no theoretical or practical guides for solving the data problem. Appropriate action, if any, depends on the particular research setting. In some instances, it pays to try valiantly to obtain the missing values. Other times it is best to use simple methods, such as interpolation, or more advanced techniques not discussed here. Finally, often the best course is simply to delete from the worksheet those observations with missing values. Many computer programs do this automatically with a "missing data" code in the appropriate cells of the worksheet. In essence, applied researchers do whatever needs to be done to get the research job done. In the resulting research it is important to report exactly what was done, not only for the benefit of the reader, but also to maintain the integrity of the applied researcher.

Terms

Conceptualization error	Missing data
Error in equations	Nonsampling error
Error in variables	Operationalization errror
Measurement error	Sampling error

Exercises

15.1 Multicollinearity is one deficiency in the sample that has implications for estimating population parameters. What are two other major deficiencies in the sample?

15.2 Describe three types of errors that may be present in a data set and their probable source.

15.3 What is a nonsampling error? Offer examples of possible causes of nonsampling error.

15.4

(a) What is the difference between "error in equations" and "error in variables"?

(b) Why does most econometric literature (including this book) spend more effort on error in equations than on error in variables?

15.5

(a) Suppose that the *dependent* variable is measured with error and that the measurement error has mean zero, a positive (but constant) variance, is uncorrelated with the population disturbance term, and is uncorrelated with the independent variable. What effects does such measurement error have on the empirical results? How serious are these effects?

(b) Suppose that an *independent* variable is measured with error, that this measurement error has mean zero, a positive (but constant) variance, and is uncorrelated with the population disturbance term. What are the consequences of this kind of measurement error for the empirical results? Are they serious?

15.6 Suppose that observations are missing from a data set because of random rather than systematic factors. Are the following observations valid or invalid? If invalid, why?

(a) The OLS estimates of the regression coefficients based on only the observations that are complete are unbiased estimators of the population parameters.

(b) When observations are deleted from OLS calculations because of missing data, the efficiency of the OLS estimators is reduced.

(c) Efficiency increases if you replace missing observations on the independent variable in a simple regression with their mean values to increase the sample size on which the OLS results can be obtained.

(d) The best way to handle the problem of missing observations is to regress the available observations on time, use the estimated equation to interpolate missing values, and then to regress the dependent variable on all the values (real and generated) of the independent variables.

IV

Time in Regression

Because time-series data sets are often used in regression estimation, this part addresses issues relating to time. Chapter 16 covers trend estimation and using time as an independent variable in a regression equation. Chapter 17 shows how to use regression to estimate seasonal indexes. Chapter 18 discusses forecasting, with primary emphasis on the forecast error.

Time in Regression Analysis

Change over time is something everyone takes for granted. People are much aware of and often keenly interested in changes that occur in variables such as unemployment rates, commodity prices, housing starts, exports, imports, and the like. Moreover, interest sometimes centers on how variables change over specific time periods, such as day-to-day price changes, month-to-month export changes, year-to-year production changes, or decade-to-decade population changes. In many cases, these changes occur with a regularity that permits them to be estimated, or quantified, in such a way that the results can be used for forecasting or developing policies of one type or another. For example, knowledge of the seasonal (month-to-month) pattern in housing starts could be of value to lending institutions for determining when the demand for loans is likely to be high or to government agencies responsible for administering unemployment compensation programs. Similarly, an awareness of regularly recurring time patterns in grain exports can be used by transportation firms for anticipating when their services will be needed.

"Time" in this sense has not been considered in previous chapters. In earlier chapters, time has entered only in the context of a *time-series* data set used for estimating population regression coefficients. In this and the following two chapters, attention turns to the types of time changes mentioned above. Sometimes the objective of applied research is to analyze the "time" component of a variable, looking for both systematic and random time patterns without attempting to assign causality. This is often referred to as *descriptive* research, since the objective is not so much to explain time patterns as it is to identify and estimate them. The research question might be: Is there a seasonal pattern in housing starts, and does it occur with sufficient regularity over time that it can be estimated? There are three basic methods that can be used for this type of analysis: regression analysis, stochastic models, and spectral analysis. *Stochastic models*, usually referred to as *autoregressive, moving average* (ARIMA) *models*, use advanced statistical procedures for estimating the autoregressive and moving average coefficients of the observed time series. Estimated ARIMA models are frequently used for forecasting. *Spectral analysis* is essentially a mathematical technique used to decompose an observed time series into a number of fundamental components of varying time periods, depending on the underlying structure of the particular time series. Because neither of the latter two methods are fundamentally linear regression models, they are not considered here.

Regression is used to estimate trends in this chapter. Of secondary interest in this chapter is using "trend" as an independent variable in a regression equation. In Chapter 17 we focus on using regression to estimate seasonal patterns, or "seasonals." In Chapter 18 we consider forecasting, predicting the value of variables over time.

Finally, we do not discuss estimating cycles in this chapter, primarily because regression analysis is not particularly useful for estimating a cyclical time component. Cycle estimation often requires data for a long period. For example, the biological nature of the hog and cattle sectors is such that the underlying cycle can require anywhere from 4 to 8 years to work itself out. Thus a typical time-series data set of 15 to 25 years permits only three to five "observations" on the cycle, making estimation of the empirical nature of the cycle a bit difficult. Something other than regression should be used for studying cycles, such as the two methods (ARIMA and spectral analysis) mentioned above.

Linear Trends

Trend refers to a systematic movement of a variable that persists over a period of time. Although this definition is conceptually satisfactory, it leaves much to be desired as a guide for empirical work. How long, for example, is a "period of time"? This vagueness notwithstanding, researchers do talk about and actually estimate trends as summary statements of steady changes in variables of interest. In this section we illustrate how to estimate trends using data on expenditures and prices for natural gas used for home heating. These are actual expenditures, at least they were for one of the authors who paid the bills.

A consumer's monthly gas bill has just arrived. He is suddenly struck by its uncomfortably large size and decides to dig out the last eight years' monthly bills to see if indeed the bills have been increasing over time. Because it would be difficult to get much from simply looking at the stack of 96 bills, the consumer decides to prepare a time-series plot to see if that will provide a clear picture of the general movement ("trend") in the gas bill. The plot is presented in Figure 16.1. At first, this figure is confusing. The bottoms are constant, the tops are rising, and there is a definite wave-type pattern in the expenditures. However, since the consumer's initial interest is simply the "big picture," the question arises regarding how to capture in a simple statement what has happened to the consumer's monthly bill over time. This type of equation leads to *trend analysis*, or *trend estimation*, using regression. The basic trend equation is written as

$$Y = b_0 + b_1 \text{Time} + e \qquad (16.1)$$

which can be estimated by OLS procedures, the only question being how to quantify "time." The conventional method in applied work is to assign time the value of 1

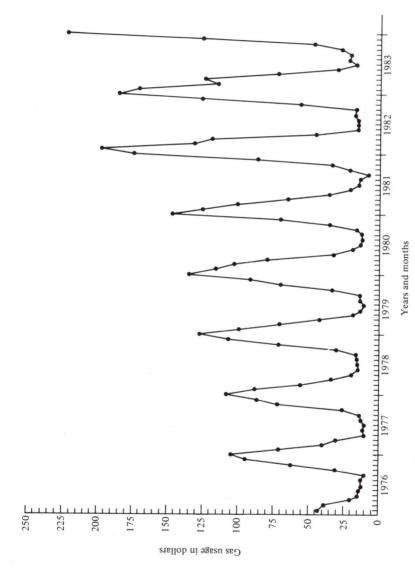

Figure 16.1 Monthly Natural Gas Usage in Dollars, January 1972 to December 1983.

342

TIME IN REGRESSION

for the first observation, the value of 2 for the second, and so on to the end of the time period. For the problem at hand, the worksheet would have the following structure:

Year	Month	Expenditure	Time-M
1976	January	43.13	1
1976	February	38.87	2
.	.	.	.
.	.	.	.
.	.	.	.
1976	November	94.39	11
1976	December	104.74	12
1977	January	71.11	13
1977	February	40.31	14
.	.	.	.
.	.	.	.
.	.	.	.
1983	November	125.57	95
1983	December	221.40	96

In this worksheet, "time" is treated like the independent variables encountered in previous chapters. The estimated equation is

$$\text{monthly expenditures} = 30.55 + .542\text{Time-M} + e \qquad (16.2)$$
$$(9.98) \quad (.179)$$

where the numbers below the coefficients are the respective standard deviations of the coefficients; "Time-M" refers to using monthly data to distinguish from equations below that use annual data. The coefficient on Time-M is positive and statistically significant; hence one can say that the consumer's monthly bill has been increasing over time. Moreover, the trend coefficient of .5426 says that on average the gas bill increased about 54 cents per *month*, since monthly data are used to estimate the equation. This is the type of summary statement referred to earlier, a statement that suppresses a lot of obvious movement (shown in Figure 16.1) to give a picture of the general movement in expenditure.

Before moving on, a brief comment on the nature of the time-series data sets used to estimate trend coefficients. In our example, the basic data are available on a monthly basis, which means that the trend coefficient is interpreted as a month-to-month change over time. But the applied researcher does not always have monthly data. Many time series are available only on a quarterly basis, others only on an annual basis, and so on. This, in principle, creates no problem, the only caution being that the estimated trend coefficient must be interpreted according to the data used, such as "quarterly trend" or "annual trend." There is often, however, the temptation to infer a period-to-period change different from the one used to estimate the trend coefficient. For example, since there are 12 months in a year, it would seem logical to multiply a monthly trend coefficient by 12 to obtain the annual trend coefficient. This may or

may not be good practice, depending on the intricate relationship between the underlying changes within years and across years in the particular series at hand. There is
nothing to guarantee that monthly and annual trend coefficients *must* bear a 1:12
relationship. In the following, monthly coefficients are estimated, and the inferred
annual trend coefficient is computed by multiplying the monthly coefficient by 12.
This inferred trend coefficient is then compared to the annual trend coefficient obtained
directly using annual average data. It turns out that the former estimates can be very
close to or very different from the direct estimates of annual trend.

The annual trend coefficient for expenditure can be inferred from the estimated
monthly coefficient as .5426 × 12 = $6.51. This says that based on the month-to-
month change of .5426, the inferred, or implied, year-to-year change is $6.51. The
worksheet for directly estimating the *annual* trend coefficient is as follows:

Year	Average Annual Expenditure	Time-A
1976	$38.19	1
1977	41.24	2
1978	49.63	3
1979	51.17	4
1980	54.64	5
1981	58.58	6
1982	78.63	7
1983	82.90	8

where "Time-A" denotes annual data and annual expenditure is average of monthly
expenditures. The estimated equation is

$$\text{annual average expenditures} = 28.47 + 6.312\text{Time-A} + e \qquad (16.3)$$
$$\qquad\qquad\qquad\qquad (4.07) \quad (.806)$$

where the numbers below the coefficients are the respective standard deviations. The
direct estimate of the year-to-year change (annual trend coefficient) is $6.31, which
is slightly different from the yearly coefficient derived from the estimated trend coefficient in (16.2).

Now that the consumer has statistically confirmed a suspicion of increasing gas
expenditures, curiosity compels the consumer to seek the possible causes. There are
at least three possibilities: increasingly cold winters; increasing gas use, due either to
colder winters or to a desire to be warmer; and increasing gas price. These three
possible causes may be checked by estimating linear trends for each of the three
variables.

The number of degree days per month is plotted in Figure 16.2, where degree days
are calculated such that higher values are associated with colder temperatures. Casual
observation of Figure 16.2 suggests no trend in the weather (probably not a surprising
result). This is confirmed by the following trend equation:

$$\text{monthly degree days} = 701.0 - .734\text{Time-M} + e \qquad (16.4)$$
$$\qquad\qquad\qquad (114.9) \quad (2.10)$$

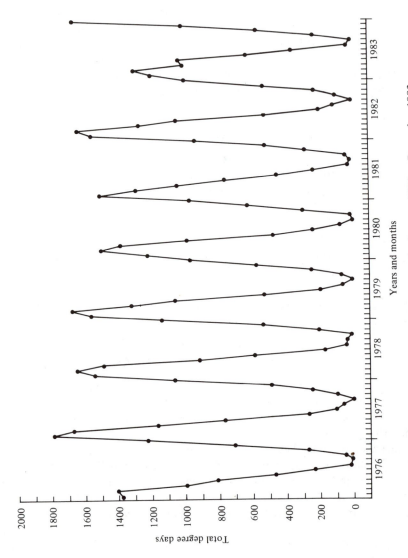

Figure 16.2 Monthly Degree Days in Madison, Wisconsin, January 1972 to December 1983.

where the numbers below the coefficients are the respective standard deviations. Although the monthly trend coefficient is $-.734$, it is not significantly different from zero. Consequently, there is no evidence that the increase in the gas bill was due to weather changes. The computed annual coefficient is $-.734 \times 12 = -8.808$. The directly estimated annual coefficient is given by

$$\text{average annual degree days} = 633.90 + 7.004\text{Time-A} + e \qquad (16.5)$$
$$(36.68) \quad (7.296)$$

with the standard deviations in parentheses. The slope is the "same" in that each is not significantly different from zero; however, there is a substantial difference between the computed and directly estimated annual trend coefficients.

Monthly gas use, measured in 100 cubic feet per month, is plotted in Figure 16.3. There is some tendency for the peak monthly use to decrease over time, suggesting a downtrend in gas use. The trend equation is

$$\text{monthly gas use} = 170.75 - .4928\text{Time-M} + e \qquad (16.6)$$
$$(25.79) \quad (.461)$$

where the numbers below the coefficients are the respective standard deviations. The trend coefficient does have a negative sign, but the low t-ratio says that the coefficient is not significantly different from zero at the .95 probability level. Consequently, there is no statistically significant monthly trend in gas use. The implied annual trend coefficient is $12 \times -.4928 = -5.9136$. The directly estimated annual coefficient is obtained from

$$\text{annual average gas use} = 177.40 - 6.789\text{Time-A} + e \qquad (16.7)$$
$$(10.33) \quad (2.108)$$

The two annual coefficients have the same sign but differ somewhat in numerical value. However, the interesting result is the insignificance of the monthly coefficient (and hence the computed annual coefficient) and the significance of the directly estimated coefficient.

The consumer now knows that there has been no trend in the weather, but that gas consumption has declined over time. The explanation for the increasing gas bill must be a rising gas price. This is confirmed by the time-series plot of gas price in Figure 16.4, which exhibits a rising price. The estimated trend equation is

$$\text{monthly gas price} = .15919 + .0055\text{Time-M} + e \qquad (16.8)$$
$$(.01081) \quad (.0002)$$

The computed annual coefficient is .0060, and the directly estimated coefficient is given by

$$\text{annual average gas price} = .12879 + .0061\text{Time-A} + e \qquad (16.9)$$
$$(.02800) \quad (.0005)$$

which shows the two annual coefficients to be identical. The simple trend analysis designed to search for the explanation for a rising gas bill is complete.

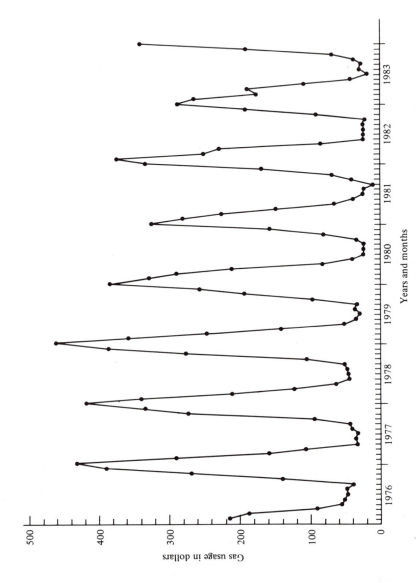

Figure 16.3 Monthly Natural Gas Usage in Dollars, January 1972 to December 1983.

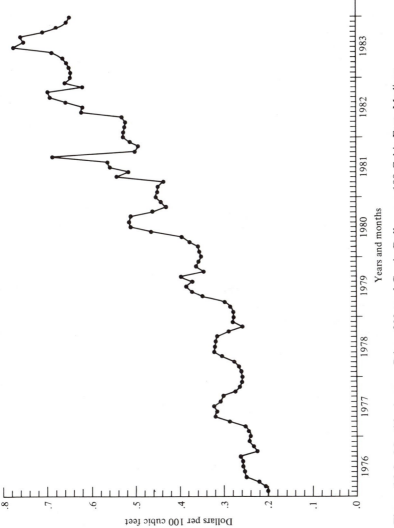

Figure 16.4 Monthly Average Price of Natural Gas in Dollars per 100 Cubic Feet, Madison, Wisconsin, January 1972 to December 1983.

In summary, this section has shown how to estimate and interpret trend coefficients, where the independent variable "time" is quantified by assigning the first observation the value 1, the second with the value 2, and so on to the end of the time series. Trend coefficients were estimated using both monthly and annual data and it was shown that using a coefficient estimated with one type of data set may not yield an equivalent computed value for some other period-to-period change.

Finally, note that this section has considered only linear trend. This approach was chosen to keep the illustrations simple and to focus on the procedure. Second, and perhaps more important, there was no theory to indicate what trend should "look like." Trend estimation, the results of which are very useful in much applied work, is an ad hoc procedure. One looks at the time plot and fits a line to capture the general movement in the variable of interest. In the absence of overwhelming arguments to the contrary, a linear summary is usually good enough. Often one is tempted to fit, say, a quadratic because the "statistics" might be better. But if a quadratic, why not a cubic. Indeed, why not a polynomial of degree equal to the number of observations, in which case the statistical fit is perfect? The point is simply that trend analysis should be used as only a crude attempt to summarize a *general* movement and to get the "big picture." The consciously suppressed minutia should be left for more sophisticated analysis.

A Segmented Trend

Although the caution against using complicated trend formulations is valid, applied researchers often encounter data sets that seem to demand something other than a simple linear trend formulation. Consider, for example, the plot of monthly gas prices in Figure 16.4, a close examination of which suggests an increase in the trend slope beginning in 1979. This trend relationship could be written

$$\text{monthly gas price} = b_0 + b_1 E + b_2 L + e \qquad (16.10)$$

where E represents the "early" period prior to 1979 and L the "late" period from 1979 on. Based on visual examination of Figure 16.4, January 1979 is selected to illustrate the method of estimating a *segmented trend line*. There are statistical procedures for selecting the precise point of change if this precise point must be known. However, as stressed above, the objective of trend analysis is usually to capture broad moves, in which case visual inspection is an acceptable expedient. In this setting, b_1 is the monthly trend slope through December 1978 and b_2 is the monthly trend slope from January 1979 through December 1983.

Before estimating (16.10), a researcher must specify what b_0, the intercept term, is to measure. There are two options: b_0 can be the point where the equation intersects the Y-axis (this is the way in which b_0 has been interpreted all along), or b_0 can be the trend value at the point of slope change, January 1979. Both are illustrated below.

b_0 *as the Y-Intercept*

For this option on b_0, the worksheet has the following structure:

Year	Month	Gas Price	Early	Late
1976	January	.2006	1	0
1976	February	.2068	2	0
.	.	.	.	.
.	.	.	.	.
.	.	.	.	.
1978	December	.2757	36	0
1979	January	.2775	37	0
1979	February	.2853	37	1
1979	March	.2969	37	2
.	.	.	.	.
.	.	.	.	.
.	.	.	.	.
1983	November	.6540	37	58
1983	December	.6474	37	59

The estimated regression equation is

$$\text{price} = .2332 + .0020E + .0072L + e \qquad (16.11)$$
$$(.0126) \quad (.0005) \quad (.0003)$$

where the numbers below the coefficients are the respective standard deviations. The slope coefficients are statistically significant and b_2 is larger than b_1, as would be expected based on visual examination of Figure 16.4. Since gas price is measured in dollars per 100 cubic feet, (16.11) says that the price rose by about .20 cent per cubic foot through December 1978 and by about .72 cent per cubic foot thereafter.

b_0 *as the Trend Price at the Point of Slope Change*

The data for equation (16.10) can also be structured so that b_0 is interpreted as the trend price at the point where the slope changes. For this interpretation of the intercept term, the worksheet has the following structure:

Year	Month	Gas Price	Early	Late
1976	January	.2006	− 36	0
1976	February	.2068	− 35	0
.	.	.	.	.
.	.	.	.	.
.	.	.	.	.
1978	December	.2757	− 1	0
1979	January	.2775	0	0
1979	February	.2853	0	1

Year	Month	Gas Price	Early	Late
1979	March	.2969	0	2
.	.	.	.	.
.	.	.	.	.
.	.	.	.	.
1983	November	.6540	.	58
1983	December	.6474	.	59

The estimated equation is

$$\text{gas price} = .30781 + .0020E + .0071L + e \tag{16.12}$$
$$(.0083) \quad (.0005) \quad (.0003)$$

The trend coefficients are identical to those shown in (16.11), but the intercept terms are different by virtue of the different specifications. In (16.11), .2332 is the point where the regression line intersects the Y-axis. In (16.12), .3078 is the "predicted" gas price for January 1979, the point chosen for the trend coefficient to change. To see that these two equations are consistent, compute the "predicted" price for (16.11) at January 1979:

$$\text{predicted gas price} = .2332 + .0020(37) + .0072(0)$$
$$= .3078$$

where the value for the E-variable is 37 and the value for the L-variable is 0 at the point of slope change. These results, (16.11) and (16.12), show that exactly the same trend coefficients are obtained whether the trend variable is coded to interpret the intercept as the point where the regression line intersects the Y-axis or to interpret it as the "predicted" price at the point of a change in trend.

Percentage Rates of Change

In the preceding section we estimated linear trends, where the trend coefficients provided an estimate of constant growth rates. But not all things exhibit a constant unit change from one period to the next. Indeed, many do not. This section shows how to estimate percentage growth rates.

The rate of change in a variable (V) between two time periods $(V_0$ and $V_1)$ is the change in V divided by its original value:

$$r = \frac{\Delta V}{V_0} = \frac{V_1 - V_0}{V_0} = \frac{V_1}{V_0} - 1 \tag{16.13}$$

For example, in Table 16.1 over the 13 years between the first quarter of 1970 and the end of 1982, per capita disposable (PCPI) income increased from \$3272 to \$9549. By (16.13), PCDI increased 192 percent:

$$r = \frac{9549 - 3272}{3272} = \frac{9549}{3272} - 1 = 1.92 = 192\%$$

This formula for calculating rates of growth is equally valid for other time periods—years, quarters, months, decades—as long as there are only two observations: a beginning point and an ending point. Often, however, there are more than two observations and, more important, researchers are interested in calculating the trend in easily understood terms. Trends, after all, are most commonly expressed in monthly,

Table 16.1. U.S. Quarterly per Capita Personal Income and Other Variables for Estimating Rates of Growth, 1970 to 1982

Year	Quarter	PCPI	LPCDI (Y_t^*)	Time (X_t^*)
1970	1	3272	8.09316	1
	2	3353	8.11761	2
	3	3358	8.13006	3
	4	3410	8.13447	4
1971	1	3517	8.16536	5
	2	3592	8.18646	6
	3	3620	8.19423	7
	4	3594	8.20221	8
1972	1	3711	8.21906	9
	2	3765	8.23350	10
	3	3831	8.25088	11
	4	3816	8.28274	12
1973	1	4143	8.32918	13
	2	4244	8.35326	14
	3	4339	8.37540	15
	4	4641	8.40111	16
1974	1	4513	8.41472	17
	2	4574	8.42814	18
	3	4697	8.45468	19
	4	4641	8.47199	20
1975	1	4809	8.47824	21
	2	5102	8.53739	22
	3	5105	8.53798	23
	4	5061	8.56159	24
1976	1	5347	8.58933	25
	2	5462	8.60557	26
	3	5540	8.61975	27
	4	5510	8.64206	28
1977	1	5772	8.66077	29
	2	5934	8.68845	30
	3	6077	8.71227	31
	4	6008	8.74034	32

Table 16.1. Continued

Year	Quarter	PCPI	LPCDI (Y_t^*)	Time (X_t^*)
1978	1	6402	8.76437	33
	2	6584	8.79240	34
	3	6749	8.81715	35
	4	6672	8.84722	36
1979	1	7186	8.87989	37
	2	7320	8.89837	38
	3	7533	8.92705	39
	4	7440	8.95183	40
1980	1	7785	8.95995	41
	2	7848	8.96801	42
	3	8074	8.99640	43
	4	8299	9.02389	44
1981	1	8551	9.05380	45
	2	8698	9.07085	46
	3	8951	9.09952	47
	4	9107	9.11680	48
1982	1	9155	9.12206	49
	2	9285	9.13616	50
	3	9461	9.15493	51
	4	9549	9.16419	52

quarterly, or annual rates of change. To see how regression can help estimate percentage rates of change from time-series data requires a brief review on the workings of compound growth.

The value of V in any time period (V_t) is equal to its value in the preceding period (V_{t-1}) plus the change in its value (ΔV) over the single time period:

$$V_t = V_{t-1} + \Delta V \tag{16.14}$$

Because, rewriting (16.13)

$$\Delta V = rV_{t-1} \tag{16.15}$$

it follows that

$$V_t = V_{t-1} + rV_{t-1} = (1 + r)V_{t-1} \tag{16.16}$$

Extending the argument above back one additional period yields

$$V_{t-1} = (1 + r)V_{t-2} \tag{16.17}$$

which, when substituted in (16.16), yields

$$V_t = (1 + r)(1 + r)V_{t-2} = (1 + r)^2 V_{t-2} \tag{16.18}$$

Extending back through time to some "original" or starting value (V_0) yields the usual compound interest formula:

$$V_t = V_0(1 + r)^t \qquad (16.19)$$

where t is the number of elapsed time periods since the beginning value. Now if only the world worked like a bank account where savings grow at a known rate r as long as they are on account, a researcher could calculate the rate of growth for the time period by using only the beginning and end points. The equation for this computation, obtained by solving (16.19) for r, is

$$r = \sqrt[t]{\frac{V_t}{V_0}} - 1 \qquad (16.20)$$

The mathematical precision of (16.20) is possible only in a deterministic world. Since most economic variables depend, at least in part, on random shocks, using (16.20) is not a particularly good way to calculate rates of growth. It would yield an answer, of course. For example, the annual rate of growth in PCDI between 1970 and 1982 could be calculated by (16.20) as

$$r = \sqrt[13]{\frac{9549}{3272}} - 1 = .0859 \quad \text{or} \quad 8.59\%$$

Similarly, the quarterly rate of growth could be calculated by taking the fifty-second rather than the thirteenth root in (16.20).

$$r = \sqrt[52]{\frac{9549}{3272}} - 1 = .0208 \quad \text{or} \quad 2.08\%$$

The practical problem with (16.20), and the reason to be suspicious of these computed rates of growth, is that the computed values rely exclusively on the beginning value and the ending value. What if these values are not representative of the beginning and the end? In technical terms, what if the two extreme values happen to involve large disturbance terms? If V_0 is "too high" and V_t is "too low" because of large positive and negative disturbance terms (respectively), the estimate of annual r using (16.20) will be biased downward. It could just as easily be biased upward if the disturbance terms were reversed. To acquire more confidence in the estimates of the rate of growth, one should use all the observations available on V to find a representative rate of growth based on some measure of central tendency. Regression will help.

The basic formula (16.19) provides a good place to begin searching for a linear and additive form with which to estimate r. Specifically, taking the natural logarithm, the logarithm to the base e of both sides yields

$$\ln V_t = \ln V_0 + t \ln (1 + r) \qquad (16.21)$$

which may be written

$$Y_t^* = \beta_0^* + \beta_1^* X_t^* \qquad (16.22)$$

where $Y_t^* = \ln V_t$ and $X_t^* = t =$ number of time periods since beginning. Note that (16.22) is linear and additive in X_1^*, that both Y_t^* and X_t^* can be calculated from basic data, Y_t^* is a simple logarithmic transformation, and X_t^* is the familiar variable called time. Finally,

$$\beta_0^* = \ln V_0 \quad \text{and} \quad \beta_1^* = \ln (1 + r) \tag{16.23}$$

The rate of growth can always be computed by manipulating the second part of (16.17) or by solving (16.23) for r:

$$r = e^{\beta_1^*} - 1 \tag{16.24}$$

All that is required is an estimate of β_1^*.

To proceed, simply attach a disturbance term to the appropriate log-linear mathematical form

$$\ln Y_t = \beta_0^* + \beta_1^* t + U_t \tag{16.25}$$

and use OLS to estimate β_0^* and β_1^*. It turns out $b_1^* = .022179$, and $b_0^* = 8.03836$, so the quarterly rate of growth was 2.24 percent:

$$r = e^{.022179} - 1 = .0224 \quad \text{[using (16.24)]} \tag{16.26}$$

Note that this estimate of r is different from the rate calculated using only the beginning and end points. This is because the "representative" income level for the first quarter of 1970 is \$3098 ($e^{8.03836} = 3098$) and the representative level for the last quarter of 1982 is \$9815 ($e^{8.03836 + 52(.022179)} = 9815$). These representative values are lower than the beginning observed beginning value (\$3272) and higher than the observed ending value (\$9549).

Occasionally, students and even experienced applied researchers will make the mistake of assuming that the b_1^* associated with (16.24) is the BLUE of the rate of growth. Technically, this b_1^* coefficient is the estimate of the continuous rate of growth, the "instant interest" banks occasionally quote in advertisements.

Thus estimating compound rates of growth from time-series date is a tricky but mechanical process. Use the log-linear form (16.25) and convert the estimate from continuous to discrete rates of growth by using (16.24). This instant rate needs to be compounded over the appropriate period in order to find the discrete rate of growth, the "effective yield" in bank terminology. Equation (16.24) is the method by which the effective r can be found from b_1^*. Generally, r is slightly larger than b_1^*.

Time as an Independent Variable

Time, or trend, was used as an independent variable earlier in the chapter in our discussion of linear trends. It was stressed there that the trend coefficient should be interpreted descriptively because it "describes" but does not "explain" broad movements in a variable over time. For example, there was a statistically significant, positive trend in natural gas prices during the 1976 to 1983 period, with a change in trend occurring in 1979. Although the estimated trend coefficients are valuable as summary, or quantitative, measures of the observed change in gas price, they provide no clue as to what "caused" the observed change. In this section we consider using a trend variable together with other variables in the equation.

Suppose that time-series data were used to estimate the equation

$$P = 30.69 - 17.06Q_p + 2.18Q_b + 18.16Q_c + e \qquad \bar{R}^2 = .53 \qquad (16.27)$$
$$(23.75) \quad (-3.41) \qquad (3.18) \qquad (2.58)$$

where P is pork price, Q_p is pork production, Q_b is beef production, Q_c is chicken production, and the numbers below the coefficients are the respective standard deviations. This equation has been used a number of times—in Chapters 8, 13, and 14—so what is wrong with it is pretty clear, but it can serve once again to illustrate still another point.

The signs of Q_b and Q_c are positive, whereas it is reasonable to expect the signs in this formulation to be negative. Moreover, the coefficient of Q_c is statistically significant. It is, of course, possible that beef and chicken are not substitutes for pork, and this may be exactly what (16.27) is saying.

When confronted by such disturbing results, the applied researcher often plots the OLS residuals against time to see if any pattern is present. The plot of the residuals from (16.27) is shown in Figure 16.5. It is clear that after accounting for the effect of changes in the quantity variables, price showed a definite upward trend over the period of analysis.

At this juncture, a trend variable could be added to the equation to see what happens. The coefficient of a trend variable, when used in conjunction with other independent variables, is interpreted exactly as it was interpreted above. Specifically, it measures (describes) the amount of period-to-period change in the dependent variable after "controlling" for the effect on the dependent variable of all other variables in the equation. Before introducing a trend variable into (16.27), consider two important issues.

First, it is the typical case that adding a trend variable to an equation increases the multiple correlation coefficient. Taken on face value, this means that the equation is "better" because it explains more of the variation in the dependent variable. But considering the interpretation of the trend coefficient presented in the preceding paragraph, this is an improper view of the increase in the multiple correlation coefficient. Trend has improved the *descriptive* but not the *explanatory* power of the equation.

Second, drawing on the omitted relevant variable problem (Chapter 13), it may be possible to make a defensible case for including a trend variable in the following way. If one or more relevant variables are omitted from the estimated equation, the coefficients of the included variables may be biased, the nature and degree of bias depending on the correlation between the included and omitted variables. In other words, the coefficients of one or more of the included variables may be picking up the effect of one or more omitted variables. This, of course, is a theoretical proposition because in a practical research setting it is not possible to make the kind of precise calculations required by the theory to determine if this is indeed the case. The solution to this problem is to include the relevant variable or variables, a solution that is not always forthcoming.

Consequently, the applied researcher might use the following line of reasoning to include a trend variable. Given that many variables, such as technology or tastes and preferences, some of which may be relevant to but omitted from the equation at hand, do exhibit trends over time, it may be reasonable to argue that a trend coefficient

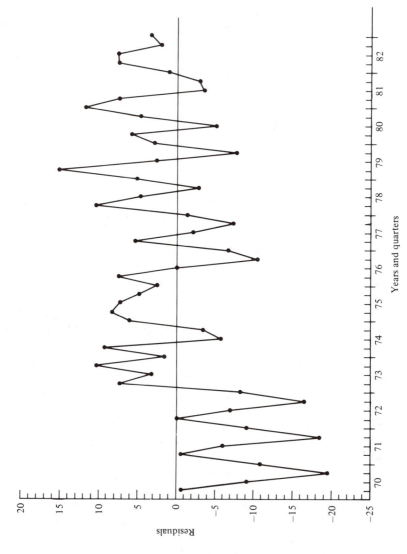

Figure 16.5 Residuals from the Pork-Price Regression Equation (16.27).

356

picks up the effect of these omitted variables and thereby reduces the potential bias in the coefficients of the other variables included in the equation. To the extent this is the case, and there is no way of knowing with certainty if it is, an equation with a significant trend coefficient is better, not because of the higher multiple correlation coefficient but because the potential for bias in the other coefficients is reduced.

To introduce a trend variable is to *detrend* the data in the sense that the coefficients of the other variables in the equation will be explaining not changes in the level of the dependent variable, but instead explaining deviations of the dependent variable from its trend value. This can be accomplished in either of two ways, by first removing the trend from all the variables ("detrending") and using the detrended values to estimate the equation, or by simply treating trend as an independent variable, as was done in previous sections. For completeness, each procedure is demonstrated. The two methods produce identical results, except for the intercept term (which is seldom, if ever, of substantive interest). Consequently, the second, simpler method is typically used in applied research.

The first detrending procedure involves obtaining values for each variable in the equation that seem "free" of trend. This is done in the following way. Let the simple trend equation be

$$Y_i = b_0 + b_1 T_i + e_i \qquad (16.28)$$

where Y_i is the dependent variable measured in its original values, T_i is the trend variable as defined earlier in this chapter, and e_i is the error term that measures the difference between each observed Y and its respective trend (or "equation") value. First estimate (16.28) to get the trend values of Y according to

$$\hat{Y}_i = b_0 + b_1 T_i \qquad (16.29)$$

where $\hat{Y}_i$ is the calculated trend value. The deviation of Y_i from its trend value can then be expressed as

$$Y_i - \hat{Y}_i = Y_i - b_0 - b_1 T_i = e_i \qquad (16.30)$$

which shows, like (16.28), that the OLS residuals measure the amount by which the Y-values deviate from their respective trend values. Similar trend equations are estimated for each of the independent variables in the equation.

The estimated linear trend equations for each of the variables in (16.27) are presented in Table 16.2. These are the respective estimates of (16.28) from which the values for (16.29) and (16.30) can be computed. The values computed by (16.30) are used to estimate the detrended version of (16.27). Note that the means of the variables are zero since the OLS residuals average zero over the sample observations. If a researcher wants the estimated equation to go through the midpoint of the original values of the variables, the proper approach is to add the mean of each variable to its respective values in (16.30) and use the resulting values to estimate the detrended version of (16.27). Thus

$$\hat{Y}_t^* = \hat{Y}_t + \bar{Y} \qquad \text{and} \qquad \hat{X}_t^* = \hat{X}_1 + \bar{X}$$

Table 16.2. Linear Trend Equations for the Variables in Equation (16.27)

Variable	Intercept	Trend Coefficient[a]
Pork price, p	24.72	.554
		(.077)
Pork quantity, Q_p	3.14	.011
		(.004)
Beef quantity, Q_b	5.58	.003
		(.003)
Chicken quantity, Q_c	2.28	.028
		(.008)

[a] Numbers in parentheses are t-ratios.

The estimates are presented in Table 16.3. These two ways of detrending yield identical estimates of the slope coefficients. They differ only by the value of the constant term.

The second method, and the preferred one in practice because it is easier to use, is to include a trend variable as an additional variable in the regression equation. As above, the trend variable is coded 1, 2, through to the last time period in the data set. The results of estimating this equation are as follows:

$$\hat{Y} = 124.68 - 20.643Q_p - 4.901Q_b - 3.379Q_c + .896T$$
$$\phantom{\hat{Y} = } (13.82) \quad (1.69) \quad\quad (1.65) \quad\quad (2.14) \quad\quad (.072) \quad (16.31)$$
$$R^2 = .90$$

The first thing to note is that the slope coefficients on the three quantity variables in equation (16.31) are identical to those in Table 16.3. In equation (16.31), however, a researcher obtains a direct estimate of the trend effect. The trend coefficient says that after accounting for the effect on price of changes in the three quantity variables, price increased .896 dollar per year due to trend factors. Remember, however, that adding a trend variable does not add to the explanatory power of the equation. In this case, pork price changed in a positive direction but the results shed no light on what

Table 16.3. Estimates of Equation (16.27) Using Detrended Variables[a]

Equation[b]	$\overline{R}^2$	Intercept	Q_p	Q_b	Q_c
1	.78	0	− 20.643	− 4.901	− 3.378
			(1.667)	(1.639)	(2.125)
2	.78	148.41	− 20.643	− 4.901	− 3.378
			(1.667)	(1.639)	(2.125)

[a] Numbers in parentheses are standard deviations.
[b] Equation 1 uses the OLS residuals [equation (16.30)]; equation 2 uses the OLS residuals adjusted for the respective sample means of the variables.

caused that change. Alternatively, the statistically significant trend coefficient may be indicating that a relevant variable has been omitted from the equation, but it does not reveal what that variable is.

The trend-adjusted equations are preferable to the base equation (16.27) if for no other reason than the coefficients of the quantity variables now have the expected negative signs. In the context of omitted relevant variables, it could be argued that the trend coefficient is picking up the effect of the omitted variable(s) and thereby purging the bias from the coefficients of the quantity variables. At this point, you might want to return to Chapter 13, where this same data set was used to illustrate the omitted relevant variable problem. Note that equation (16.31) is very similar to equation 4 in Table 13.4, where income was added to the equation. The point is that trend in (16.31) is probably picking up the effect of the omitted income variable.

Summary

In equation (16.31), it is preferable to use the income variable instead of the trend variable. However, there are many cases where the omitted variable is not as obvious, and it is best to use the trend variable. Trend analysis can be used directly to obtain a summary measure of the general movement of a variable over time, or a trend variable can be used on conjunction with other independent variables in a regression equation. But in either case, the trend coefficient must be treated as simply a descriptive statement of how the dependent variable has changed over time. There may be, of course, specific research settings where information extraneous to the sample will permit a more sophisticated interpretation of the coefficient. However, it is the responsibility of the applied researcher to defend such an interpretation.

Terms

ARIMA	Spectral analysis
Cycle	Time-series analysis
Detrend	Time-series plot
Growth rate (r)	Time-series regression
Seasonal	Trend
Segmented trend	Trend variable

Exercises

16.1 What are the three basic components of time that are of interest to applied researchers?

16.2 Are the following statements true or false? If false, why?
  (a) Trend refers to a systatic movement in a particular direction that persists over a substantial period of time.
  (b) Trends are always linear.
  (c) Trends are always positive.
  (d) Cycles take more than a year to work themselves out.
  (e) Seasonal time patterns occur within a year, but repeat themselves from year to year.
  (f) Time-series analysis and regression on time-series data are technically the same thing.

16.3 Consider the following data set.

Year	Current Price	Quantity (Millions of Pounds)	Price Index	Population (Millions)
1975	10	100	.98	50
1976	12	102	1.00	51
1977	14	97	1.10	51
1978	13	105	1.15	52
1979	16	101	1.25	53
1980	19	96	1.40	54
1981	20	100	1.50	54

  (a) Plot nominal price versus year and draw in a freehand linear trend line.
  (b) Plot quantity versus year and draw in a freehand linear trend line.
  (c) Calculate a linear trend for nominal price and interpret the coefficient of time.
  (d) Calculate a linear trend for quantity and interpret the coefficients of the equation.
  (e) Calculate a linear trend for per capita quantity.
  (f) Calculate a linear trend for real price.
  (g) Calculate the regression of per capita quantity as a function of real price and time.
  (h) How do you justify the large change in the coefficient of time when compared to part (e)?

16.4 Consider the following data set.

Year	Quarter	Price
1980	1	100
	2	98
	3	95
	4	93
1981	1	90
	2	89
	3	86
	4	85

Year	Quarter	Price
1982	1	83
	2	84
	3	82
	4	85
1983	1	98
	2	92
	3	96
	4	100

(a) Plot price versus trend. What would you conclude about the advisability of using a linear time trend?
(b) Study your plot and determine approximately the quarter and year that the downward trend in price reversed.
(c) Estimate a simple linear trend for price.
(d) Set up a worksheet with a segmented linear trend using two time variables and the first quarter of 1982 as the beginning of the second segment. Estimate the trend equation.
(e) Draw both the estimated linear and segmented trend lines on your plot for part (a). Which fits the observations on price better?
(f) Refer to Chapter 11 and use a quadratic trend specification to find the turning point in the data set.

16.5 Consider the following data set.

Year	Price	Quantity	Price Index
1950	10	100	1.00
1951	11	98	1.01
1952	12	99	1.03
1953	14	92	1.02
1954	16	94	1.04
1955	19	87	1.06
1956	23	86	1.05
1957	28	81	1.09
1958	27	84	1.10
1959	30	75	1.10
1960	33	50	1.12

Use regression to estimate the annual rate of change in
(a) Price.
(b) Quantity
(c) Price index.
(d) Using your equation in part (c), what is the estimated price index for 1949?

16.6 Suppose that you are given the following beginning and ending values *only*.

Year	P	Q	PI
1950	10	100	1.00
1960	33	50	1.12

(a) What is the general formula for calculating an annual rate of growth for these cases?

(b) Using your answer to part (a), what is the annual rate of growth in P, Q, and PI?

(c) Comparing your answers in part (b) to your answers in Exercise 16.5, what can you conclude about the two methods?

16.7 Are the following statements true or false? If false, why?

(a) A trend variable should be included in all regression equations that are estimated using time-series data.

(b) One possible reason for including a trend variable in a regression equation is to pick up the effects of other variables that we must omit.

(c) Another frequently used argument for including trend in a regression equation is that the trend variable picks up unobservable phenomena (such as tastes and technology) that change slowly but steadily over time.

(d) One danger of including trends in a regression equation is that you will introduce severe multicollinearity and thereby "muddy the water" with respect to your other included variables.

16.8 Given the following data:

Y	X
13	−5
4	−3
4	1
21	5
70	10

Fit the following model and comment on your results.

$$Y = b_0 + b_1X + b_2X^2 + b_3X^3 + e$$

16.9 You have data measured on a price variable for the following dates: July 15, 17, 18, 20, 24, 27, 28, and 31; August 1, 5, 7, and 9. You want to estimate a linear trend for the data. What are two specific forms of the time variable?

Estimating Seasonal Patterns

Occasionally, the radio or the newspaper will report such things as "The unemployment rate in May increased from 9.38 percent in April to 10.4 percent on a seasonally adjusted basis" or "Housing starts during the first quarter were running at 1.2 million on an annual basis." Behind statements like these are seasonal patterns, frequently referred to as "seasonals." In this chapter we show how to use regression to estimate seasonals and how to test for a significant seasonal pattern. Before doing that, a brief discussion of what seasonals are and how they can be used is in order.

What Are Seasonals?

The word *seasonal* refers to a time pattern in a variable that occurs within a 12-month period, such as a calendar year, a crop production and marketing year, or a fiscal year that spans two calendar years. The pattern of interest may be weekly (a weekly seasonal in grain exports), monthly (a monthly seasonal in the unemployment rate), or quarterly (a quarterly seasonal in housing starts). The *seasonal index* for a particular time period, say a month, is a measure of how much the value for that month deviates from the average for the 12-month period, where the deviation is usually measured in percentage terms. For example, a seasonal index for June of 105 means that due to seasonal factors, the June value of the variable is, on average, 5 percent higher than the 12-month average of the variable. A similar interpretation is given to weekly and quarterly seasonals.

Many variables of interest exhibit seasonal patterns: gross national product, unemployment rates, housing starts, production and prices of agricultural commodities, exports, imports, construction activity, natural gas prices, and so on. The key question is whether these patterns are stable, that is, whether they occur with regular periodicity from one year to the next. If they are stable in this sense, they can be estimated and used in a number of ways. For example, a stable seasonal can be computed that shows how the unemployment rate changes from one month to the next due to underlying *seasonal factors*, such as the opening and closing of schools, or the curtailment of construction activity due to cold weather. Armed with this knowledge, one can determine whether a particular observed month-to-month change in unemployment was due strictly to normal seasonal forces or to something else. This sort of analysis lies behind a statement like "The unemployment rate increased from 9.3 percent in April to 14.4 percent in May on a seasonally adjusted basis," which says that after adjusting for the "normal" month-to-month seasonal change, there was a "real" increase of 5.1 percentage points in unemployment in May. In this way, knowledge of seasonal patterns permits the monitoring of many sectors of the economy to see if real changes or only normal month-to-month changes are occurring.

Estimating Seasonals by OLS

In this section we show how to set up the worksheet for estimating monthly seasonals and how to obtain the seasonal indexes from the OLS coefficients. The monthly gas use data plotted in Figure 16.1 are used to illustrate obtaining seasonal indexes from regression analysis. The worksheet for estimating weekly or quarterly seasonals would be set up in a similar fashion.

The basic seasonal model is

$$CCF/m = b_0 + b_1 J + b_2 F + \cdots + b_{12} D + e \qquad (17.1)$$

where CCF/m = monthly gas use, cubic feet
  J,F, . . ., D = months
  b_0 = constant term
  b_i = amount that price deviates from the overall
      average for the ith month

Because the independent variables, months, are classificatory variables, this equation can be estimated by OLS procedures using dummy variables, as developed in Chapter 9. The worksheet looks as follows:

b_0	J	F	$\cdots$	N	D
1	1	0	$\cdots$	0	0
1	0	1	$\cdots$	0	0
.					
.					
.					
1	0	0		1	0
1	0	0	$\cdots$	0	1

and so on. The column headed with b_0 is included as a reminder that the constant term is the coefficient of a special variable, one that has a value of 1 over all observations. It is not, of course, included on the researcher's worksheet, but it is recognized by the computer program when the calculations are made. It is included here as a reminder of the dummy variable trap, which means that a restriction must be imposed in order to estimate the regression equation. To illustrate the flexibility of dummy variables, the two restrictions, one on the dummy variables and one on the coefficients of the dummy variables developed in Chapter 9, are used.

Omit One Period

The dummy variable portion of the worksheet with January omitted looks as follows:

b_0	Feb.	Mar.	$\cdots$	Nov.	Dec.	
1	0	0	$\cdots$	0	0	For January observations
1	1	0	$\cdots$	0	0	For February observations
.	.	.		.	.	
.	.	.		.	.	
.	.	.		.	.	
1	0	0	$\cdots$	1	0	For November observations
1	0	0	$\cdots$	0	1	For December observations

The equation to estimate is

$$CCF/m = b_0 + b_2F + b_3M + \cdots + b_{11}N + b_{12}D + e \qquad (17.2)$$

Notice that by this coding scheme, b_0 is the regression price for January since the value for each of the other monthly dummy variables is zero for January observations.

The monthly indexes will be computed from these regression coefficients after an alternative restriction for avoiding the dummy variable trap is used. But first some comments on the regression results in Table 17.1. By the formulation of (17.2), the

Table 17.1.   Estimated Seasonal Coefficients of Monthly Gas Use; January Omitted

Variable	Coefficient	Standard Deviation of Coefficient	t-ratio
Constant	306.37	18.43	16.61
February	− 87.62	26.07	− 3.36
March	− 150.50	26.07	− 5.77
April	− 237.25	26.07	− 9.09
May	− 266.37	26.07	− 10.21
June	− 274.37	26.07	− 10.52
July	− 271.62	26.07	− 10.41
August	− 273.50	26.07	− 10.48
September	− 233.62	26.07	− 8.95
October	− 140.62	26.07	− 5.39
November	− 46.12	26.07	− 1.76
December	67.37	26.07	2.58

coefficient of each variable measures the amount by which gas use in that month deviates from January, the omitted category. For example, the May gas use is, on average, 266.37 CCF smaller than the January use.

The standard deviations of the monthly coefficients are the same, which may be surprising. It is difficult to show exactly why this is the case without using matrix algebra, but it is possible to get an intuitive feel of what is going on. Suppose that there are an equal number of observations on three categories and one is eliminated in order to estimate an equation. If the equation is written in deviation form, then, from Chapter 4,

$$S_{b_1}^2 = \frac{\Sigma e^2}{n - 3} \frac{\Sigma x_2^2}{(\Sigma x_1^2)(\Sigma x_2^2) - (\Sigma x_1 x_2)^2} \tag{4.41}$$

and

$$S_{b_2}^2 = \frac{\Sigma e^2}{n - 3} \frac{\Sigma x_1^2}{(\Sigma x_1^2)(\Sigma x_2^2) - (\Sigma x_1 x_2)^2} \tag{4.42}$$

Each of the two dummy variables, x_1 and x_2, has the same number of 1's and 0's in its respective column. Consequently, the means and sum of squared deviations are the same for each variable. Moreover, by the coding scheme, the 1's and 0's are located in the respective columns such that the sum of cross products is zero (see worksheet above). In other words, $\Sigma x_1^2 = \Sigma x_2^2$ and $\Sigma x_1 x_2 = 0$. Using these results, (4.41) and (4.42) yields $S_{b_1} = S_{b_2}$. This extends to the general case for (17.2). Thus the standard deviations of the dummy variable coefficients will all be equal, as shown in Table 17.1.

Seasonals Sum to Zero

The second method for avoiding the dummy variable trap is to restrict the coefficients to sum to zero (see Chapter 9):

$$\sum_{i=1}^{12} d_i = 0 \quad \text{or} \quad d_1 = -\sum_{i=2}^{12} d_i$$

The basic equation to be estimated is

$$\text{monthly gas use} = d_0 + d_1 J + d_2 F + \cdots + d_{12} D + e \tag{17.3}$$

where the regression coefficients are different from those in (17.1) (see Chapter 9). In this case d_0 is the average gas use in the sample because "on average" the monthly coefficients are zero. To see the coding scheme implied by this restriction, substitute $d_1 = -\sum_{i=2}^{12} d_i$ into (17.3) to obtain

$$\begin{aligned} \text{monthly gas use} &= d_0 + (-d_2 - d_3 \ldots - d_{12})J \\ &\quad + d_2 F + \cdots + d_{12} D + e \\ &= d_0 + d_2(F - J) + d_3(M - J) \\ &\quad + \cdots + d_{12}(D - J) + e \end{aligned} \tag{17.4}$$

This implies the following worksheet:

d_0	F	$\cdots$	N	D	
1	-1	$\cdots$	-1	-1	For January observations
1	1	$\cdots$	0	0	For February observations
.					
.					
.					
1	0	$\cdots$	0	1	For December observations

Coding in this way eliminates the linear dependence since the sum over the columns for the months no longer equals a column of 1's. As a consequence of this adjustment, the equation actually estimated is

$$\text{monthly gas use} = d_0 + d_2 F + \cdots + d_{12} D + e$$

and once we have estimated the coefficients of this equation we obtain the estimate of d_1, the coefficient for January, from the restriction

$$d_1 = -d_2 - d_3 - \cdots - d_{12}$$

This coding procedure yields the estimates shown in Table 17.2. Note that the estimated regression coefficients are different from those in Table 17.1, since a different coding scheme was used. However, the overall regression results are the same.

In fact, the results of Table 17.1 are obtainable from Table 17.2, or vice versa. Remember that the coefficients in Table 17.1 are interpreted as the deviations of month

Table 17.2. Estimated Seasonal Coefficients of Gas Use; Coefficients Sum to Zero

Variable	Estimated Coefficient	Standard Deviation of Coefficient	t-ratio
Constant	146.85	5.32	13.93
January[a]	159.51	17.65	9.04
February	71.89	17.65	4.07
March	9.02	17.65	.51
April	-77.72	17.65	-4.40
May	-106.85	17.65	-6.05
June	-114.85	17.65	-6.50
July	-112.10	17.65	-6.35
August	-113.97	17.65	-6.45
September	-74.10	17.65	-4.19
October	18.89	17.65	1.07
November	113.39	17.65	6.42
December	226.89	17.65	12.85

[a]Derived from restriction that $\sum_{i=1}^{12} d_i = 0$.

i from January, the omitted category. Thus the February coefficient minus the January coefficient in Table 17.2 is the same as the February coefficient in Table 17.1.

$$-71.89 - (159.51) = -87.62 \text{ for February}$$
$$9.02 - (159.51) = -150.49 \text{ for March}$$

The point is that the researcher can use whichever method is more convenient and obtain the same results.

Computing Seasonal Indexes

The seasonal for a particular month measures how much the value for that month deviates from the average, usually expressed in percentage terms. So the general formula for computing the seasonal index, S_i, for the *i*th month is

$$S_i = \frac{\text{price}_i}{12\text{-month average price}} \tag{17.5}$$

The results obtained from using the equations above are presented in Table 17.3, where price$_i$ is computed from the appropriate regression equation. Note that the two restrictions yield exactly the same seasonal indexes.

Table 17.3. Computation of Estimated Monthly Gas Usage and the Corresponding Seasonal Index

| | Estimated Monthly Gas Use | | Seasonal Index[a] | |
Month	Omit Jan. Dummy[b]	$\Sigma\, d_i = 0$[c]	Omit Jan. Dummy	$\Sigma\, d_i = 0$
January	306.37	306.36	208.6	208.4
February	218.75	218.74	149.0	149.0
March	155.87	155.87	106.1	106.1
April	69.12	69.13	47.1	47.1
May	40.00	40.00	27.2	27.2
June	32.00	32.00	21.8	21.8
July	34.75	34.75	23.7	23.7
August	32.87	32.88	22.4	22.4
September	72.75	72.75	49.5	49.5
October	165.75	165.74	112.9	112.9
November	260.25	260.74	177.2	177.2
December	373.74	373.74	254.5	254.5
Average	146.85	146.85	100.0	100.0

[a] Computed by (17.5)
[b] Computed from regression results in Table 17.1.
[c] Computed from regression results in Table 17.2.

A final comment is in order. The regression results above present an average for the monthly indexes. Because the indexes are computed to express each month's value as a percent of the annual average, it follows that the twelve indexes must average 100.0. It is good practice to make this check before using the indexes for any calculations. All researchers make mistakes, so it is a good idea to use every check possible before proceeding with the analyses.

Using Seasonal Indexes

The estimated equations above show that there is a statistically significant seasonal pattern in gas use. The seasonal indexes in Table 17.3 can be used to illustrate how knowledge of a seasonal pattern can be helpful. One illustration is "forecasting" future gas use and the other is "monitoring" for gas use changes due to something other than normal seasonal changes.

Suppose that the consumer receives the January gas bill and the gas use is 250 cubic feet. Table 17.3 indicates that typically January use is 208.6 percent of the annual average use. These two bits of information can be used to "forecast" the average gas use for the year by

$$\text{forecast annual average} = \frac{\text{value for month}}{\text{seasonal for month}} = \frac{250}{2.086} = 119.85 \quad (17.6)$$

This forecast, in turn, can be used to forecast gas use for a particular month, say August. Table 17.3 shows the August seasonal to be 22.4. Consequently, forecast annual average × august seasonal yields to August forecast

$$\text{August gas use forecast} = 119.85 \times .224 = 26.85 \quad (17.7)$$

Similar forecasts could be made for any other month.

Finally, seasonals can be used to monitor for "real" changes, changes due to something other than normal seasonal forces. Suppose that gas use in May is 52.6 units. This implies that use in May an annual average rate of 193.38 CCF.

$$\text{annual rate in May} = \frac{52.6}{.272} = 193.38 \text{ CCF} \quad (17.8)$$

The use in June is 45.5. If the use change from May to June were due to seasonal factors only, the expected June usage based on the actual May usage would be

$$\text{expected June use} = 193.38 \times .218 = 42.16 \quad (17.9)$$

Since the actual June usage of 45.5 is higher than the use expected from a normal seasonal change, it is reasonable to conclude that there was a real increase in June gas use. It is computations like these that lie behind such statements as "Consumer income did not increase in September on a seasonally adjusted basis" and "Housing starts in February were at a higher annual rate than they were in January."

Adjusting for Trend

When estimating one time component, such as seasonal indexes, it is sometimes necessary to remove another time component, such as trend. This is illustrated here using the gas price data plotted in Figure 16.4. The data are used for illustrations only and nothing is to be inferred concerning public utility pricing.

The estimates of the seasonal coefficients under alternative restrictions on the equations are presented in Tables 17.4 and 17.5. The seasonal indexes are given in Table 17.6. As the regression results show, there is no significant seasonal pattern in gas price.

In Chapter 16 the same data set was used for estimating trend equations, and a significant trend appeared in this price series, one that is not recognized in estimating the seasonals above. This may be the reason for finding no significant seasonal: It was masked by the price trend. To see how this is possible, first introduce a *linear* trend variable. The model to be estimated is then given by

$$p = b_0 + d_1 J + \cdots + d_{12} D + tT + e$$

where the variables are defined as in (17.3) and T is the trend variable. The worksheet for this problem is

b_0	F	$\cdots$	D	T
1	-1	$\cdots$	-1	1
1	1	$\cdots$	0	2
.				
.				
.				
1	0	$\cdots$	1	96

The trend is entered by coding the first observation with a 1 and increasing by 1 for each observation until 96 is reached at the end of the data, just as in the trend analysis of Chapter 16. The regression results are presented in Table 17.7.

Comparing these results to those in Tables 17.4 and 17.5 shows that adjusting for the monthly trend in gas price results in a significant seasonal pattern. In the previous tables, the underlying trend was so strong that it masked the seasonal pattern and consequently, nonsignificant seasonal coefficients were obtained. The impact of removing the monthly trend on the estimated seasonal coefficients is demonstrated in Table 17.7. Because the trend was positive, the seasonals were understated for the early part of the year and overstated in the latter part of the year. Compare January of 86.8 versus 93.9 and December of 99.6 versus 92.5. On the other hand, the indexes for June and July are relatively close. These results make the important point that when estimating one time component, it is necessary to adjust for the possibility of other time components in the data series.

Table 17.4. Estimated Seasonal Coefficients for the Price of Natural Gas January 1976 to December 1983, January Price Omitted

Variable	Estimated Coefficient	Standard Deviation of Estimate	t-ratio
Constant	.36964	.05929	6.23
February	.00301	.08384	.03
March	.01355	.08384	.16
April	.04884	.08384	.58
May	.07377	.08384	.09
June	.09769	.08384	1.16
July	.09752	.08384	1.16
August	.12019	.08384	1.43
September	.06637	.08384	.79
October	.04622	.08384	.55
November	.05490	.08384	.65
December	.05469	.08384	.65

$\overline{R}^2 = -.073$, computed F-ratio $= .028$

In Chapter 16 we saw that there was a trend shift in gas price beginning in 1979. The effect on the seasonal indexes from adjusting for this trend change is shown in Table 17.8. Notice that the results are similar to those in the Table 17.7. However, these differences may be sufficient to make the latter indexes preferable.

Finally, the data may be "deseasonalized" just as they can be detrended, by dividing by the seasonal value (see Chapter 16). In applied work the effect of seasonal movement is sometime suppressed in order to better study the effect of other variables.

Table 17.5. Estimated Seasonal Coefficients, Coefficients Sum to Zero for the price of Natural Gas, January 1976 to December 1983

Variable	Estimated Coefficient	Standard Deviation of Estimate	t-ratio
Constant	.42604	.01711	24.89
February	-.05338	.05676	-.94
March	-.04284	.05676	-.75
April	-.00755	.05676	-.13
May	.01737	.05676	.30
June	.04129	.05676	.72
July	.04112	.05676	.72
August	.06379	.05676	1.12
September	.00996	.05676	.17
October	-.01017	.05676	-.17
November	-.00149	.05676	-.02
December	-.00170	.05676	-.03

$\overline{R}^2 = -.073$, computed F-ratio $= .028$

Table 17.6. Computation of Monthly Seasonal Prices and Seasonal Indexes; Natural Gas Price

Month	Monthly Price		Seasonal Index[a]	
	Omit Jan. Dummy[b]	$\Sigma d_i = 0$[c]	Omit Jan. Dummy	$\Sigma d_i = 0$
January	.36964	.36964	86.8	86.8
February	.37265	.37266	87.5	87.5
March	.38319	.38320	89.9	89.9
April	.41848	.41849	98.2	98.2
May	.44341	.44341	104.1	104.1
June	.46733	.46733	109.7	109.7
July	.46716	.46716	109.7	109.7
August	.48983	.48983	115.0	115.0
September	.43601	.43600	102.3	102.3
October	.41586	.41587	97.6	97.6
November	.42454	.42455	99.6	99.6
December	.42433	.42434	99.6	99.6
Average	.42604	.42604	100.0	100.0

[a] Computed by (17.5).
[b] Computed from regression results in Table 17.4.
[c] Computed from regression results in Table 17.5.

Table 17.7. Monthly Gas Price Seasonals Adjusted for Linear Trend

Variable	Coefficient	t-ratio	Monthly Price[a]	Seasonal Index[b]
Constant	.15906	17.33	—	
January[c]	− .02613	− 1.74	.39997	93.9
February	− .02861	− 1.90	.39943	93.3
March	− .02358	− 1.57	.40246	94.5
April	.00620	0.41	.43224	101.5
May	.02563	1.70	.45167	106.0
June	.04405	2.93	.47009	110.3
July	.03837	2.55	.46441	109.0
August	.05553	3.70	.48157	113.0
September	− .00379	− 0.25	.42225	99.1
October	− .02943	− 1.96	.39661	93.1
November	− .02626	− 1.74	.39978	93.8
December	− .03198	− 2.12	.39406	92.5
Trend	.00550	33.45	—	—
Average			.42604	100.0

[a] Computed as sample average price of .42606 + monthly coefficient, since monthly coefficients sum to zero.
[b] Computed with equation (17.5), where sample average price = .42604.
[c] Derived from restrictions that monthly coefficients sum to zero.

Table 17.8. Monthly Gas Price Seasonals Adjusted for a Segmented Trend

Variable	Coefficient	t-ratio	Monthly Price[a]	Seasonal Index[b]
Constant	.23332	27.62	—	—
January[c]	−.02961	−3.00	.39843	93.5
February	−.02982	−3.23	.39622	93.0
March	−.02452	−2.66	.40152	94.2
April	.00553	0.60	.43158	101.3
May	.02523	2.74	.45127	105.9
June	.04392	4.77	.46996	110.3
July	.03851	4.18	.46455	109.0
August	.05594	6.07	.48196	113.1
September	−.00312	−0.33	.42292	99.3
October	−.02850	−3.09	.39754	93.3
November	−.02506	−2.71	.40096	94.1
December	−.03051	−3.30	.39553	92.8
Trend: 1976–1979	.00201	6.43	—	—
Trend: 1979–1983	.00717	41.29	—	—
Average			.42604	99.98

[a] Computed as sample average of .42604 + monthly coefficient, since monthly coefficients sum to zero.
[b] Computed using equation (17.5), where sample average price = .42604.
[c] Derived from restriction that monthly coefficients sum to zero.

The standard procedure is to include seasonal dummies in the equation rather than deseasonalizing the variables and using the resulting values for estimating the regression equation. The actual gas price and the deseasonalized gas price using the equation in Table 17.8 are plotted in Figure 17.1.

Summary

In this chapter, as in Chapter 16, we have demonstrated the use of regression analysis for estimating a time component in a variable. Seasonal indexes may be of interest in themselves for forecasting changes or monitoring for real changes. In other cases the interest in seasonals may simply be to remove their effect in order that the effect of other variables may be studied. Finally, seasonal coefficients, like trend coefficients must be interpreted for what they are, namely, descriptions of how a variable has changed over time.

374

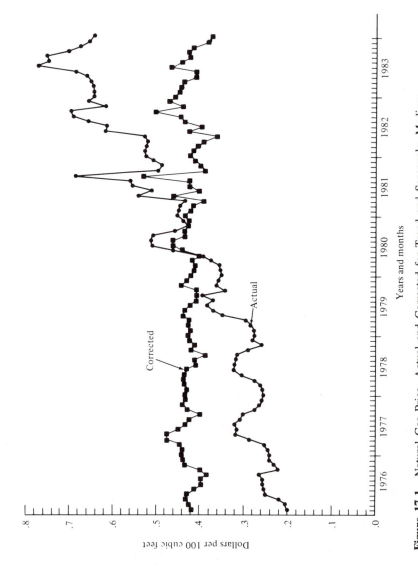

Figure 17.1 Natural Gas Price, Actual and Corrected for Trend and Seasonals, Madison, Wisconsin, January 1972 to December 1983.

Terms

Deseasonalizing data   Seasonally adjusted

Seasonal   Seasonal variaiton

Seasonal Index

Exercises

17.1 Consider the following regression results:

$$P = 100 - 4Q_2 + 2Q_3 + 3Q_4 + e \qquad R^2 = .48$$
$$ (1) \quad\ (.5) \quad\ (.6) \qquad\qquad n = 40$$

where $Q_2 = -1$ if first quarter; 1 if second quarter; 0 otherwise

$Q_3 = -1$ if first quarter; 1 if third quarter; 0 otherwise

$Q_4 = -1$ if first quarter; 1 if fourth quarter; 0 otherwise

and the standard errors are in parentheses.

(a) What is d_1, the coefficient for the first quarter?

(b) What is the seasonal price index for each quarter?

(c) Due to seasonal factors, we would expect first-quarter prices to be _____ percent (higher, lower) than the 12-month average price.

(d) Due to seasonal factors, we would expect fourth-quarter prices to be _____ percent (higher, lower) than the 12-month average price.

(e) If an appropriate agency announced that the price in the first quarter was $120, you would say that "the price in the first quarter was _____ on an annual basis."

(f) If prices increased from 130 in the second quarter to 135 in the third quarter, you would say that prices on a seasonally adjusted basis (increased, decreased) from _____ to _____. This is a(n) (increase, decrease) of _____ percent in price on a seasonally adjusted basis.

(g) If prices declined from $115 in the fourth quarter to $105 in the first quarter, you would say that, on a seasonally adjusted basis, prices (increased, decreased) from _____ to _____. This is a(n) (increase, decrease) of _____ percent in price on a seasonally adjusted basis.

(h) If prices decreased from $103 in the fourth quarter to $99 in the first quarter of the next year, then you would say that, on a seasonally adjusted basis, prices (increased, decreased) from _____ to _____. This is a(n) (increase, decrease) of _____ percent in price on a seasonally adjusted basis.

17.2 Consider the following regression equation on quarterly prices for the years 1973 through 1984.

$$P = 80 + 2Q_2 + 3Q_3 - 1Q_4 + .5T + e \qquad R^2 = .64$$
$$ (.5) \quad (1) \quad\;\; (.2) \qquad\qquad\quad n = 48$$

where Q's and values in parentheses are like those in Exercise 17.1 and $T =$ trend variable (1–48). Answer the following questions using T at its mean value of 24.5.

(a) What is the average price $\bar{P}$?
(b) What are the quarterly seasonal price indexes?
(c) If the local newspaper reported that the price in the first quarter of 1985 was 120, what is the seasonally adjusted price?
(d) If price decreased from \$103 in the fourth quarter of 1984 to \$101 in the first quarter of 1985, did seasonally adjusted prices decrease or increase, and by how much?

17.3 Assume that you want to estimate the seasonal component for the following model.

$$P = \beta_0 + \beta_1 Q_1 + \beta_2 Q_2 + \beta_3 Q_3 + \beta_4 Q_4 + U$$

where P = monthly price
Q_1 = 1 for January, February, or March; 0 otherwise
Q_2 = 1 for April, May, or June; 0 otherwise
Q_3 = 1 for July, August, or September; 0 otherwise
Q_4 = 1 for October, November, or December; 0 otherwise

(a) Assume that $Q_1 + Q_2 + Q_3 + Q_4 = 1$ and develop the appropriate statistical model.
(b) Assume that $\beta_1 + \beta_2 + \beta_3 + \beta_4 = 0$ and develop the appropriate statistical model.
(c) Complete the following worksheet for the first 12 observations under the assumption of parts (a) and (b).

Month	b_0	Part (a)			Part (b)		
		Q_2	Q_3	Q_4	Q_2^*	Q_3^*	Q_4^*
January							
February							
March							
April							
May							
June							
July							
August							
September							
October							
November							
December							

17.4 The data set for Exercise 17.1 was used to estimate the same equation under the assumption that $Q_1 + Q_2 + Q_3 + Q_4 = 1$. The resulting estimated equation is

$$P = 99 - 3Q_2 + 3Q_3 + 4Q_4 \qquad R^2 = .48$$
$$n = 40$$

(a) What is the estimate of β_1, the population slope of Q_1?
(b) What is the seasonal price index for each quarter?
(c) If prices increased from \$130 in the second quarter to \$135 in the third quarter, what happened to seasonally adjusted price?

17.5 Consider the following results:

Month	Coefficient
Constant	200
February	2
March	4
April	6
May	5
June	2
July	1
August	−1
September	−4
October	−7
November	−5
December	−3

where the standard error for each regression coefficient is 2 and the results are based on 120 observations.

(a) What is the seasonal price index for each month?
(b) Which months have statistically significant seasonal coefficients?

17.6 Assume that the following regression equation was estimated under the assumption that the seasonal coefficients sum to zero.

$$P = a_0 + d_2 M_2^* + d_3 M_3^* + \cdots d_{12} M_2^* + b_1 X_1 + \cdots + b_i X_i + e$$

where P = monthly price
M_i^* = dummy varible from $M_i - M_1$
X_i = independent variables

(a) What is the seasonal price index for each month given the following estimated coefficients for each month?

Month	Coefficient
Constant	100.0
February	2.0

Month	Coefficient
March	4.0
April	6.0
May	5.0
June	3.0
July	1.0
August	−1.0
September	−3.0
October	−5.0
November	−4.0
December	−2.0

(b) What are the seasonally adjusted prices if the published monthly prices are as follows:

Month	Price
January	190
February	212
March	218
April	218
May	210
June	206
July	202
August	200
September	196
October	192
November	194
December	198

(c) Plot the unadjusted and adjusted prices. What do you conclude?

17.7 Given the following data on pork demand:

Year	Quarter	Price of Pork (per Hundred weight)	Quantity of Pork (Billions of Pounds)	Per Capita Personal Income
1970	1	$27.19	30.56	$7382
	2	23.86	31.33	7515
	3	22.52	31.54	7589
	4	16.32	39.04	7543
1971	1	17.80	36.71	7667
	2	17.33	36.78	7732
	3	19.27	34.41	7750
	4	20.06	38.16	7795

Year	Quarter	Price of Pork (per Hundred weight)	Quantity of Pork (Billions of Pounds)	Per Capita Personal Income
1972	1	24.67	35.03	7847
	2	25.00	33.86	7914
	3	28.84	30.64	8039
	4	28.89	35.07	8251
1973	1	35.63	32.62	8410
	2	36.82	31.78	8508
	3	49.04	27.91	8578
	4	40.29	33.47	8619
1974	1	38.40	33.78	8533
	2	28.00	35.31	8511
	3	36.59	32.42	8507
	4	39.06	34.31	8394
1975	1	39.35	30.44	8255
	2	46.11	29.23	8671
	3	58.83	25.12	8583
	4	52.20	28.35	8649
1976	1	47.99	28.95	8775
	2	49.19	27.83	8812
	3	43.88	29.53	8884
	4	34.25	35.90	8967
1977	1	39.08	32.94	9036
	2	40.87	31.86	9125
	3	43.85	30.74	9280
	4	41.38	34.99	9399
1978	1	47.44	32.43	9487
	2	47.84	32.65	9530
	3	48.52	31.58	9622
	4	50.05	35.40	9732
1979	1	51.98	33.98	9813
	2	48.04	37.58	9778
	3	38.52	38.59	9809
	4	36.39	43.47	9867
1980	1	36.31	41.24	9958
	2	31.18	43.00	9805
	3	46.23	37.57	9882
	4			

(a) Estimate a model in which the quantity of pork slaughtered is a function of price and per capita income and includes an adjustment for seasonality.

(b) What is the seasonal index for pork slaughter if mean pork slaughter is 33.68?

(c) Why would you expect the coefficients on pork price and per capita income to be biased and inefficient if the seasonal variables were excluded from the statistical model?

18

Forecasting

The regression theory of previous chapters centers on the linear, unbiased, minimum-variance porperties of OLS estimators. Much attention is placed on whether these properties are maintained when the underlying assumptions of the classical model are violated. For example, in the presence of an autoregressive disturbance term, the OLS coefficient estimators are linear and unbiased, but they are no longer minimum-variance estimators. Consequently, the equation must be transformed into one with a nonautoregressive disturbance term before using the OLS formulas to obtain estimates of the regression coefficients. Loosely speaking, then, regression theory is concerned with the purity of the OLS estimates, where purity is defined by the linear, unbiased, minimum-variance properties. This concern is important. Regression coefficients are response parameters. An income coefficient is a quantitative measure of change in, say, consumption in response to a change in income. The researcher needs to know whether the estimates of these coefficients obtained in a specific research setting are linear, unbiased, minimum-variance estimates. If they are not, the researcher cannot make valid probability (statistical) statements about the numerical values of the unobservable population regression coefficients.

In this chapter attention shifts from estimating and interpreting regression coefficients to using a regression equation for forecasting and predicting. Interest shifts from the properties of regression coefficients to the properties of forecasts or predictions made with the regression equation. In the next section we give a precise but modest definition of forecasting. In the second section we derive the forecast error under different assumptions about what is known at the time a forecast is made. Incorporating available knowledge of an autoregressive structure (see Chapter 14) is covered in the final section.

Definition and Some Distinctions

Thinking about forecasting, especially from a statistical standpoint, is rather difficult because several distinctions have to be made simultaneously. The verbs *predicting* and *forecasting* can be used interchangeably. Each refers to the act of making a statement about an event before that event occurs. For example, one might say "The retail price of oranges will be 10 percent higher next year," or "If the tax base in the Stetson Consolidated School District were to increase 10 percent, school expenditures per pupil would increase 8 percent." Formally, forecasting and prediction involve making a "statement in advance" of the occurrence of an event. Moreover, it is a statement in advance made on the basis of special knowledge, particularly on the basis of something other than divine inspiration. One should aspire to being a good applied forecaster, not a Delphic oracle.

For current purposes, that "special knowledge" is the regression equation

$$Y = \beta_0 + \beta_1 X + U \tag{18.1}$$

In this context, the "statement in advance" has the following structure: if X were to take on the value X_{T+1}, the associated value of Y would be

$$\hat{Y}_{T+1} = \beta_0 + \beta_1 X_{T+1} \tag{18.2}$$

In other words, forecasting or predicting is concerned with the value of Y, given that $X = X_{T+1}$. This forecasted value of Y has a variance, the square root of which is the *forecast error*, to which our attention turns in the next section.

Elsewhere in this book, the subscript i is generally used to identify the sample points, a notation that makes no explicit reference to the type of data set used for estimation. Most of the derivations therefore apply equally to time-series and cross-sectional data sets. What follows also applies equally to either type of data set, but the discussion is easier to follow if it is cast in terms of "time." This is done by using a t subscript.

Two basic distinctions must be made: *ex post* versus *ex ante forecasting* and *conditional* versus *unconditional forecasting*. It is helpful to think of a time continuum consisting of three segments. The first represents the time period used for estimating the regression equation (the years from 1961 to 1980, for example). The second segment refers to the period of time from the last year of the estimation period to the "present" (1981 to 1984, for example). The third period represents the "future" (all years following 1984). This is shown schematically in Figure 18.1. The distinction between *ex post* forecasting and *ex ante* forecasting is clear. During the $(T_1 - T_2)$ time interval, forecast values for the dependent variable can be obtained, but the forecasting is over a time interval for which the values of all the independent variables are known. This may not seem to be true forecasting in the sense of making advance

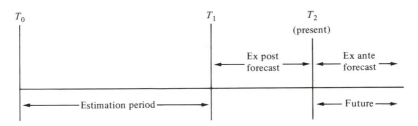

Figure 18.1   Types of Forecasts.

statements, and indeed it is not, but making *ex post* forecasts is nevertheless an important exercise. Checking the forecasted values of the dependent variable with the known values of the dependent variable provides an assessment of the forecasting reliability of the estimated equation. If there exist sufficient time-series data points for estimating the equation, it is good practice to "save" a few observations to be used for checking the equation via *ex post* forecasting. If this check uncovers no obvious deficiencies, the equation may be reestimated using the additional data in the $(T_1 - T_2)$ interval. If deficiencies are uncovered, it is back to a reassessment of the model estimated for forecasting.

Finally, *ex ante* forecasting involves making statements about the period following the time ("present") the forecast is made. This leads to a second important distinction. If, at the time of forecasting, the values of the independent variables are known with certainty, an *unconditional* forecast can be made. If, on the other hand, the values of the independent variables are not known with certainty, a *conditional* forecast is made, a forecast conditional on the assumed values of the independent variables. Note that *ex post* forecasts are unconditional forecasts; *ex ante* forecasts may be either, depending on the structure of the forecasting equation.

With these distinctions out of the way, forecasting under various situations, with particular emphasis on the forecasting error, will be discussed.

Forecast Error Under Alternative Assumptions

The magnitude of the forecast error depends on what is known at the time the forecast is made. In particular, the magnitude of the forecast error depends on whether the regression coefficients are known or must be estimated (as they must be in applied forecasting) and on whether the value of the forecasting variable, X_{T+1}, is known with certainty or is measured with error. To keep the exposition simple, yet demonstrate the danger of ignoring the correct formula for computing the forecast error, the problem is investigated using a simple regression equation.

β_i *Known*, X_{T+1} *Known*

This case is not relevant to applied forecasting because the population regression coefficients are never known. Nevertheless, it is a good beginning point, as it provides a reference point for seeing what happens to the forecast error when using OLS coefficients.

The population regression equation is

$$Y_t = \beta_0 + \beta_1 X_t + U_t, \qquad t = 1, \ldots, T \qquad (18.3)$$

Since this holds for all t, it is possible to write

$$Y_{T+1} = \beta_0 + \beta_1 X_{T+1} + U_{T+1} \qquad (18.4)$$

Suppose that a forecast of Y_{T+1} is made at time T with X_{T+1} known with certainty.

In this case the forecasted value of Y_{T+1} is

$$\hat{Y}_{T+1} = \beta_0 + \beta_1 X_{T+1} \qquad (18.5)$$

The forecast error is defined as the difference between actual Y in $T+1$ [equation (18.4)] and the value for T_{T+1} forecasted at time T, equation (18.5). This can be written as

$$Y_{T+1} - \hat{Y}_{T+1} = (\beta_0 + \beta_1 X_{T+1} + U_{T+1}) - (\beta_0 + \beta_1 X_{T+1}) = U_{T+1} \qquad (18.6)$$

Finally, squaring (18.6) and taking the expected value yields the variance of the forecast error:

$$\sigma_f^2 = E(Y_{T+1} - \hat{Y}_{Y+1})^2 = E(U_{T+1}^2) = \sigma^2 \qquad (18.7)$$

It is important to notice that for this case, where the regression coefficients are assumed known, the variance of the forecast, σ_f^2, is equal to the variance of the population disturbance term, σ^2. In other words, as long as there is a stochastic element in the system, represented by U_t, the variance of the forecast error will be positive. The square root of σ^2 is the standard deviation of Y about the regression equation developed in Chapter 3. In the context of forecasting, this is called the *standard error of the forecast* and is written as σ_f. The relationship between σ_f and the regression equation is shown in Figure 18.2, where $\hat{Y}_{T+1}$ is the forecasted value of Y. The interval $(\hat{Y}_{T+1} - 2\sigma_f)$ to $(\hat{Y}_{T+1} + 2\sigma_f)$ is the .95 confidence interval around the forecast $\hat{Y}_{T+1}$ and is interpreted as any confidence interval.

β_i *Estimated,* X_{T+1} *Known*

Because population regression coefficients are not known, forecasts must be based on the OLS coefficient estimates. The OLS estimate of the population regression equation (18.3) is

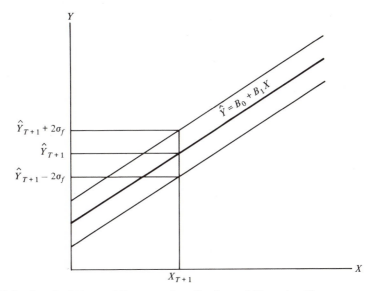

Figure 18.2 Standard Error of Forecast when β_0, β_1, and X_{T+1} Are Known.

$$Y_t = b_0 + b_1 X_t + e_t \tag{18.8}$$

Assuming, as above, that X_{T+1} is known with certainty at T, when the forecast is made, the forecast of Y for $T + 1$ using the estimated equation is

$$\hat{Y}_{T+1} = b_0 + b_1 X_{T+1} \tag{18.9}$$

The forecast error, the actual value of Y_{T+1} minus the forecasted value $\hat{Y}_{T+1}$, is

$$Y_{T+1} - \hat{Y}_{T+1} = (\beta_0 + \beta_1 X_{T+1} + U_{T+1}) - (b_0 + b_1 X_{T+1}) \tag{18.10}$$
$$= (\beta_0 - b_0) + (\beta_1 - b_1)X_{T+1} + U_{T+1}$$

Notice that the expected value of the forecast error is zero since the expected value of each term on the right-hand side of (18.10) is zero. Hence the OLS equation yields unbiased forecasts. The variance of this forecast error is

$$\sigma_f^2 = E(Y_{T+1} - \hat{Y}_{T+1})^2 = E[(\beta_0 - b_0) + (\beta_1 - b_1)X_{T+1} + U_{T+1}]^2 \tag{18.11}$$
$$= V(b_0) + V(b_1)X_{T+1}^2 + 2\,\text{Cov}\,(b_0, b_1)X_{T+1} + \sigma^2$$

which after tedious but straightforward manipulations can be written as

$$\sigma_f^2 = E(Y_{T+1} - \hat{Y}_{T+1})^2 = \sigma^2 \left[1 + \frac{1}{T} + \frac{(X_{T+1} - \bar{X})^2}{\sum_{t=1}^{T} (X_t - \bar{X})^2} \right] \tag{18.12}$$

Equation (18.9) shows that the forecast is a linear function of the sample points. The expected value of (18.10) shows that the forecast is unbiased; "on average," the forecast error is zero. Finally, (18.12) is the variance of the forecast error. By a theorem, which is not proved here, this is a minimum variance forecast. Consequently, in the context of the classical regression model (18.3), the ordinary least squares forecast is a linear (18.9), unbiased (18.10), minimum-variance (18.12) forecast.

An estimate S_f^2 of σ_f^2 is obtained by substituting S^2 for σ^2 in (18.11) or (18.12). It is called the *standard error of forecast*. The equation comparable to (18.11) for the standard error of forecast in the multiple regression case for three independent variables is

$$S_f^2 = V(b_0) + V(b_1)X_{1,T+1}^2 + V(b_2)X_{2,T+1}^2 + V(b_3)X_{3,T+1}^2$$

$$+ 2\text{Cov}\,(b_1 b_2)X_{1,T+1}X_{2,T+2} + 2\text{Cov}\,(b_1 b_3)X_{1,T+1}X_{3,T+1} \tag{18.13}$$

$$+ 2\text{Cov}\,(b_2 b_3)X_{2,T+1}X_{3,T+1} + S^2$$

The relationship between the estimated regression equation and the standard deviation of the forecast error, σ_f, is shown graphically in Figure 18.3.

Several comments are in order. Note first that (18.12) is the variance of the preceding section multiplied by an expression that is positive. Thus the variance of the forecast error reflects not only the stochastic element in the system, σ^2, but also variance arising as a consequence of having to use estimated coefficients. CAUTION: *Do not* use the standard deviation of the regression equation, a statistic normally printed as part of the standard regression output, as a measure of the standard deviation of the forecast error. It will understate the true standard deviation because the term on the right-hand side of (18.12) is not included in the computation. The forecast will be less precise than the standard error of the regression indicates.

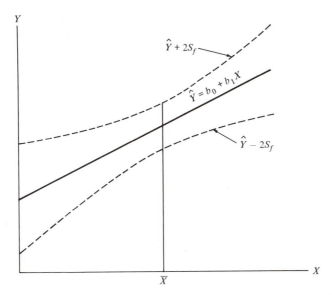

Figure 18.3 Forecast Interval when β_0, β_1 Are Unknown and Estimated by OLS.

The $\overline{X}$ term in the numerator of (18.12) is the mean of X computed over the data set used to estimate the regression equation, and X_{T+1} is the value of X used to forecast Y. Thus the greater the difference between the value of the forecasting variable and the mean of that variable in the sample, the greater the variance of the forecast error. The farther X_{T+1} is from $\overline{X}$, the fewer the sample observations on how Y responds to changes in X. The cost of this limited amount of information in the relevant range is a larger forecast error. This is frequently a problem with time-series data where the independent variables often exhibit pronounced time trends.

Finally, equation (18.12) shows that, all else constant, the larger the sample, the smaller the variance of the forecasting error. Although one should not passively subscribe to the often-made statement that the greater the number of observations the better (what if the structure of the population regression function is changing over time?), it is clear on both intuitive and statistical grounds that large samples are desirable when forecasting is the research objective.

β_i *Estimated,* X_{T+1} *Not Known with Certainty*

This case is the one applied forecasters must live with: Regression coefficients are estimated and the exact values of the forecasting variables are seldom, if ever, known with certainty. The steps involved in deriving the implications of "error" in the value of the forecasting variable are tedious, and they are not reproduced here.

Assume that the forecasting value of X_{T+1}, X_{T+1}^*, is not known with certainty, and assume further that it is related to its true value by

$$X_{T+1}^* = X_{T+1} + V_{T+1} \qquad \text{where } V \sim N(0, \sigma_v^2) \qquad (18.14)$$

which states that the unknown value deviates from its true value by a random term with zero mean and nonzero variance. Applying here the same type of analysis as in the preceding section yields the following equation for the variance of the forecast error:

$$\sigma_f^2 = \sigma^2\left[1 + \frac{1}{T} + \frac{(X_{T+1}^* - \overline{X})^2}{\Sigma_{t=1}^T (X_t - \overline{X})^2} + \frac{\overline{X}_{T+1}\sigma_v^2}{\Sigma_{t=1}^T (X_t - \overline{X})^2}\right] + \beta_1^2\sigma_v^2 \quad (18.15)$$

Careful examination of this equation reveals that it contains, in addition to all the terms of (18.12), the variance of the error in X_{T+1}^*, σ_v^2. Because the new terms in (18.15) are all positive, the variance of the forecast error has increased. An additional cost is incurred in terms of higher variance for the lack of information about the true value of X_{T+1}.

This real-world situation is even worse than it seems. In the previous case, where the value of the forecasting variable was known, the variance, and hence the standard deviation of the forecast error, can be computed from equation (18.13) by replacing the population variance with its estimate from the sample. In other words, with X_{T+1} known, the sample provides sufficient information to compute the needed standard deviation. This is not so in the present case because the sample provides no information about the variance of X_{T+1}^*. To make matters even worse, the value of β_1 in (18.15) is unknown.

Since σ_v^2 and β_1 are not known, about all that can be done is base the variance of the forecast error on (18.11) or (18.12), which at least takes into account the sample size and the distance of the value of the forecasting variable from the center of the data. It is important to remember, however, that (18.11), (18.12), and (18.15) understate the true value of the standard error of the forecast when X_{T+1} is not known with certainty.

Autoregressive Structure and Forecasting

Since the derivations above are cast in terms of time-series data, it is instructive to look at autocorrelation in the context of forecasting. Autoregression and its implication for estimating parameters are covered in Chapter 14. In the context of forecasting, however, the question becomes: If the disturbance scheme follows an autoregressive structure, can the forecasting ability of an estimated equation be improved by taking advantage of the autoregressiveness? Let the properly specified system be

$$Y_t = \beta_0 + \beta_1 X_t + U_t \quad (18.16)$$

with a first-order autoregressive structure given by

$$U_t = \rho U_{t-1} + V_t, \quad \text{where } V_t \sim N(0, \sigma_v^2), \quad |\rho| < 1 \quad (18.17)$$

where ρ is the autoregressive coefficient. To isolate the implication of this model for forecasting, assume that all the coefficients are known. In this case, the value of Y is

$$Y_{T+1} = \beta_0 + \beta_1 X_{T+1} + U_{T+1} \qquad (18.18)$$

By the autoregressive specification, the forecasted value for U_{T+1} made at T can be written as

$$\hat{U}_{T+1} = \rho U_T \qquad (18.19)$$

This yields as the forecast

$$\hat{Y}_{T+1} = \beta_0 + \beta_1 X_{T+1} + \rho U_T \qquad (18.20)$$

where

$$E(\rho U_T) = \rho E(U_T) = 0 \qquad (18.21)$$

implies an unbiased forecast, since by assumption above, ρ is a constant. The forecast error is given by

$$Y_{T+1} - \hat{Y}_{T+1} = (\beta_0 + \beta_1 X_{T+1} + U_{T+1}) - (\beta_0 + \beta_1 X_{T+1} + \rho U_T)$$

$$= U_{T+1} - \rho U_T \qquad (18.22)$$

$$= V_{T+1}$$

with variance

$$E(Y_{T+1} - \hat{Y}_{T+1})^2 = E(U_{T+1} - \rho U_T)^2 \qquad (18.23)$$

which yields, after considerable but straightforward manipulation,

$$E(Y_{T+1} - \hat{Y}_{T+1})^2 = (1 - \rho^2)\sigma^2 \qquad (18.24)$$

This is an important result: If the disturbance term follows a first-order autoregressive scheme, a smaller standard deviation of the forecast is obtained if the forecasting equation explicitly recognizes the autoregression. This result is really no surprise. Since more information about the structure of the system is used, more precise forecasts should be forthcoming. As a general rule, the applied forecaster should take advantage of autoregressiveness if it exists in the sample.

Summary

Forecasting is a way of life in many sectors of the economy, especially in agriculture, where substantial economic and policy decisions are based on forecasts of production, prices, exports, and the like. Because many dollars are often involved, accurate forecasts are crucial. Yet the analysis in this chapter shows that the variance of forecasts is quite sensitive to what is known at the time the forecast is made and the distance of the forecast from the data centroid. Consequently, the careful forecaster must pay considerable attention to computing the correct forecast error; unfortunately, we fear that many do not.

Terms

Conditional forecast	Forecast interval
Ex ante forecasting	Prediction
Ex post forecasting	Standard error of forecast
Forecast	Unconditonal forecast
Forecast error	

Exercises

18.1 Given a set of OLS regression results,

$$Y_t = 16 + 3X_t + e_i$$

what would $\hat{Y}$ be for
(a) $X_t = 2$?
(b) $X_t = 3$?
(c) $X_t = 20$?
(d) $X_t = 0$?

18.2 The following OLS regression results were based on a sample of 25 observations:

$$Y_t = 58 - 4X_t + e_t \qquad R^2 = .81$$

$$\overline{X} = 10$$

(a) What is the Pearson correlation coefficient between Y_t and X_t?
(b) What would be the predicted value for Y_t at $X_t = 12$?
(c) Would you have more confidence in a forecast based on $X_t = 10$ or $X_t = 20$? Why?

18.3 Consider the following forecasting equation with standard errors in parentheses.

$$Y_t = 24 + .63X_t + e_t \qquad R^2 = .64$$
$$\quad\;\; (4.2)\;(.14)$$

$$N = 20 \qquad\qquad S^2 = 6$$

$$\overline{X} = 42 \qquad\qquad \Sigma\, x^2 = 3.76$$

$$\overline{Y} = 50.46$$

(a) If you knew for certain that $X_{T+1} = 40$, what point forecast would you make for Y_{T+1}?
(b) What is the 95 percent confidence interval for Y_T?
(c) Would the 95 percent confidence interval about the point forecast be *smaller* if $X_{T+1} = 43$ or if $X_{T+1} = 35$? Why?

18.4 Suppose that we wanted to forecast state income tax revenues (R_{T+1}) in time period $T + 1$ as a function of aggregate personal income in the state (I_{T+1}). OLS regression analysis yields the following forecasting equation:

$$\hat{R}_t = 2{,}000{,}000 + .12I_t$$

$$R^2 = .64$$

$$T = 20$$

$$\Sigma (I - \bar{I})^2 = \$1 \text{ billion} \qquad \bar{I} = \$410 \text{ million}$$

$$S = \$1.6 \text{ million}$$

The State Planning Department estimates the I_{T+1} will be \$420 million. (NOTE: In answering, watch units carefully.)
  (a) How much state income tax revenues would you forecast for $T + 1$ (the point forecast)?
  (b) What is the 99 percent confidence interval for the forecast?
  (c) Is your forecast in part (a) *ex ante* or *ex post*?
  (d) Is your forecast *conditonal* or *unconditional*? Why
  (e) Is your forecast unbiased? Will it be correct? Why?
  (f) If R_{T+1} turns out to be \$52 million, what is your forecast error?

18.5 Are the following statements true or false? If false, why?
  (a) Both forecasting and predicting involve making statements in advance of an event.
  (b) *Ex post* forecasting is unnecessary.
  (c) All *ex post* forecasts are unconditional forecasts.
  (d) All *ex ante* forecasts are unconditional forecasts.
  (e) Forecasts errors tend to increase as we use estimated values for the regression coefficients and for independent variables.
  (f) One can use the standard deviation of the regression equation shown on the OLS printout as a good proxy for the standard deviation of your forecast error.
  (g) The farther the values of the forecasting variables are from the data centroid, the more reliable the forecast.
  (h) Based on the same data, conditional forecasts have greater variance of forecasting errors than unconditional forecasts.
  (i) Unconditional forecasts based on a lagged independent variable are better than conditional forecasts based on estimated independent variables.
  (j) If the disturbance term follows a first-order autoregressive scheme, a smaller standard deviation of the forecast is obtained if the forecasting equation explicitly recognizes the autoregression.

18.6 The following equation estimates Y as a function of three independent variables. The OLS equation with standard errors in parentheses is

$$Y = 1.508 + .60X_1 - .70X_2 - .94X_3 + e$$
$$(.271) \quad (.12) \qquad (.50) \qquad (.40)$$

$$N = 10 \qquad \overline{X}_1 = 1.6 \qquad \text{Cov } (b_1 b_2) = .0048$$

$$R^2 = .97 \qquad \overline{X}_2 = .4 \qquad \text{Cov } (b_1 b_3) = .0100$$

$$S^2 = .20 \qquad \overline{X}_3 = .3 \qquad \text{Cov } (b_2 b_3) = -.200$$

(a) What is the calculated value of Y in each of the following situations?

	X_1	X_2	X_3
(i)	2	0	0
(ii)	3	0	1
(iii)	1	1	1

(b) What is the 90 percent forecast interval when $X_1 = 2$, $X_2 = 1$, and $X_3 = 0$?

(c) In part (b), could the predicted value of Y be zero? Why or why not?

V

Miscellany

Books on applied research overlook what is perhaps the most difficult and most time-consuming element of applied research—writing up the results. In Chapter 19 we discuss writing research reports, emphasizing the need for writing and rewriting. A prototype timetable for conducting a research project and writing the final report during a semester is presented.

Finally, in Chapter 20 we cover the basic theorems of matrix algebra and present the general treatment of single-equation regression theory. This chapter can be used as a reference for those who would like to see the material in the earlier chapters presented in matrix algebra. It can also be used directly for those who want to learn regression theory using the powerful notational advantage of matrix algebra.

Preparing a Research Report

Applied econometrics involves using regression techniques to tackle research questions. Preparing a research paper is one of the best ways to practice the things preached in this book. The purpose of the chapter is to give beginning researchers a practical guide for preparing a research report in which the econometric tools presented in this book are used to address a research problem. This chapter may be read first, last, or anywhere in the middle of one's study of econometrics.

Anyone who can handle the econometric material in this book can at least read, write, and understand theory. There are no secret steps to improving your reading, your writing, or your understanding of theory. (If we actually had such secrets, we would write some other, better-selling book. Or, if we dared, we would just claim to possess these secrets to self-improvement, do some advertising, and start a brisk mail-order business.) What this chapter offers is a way of starting the creative act of combining economics, econometrics, data, writing, and common sense into a research paper that others can read and understand. The suggestions offered here are not perfect, but they work. Following these suggestions would enable beginning researchers to get started on a research project of their own and to finish it in a businesslike way.

What follows is a beginner's guide to preparing a research report. First the components of the applied research are briefly discussed. Less formally, in the first section we address the question: What does one need in order to write an empirical research paper? In the second section we mention some things researchers must consider when choosing a topic to research. In the third section we go through, step by step, one workable way to prepare a piece of empirical work. Finally, in the last section we outline what should be included in five increasingly complex drafts of a research paper, from a topic statement through to a complete, professional research paper. Together the four sections are designed to provide a good understanding of what goes into making a research paper.

The material in this chapter, however, can offer nothing more than a good start. Good research, like good piano playing or good photography, requires the magic act of creation. Technique is important in creating, but practice and talent (the dynamic duo a high school athletic coach might dub "perspiration and inspiration") also play big parts. People cannot be told how to do good research anymore than people can be told how to play the piano like Arthur Rubinstein or how to take pictures like Ansell Adams. This "artistic" side of research is the topic of a thought-provoking article by George W. Ladd that you must read (see Suggested Readings in the Appendix). This chapter has the more modest goal of describing one way to try to do good research. Whether the resulting research report is good or bad, interesting or boring, imaginative or mechanical, useful or arcane is up to the researcher.

Components of Applied Research

The first thing a researcher needs is an objective. This is the goal, the idea kept in the back of a researcher's mind throughout the whole research process. Many practicing economists try to cast the research goal or objective in the form of a research question. For example, what is the price elasticity of demand for pork in the United States? Why do some school districts spend more per pupil than other school districts? How will the quantity of milk consumed respond to an advertising campaign? These are just three of an endless number of possible research questions. In a later section we discuss what a researcher considers while developing research questions, but for now, assume that a research question has been concocted.

Once a research question has been asked, it should be kept firmly in mind. It is the guiding light to research. All too often students, and even experienced researchers, say that they are going to "look at" this problem or to "study" some broad topic. That is a fine way to express general interest, to get started on reading and thinking about a project, but it is a very poor way to begin doing empirical research. One must formulate a specific research question before developing a model, collecting data, and running regressions. Being anxious to start and to complete a research project is a common feeling among both experienced and beginning researchers. However, experienced researchers know they must have a specific notion of what they are trying to accomplish before they begin. Novices, on the other hand, tend to think a general idea is all one needs. They charge ahead, only to flounder helplessly and hopelessly the first time they face the unending questions in applied research: Cross-sectional or time-series data? What should the sample include? Should data be collected on this variable or that variable or both? What functional form should be used? And so on. When faced (as researchers inevitably are) with these and related questions, the best approach is to begin by asking: "What is my research question?"

But research questions are not written in stone. They, like the researcher asking them, evolve as the research proceeds. After all, people learn by doing. As the research project proceeds, the research question comes ever sharper into focus. Mucking around in a mire of data is an excellent way to sharpen a research question. Although from a distance it may seem a terrible waste of resources, it is usually best to start with a research question and then continually refine that question while wrestling with all the exigencies of applied research. Most beginning researchers start with an extremely broad research question (e.g., "What can be done about the energy crisis?") and end up, by natural evolution, answering a rather precise research question (e.g., "What was the retail price elasticity of demand for regular gasoline in Minnesota between 1972 and 1982?").

Once a researcher has a beginning research question in mind, a plan is needed. A plan is nothing more than a statement of how a researcher is going to go about doing what needs to be done. A plan is a road map to guide the researcher on the journey. Like any map, a plan can only keep one headed in the right direction. It cannot show every little hill, valley, and turn that are the inevitable parts of any journey. The plan in this chapter, for example, is to provide a general outline for doing empirical research in a later section called "Steps in a Research Process." For now, just note that you must have a specific step-by-step plan of action written out and by your side while doing research. Of course, plans, like research questions, evolve as more is learned about the problem at hand. Writing down and revising plans is a bit of a nuisance, but it is not nearly as annoying as spending several frustrating hours trying to do something (find some numbers, read a journal article, enter a large data set into the computer) only to finish and face an unanswerable question: *Why* did I waste all my time doing *that*? A written plan keeps a researcher on track.

With a research question to answer and a plan for answering it, attention should turn to the toolkit. First a researcher needs *theory* to indicate what variables to consider, what the direction of causality is, how the variables should be defined empirically, what an appropriate functional form for the estimating equation might be, and many other practical questions. Theory as a tool is stressed in Chapters 8 to 11. Remember here that many applied researchers are fond of saying "There is nothing as practical as a good theory." *Mathematics* is another tool that applied researchers use to manipulate equations, to express their models in symbolic form, and to understand related work by other researchers. *Statistics*, or econometrics narrowly defined, is the tool used to help quantify relationships, test hypotheses, explain behavior, make predictions about the future, and generally obtain quantitative answers to research questions.

Besides theory, mathematics, and statistics, researchers need an assortment of *materials*. Pencils, pens, paper, note cards, graph paper, a calculator, and, ultimately, a computer are necessary tools of the trade. So is the library, where one can find other people's writings on topics related to the research question. A quiet place to work, to think, and to record thoughts is also nice.

The final, and perhaps the most important tool, is personal knowledge. Everyone has a view of the world that is unique. Moreover, as Dr. Spock assured a generation of frightened parents, "you know more than you think you know." No matter what problem is chosen for study, everyone has accumulated a surprisingly powerful assortment of ideas about that problem from reading, going to class, watching television, traveling, and just bumping along through life. Use what you know. Of course, lots of your knowledge is rather vague and perhaps will not stand up under the critical scrutiny of empirical research. Use it anyway and refine it along the way. Finally, make sure that what you find and report makes sense to you: rigorous nonsense is still nonsense.

With an objective, a plan, and some tools, a researcher next needs some *data*. Data, or what researchers often refer to as "the numbers," are the clay to sculpt into an empirical view of the world. The mechanics of data collection and manipulation are discussed in Chapters 7 to 11. Remember here the platitude "get good numbers" and hope for good luck in your hunt.

Finally, a researcher needs to know how to actually use an objective, a plan, some tools, and some data to answer a research question. Such research technique is both easy and hard to acquire. Once all the pieces (the objective, plan, tools, and data) are laid out, assembling them to answer the research question is simple, almost mechanical. Yet figuring out a manageable objective, a practical plan, the appropriate tools, and where to find good numbers is technique too, and these are artistic, not mechanical, problems. Research technique comes naturally to few people. The rest of us get better with practice. To begin practicing, one needs a research question.

Refining the Research Question

Often research topics just appear. Your boss might tell you what to work on. Maybe there is a question you just know needs to be answered. Maybe there is some topic that you are simply curious about. After playing the empirical research game awhile, most people find that there are more interesting questions than there is time and energy to address. In all the cases above, choosing a research topic is not a major problem.

Often, though, especially for tyros, choosing a research topic is difficult. The problem is not lack of curiosity, but lack of a special kind of knowledge, the kind of knowledge, gained from theory and experience, about what kinds of questions are and are not researchable, about what can and cannot be done, especially with regard to econometrics. It is scary to commit yourself to work hard on something for a long time when you are not sure just what econometrics is all about. Even after formal training in regression, there still is that terrible moment when every beginning researcher is left alone with a nasty question: What am I going to do with all that fancy stuff I have learned? Although what follows does not include a list of possible topics to choose from, it does offer several ideas for developing original topics.

1. Accept that the research topic is your choice.   Committing yourself to a research topic is rather like going out on a first date: it is usually not forever (although it may seem like it if you choose badly) and what is interesting and attractive depends on personal preferences. It is best for beginners to start by dreaming up several interesting economic questions. Do this without worrying about whether the question can be answered with the research components you can assemble. Then take the list of possible research questions to an old hand and stir the ideas around a little: Are they roughly manageable? Are data likely to be available? How can the questions be sharpened? Old hands can reassure beginners that they are on the right track, but unfortunately, nobody can ever guarantee that a topic will pan out. Applied research is that way.

2. Choose an interesting question.   Only interest can sustain you through the misfortunes that are an unavoidable part of doing empirical research. Also, you will learn a lot about whatever topic you choose and you might as well learn a lot about a topic that interests you. If your boss keeps assigning research questions that are not

very interesting, it might be time to find a new boss or a new job. If you have a choice in selecting topics, choose those you really are interested in rather than those you think might impress others.

3. Some prior knowledge helps.   If you know a little about the structure of an industry, the nature of a crop, or the workings of a system, this is a big advantage. Again, you know more than you think. Other economic classes, jobs, economic situations of friends or family members, reading in the popular or the technical press, and hobbies combine to provide a great deal of basic economic knowledge.

Early in the process (perhaps even before talking with any experienced researchers), several basic questions need to be addressed. What commodity is of interest? Corn, cows, cars, teachers, taxes, trucking, or what? What characteristic of the commodity is of interest? Its price, quantity supplied, quantity demanded, amount spent on it, profits, level of export or import, profitability, number, or what? What geographical or jurisdictional area is of interest? What households, cities, counties, states, regions, countries, or universes do you want to consider? Are data available? When some of these basic questions are answered, it is time to mull over the prospects for good research alone, with fellow students, and with old hands at the empirical research game. When you feel only mildly apprehensive about the answers to these questions (holding out for perfect comfort means never starting!), it is time to plunge into the actual work.

A personal aside to show how a Tyro chose a research topic. Once upon a time one of the authors faced the prospect of writing an undergraduate thesis. He wanted to do some empirical work and he wanted it to be good. So he dreamed up all kinds of impressive-sounding topics, things like "The Economic Future of the Common Market" and "The Effect of Monopoly Power in the Automobile Industry." Tyro's problem was that he did not have any basic knowledge about these fancy topics and was not really interested in learning about them. Fall turned into winter and the spring of 1972 loomed. No thesis meant no degree in June. Trouble was brewing.

One day at lunch Buddy asked Tyro "What are you going to write your thesis on?" Not having a serious answer to offer, Tyro decided to make a joke. The first thing that came into his head was something from that morning's sports page, so he said in a mock-serious tone: "I'm going to determine what economics says Vida Blue should be paid." (For those who are not baseball fans or are too young to remember, Vida Blue was a rookie pitching sensation for Charley Finley's Oakland Athletics in 1971. Mr. Blue was threatening, as were the ways of players back in the days before free-agents, not to pitch in 1972 unless he got a big raise.) Buddy, a fellow economics major, did not laugh at the joke. In fact, he looked awfully envious. Tyro was green, but he knew enough to pretend he really was working on Vida Blue so that Buddy would not steal the idea.

Later, while thinking in the quiet of the library, Tyro realized that the idea made a lot of sense. It was an interesting research question. As a lifelong baseball fan, a former minor-league batboy, and an avid fastpitch softball player, Tyro even had a little basic information. Maybe he would study the value (the "characteristic") of Vida Blue (the "commodity") to baseball's Charlie Finley (the "market").

But how about data? Two basic principles from undergraduate economics courses seemed relevant: opportunity wage and the value of marginal product. A guess could be made about Vida Blue's opportunity wage by learning a little about the man, his background and education, and the job prospects for unemployed jocks. The value of Vida Blue's marginal product would be trickier. His marginal physical product, a prime component of value of marginal product, could be defined in terms of extra fans who went to the ballpark when he pitched. Attendance at each Oakland game in 1971 and whether Vida Blue pitched a particular game could be found in the old *New York Times* on microfilm in the bowels of the library. The amount of extra revenue each fan generated could be approximated by learning a little about ticket prices, concession proceeds, and sharing agreements among owners. Tyro decided he had indeed found an interesting topic that was researchable.

Then came the usual assortment of conceptual problems, data problems, mistakes and false starts, annoyingly restrictive assumptions, deadline pressures, and difficulties in getting things down sensibly on paper. The results were not particularly profound or useful, but the research question got answered as well as Tyro could answer it with the techniques he possessed. No longer quite so much a rookie, Tyro found he learned a lot and enjoyed doing it.

A short epilogue. One day, years later, when Tyro had become Bearded Professor, he was lecturing an econometrics class. Just as he was switching from talking about Best Linear Unbiased Estimators to discussing the difficult task of choosing a research topic, one of his favorite students fell fast asleep. Toward lecture's end, the sleepy but diligent student woke up, heard mention of Vida Blue, and asked: "What kind of an estimator is a Vida?"

Steps in the Research Process

Doing quantitative research means going from theory to numbers, from abstract to empirical propositions. There are two types of basic skills needed to do empirical work on a research problem. The first set of skills are practical, things like knowing how to manipulate data, run regressions, deal with computers, and present findings. Believe it or not, this is the relatively easy set of skills to develop. Anyone (well, anyone who has read this text at least) can get some numbers and crunch out regression equations by the score. The hard part is conceptualizing a problem in such a way that the leap from theory to empirical work is manageable. It can be done, however. Anyone who is game to try can apply theory to data and get results. In this section we discuss what to do to try to answer any research question, however tentative.

The first step involves *defining the problem*. The research question is, of course, an important first step. In econometric research, as in research generally, the ability to ask the right question is a highly prized attribute. The equally important second step is identifying what information is needed to answer the research question. Here is where a researcher needs a theory, whether it be original or cadged from others, that formalizes the important workings of the economic world being studied. What other people have written on similiar topics, often referred to as "the literature," is a valuable resource in developing such a model. It is not very likely that you are the first person to worry about any research question, and there is a great deal to be learned about any topic, as well as about applied research generally, by perusing the literature surrounding the topic. Empirical research is seldom totally original, so novices might as well stand on the shoulders of the professionals, be they giants or midgets, who have been there before.

To get started on a literature review, look in the *Journal of Economic Literature* and similar bibliographical publications for several recent articles on the topic. Some libraries have the capability of doing an electronic literature search for citations to relevant articles. However these initial citations are generated, find the articles and, if their content seems relevant, read them. Be sure to take note of the articles listed in the back. Read those articles as well. Be sure to record on notecards the citations (in proper bibliographic form) and the major findings of each work. Working backward from the most recent literature in this fashion is an efficient way to do a thorough literature search. The sure-fire indicator that one is finished with a literature review is when references stop citing any new articles.

Defining a problem is really not the lonely business described above. In fact, the best way to get started is to talk with someone who has done work in the area of interest. Some important and some recent references will no doubt come up in the conversation that will provide a start on your literature review. Such brainstorming sessions also are excellent ways to get a feel for what questions are interesting, manageable, and timely in the area of interest. If you cannot find the perfect source, talk with anyone who is willing to listen: they probably will either help or send you to someone who can.

The next step is to formulate a model. As noted, a model is just a formal statement of the relationship among the variables that are important. Models can be expressed in prose, pictures (charts, diagrams, or flowcharts), or equations. One should try to express models in all three media. Try words first because that is the easiest and least formal approach. Then try drawing some pictures. Pictures are more concise than words and have more visual impact. Finally, try to state your key insights in mathematical symbols and equations. Such symbols are the most concise, brief, dense, and useful form of expression for applied research. Out of this model formulation, some working hypotheses will emerge. What signs do you expect each of the coefficients to take? What functional form might be appropriate? These hypotheses can be abandoned later as the evidence warrants.

The next step is to obtain some data. The mechanics of data collection are discussed in Chapters 7 and 8. Remember here to record sources carefully, copy numbers accurately, verify that the numbers have been entered into the computer accurately, and let the computer do any transformations that need to be made. A word of warning is in order: It is often difficult to find relevant data for specific problems. This is especially true when studying countries that do not have sophisticated data collection systems. Even if the good old data-loving United States is the area of interest, beginning researchers are often disappointed to discover that there have not been little elves collecting data for the last 30 years on a variable that is important to today's research question. Imagination, patience, and a willingness to root around are the hallmarks of a good researcher.

While considering warnings, consider one more: Do not have complete faith in the validity of some numbers just because they are written in a book under an appropriate sounding column heading. Be suspicious. Ask questions. Exactly what do these numbers mean? How were they collected? How reliable are they? Researchers often have to accept and use whatever numbers they can get their hands on, but good researchers do not have to assume that these numbers represent perfect truth.

Finally, you come to what is (or will be) the easiest step for anyone who has read and understood this text: using econometrics to quantify your results. The previous chapters deal with the theory and practice of econometrics, so we will offer only one parting shot here: Do the best you can and do not worry about it. No piece of empirical research is perfect. As long as you fully understand what is strong and what is weak in the work—and do not try to fool anybody about which is which—you have nothing to worry about. Of course, while doing research, you want to do everything possible to improve the empirical results.

After generating some empirical results, the next step is to evaluate what you have wrought. What do the results mean? Do they agree with the working hypotheses? If not, is the model wrong, are the data suspicious, or is the world different from the theory? How can the research be improved? Armed with answers to these questions, you can go back and work some more on the research question, the data, and the empirical findings. This iterative process goes on until you run out of time, ideas, data, technique, or energy.

If doing empirical research were a neat, clean business, the next sentence in this chapter might read something like "When a researcher runs out of the iterations described above, the empirical research is done and all one needs to do is write up the results." Unfortunately, applied research is not like that. Writing-up results is an important part of the iterative learning process called research. More directly, you learn a lot by writing about research findings, as Ladd points out so ably in his paper. Good research reports are rewritten research reports. One approach to writing research reports is described in the next section.

Writing the Paper

Beginning courses in econometrics often require students to prepare a research paper based on their econometric work. Other people get their first chance to use econometrics for a paper for another class, a thesis or dissertation, a report that must be done at work, or some other professional assignment. Whatever the situation, doing something for the first time is often difficult. What follows is one possible schedule for organizing the work involved in a first paper using econometrics.

The particular schedule presented below may not be directly applicable to every situation, but it can be modified to meet special circumstances. The main message here is that good writing is rewriting, so you must plan to allow time for this often-ignored aspect of research. Some sort of deadline helps make time for writing and rewriting. Meeting the deadlines discussed below is one way an econometric novice may be transformed into an author of a 20-page paper that looks, and maybe even reads, like a professional journal article.

The three keys to the following system are writing under deadlines, doing things incrementally, and rewriting. These are hardly breathtaking breakthroughs in writing, but sometimes it is helpful to strengthen your grip on the obvious. One accepts deadlines because the work needs to be spread out over time in order to get done properly. Cramming may work for exams on occasion, but it never works for doing empirical research. There are too many unavoidable snags in conceiving a problem, finding data, making the computer work, and trying to unearth the root of surprising results. Besides, most people write only under the pressure of deadlines.

So suppose that you wanted (or needed) to have a research report completed 15 weeks from today. One possible schedule, the one the authors impose on their students, follows.

By the end of week 2, you should prepare a *topic report* containing a brief statement of (1) the general topic, (2) a beginning research question, (3) a list of possible relevant economic variables, and (4) whatever you know about possible data sources. You should spend your time the first few weeks thinking about what interests you, talking with other people who know something useful, and reading research papers to get a feel for what the final paper should look like.

A month later, by the end of week 6, you should prepare a *preliminary report*. This report should summarize the work up to, but not including, the first regressions. Its first paragraph should contain an up-to-date statement of the research area and a revised version of the research question. Next it should present a list of conceptual variables that seem relevant to the problem. The data used should be described and carefully documented. Then the report should discuss each of the specific variables that will be tried and should argue why each specific variable might be a good proxy for the conceptual variable identified in the previous section of the report. Finally, the preliminary report should contain a formal annotated bibliography of several (at least five) articles on the topic area. Pertinent articles that do not include regression analysis may still be helpful for other aspects of the research, such as identifying conceptual and empirical variables, interpreting regression results, and the like. Each entry in the bibliography should specifically note (1) the author's research question, (2) how regression was used to answer the research question, (3) relevant findings for your research, and (4) citations in proper bibliographic form.

By the end of week 10, after about a month's more work, an interim report should be prepared. This report, unlike the previous two, would be an early draft of the final paper, summarizing your empirical work and putting it into context. The following outline may help.

Outline for Preliminary Report
Title

I. Introduction
  A. Research Area and Research Question
  B. Literature Review
    1. Other relevant work
    2. Finding of other researchers
  C. Theory (verbal, graphical, mathematical)

    D. Variables Included
      1. Why selected
      2. Sources of data
    E. Other Possible Variables
      1. Why possible
      2. Why not included
    F. Working Hypotheses
  II. Preliminary Analysis
    A. Results of Early Regressions
    B. Interpret Findings
    C. Evalute Results
  III. Summary and Implication
    A. What You Learned About Research Question
    B. Plans for Future Reading, Data Collection, and Regressions

Three weeks later, by the end of week 13, you should write a *first draft* of your complete research paper, which will draw heavily from your preliminary report. No doubt you will not have completed your empirical work, but you still should stop and write a complete report. Preparing a complete first draft of the final paper (described below) enables you to see just what needs to be done during the final two weeks, it forces you to begin putting your work into a broader framework, and it allows you to solicit critical comments and suggestions from others. This is the hardest step toward finishing your research paper, but it is also the most important. Make the time to write a good first draft, to think about what you write, and to take advantage of whatever suggestions others might make. Avoid, however, embarking on new campaigns involving different topics or new data. When you get this far, it is time to put the best face possible on whatever you have done.

Sooner than seems possible, the 15-week final deadline will be upon you and it will be time to write the final report. This report can be organized in many different ways. One rather standard outline is offered below, but you should develop and use an outline that best fits your material and your style.

Outline for Final Paper
Title

  I. Introduction
    A. Identify Problem and Research Question
    B. Background of System Being Studied, Including Literature Review
    C. Graphical Overview (e.g., time series of dependent variable, frequency distribution for cross-sectional variable)
    D. Brief Outline of What Is Coming
  II. Model
    A. Conceptual Variables
    B. Relationship Among Variables
    C. Transformations and Other Adjustments of Variables
    D. Working Hypotheses/Expected Signs
    E. Functional Form for Equations

On Writing Reports

By the time you sit down to write a final report, you have done a great deal of good work. You know something that others want and need to know. Now it is time to write up your results. Do not blow it! If you do a lousy job writing the final report, others will not want or even be able to read about what you have done. Good research in reports nobody is able to read is useless research. Writing well is at least as (debatably more) important as regression technique in doing applied research.

We really do not have anything new to say about writing style or technique, but we do urge you to write as well as you can and strive always to write better. Books on good writing are helpful. Our personal favorites, in order, are Strunk and White's *Elements of Style*, Zinsser's *On Writing Well*, and Baker's *The Practical Stylist*. A style manual is also useful to make sure that the format of your paper is proper: Turabian's *A Manual for Writers of Term Papers, Theses, and Dissertations* does this tedious job nicely and cheaply.

There are two practical suggestions, specific to empirical research papers, that might be useful.

First, remember that econometrics is only a tool that is useful in answering research questions and should *not* be the focus of written reports. People reading research reports are going to assume that the researcher knows how to do regression analysis until shown differently. Do not try to show how much you know about econometrics. Instead, just answer the research question as well as possible, using regression fanfare only when its useful. Just write the story as well as possible.

Second, write about only the best regression results. Funnel all your results into three, four, or maybe five equations, each with different strengths and weaknesses. Present these equations in a summary table similar to Table 19.1.

Finally, remember your audience when you present empirical findings. A release for possible newspaper use, for example, would contain only a verbal interpretation on your findings, while a paper to be submitted to an economics journal would be far more technical.

Table 19.1. Typical Format for Presenting Regression Results

Equation	N	S	R^2	b_0	b_1	b_2	b_3	b_4	b_5
1	52	4.45	.86	95.38	-21.27* (1.89)	1.37 (1.77)	-3.85 (1.57)	-28.38* (.65)	—
2	52	3.86	.89	-237.50	-20.80* (1.68)	-5.08* (1.81)	-3.17 (2.21)	-4.78 (8.50)	.0018* (.0004)
3	52	4.13	.89	113.01	-4.67 (.38)	-.63 (.38)	-.80 (.50)	4.84 (.48)	—

Regression Theory and Matrix Algebra

This chapter is organized into three major parts. The first develops the subset of matrix algebra needed to handle regression theory at the level of this book. To keep the presentation as simple as possible, yet as complete as necessary, various properties of matrices are used without demonstrating their validity. More advanced students should be able to derive these properties. Part B gives the general treatment of the classical regression model. The material in Chapters 3 to 6 is covered here. Part C covers specification errors and includes omitted relevant variables and included irrelevant variables, the subjects of Chapter 13. We also introduce generalized least squares as a framework for treating the heteroscedasticity and autocorrelation problems covered in Chapter 14.

PART A

Matrix Algebra

In this part the basic matrices and vectors needed for regression theory are defined, the basic matrix manipulations of addition and multiplication are illustrated, and a selected number of basic properties of matrices are presented. Additional properties are introduced as needed in later sections.

The worksheet was introduced in Chapter 7 as a device for recording the values of variables used to estimate a regression equation. The columns of the worksheet identified the variables and the rows contained the n sample values ("observations") for each variable. In other words, the data were recorded in a two-dimensional (rectangular) array, where the vertical dimension (columns) referred to the variables and the horizontal dimension (rows) referred to the sample values of the variables. Now a formal definition: A *matrix* is a rectangular array of numbers.

The General Structure of Matrices

The general matrix is written as follows:

$$\begin{bmatrix} x_{11} & x_{12} & \cdots & x_{1K} \\ x_{21} & x_{22} & \cdots & x_{2K} \\ \vdots & \vdots & & \vdots \\ x_{n1} & x_{n2} & \cdots & x_{nK} \end{bmatrix}$$

In the context of a worksheet for regression analysis, this is the portion of the worksheet that records the n sample values for each of the K independent variables. Each element in the worksheet, x_{ik}, has a "double subscript," which permits identification of any particular number in the worksheet. The first subscript, i, refers to the ith row in the matrix (the ith observation in the worksheet), where, because there are n sample observations, the subscript i takes on the values 1, 2, . . ., n. The second subscript, k, refers to the kth column in the matrix (the kth indpendent variable in the worksheet). Because there are K independent variables, the subscript k takes on the values 1, 2, . . ., K. For example, x_{11} is the first observation on the first independent variable in the worksheet. In general, x_{ik} is the ith sample value for the kth independent variable. These ranges on the subscripts, $i = 1, . . , n$ and $k = 1, . . ., K$, define the *dimensions* of the matrix. The matrix above is an $n \times K$ matrix, a matrix with n rows and K columns. The dimensions of a matrix are very important in matrix algebra.

In summary, a matrix is a rectangular array of numbers with n rows and K columns, like the independent variable portion of the worksheet in Chapter 7. In the following paragraphs we discuss a number of special matrices that are useful in later sections.

A *scalar matrix* is a 1×1 matrix. It is a single number and is treated as such in matrix algebra.

A *column vector* is the special $n \times 1$ matrix. An example is the column of the n values of the independent variable X_1:

$$\begin{bmatrix} x_{11} \\ x_{21} \\ \cdot \\ \cdot \\ \cdot \\ x_{n1} \end{bmatrix}$$

A *row vector* is the special $1 \times K$ matrix. An example is

$$[x_{21} \quad x_{22} \quad \cdots \quad x_{2K}]$$

the worksheet row containing the second observations on each of the independent variables.

The *null matrix* is a matrix of any dimension where all elements are 0's. The null matrix, often denoted Φ, functions in matrix algebra like a zero in scalar algebra.

A *square matrix* is a matrix of dimensions $n \times n$, a matrix with the same number of rows and columns. A square matrix plays a major role in matrix algebra, especially in its application to regression theory.

A *diagonal matrix* is a square matrix that has nonzero elements on the principal diagonal (the northwest-southeast line) and 0's elsewhere. An example is

$$\begin{bmatrix} 1 & 0 & 0 & \cdots & 0 \\ 0 & 6 & 0 & \cdots & 0 \\ & \cdot & \cdot & & \cdot \\ & \cdot & \cdot & & \cdot \\ 0 & 0 & 0 & \cdots & 4 \end{bmatrix}$$

A special case of a diagonal matrix is the *identity* matrix, with 1's on the principal diagonal and 0's elsewhere. This matrix is written I_n as a reminder that it is a square matrix of dimensions $n \times n$. Generally, the n is suppressed because the dimensions of I are usually clear from the context. The identity matrix plays a role in matrix algebra analogous to "1" in scalar algebra.

The *transpose matrix* is obtained by interchanging the rows and columns of the original matrix. Notationally, if X is an $n \times K$ matrix, its transpose, written as X' (read "X-prime") is a $K \times n$ matrix. An example is

$$X = \begin{bmatrix} x_{11} & x_{12} & x_{13} \\ x_{21} & x_{22} & x_{23} \end{bmatrix} \qquad X' = \begin{bmatrix} x_{11} & x_{21} \\ x_{12} & x_{22} \\ x_{13} & x_{23} \end{bmatrix}$$

where the rows of X become the columns of X'. The transpose of the transpose yields the original matrix. In general, the dimensions of X' will be different from the dimensions of X. The important exception being the special case of an $n \times n$ matrix, in which case its transpose will also be $n \times n$. Observe the conventional notations of using a capital letter to denote a matrix (e.g., X) and a lowercase letter, usually subscripted (e.g., x_{23}), to denote an element in a matrix. The exceptions to this notation are the use of b and e in OLS regression to denote matrices of coefficients and residuals.

A matrix is *symmetric* if the matrix is square and if the elements in the upper right-hand triangle above the principal diagonal are equal to the elements in the lower left-hand triangle below the principal diagonal, that is, if $X_{ik} = X_{hi}$. An example of a symmetric matrix is

$$\begin{bmatrix} x_{11} & x_{12} & x_{13} & x_{14} \\ x_{12} & x_{22} & x_{23} & x_{24} \\ x_{13} & x_{23} & x_{33} & x_{34} \\ x_{14} & x_{24} & x_{34} & x_{44} \end{bmatrix}$$

The special characteristic of a symmetric matrix is that the first row contains the same elements as the first column, the second row the same as the second column, the third row the same as the third column, and the fourth row is the same as the fourth column, and so on. This characteristic of a symmetric matrix means that it is equal to its transpose. Symmetric matrices are important in regression theory.

A matrix that is grouped into submatrices is called a *partitioned matrix*. The $n \times (p + q)$ matrix

$$
Z = \begin{bmatrix}
x_{11} & \cdots & x_{1p}w_{11} & \cdots & w_{1q} \\
\cdot & \cdots & \cdot & & \cdot \\
\cdot & & \cdot & & \cdot \\
\cdot & & \cdot & & \\
x_{n1} & \cdots & x_{np}w_{n1} & \cdots & w_{nq}
\end{bmatrix}
$$

can be be partitioned as

$$
Z = \left[\begin{array}{ccc|ccc}
x_{11} & \cdots & x_{1p} & w_{11} & \cdots & w_{1q} \\
\cdot & & \cdot & & & \cdot \\
\cdot & \cdot & \cdot & & \cdot & \\
\cdot & & \cdot & & & \\
x_{11} & \cdots & x_{np} & w_{n1} & \cdots & w_{nq}
\end{array}\right] = [x{:}w]
$$

where the submatrix X is $n \times p$ and the submatrix W is $n \times q$. The dimensions of X and W taken together must equal the dimensions of Z. In general, a $p \times q$ matrix can be written as

$$
Z = \begin{bmatrix}
A & B \\
C & D
\end{bmatrix}
$$

where the dimensions of the matrices A, B, C, D must be such that the $p \times q$ dimensions of Z are preserved. Partitioned matrices can be multiplied, with the submatrices treated like the matrix "elements" as long as the submatrices are of proper dimensions for matrix multiplication (see below).

Matrix Manipulations

There are four basic arithmetic operations: addition, subtraction, multiplication, and division. These can be compressed into the two fundamental operations of addition and multiplication. A number can be subtracted from another by "adding" the negative of the number. A number can be divided by another number by multiplying it by the reciprocal of that number. Similarly, matrices can be added and multiplied, where careful attention must be paid to the dimensions of the matrices.

Addition

Adding matrices requires that the matrices be of exactly the same dimensions, because matrix algebra addition involves adding corresponding elements. Let the matrices X and W be of dimensions 2×2. The matrix sum $X + W$ is given by

$$
\begin{bmatrix}
x_{11} & x_{12} \\
x_{21} & x_{22}
\end{bmatrix} + \begin{bmatrix}
w_{11} & w_{12} \\
w_{21} & w_{22}
\end{bmatrix} = \begin{bmatrix}
x_{11} + w_{11} & x_{12} + w_{12} \\
x_{21} + w_{21} & x_{22} + w_{22}
\end{bmatrix} = \begin{bmatrix}
z_{11} & z_{12} \\
z_{21} & z_{22}
\end{bmatrix}
$$

where $z_{11} = x_{11} + w_{11}$, $z_{12} = x_{12} + w_{12}$, and so on. Because corresponding elements are added to form the matrix sum, the dimensions of the resulting matrix, Z, are the same as the dimensions of the two matrices being added. There is no restriction on the number of matrices added as long as all matrices are of the same dimension.

Multiplication

In arithmetic, $2 \times 4 = 4 \times 2 = 8$, where the order of multiplication is of no consequence. However, when working with matrices, the order of multiplication is important. For example, the matrix product XW may exist but not the matrix product WX. This is demonstrated with several examples.

To multiply a *matrix* by a *scalar* is to multiply each element of the matrix by the scalar. Let a by a scalar and X be a 2×2 matrix and write

$$[a]\begin{bmatrix} x_{11} & x_{12} \\ x_{21} & x_{22} \end{bmatrix} = \begin{bmatrix} ax_{11} & ax_{12} \\ ax_{21} & ax_{22} \end{bmatrix}$$

In general, if a is a scalar and X is a matrix of any dimensions, the matrix product is aX, with the dimension of X.

Matrix multiplication distinguishes between premultiplication and postmultiplication. The matrix product XW consists of *premultiplying* W by X or *postmultiplying* X by W. Similarly, the matrix product WX consists of premultiplying X by W or postmultiplying W by X. It is important to understand that the matrix product XW may or may not exist and the matrix product WX may or may not exist. If X and W are square matrices, the products XW and WX exist but their respective elements will not necessarily be the same. The product XW may not exist if the dimensions of X and W are inconsistent. More on this below.

Matrix addition requires the matrices to have the same dimensions. For matrix multiplication, the basic condition is that the number of *columns* of the ''lead'' matrix is the same as the number of *rows* in the ''following'' matrix. For example, to obtain the matrix product XW, the number of columns in X must be the same as the number of rows in W. Similarly, to form the matrix product WX, the number of columns in W must be the same as the number of rows in X. It is important to notice that the dimensions of the matrices determine the order of matrix multiplication.

Matrix multiplication involves multiplying a row vector by a column vector. For example, the product obtained by premultipling a 2×3 matrix by a 2×2 matrix is

$$\begin{bmatrix} x_{11} & x_{12} \\ x_{21} & x_{22} \end{bmatrix}\begin{bmatrix} w_{11} & w_{12} & w_{13} \\ w_{21} & w_{22} & w_{23} \end{bmatrix}$$

$$= \begin{bmatrix} x_{11}w_{11} + x_{12}w_{21} & x_{11}w_{12} + x_{12}w_{22} & x_{11}w_{13} + x_{12}w_{23} \\ x_{21}w_{11} + x_{22}w_{21} & x_{21}w_{12} + x_{22}w_{22} & x_{21}w_{13} + x_{22}w_{23} \end{bmatrix}$$

$$= \begin{bmatrix} z_{11} & z_{12} & z_{13} \\ z_{21} & z_{22} & z_{23} \end{bmatrix}$$

where X is 2×2, W is 2×3, and Z is 2×3. Note that the matrix product WX does not exist because the W has three columns and X has two rows.

Let X be $n \times K$ and W be $n \times K$. The product XW cannot be formed, because X

has K columns and W has n rows and the condition stated for matrix multiplication is not satisfied. Similarly, we cannot form the matrix product WX because W has K columns and X has n rows. In this case, the matrices do not conform for multiplication.

Let X be $n \times K$ and W be $K \times p$. The product XW exists because X has K columns and W has K rows. However, the product WX does not exist because W has p columns and X has n rows. Note that an $n \times K$ matrix postmultiplied by a $K \times p$ matrix yields an $n \times p$ matrix.

Finally, let X be $n \times K$ and W be $K \times n$. Both matrix products XW and WX exist. The dimension of the matrix product will be different, however, depending on the order of multiplication: The product XW will be $n \times n$ and the product WX will be $K \times K$.

In general, premultiplying a $p \times q$ matrix by an $n \times p$ matrix (or postmultiplying an $n \times q$ matrix by a $p \times q$ matrix) results in an $n \times q$ matrix. The nqth element of the matrix product is the sum of products of x_{np} and x_{pq} summed over p.

These general rules of matrix addition and multiplication apply directly to the special cases of adding and multiplying vectors and to multiplying vectors or vectors and general matrices.

Inverse and Nonsingular Matrices

As stated above, dividing one number by another number is the same as multiplying the first number by the *reciprocal*, or *inverse*, of the second number. Similarly, a matrix is "divided" by multiplying it by the inverse of another matrix. But how is the matrix inverse obtained? To answer this question properly requires a lengthy detour to develop the important concept of a *determinant*. Alternatively, a simple example can illustrate what a determinant is and show how it is used in matrix division. The latter option is pursued here. Doing so requires that the reader accept the generality of the results obtained from the example, much the same as one might accept that $2 + 2 = 4$ without first developing a theory of numbers. It is sufficient here for the reader to know that the inverse of a matrix X is a matrix such that when multiplied by X yields the identity matrix, and that the existence of an inverse matrix depends on something called a determinant, an example of which is given below.

The reciprocal, or inverse, of the number 2 is $1/2$, so it follows that multiplying 2 by its inverse yields 1. Indeed, any number, n, multiplied by its inverse, $1/n$, yields 1. This inverse relationship is used in matrix algebra to "divide" matrices, but *its use is limited to a square matrix*. The inverse of a square matrix, X, is a matrix such that when multiplied by X yields the identity matrix. The inverse of X is written as X^{-1}. (Whether the inverse matrix exists, and it may not, is discussed below.) Note that "-1" is not an exponent in the true sense of the word, it is simply matrix notation for an inverse matrix.

Consider an example:

$$X = \begin{bmatrix} 2 & 5 \\ 3 & 1 \end{bmatrix}, \quad X^{-1} = \begin{bmatrix} a & b \\ c & d \end{bmatrix} \quad \text{where } XX^{-1} = X^{-1}X = I = \begin{bmatrix} 1 & 0 \\ 0 & 1 \end{bmatrix}$$

The problem is to find values for a, b, c, and d, the elements of the inverse matrix, such that $X^{-1}X = I$, the identity matrix. Applying the multiplication rules defined above, we obtain the following equations:

$$2a + 5c = 1$$

$$2b + 5d = 0$$

$$3a + 1c = 0$$

$$3b + 1d = 1$$

which after the appropriate substitutions yields the values

$$a = -\frac{1}{13}$$

$$b = \frac{5}{13}$$

$$c = \frac{3}{13}$$

$$d = -\frac{2}{13}$$

and by substitution into X^{-1} above we get

$$\begin{bmatrix} 2 & 5 \\ 3 & 1 \end{bmatrix} \begin{bmatrix} -\dfrac{1}{13} & \dfrac{5}{13} \\ \dfrac{3}{13} & -\dfrac{2}{13} \end{bmatrix} = \begin{bmatrix} 1 & 0 \\ 0 & 1 \end{bmatrix}$$

These manipulations illustrate the importance of the square matrix. In the example, there are four unknowns (a, b, c, and d) and four equations. This "fully specified" system can in principle be solved for the unknowns.

It is easy to see what is going on in this simple example. But if the X-matrix is very large, say 20×20, the solution to the 20 equations would be a very cumbersome, if not impossible, procedure for obtaining the elements of the inverse matrix. This is where determinants, a subject not developed here, enter to provide a powerful method for finding the inverse matrix. For practical reasons, inverses must be computed with the aid of a computer when the dimension of the matrix is, say, 4×4 or larger.

Notice in the specific example above that each element in the inverse matrix is divided by "-13." This *number* is called the determinant of the primary matrix and it plays a very important role in matrix inversion. Although how a determinant is computed is not important here, it is extremely important to know that the determinant of an X-matrix can be zero. The condition under which this can happen is a subject for more advanced texts, but the implication of a zero determinant is immediately apparent. The inverse of the X-matrix does not exist if its determinant is zero, because dividing by zero is an undefined arithmetic operation. If the determinant of a matrix is zero, the matrix is called *singular* and its inverse does not exist. If the determinant is not zero, the matrix is called *nonsingular* and its inverse exists. In summary, if X is nonsingular, its inverse exists and the matrix product $X^{-1}X$ equals I, the identity matrix.

The Quadratic Form

Terms such as $\sum_i e_i^2$, $\sum_i x_i^2$, and so on, are encountered many times in this book. These terms are often referred to as *quadratic terms* because they are obtained from expressions like

$$\sum_i (X_i + Y_i)^2 = \sum_i X_i^2 + 2 \sum_i X_i Y_i + \sum_i Y_i^2$$

which contain terms in X^2, XY, and Y^2. In matrix algebra, the *quadratic form of the matrix* is used to write such expressions.

In general, if X is an $n \times 1$ column vector and A an $n \times n$ symmetric, nonsingular matrix, the quadratic form is written as $X'AX$, which is a 1×1 matrix, or a scalar. An example. Let X be an $n \times 1$ column vector and let A be an $n \times n$ identity matrix I. The quadratic form is $X'IX$, written out as

$$X'IX = [x_1 \cdots x_n] \begin{bmatrix} 1 & 0 & \cdots & 0 \\ 0 & 1 & \cdots & 0 \\ \cdot & \cdot & & \cdot \\ \cdot & \cdot & & \cdot \\ \cdot & \cdot & & \cdot \\ 0 & 0 & \cdots & 1 \end{bmatrix} \begin{bmatrix} x_1 \\ \cdot \\ \cdot \\ \cdot \\ x_n \end{bmatrix} = [x_1^2 + \cdots + x_n^2] = \sum_{i=1}^{n} x_i^2$$

which is the sum of squared values of x.

Positive Definite Matrix

A symmetric, nonsingular matrix A is said to be *positive definite* if $X'AX > 0$ for all X. Applying this definition to the example above, I is seen to be positive definite because every element in $X'IX$ is positive. The matrix A is said to be *positive semi-definite* if $X'AX \geqq 0$ for all X. An important consequence of this property is the existence of a nonsingular matrix P such that $PP' = A$ if A is positive definite. This matrix property is elaborated upon when it is used below.

PART B

Regression Theory

The material is earlier chapters may now be redone using matrix algebra. The first task is to develop OLS regression, beginning with the population regression function and ending with hypothesis testing. This covers the material in Chapters 3 to 6.

The OLS Estimators

The population regression function is

$$Y = \beta_0 + \beta_1 X_1 + \cdots + \beta_k X_k + U \qquad (20.1)$$

which is written in matrix notation as

$$Y = X\beta + U \tag{20.2}$$

where $Y = n \times 1$ vector of observations on the dependent variable

$X = n \times (K + 1)$ matrix of observations on the independent variables, where the first column contains all 1's to allow for the intercept term, β_0

$\beta = (K + 1) \times 1$ vector of coefficients to be estimated, where the first element is β_0

$U = n \times 1$ vector of disturbance terms

The statistical specifications are

$$E\begin{bmatrix} U_1 \\ U_2 \\ \cdot \\ \cdot \\ \cdot \\ U_n \end{bmatrix} = \begin{bmatrix} E(U_1) \\ E(U_2) \\ \cdot \\ \cdot \\ \cdot \\ E(U_n) \end{bmatrix} = \begin{bmatrix} 0 \\ 0 \\ \cdot \\ \cdot \\ 0 \end{bmatrix} = [0], \quad \text{an } n \times 1 \text{ null vector} \tag{20.3}$$

$$E(UU') = E\begin{bmatrix} U_1 \\ U^2 \\ \cdot \\ \cdot \\ \cdot \\ U_n \end{bmatrix} [U_1 \quad U_2 \quad \cdots \quad U_n]$$

$$= E\begin{bmatrix} U_1^2 & U_1U_2 & \cdots & U_1U_n \\ U_2U_1 & U_2^2 & \cdots & U_2U_n \\ \cdot & \cdot & & \cdot \\ \cdot & \cdot & & \cdot \\ \cdot & \cdot & & \cdot \\ U_nU_1 & U_nU_2 & \cdots & U_n^2 \end{bmatrix} \tag{20.4}$$

$$= \begin{bmatrix} E(U_1^2) & E(U_1U_2) & \cdots & E(U_1U_n) \\ E(U_2U_1) & E(U_2^2) & \cdots & E(U_2U_n) \\ \cdot & \cdot & & \cdot \\ \cdot & \cdot & & \cdot \\ \cdot & \cdot & & \cdot \\ E(U_nU_1) & E(U_nU_2) & \cdots & E(U_n^2) \end{bmatrix}$$

By definition, the variance of U, a random variable, is $E[U - E(U)]^2$. By (20.3), $E(U) = 0$, so the variance of U can be written simply as $E(U^2)$. By definition, the covariance of U_iU_j is $E[(U_i - E(U_i))(U_j - E(U_j))]$, which by (20.3) may be written as $E[U_iU_j]$. Consequently, the variances of the conditional distributions discussed in Chapter 3 are along the principal diagonal of this matrix and the covariances across the conditional distributions are the off-diagonal elements. Under the assumptions used in Chapters 3 and 4, the variances of the conditional distributions are all equal to σ^2 and all the covariances are zero. Thus (20.4) can be written as

$$E(UU') = \begin{bmatrix} \sigma^2 & 0 & \cdots & 0 \\ 0 & \sigma^2 & \cdots & 0 \\ \cdot & \cdot & & \cdot \\ \cdot & \cdot & & \cdot \\ 0 & 0 & \cdots & \sigma^2 \end{bmatrix} = \sigma^2 I \qquad (20.5)$$

where I is the $n \times n$ identity matrix.

Given these assumptions, turn now to the estimator. The sample regression function is

$$Y = b_0 + b_1 X_1 + \cdots + b_K X_K + e \qquad (20.6)$$

which may be written in matrix notation as

$$Y = Xb + e \qquad (20.7)$$

where the matrices are of the same order as in (20.1), b is the $(K + 1) \times 1$ vector of OLS coefficients, including b_0, the intercept term, and e is the $n \times 1$ vector of OLS residuals. To derive the OLS estimators, rewrite (20.7) as

$$e = Y - Xb \qquad (20.8)$$

and form the sum of squared residuals, ESS, as

$$e'e = (Y - Xb)'(Y - Xb) \qquad (20.9)$$

Because e is an $n \times 1$ column vector, the vector product $e'e$ is a 1×1 matrix, or a *scalar*.

The term $(Y - Xb)'$ is the *transpose* of a sum, and the sum involves the *matrix product, Xb*.

Property 1

The transpose of a sum is the sum of the transposes. Hence $(Y - Xb)' = Y' - (Xb)'$.

Property 2

The transpose of a matrix product is equal to the transposed elements taken in reverse order. Hence $(Xb)' = b'X'$.

If we use these properties, (20.9) can be written as

$$e'e = (Y' - b'X')(Y - Xb) \qquad (20.10)$$

from which derive the OLS estimators. Applying the distributive law of multiplication, (20.10) becomes

$$e'e = Y'Y - Y'Xb - b'X'Y + b'X'Xb \qquad (20.11)$$

Since $e'e$ is a scalar, each of the four elements on the right-hand side of (20.11) is a scalar. This expression can be simplified by writing $Y'Xb$ as $b'X'Y$, which reduces (20.11) to

$$e'e = Y'Y - 2b'X'Y + b'X'Xb \qquad (20.12)$$

from which the desired b-vector is obtained by minimizing $e'e$, the sum of squared residuals. Note that $b'X'Y$ is a scalar, because the transpose of a scalar equals itself $b'X'Y' = Y'Xb$. Rather than digressing on matrix calculus, we assert the following result:

$$\frac{\partial e'e}{\partial b} = -2X'Y + 2X'Xb = 0 \tag{20.13}$$

[The suspicious reader might find it fun to try to reproduce these results by "writing out" (20.12) and applying a little differential calculus to see what is going on.]

Equation (20.13) yields

$$X'Xb = X'Y \tag{20.14}$$

These are the normal equations derived in Chapters 3 and 4. For simple regression, (20.14) is written out as

$$\begin{bmatrix} n & \Sigma\, X_i \\ \Sigma\, X_i & \Sigma\, X_i^2 \end{bmatrix} \begin{bmatrix} b_0 \\ b_1 \end{bmatrix} = \begin{bmatrix} \Sigma\, Y_i \\ \Sigma\, X_i Y_i \end{bmatrix}$$

or

$$b_0 n + b_1 \Sigma\, X_i = \Sigma\, Y_i$$
$$b_0 \Sigma X_i + b_1 \Sigma\, X_i^2 = \Sigma\, X_i Y_i$$

as the normal equations derived in Chapter 3.

In scalar algebra, the value for b in (20.14) would be obtained simply by dividing through by $X'X$. In matrix algebra b is obtained by premultiplying (20.14) by the inverse of $X'X$. By assumption, $X'X$ is nonsingular (its inverse exists), so premultiplying through by $(X'X)^{-1}$, a valid operation, yields

$$(X'X)^{-1}(X'X)b = (X'X)^{-1}(X'Y) \tag{20.15}$$

or

$$b = (X'X)^{-1}X'Y \tag{20.16}$$

since by definition $(X'X)^{-1}(X'X) = I$, the identity matrix.

Equation (20.14) is the matrix representation of the "normal equations" derived in Chapters 3 and 4, and equation (20.16) is the matrix representation of the solution of those equations, showing how to use the observed values of Y and the X-variables to compute the OLS coefficients. In Chapters 3 and 4 the b's were written in terms of cross-product terms in the X-variables, the $(X'X)^{-1}$ part of (20.16), and cross-product terms of the X-variables with Y the $X'Y$ part of (20.16). Equation (20.16) shows exactly the same thing, but in the more compact matrix notation.

Equation (20.16) shows that b is a linear function of the sample values of Y. Since the X-values are assumed to be fixed in repeated sampling, the b vector will change as the Y vector changes from sample to sample. To see that the b vector can be written as a linear function of the population disturbance values, which necessarily change as Y changes in repeated sampling, substitute (20.2) into (20.16) to obtain

$$b = (X'X)^{-1}X'(X\beta + U) \tag{20.17}$$

which, by applying the distributive law of multiplication and using the property of the inverse matrix, yields

$$b = \beta + (X'X)^{-1}X'U \qquad (20.18)$$

Because β is a population parameter and the X matrix is fixed in repeated sampling, this equation shows b changing linearly as U changes across samples.

The expected value of (20.18) is

$$E(b) = \beta + (X'X)^{-1}X'E(U) \qquad (20.19)$$

which, by (20.3), reduces to

$$E(b) = \beta \qquad (20.20)$$

The $(K + 1) \times 1$ OLS vector b is an unbiased estimator of the $(K + 1) \times 1$ vector of population regression coefficients.

In Chapter 3, the variance of the OLS slope, b_1, was written in scalar algebra as

$$\text{Var } (b_1) = E[b_1 - E(b_1)]^2 \qquad (20.21)$$

or   (20.22)

$$\text{Var } (b_1) = E(b_1 - \beta_1)^2$$

The analogous statement for the general regression model in matrix algebra is

$$\text{Var-cov } (b) = E[(b - \beta)(b - \beta)'] \qquad (20.23)$$

where b and β are the $(K + 1) \times 1$ vectors defined above and $(b - \beta)(b - \beta)'$ is a $(K + 1) \times (K + 1)$ matrix of terms in b and β. The expression (20.23) is called the variance-covariance matrix of b, the vector of OLS estimates. The basis for this designation can be seen by writing out (20.23) as follows:

$$E(b - \beta)(b - \beta)' = E \begin{bmatrix} b_0 - \beta_0 \\ b_1 - \beta_1 \\ \vdots \\ b_K - \beta_K \end{bmatrix} [(b_0 - \beta_0)(b_1 - \beta_1) \cdots (b_K - \beta_K)]$$

which has the product

$$\begin{bmatrix} E(b_0 - \beta_0)^2 & E(b_0 - \beta_0)(b_1 - \beta_1) & \cdots & E(b_0 - \beta_0)(b_K - \beta_K) \\ E(b_1 - \beta_1)(b_0 - \beta_0) & E(b_1 - \beta_1)^2 & \cdots & E(b_1 - \beta_1)(b_K - \beta_K) \\ \vdots & \vdots & & \vdots \\ E(b_K - \beta_K)(b_0 - \beta_0) & E(b_K - \beta_K)(b_1 - \beta_1) & \cdots & E(b_K - \beta_K)^2 \end{bmatrix}$$

The variances of the OLS coefficients are the diagonal elements and the covariances of the coefficients are the off-diagonal elements.

The formal derivation is as follows:

$$\text{Var-cov } (b) = E\{[(X'X)^{-1}X'U][(X'X)^{-1}X'U]'\} \qquad (20.24)$$

by (20.18). Using Property 2, it is possible to write

$$\text{Var-cov } (b) = E\{(X'X)^{-1}X'UU'X(X'X)^{-1}\} \qquad (20.25)$$

Because X is fixed in repeated sampling, the E-operator applies only to the UU' term,

$$\text{Var-cov } (b) = (X'X)^{-1}X'E(UU')X(X'X)^{-1} \qquad (20.26)$$

Substituting (20.4) yields

$$\text{Var-cov } (b) = (X'X)^{-1}X'\sigma^2IX(X'X)^{-1} \qquad (20.27)$$

Because σ^2 is a scalar and I is the identity matrix,

$$\text{Var-cov } (b) = \sigma^2[(X'X)^{-1}X'X(X'X)^{-1}] \qquad (20.28)$$

Finally,

$$\text{Var-cov } (b) = \sigma^2(X'X)^{-1} \qquad (20.29)$$

is the variance-covariance matrix of the OLS coefficients. In Chapters 3 and 4, variances of the OLS coefficients are expressed as the variance of the population disturbance term divided by the sum-of-squares terms in the X-variables. Equation (20.29) gives the general case for K independent variables.

The Gauss–Markov Theorem

In Chapters 3 and 4, the Gauss–Markov theorem was used to claim the linear, unbiased, minimum-variance properties for the OLS estimators. Here this theorem is proved.

Begin with the population regression equation

$$Y = X\beta + U \qquad (20.2)$$

and propose

$$c = C'Y \qquad (20.30)$$

as an arbitrary estimator for the population regression coefficients. C' is a $(K + 1) \times n$ matrix of known constants and Y is the $n \times 1$ column vector of observations on the dependent variable. This makes the estimator c a linear function of the sample points. Substituting (20.2) into (20.30) yields

$$c = C'(X\beta + U) = C'X\beta + C'U \qquad (20.31)$$

which expresses the estimator as a linear function of the population disturbance term. The expected value of this arbitrary estimator is

$$E(c) = C'X\beta \qquad (20.32)$$

using the assumption on the mean of the conditional distributions of the disturbance term. For this to be an unbiased estimator, that is, for $E(c) = \beta$, the following condition must hold:

$$C'X = I, \quad \text{which yields } (c - \beta) = C'U, \text{ from (20.31)} \qquad (20.33)$$

Assume for the moment that this condition is satisfied and write the variance-covariance matrix for the estimator as

$$\text{Var-cov } (c) = E[(c - \beta)(c - \beta)'] = E(C'UU'C) = \sigma^2 C'C \qquad (20.34)$$

using (20.33) and the assumption on the disturbance term. Now let

$$C' = (X'X)^{-1}X' \qquad (20.35)$$

where, because the values of the X-variable are fixed in repeated sampling, C' is a matrix of constants. Equations (20.31) to (20.35) become, respectively,

$$c = (X'X)^{-1}X'Y \qquad (20.36)$$

$$c = \beta + (X'X)^{-1}X'U \quad \text{or} \quad c - \beta = (X'X)^{-1}X'U \qquad (20.37)$$

$$E(c) = \beta \qquad (20.38)$$

$$(X'X)^{-1}X'X = I \qquad (20.39)$$

$$\text{Var-cov } (c) = \sigma^2(X'X)^{-1} \qquad (20.40)$$

But these are the OLS formulas of the preceding section, which means that c is the OLS estimator b of the preceding section. This shows that the OLS estimator b is a linear and unbiased estimator. Remaining is to determine if (20.40) is a minimum variance. This is done by finding another linear, unbiased estimator and comparing its variance to (20.41).

Consider some other arbitrary estimator A', also a matrix of known constants, and write

$$A'X = [(X'X)^{-1}X' + D']X = (X'X)^{-1}X'X + D'X = I + D'X \qquad (20.41)$$

which expresses A' as C' in (20.36) plus D', a matrix of known constants. A' is written this way because interest centers on comparing the properties of C', the OLS estimator, with the properties of A', a general estimator, since the elements of D' can be any known constants. In the special case where D' is a null matrix, the elements of A' will equal the elements of C'; otherwise, the elements will be different. (20.41) will be an unbiased estimator if the following holds:

$$D'X = 0 \qquad (20.42)$$

Because interest centers on comparing the variances of two linear, unbiased estimators, (20.42) is assumed to hold.

The variance-covariance matrix for (20.42) is given by

$$\text{Var-cov } (A) = E\{[(X'X)^{-1}X' + D']U\}\{[(X'X)^{-1}X' + D']U\}' \qquad (20.43)$$
$$= \sigma^2(X'X)^{-1} + D'D = \text{Var-cov } (b) + D'D$$

where $D'D$ is a positive semidefinite matrix, since all its elements are zero or positive. To illustrate, D is a 3×1 column vector for the two-independent variable case. Assume that its elements are 2, 0, and -4. In (20.44) $D'D$ is a scalar, the value of which is

$$D'D = [2 \quad 0 \quad -4] \begin{bmatrix} 2 \\ 0 \\ -4 \end{bmatrix} = [4 + 0 + 16] = 20$$

where the elements of $D'D$ are either zero or positive.

The variance-covariance of the estimator A', (20.44), is equal to or greater than the variance-covariance of C', the OLS estimator. Therefore, the OLS estimator is a minimum-variance estimator. Chapter 3 presents a nonmatrix proof for the special case of simple regression.

In summary, under the assumptions (20.3) to (20.6), the OLS estimators are *Best, Linear, Unbiased Estimators* of the population regression coefficients. This proves the Gauss–Markov theorem used in Chapters 3 and 4.

Variances of the OLS Coefficients

The variance of b, which plays a crucial role in hypothesis testing, depends on the variance of the population disturbance term. Since this variance is an unobservable population parameter, it must be estimated from the sample data. The procedure, as outlined in Chapter 3 for simple regression, is to "link" the observable OLS error term with the unobservable population disturbance term.

The vector of OLS residuals was given above as

$$e = Y - Xb \tag{20.8}$$

Substituting (20.2) for Y and (20.17) for b yields

$$e = X\beta + U - X[(X'X)^{-1}X'(X\beta + U)]$$
$$= X\beta + U - X\beta - X(X'X)^{-1}X'U \tag{20.44}$$
$$= U - X(X'X)^{-1}X'U$$

as the connection between the OLS residuals and the population disturbance terms. The U term can be factored out to obtain

$$e = [I_n - X(X'X)^{-1}X']U \tag{20.45}$$

where I is the $n \times n$ identify matrix. This is an important equation in econometrics because it provides the link between the computed (observable) values of the OLS error term and the unobservable population disturbance term. This, in turn, permits us to use the sample data to estimate σ^2, the variance of the population disturbance term that appears in (20.41).

The expression $[I_n - X(X'X)^{-1}X']$ is a special matrix called an *idempotent matrix*, with the special property that when premultiplied by its transpose it equals itself:

Property 3

A matrix such as $[I_n - X(X'X)^{-1}X']$, often written as M, is a symmetric, idempotent matrix that has the special property $M'M = M$.

Since e is an $n \times 1$ column vector, the right-hand-side of (20.45) must also be $n \times 1$.

$$e'e = U'M'MU \tag{20.46}$$

which shows the sum of squared OLS residuals as a function of the population disturbance terms. Consequently,

$$e'e = U'MU \tag{20.47}$$

$$E(e'e) = E(U'MU) \tag{20.48}$$

the evaluation of which requires additional matrix properties.

Property 4

The *trace* (written "tr") of a matrix is the sum of the elements on its main diagonal. Note that this applies only to a square $n \times n$ matrix.

Property 5

If A and B are matrices of dimensions $n \times n$,

$$\text{tr}(A + B) = \text{tr}(A) + \text{tr}(B)$$

Property 6

If A and B are matrices such that the matrix products AB and BA exist, tr (AB) = tr (BA). This holds for more than two matrices as long as all the relevant matrix products exist.

Property 7

If $E(U_i) = 0$, all i; $E(U_i^2) = \sigma^2$, all i; and $E(U_i U_j) = 0$, $i \neq j$, then $E(U'MU) = \sigma^2 \text{ tr } M$.

Given these properties, rewrite (20.48) as

$$
\begin{aligned}
E(e'e) &= E\{U'[I_n - X(X'X)^{-1}X']U\} \\
&= \sigma^2 \text{ tr } [I_n - X(X'X)^{-1}X'] \quad \text{by Property 7} \\
&= \sigma^2\{\text{tr}(I_n) - \text{tr}[X(X'X)^{-1}X']\} \quad \text{by Property 5} \\
&= \sigma\{\text{tr}(I_n) - \text{tr}[(X'X)^{-1}X'X]\} \quad \text{by Property 6}
\end{aligned}
\tag{20.49}
$$

I is the $n \times n$ identity matrix, and the sum of the terms on its principal diagonal is n. The second term in brackets, by the property of inverse matrices, is also an identity matrix with 1's on its main diagonal. Because X is the matrix of independent variables from the work sheet with an added column for the intercept term, the identity matrix here is of dimension $(K + 1) \times (K + 1)$. Consequently, its trace is $K + 1$, and (20.49) can be written as

$$E(e'e) = \sigma^2[n - (K + 1)] \tag{20.50}$$

which yields

$$S^2 = \frac{e'e}{n - (K + 1)} \tag{20.51}$$

an unbiased estimator of the population variance, the general result of the special cases developed in Chapters 3 and 4. Finally, the estimated variance-covariance matrix for the OLS coefficients is

$$S_b^2 = \{(X'X)^{-1}\} \frac{e'e}{n - (K + 1)} \tag{20.52}$$

by substituting (20.53) into (20.30).

To summarize the results so far:

Population regression function: $Y = X\beta + U$
Sample regression function: $Y = Xb + e$
Vector of OLS coefficients: $b = (X'X)^{-1}X'Y$
Variance-covariance matrix of OLS coefficients: Var-cov $(b) = (X'X)^{-1}\sigma^2$
Unbiased estimator of σ^2: $S^2 = e'e/[n - (K + 1)]$
Estimated variance-covariance matrix of coefficients:

$$S_b^2 = (X'X)^{-1} \frac{e'e}{n - (K + 1)}$$

Variables Expressed as Deviations

Much of the development in the previous chapters was carried out using the variables expressed as deviations from their respective means. This was done simply to make the writing easier, as it in effect "eliminated" the intercept, which can be quickly recovered simply by "adding the mean back in." The results of using variables as deviations from means in matrix notation would look exactly like the results above. The substantive differences would be that the elements of the Y and X matrices would be written in deviation form, the X-matrix would be of dimension $n \times K$ because it would not have the column of 1's for the intercept term, and b would be a $K \times 1$ column vector because it would not contain the OLS intercept term.

Coefficient of Determination, R^2

In Chapter 5 the variance of the dependent variable was written as the sum of the variance due to regression plus the variance due to the error term. Expressing the variables in deviation form yields, via equation (20.12),

$$Y'Y = 2b'X'Y - b'X'Xb + e'e \qquad (20.53)$$

where $Y'Y$ is TSS, the total sum of squares. By equation (20.14), $X'Xb = X'Y$, which permits (20.53) to be rewritten as

$$Y'Y = b'X'Y + e'e \qquad (20.54)$$

where $b'X'Y$ = RSS, the sum of squares due to regression, and $e'e$ = ESS, the sum of squares due to the error term. The coefficient of determination (R^2) is defined as the percent of variation in the dependent variable explained by the regression equation and can be calculated from (20.54) as

$$R^2 = \frac{b'X'Y}{Y'Y} \qquad (20.55)$$

Finally, by (20.55),

$$b'X'Y = Y'YR^2 \qquad (20.56)$$

and, after a little manipulation,

$$e'e = Y'Y(1 - R^2) \qquad \text{or} \qquad \frac{e'e}{Y'Y} = 1 - R^2 \qquad (20.57)$$

as alternative expressions for RSS and ESS, respectively, which can be substituted in the analysis-of-variance table to form the F-statistic written in terms of R^2 (see Chapter 6).

PART C

Specification Errors

This section presents the matrix, or general, treatment of omitted relevant variables, included irrelevant variables, heteroscedasticity, and autoregression disturbances—subjects treated in Chapters 13 and 14 using special cases. To do this requires a brief detour to derive the inverse of a partitioned matrix.

Inverse of a Partitioned Matrix

To motivate interest in the inverse of a partitioned matrix, consider the population regression equation

$$Y = X\beta + U \qquad (20.58)$$

to be estimated by

$$Y = Xb + e \qquad (20.59)$$

with the coefficient estimators given by

$$b = (X'X)^{-1}X'Y \qquad (20.60)$$

Without losing any generality, X, β, and b can be *partitioned* as

$$X = [X_1 : X_2] \qquad \beta = \begin{bmatrix} \beta_1 \\ \cdots \\ \beta_2 \end{bmatrix} \qquad b = \begin{bmatrix} b_1 \\ \cdots \\ b_2 \end{bmatrix} \qquad (20.61)$$

and write (20.60) as

$$\begin{bmatrix} b_1 \\ \cdots \\ b_2 \end{bmatrix} = \left(\begin{bmatrix} X_1' \\ \cdots \\ X_2' \end{bmatrix} [X_1 : X_2] \right)^{-1} \begin{bmatrix} X_1' \\ \cdots \\ X_2' \end{bmatrix} [Y]$$

$$= \begin{bmatrix} X_1'X_1 : X_1'X_2 \\ \cdots\cdots\cdots \\ X_2'X_1 : X_2'X_2 \end{bmatrix}^{-1} \begin{bmatrix} X_1'Y \\ X_2'Y \end{bmatrix} \qquad (20.62)$$

where the matrix elements are submatrices of the original X-matrix, partitioned such that their dimensions permit the indicated matrix multiplications. It can be shown that the inverse matrix in (20.62) exists, so nothing is lost by partitioning. The value of partitioning the X-matrix derives from the analytical insights provided with regard to the implication of adding and deleting independent variables on the properties of the OLS estimators. This is illustrated in the following two sections.

Omitted Relevant Variables

Let the properly specified model be given by

$$Y = X\beta + U \qquad (20.63)$$

where U statisfies the classical assumptions. Now partition $X\beta$ according to

$$Y = [X_1 \quad X_2]\begin{bmatrix} \beta_1 \\ \beta_2 \end{bmatrix} + U \qquad (20.64)$$

to obtain

$$Y = X_1\beta_1 + X_2\beta_2 + U \qquad (20.65)$$

Now suppose, for reasons discussed in Chapter 13, that the relevant variables in X_2 are omitted, yielding the estimating equation

$$Y = X_1b_1 + e^* \qquad (20.66)$$

where e^* is different from e in (20.59). Under this specification.

$$b_1 = (X_1'X_1)^{-1}X_1'Y \qquad (20.67)$$

is the vector of the OLS coefficients. Substituting (20.65) for Y yields

$$b_1 = (X_1'X_1)^{-1}X_1'(X_1\beta_1 + X_2\beta_2 + U) \tag{20.68}$$

with an expected value of

$$E(b_1) = \beta_1 + (X_1'X_1)^{-1}X_1'X_2\beta_2 \tag{20.69}$$

which suggests that the OLS estimators are biased, since $E(b_1) \neq \beta_1$ and $\beta_2 \neq 0$ by assumption [see (20.65)]. Whether b_1 is biased depends on the expression

$$(X_1'X_1)^{-1}X_1'X_2 \tag{20.70}$$

But notice that this term is the OLS regression of the values of the variables in X_2 on the values of the variables in X_1. It is the regression of the "omitted" variables on the "included" variables. These regressions, usually referred to as *auxiliary regressions*, must be viewed as descriptive only, since the X_1-values and the X_2-values are by the usual assumptions fixed in repeated sampling.

Consequently, for b_1 to be an unbiased estimator of β_1, the full set of the OLS coefficients of all the auxiliary regressions must be *zero*. Alternatively, b_1 is unbiased only if all the correlations between the included and omitted variables are zero. If this condition is not satisfied, the OLS coefficients are biased.

The bias has two components: the coefficients of the OLS auxiliary regressions and the population regression coefficients of the omitted variables. This shows that the OLS coefficients not only estimate the effect of the included variables X_1, they also pick up the effect of the omitted variables X_2 by virtue of the presence of β_2 in (20.68). This can lead to such things as coefficients with wrong signs or coefficients with outrageous values. Finally, the standard statistical tests cannot be used because they are valid only for unbiased estimators.

Included Irrelevant Variables

Let the properly specified population regression equation be

$$Y = X\beta + U \tag{20.71}$$

partitioned as

$$Y = [X_1 \quad X_2]\begin{bmatrix} \beta_1 \\ 0 \end{bmatrix} + U \tag{20.72}$$

where $\beta_2 = 0$, which says that the X_2-variables are "irrelevant." But suppose that you estimate

$$Y = Xb + e = [X_1 \quad X_2]\begin{bmatrix} b_1 \\ b_2 \end{bmatrix} + e \tag{20.73}$$

That is, the irrelevant variables are included and the specification that $\beta_2 = 0$ is ignored. Using a complicated rule for inverting a partitioned matrix yields

$$E(b_1) = \beta_1 + X_2'X_1\beta_1 - X_2'X_1\beta_1 = \beta_1 \tag{20.74}$$

and

$$E(b_2) = X_2'X_1\beta_1 - X_2'X_1\beta_1 = 0 \tag{20.75}$$

or

$$E\begin{bmatrix} b_1 \\ \cdots \\ b_2 \end{bmatrix} = \begin{bmatrix} E(b_1) \\ \cdots \\ E(b_2) \end{bmatrix} = \begin{bmatrix} \beta_1 \\ \cdots \\ 0 \end{bmatrix} \tag{20.76}$$

which shows that the OLS coefficients are unbiased when irrelevant variables are included in the equation. However, as was shown in Chapter 13, the variances of the coefficients of the relevant variables are larger with the irrelevant variables in the equation, increasing the likelihood of accepting the null hypothesis when it should be rejected. Remember the caveat: Beware the kitchen sink regression.

Generalized Least Squares

Chapter 14 discussed the problems of heteroscedasticity and autoregressiveness among the population disturbance terms. These two problems are treated here using the generalized least squares model. Let the population function be

$$Y = X\beta + U \tag{20.77}$$

where all the classical assumptions hold, except for the variance-covariance matrix of the disturbance terms, specified as

$$E(UU') = \sigma^2 \Omega \tag{20.78}$$

where σ^2 is the variance of the population disturbance term. To gain perpective on the general model, first specify that Ω is the identity matrix, so that (20.78) becomes simply σ^2, the OLS assumption. A reminder of some of its properties is pertinent to what is done below: The identity matrix is a symmetric matrix because it is equal to its transpose, and more important, it is a positive definite matrix because every element it its quadratic form $x'Ix$ is positive for any nonzero x-vector. This is shown by

$$[\sigma_1 \cdots \sigma_2] \begin{bmatrix} 1 & 0 & \cdots & 0 \\ 0 & 1 & \cdots & 0 \\ \cdot & \cdot & & \cdot \\ \cdot & \cdot & & \cdot \\ \cdot & \cdot & & \cdot \\ 0 & 0 & \cdots & 1 \end{bmatrix} \begin{bmatrix} \sigma_1 \\ \cdot \\ \cdot \\ \cdot \\ \sigma_n \end{bmatrix} = \sigma_1^2 + \cdots + \sigma_n^2 \tag{20.79}$$

The implication of (20.78) and these properties of the identity matrix is a homosce-dastistic and nonautoregressive disturbance term, key conditions for claiming the BLUE properties of the OLS estimators. With this brief review, we can examine the consequences of using OLS estimators when Ω is not the identity matrix, in other words, when the classical assumptions on the disturbance term do not hold. First, derive the minimum-variance estimator for (20.77), where Ω is not an identity matrix in (20.78).

Let

$$c = C'Y \qquad (20.80)$$

be a linear estimator of β in (20.77), where C' is a matrix of known constants defined such that c is a minimum-variance estimator. Substituting (20.77) yields

$$c = C'(X\beta + U) = C'X\beta + C'U \qquad (20.81)$$

with expected value given by

$$E(c) = C'X\beta \qquad (20.82)$$

which is unbiased if $C'X = I$. Assume that this is the case and derive the variance-covariance matrix of c, the minimum-variance estimator. By specification:

$$\text{Var-cov }(c) = E[(c - \beta)(c - \beta)'] = \sigma^2 C'\Omega C \qquad \text{[from (20.34)]} \qquad (20.83)$$

To determine if the OLS estimator is a minimum-variance estimator in this case, let $C' = (X'X)^{-1}X'$, the OLS weights. Substitution into (20.82) shows that the least squares estimator is an unbiased estimator. However, substitution into (20.83) yields

$$\text{Var-cov }(b) = (X'X)^{-1}X'\Omega(X'X)^{-1}X'\sigma^2 > (X'X)^{-1}\sigma^2 \qquad (20.84)$$

In practical terms this means that using OLS in this case results in variances larger than they should be, a major consequence being not rejecting the null hypothesis when it should be rejected. Of greater consequence is that the OLS estimator of the population variance, equation (20.51), is a biased estimator, rendering invalid the standard tests.

To recap quickly, if OLS estimators are used when Ω is not the identity matrix, unbiased estimates of the population regression coefficients are obtained, but they are inefficient estimates. Finally, the OLS estimate of σ^2 (S^2) is biased, rendering invalid the standard statistics for hypothesis testing. These results provide the motivation for examining the generalized least squares model.

In the general case, the structure of Ω is given by

$$\Omega = \begin{bmatrix} \sigma_1^2 & \sigma_{12} & \cdots & \sigma_{1n} \\ \sigma_{22} & \sigma_2^2 & \cdots & \sigma_{2n} \\ \cdot & \cdot & & \cdot \\ \cdot & \cdot & & \cdot \\ \cdot & \cdot & & \cdot \\ \sigma_{n1} & \sigma_{n2} & \cdots & \sigma_n^2 \end{bmatrix} \qquad (20.85)$$

which allows for the variances to differ across the conditional distributions of U, as shown by the diagonal elements, and allows for correlation among the disturbance terms, as shown by the off-diagonal terms.

Proceed, as was done in Chapter 14, by trying to find a transformation of (20.77) that produces an equation with a disturbance term satisfying the OLS assumptions in which case OLS procedures can be applied to the transformed equation to obtain BLUE of the population regression coefficients.

Because the variance-covariance matrix Ω is positive definite, there exists a matrix P, such that $\Omega = PP'$. Premultiplying Ω by P^{-1} and postmultiplying by $P^{-1'}$ yields $P^{-1}\Omega P^{-1'} = I$, the identity matrix. In addition, we can write $\Omega^{-1} = P^{-1'}P^{-1}$. Premultiply (20.77) by P^{-1} to obtain

$$P^{-1}Y = P^{-1}X\beta + P^{-1}U \tag{20.86}$$

where it can be shown that

$$E(P^{-1}UU'P^{-1'}) = \sigma^2 P^{-1}\Omega^{-1}P^{-1'} = \sigma^2 I \tag{20.87}$$

This shows that the disturbance term of the transformed equation, (20.86), satisfies the classical assumptions for best, linear, unbiased estimators. The generalized least squares estimator is given by

$$b = (X'P^{-1'}P^{-1}X)^{-1}(X'P^{-1'}P^{-1}Y) = (X'\Omega^{-1}X)^{-1}(X'\Omega^{-1}Y) \tag{20.88}$$

with variance-covariance matrix

$$\text{Var-cov }(b) = (X'\Omega^{-1}X)^{-1}\sigma^2 \tag{20.89}$$

As presented here, the generalized least squares model is seen as a two-step process: First transform the population regression function to one with the desired disturbance term, and then apply OLS procedures to the transformed variables. This is the notion of generalized least squares. By Aitken's generalized Gauss–Markov least squares theorem, the BLUE properties may be claimed for these estimators.

Two comments on the matrix Ω. First, it is a "general" matrix, meaning that the variances on the main diagonal are not necessarily all the same and some or all of the off-diagonal elements can be nonzero. Note that if the variances are all equal and if all the off-diagonal elements are zero, the generalized model "collapses" to the classical model discussed above.

Second, the derivations above assume that Ω is known. In practice, the elements of this matrix will not be known. Consequently, to obtain estimates of the regression coefficients, the elements of Ω will have to be determined. Equation (20.86) provides the general framework. Each variable is transformed so that (20.87) holds for the transformed data. If $Y^* = P^{-1}Y$ and $X^* = P^{-1}X$, then (20.86) can be estimated by OLS using the transformed variable matrices Y^* and X^*. The problem is finding an appropriate estimate of Ω from which p can be calculated and then used to transform Y and X. Because we discussed in detail in Chapter 14 how to proceed in the presence of heteroscedasticity and autocorrelation, the problems of estimation need not be pursued further here.

Appendix: Statistical Tables

Table A.1. Normal Distribution

$$Z = \frac{X - \mu}{\sigma} \text{ (standardized normal)}$$

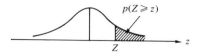

Z	.00	.01	.02	.03	.04	.05	.06	.07	.08	.09
.0	.5000	.4960	.4920	.4880	.4840	.4801	.4761	.4721	.4681	.4641
.1	.4602	.4562	.4522	.4483	.4443	.4404	.4364	.4325	.4286	.4247
.2	.4207	.4168	.4129	.4090	.4052	.4013	.3974	.3936	.3897	.3859
.3	.3821	.3783	.3745	.3707	.3669	.3632	.3594	.3557	.3520	.3483
.4	.3446	.3409	.3372	.3336	.3300	.3264	.3228	.3192	.3156	.3121
.5	.3085	.3050	.3015	.2981	.2945	.2912	.2877	.2843	.2810	.2776
.6	.2743	.2700	.2676	.2643	.2611	.2578	.2546	.2514	.2483	.2451
.7	.2420	.2389	.2358	.2327	.2296	.2266	.2236	.2206	.2177	.2148
.8	.2119	.2090	.2061	.2033	.2005	.1977	.1949	.1922	.1894	.1867
.9	.1841	.1814	.1788	.1762	.1736	.1711	.1685	.1660	.1635	.1611
1.0	.1587	.1562	.1539	.1515	.1492	.1469	.1446	.1423	.1401	.1379
1.1	.1357	.1335	.1314	.1292	.1271	.1251	.1230	.1210	.1190	.1170
1.2	.1151	.1131	.1112	.1093	.1075	.1056	.1038	.1020	.1003	.0985
1.3	.0968	.0951	.0934	.0918	.0901	.0885	.0869	.0853	.0838	.0823
1.4	.0808	.0793	.0778	.0764	.0749	.0735	.0721	.0708	.0694	.0681
1.5	.0668	.0655	.0643	.0630	.0618	.0606	.0594	.0582	.0571	.0559
1.6	.0548	.0537	.0526	.0516	.0505	.0495	.0485	.0475	.0465	.0455
1.7	.0446	.0436	.0427	.0418	.0409	.0401	.0392	.0384	.0375	.0367
1.8	.0359	.0351	.0344	.0336	.0329	.0322	.0314	.0307	.0301	.0294
1.9	.0287	.0281	.0274	.0268	.0262	.0256	.0250	.0244	.0239	.0233
2.0	.0228	.0222	.2017	.0212	.0207	.0202	.0197	.0192	.0188	.0183
2.1	.0179	.0174	.0170	.0166	.0162	.0158	.0154	.0150	.0146	.0143
2.2	.0139	.0136	.0132	.0129	.0125	.0122	.0119	.0116	.0113	.0110
2.3	.0107	.0104	.0102	.0099	.0096	.0094	.0091	.0089	.0087	.0084
2.4	.0082	.0080	.0078	.0075	.0073	.0071	.0069	.0068	.0066	.0064
2.5	.0062	.0060	.0059	.0057	.0055	.0054	.0052	.0051	.0049	.0048
2.6	.0047	.0045	.0044	.0043	.0041	.0040	.0039	.0038	.0037	.0036
2.7	.0035	.0034	.0033	.0032	.0031	.0030	.0029	.0028	.0027	.0026
2.8	.0026	.0025	.0024	.0023	.0023	.0022	.0021	.0021	.0020	.0019
2.9	.0019	.0018	.0018	.0017	.0016	.0016	.0015	.0015	.0014	.0014
3.0	.0013	.0013	.0013	.0012	.0012	.0011	.0011	.0011	.0010	.0010

Note: The table plots the cumulative probability $Z \geq z$.
Source: Based on *Biometrika Tables for Statisticans*, Vol. 1, 3rd ed. (1966), with the permission of the Biometrika trustees.

Table A.2. *t*-Distribution

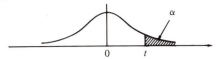

Degrees of Freedom	α: .1 $\alpha/2$: .2	.05 .10	.025 .05	.01 .02	.005 .01
		Probability of a Value at Least as Large as the Table Entry[a]			
1	3.078	6.314	12.706	31.821	63.657
2	1.886	2.920	4.303	6.965	9.925
3	1.638	2.353	3.182	4.541	5.841
4	1.533	2.132	2.776	3.747	4.604
5	1.476	2.015	2.571	3.365	4.032
6	1.440	1.943	2.447	3.143	3.707
7	1.415	1.895	2.365	2.998	3.499
8	1.397	1.860	2.306	2.896	3.355
9	1.383	1.833	2.262	2.821	3.250
10	1.372	1.812	2.228	2.764	3.169
11	1.363	1.796	2.201	2.718	3.106
12	1.356	1.782	2.179	2.681	3.005
13	1.350	1.771	2.160	2.650	3.012
14	1.345	1.761	2.145	2.624	2.977
15	1.341	1.753	2.131	2.602	2.947
16	1.337	1.746	2.120	2.583	2.921
17	1.333	1.740	2.110	2.567	2.898
18	1.330	1.734	2.101	2.552	2.878
19	1.328	1.729	2.093	2.539	2.861
20	1.325	1.725	2.086	2.528	2.845
21	1.323	1.721	2.080	2.518	2.831
22	1.321	1.717	2.074	2.508	2.819
23	1.319	1.714	2.069	2.500	2.807
24	1.318	1.711	2.064	2.492	2.797
25	1.316	1.708	2.060	2.485	2.787
26	1.315	1.706	2.056	2.479	2.779
27	1.314	1.703	2.052	2.473	2.771
28	1.313	1.701	2.048	2.467	2.763
29	1.311	1.699	2.045	2.462	2.756
30	1.310	1.697	2.042	2.457	2.750
40	1.303	1.684	2.021	2.423	2.704
60	1.296	1.671	2.000	2.390	2.660
120	1.289	1.658	1.980	2.358	2.617
Normal ∞	1.282	1.645	1.960	2.326	2.576

[a] The first probability at the head of each column (the smaller number) is the probability for a one-tailed test. The second (larger) probability is the probability for a two-tailed test.

Source: Reprinted from Table IV in Sir Ronald A. Fisher, *Statistical Methods for Research Workers*, 14th ed. (copyright 1972 by Hafner Press, a Division of Macmillan Publishing Co., Inc) with the permission of the publisher and the late Sir Ronald Fisher's Literary Executor.

431

Table A.3. Percentage Points for the F-Distribution[a]

a. Upper 5% Points

v_2	| v_1																		
	1	2	3	4	5	6	7	8	9	10	12	15	20	25	30	40	60	120	∞
1	161.4	199.5	215.7	224.6	230.2	234.0	236.8	238.9	240.5	241.9	243.9	245.9	248.9	249.1	250.1	251.1	252.2	253.3	254.3
2	18.51	19.00	19.16	19.25	19.30	19.33	19.35	19.37	19.38	19.40	19.41	19.43	19.45	19.45	19.46	19.47	19.48	19.49	19.50
3	10.13	9.55	9.28	9.12	9.01	8.94	8.89	8.85	8.81	8.79	8.74	8.70	8.66	8.64	8.62	8.59	8.57	8.55	8.53
4	7.71	6.94	6.59	6.39	6.26	6.16	6.09	6.04	6.00	5.96	5.91	5.86	5.80	5.77	5.75	5.72	5.69	5.66	5.63
5	6.61	5.79	5.41	5.19	5.05	4.95	4.88	4.82	4.77	4.74	4.68	4.62	4.56	4.53	4.50	4.46	4.43	4.40	4.36
6	5.99	5.14	4.76	4.53	4.39	4.28	4.21	4.15	4.10	4.06	4.00	3.94	3.87	3.84	3.81	3.77	3.74	3.70	3.67
7	5.59	4.74	4.35	4.12	3.97	3.87	3.79	3.73	3.68	3.64	3.57	3.51	3.44	3.41	3.38	3.34	3.30	3.27	3.23
8	5.32	4.46	4.07	3.84	3.69	3.58	3.50	3.44	3.39	3.35	3.28	3.22	3.15	3.12	3.08	3.04	3.01	2.97	2.93
9	5.12	4.26	3.86	3.63	3.48	3.37	3.29	3.23	3.18	3.14	3.07	3.01	2.94	2.90	2.86	2.83	2.79	2.75	2.71
10	4.96	4.10	3.71	3.48	3.33	3.22	3.14	3.07	3.02	2.98	2.91	2.85	2.77	2.74	2.70	2.66	2.62	2.58	2.54
11	4.84	3.98	3.59	3.36	3.20	3.09	3.01	2.95	2.90	2.85	2.79	2.72	2.65	2.61	2.57	2.53	2.49	2.45	2.40
12	4.75	3.89	3.49	3.26	3.11	3.00	2.91	2.85	2.80	2.75	2.69	2.62	2.54	2.51	2.47	2.43	2.38	2.34	2.30
13	4.67	3.81	3.41	3.18	3.03	2.92	2.83	2.77	2.71	2.67	2.60	2.53	2.46	2.42	2.38	2.34	2.30	2.25	2.21
14	4.60	3.74	3.34	3.11	2.96	2.85	2.76	2.70	2.65	2.60	2.53	2.46	2.39	2.35	2.31	2.27	2.22	2.18	2.13
15	4.54	3.68	3.29	3.06	2.90	2.79	2.71	2.64	2.59	2.54	2.48	2.40	2.33	2.29	2.25	2.20	2.16	2.11	2.07
16	4.49	3.63	3.24	3.01	2.85	2.74	2.66	2.59	2.54	2.49	2.42	2.35	2.28	2.24	2.19	2.15	2.11	2.06	2.01
17	4.45	3.59	3.20	2.96	2.81	2.70	2.61	2.55	2.49	2.45	2.38	2.31	2.23	2.19	2.15	2.10	2.06	2.01	1.96
18	4.41	3.55	3.16	2.93	2.77	2.66	2.58	2.51	2.46	2.41	2.34	2.27	2.19	2.15	2.11	2.06	2.02	1.97	1.92
19	4.38	3.52	3.13	2.90	2.74	2.63	2.54	2.48	2.42	2.38	2.31	2.23	2.16	2.11	2.07	2.03	1.98	1.93	1.88
20	4.35	3.49	3.10	2.87	2.71	2.60	2.51	2.45	2.39	2.35	2.28	2.20	2.12	2.08	2.04	1.99	1.95	1.90	1.84
21	4.32	3.47	3.07	2.84	2.68	2.57	2.49	2.42	2.37	2.32	2.25	2.18	2.10	2.05	2.01	1.96	1.92	1.87	1.81
22	4.30	3.44	3.05	2.82	2.66	2.55	2.46	2.40	2.34	2.30	2.23	2.15	2.07	2.03	1.98	1.94	1.89	1.84	1.78
23	4.28	3.42	3.02	2.80	2.64	2.53	2.44	2.37	2.32	2.27	2.20	2.13	2.05	2.01	1.96	1.91	1.86	1.81	1.76
24	4.26	3.40	3.01	2.78	2.62	2.51	2.42	2.36	2.30	2.25	2.18	2.11	2.03	1.98	1.94	1.89	1.84	1.79	1.73
25	4.24	3.39	2.99	2.76	2.60	2.49	2.40	2.34	2.28	2.24	2.16	2.09	2.01	1.96	1.92	1.87	1.82	1.77	1.71
26	4.23	3.37	2.98	2.74	2.59	2.47	2.39	2.32	2.27	2.22	2.15	2.07	1.99	1.95	1.90	1.85	1.80	1.75	1.69
27	4.21	3.35	2.96	2.73	2.57	2.46	2.37	2.31	2.25	2.20	2.13	2.06	1.97	1.93	1.88	1.84	1.79	1.73	1.67
28	4.20	3.34	2.95	2.71	2.56	2.45	2.36	2.29	2.24	2.19	2.12	2.04	1.96	1.91	1.87	1.82	1.77	1.71	1.65
29	4.18	3.33	2.93	2.70	2.55	2.43	2.35	2.28	2.22	2.18	2.10	2.03	1.94	1.90	1.85	1.81	1.75	1.70	1.64
30	4.17	3.32	2.92	2.69	2.53	2.42	2.33	2.27	2.21	2.16	2.09	2.01	1.93	1.89	1.84	1.79	1.74	1.68	1.62
40	4.08	3.23	2.84	2.61	2.45	2.34	2.25	2.18	2.12	2.08	2.00	1.92	1.84	1.79	1.74	1.69	1.64	1.58	1.51
60	4.00	3.15	2.76	2.53	2.37	2.25	2.17	2.10	2.04	1.99	1.92	1.84	1.75	1.70	1.65	1.59	1.53	1.47	1.39
120	3.92	3.07	2.68	2.45	2.29	2.18	2.09	2.02	1.96	1.91	1.83	1.75	1.66	1.61	1.55	1.50	1.43	1.35	1.25
∞	3.84	3.00	2.60	2.37	2.21	2.10	2.01	1.94	1.88	1.83	1.75	1.67	1.57	1.52	1.46	1.39	1.32	1.22	1.00

432

b. Upper 1% Points

v_1

v_2	1	2	3	4	5	6	7	8	9	10	12	15	20	25	30	40	60	120	∞
1	4052.	4999.5	5403.	5625.	5764.	5859.	5928.	5981.	6022.	6056.	6106.	6157.	6209.	6235.	6261.	6287.	6313.	6339.	6366.
2	98.50	99.00	99.17	99.25	99.30	99.33	99.36	99.37	99.39	99.40	99.42	99.43	99.45	99.46	99.47	99.47	99.48	99.49	99.50
3	34.12	30.82	29.46	28.71	28.24	27.91	27.67	27.49	27.35	27.23	27.05	26.87	26.69	26.60	26.50	26.41	26.32	26.22	26.13
4	21.20	18.00	16.69	15.98	15.52	15.21	14.98	14.80	14.66	14.55	14.37	14.20	14.02	13.93	13.84	13.75	13.65	13.56	13.46
5	16.26	13.27	12.06	11.39	10.97	10.67	10.46	10.29	10.16	10.05	9.89	9.72	9.55	9.47	9.38	9.29	9.20	9.11	9.02
6	13.75	10.92	9.78	9.15	8.75	8.47	8.26	8.10	7.98	7.87	7.72	7.56	7.40	7.31	7.23	7.14	7.06	6.97	6.88
7	12.25	9.55	8.45	7.85	7.46	7.19	6.99	6.84	6.72	6.62	6.47	6.31	6.16	6.07	5.99	5.91	5.82	5.74	5.65
8	11.26	8.65	7.59	7.01	6.63	6.37	6.18	6.03	5.91	5.81	5.67	5.52	5.36	5.28	5.20	5.12	5.03	4.95	4.86
9	10.56	8.02	6.99	6.42	6.06	5.80	5.61	5.47	5.35	5.26	5.11	4.96	4.81	4.73	4.65	4.57	4.48	4.40	4.31
10	10.04	7.56	6.55	5.99	5.64	5.39	5.20	5.06	4.94	4.85	4.71	4.56	4.41	4.33	4.25	4.17	4.08	4.00	3.91
11	9.65	7.21	6.22	5.67	5.32	5.07	4.89	4.74	4.63	4.54	4.40	4.25	4.10	4.02	3.94	3.86	3.78	3.69	3.60
12	9.33	6.93	5.95	5.41	5.06	4.82	4.64	4.50	4.39	4.30	4.16	4.01	3.86	3.78	3.70	3.62	3.54	3.45	3.36
13	9.07	6.70	5.74	5.21	4.86	4.62	4.44	4.30	4.19	4.10	3.96	3.82	3.66	3.59	3.51	3.43	3.34	3.25	3.17
14	8.86	6.51	5.56	5.04	4.69	4.46	4.28	4.14	4.03	3.94	3.80	3.66	3.51	3.43	3.35	3.27	3.18	3.09	3.00
15	8.68	6.36	5.42	4.89	4.56	4.32	4.14	4.00	3.89	3.80	3.67	3.52	3.37	3.29	3.21	3.13	3.05	2.96	2.87
16	8.53	6.23	5.29	4.77	4.44	4.20	4.03	3.89	3.78	3.69	3.55	3.41	3.26	3.18	3.10	3.02	2.93	2.84	2.75
17	8.40	6.11	5.18	4.67	4.34	4.10	3.93	3.79	3.68	3.59	3.46	3.31	3.16	3.08	3.00	2.92	2.83	2.75	2.65
18	8.29	6.01	5.09	4.58	4.25	4.01	3.84	3.71	3.60	3.51	3.37	3.23	3.08	3.00	2.92	2.84	2.75	2.66	2.57
19	8.18	5.93	5.01	4.50	4.17	3.94	3.77	3.63	3.52	3.43	3.30	3.15	3.00	2.92	2.84	2.76	2.67	2.58	2.49
20	8.10	5.85	4.94	4.43	4.10	3.87	3.70	3.56	3.46	3.37	3.23	3.09	2.94	2.86	2.78	2.69	2.61	2.52	2.42
21	8.02	5.78	4.87	4.37	4.04	3.81	3.64	3.51	3.40	3.31	3.17	3.03	2.88	2.80	2.72	2.64	2.55	2.46	2.36
22	7.95	5.72	4.82	4.31	3.99	3.76	3.59	3.45	3.35	3.26	3.12	2.98	2.83	2.75	2.67	2.58	2.50	2.40	2.31
23	7.88	5.66	4.76	4.26	3.94	3.71	3.54	3.41	3.30	3.21	3.07	2.93	2.78	2.70	2.62	2.54	2.45	2.35	2.26
24	7.82	5.61	4.72	4.22	3.90	3.67	3.50	3.36	3.26	3.17	3.03	2.89	2.74	2.66	2.58	2.49	2.40	2.31	2.21
25	7.77	5.57	4.68	4.18	3.86	3.63	3.46	3.32	3.22	3.13	2.99	2.85	2.70	2.62	2.54	2.45	2.36	2.27	2.17
26	7.72	5.53	4.64	4.14	3.82	3.59	3.42	3.29	3.18	3.09	2.96	2.81	2.66	2.58	2.50	2.42	2.33	2.23	2.13
27	7.68	5.49	4.60	4.11	3.78	3.56	3.39	3.26	3.15	3.06	2.93	2.78	2.63	2.55	2.47	2.38	2.29	2.20	2.10
28	7.64	5.45	4.57	4.07	3.75	3.53	3.36	3.23	3.12	3.03	2.90	2.75	2.60	2.52	2.44	2.35	2.26	2.17	2.06
29	7.60	5.42	4.54	4.04	3.73	3.50	3.33	3.20	3.09	3.00	2.87	2.73	2.57	2.49	2.41	2.33	2.23	2.14	2.03
30	7.56	5.39	4.51	4.02	3.70	3.47	3.30	3.17	3.07	2.98	2.84	2.70	2.55	2.47	2.39	2.30	2.21	2.11	2.01
40	7.31	5.18	4.31	3.83	3.51	3.29	3.12	2.99	2.89	2.80	2.66	2.52	2.37	2.29	2.20	2.11	2.02	1.92	1.80
60	7.08	4.98	4.13	3.65	3.34	3.12	2.95	2.82	2.72	2.63	2.50	2.35	2.20	2.12	2.03	1.94	1.84	1.73	1.60
120	6.85	4.79	3.95	3.48	3.17	2.96	2.79	2.66	2.56	2.47	2.34	2.19	2.03	1.95	1.86	1.76	1.66	1.53	1.38
∞	6.63	4.61	3.78	3.32	3.02	2.80	2.64	2.51	2.41	2.32	2.18	2.04	1.88	1.79	1.70	1.59	1.47	1.32	1.00

Source: This table is based on Table 18 of Biometrika Tables for Statisticians, Vol. 1, edited by E. S. Pearson and H. O. Hartley (1970). By permission of the Biometrika trustees.

[a] v_1, Numerator degrees of freedom; v_2, denominator degrees of freedom.

Table A.4. Durbin–Watson Statistic, d: Significance Points of d_L and d_U[a]

a. 5% Level

n	$k' = 1$		$k' = 2$		$k' = 3$		$k' = 4$		$k' = 5$	
	d_L	d_U	d_L	d_U	d_L	d_U	d_L	d_U	d_L	d_U
15	1.08	1.36	.95	1.54	.82	1.75	.69	1.97	.56	2.21
16	1.10	1.37	.98	1.54	.86	1.73	.74	1.93	.62	2.15
17	1.13	1.38	1.02	1.54	.90	1.71	.78	1.90	.67	2.10
18	1.16	1.39	1.05	1.53	.93	1.69	.82	1.87	.71	2.06
19	1.18	1.40	1.08	1.53	.97	1.68	.86	1.85	.75	2.02
20	1.20	1.41	1.10	1.54	1.00	1.68	.90	1.83	.79	1.99
21	1.22	1.42	1.13	1.54	1.03	1.67	.93	1.81	.83	1.96
22	1.24	1.43	1.15	1.54	1.05	1.66	.96	1.80	.86	1.94
23	1.26	1.44	1.17	1.54	1.08	1.66	.99	1.79	.90	1.92
24	1.27	1.45	1.19	1.55	1.10	1.66	1.01	1.78	.93	1.90
25	1.29	1.45	1.21	1.55	1.12	1.66	1.04	1.77	.95	1.89
26	1.30	1.46	1.22	1.55	1.14	1.65	1.06	1.76	.98	1.88
27	1.32	1.47	1.24	1.56	1.16	1.65	1.08	1.76	1.01	1.86
28	1.33	1.48	1.26	1.56	1.18	1.65	1.10	1.75	1.03	1.85
29	1.34	1.48	1.27	1.56	1.20	1.65	1.12	1.74	1.05	1.84
30	1.35	1.49	1.28	1.57	1.21	1.65	1.14	1.74	1.07	1.83
31	1.36	1.50	1.30	1.57	1.23	1.65	1.16	1.74	1.09	1.83
32	1.37	1.50	1.31	1.57	1.24	1.65	1.18	1.73	1.11	1.82
33	1.38	1.51	1.32	1.58	1.26	1.65	1.19	1.73	1.13	1.81
34	1.39	1.51	1.33	1.58	1.27	1.65	1.21	1.73	1.15	1.81
35	1.40	1.52	1.34	1.58	1.28	1.65	1.22	1.73	1.16	1.80
36	1.41	1.52	1.35	1.59	1.29	1.65	1.24	1.73	1.18	1.80
37	1.42	1.53	1.36	1.59	1.31	1.66	1.25	1.72	1.19	1.80
38	1.43	1.54	1.37	1.59	1.32	1.66	1.26	1.72	1.21	1.79
39	1.43	1.54	1.38	1.60	1.33	1.66	1.27	1.72	1.22	1.79
40	1.44	1.54	1.39	1.60	1.34	1.66	1.29	1.72	1.23	1.79
45	1.48	1.57	1.43	1.62	1.38	1.67	1.34	1.72	1.29	1.78
50	1.50	1.59	1.46	1.63	1.42	1.67	1.38	1.72	1.34	1.77
55	1.53	1.60	1.49	1.64	1.45	1.68	1.41	1.72	1.38	1.77
60	1.55	1.62	1.51	1.65	1.48	1.69	1.44	1.73	1.41	1.77
65	1.57	1.63	1.54	1.66	1.50	1.70	1.47	1.73	1.44	1.77
70	1.58	1.64	1.55	1.67	1.52	1.70	1.49	1.74	1.46	1.77
75	1.60	1.65	1.57	1.68	1.54	1.71	1.51	1.74	1.49	1.77
80	1.61	1.66	1.59	1.69	1.56	1.72	1.53	1.74	1.51	1.77
85	1.62	1.67	1.60	1.70	1.57	1.72	1.55	1.75	1.52	1.77
90	1.63	1.68	1.61	1.70	1.59	1.73	1.57	1.75	1.54	1.78
95	1.64	1.69	1.62	1.71	1.60	1.73	1.58	1.75	1.56	1.78
100	1.65	1.69	1.63	1.72	1.61	1.74	1.59	1.76	1.57	1.78

Table A.4. (*continued*)

b. 1% Level

	$k' = 1$		$k' = 2$		$k' = 3$		$k' = 4$		$k' = 5$	
n	d_L	d_U	d_L	d_U	d_L	d_U	d_L	d_U	d_L	d_L
15	.81	1.07	.70	1.25	.59	1.46	.49	1.70	.39	1.96
16	.84	1.09	.74	1.25	.63	1.44	.53	1.66	.44	1.90
17	.87	1.10	.77	1.25	.67	1.43	.57	1.63	.48	1.85
18	.90	1.12	.80	1.26	.71	1.42	.61	1.60	.52	1.80
19	.93	1.13	.83	1.26	.74	1.41	.65	1.58	.56	1.77
20	.95	1.15	.86	1.27	.77	1.41	.68	1.57	.60	1.74
21	.97	1.16	.89	1.27	.80	1.41	.72	1.55	.63	1.71
22	1.00	1.17	.91	1.28	.83	1.40	.75	1.54	.66	1.69
23	1.02	1.19	.94	1.29	.86	1.40	.77	1.53	.70	1.67
24	1.04	1.20	.96	1.30	.88	1.41	.80	1.53	.72	1.66
25	1.05	1.21	.98	1.30	.90	1.41	.83	1.52	.75	1.65
26	1.07	1.22	1.00	1.31	.93	1.41	.85	1.52	.78	1.64
27	1.09	1.23	1.02	1.32	.95	1.41	.88	1.51	.81	1.63
28	1.10	1.24	1.04	1.32	.97	1.41	.90	1.51	.83	1.62
29	1.12	1.25	1.05	1.33	.99	1.42	.92	1.51	.85	1.61
30	1.13	1.26	1.07	1.34	1.01	1.42	.94	1.51	.88	1.61
31	1.15	1.27	1.08	1.34	1.02	1.42	.96	1.51	.90	1.60
32	1.16	1.28	1.10	1.35	1.04	1.43	.98	1.51	.92	1.60
33	1.17	1.29	1.11	1.36	1.05	1.43	1.00	1.51	.94	1.59
34	1.18	1.30	1.13	1.36	1.07	1.43	1.01	1.51	.95	1.59
35	1.19	1.31	1.14	1.37	1.08	1.44	1.03	1.51	.97	1.59
36	1.21	1.32	1.15	1.38	1.10	1.44	1.04	1.51	.99	1.59
37	1.22	1.32	1.16	1.38	1.11	1.45	1.06	1.51	1.00	1.59
38	1.23	1.33	1.18	1.39	1.12	1.45	1.07	1.52	1.02	1.58
39	1.24	1.34	1.19	1.39	1.14	1.45	1.09	1.52	1.03	1.58
40	1.25	1.34	1.20	1.40	1.15	1.46	1.10	1.52	1.05	1.58
45	1.29	1.38	1.24	1.42	1.20	1.48	1.16	1.53	1.11	1.58
50	1.32	1.40	1.28	1.45	1.24	1.49	1.20	1.54	1.16	1.59
55	1.36	1.43	1.32	1.47	1.28	1.51	1.25	1.55	1.21	1.59
60	1.38	1.45	1.35	1.48	1.32	1.52	1.28	1.56	1.25	1.60
65	1.41	1.47	1.38	1.50	1.35	1.53	1.31	1.57	1.28	1.61
70	1.43	1.49	1.40	1.52	1.37	1.55	1.34	1.58	1.31	1.61
75	1.45	1.50	1.42	1.53	1.39	1.56	1.37	1.59	1.34	1.62
80	1.47	1.52	1.44	1.54	1.42	1.57	1.39	1.60	1.36	1.62
85	1.48	1.53	1.46	1.55	1.43	1.58	1.41	1.60	1.39	1.63
90	1.50	1.54	1.47	1.56	1.45	1.59	1.43	1.61	1.41	1.64
95	1.51	1.55	1.49	1.57	1.47	1.60	1.45	1.62	1.42	1.64
100	1.52	1.56	1.50	1.58	1.48	1.60	1.46	1.63	1.44	1.65

[a] n, Number of observations; k', = number of explanatory variables excluding constant term.

Source: J. Durbin and G. S. Watson. "Testing for Serial Correlation in Least Squares Regresison," *Biometrika*, Vol. 38, p. 159–177 (June 1951). Reproduced with permission of the Biometrika trustees.

Glossary

Adaptive Expectations Model. A model growing out of the assumption that changes in the dependent variable depend on the expected value of an independent variable rather than on its actual value. The resulting statistical equation includes both a lagged dependent and independent variable.

Additive in X_i. The marginal effect of an independent variable (X_i) on the dependent variable does not depend on the level of other independent variables in the equation. The first derivative of the equation with respect to X_i is not a function of X_j, $j \neq i$, in the model.

Adjusted Coefficient of Multiple Determination ($\overline{R}^2$). An R^2 adjusted for degrees of freedom. It can be used to compare explanatory power of regression equations with different independent variables or using a different number of observations.

Alternative Hypothesis (H_a). The counter proposition to the null hypothesis (H_0). It states the likely alternative value for the statistic under test, for example,

$$H_0: \beta = 10 \quad \text{versus} \quad H_a: \beta \neq 10$$

$$H_0: \overline{X} = \mu \quad \text{versus} \quad H_a: \overline{X} \neq \mu$$

$$H_0: S^2 = \sigma_\mu^2 \quad \text{versus} \quad H_a: S^2 \neq \sigma_\mu^2$$

Analysis-of-Variance Table. A standardized table that decomposes the variance of the dependent variable into sources of variance due to regression and to a random component. It serves as a useful framework for hypothesis testing.

ARIMA. An abbreviation for autoregressive, moving average model.

Autocorrelation. The presence of correlation among the disturbance terms. This violation of one of the assumptions of the Guass–Markov theorem is usually associated with time-series data. It results in unbiased but inefficient OLS estimators.

Autoregression. *See* Autocorrelation; First-Order Autoregression.

Autoregression Coefficient. It indicates the nature of the relationship between disturbance terms μ_t and μ_{t-i}, where i is the order of the lag (e.g., in a first-order autoregressive process, $\mu_t = \rho\mu_{t-1} + V_t$. It is usually denoted as ρ (rho).

Auxiliary Regresssions. The regression of an independent variable on the other $K - 1$ independent variables in the regression model.

Best Estimator. The estimator producing estimates with the smallest variance about the population parameter being estimated. If θ^*, the estimator, produces estimate $\hat{\theta}$ of θ, then $E(\hat{\theta} - \theta)^2$ will be a minimum.

Beta Coefficients. The regression coefficients that result from estimating a regression using standardized variables. The coefficient is interpreted as the number of standard deviation changes in the dependent variable for 1-standard-deviation change in the independent variable.

Biased Estimator. An estimator whose expected value is not equal to the parameter it is designed to estimate. For example, if θ^* is an estimator yielding $\hat{\theta}$ as an estimate of θ, then $E(\hat{\theta}) \neq \theta$.

Binary Variable. *See* Dummy Variable.

BLUE. Acronym for ''best linear and unbiased estimator.''

Bruesch–Pagan Test. A test for the presence of heteroscedasticity.

Calculated Y. *See* Y-Hat.

Causal Relationship. An assertion, embodied in single-equation regression models, that the values for the independent variables affect the values for the dependent variable but the converse is not true. Causality is derived from the theory guiding the empirical research.

Census. Obtaining information by enumerating all the elements in a population.

Central Limit Theorem. A statistical theorem that says if X has any distribution with a mean of μ and variance of σ^2, then the distribution of $\overline{X}$ approaches the normal distribution with mean of μ and variance of σ^2/n as n (the sample size) increases.

Centroid. The point in the data cluster represented by the means of all the variables.

Chi-Square Distribution. The distribution of the sum of a squared standardized normal variable with mean zero and a variance S_x^2. It is the distribution of variables such as TSS, RSS, and ESS divided by their respective degrees of freedom.

Classical Linear Regression Model. A (simple or multiple) regression equation plus assumed statistical properties for the disturbance term and the independent variables; the basis for regression analysis.

Cobb–Douglas Function. A well-known equation in which the value of dependent variable is a multiplicative function of the independent variables. It is frequently used in applied research because the coefficients are elasticities.

Cobweb Model. The output decisions for time t depend on price in time $t - 1$. An early theoretical justification for including a lagged variable in an OLS equation to explain a dependent variable.

Coefficient of Multiple Determination (R^2). The percent of variation in the dependent variable associated with or explained by variation in the independent variables in the regression equation.

Coefficient of Variation.   The standard deviation of a variable divided by its mean. A unit-free statistic measuring relative variation in a variable.

Column Vector.   A set of numbers or symbols (e.g., annual prices from 1960 to 1963) written as a column of numbers. For example, the numbers [24.47   30.98   26.12   32.57] can be represented by a single symbol, P.

$$P = \begin{bmatrix} 24.47 \\ 30.98 \\ 26.12 \\ 32.57 \end{bmatrix}$$

Conceptual Error.   The data used to measure a variable do not measure the relevant conceptual variable identified by the theory.

Conceptual Variable.   The general theoretical variables described by the theory supporting the statistical model, such as income, price, consumption, substitutes for pork, etc.

Conditional Distribution.   The distribution of a variable based on a specified condition, for example, the distribution of values of Y for a specific X, say X^*, $(Y|X^*)$. In simple regression the distribution of $Y|X^* = \beta_0 + \beta_1 X^*$.

Conditional Forecast.   A forecast based on assumed rather than known values for the independent variables. The forecasted values depend in part (are "conditional on") the values assigned the independent variables in the forecasting equation.

Conditional Mean.   The mean calculated while holding other variables fixed. For example, if $Y = f(X_1, X_2)$, there are two conditional means of Y: $E(Y|X_1)$ and $E(Y|X_2)$.

Confidence Interval.   The numerical range around a sample statistic that contains the parameter value with some prestated level of probability.

Confidence Level.   The percent of the times that the constructed confidence level will include the population parameter.

Constrained Estimation.   Multiple regression where linear constraints (e.g., $b_2 = 5$ or $b_1 + b_2 = 16$) are imposed on the regression coefficients prior to estimation.

Correlation Coefficient.   A measure or index of association, or covariation, between two variables, also known as r, or the Pearson correlation coefficient; the coefficient ranges between -1 and $+1$.

Covariance.   A measure of the degree to which the values of two variables vary together. It is the expected value of the cross product of the differences of each variable from its respective mean.

Covariance Analysis.   A regression equation in which the slopes or intercepts are permitted to vary by the class of one or more qualitative variables.

Critical Value.   The value from a statistical table that when compared to a statistic, provides the basis for rejecting or not rejecting the null hypothesis.

Cross Products. The result of multiplying the deviations of two variables, (e.g., if $x_{1i} = (X_{1i} - \overline{X})$ and $x_{2i} = (X_{2i} - \overline{X})$, then the cross product is $x_{1i}x_{2i}$.

Cross-Sectional Data. Numbers collected on a set of observational units at a single period of time, for example, data collected on budget, tax rate, and enrollment for a sample of school districts during the 1984 school year or on how much a sample of U.S. households spent on dairy products last week.

Cycle. A pattern of change in a variable that repeats periodically.

Deflation. Dividing one data series by another to measure how the numerator has moved relative to the deflator (the denominator).

Degrees of Freedom. The number of linearly independent prices of information in n observations.

Dependent Variable. The variable on the left-hand side of the regression equation, where theory suggests that its value depends on the values of the independent variables.

Deseasonalizing. Removing the seasonal variation in a variable.

Detrend. Removing the period-to-period change in a variable due to the passage of time (trend).

Deviations. Values for a variable expressed as a deviation from its mean (e.g., $x_i = X_i - \overline{X}$). Lowercase letters are used to represent a variable in deviation units.

Distribution. *See* Frequency Distribution; Probability Distribution.

Disturbance Term (U). The term attached to the population regression equation to make it mathematically correct. It is included because relevant variables are omitted from the equation, the system under study has an inherently random component, or Y is measured with error.

Dummy Variable. A variable that takes the value 1 if an observation fits in a predefined category and the value 0 otherwise. It is used to quantify classificatory variables. Also called a zero-one or binary variable.

Dummy Variable Trap. Including dummy variables for all possible categories in a regression equation. The OLS computational procedure breaks down because of perfect correlation across the dummy variables.

Durbin–Watson Statistic. The most common test for the presence of first-order autoregression in the OLS residuals. It is also the name for the special table that contains the critical values for the test.

Econometric Equation. A formal statement of the relationship between a dependent variable and a set of independent variables plus a disturbance term; not reversible.

Econometrics. The study of the quantitative measurement of economic relationships combining economic theory, mathematics, and statistics.

Efficient Estimate. The estimator producing estimates with the smallest variance. *See* Best Estimator.

Elasticity. The percentage change in a dependent variable associated with a 1 percent change in an independent variable.

Error-in-Equations. Error asssociated with the inexact nature of the relationship being studied.

Error-in-Variables. Error in measuring the independent and dependent variables.

Error Sum of Squares (ESS). The sum of the squared differences between observed and regression values of the dependent variable in a regression equation; the sum of squared residuals.

Error Term. Difference between the actual and calculated Y. *See* Residual.

Error Variance. *See* Standard Error of Regression.

ESS. *See* Error Sum of Squares.

Estimate. A number used to approximate the value of a parameter, calculated from a formula (an estimator) using sample data.

Estimated Error Variance. *See* Estimated Variance of Regression.

Estimated Variance of Regression. An unbiased estimator of the variance of the population disturbance term σ^2. It is computed by dividing the sum of the squared residuals by the appropriate degrees of freedom $(n - k - 1)$.

Estimator. A formula applied to the data of a specific sample to calculate a sample statistic, or estimate of a population parameter.

Ex-Ante Forecasting. Forecasting the dependent variable for a time period beyond the current period.

Expectation Operator. A linear operator used to compute the expected value of a random variable.

Expected Value. The mean value of a random variable. Calculated as the sum of the product of each possible value of the variable times that value's relative frequency of occurrence in the population.

Explanatory Variable. *See* Independent Variable.

Ex-Post Forecasting. Forecasting values for the time period after the estimation period but over a period when values of all variables are known. Used to assess the reliability of the estimated equation for true, or *ex ante*, forecasting.

Fail to Reject Null Hypothesis. To decide that a hypothesized value, β^*, is consistent with the data used to test it.

F-Distribution. The distribution formed by the ratio of two independent variables each distributed according to the chi-square distribution.

First-Order Autoregression. The simplest model of serial correlation. Each disturbance term is equal to some fraction (rho) of the previous disturbance term plus a new independent disturbance term that conforms to all the Gauss–Markov assumptions.

Forecast. To make a statement about an event before the event occurs. In econometrics a statement made in advance about the value of a dependent variable using regression results.

Forecast Error. The difference between the forecasted value for the dependent variable ($\hat{Y}_{T+1}$) and the value that variable actually takes Y_{T+1}; $(Y_{T+1} - \hat{Y}_{T+1})$.

Forecast Interval. Assuming some level of probability, it is the range of values in which it is predicted that the actual value of the dependent variable will fall.

Frequency Distribution. A table or graph showing the number of times each possible value of a variable appears in the population or sample.

F-Statistic. The calculated ratio of two independent sample statistics, each with a chi-square distribution.

Functional Form. The specific mathematical relationship among the variables in a regression equation (e.g., linear, log-log, quadratic form, etc.).

Gauss–Markov Theorem. Says that OLS estimators of the regression coefficients in the classical regression model are best, linear, unbiased estimators.

General Form. A nonspecific mathematical or econometric equation. The relevant variables are specified but the specific form of the relationship among them is not [e.g., $Y = f(X)$ or $Y = F(X, U)$].

Generic Variable. A general variable used to represent a theoretical variable. It includes many possible specific counterparts. For example, "income" is a generic variable that includes per capita disposable income, per capita net national product, take-home pay, etc.

Goldfeld–Quandt Test. A test for the presence of heteroscedasticity.

Growth Rate. The compound percentage rate of change in a variable over time, usually denoted by r.

Heteroscedasticity. The variance of the disturbance term in OLS is not constant. The OLS estimators are unbiased but inefficient in the presence of heteroscedasticity.

Hildreth–Lu Procedure. A procedure for estimating the autocorrelation coefficient ρ (rho) in a first-order autoregressive model. It requires interating over many possible values of ρ in search of the one that yields the smallest residual sum of squares.

Homoscedasticity. The assumption in the classical linear regression model that the variance of the disturbance term is constant across the data set.

Hypothesis. A conjecture or assumption about one or more parameters of a population.

Hypothesis Test. An evaluation, on the basis of probabilities, as to whether the sample evidence supports an a priori value of the population parameter.

Independent Variable. A variable on the right-hand side of a regression equation, because theory suggests that variation in its value influences the value of the dependent variable, sometimes called an explanatory variable and usually denoted by X_i.

Instrumental Variables. A procedure used to correct OLS estimates when an explanatory variable is not independent of the disturbance term. It involves substituting another variable that is minimally correlated with the disturbance term for the highly correlated one.

Interaction Variable or Term.   An independent variable formed by multiplying two independent variables together. A useful transformation for modeling nonadditivity in an equation.

Intercept.   The point where a linear regression line intersects the Y axis; denoted by β_0 or b_0.

Intercept Dummy.   A binary variable formulation that allows the intercept of the equation to change across categories of a classificatory variable.

Intrinsically Linear and Additive Equation.   An equation that can be transformed so that it is linear and additive in all the transformed variables and the transformed variables can be computed from the sample data. An essential requirement of an economic model if it is to be estimated by OLS.

Irrelevant Variable.   An independent variable included in a regression equation that theory says is not a relevant explanatory variable of Y. Including such a variable is a possible source of inefficiency but not bias in the OLS estimates.

Joint Test.   Test of a null hypothesis involving more than one regression coefficient.

Lagged Variable.   A variable in a time-series model that takes a value from a time period previous to that of the dependent variable (e.g., $Y_t = b_0 + b_1 X_{t-1}$).

Law of Large Numbers.   As the sample size increases, the difference between the sample statistic and its population counterpart decreases.

Least Squares.   A mathematical technique for calculating the values for the coefficients of a linear equation from a set of data by minimizing the sum of the squared residuals. *See* Ordinary Least Squares.

Least Squares Line.   The line (on a graph) or the equation representing the calculated value of Y_i (the dependent variable), for the sample values of X_{ik}.

Least Squares Residuals.   *See* Residual.

Linear Estimator.   A formula for calculating a statistic from sample observations (an estimator) that is a linear function of the values of the sample variables, and thus follows the general from $X^* = w_1 X_1 + w_2 X_2 + \cdots + w_n X_n$, where X^* is the statistic; $X_1, X_2, \ldots, X_n$ are the sample observations; and $w_1, w_2, \ldots, w_n$ are the weights applied to each observation.

Linear Form.   A mathematical specification that is linear and additive in all X's. The form requires no transformations of the data and implies constant marginal effects and varying elasticities. The conventional mathematical specification for a regression equation.

Linear in X.   An equation in which the marginal effect of an independent variable, X_i, on the dependent variable does not depend on the magnitude of X_i (i.e., the first derivative of the equation with respect to X_i is not a function of X_i itself).

Linear-Log.   A functional form where the dependent variable is in its original form and the independent variables are expressed in logarithms. It implies that a percentage change in the independent variable has the same absolute effect on the dependent variable irrespective of the level of X.

Linear Regression Model.   The linear equation $Y = \beta_0 + \beta_1 X_1 + \cdots + \beta_k X_k + U$; the assumptions on the error term used in ordinary least squares (OLS).

Log-Linear. A functional form in which the dependent variable is expressed in logarithms and independent variables are in their original form. This transformation of an exponential function is useful for estimating rates of growth in the dependent variable.

Log-Log. A functional form where both the independent and the dependent variables are expressed as the logarithm of the original values. This form implies constant elasticities and varying marginal effects.

Marginal Physical Product. In production economics, the amount contributed to output by one additional unit of input.

Mathematical Form. A formal statement of the relationship among variables without any disturbance term. The statement is reversible, implying no direction of causality.

Matrix. A set of columns of numbers (column vectors) treated as an entity.

Mean. The "average" value of a variable. It is defined as the expected value of a variable.

Mean Square. The average variation associated with a specific source of variation. It is calculated as the appropriate sum of squares divided by degrees of freedom (e.g., mean-squared error).

Measurement Errors. Nonsampling errors in data arising out of inaccurate data generation procedures (e.g., poor questions, faulty equipment, and human recording errors) resulting in inaccurate measurement of variables.

Minimum-Variance Estimator. The estimator having a distribution with the smallest variance. *See* Best Estimator.

Missing Data. Gaps in a data set because values of the independent or dependent variables are missing.

Misspecification. An incorrect formulation of the regression equation due to omitting a relevant variable(s), including an irrelevant variable, using an incorrect functional form, or incorrectly specifying the disturbance term.

Moment. Deviation, or distance of a variable from its mean (e.g., $x_i = X_i - \overline{X}$).

Multicollinearity. The lack of independence among the explanatory variables in a data set. It is a sample problem that results in relatively large standard errors for the estimated regression coefficients, but not biased estimates.

Multiple Regression. A regression equation containing more than one independent variable.

Net Regression Coefficient. *See* Partial Regression Coefficient.

Nominal Data. Data expressed in natural units (i.e., no correction for changing general price level, population, etc.).

Nonadditive in X. The marginal effect of an independent variable, X_i, on the dependent variables depends on the magnitude of other independent variables in the equation. Mathematically, the first derivative of the dependent variable with respect to X is a function of at least one other X in the equation.

Nonlinear in X. The marginal effect of X_i on Y depends on the level of X. The first derivative of the dependent variable with respect to X_i is a function of X_i itself.

Nonsampling Error. Differences between the survey value of a statistic and its population counterpart due to measurement or response errors.

Normal Distribution. A frequency distribution commonly used in statistics. Its graph is a "bell-shaped" curve.

Normal Equations. The set of equations that when solved simultaneously yield the formulas for computing the least squares estimates of regression coefficients (OLS estimates).

Null Hypothesis. A testable statement (usually denoted H_0:) that the value of a statistic is equal to some prespecified value. For example, H_0: $\beta_1 = 25$ or H_0: $b_1 - \beta_1 = 0$.

Omitted Variable. A variable affecting the dependent variable but is excluded from the estimated regression equation. It is thus assumed to be in the error or disturbance term.

One-Tailed Test. The alternative hypothesis is specified as an inequality (e.g., $\beta_1 < 0$). It is used when theory suggests that only one end of the distribution of the statistic is of interest.

Operationalization Error. Errors caused by the use of an improper rule of correspondence to link a theoretical concept to an observable phenomena (e.g., a set of numbers that do not reflect what is expressed or implied by "income").

Ordinary Least Squares (OLS). The method of calculating the coefficients of an inexact linear function by minimizing the sum of the squared residuals [i.e., minimize $\Sigma\ e_i^2 = \Sigma\ (Y_i - \hat{Y}_i)^2$].

Outlier. A data point (observation) that is outside the normal range of points (e.g., an extreme value).

Parameter. The constant of a population, usually an unknown value that must be estimated on the basis of a sample.

Partial Adjustment Model. A model that includes a lagged dependent variable. The model assumes that complete adjustment to changing conditions is not always possible within one time period.

Partial Regression Coefficient. β_i (for a population) or b_i (for a sample) in a multiple regression equation. It measures the change in $E(Y)$ or $\hat{Y}$ corresponding to a 1-unit change in X_i, holding all other explanatory variables constant. Also called regression slope.

Pearson Correlation Coefficient. *See* Correlation Coefficient.

Per Capita. Data expressed as per unit of the population in the sample. For example, income is often divided by the relevant population (numbers of people, households, factories, establishments, etc.) to express the values in income per unit.

Pooled Data. Combining data sets.

Population. The complete collection of elements about which information is desired.

Population Parameters. Characteristics of the population about which information is sought via statistical and econometric procedures.

Population Regression Equation. The hypothesized functional relationship between Y and a set of X_i's in the population, generally denoted $Y = \beta_0 + \beta_1 X_1 + \beta_2 X_2 + \cdots + \beta_k X_k + U$.

Population Regression Parameter. The coefficients of the population regression equation (e.g., β_0, β_1, β_2, σ_μ^2).

Prediction. To make a statement about an event before the event occurs. To forecast based on a regression equation.

Quadratic in X. A functional form involving both X_i and X_i^2. It is useful in modeling turning points.

Qualitative Variables. A variable whose values reflect groups that cannot be unambiguously ordered. They are usually represented by binary variables in an OLS equation.

Quantitative Variable. A variable that is measured on a continuous scale (i.e., it is cardinal). The numerical value of each data point indicates an exact relationship to other values (e.g., \$10 is \$1 more than \$9 and \$2 less than \$12).

R^2. *See* Coefficient of Multiple Determination.

Random Error. *See* Stochastic Disturbance.

Random Variable. A variable that takes on different values with known frequency, but where the probability of a particular outcome on a given trial is not known or predictable.

Real Data. A variable expressed in relative units (e.g., relative to changes in some base variable). For example, in order to eliminate the general change in price from a variable, the nominal value might be divided by the values of an index of general prices, such as the CPI, to obtain new variable, ''real prices.''

Reciprocal in X. A functional form in which an independent variable is the reciprocal of its observed value $(1/X_i)$. It is useful for modeling nonlinear relations with satiation or minimum-acceptable levels of the dependent variable.

Regression Coefficient. The values of the slope (b_i) or intercept (b_0) in a regression equation.

Regression Equation. The estimated equation obtained by the method of least squares.

Regression line. The predicted values of the dependent variable Y for each (set of) value(s) for the independent variable(s), X_i (e.g., $\hat{Y} = b_0 + b_1 X$).

Regression Slopes. *See* Partial Regression Coefficient.

Regresssion Sum of Squares (RSS). The sum of the squared deviations of the regression values of the dependent variable (the $\hat{Y}_i$) about the sample mean of the dependent variable, $\Sigma (\hat{Y}_i - \bar{Y})^2$.

Regression Values. *See* Y-Hat $(\hat{Y})$.

Reject Hypothesis. To decide, based on statistical interference, that the data do not support the null hypothesis about the value of a parameter.

Relative Frequency Distribution. A table or graph showing the proportion of the observations in the population or sample that take on each possible value.

Relevant Variable. On the basis of the theoretical foundation of the model, an independent variable that should be included in a regression equation. If such a variable is not included, there is a potential source of bias in the OLS estimators.

Research Question. The query that motivates and guides empirical research.

Residual. The difference (positive or negative) between the observed value for the dependent variable (Y_i) and the value calculated by the estimated regression equation ($\hat{Y}$); $e_i = Y_i - \hat{Y}_i$.

Residual Plot. A plot of the residuals (e_i) against time or an independent variable.

Residual Sum of Squares. *See* Error Sum of Squares.

Reversibility. A property of mathematical equations which says that if $Y = f(X)$, then an inverse function $[X = f^{-1}(Y)]$ exists.

Row Vector. Data expressed in sequence in a row and treated as a single entity. For example, the annual income of three families, 25,000; 12,197 and 18,221 is represented by a single symbol such as I, for example,

$$I = [25,000 \quad 12,197 \quad 18,221]$$

RSS. *See* Regression Sum of Squares.

Sample. A subset of observations drawn from a population.

Sample Regression Equation. An estimate of the population regression equation, generally denoted

$$Y = b_0 + b_1X_1 + b_2X_2 + \cdots + b_kX_k + e$$

Sample Regression Slope. The estimate of a population regression slope obtained using OLS on sample data (e.g., b_i).

Sampling Distribution. Distribution of values of a statistic computed from a specific size sample of observations drawn from a population.

Sampling Error. The difference between a sample statistic and its population counterpart attributable to using a sample instead of a census.

Scaling. Changing the units of measurement of a variable (i.e., multiplying by 100, dividing by 1000, etc.).

Scatter Diagram. A plot of observed data points, usually with the dependent variable on the vertical axis and the independent variable on the horizontal axis.

Seasonal. A pattern of change that occurs within a 12-month period.

Seasonal Index. A measure of seasonal variation, usually expressed as the percentage deviation of a variable in a particular week, month, and so on, from its average value over the entire 12-month period.

Seasonally Adjusted. Adjective referring to the value for an economic variable after the regular within-year (seasonal) variation has been eliminated.

Seasonal Variation. A 12-month pattern in the observations that repeats itself from year to year; also refers to the average deviation of the variable during a "season" (day, week, month, or quarter) from the annual average.

Segmented Trend. A trend that is broken into two or more parts to capture different long-term movements in the dependent variable.

Serial Correlation. A special type of autocorrelated disturbance where the error term for observation t is related to the error term for observation $t - 1$.

Significance Level. The probability of rejecting a true null hypothesis.

Simple Regression. A technique for estimating the parameters of an equation containing only one independent variable.

Slope Dummy. A type of binary variable constructed so that it allows the slope of a continuous independent variable, X, to be different across different categories of a classificatory variable.

Slope Regression Coefficients (b_i). They measure the change in the dependent variable per unit change in an independent variable. Also called partial or net regression coefficients.

Sources of Variation. In regression analysis, the division of the total variation in the dependent variable (TSS) into components associated with variation in the independent variables (RSS) and unexplained variation (ESS).

Specific Variable. A variable that is used to represent a theoretical or generic variable in a statistical model. For example, the quantity of beef produced might be used as a specific variable to represent the generic variable "substitute for pork."

Spectral Analysis. The decomposition of a time series into components that are associated with the frequency of their occurrence across a data set that can be ordered in some manner (e.g., time of observation).

Standard Deviation. A measure of the dispersion of a variable about its mean. It is the square root of the variance of the variable.

Standard Deviation of Regression. *See* Standard Error of Regression.

Standard Error. Square root of a variance; standard deviation.

Standard Error of b_i. *See* Variance of a Regression Coefficient.

Standard Error of Estimate. *See* Standard Error of Regression.

Standard Error of Forecast. The standard deviation of the forecast error. It is almost always larger than the standard error of regression.

Standard Error of Regression. An estimate of the standard deviation of the population disturbance term. It is calculated as the positive square root of the estimated variance of regression S. It is also called the standard error of the estimate, standard deviation of the estimate, and standard deviation of the regression.

Standardized Coefficients. *See* Beta Coefficient.

Standardized Normal Distribution. The distribution of a standardized normal variable; the distribution will have a mean of 0 and variance of 1.

Standardized Normal Variable. A standardized variable that has a normal distribution [i.e., $Z = (X - \overline{X})/S_x$ and $\overline{Z} = 0$, $S_Z^2 = 1$].

Standardized Regression. Regression with all variables expressed as standardized variables.

Standardized Variable. A transformation on a random variable obtained by subtracting its mean and dividing by its standard deviation; standardized variables have a mean of a zero and a variance of 1.

$$x_i = \frac{X_i - \overline{X}}{S_x}$$

Statistic. A number computed from sample data by an estimator and used as an estimate of a population parameter.

Statistical Interference. Procedures to estimate the value of a population parameter from the information in a sample.

Stochastic Disturbance. Inclusion of U in the population regression equation because of an inherent random indeterminacy in the systems behavior.

Structural Shift. A shift in the parameters of the underlying population regression function.

Student's t. A distribution used to test hypotheses about standardized random variables; approaches the normal distribution as the number of degrees of freedom increases.

Sum of Squared Residuals (ESS). The value minimized by the method of least squares. Calculated by obtaining the residual for each observation, squaring it, and summing the square. Also called the error sum of squares. $\Sigma (Y_i - \hat{Y}_i)^2 = \Sigma e_i^2$.

t-Distribution. The distribution of a standard normal variable when the sample standard deviation S_x is used in place of σ_x in the estimator.

Theory. An abstract description of some phenomena. It is the foundation upon which empirical research in economics is based.

Time-Series Analysis. The analysis of a variable subject to change over time in order to isolate periodic changes such as trend, cycles, and seasonals.

Time-Series Data. Data collected over several periods of time (e.g., a data set containing quarterly observations on prices, quantities, and consumer incomes in the aggregate U.S. market between 1950 and 1983).

Time-Series Plot. A plot of the values of a variable against time (e.g., values of the variable on the vertical axis and time on the horizontal axis).

Time-Series Regression. One type of time-series analysis. Others are ARIMA, spectral analysis, and so on.

Total Sum of Squares (TSS). The total sum of the squared deviations of the sample values of the dependent variable about the sample mean of the dependent variable: $\Sigma (Y_i - \overline{Y})^2$.

Transpose. To change a vector or a matrix by interchanging its rows and columns. Usually noted by attaching a prime to the symbol (e.g., if V is a column vector, its transpose, V', is a row vector).

Trend.   A systematic change in a variable that persists over time.

Trend Variable.   A regression equation incorporating time as an independent variable. It is designed to capture the systematic movement in the dependent variable.

TSS.   *See* Total Sum of Squares.

t-Statistic.   A standardized variable used in hypothesis testing calculated as $t = (\hat{\theta} - \theta^*)/S_{\hat{\theta}}$, where θ is the sample statistic, θ^* is the hypothesized value, and $S_{\hat{\theta}}$ is the standard error of $\hat{\theta}$ computed from the sample.

t-Table.   A table containing the critical values for the t-statistic at various degrees of freedom and levels of significance.

Two-Stage Least Squares.   An OLS technique that substitutes calculated values of an independent variable for its raw counterpart. Used when an explanatory variable is not independent of the disturbance term.

Two-Tailed Test.   The alternative hypothesis is specified as not equal to the value stated in the null hypothesis (e.g., H_0: $\beta_1 = 0$, H_a: $\beta_1 \neq 0$). Used when theory suggests that both ends of the distribution of the statistic are of interest.

Type I Error.   Rejecting the null hypothesis when it is true.

Type II Error.   Not rejecting the null hypothesis when it is false.

Unbiased Estimator.   An estimator producing estimates whose expected value is equal to the parameter it is designed to estimate. If θ^* is an estimator yielding $\hat{\theta}$ as an estimate of θ, then $E(\hat{\theta}) = \theta$.

Unconditional Forecasting.   Predictions or forecasts made using values for the independent variables that are known with certainty at the time of the forecast.

Variable.   Characteristic of a population that can be expressed in quantitative terms. The numerical values of the characteristic vary across units of the population.

Variance.   A measure of the dispersion of individual values of a random variable around its mean value. It is calculated as the expected value of the squared deviation of the random variable from its mean.

Variance of a Regression Coefficient (S_b^2).   A measure of the sampling variability of an estimated regression coefficient about it expected value. S_{b_1} is the "standard error" of the OLS regression parameter estimate b_1.

Vector.   An ordered set of numbers.

Weighted Regression.   A procedure whereby the values of the variables in an OLS equation are weighted. The procedure is used to deal with heteroscedasticity by transforming all variables in the regression equation by some other variable by "weighting" them and then applying OLS to the weighted observations.

Worksheet.   A table containing the data used for regression analysis; usually, the columns identify the variable and each row represents one observation.

Y-Hat ($\hat{Y}$).   The calculated value of the dependent variable, Y, obtained by using the estimated OLS equation and the values of the independent variables:

$$\hat{Y} = b_0 + b_1X_1 + b_2X_2 + \cdots + b_kK_k$$

Suggested Readings

A large number of econometrics books, differing substantially by degree of sophistication, readability, and focus on specific applied research questions, are available. To cite further readings in each of these books would be a monumental task. To identify the "best" subset of these books for suggested readings would be an impossible task. Nevertheless, we felt that the user of this book should be steered toward additional readings, either for further clarification or for a more rigorous treatment of a particular topic. For this reason, citations to the following two books are provided:

> Kmenta, Jan, *Elements of Econometrics,* Macmillan Publishing Company, New York, 1971.
>
> Judge, George, R. Carter Hill, William Griffiths, Helmut Lutkepohl, and Tsoung-Chao Lee, *Introduction to the Theory and Practice of Econometrics*, John Wiley & Sons, Inc., New York, 1982.

The selection of these books was not arbitrary. Readers who can handle the material in this book will find the Kmenta book a natural next step. Many topics are covered in greater depth and new topics are introduced, yet the presentation, as in this book, does not use matrix algebra. The book by Judge et al. on the other hand, is probably the current "frontier" econometrics textbook. The material in this book can be handled only by those with a strong statistical background and an easy facility with matrix algebra.

CHAPTER 1
Least Squares Principle and Normal Equations
Kmenta: pp. 206–207
Judge et al.: pp. 24–25
Writing Variables in Deviation Form
Kmenta: pp. 207–208

CHAPTER 2
What Is Econometrics?
Judge et al.: pp. 1–5
Statistical Inference
Kmenta: pp. 1–15
Estimations and Properties of Estimators
Kmenta: pp. 154–186
Judge et al.: pp. 26–32

Autocorrelation
  Kmenta: pp. 269–297
  Judge et al.: pp. 435–472

CHAPTER 15
Measurement Error
  Kmenta: pp. 307–322
  Judge et al.: p. 227; pp. 532–537
Missing Observations
  Kmenta: pp. 336–345
  Judge et al.: pp. 328–330

CHAPTER 17
  Kmenta: pp. 422–424
  Judge et al.: pp. 507–509

CHAPTER 18
  Kmenta: pp. 239–242; pp. 374–376
  Judge et al.: pp. 143–148; pp. 395–397

CHAPTER 19
On Writing
  Baker, Sheridan, *The Practical Stylist*, 4th ed., Harper & Row, New York, 1977.
  Strunk, William, Jr., and E. B. White, *The Elements of Style*, 3rd ed., Macmillan
    Publishing Company, New York, 1979.
  Zinsser, William, *On Writing Well*, 3rd ed., Harper & Row, New York, 1985.
Style Manual
  Turabian, Kate L., *A Manual for Writers of Term Papers, Theses, and Dissertations*,
    4th ed., The University of Chicago Press, Chicago, 1973.
  Words Into Type (based on studies by Marjorie E. Skillin, Robert M. Gay, and other
    authorities), 3rd ed., Prentice-Hall, Englewood Cliffs, N.J., 1974.
On Research
  Ladd, George W., "Artistic Research Tools for Scientific Minds," *American Journal
    of Agricultural Economics*, Vol. 61, No. 1, (1979), pp. 1–11.

CHAPTER 20
  Kmenta: Appendix B, pp. 604–613
  Judge et al.: pp. 207–213

Answers to Selected Exercises

CHAPTER 1

1.1 (d) $b_1 = .20625; b_0 = 8.125$

1.2 (g) $e_H = 1; e_J = -1; e_K = 1; e_L = -3; e_M = 2$

    (i) No line leads to a smaller sum of squared residuals than the least squares line; most likely, any freehand line will produce a larger sum of squared residuals than $\Sigma\, e_i^{*2}$.

1.3 (a) $\Sigma\, e_i^* = 0$

    (c) Yes. As long as $b_0 = \bar{Y} - b_1\bar{X}$, the line will go through the controid. The residuals from a line through the centroid (with any slope) will sum to zero.

1.4 (c) $b_1 = .55; b_0 = -35$

    (e) Centroid $= (\bar{X}, \bar{Y}) = (120, 31)$; yes: $31 = -35 + (.55)(120)$

    (g) $b = \dfrac{\Sigma\, x_i y_i}{\Sigma\, x_i^2} = .55$

    (i) The intercept of the line is zero.

1.5 (a) 56

    (c) 26

    (e) 24

    (g) 328

1.6 (a) $b_1 = \dfrac{\Sigma\, x_i y_i}{\Sigma\, x_i^2} = -10.9$

1.7 (a) $(\bar{Y}, \bar{X}) = (5, 3)$

    (c) $b_0 = 2.429$

1.9 (a) b_1

    (c) 0

1.10 (c) No; $562 \neq 3024$

    (e) $b_1 = 2.231$

(h)

	y_i	x_i
Al	-8	-2
Betty	-2	-2
Chuck	-6	-1
Doris	$+2$	0
Elvis	$+8$	$+1$
Fran	$+6$	$+4$

(k) $b_1 = 2.231$
(m) Yes
(o) Intercept $= 0$, slope $= 2.231$
(q) Yes; the slopes are the same, but the intercepts are different.
(s) Yes

CHAPTER 2
2.1 (a) 2

(c)

Possible Sample Means	Frequency	Relative Frequencies
0	3	.3
2	3	.3
3	3	.3
5	$\frac{1}{10}$	$\frac{.1}{1.0}$

(e)

Possible Sample Means	Frequency	Relative Frequencies
1.0	1	.2
1.5	1	.2
2.5	$\frac{3}{5}$	$\frac{.6}{1.0}$

$$\text{mean} = (1)(.2) + (1.5)(.2) + (2.5)(.6)$$
$$= .2 \quad + \quad .3 \quad + \quad 1.5$$
$$= 2.0$$
$$\text{Var} = [(1 - 2)^2(.2)] + [(1.5 - 2)^2(.2)] + [(2.5 - 2)^2(.6)]$$
$$= \quad (1)(.2) \quad + \quad (.25)(.2) \quad + \quad (.25)(.6)$$
$$= .2 + .05 + .15$$
$$= .40$$

(g) Yes, because in both cases the expected value of the sample mean is equal to 2.

(i) $\text{Var}(\overline{X}) = \Sigma \; [\overline{X}_i - E(\overline{X})]^2 \; f(\overline{X}_i)$

for $n = 2$; $\text{var}(\overline{X}) = 2.4$
for $n = 4$; $\text{var}(\overline{X}) = .4$

2.2. (a) Variance

(c) Standard deviation

2.3. $E(r) = 6.0$

2.4. (a) 2.4

(c) 3.0

(e) 6.3

(g) 1.04

(i) 1.00

(k) 5.1

(m) 26.4

2.5. $3200

2.6. (a) $E[X - E(X)^2 = E\{X^2 - 2XE(X) + [E(X)]^2\}$
$= E\{(X)^2 - 2[E(X)]^2 + [E(X)]^2\}$
$= E(X)^2 - [E(X)]^2$
$= \sigma^2$

2.7. (a) $28.44 \le \mu \le 71.56$

(c) $37.35 \le \mu \le 62.65$

2.8. (a) .67

(c) .95

(e) .025

2.9. (a) $\text{var}(X + Y) = \sigma_x^2 + \sigma_y^2 + 2\sigma_{xy}^2$.

2.10. (a) $\overline{W} = 16$, $\text{var}(W) = 36$

(c) $\overline{W} = 8$, $\text{var}(W) = 36$

2.11. (a) $E(Y) = a + b\mu$
$\text{var}\;(Y) = E[Y - E(Y)]^2 = b^2 \; \text{var}(X)$

(c) It will have a mean of zero and var $= 1$.

CHAPTER 3

3.1 $Y_i = \beta_0 + \beta_1 X_i + U_i, \; i = i, \ldots, n$

where $E(U_i) = 0$

$E(U_i^2) = \sigma^2$ where σ^2 is a constant

$E(U_i U_j) = 0$ for all $i \ne j$

The values of X are fixed in repeated sampling, or $E(XU) = 0$.

3.3 (a) 2.042

(c) 1.645

(e) 2.518

(g) 2.576

(i) 1.645

3.4 (a) $Y_i = \beta_0 + \beta_1 X_i + U_i$

(c) $b_1 = \dfrac{\Sigma\, xy}{\Sigma\, x^2} = -.1330$; $b_0 = \overline{Y} - b_1\overline{X} = 7.9950$

(e) $S = .4472$

(g) $S_{g_1} = .02$

3.5 (a) $\overline{X} = \dfrac{\Sigma\, X}{n} = \$3 \text{ per galllon}$

(c) $b_1 = \dfrac{\Sigma\, xy}{\Sigma\, x^2} = -22 \text{ gallons}$

(e) $S^2 = \dfrac{\Sigma\, e^2}{n-2} = \dfrac{528}{10} = 52.8 \text{ gallons}$

(g) $S_{b_1}^2 = \dfrac{S^2}{\Sigma\, x^2} = 2.64 \text{ gallons}$

(i) $H_0\!: b_1 = 0$

$H_a\!: b_1 \neq 0$

Critical t-value $= 2.22$

$t = \dfrac{-22}{1.62} = 13.6$

Conclusion: reject H_0

3.6 (b) $\overline{Y} = 80 \text{ hours}$

(d) $b_0 = 20 \text{ points}$

(f) $S_{b_1} = 2 \text{ points}$

(h) It is a measure of the dispersion of actual Y-values about the population regression function. It is the variation in Y-values not explained by X, hours studied.

3.7 (a)

i	Y	X	$\hat{Y}$	e	e^2
1	1	1	1.3	$-.3$	.09
2	3	2	2.1	.9	.81
3	2	3	2.9	$-.9$	.81
4	4	4	3.7	.3	.09
	10	10	10.0	0.0	1.80

(c) $S = $ standard deviation of regression $= .9487$

(e) The sums of $\hat{Y}$'s and e's are identical, but $\Sigma\, e^2$ is larger in part (d) than in part (a).

3.8 (a) All the values for the dependent variable lie on the estimated regression line.

(c) $b_0 = \overline{Y}$ and $b_1 = 0$

3.9 (a)

Y	X	x_i	y_i	x_iy_i	x_i^2	y_i^2
0	0	-1.6	-1.9	3.04	2.56	3.61
2	1	$-.6$	.1	$-.06$	.36	.01
1	2	.4	$-.9$	$-.36$	.16	.81
3	1	$-.6$	1.1	$-.66$	.36	1.21
1	0	-1.6	$-.9$	1.44	2.56	.81
3	3	1.4	1.1	1.54	1.96	1.21
4	4	2.4	2.1	5.04	5.76	4.41
2	2	.4	.1	.04	.16	.01
1	2	.4	$-.9$	$-.36$	.16	.81
2	1	$-.6$	.1	$-.06$	.36	.01
19	16	0.0	0.0	9.60	14.40	12.90

(c) $b_0 = .833$

(e) $S^2 = .812; S = .901$

3.11   Numerator:

$$\Sigma\, x_iy_i = \Sigma\, (Y_i - \bar{Y})(X_i - \bar{X})$$

$$= \Sigma\, (Y_iX_i - \bar{X}Y_i - \bar{Y}X_i + \bar{Y}\bar{X})$$

$$= \Sigma\, Y_iX_i - \bar{X}\,\Sigma\, Y_i - \bar{Y}\,\Sigma\, X_i + n\bar{Y}\bar{X}$$

$$= \Sigma\, Y_iX_i - \frac{\Sigma\, X_i\,\Sigma\, Y_i}{n} - \frac{\Sigma\, Y_i\,\Sigma\, X_i}{n} + \frac{\Sigma\, Y_i\,\Sigma\, X_i}{n}$$

$$= \Sigma\, Y_iX_i - \frac{\Sigma\, Y_i\,\Sigma\, X_i}{n}$$

Denominator:

$$\Sigma\, x_i^2 = \Sigma\, (X_i - \bar{X})^2$$

$$= \Sigma\, (X_i^2 - 2X_i\bar{X} + \bar{X}^2)$$

$$= \Sigma\, X_i^2 - 2\bar{X}\,\Sigma\, X_i + n\bar{X}^2$$

$$= \Sigma\, X_i^2 - \frac{2(\Sigma\, X_i)^2}{n} + \frac{(\Sigma\, X_i)^2}{n}$$

$$= \Sigma\, X_i^2 - \frac{(\Sigma\, X_i)^2}{n}$$

CHAPTER 4

4.1 (a) $Y_i = \beta_0 + \beta_1 X_{1i} + \beta_2 X_{2i} + U_i$ where $i = 1, \ldots, n$

$E(U) = 0$

$E(U^2) = \sigma^2$

$E(U_iU_j) = 0$ for $i \neq j$

$E(U_iX_{ki}) = 0$ for $i \neq j$ and $k = 1, 2$

No exact linear relationship exists betweeen X_1 and X_2.

(c) The OLS estimators are minimum variance, linear, and unbiased (BLUE).

4.2 (a)

i	y	x_1	x_2	yx_1	yx_2	x_1x_2	x_1^2	x_2^2
1	-20	-3	0	60	0	0	9	0
2	-10	0	-1	0	10	0	0	1
3	10	-2	0	-20	0	0	4	0
4	0	3	1	0	0	3	9	1
5	20	2	0	40	0	0	4	0
	0	0	0	80	10	3	26	2

(c) $b_2 = \dfrac{\Sigma\, yx_2}{\Sigma\, x_2^2} = 5.00;\ b_0 = \bar{Y} - b_2\bar{X}_2 = 25.00$

(e) $b_{y1.2}$ is the unit change in Y associated with a 1-unit increase in X_1, holding X_2 constant; in this case, a 1-unit increase in X_1 tends to increase Y by 3.02 units, holding X_2 constant.

$b_{y2.1}$: a 1-unit increase in X_2 is associated with a .47-unit increase in Y, holding X_1 constant.

4.3 (a)

	y	x_1	x_2	yx_1	yx_2	x_1x_2	x_1^2	x_2^2
1	-60	0	10	0	-600	0	0	100
2	-40	0	10	0	-400	0	0	100
3	0	-30	0	0	0	0	900	0
4	50	10	0	500	0	0	100	0
5	50	20	-20	1000	-1000	-400	400	400
	0	0	0	1500	-2000	-400	1400	600

(c) $b_2 = \dfrac{\Sigma\, yx_2}{\Sigma\, x_2^2} = \dfrac{-2000}{600} = -3.33;\ b_0 = 100 - (-3.33)(20) = 166.60$

(e) $b_{Y1.2}$; a 1-acre increase is associated with a \$150 increase in land value, holding distance from city constant.

$b_{Y2.1}$; a 1-mile increase in distance from the city is associated with a \$3230 decrease in property values, holding acres constant.

4.4 (a) $Y = 166.0 - 1.21X_1 - 3.89X_2$

(c) (4.20); ESS $= \Sigma\, e_i^2 = \Sigma\,(Y_i - \hat{Y}_i)^2 = 91.18$

(e) $S_{b_{y1.2}}^2 = .18;\ S_{b_{y2.1}}^2 = .12$

4.5 (a) $S^2 = 2.01$

(c) 14 observations

(e) $b_0 = \bar{Y} - b_{y1.2}\bar{X}_1 - b_{y2.1}\bar{X}_2 = 19.73$

4.6 (a) 8.28

(c) 3.80

(e) 702.89

4.7 (a) $S_{b_1} = 8; S_{b_2} = 24$

(c) $S_{b_1} = 40; S_{b_2} = 120$

(e) $S_{b_1} = \dfrac{K}{2.5}; S_{b_2} = \dfrac{K}{.833}$

4.8 (a) The following interpretations assume that other factors are held constant.

b_0: intercept

b_1: annual teacher salaries tend to increase by \$4.80 for every dollar increase in monthly opportunity wages

b_2: annual teacher salaries tend to increase as class size increases; salaries tend to decrease by \$14.37 for every additional teacher hired per 1000 students

b_3: annual teacher salaries tend to increase by \$235.77 with each year of experience

(c) Cannot ever know

CHAPTER 5

5.1 (a) .130

(c) .848

5.2 (a) Very difficult without plotting the data

5.3

Y_i	$= \bar{Y}$	$+ (\hat{Y}_i - \bar{Y})$	$+ (Y_i - \hat{Y}_i)$
(a) 22	18	0	4
(c) 26	18	8	0
(e) 8	18	−6	−4
(g) 18	18	−2	2

5.4 (a) $b_0 = 17.8; b_1 = -2.6$

(c) $TSS = \Sigma (Y_i - \bar{Y})^2 = 94; RSS = \Sigma (\hat{Y}_i - \bar{Y})^2 = 67.6;$
$ESS = \Sigma (Y_i - \hat{Y})^2 = \Sigma e_i^2 = 26.4$

(e) $r_{\hat{Y}Y} = .848$

(g) $R^2 = (r_{\hat{Y}Y})^2$

(i) No, $r_{Y\hat{Y}}$ is always positive, but $(r_{\hat{Y}Y})^2 = (r_{YX})^2$.

5.5. (a) $R^2 = .67$

(c) $S_Y^2 = 28.2, \quad S_e^2 = 9.4$

(e) $S^2 = \dfrac{n}{(n - K - 1)} S_e^2$

5.6 (a) $\bar{R}^2 = .56$

(c) $\bar{R}^2 = .20$

(e) $\bar{R}^2 = .89$

CHAPTER 6

6.1 (a) False; statistics allows us only to reject hypotheses on probability grounds.
   (c) True
   (e) True
   (g) True
   (i) False; they are chi-squared distributed.
   (k) True

6.2 (a) 50
   (c) 400
   (e) $ESS/n - (k + 1)$
   (g) 2.98
   (i) 24.49
   (k) 22.5; therefore, reject H_0

6.3 (a) 2.042
   (c) 1.96
   (e) 2.518
   (g) 2.576
   (i) 1.645

6.4 (a) 2.92
   (c) 2.17
   (e) 5.78
   (g) 2.80
   (i) 1.57

6.5 (a) $P[1.07 < \beta_1 < 3.13] = .95$
   (c) $t_c = 1.708$, $t = 2.20$, reject H_0

6.6 (a) $b_0 = -7.6682$; $b_1 = 51.0918$; $b_2 = 41.4607$
   (c) $S = 19.2$
   (e) 35.24 nd 66.94
   (g) $t = 3.47 > t_c = 2.898$; so reject H_0
   (i) $t = 1.58 < t_c = 2.110$; do not reject H_0
   (k) $\bar{R}^2 = 69.9\%$

6.7 (a)

Source of Variation	Degrees of Freedom	Sum of Squares	Mean Square
All variables (X1, X2, X3, X4)	4	800	200
First two variables (X1, X2)	2	300	150
Difference	2	500	250
Residual	21	700	33.3
Total	25	1500	

   (c) $F = \dfrac{300/2}{1200/23} = 28.75$; $F_c = 3.42$; reject H_0

6.8 (a) $r_{y1} = .623$; $r_{y2} = .703$; $r_{12} = -.083$

(c) $b_{02} = 54.44$; $b_{y2} = 15.185$

(e) $S^2 = 135.26$

(g) $R^2 = .962$; $\overline{R}^2 = .952$

(i) $t = \dfrac{16.424}{1.588} = 10.34$; reject H_0 in favor of H_a

6.9 Analysis-of-Variance Table Testing the Significance of the Difference in the Regression Coefficients of Two Data Sets

Source of Variation	d.f.	S.S.	M.S.
Residual in pooled	225	10,760.1750	
Less: residuals in set I + set II	222	4,948.3800	22.290
Difference	3	5,811.7950	1,937.2650

$$F = \frac{1937.2650}{22.290} = 86.9; \quad F^{01}_{3,222} = 3.78$$

Reject the hypothesis that the effect of income on housing expenditures is the same in the two regions.

CHAPTER 7

7.1 (a) $b_0 = -7.6682$; $b_1 = 51.0918$; $b_2 = 41.4607$

(c) $S_{b_0} = 13.1408$; $S_{b_1} = 7.5179$; $S_{b_2} = 36.9885$

(e) 35.23 and 66.96

(g) Accept H_0

(i) -65.73 to 148.65

(k) $\overline{R}^2 = .70$

7.2 In time series, conditions change over the length of time of the data set. In cross-sectional data, conditions change over the observations in the data set.

7.3 (a) Time series

(c) Time series

(e) Cross-sectional

7.4 (a)

Name	Height (Inches)	Weight (Pounds)	Age (Years)	Sex[b]	Amount
John	72	180	22	0	$1.35
Mary	65	110	23	1	.97
.	.	.	.	.	.
.	.	.	.	.	.
.	.	.	.	.	.

[b] 0 = male; 1 = female.

(c) Set (a) is cross-sectional; it records observations at one point in time (i.e., one day). Set (b) is a time series; it records data at several different time periods.

7.5 (a) $\begin{bmatrix} 5 \\ 9 \\ 14 \end{bmatrix}$ (c) $\begin{bmatrix} 4 \\ 8 \\ 12 \end{bmatrix}$

(e) [3 5 8]

7.6 (a) [6 8]

(c) [2 2]

(e) undefined

(g) $[4 \quad 5]\begin{bmatrix} 2 \\ 3 \end{bmatrix} = 23$

7.7 $X_2 = [2 \quad 3 \quad 5]$

7.8 (a) $Q = [6 \quad 10 \quad 5]; P = [30 \quad 25 \quad 50]$

7.9 (a) [8 6 12]

(c) 174

(e) 244

(g) *Rules*

(i) $(X_1 + X_2)' = X_1' + X_2'$

(ii) $(X_1 + X_2)'X_1 = (X_1' + X_2')X_1 = X_1'X_1 + X_2'X_1$

(iii) $(X_1 + X_2)'(X_1 + X_2) = (X_1' + X_2')X_1 + (X_1' + X_2')X_2$
$$= X_1'X_1 + X_2'X_1 + X_1'X_2 + X_2'X_2$$

7.10 (a) $X_1 + A_1 = \begin{bmatrix} 8 & 7 \\ 6 & 2 \end{bmatrix}$

(c) $X_1 - A_1 = \begin{bmatrix} 4 & 1 \\ -2 & -8 \end{bmatrix}$

(e) $A_1X_1 = \begin{bmatrix} 18 & -1 \\ 34 & 1 \end{bmatrix}$

(g) $A_2X_2 = \begin{bmatrix} 28 & 4 & 21 \\ 53 & 23 & 42 \end{bmatrix}$

(i) $X_2A_2' = \begin{bmatrix} 36 & 63 \\ 0 & 18 \\ 17 & 37 \end{bmatrix}$

7.11 (a) $A' = \begin{bmatrix} 2 & 4 \\ 3 & 5 \end{bmatrix}$

(c) $(A + B)' = \begin{bmatrix} \begin{bmatrix} 2 & 3 \\ 4 & 5 \end{bmatrix} + \begin{bmatrix} 3 & 1 \\ 2 & 5 \end{bmatrix} \end{bmatrix}' = \begin{bmatrix} 5 & 4 \\ 6 & 10 \end{bmatrix}' = \begin{bmatrix} 5 & 6 \\ 4 & 10 \end{bmatrix}$

(e) $(AB)' = \begin{bmatrix} 12 & 17 \\ 22 & 29 \end{bmatrix}' = \begin{bmatrix} 12 & 22 \\ 17 & 29 \end{bmatrix}$

(g) $(A + B)' = A' + B'$
$(AB)' = B'A'$

7.12 (a) [220   110   55   0   165]′

    (c) [210.6   53.6   36.2 -28.2 118.0]′

    (e) [43.7 140.7 -21.9 -17.5 -183.7]′

$$\text{(g)} \begin{bmatrix} 420 \\ 360 \\ 180 \\ 120 \\ 100 \end{bmatrix} = \begin{bmatrix} 1 & 40 & 1 \\ 1 & 20 & 6 \\ 1 & 10 & 2 \\ 1 & 0 & 3 \\ 1 & 30 & 5 \end{bmatrix} \begin{bmatrix} 165.7 \\ 5.5 \\ -9.4 \end{bmatrix} + \begin{bmatrix} 43.7 \\ 140.7 \\ -21.9 \\ -17.5 \\ -183.7 \end{bmatrix}$$

CHAPTER 8

8.3 (a), (b), (c) There are trends in the plots and also cycles.

(d), (e), (f)

	Maximum	Minimum	Mean	Standard Deviation	Coefficient of Variation
Y	462	33	167	139	.83
X_1	.32	.20	.27	.03	.11
X_2	1790	6	658.3	586.3	.89

8.4 $Y = 475.6 - 1318.3X_1 + .0728X_2 + e$

          (188.4)   (648.1)   (.038)

    $S = 120.2$

    $R^2 = .288$

    (a) $t = -2.03$; reject H_0

    (c) $t_{.80} = 1.310$; reject both null hypotheses

CHAPTER 9

9.1 (a) Continuous

    (c) Classifactory

    (e) Continuous

    (g) Classifactory

    (i) Continuous

9.2 Too many dummy variables are included in the regression equation. As a result, they sum to 1 and thus are perfectly correlated with the implicit set of 1's for the constant term. The OLS estimates breakdown.

9.3 (a) To avoid the dummy variable trap

    (c) $9000

    (e) Yes, reject H_0: $\beta_1 = 0$ in favor of H_a: $\beta_1 \neq 0$, where $\beta_1 = \beta_{MS} - \beta_{BA}$

    (g) $S = 20,000 - 8,000X_3 - 11,000X_1 + e$

9.4 (a) $19,000

    (c) $18,000

    (e) $1500 more to a woman

9.5 (a) $17,000

    (c) $b_1 = $3000

    (e) No; accept H_0: $\beta_1 = 0$

9.6 (a) $8000 for men and $6500 for woman
   (c) $r = -.40$
9.7 (a) $7000
   (c) Yes; reject H_0 that the coefficeint on $D_2 = 0$
   (e) Yes; reject H_0 that the coefficient for $S_2D_2 = 0$
9.8 (b) This may be done via different intercepts using

$$Y = a + b_1X_1 + b_2D_1 + e$$

$$D_1 = 1 \text{ for households with working spouse}$$

$$= 0 \text{ otherwise}$$

   or via (different slopes and intercepts) using

$$Y = a + b_1X_1 + b_2D_1 + b_3(D_1X_1) + e$$

9.9 (b) 145,000 units

CHAPTER 10
10.1 (a) $b_0 = 3; b_1 = .2$
   (c) $b_0 = 13; b_1 = 2$
   (e) $b_0 = 11; b_1 = 2$
   (g) $b_0 = .01; b_1 = .02$
   (i) $b_0 = .11; b_1 = .2$
10.2 (a) $b_1^* = (1/f)b_1; b_0^* = b_0$
   (c) $b_1^* = b_1; b_0^* = b_0 + b_1h$
   (e) $b_1^* = b_1; b_0^* = b_0 + k - b_1h$
   (g) $b_1^* = gb_1; b_0^* = gb_0 + k$
   (i) $b_1^* = (g/f)(b_1); b_0^* = gb_0 + k - (g/f)(b_1)(h)$
10.3 (a) $b_I = .0012$
   (c) $b_k = 150$
10.4 (a) Invalid because scaling affects size of b_i
   (c) Invalid; size of t measures ratio of b to its standard error
   (e) Valid; for a percentage comparison

10.5 (b)

	G/P	P
P	$-.711$	
V/P	.642	$-.905$

   (d) $G = -13.267 + .696P + .081V + e \qquad R^2 = .998$
       $\qquad\quad (8.17) \quad (.066) \quad (.040)$
       Each million dollars in property value adds $81 to city spending on public safety. Not significant, $t = 2.00 < t_c$.
   (f) Depends on the objective of the research

10.6 (a)

	R	I	P	R/P
I	− .85			
P	.80	− .91		
R/P	− .42	.68	− .87	
I/P	− .85	.88	− .98	.82

The R has a lower correlation with the variables specified in per capita terms.

(c) $R = 3290 - 11.66I + 9.93P + e \quad R^2 = .73$
$\quad (2458) \quad (9.96) \quad (47.0)$

Each $1000 increase in income is associated with a 11.66-pound *decrease* in rice consumption.

(e) In part (b), as income increase, holding population constant, per capita income decrease. Hence parts (b) and (c) are consistent.

10.7 (b) $Q = -6.15 + .80P + e \quad R^2 = .77$
$\quad (3.87) \quad (.15)$

There is a positive relationship between Q and P, which is contrary to theoretical expectations.

(d) $Q = 21.77 - .49(P/G) + e \quad R^2 = .62$
$\quad (1.93) \quad (.13)$

(f) $Q = -1.74 + .523P + 1.380G + e \quad R^2 = .81$
$\quad (5.1) \quad (.26) \quad (1.09)$

In part (d) Q decreases .49 unit for each unit increase in P *relative* to the general price level. In part (f), Q increases .52 unit for each unit increase in P *holding G constant*.

10.8 (a) There is a dampening oscillation between Q and P_t as Q moves closer and closer to a value between 0 and 80 while P_t approaches 5 to 6.

(c) $Q_t = 122.78 - 7.50P_t + e \quad R^2 = .85$
$\quad (8.30) \quad (1.28)$

(e) $Q_t = 34.34 + 7.06P_{t-1} + e \quad R^2 = .87$
$\quad (7.95) \quad (1.22)$

CHAPTER 11

11.1 (a) Explicit
(c) Specific
(e) Specific

11.2 (a) Econometric
(c) Mathematical

11.3 (a), (b), (c)

11.5 (a), (b), (c), (e), (f), (g)

11.6 (a) $E_{QP} = \beta_1(\overline{P}/\overline{Q}) = .44$

11.7 (a) Plodder's model: $T = \beta_0 + \beta_1 M + U$

Expected signs: $\beta_0 > 0,\ \beta_1 < 0$

Null hypothesis: $H_0:\ \beta_1 = 0$

(c) Champ's model: $\ln T = \beta_0 + \beta_1 \ln M + U$

Expected signs: $\beta_1 < 0$

Null hypothesis: $\beta_1 = -.2$

11.8 (a) Model I: $\dfrac{\partial A}{\partial P} = -1000$ tickets

Model II: $\dfrac{\partial A}{\partial P} = .6\,\dfrac{8000}{12} = -400$ tickets

(c) Model I: $\dfrac{\partial A}{\partial W} = b_1 = 1200$ tickets

Model II: $\dfrac{\partial A}{\partial W} = b_1\left(\dfrac{\overline{A}}{\overline{W}}\right) = 900$ tickets

11.9 (a) Moe's model: $\quad G = \beta_0 + \beta_1 \ln H + U$

$\qquad\qquad H_0:\ \beta_1 = 14.427$

$\qquad\qquad H_a:\ \beta_1 \neq 14.427$

Curly's model: $\quad G = \beta_0 + \beta_1(1/H) + U$

$\qquad\qquad H_0:\ \beta_1 = 0$

$\qquad\qquad H_a:\ \beta_1 < 0$

Shemp's model: $G = \beta_0 + \beta_1 H + \beta_2 H^2 + U$

$\qquad\qquad H_0:\ \beta_1 = 0;\ H_a:\ \beta_1 > 0$

$\qquad\qquad H_0:\ \beta_2 = 0;\ H_a:\ \beta_2 < 0$

Hardy's model: $\ G = \beta_0 + \beta_1 H + \beta_2 W + U$

$\qquad\qquad H_0:\ \beta_1 = 0 \text{ and } \beta_2 = 0$

$\qquad\qquad H_a:\ \beta_1 \neq 0 \text{ or } \beta_2 \neq 0$

(b) *Larry*: $\ln G = 4.16 + .158 \ln H + e \qquad \overline{R}^2 = .84$

$\qquad\qquad\ (.043)\quad (.023) \qquad\qquad\qquad S\ = .06$

$t = \dfrac{.158 - .500}{.023} = -14.9;\ t_{05} = 2.306;\ \text{reject } H_0$

Shemp: $G = 63.5 + 4.25H - .124H^2 + e \qquad \overline{R}^2 = .78$

$\qquad\qquad\ (4.52)\ \ (1.13)\quad\ (.054) \qquad\qquad S\ = 5.66$

$t = \dfrac{4.25 - 0}{1.13} = 3.7;\ t = \dfrac{-.124 - 0}{.054} = -2.3$

$t_{05} = 1.86;\ \text{reject } H_0$

Hardy: $G = 52.5 + 1.616H + .128W + e \qquad \overline{R}^2 = .745$

$\qquad\qquad\ (10.67)\ (.36)\qquad (.069) \qquad\qquad S\ = 6.15$

$F = \dfrac{534.44}{37.81} = -14.31$

$F_{2,7} = 4.74;\ \text{therefore, reject } H_0$

11.10 (a) Moe: $\dfrac{12.567}{6} = 2.09$

Curly: $\dfrac{37.293}{36} = 1.04$

(b) Moe: No maximum grade
Larry: No maximum grade
Curly: Maximum = 94.5
Shemp: Maximum = 99.9

(d) 17.15

CHAPTER 12

12.1 (a) False; the expected value of an OLS estimator does not change if there is multicollinearity between independent variables.

(c) False; eliminating *all* multicollinearity is unnecessary and is often impossible to achieve.

12.2 X_1 (2, -3, 1, -1, 2) and X_2 = (3, 2, 8, 4, -2) is one example. Such combinations of data are *not* likely to occur naturally because there is always some correlation between variables.

12.4 (a)

	Case I	Case II
Y^*	$Y - 4X_2$	$Y - 3X_1$
X^*	X_1	$4X_1 + X_2$

12.5 (a) Reasonable if possible and affordable

(c) Not reasonable; β_1 is significantly different from zero.

(e) Unreasonable; new variables can only add to (never solve) multicollinearity problems.

12.6 (a) Since $\Delta Y = Y_t - Y_{t-1}$ the third variable is perfectly linearly related to $Y_t + Y_{t-1}$.

(c) No, three parameters and only two independent variables

12.7 (a) Yes, $L_2 + K = \$30,000$; L_2 and K are perfectly collinear.

CHAPTER 13

13.1 (a) Only if the bias term in (13.7) is equal to zero

13.2 (a) Yes

(c) $E(b_2) = \beta_2 = 0$

13.3 (a) Theory indicates that some variables are relevant and must be included in the equation; otherwise, one never knows for sure if a variable is relevant or not.

13.4 (a) 11

(c) 5

13.5 (a) Perhaps, but the unexpected sign may also be due to sampling error or faulty measurement of income.

(c) Disagree; it is possible but not guaranteed.

13.6 (a) The statement is true statistically but suspicious theoretically. This might be one of the rare (95%) cases where the null hypothesis is incorrectly accepted.

(c) True, if you are convinced P is truly irrelevant to test scores and it is not a proxy for some other important variable.

13.7 (a) $E(b_{pw}) = \beta_w + \beta_m b_{mw}$

$E(b_{pk}) = \beta_k + \beta_m b_{mk}$

(b) The coefficient of W_i is negatively biased:

$E(b_{pw}) = \beta_w + \cdots + \beta_m^+ b_{mw}^- \ mb - mw = \beta_w - \text{(bias term)}$

(c) The coefficient of K_i is positively biased:

$E(b_{pk}) = \beta_k^+ + \beta_m^+ b_{mk}^+ = \beta_k + \text{(bias term)}$

13.8 (a) $E(b_1) = \beta_1 + \beta_2 b_{21}$

The direction of bias depends on the sign of β_2, since b_{21} is greater than zero.

(i) If $\beta_2 > 0$ (i.e., y is an increasing function of X_2), b_1 will be negatively biased.

(ii) If $\beta_2 < 0$ (i.e., y is a decreasing function of X_2), b_1 will be positively biased.

13.9 (a) Disagree; t-tests are not valid when relevant variables are omitted.

(c) Disagree; it is not clear what is the direction and magnitude of the bias until the magnitude of β_v, β_a, etc., are known.

(e) Disagree; new variables will cause b_s to change, but the direction is not clear.

CHAPTER 14

14.1 (a) Heteroscedasticity

(c) Only the best or minimum-variance property

(e) Heteroscedasticity is more likely to occur in cross-sectional data; autocorrelation is more likely to occur in time-series data, but either problem can be found in either type of data.

(g) Positive

14.2 (a) The OLS estimators of b_0, b_1, b_2 are unbiased but $E(S^2) \neq \sigma^2$.

(c) No, since $S_{b_i}^2$ is a biased estimate of the variance of b_i.

14.3 (a) $E(e^2) = X_2 \sigma^2$

(c) The OLS estimates b_0^*, b_1^* are the best linear unbiased estimates of β_0 and β_i and $E[(S^*)^2] = \sigma^2$.

(e)

Y^*	X_0^*	X_1^*	X_2^*
2,857.14	1/35	13,828.57	35
1,565.22	1/23	8,347.83	23
33,073.02	1/315	157,498.41	315

14.4 (a) $E(e^2) = X_2^2\sigma^2$.

(c)

$Y*$	X_0^*	X_1^*	X_2^*
81.63	1/1225	395.10	1
68.05	1/529	362.95	1
104.99	1/99,225	499.99	1

14.5

$$\frac{C_t}{E(C_t)} = b_0 \frac{1}{E(C_t)} + b_1 \frac{I_t}{E(C_t)} + b_2 \frac{W_t}{E(C_t)} + \frac{e_t}{E(C_t)}$$

Note: $E(C_t) = \hat{C}_t = \hat{C}_0 + \hat{C}_1 I_t + \hat{C}_2 W_t + V_t$

Steps

1. By OLS, estimate the equation and compute $\hat{C}_t$.
2. Transform each variable by dividing by $\hat{C}_t$.

$$C_t^* = \frac{C_t}{\hat{C}_t};\ C_0^* = \frac{1}{\hat{C}_t};\ I_t^* = \frac{I_t}{\hat{C}_t};\ W_t^* = \frac{W_t}{\hat{C}_t}$$

3. Estimate the following equation by OLS with no constant in the equation:

$$C_t^* = b_0 C_0^* + b_1 I_t^* + b_2 W_t^*$$

14.7 (a) Yes; $d_L = 1.44$, $d_U = 1.54$, $4 - d_U = 2.46$, and $4 - d_L = 2.56$.

(c) Cannot say because autocorrelation makes the hypothesis test invalid

14.8 (a) Yes; still unbiased

(c) No; it is biased (usually downward).

(e) $Y_t^* = Y_t - .5Y_{t-1}$; $X_t^* = X_t - .5X_{t-1}$

	Y_t^*	X_{1t}^*
1	*	*
2	160	10
3	257	13.5

(g) Yes

(i) Yes

14.9 (a) $Y_t - Y_{t-1} = \beta_1(X_t - X_{t-1}) + U_t - U_{t-1}$ or $Y_t^* = \beta_1 X_t^* + V_t^*$

(c) If the original equation includes a time trend (i.e., $T = 1, 2, 3, \ldots,$) $T_i - T_{i-1} = 1$ and a constant term would be appropriate.

14.10 (a) Yes

14.11   Durbin–Watson worksheet

Obs.	Y	X	$\hat{Y}$	e_t	e_{t-1}	$(e_t - e_{t-1})^2$	e_t^2
1	2.4	1.0	1.0	1.4	—	—	1.96
2	2.5	2.0	2.0	.5	1.40	.81	.25
3	2.5	3.0	3.0	−.5	.50	1.00	.25
4	1.6	4.0	4.0	−2.4	−.050	3.61	5.76
5	3.7	5.0	5.0	−1.3	−2.40	1.21	1.69
6	5.8	6.0	6.0	−.2	−1.30	1.21	.04
7	6.9	7.0	7.0	−.1	−.20	.01	.01
8	7.0	8.0	8.0	−1.0	−.10	.81	1.00
9	11.1	9.0	9.0	2.1	−1.00	9.61	4.41
10	11.2	10.0	10.0	1.2	2.10	.81	1.44
11	11.3	11.0	11.0	.3	1.20	.81	.09
12	13.4	12.0	12.0	1.4	.30	1.21	1.96
13	16.5	13.0	13.0	3.5	1.40	4.41	12.25
14	11.5	14.0	14.0	−2.5	3.50	36.00	6.25
15	12.6	15.0	15.0	−2.4	−2.50	.01	5.76
						61.52	43.12

$$\text{D. W.} = \frac{\Sigma (e_t - e_{t-1})^2}{\Sigma e_t^2} = \frac{61.52}{43.12} = 1.42$$

The Durbin–Watson d_L, d_U at .05 with $K = 1$, $n = 15$

$$d_L = 1.08 \qquad d_U = 1.36$$

H_0 is not rejected because $d_U < 1.42$

CHAPTER 15

15.1   Measurement errors and missing data

15.3   Data errors due to problems other than the sampling method. Examples are: improperly structured questionnaires; improperly trained interviewers; improperly calibrated measuring devices; reporting and recording errors; and others.

15.4 (b) Assumptions on the stochastic disturbance term (errors in equation) are the foundation of modern econometric estimation techniques. In contrast, errors in variables are difficult to detect and few practical solutions exist to the problem. Nevertheless, researchers must constantly be aware of the damage that variable errors can do to their estimate.

15.5 (b) The measurement error in an independent variable causes that variable and the disturbance term to be correlated, hence the OLS estimates of the regression slope, are biased. Yes, it has serious consequences, but applied researchers must routinely deal with it.

15.6 (a) Valid, but they are not minimum variance.

(c) Valid; efficiency increases in *most* cases.

CHAPTER 16

16.1   Trend, cycles, and seasonality

16.2 (a) True

(c) False; trends can be negative.

(e) True

16.3 (c) $P = 8.29 + 1.64T + e$; price increases by \$1.64 per year.

(e) $Q/P = 2.05 - .03T + e$

(g) $Q/P = 2.61 - .007T - .054RP + e$

16.4 (a) Not advisable; a linear trend has very little relationship to the form of the data in the plot.

(c) $P = 92.15 - .13T + e$; $R^2 = .01$

(e) The segmented line obviously fits better.

16.5 (a) $\ln P = 2.155 + .1288T + e$; r = estimated annual rate of growth = 13.7%

(c) $\ln PI = -.0139 + .0113T + e$; $r = 1.1\%$

16.6 (a) $r = \sqrt[10]{\dfrac{V1960}{V1950}} - 1$

(c) The two methods yield different answers *most of the time*; the regression method is less sensitive to values for the first and last observation, since it averages over the whole data series.

16.7 (a) False, a trend variable should not be included unless the researcher has a very good, explicit reason for including it—even then it is not often a good practice.

(c) True, although you should be prepared to defend using such a technique.

16.9   One of many possibilities is

$$1, 3, 4, 6, 10, 13, 14, 17, 18, 22, 24, 26$$

Another is

$$-16, -14, -13, -11, -7, -4, -3, 0, 1, 5, 7, 9$$

CHAPTER 17

17.1 (a) -1

(c) 1% lower

(e) \$121.21

(g) Decreased from \$111.65 to \$106.06, a decrease of 5.0%

17.2 (a) $\bar{P} = 80 + (24.5)(.5) = 92.25$

(c) 125.44

17.3 (a) $P = b_0^* + b_2^* Q_2 + b_3^* Q_3 + b_4^* Q_4 + e$

$$\text{where } b_0^* = E(\beta_0 + \beta_1)$$
$$b_2^* = E(\beta_2 - \beta_1)$$
$$b_3^* = E(\beta_3 - \beta_1)$$
$$b_4^* = E(\beta_4 - \beta_1)$$

(c)

Month	b_0	Part (a)			Part (b)		
		Q_2	Q_3	Q_4	Q_2^*	Q_3^*	Q_4^*
January	1	0	0	0	−1	−1	−1
February	1	0	0	0	−1	−1	−1
March	1	0	0	0	−1	−1	−1
April	1	1	0	0	1	0	0
May	1	1	0	0	1	0	0
June	1	1	0	0	1	0	0
July	1	0	1	0	0	1	0
August	1	0	1	0	0	1	0
September	1	0	1	0	0	1	0
October	1	0	0	1	0	0	1
November	1	0	0	1	0	0	1
December	1	0	0	1	0	0	1

17.4 (a) 99

(c) They declined from $135.42 in the second quarter to $132.35 in the third quarter.

17.5 (a)

January	100	July	100.5
February	101.0	August	99.5
March	102	September	98.0
April	103	October	96.5
May	102.5	November	97.5
June	101.0	December	98.5

17.6 (a)

Month	Index
January	94
February	102
March	104
April	106
May	105
June	103
July	101
August	99
September	97
October	95
November	96
December	98

(c) Much of the observed change in prices from month to month represented seasonal changes.

17.7 (a) Estimated under the assumption that $\sum\limits_{i=1}^{4} d_i = 0$;

$$Q = .704 - .420P + .0056I - .5046Q_2^* - 1.1448Q_3^* + 1.5670Q_4^*, \; + e$$
where $Q_i^* = Q_i - Q_1$

(c) Because there would be relevant variables excluded from the equation (see Chapter 13)

CHAPTER 18

18.1 (a) 22

(c) 76

18.2 (a) $-.9$

(c) More confidence in a forecast based on $X_i = 10$ (the sample mean) because the standard error of forecast is smallest at the sample mean of X.

18.3 (a) 49.20

(c) The 95% confidence level would be smaller if $X_{t+1} = 43$ because 43 is closer to $\bar{X}$ than 35.

18.4 (b) $P[47,461,000 \leq R_{T+1} \leq 57,339,000] = .99$

(d) Conditional because I_{T+1} is an estimate

(f) $400,000

18.5 (a) True

(c) True

(e) True

(g) False; the standard deviation of the regression increases with the distance between the value of the forecasting variables and their means.

(i) False; lagging independent variables is just one—and not necessarily the best—technique for estimating the appropriate value of the independent variable.

18.6 (a) (i) $= 2.71$; (ii) $= 2.37$; (iii) $= .468$

(c) No, because the 90 percent confidence interval does not include zero. Nonetheless, there is always some probability that Y_{T+1} is really zero.

Index
